P9-BBU-930

Cambodia

Temples of
Angkor
p132

Siem Reap
p96

Northwestern
Cambodia
p231

Eastern Cambodia
p272

Phnom Penh
p40

South Coast
p175

Nick Ray, Ashley Harrell

Contents

DANCERS AT ANGKOR WAT
P147

TA PROHM TEMPLE P159

RAWPIXEL.COM/SHUTTERSTOCK ©

GUITAR PHOTOGRAPHER/SHUTTERSTOCK ©

Contents

Welcome to Cambodia

There's a magic about this charming yet confounding kingdom that casts a spell on visitors. In Cambodia, ancient and modern worlds collide to create an authentic adventure.

An Empire of Temples

Contemporary Cambodia is the successor state to the mighty Khmer empire, which, during the Angkorian period, ruled much of what is now Laos, Thailand and Vietnam. The remains of this empire can be seen at the fabled temples of Angkor, monuments unrivalled in scale and grandeur in Southeast Asia. The traveller's first glimpse of Angkor Wat, the ultimate expression of Khmer genius, is sublime and is matched by only a few select spots on earth, such as Machu Picchu or Petra.

The Urban Scene

Just as Angkor is more than its wat, so too is Cambodia more than its temples, and its urban areas can surprise with their sophistication. Chaotic yet charismatic capital Phnom Penh is a revitalised city earning plaudits for its sumptuous riverside setting, cultural renaissance, and world-class wining-and-dining scene. Second city Siem Reap, with cosmopolitan cafes and a diverse nightlife, is as much a destination as the nearby iconic temples. And up-and-coming Battambang, reminiscent of Siem Reap before the advent of mass tourism, charms with graceful French architecture and a thriving contemporary art scene.

Upcountry Adventures

Experience the rhythm of rural life and landscapes of dazzling rice paddies and swaying sugar palms in Cambodia's countryside. The South Coast is fringed by tropical islands dotted with the occasional fishing village. Inland lie the Cardamom Mountains, part of a vast tropical wilderness providing a home to elusive wildlife and a gateway to emerging ecotourism adventures. The mighty Mekong River cuts through the country and hosts some of the region's last remaining freshwater dolphins. The northeast is a world unto itself, its wild and mountainous landscapes home to Cambodia's ethnic minorities and an abundance of natural attractions and wildlife.

The Cambodian Spirit

Despite having the eighth wonder of the world in its backyard, Cambodia's real treasure is its people. The Khmers have been to hell and back, struggling through years of bloodshed, poverty and political instability. Thanks to an unbreakable spirit and infectious optimism, they have prevailed with their smiles intact. No visitor comes away without a measure of admiration and affection for the inhabitants of this enigmatic kingdom.

Why I Love Cambodia

By Nick Ray, Writer

Dating right back to my first trip in 1995, it has been the people that are the most memorable part of a journey through Cambodia, their sense of humour mischievous and their smiles infectious. The temples of Angkor are undoubtedly spectacular and deservedly top the annual travel lists of the world's most impressive sites. However, the coastline is beautiful and blissfully undeveloped compared with some of the region. And it remains a frontier for motorbike rides from the Cardamoms in the southwest to Mondulkiri in the northeast. Even as it develops, Cambodia remains an authentic adventure.

For more about our writers, see p384.

Above: Entrance to Preah Khan temple (p162)

Cambodia

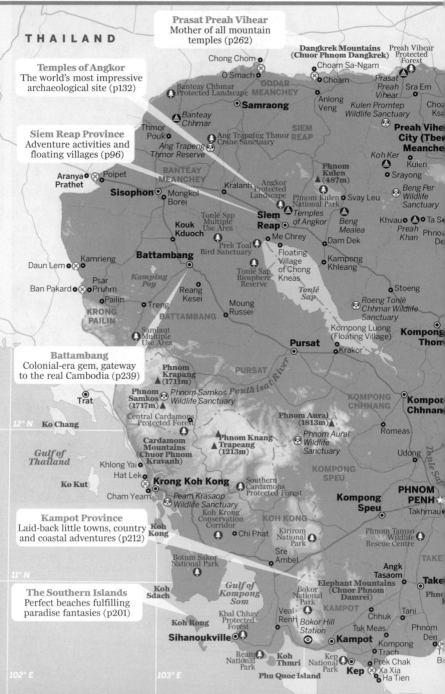

THAILAND

Prasat Preah Vihear
Mother of all mountain temples (p262)

Temples of Angkor
The world's most impressive archaeological site (p132)

Siem Reap Province
Adventure activities and floating villages (p96)

Battambang
Colonial-era gem, gateway to the real Cambodia (p239)

Kampot Province
Laid-back little towns, country and coastal adventures (p212)

The Southern Islands
Perfect beaches fulfilling paradise fantasies (p201)

Chong Chom
O Smach
Choam Sa-Ngam
Choam
Dangkrek Mountains (Chuor Phnom Dangkrek)
Preah Vihear Protected Forest
Prasat Preah Vihear
Sra Em
ODDAR MEANCHEY
Banteay Chhmar Protected Landscape
Anlong Veng
Kulen Promtep Wildlife Sanctuary
Choa Ks
Samraong
Banteay Chhmar
SIEM REAP
Preah Vihe City (Tber Meanche
Thmor Pouk
Ang Trapaing Thmor Crane Sanctuary
Koh Ker
Kulen
Ang Trapeng Thmor Reserve
Srayong
BANTEAY MEANCHEY
Angkor Protected Landscape
Phnom Kulen (487m)
Beng Per Wildlife Sanctuary
Aranya Prathet
Poipet
Kralanh
Phnom Kulen National Park
Svay Leu
Khvau
Ta S
Sisophon
Mongkol Borei
Preah Khan
Phno De
Tonlé Sap Multiple Use Area
Siem Reap
Temples of Angkor
Beng Mealea
Kouk Kduoch
Prek Toal Bird Sanctuary
Me Chrey
Dam Dek
Daun Lem
Kamrieng
Battambang
Floating Village of Chong Kneas
Kampong Khleang
Tonlé Sap Biosphere Reserve
Psar Pruhm
Ban Pakard
Reang Kesei
Stoeng
Pailin
KRONG PAILIN
Treng
Moung Russei
Tonlé Sap
Roeng Tonlé Chhmar Wildlife Sanctuary
Samlaut Multiple Use Area
Kompong Luong (Floating Village)
Kompong Thom
Pursat
Krakor
PURSAT
Phnom Krapang (1711m)
Pouthisat River
Trat
Phnom Samkos (1717m)
Phnom Samkos Wildlife Sanctuary
KOMPONG CHHNANG
Kompor Chhnan
Central Cardamoms Protected Forest
Phnom Aural (1813m)
Gulf of Thailand
Ko Chang
Cardamom Mountains (Chuor Phnom Kravanh)
Phnom Knang Trapeang (1213m)
Phnom Aural Wildlife Sanctuary
Romeas
Ko Kut
Khlong Yai
Hat Lek
KOMPONG SPEU
Udong
Krong Koh Kong
Southern Cardamons Protected Forest
PHNOM PENH
Cham Yeam
Peam Krasaop Wildlife Sanctuary
Kompong Speu
Takhmau
Koh Krong Conservation Corridor
KOH KONG
Phnom Tamao Wildlife Rescue Centre
Koh Kong
Chi Phat
Kirirom National Park
Angk Tasaom
Take
Botum Sakor National Park
Sre Ambel
Elephant Mountains (Chuor Phnom Damrei)
Phno
Koh Sdach
Gulf of Kompong Som
Bokor National Park
KAMPOT
Tani
Kbal Chhay Protected Forest
Veal Renh
Bokor Hill Station
Chhuk
Phnom Den
Koh Rong
Tuk Meas
Kompong Trach
Sihanoukville
Kampot
Ream National Park
Koh Thmri
Kep National Park
Prek Chak
Kep
Xa Xia
Phu Quoc Island
Ha Tien

12° N
11° N
102° E
103° E

0   100 km
0   50 miles

LAOS

Muang
Khong

Anlong
Cheuteal

Siem
Pang

Virachey
National
Park

RATANAKIRI

Voen Sai

Tonlé San

Le Thanh

REAH
HEAR

Stung Treng
Ramsar Site

Preah
Rumkel

STUNG
TRENG

Ban Lung

Bokheo

O Yadaw

vay Pak

Thala Boravit

Tonlé Srepok

**Stung
Treng**

*Boeng Yeak
Lom*

Rovieng

Mekong River

Lumphat

*Lumphat
Wildlife
Sanctuary*

Mondulkiri
Where the wild things
are (p295)

Sen River

KOMPONG
THOM

KRATIE

Koh Nhek

*Sambor
Prei Kuk*

Sambor

Sandan

*Phnom Prech
Wildlife
Sanctuary*

MONDULKIRI

*Mondulkiri
Protected
Forest*

Baray

Spoe
Tbong

Kratie

**Sen
Monorom**

*Nam Lear
Wildlife Sanctuary*

Stung
Trang

Chhlong

*Seima
Protected
Forest*

Sre
Kthum

Skuon

**Kompong
Cham**

TBONG
KHMUM

Snuol

Trapeang
Sre

Kratie
Rare dolphins in the
Mekong River (p279)

KOMPONG
CHAM

Chup

Suong

Trapeang
Plong

Memot

Loc Ninh

PREY
VENG

Xa Mat

VIETNAM

KÂNDAL

**Prey
Veng**

SVAY
RIENG

Tay Ninh

Phnom Penh
The 'pearl of Asia'
is back (p40)

Neak
Luong

Ba Phnom

Kaam
Samnor

Banteay
Chakrey

**Svay
Rieng**

Chiphu

Moc Bai

Bavet

Vinh
Luong

Khanh
Binh

ELEVATION

1500m
1000m
500m
250m
0

Chau Doc

**Ho Chi
Minh City**

*SOUTH
CHINA SEA*

107° E

108° E

Cambodia's
Top 10

1

Temples of Angkor

1 One of the world's most magnificent sights, the temples of Angkor (p132) are so much better than the superlatives suggest. Choose from Angkor Wat, the world's largest religious building; Bayon, one of the world's weirdest, with its immense stone faces; or Ta Prohm, where nature runs amok. The ancient Khmers packed the equivalent of all Europe's cathedrals into an area the size of Los Angeles, so there are plenty of temples to choose from: the beautiful carvings of Banteay Srei, the jungle ruin of Beng Mealea and the Mayan-style pyramid temple of Koh Ker. Angkor Wat (p147)

The Southern Islands

2 In Cambodia's up-and-coming southern islands (p201) your best chances to fulfil those paradise fantasies are Koh Rong and Koh Rong Sanloem. Off the coast of Sihanoukville, Koh Rong is party central, with its hippy trippy Koh Tuch village; the rest of the island, fringed by silicon sand and clad in dense jungle, is an escape. Just south and slightly mellower is Koh Rong Sanloem, with tropical hideaway resorts and gentle, shallow bays. There are more islands along the coast, including the Koh Sdach archipelago and the large, almost undeveloped, Koh Kong. Koh Rong Sanloem (p207)

GUITAR PHOTOGRAPHER/SHUTTERSTOCK ©

NATALIA MAROZ/SHUTTERSTOCK ©

Phnom Penh

3 The Cambodian capital is a chaotic yet charming city that has stepped out of the shadows of the past to embrace a brighter future. Boasting one of the most beguiling riverfronts in the region, Phnom Penh (p40) is surprisingly sophisticated thanks to its hip hotels, epicurean eateries and boho bars ready to welcome urban explorers. Experience emotional extremes at the inspiring National Museum and the depressing Tuol Sleng prison, showcasing the best and worst of Cambodian history.
National Museum of Cambodia (p43)

Siem Reap Province

4 Siem Reap town (p52) only came into existence as a gateway to the temples of Angkor, but has emerged as a world class destination in its own right, with a superb selection of restaurants, cafes and bars, not to mention markets, boutiques and galleries. Beyond the town lie other-worldly floating villages on the Tonlé Sap lake, adventure activities such as quad biking and ziplining, and cooking classes. There are also some traditional villages where you can experience local life in a homestay. Pub St (p117)

Kampot Province

5 Kampot Province (p212) has atmospheric towns, national parks, cave pagodas and tropical beaches. In laid-back Kampot town, choose from backpacker hostels, riverside resorts or boutique hotels to take in the wonderful French architectural legacy, or explore the pretty river by paddleboard or kayak. Sleepier Kep has its famous Crab Market, hiking in Kep National Park and nearby Koh Tonsay (Rabbit Island). Trips include the winding ascent to Bokor Hill Station (pictured) or exploring the working pepper farms for which Kampot is justly famous.

Battambang

6 This is the real Cambodia, unfurling along the banks of the Sangker River, Battambang (p239) is one of the country's best-preserved colonial-era towns. Streets of French shophouses host everything from fair-trade cafes to art galleries. Beyond the town is the countryside and a cluster of ancient temples, which, although not exactly Angkor Wat, do, mercifully, lack the crowds. Then there's the Phare Ponleu Selpak, a wildly successful nonprofit that puts on an awe-inspiring local circus. Phnom Sampeau temple (p250)

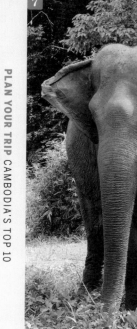

SNUDJ.WELA/SHUTTERSTOCK ©

Mondulkiri

7 Eventually the endless rice fields and sugar palms that characterise the Cambodian landscape give way to rolling hills and the wild east of Mondulkiri (p295), home to the hardy Bunong people, who still practise animism and ancestor worship. Wildlife is a big draw here with the opportunity to 'walk with the herd' at Elephant Valley Project (pictured) or spot doucs or gibbons on a trek through the Seima Protected Forest. Add thunderous waterfalls and a jungle zipline to the mix and you have the perfect ingredients for an authentic adventure.

Prasat Preah Vihear

8 The mother of all mountain temples, Prasat Preah Vihear (p262) stands majestically atop the Dangkrek Mountains, forming a controversial border post between Cambodia and Thailand. The temple's foundation stones stretch to the edge of the cliff that falls away to the plains below; the views across northern Cambodia are incredible. The 300-year chronology of its construction also offers an insight into carving and sculpture during the Angkorian period. It's all about location, though, and it doesn't get better than this.

Kratie

9 Gateway to the rare freshwater Irrawaddy dolphins of the Mekong River, Kratie (p279) is a busy crossroads on the route between Phnom Penh and northeastern Cambodia or southern Laos. The town has a certain decaying colonial grandeur and boasts some of the country's best Mekong sunsets. Nearby Koh Trong is a relaxing place to experience a homestay or explore by bike. North of Kratie lies the Mekong Discovery Trail, including community-based homestays, bicycle rides and boat trips. Phnom Sombok (p279)

Khmer Cuisine

10 Everyone has tried Thai and Vietnamese specialities before they hit the region, but Khmer cuisine (p341) remains under the culinary radar. *Amok* (baked fish with lemongrass, chilli and coconut) is the national dish, but seafood and freshwater-fish dishes are plentiful, including Kep crab infused with Kampot pepper. It wouldn't be Asia without street snacks, and Cambodia delivers everything from noodles (*mee*) and congee (*bobor*) to deep-fried tarantulas and roasted crickets. *Amok*

JM TRAVEL PHOTOGRAPHY/SHUTTERSTOCK ©

Need to Know

For more information, see Survival Guide (p349).

Currency
riel (r); US dollars (US$) universally accepted

Language
Khmer, English, Chinese, French

Visas
One-month tourist visa is US$30 on arrival; requires one passport-sized photo. Easily extendable business visas are available for US$35. E-visas can be arranged online at www.evisa.gov.kh.

Money
ATMs widely available, including all major tourist centres and pro-vincial capitals. Credit cards accepted by many hotels and restaurants in larger cities.

Mobile Phones
Local SIM cards and unlocked mobile phones are readily available.

Time
Indochina Time Zone (GMT/UTC plus seven hours)

When to Go

Siem Reap •
GO Nov–Aug

Sen Monorom •
GO Year-round

Phnom Penh •
GO Year-round

Sihanoukville •
GO Nov–Jun

• Kep
GO Nov–Jul

◼ Tropical climate, wet & dry seasons

High Season
(Nov–Feb)

➡ Cooler and windy, with almost Mediterranean temperatures.

➡ Book accommodation in advance during the peak Christmas and New Year period.

Shoulder
(Apr & Oct)

➡ In April and May the mercury hits 40°C and visitors melt.

➡ October and November are an excellent time for exploration as rains taper off while the dusty dry season has yet to begin.

Low Season
(May–Sep)

➡ Big accommodation discounts and protective cloud cover make this a great time to visit the temples.

➡ South Coast can be busy as Western visitors escape for summer holidays while school is out.

Useful Websites

Lonely Planet (www.lonelyplanet.com/cambodia) Destination information, hotel bookings, traveller forum and more.

Phnom Penh Post (www.phnompenhpost.com) Cambodia's newspaper of record.

Travelfish (www.travelfish.org) Opinionated articles and reviews.

Move to Cambodia (www.movetocambodia.com) Insightful guide to living and working in Cambodia.

Cambodia Tribunal Monitor (www.cambodiatribunal.org) Detailed coverage of the Khmer Rouge trials.

Important Numbers

Drop the 0 from a regional (city) code when calling Cambodia from another country.

Ambulance	☏119
Cambodia code	☏855
Fire	☏118
International access code	☏001
Police	☏117

Exchange Rates

Australia	A$1	3100r
Canada	C$1	3050r
Euro zone	€1	4900r
Japan	¥100	3750r
New Zealand	NZ$1	2900r
Thailand	1B	128r
UK	UK£1	5560r
USA	US$1	4000r

For current exchange rates see www.xe.com.

Daily Costs

Budget: Less than US$50

➡ Cheap guesthouse room: US$5–10

➡ Local meals and street eats: US$1–3

➡ Local buses (per 100km): US$2–3

Midrange: US$50–200

➡ Air-con hotel room: US$15–50

➡ Decent local restaurant meal: US$5–10

➡ Local tour guide per day: US$25–35

Top End: More than US$200

➡ Boutique hotel or resort: US$50–500

➡ Gastronomic meal with drinks: US$25–50

➡ 4WD rental per day: US$60–120

Opening Hours

Everything shuts down during the major holidays: Chaul Chnam Khmer (Khmer New Year), P'chum Ben (Festival of the Dead) and Chaul Chnam Chen (Chinese New Year).

Banks 8am to 3.30pm Monday to Friday, Saturday mornings

Bars 5pm to late

Government offices 7.30am to 11.30am and 2pm to 5pm Monday to Friday

Local markets 6.30am to 5.30pm daily

Museums Hours vary, but usually open seven days a week

Restaurants (international) 7am to 10pm or meal times

Restaurants (local) 6.30am to 9pm

Shops 8am to 6pm daily

Arriving in Cambodia

Phnom Penh International Airport The airport is 7km west of city centre. Official taxis/*remork-motos (tuk tuks)* to anywhere in the city cost US$12/9 (30 minutes to one hour). Flag a *moto* (motorcycle taxi) outside for about US$3 one-way.

Siem Reap International Airport The airport is 7km from the town centre; taxis/*remorks* cost US$9/7 (15 to 30 minutes). A trip to the town centre on a *moto* is about US$3. Many hotels and guesthouses offer free airport pick-up.

Land borders Shared with Laos, Thailand and Vietnam; Cambodian visas are available on arrival. Most borders are open 7am to 5pm. Overcharging for visas is common at the Poipet and Cham Yeam (Koh Kong) border crossings, so arrange an e-visa in advance.

Getting Around

Bus The most popular form of transport for most travellers, connecting all major towns and cities.

Car Private car or 4WD is an affordable option for those who value time above money.

Motorbike An amazing way to travel for experienced riders.

Air Domestic flights link Phnom Penh and Siem Reap, and Siem Reap and Sihanoukville.

Boat Less common nowadays, but Siem Reap to either Battambang or Phnom Penh remain popular routes.

Train Newly resumed service has sporadic and slow services linking Phnom Penh with Kampot and Sihanoukville.

For much more on **getting around**, see p361.

First Time Cambodia

For more information, see Survival Guide (p349).

Checklist

➡ Make sure your passport is valid for at least six months beyond the date of arrival.

➡ Arrange any recommended inoculations.

➡ Arrange for appropriate travel insurance.

➡ Check the airline baggage restrictions.

➡ Inform your debit-/credit-card company you're heading away.

➡ Check to make sure you can obtain a visa-on-arrival in Cambodia.

What to Pack

➡ Lightweight, light-coloured clothing to reflect the sun

➡ Comfortable sandals or shoes

➡ Refillable water bottle

➡ Powerful sunscreen and long-lasting deodorant

➡ Earplugs to block out the noise

➡ Universal travel adaptor

➡ Unlocked mobile phone for use with a Cambodian SIM card

➡ Rain coat if travelling in wet season

Top Tips for Your Trip

➡ Do your homework on land border crossings before you cross to ensure you don't great stranded in a remote location after dark.

➡ Overnight sleeper buses are generally pretty comfortable in Cambodia and will save the cost of a night's accommodation.

➡ If time is more important than money, consider domestic flights between Siem Reap and Sihanoukville, as the road is long.

➡ Most basic supplies such as toiletries, sanitary pads, shaving foam, insect repellent and sunscreen can be purchased in major towns.

➡ Dress appropriately around the countryside, as Cambodia remains a conservative country and not a beach destination.

➡ Buy a *krama,* a checked traditional local scarf, for your travels, as it is a multipurpose travel towel that the locals use in a multitude of ways.

What to Wear

Lightweight and loose-fitting clothes are best, including cottons and linens to combat the humidity. Cambodia is not a very dressy place, so smart clothes are not really a necessity. If heading to the upland northeast in November to March pack a jacket and/or sweater for the cool nights. Shorts are acceptable throughout the country, but have something to cover elbows and knees for temple visits. At beach destinations, cover up with a sarong or something similar when not on the beach

Sleeping

It's worth booking in advance in popular destinations during peak-season months and around major holidays.

Guesthouses Usually family-run, locally-owned; offer good-value rooms.

Hotels Cambodia offers everything from cheap business pads to luxury heritage hotels.

Hostels Hostels offer a mix of dorm beds and private rooms, sometimes with a pool, but are concentrated in Phnom Penh, Siem Reap and the South Coast.

Homestays These usually involve staying with a family in a village in rustic facilities.

Bargaining

Haggling is de rigueur for Cambodia. See p353 for more information.

It's important to haggle in markets in Cambodia, otherwise the stallholder may 'shave your head' (local vernacular for 'rip you off'). As well as in markets, bargaining is the rule when arranging share taxis and pick-ups, and in some guesthouses. The Khmers are not ruthless hagglers, so a persuasive smile and a little friendly quibbling is usually enough to get a price that's acceptable to both you and the seller.

Tipping

Tipping is not traditionally expected, but in a country as poor as Cambodia, tips can go a long way

Etiquette

The Cambodian people are very gracious hosts, but there are some important spiritual and social conventions to observe.

➡ **Buddhism** When visiting temples, cover up to the knees and elbows, and remove your shoes and any head covering when entering temple buildings. Sit with your feet tucked behind you to avoid pointing them at Buddha images. It's also good to leave a small donation. Women should never touch a monk or his belongings.

➡ **Meet & Greet** Called the *sompiah*, the local greeting in Cambodia involves putting your hands together in a prayer-like manner. Use this when introduced to new Khmer friends. When beckoning someone over, always wave towards yourself with the palm down.

➡ **Modesty** Avoid wearing swimsuits or scanty clothing around towns in Cambodia, even in beach destinations. Wear a sarong to cover up.

➡ **Saving face** Never get into an argument with a Khmer person. It's better to smile through any conflict.

Eating

Unlike the culinary colossi that are its neighbours Thailand and Vietnam, Cambodia is not that well known in international food circles. But Cambodian cuisine is also quite special, with a great variety of national dishes, some drawing on the cuisine of its neighbours, but all with a unique Cambodian twist. You are bound to find something that takes your fancy, whether your tastes run to spring rolls or curry.

What's New

Domestic Airlines Taking Off

New airlines are, quite literally, taking off at frequent intervals and this is driving down the price of domestic flights and opening up smooth connections between the temples and the beach.

Homestays in Siem Reap

Homestays are popping up all over Cambodia, but one of the easiest places to experience a slice of local life is Siem Reap Province thanks to its proximity to the one and only Angkor Wat.

BeTreed Adventures

A remote new eco-stay on 7000 acres of forestland in Preah Vihear Province, run by two former NGO workers aiming to protect wildlife while hosting guests in fabulous tree house and bungalow accommodations. (p269)

Craft Beer in the Capital

Microbrew is taking off in Phnom Penh with several new craft-beer emporiums opening up in the past couple of years, including Hops and Botanico. Cheers! (p75)

Kampot Dining Scene

An ever-evolving culinary capital, Kampot's best new restaurants include Twenty Three Bistro (haute cuisine), Thai Fire (Thai/Laotian food) and Jetzt (delicious burgers). (p217)

Angkor Ticket Prices

The price of admission to the majestic temples of Angkor has risen dramatically to US$37/62/72 for 1/3/7 days, although you can use a 3-day pass over one week and a 7-day pass over one month.

Octopuses Garden Diving Center

On Koh Sdach, this dive shop runs excellent trips to reefs around the archipelago, good lodgings and tasty meals. (p211)

Sambor Prei Kuk

These vine-entwined brick temples recently became the country's third Unesco World Heritage Site and represent the most important pre-Angkorian city in Cambodia. (p269)

New Night Buses

Night buses are a cost-effective way to travel around Cambodia: new routes include Siem Reap to Sen Monorom in Mondulkiri, via the capital Phnom Penh.

Osoam Cardamom Community Centre

This excellent community tourism project in the northern Pursat region of the Cardamom Mountains, is growing more popular with travellers for its entertaining hosts and incredible hikes. (p238)

Sunset Beach on Koh Rong Sanloem

A handful of charming accommodations and activities have quietly sprung up on the jungle-clad shores of Koh Rong Sanloem's lesser-explored western coastline. It's well worth the trek. (p208)

For more recommendations and reviews, see lonelyplanet.com/cambodia

If You Like...

Temples

Angkor Wat The mother temple that puts all others in the shade, with epic bas-reliefs and iconic *apsaras* (nymphs). (p147)

Ta Prohm The stuff of Indiana Jones fantasies, iconic tree roots are locked in a muscular embrace with ancient stones. (p159)

Prasat Preah Vihear The most mountainous of the Khmer mountain temples, perched imperiously on the cliff-face of the Dangkrek Mountains. (p262)

Angkor Thom The great walled city of Angkor with the enigmatic faces of Bayon temple at its exact centre. (p153)

Sambor Prei Kuk The first temple city in the region, recently named Cambodia's third UNESCO World Heritage Site. (p269)

Banteay Chhmar Angkor's pre-eminent king, Jayavarman VII, ran riot in this jungle backwater, erecting a clutch of temples festooned with his image. (p256)

Islands & Beaches

Koh Rong & Koh Rong Sanloem Up-and-coming islands near Sihanoukville with long and lonely white-sand beaches, plus snorkelling and diving. (p202)

Kep Cambodia's original resort, Kep offers boutique resorts, seafood specialities and the backpacker beach of Koh Tonsay (Rabbit Island). (p223)

Koh Sdach A castaway-cool archipelago with just a few authentic restaurants and stays, and some vibrant undersea life. (p211)

Sihanoukville King of the Cambodian beach resorts, with a headland ringed by squeaky white sands and azure waters. (p186)

Koh Kong Island Empty stretches of sand on practically uninhabited Koh Kong Island and a hidden lagoon. (p182)

Epicurean Experiences

Phnom Penh Dine to make a difference at one of Phnom Penh's many training restaurants to help the disadvantaged. (p66)

Siem Reap Try one of the new specialist foodie tours or browse the lively restaurants of the Old Market area. (p112)

Kep Famous for its succulent crab with Kampot pepper, sample it fresh at the the iconic Crab Market. (p223)

Battambang Discover the delights of Cambodian cooking with a cheap and cheerful cooking class in this relaxed riverside town. (p239)

Sihanoukville Sample succulent seafood at Cambodia's leading resort, including fresh fish, prawns and squid barbecued on the beach. (p195)

Water Features

Mekong Discovery Trail See rare freshwater dolphins, cycle around remote Mekong islands or experience a local family homestay. (p284)

Tonlé Sap lake Discover floating villages, bamboo skyscrapers, flooded forests and rare birdlife with a boat trip on Cambodia's Great Lake. (p127)

Boeng Yeak Lom This jungle-clad crater lake is Cambodia's most inviting natural swimming pool, located in Ratanakiri Province. (p288)

Bou Sraa Waterfall One of Cambodia's largest falls in remote Mondulkiri Province and is spanned by the breathtaking Mayura Zipline. (p296)

Tatai River Entices with sublime jungle scenery, thundering waterfalls and dreamy ecolodges nestled in the rainforest. (p181)

Markets & Shopping

Russian Market and **Psar Thmei** Phnom Penh is home to the iconic Psar Thmei and the shopping magnet that is the Russian Market. (p81; p80)

Psar Chaa and **Psar Leu** Siem Reap is a major shopping destination thanks to Psar Chaa (Old Market) and authentic Psar Leu (Main Market). (p120; p195)

Battambang's Galleries There's an emerging art scene in Battambang, with several galleries selling local artists' work. (p248)

Otres Market Sihanoukville's Otres Village hosts the weekend Otres Market, more Camden than Cambodia. (p197)

Crab Market Shopping for seafood is the name of the game and this traditional Kep seafront market does not disappoint at dawn. (p227)

Nightlife

Phnom Penh Warm up with a riverfront happy hour, bar crawl around the Bassac Lane area and end up in a nightclub. (p75)

Siem Reap There are so many bars around the Old Market that one strip has earned itself the accolade of Pub St. (p117)

Koh Rong Anything goes on the backpacker strip of Koh Tuch Beach, where – full moon or not – all-night parties are the norm. (p206)

Sihanoukville The beachfront strips of Serendipity and Ochheuteal have long been party central. (p196)

Battambang It's a mellow scene compared with party heavyweights such as Phnom Penh, but there are some atmospheric old bars. (p247)

Top: Masks at a stall in Psar Chaa (Old Market), Siem Reap (p120)

Bottom: Snorkelling off Koh Rong (p202)

Month by Month

January

This is peak tourist season in Cambodia with Phnom Penh, Siem Reap and the South Coast heaving. Chinese and Vietnamese New Years sometimes fall in this month too.

✯ Chaul Chnam Chen (Chinese New Year)

The Chinese inhabitants of Cambodia celebrate their New Year somewhere between late January and mid-February – for the Vietnamese, this is Tet. As many of Phnom Penh's businesses are run by Chinese-Khmers, commerce grinds to a halt around this time and there are dragon dances all over town.

February

Still one of the busiest times of year for tourist arrivals, February is also often the month for Chinese and Vietnamese New Years.

✯ Giant Puppet Parade

This colourful annual fundraising event (www.giantpuppetproject.com) takes place in Siem Reap. Local organisations, orphanages and businesses come together to create giant puppets in the shape of animals, deities and contemporary characters, and the whole ensemble winds its way along the Siem Reap River.

April

This is the most important month in the calendar for Khmers, as the New Year comes in the middle of April. For tourists it's a possible month to avoid, as the mercury regularly hits 40°C.

✯ Chaul Chnam Khmer (Khmer New Year)

This is a three-day celebration of the Khmer New Year. Cambodians make offerings at wats, clean out their homes and exchange gifts. It is a lively time to visit the country as the Khmers go wild with water in the countryside.

May

This is the beginning of the low season for visitors as the monsoon arrives (and lasts till October), but there may be a last blast of hot weather to welcome mango season and some delicious ripe fruits.

✯ Chat Preah Nengkal (Royal Ploughing Ceremony)

Led by the royal family, the Royal Ploughing Ceremony is a ritual agricultural festival held to mark the traditional beginning of the rice-growing season. It takes place in early May in front of the National Museum, near the Royal Palace in Phnom Penh.

TANG CHHIN SOTHY/AFP/GETTY IMAGES ©

TIM GERARD BARKER/GETTY IMAGES ©

Top: Fireworks display during Bon Om Tuk, Phnom Penh
Bottom: Giant Puppet Parade (p21), Siem Reap

✨ Visakha Puja (Buddha Day)

A celebration of Buddha's birth, enlightenment and *parinibbana* (passing). Activities are centred on wats. It falls on the eighth day of the fourth moon (May or June) and is best observed at Angkor Wat, where you can see candle-lit processions of monks.

September

Traditionally the wettest month in Cambodia, September is usually a time of sporadic flooding along the Mekong. The calendar's second most important festival, P'chum Ben, usually falls in this month.

✨ P'chum Ben (Festival of the Dead)

This festival is a kind of All Souls' Day, when respects are paid to the dead through offerings made at wats. P'chum Ben lasts for several days and devout Buddhists are expected to visit seven wats during the festival.

October

The rains often linger long into October and this has led to some major flooding in Siem Reap in recent years. However, the countryside is extraordinarily green at this time.

✨ Bon Om Tuk (Water Festival)

Celebrating the victory of Jayavarman VII over the Chams, this festival also marks the extraordinary natural phenomenon of the reversal of the current of Tonlé Sap River. It's one of the most important festivals in the Khmer calendar and is a wonderful, chaotic time to be in Phnom Penh or Siem Reap.

November

November brings the dry, windy season and signals the start of the best period to be in the country (which extends through until January or February). Bon Om Tuk often comes around in November.

✨ Angkor Photo Festival

In Siem Reap, resident and regional photographers descend on the temples and team up with local youths to teach them the tricks of the trade (www.angkor-photo.com). Photography exhibitions are staged all over town.

✨ Kampot Writers & Readers Festival

Launched in 2015, this festival (www.kampotwritersfestival.com) brings four days of literary discussions, poetry readings, art exhibitions, concerts and creative workshops to Kampot.

December

Christmas and New Year are the peak of the peak season at Angkor and leading beach resorts; book a long way ahead. Sign up for a half marathon or cycle ride if you fancy doing something for charity.

✨ Angkor Wat International Half Marathon

This half marathon (www.angkormarathon.org) has been a fixture in the Angkor calendar for more than 15 years. Choose from a 21km half marathon, a 10km fun run or various bicycle races. It's hard to imagine a better backdrop to a road race than the incredible temples of Angkor.

Plan Your Trip
Itineraries

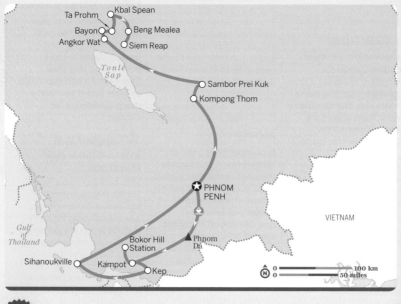

Ta Prohm
Kbal Spean
Bayon
Beng Mealea
Angkor Wat
Siem Reap
Tonle Sap
Sambor Prei Kuk
Kompong Thom
PHNOM PENH
Gulf of Thailand
VIETNAM
Bokor Hill Station
Phnom Da
Sihanoukville
Kampot
Kep
0 — 100 km
0 — 50 miles
N

2 WEEKS — The Best of Cambodia

This is the ultimate journey, via temples, beaches and the capital. It can be run in any direction, but it is best followed to the letter, starting in the capital, exploring the coastline and winding up at the world's most impressive collection of temples, Angkor.

Hit **Phnom Penh** for its impressive National Museum and stunning Silver Pagoda. It's home to the most eclectic dining scene in Cambodia, with fine-dining Khmer restaurants, an international array of eateries and some safe street-food eating. There's also superb shopping at Russian Market, and a night shift that never sleeps.

Take a fast boat to the hilltop temple of **Phnom Da**, dating from the pre-Angkorian time, and then continue south to the colonial-era town of **Kampot**, which makes a good base for this area. From here, visit the seaside town of **Kep** (and Rabbit Island, just off the coast) and nearby cave pagodas. It is also possible to make a side trip to **Bokor Hill Station** or visit a pepper plantation.

Sambor Prei Kuk (p269)

Go west to the beach town of **Sihanoukville**, the jumping-off point to explore Cambodia's idyllic islands, Koh Rong and Koh Rong Sanloem, where you can feast on seafood, dive or snorkel the nearby waters, or just relax in a hammock. Then backtrack via Phnom Penh to **Kompong Thom** and visit the pre-Angkorian brick temples of **Sambor Prei Kuk**.

Finish the trip at Angkor, a mind-blowing experience that few other sights can compare with. See **Angkor Wat**, perfection in stone; **Bayon**, weirdness in stone; and **Ta Prohm**, nature triumphing over stone – before venturing further afield to **Kbal Spean** or jungle-clad **Beng Mealea**.

Save some time for soaking up **Siem Reap**, one of the most diverse destinations in Cambodia, with a host of activities on tap. Everything from cooking classes to Vespa tours is on offer, and some of these activities are a great way to punctuate the temple tours.

This trip can take two weeks at a steady pace or three weeks at a slow pace. Public transport serves most of this route, although some of the side trips will require chartered transport or a motorbike trip.

 A Tale of Two Cities

If time is tight, focus on the big hitters of Phnom Penh and Siem Reap. With two nights in the capital and three or four nights in temple town, discover the best of modern and ancient Cambodia.

Start out in **Phnom Penh** to encounter Cambodia's contrasting history. Relive the glories of the past at the National Museum and the Royal Palace, then discover a darker past with a visit to the Tuol Sleng Genocide Museum and the Killing Fields of Choeung Ek. Explore the excellent wining-and-dining scene by night.

From the capital, hop the short flight to **Siem Reap**, or opt for the improved overland route to see more of the Cambodian countryside. Spend a couple of days touring the nearby temples of Angkor, including headline names such as **Angkor Wat**, **Bayon** and **Ta Prohm**. Allow some time to catch the support acts, like beautiful **Banteay Srei** and immense **Preah Khan**. Add some activities to the mix with a zipline experience, a quad-bike adventure or some pampering at a sumptuous spa.

If you decide to travel overland between these two cities, the months from July to December are best for this, as the landscape is lush and green.

Top: Preah Khan (p162)
Bottom: Memorial for children at Choeung Ek (p47)

4 WEEKS The Big One

Cambodia is a small country and even though the roads are sometimes bad and travel can be slow, most of the highlights can be visited in a month.

Setting out from the hip capital that is **Phnom Penh**, pass through the bustling Mekong town of **Kompong Cham** before heading on to **Kratie** for an encounter with the elusive Irrawaddy river dolphins. Then it is time to make a tricky choice to experience the beauty of the northeast. To ensure maximum time elsewhere, choose between **Ratanakiri Province** and the volcanic crater lake of Boeng Yeak Lom, or **Mondulkiri Province** and the original Elephant Valley Project. Both offer primate experiences for those who fancy a bit of monkey business along the way. If you have a bit of extra time up your sleeve, you could combine the two in a grand loop, now that the road between Sen Monorom and Ban Lung is in good shape.

Next up, head to the South Coast. Take your time and consider a few nights in **Kep** or on one of the nearby islands, and a boat trip from **Sihanoukville** to explore the up-and-coming islands off the coast. Turning back inland, check out **Kirirom National Park**, home to pine trees, black bears and some spectacular views of the Cardamom Mountains.

Then it's time to go northwest to charming **Battambang**, one of Cambodia's best-preserved colonial-era towns and a base from which to discover rural life. Take the proverbial slow boat to **Siem Reap**, passing through stunning scenery along the snaking Sangker River, and turn your attention to the **temples of Angkor**.

Visit all the greatest hits in and around Angkor, but set aside some extra time to venture further to the rival capital of **Koh Ker**, which is cloaked in thick jungle, or **Prasat Preah Vihear**, a mountain temple perched precariously atop a cliff on the Thai border.

Overlanders can run this route in reverse, setting out from Siem Reap and exiting Cambodia by river into Vietnam or Laos. Entering from Laos, divert east to Ratanakiri before heading south. Getting around is generally easy, as there are buses on the big roads, taxis on the small roads and buzzing boats on the many rivers.

Top: Koh Ker (p172)
Bottom: Irrawaddy dolphin (p281)

Off the Beaten Track: Cambodia

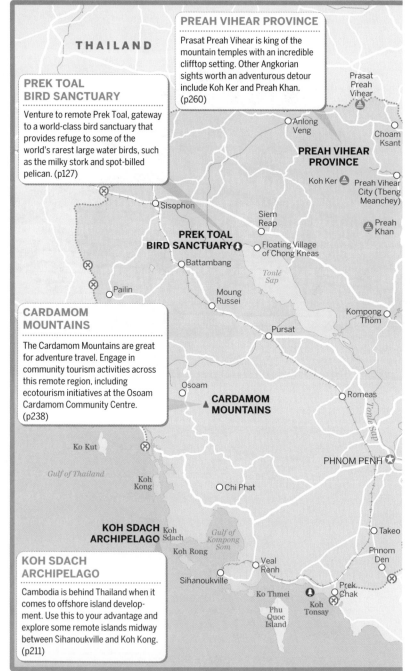

PREAH VIHEAR PROVINCE

Prasat Preah Vihear is king of the mountain temples with an incredible clifftop setting. Other Angkorian sights worth an adventurous detour include Koh Ker and Preah Khan. (p260)

PREK TOAL BIRD SANCTUARY

Venture to remote Prek Toal, gateway to a world-class bird sanctuary that provides refuge to some of the world's rarest large water birds, such as the milky stork and spot-billed pelican. (p127)

CARDAMOM MOUNTAINS

The Cardamom Mountains are great for adventure travel. Engage in community tourism activities across this remote region, including ecotourism initiatives at the Osoam Cardamom Community Centre. (p238)

KOH SDACH ARCHIPELAGO

Cambodia is behind Thailand when it comes to offshore island development. Use this to your advantage and explore some remote islands midway between Sihanoukville and Koh Kong. (p211)

THAILAND

Prasat Preah Vihear

Anlong Veng

Choam Ksant

PREAH VIHEAR PROVINCE

Koh Ker

Preah Vihear City (Tbeng Meanchey)

Sisophon

Siem Reap

Preah Khan

PREK TOAL BIRD SANCTUARY

Floating Village of Chong Kneas

Battambang

Tonlé Sap

Pailin

Moung Russei

Kompong Thom

Pursat

Osoam

CARDAMOM MOUNTAINS

Romeas

Tonlé Sap

Ko Kut

PHNOM PENH

Gulf of Thailand

Koh Kong

Chi Phat

KOH SDACH ARCHIPELAGO

Koh Sdach

Gulf of Kompong Som

Takeo

Koh Rong

Phnom Den

Veal Renh

Sihanoukville

Prek Chak

Ko Thmei

Koh Tonsay

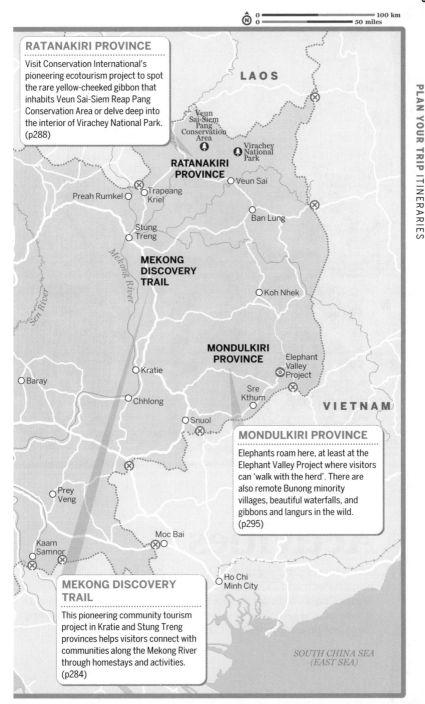

0 — 100 km
0 — 50 miles

RATANAKIRI PROVINCE

Visit Conservation International's pioneering ecotourism project to spot the rare yellow-cheeked gibbon that inhabits Veun Sai-Siem Reap Pang Conservation Area or delve deep into the interior of Virachey National Park. (p288)

MONDULKIRI PROVINCE

Elephants roam here, at least at the Elephant Valley Project where visitors can 'walk with the herd'. There are also remote Bunong minority villages, beautiful waterfalls, and gibbons and langurs in the wild. (p295)

MEKONG DISCOVERY TRAIL

This pioneering community tourism project in Kratie and Stung Treng provinces helps visitors connect with communities along the Mekong River through homestays and activities. (p284)

LAOS

VIETNAM

SOUTH CHINA SEA (EAST SEA)

Cycling tour of Angkor Thom (p153)

Plan Your Trip
Activities

Cambodia is catching up with its more-developed neighbours: Phnom Penh and Siem Reap have plenty of activities, but the South Coast offers water sports and the northeast is the place for a walk on the wild side. Whether you are hiking, biking, ascending peaks or plumbing depths, Cambodia delivers the action.

SHARPTONGUE/SHUTTERSTOCK ©

When To Go

November to February

This is the cooler dry season and the best time for strenuous activities such as trekking and cycling. Higher-altitude places like Mondulkiri and Ratanakiri are worth considering any time of year because they're always cooler, although they can get chilly at night.

March to May

The mercury regularly hits 40°C during the hot season, so this is the perfect time to cool off with some water sports such as scuba diving, stand-up paddleboarding or sailing, all on the South Coast.

June to October

The wet season is not ideal for hiking or biking due to torrential downpours and the presence of leeches in many jungle areas. However, it's a great time for boat trips and kayaking on Cambodia's extensive network of rivers.

Boat Trips

With so much water around the country, it's hardly surprising that boat trips are popular with visitors. Some of these are functional, such as travelling up the Tonlé Sap River from Phnom Penh to Siem Reap, or along the Sangker River from Siem Reap to Battambang. Particularly in the wet season, when the Mekong is in full flow and the Tonlé Sap at its maximum extent, do as the locals do and travel by boat.

Where to Go

Southern Islands Travellers can hop on boats from various launching points to explore underwater environs and islands near and far such as Koh Rong (p202), Koh Rong Sanloem (p207) and Koh Sdach (p211).

Kampot The riverside town of Kampot (p212) offers boat trips upriver to mangroves and downriver to isolated beaches and the open sea.

Mekong River The mother river flows through the heart of Cambodia and offers some rewarding opportunities for discovering tranquil islands and quiet homestays along the Mekong Discovery Trail (p284).

Tonlé Sap Lake Explore floating villages (p129), flooded forests (p130) and bird sanctuaries (p127) with a boat trip on the Great Lake.

Cycling

Cambodia is a great country for adventurous cyclists to explore. Given the country's legendary potholes, a mountain bike is the best bet. Some roads remain in poor condition, but there is usually a flat unpaved trail along the side. Travelling at such a gentle speed allows for much more interaction with the locals. Bicycles can be transported around the country on the roof of minibuses.

Cycling around Angkor is a rewarding experience as it really helps to get a measure of the size and scale of the temple complex. Mountain biking is likely to take off in Mondulkiri and Ratanakiri Provinces over the coming years, as there are some great trails. Guesthouses and hotels throughout Cambodia rent out bicycles for around US$2 per day, or US$7 to US$15 for an imported brand.

Where to Go

Battambang The beautiful countryside around Battambang (p239) is perfect for two-wheeled exploring.

Kampot Pedal along rivers, through rural landscapes and out to organic pepper farms that dot the Kampot province (p212).

Koh Dach Silk Island (p90) is the perfect place to escape the hustle and bustle of Phnom Penh on two wheels.

Mondulkiri Province The meeting of the hills is an appropriate name for this mountainous province and there are some great biking trails to Bunong villages (p296) and jungle waterfalls (p296).

Temples of Angkor The temples (p132) can get very busy in peak season, so leave the crowds behind and follow local jungle trails (p107). Organised tours available.

Dirt Biking

For experienced riders, Cambodia is one of the most rewarding off-road biking destinations in the world. The roads are generally considered some of the worst in Asia (or best in Asia for die-hard biking enthusiasts). There are incredible rides all over the country, particularly in the provinces of Preah Vihear, Mondulkiri, Ratanakiri and the Cardamom Mountains, but it is best to stay away from the main highways as traffic and dust make them a choking experience.

The advantage of motorcycle travel is that it allows for complete freedom of movement and you can stop in small villages that Westerners rarely visit. It is possible to take motorcycles upcountry for tours, but only experienced off-road bikers should take to these roads with a dirt bike.

Motorcycles are available for hire in most popular tourist destinations. Costs are US$5 to US$10 per day for a 100cc motorcycle and around US$10 to US$25 for a 250cc dirt bike.

Where to Go

Cardamom Mountains Not for the faint-hearted, the Cardamom Mountains offer some tough jungle

---

QUAD BIKING

Quad bikes or ATVs are growing in popularity in Cambodia thanks to the prevalence of dirt roads across the country. Siem Reap has three operators (p102) offering countryside tours around temple town. Phnom Penh has one quad-bike outfit (p59), which offers a very different experience to city life. Prices for quad biking range from US$25 per hour to more than US$100 for a full-day adventure.

---

trails north to Pailin or Pursat. Seek an experienced operator (p238).

Kampot The landscapes around Kampot include rice fields, salt pans, pepper farms, karst peaks and Bokor Hill Station (p221).

Mondulkiri Province The rolling hills of Mondulkiri are perfect for dirt biking, and include the stunning road that follows the Seima Protected Forest (p302) to Sen Monorom.

Preah Vihear Province Get your kicks on Cambodia's Route 66 (NH66), which runs from Beng Mealea (p168) to the remote temple of Preah Khan (p162). Or ascend to the realm of the gods at Prasat Preah Vihear (p262).

Trekking & Walking

Trekking is not the first activity most people would associate with Cambodia, due to the ongoing presence of land mines, but there are plenty of safe areas in the country – including the nascent national parks – where walking can be enjoyed. The northeastern provinces of Mondulkiri and Ratanakiri, with their wild, natural scenery, abundant waterfalls and ethnic-minority populations, are emerging as the country's leading trekking destinations.

Cambodia has an established network of national parks with visitor facilities; Bokor National Park, Kirirom National Park and Ream National Park all offer day trekking potential, while Virachey National Park in Ratanakiri has multiday treks. Chi Phat and the Cardamom Mountains also offer the possibility of a walk on the wild side.

Angkor is emerging as a good place for gentle walks between the temples; as visitor numbers skyrocket, this is one way to experience peace and solitude.

Where to Go

Koh Kong Province Coastal gateway to the Cardamoms, Koh Kong has several trekking companies offering jungle treks around Tatai (p181).

Mondulkiri Province One of the most rewarding trekking destinations in Cambodia thanks to cooler climes, Bunong minority encounters (p299) and thundering waterfalls, not to mention tracking elephants (p297) or gibbons (p302).

Ratanakiri Province Choose from gentle treks to ethnic-minority villages or hard-core treks into the heart of Virachey National Park (p294).

Red-shanked doucs

Water Sports

Snorkelling and diving are available off the coast of Sihanoukville, and while the underwater scenery may not be as spectacular as in Indonesia or the Philippines, there is still plenty out there in the deep blue yonder. It's best to venture to the more remote dive sites, such as Koh Tang and Koh Prins, staying overnight on a boat. There are many unexplored areas off the coast between Koh Kong and Sihanoukville that could one day put Cambodia on the dive map of Asia.

As the Cambodian coast takes off, there are more water sports available, including boating, windsurfing and kitesurfing off the beaches of Sihanoukville. In Kampot, stand-up paddleboarding has taken off in a big way and it's a great way to appreciate the river scenery.

Where to Go

Kep Hit the waterfront Sailing Club (p225) to rent a hobie cat sailing boat or windsurfer to explore the calm waters off the coast.

ZIPLINING IN CAMBODIA

Ziplining has recently taken off in Cambodia. Angkor Zipline (p162) offers the longest zipline course in the country with 10 lines and the chance to spot some gibbons in the wild. Mayura Zipline (p296) is a new adrenaline-fuelled adventure above the Bou Sraa Waterfall in Mondulkiri Province. There is also a zipline on Koh Rong (p204) if you need more than a beach buzz, and a super-scenic and affordable canopy tour at BeTreed Adventures (p269) near Preah Khan of Kompong Svay. Ziplining doesn't come cheap though – Angkor Zipline charges around US$99 per person and the Mayura Zipline around US$69 per person.

Temples of Angkor From a base in Siem Reap, explore Angkor Thom (p153) on foot or ascend to the River of a Thousand Lingas at Kbal Spean (p170).

ROCK CLIMBING

Rock climbing is very much in its infancy compared with neighbouring Laos, Thailand and Vietnam, but there is a climbing outfit down in Kampot Province where the landscape is peppered with karst outcrops. Climbodia (p213) offers cabled routes up Phnom Kbal Romeas, about 5km south of Kampot town, from US$35 for a half day.

Kampot Explore the river and mangrove channels on a stand-up paddleboard (p213), or laze around in an inner tube if that sounds like too much hard work.

Sihanoukville Water sports capital (p188) of Cambodia; choose from diving, snorkelling, windsurfing, wake-boarding, jet skiing and more.

Southern Islands Koh Rong (p202) and Koh Rong Sanloem (p207) provide an up-and-coming base for serious divers wanting some big-fish action.

Wildlife Spotting

Cambodia is home to rich and varied wildlife that has somehow survived the dramatic events that engulfed the country in the past decades. Big cats, small cats, elephants, primates and some curious critters all call the Cambodian jungle their home, and it's possible to see them across the country. Birdwatching is a big draw, as the country is home to some of the region's rarest large waterbirds, including adjutants, storks and pelicans.

Where to Go

Kratie Province Extremely rare freshwater river dolphins inhabit stretches of the Mekong River between Kratie (p281) and the Laos border.

Mondulkiri Province Walk with the herd at Elephant Valley Project (p297) or spot gibbons and doucs in the Seima Protected Forest (p302).

Phnom Tamao Wildlife Rescue Centre So much more than a zoo, this wildlife sanctuary (p93) offers behind-the-scenes tours to meet the animals.

Prek Toal Bird Sanctuary Cambodia's world-class bird sanctuary (p127); see rare waterbirds like the spot-billed pelican, black-headed ibis and painted stork.

Ratanakiri Province This remote jungle province is home to a pioneering gibbon-spotting project (p290).

Siem Reap Visit the Angkor Centre for Conservation of Biodiversity (p126), where rare animals, including the giant ibis, pangolin, silvery langur and leopard cat, can be seen.

Regions at a Glance

Phnom Penh, Cambodia's resurgent capital, is the place to check the pulse of contemporary life. Siem Reap, gateway to the majestic temples of Angkor, is starting to give the capital a run for its money with sophisticated restaurants, funky bars and chic boutiques. World Heritage Site Angkor houses some of the most spectacular temples on earth.

Down on the South Coast are several up-and-coming beach resorts and a smattering of tropical islands that are just beginning to take off, unlike those of neighbouring countries. Northwestern Cambodia is home to Battambang, a slice of more traditional life, and several remote jungle temples. The country's wild east is where elephants roam, waterfalls thunder and freshwater dolphins can be found.

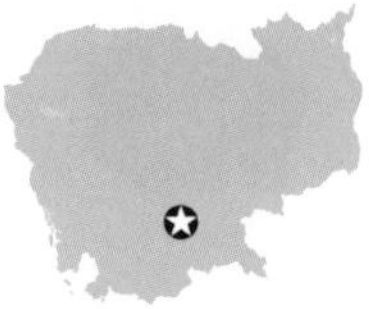

Phnom Penh

Shopping
Dining
Bars

Chic Boutiques

Choose from colourful local markets where bargains abound or check out the impressive collections of local designers. There are plenty of good-cause shops where your spending assists Cambodia.

Creative Cuisine

French bistros abound, and outstanding fusion restaurants blend the best of Cambodian and European flavours. Ubiquitous Cambodian barbecues offer a local experience, or try gourmet Khmer cuisine in a designer restaurant.

Happy Hour

Get started early in a breezy establishment overlooking the Mekong, move on to a live-music bar, and dance till dawn in a club. Phnom Penh is 24/7, one of the liveliest capitals in Asia.

p40

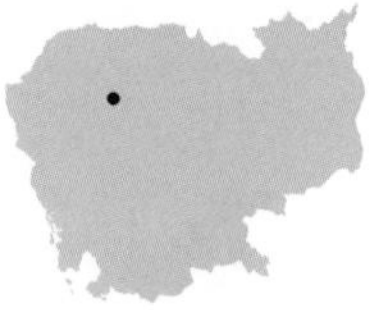

Siem Reap

Activities
Temples
Dining

Adventures Beyond Angkor

Take to the skies by helicopter to see Angkor from a different angle. Zipline through the jungle or quad bike through rice fields. Experience a cooking class or unwind with a massage.

Divine Inspiration

It's not just all about Angkor Wat. True, it's one of the world's most iconic buildings, but down the road are the enigmatic faces of the Bayon and the jungle temple of Ta Prohm.

Eclectic Epicurian Experiences

Contemporary Khmer cuisine, spiced-up street food, fine French dining and more: Siem Reap is a dining destination in itself. Continue the night along Pub St and the gentrified lanes beyond.

p96

South Coast

Activities
Dining
Beaches

Land or Sea

National parks and protected areas dot the region, offering trekking, mountain biking, kayaking, rock climbing and kitesurfing. Water sports abound or venture underwater to experience snorkelling or scuba diving.

Seafood Specialities

Each coastal town has its speciality. In Kep, it's delectable crab. In Takeo, it's river lobster. In Kampot, it's anything cooked with the region's famous pepper. Sihanoukville offers a seafood extravaganza.

Tropical Bliss

Claim a strip of sand all to yourself or relax in a beachfront bar. Choose life in the fast lane in Sihanoukville, the slow lane in Kep or forget the roads altogether and escape to the islands.

p175

Northwestern Cambodia

Temples
Boat Trips
Towns

Beyond the Crowds

Heard enough about Angkor Wat? Don't forget the pre-Angkorian capital of Sambor Prei Kuk, the jungle temples of Preah Vihear Province and atmospheric Banteay Chhmar.

Floating Villages

One of the best boat rides in Cambodia links Battambang to Siem Reap following the Sangker River. Explore the largest floating village on the Tonlé Sap lake, Kompong Luong.

The Real Cambodia

Riverside Battambang has some of the country's best-preserved French architecture, while Kompong Chhnang and Kompong Thom are off the tourist trail and offer a slice of real Cambodia.

p231

Eastern Cambodia

Culture
River Life
Wildlife

A World Apart

Northeast Cambodia is home to a mosaic of ethnic minorities. Encounter the Bunong people of Mondulkiri or venture up jungle rivers to visit the remote tribal cemeteries in Ratanakiri.

The Mighty Mekong

The Mekong cuts through the region's heart and includes the Mekong Discovery Trail, a community-based tourism initiative. Beyond the Mekong is the Tonlé Srepok tributary, as depicted in *Apocalypse Now*.

The Wild Things

View rare freshwater dolphins around Kratie, walk with a herd of elephants in Mondulkiri or spot primates in community-based forest treks around Mondulkiri or Ratanakiri.

p272

On the Road

Temples of Angkor
p132

Siem Reap
p96

Northwestern Cambodia
p231

Eastern Cambodia
p272

Phnom Penh
p40

South Coast
p175

Phnom Penh

📞 023 / POP 2 MILLION

Best Places to Eat

➡ Boat Noodle (p70)
➡ Le Bouchon (p69)
➡ Malis (p72)
➡ Romdeng (p68)
➡ Sovanna II (p73)

Best Places to Stay

➡ Eighty8 Backpackers (p61)
➡ Mad Monkey (p65)
➡ Palace Gate Hotel (p64)
➡ Pavilion (p65)
➡ Raffles Hotel Le Royal (p64)

Why Go?

Phnom Penh (ភ្នំពេញ): the name can't help but conjure up an image of the exotic. The glimmering spires of the Royal Palace, the fluttering saffron of the monks' robes and the luscious location on the banks of the mighty Mekong – this is the Asia many daydream about from afar.

Cambodia's capital can be an assault on the senses. Motorbikes whiz through laneways without a thought for pedestrians; markets exude pungent scents; and all the while the sounds of life – of commerce, of survival – reverberate through the streets. But this is all part of the enigma.

Once the 'Pearl of Asia', Phnom Penh's shine was tarnished by the impact of war and revolution. But the city has since risen from the ashes to take its place among the hip capitals of the region, with an alluring cafe culture, bustling bars and a world-class food scene.

When to Go
Phnom Penh

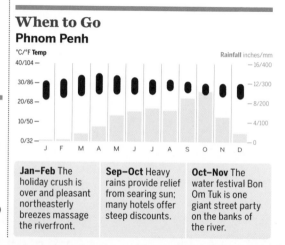

Jan–Feb The holiday crush is over and pleasant northeasterly breezes massage the riverfront.

Sep–Oct Heavy rains provide relief from searing sun; many hotels offer steep discounts.

Oct–Nov The water festival Bon Om Tuk is one giant street party on the banks of the river.

PHNOM PENH

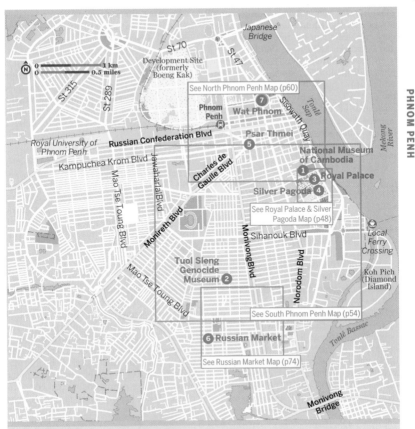

Phnom Penh Highlights

1 National Museum of Cambodia (p43) Discovering the world's finest collection of Khmer sculpture.

2 Tuol Sleng Genocide Museum (p46) Delving into the dark side of Cambodian history here and at the Killing Fields of Choeung Ek.

3 Royal Palace (p42) Exploring the striking official residence of King Sihamoni.

4 Silver Pagoda (p43) Being dazzled by the 5000 silver floor tiles, part of the Royal Palace complex.

5 Nightlife (p76) Diving into Phnom Penh's frenzied nightlife with a happy-hour cocktail at FCC, a bar crawl on Bassac Lane and a late-night cameo in one of the city's happening clubs.

6 Psar Thmei (p80)

Browsing the iconic domed Central Market, a striking 1937 building designed like a Babylonian ziggurat.

7 Russian Market (p81) Shopping till you drop (of heat exhaustion) at this bounteous market.

8 Wat Phnom (p47) Praying for luck during your trip, should you need it, at this historic hilltop temple.

History

Legend has it that the city of Phnom Penh was founded when an old woman named Penh found four Buddha images that had come to rest on the banks of the Mekong River. She housed them on a nearby hill, and the town that grew up here came to be known as Phnom Penh (Hill of Penh).

In the 1430s, Angkor was abandoned and Phnom Penh chosen as the site of the new Cambodian capital. Angkor was poorly situated for trade and subject to attacks from the Siamese (Thai) kingdom of Ayuthaya.

Phnom Penh commanded a more central position in the Khmer territories and was perfectly located for riverine trade with Laos and China via the Mekong Delta.

By the mid-16th century, trade had turned Phnom Penh into a regional power. Indonesian and Chinese traders were drawn to the city in large numbers. A century later, however, the landlocked and increasingly isolated kingdom had become little more than a buffer between the ascendant Thais and Vietnamese, until the French took over in 1863.

The French protectorate in Cambodia gave Phnom Penh the layout we know today. They divided the city into districts or *quartiers* – the French and European traders inhabited the area north of Wat Phnom between Monivong Blvd and Tonlé Sap. By the time the French departed in 1953, they had left many important landmarks, including the Royal Palace, the National Museum, Psar Thmei (Central Market) and many impressive government ministries.

The city grew fast in the post-independence peacetime years of Norodom Sihanouk's rule: by the time he was overthrown in 1970, the population of Phnom Penh was approximately 500,000. As the Vietnam War spread into Cambodian territory, the city's population swelled with refugees and reached nearly three million in early 1975. The Khmer Rouge took the city on 17 April 1975, and as part of its radical revolution immediately forced the entire population into the countryside. Whole families were split up on those first fateful days of 'liberation'.

During the time of Democratic Kampuchea, many tens of thousands of former Phnom Penhois – including the vast majority of the capital's educated residents – were killed. The population of Phnom Penh during the Khmer Rouge regime was never more than about 50,000, a figure made up of senior party members, factory workers and trusted military leaders.

Repopulation of the city began when the Vietnamese arrived in 1979, although at first it was strictly controlled by the new government. During much of the 1980s, cows were more common than cars on the streets of the capital. The 1990s were boom years for some: along with the arrival of the UN Transitional Authority in Cambodia (Untac) came US$2 billion (much of it in salaries for expats).

Phnom Penh has really begun to change in the last two decades, with roads being repaired, sewage pipes laid, parks inaugurated and riverbanks reclaimed. Business is booming in many parts of the city, with skyscrapers under development, investors rubbing their hands with the sort of glee once reserved for Bangkok or Hanoi, and swanky new restaurants opening. Phnom Penh is back, and bigger changes are set to come.

◉ Sights

A relatively small city, Phnom Penh is easy to navigate as it is laid out in a numbered grid. The most important cultural sights can be visited on foot and are located near the riverfront in the most attractive part of the city. Most other sights are also fairly central, just a short *remork-moto (tuk tuk)* ride from the riverfront.

★ **Royal Palace** PALACE
(ព្រះបរមរាជវាំង; Map p48; Samdech Sothearos Blvd; admission incl camera 40,000r, guide per hour US$10; ⊙ 7.30-11am & 2-5pm) With its classic Khmer roofs and ornate gilding, the Royal Palace dominates the diminutive skyline of Phnom Penh. It's a striking structure near the riverfront, bearing a remarkable likeness to its counterpart in Bangkok. Being the official residence of King Sihamoni, parts of the massive palace compound are closed to the public. The adjacent Silver Pagoda is open to visitors.

Visitors are allowed to visit only the throne hall and a clutch of buildings surrounding it. Visitors need to wear shorts that reach to the knee, and T-shirts or blouses that reach to the elbow; otherwise they will have to buy an appropriate sarong as a covering at the ticket booth. The palace gets very busy on Sundays, when countryside Khmers come to pay their respects, but being among crowds of locals can be a fun way to experience the place.

Visitors enter into the eastern portion of the palace compound near the **Chan Chaya Pavilion**. Performances of classical Cambodian dance were once staged in this pavilion, which is still sometimes lit up at night to commemorate festivals or anniversaries.

The main attraction in the palace compound is the **Throne Hall**, topped by a 59m-high tower inspired by the Bayon at Angkor. The Throne Hall is used for coronations and ceremonies such as the presentation of credentials by diplomats. Many of the

PHNOM PENH IN TWO DAYS

Start early to observe the aerobics sessions on the riverfront, then grab breakfast before venturing into the **Royal Palace** (p42). Next is the **National Museum of Cambodia** (p43) and the world's most wondrous collection of Khmer sculpture. After lunch at **Friends** (p68) restaurant, check out the funky architecture of **Psar Thmei** (p80), but save the serious shopping for the **Russian Market** (p81). Celebrate your shopping coups with a riverside happy-hour drink at **FCC** (p76), and then a night out on the town.

Start day two with a **Khmer Architecture Tours** (p58) walking tour of the centre, or just wander around **Wat Phnom** (p47), where Khmers pray for luck. Have lunch on the riverside, then visit the sobering **Tuol Sleng museum** (p46) before continuing on to the **Killing Fields of Choeung Ek** (p47). It is a grim afternoon, but essential for understanding just how far Cambodia has come in the intervening years. Wind up your weekend with a **sunset cruise** on the Mekong River, offering a beautiful view over the Royal Palace.

items once displayed here were destroyed by the Khmer Rouge.

South of the Throne Hall, check out the curious iron **Napoleon III Pavilion**. Given to King Norodom by Napoleon III of France, it was hardly designed with the Cambodian climate in mind.

★ Silver Pagoda   BUDDHIST TEMPLE
(ព្រះវិហារព្រះកែវមរកត; Map p48; Royal Palace compound; incl in admission to Royal Palace; ☺7.30-11am & 2-5pm) Within the Royal Palace compound is the extravagant Silver Pagoda, also known as Wat Preah Keo or Temple of the Emerald Buddha. It is so named for its floor, which is covered with five tons of gleaming silver. You can sneak a peek at some of the 5000 tiles near the entrance, but most are covered to protect them.

The staircase leading to the Silver Pagoda is made of Italian marble. Rivalling the silver floor is the Emerald Buddha, an extraordinary Baccarat-crystal sculpture sitting atop an impressive gilded pedestal. Adding to the lavish mix is a life-sized solid-gold Buddha adorned with 2086 diamonds, the largest weighing in at 25 carats. Created in the palace workshops during 1906 and 1907, the gold Buddha weighs 90kg. Directly in front of it, in a Formica case, is a miniature silver-and-gold stupa containing a relic of Buddha brought from Sri Lanka. To the left is an 80kg bronze Buddha, and to the right a silver Buddha. On the far right, figurines of solid gold tell the story of the Buddha.

The pagoda was originally constructed of wood in 1892 during the rule of King Norodom, who was apparently inspired by Bangkok's Wat Phra Kaew, and was rebuilt in 1962. It was preserved by the Khmer Rouge to demonstrate to the outside world its concern for the conservation of Cambodia's cultural riches. Although more than half of the pagoda's contents were lost, stolen or destroyed in the turmoil that followed the Vietnamese invasion, what remains is spectacular. This is one of the few places in Cambodia where bejewelled objects embodying some of the brilliance and richness of Khmer civilisation can still be seen.

Along the walls of the pagoda are examples of extraordinary Khmer artisanship, including intricate masks used in classical dance and dozens of gold Buddhas. The many precious gifts given to Cambodia's monarchs by foreign heads of state appear rather spiritless when displayed next to such diverse and exuberant Khmer art. (Note that photography is not permitted inside the Silver Pagoda.)

Ramayana Mural   PUBLIC ART
(Map p48; Royal Palace compound) The Silver Pagoda complex is enclosed by walls plastered with an extensive and, in parts, spectacular mural depicting the classic Indian epic of the *Ramayana* (known as the *Reamker* in Cambodia). The story begins just south of the east gate and includes vivid images of the battle of Lanka. The mural was created around 1900 and parts of it have recently undergone restoration.

★ National Museum of Cambodia   MUSEUM
(សារមន្ទីរជាតិ; Map p60; www.cambodiamuseum.info; cnr Sts 13 & 178; US$10; ☺8am-5pm) Located just north of the Royal Palace, the National Museum of Cambodia is housed in a graceful terracotta structure of traditional design (built from 1917 to 1920), with

Greater Phnom Penh

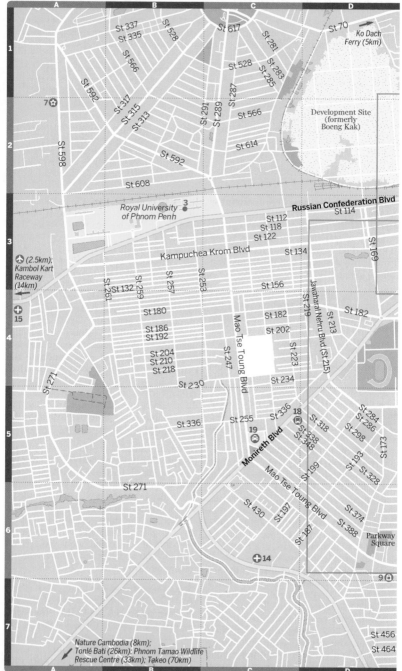

St 337
St 335
St 528
St 617
St 70
Ko Dach
Ferry (5km)
St 528
St 281
St 283
St 566
St 285
St 592
St 287
St 291
St 289
St 566
Development Site
(formerly
Boeng Kak)
St 317
St 315
St 313
7
St 614
St 592
St 598
St 608

St 112
St 118
St 122
Russian Confederation Blvd
St 114
Royal University
of Phnom Penh
3
St 169
Kampuchea Krom Blvd
St 134
(2.5km);
Kambol Kart
Raceway
(14km)
St 261
St 132
St 259
St 257
St 253
St 156
St 180
St 182
Jawaharal Nehru Blvd (St 215)
St 182
15
St 219
St 213
St 186
St 192
St 202
Mao Tse Toung Blvd
St 271
St 204
St 210
St 218
St 247
St 223
St 230
St 234
St 284
St 286
St 298
St 336
18
St 255
St 318
St 173
St 336
19
St 338
St 348
St 193
St 328
Monireth Blvd
St 199
Mao Tse Toung Blvd
St 374
St 271
St 430
St 197
St 388
Parkway
Square
14
St 187
9
Nature Cambodia (8km);
Tonlé Bati (26km); Phnom Tamao Wildlife
Rescue Centre (33km); Takeo (70km)
St 456
St 464

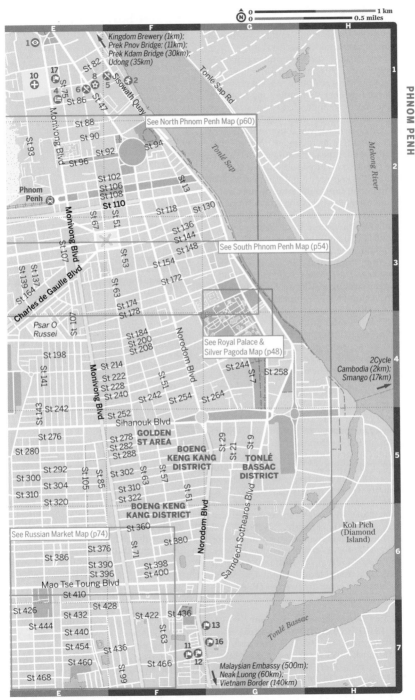

0 _____ 1 km
0 _____ 0.5 miles

Kingdom Brewery (1km);
Prek Pnov Bridge; (11km);
Prek Kdam Bridge (30km);
Udong (35km)

Tonlé Sap Rd

Mekong River

Sisowath Quay

St 82
St 86   St 47
St 75
St 88
St 90
St 96   St 92
St 94

Tonlé Sap

Monivong Blvd

St 93

Phnom
Penh

St 102
St 106
St 108
St 110
St 67   St 51

St 13
St 118   St 130

See North Phnom Penh Map (p60)

St 137
St 139
St 164

Charles de Gaulle Blvd

St 107

St 53
St 63

St 136
St 144
St 148
St 154
St 172

See South Phnom Penh Map (p54)

St 174
St 178

Norodom Blvd

St 184
St 200
St 208

St 102
St 51

Psar O
Russei

St 198

St 214
St 222
St 228
St 240
St 242   St 254
St 252

St 244   St 258

See Royal Palace &
Silver Pagoda Map (p48)

2Cycle
Cambodia (2km);
Smango (17km)

St 141
St 242

Monivong Blvd

St 141

St 51
St 7

Sihanouk Blvd
GOLDEN
ST AREA
St 278
St 282
St 288

St 276
St 280

BOENG
KENG KANG
DISTRICT

St 29
St 21
St 9

TONLÉ
BASSAC
DISTRICT

St 292
St 300   St 304
St 310   St 320

St 105
St 85

St 302
St 310
St 322

St 63
St 57
St 51

BOENG KENG
KANG DISTRICT

Samdech Sothearos Blvd

Koh Pich
(Diamond
Island)

See Russian Market Map (p74)

St 360

St 376
St 386

St 390
St 396

St 71

St 380

St 398
St 400

Norodom Blvd

Mao Tse Toung Blvd
St 410

St 426
St 444

St 432
St 440
St 454
St 460

St 428

St 422   St 436

St 63

St 436

St 466

St 468

St 99

Tonlé Bassac

13
16
11
12

Malaysian Embassy (500m);
Neak Luong (60km);
Vietnam Border (140km)

an inviting courtyard garden. The museum is home to the world's finest collection of Khmer sculpture: a millennium's worth and more of masterful Khmer design.

Most visitors start left and continue in a clockwise, chronological direction. The first significant sculpture to greet visitors is a large fragment – including the relatively intact head, shoulders and two arms – of an immense bronze reclining Vishnu statue, which was recovered from the Western Mebon temple near Angkor Wat in 1936. Continue into the southern pavilion, where the pre-Angkorian collection begins, illustrating the journey from the human form of Indian sculpture to the more divine form of Khmer sculpture from the 5th to 8th centuries. Highlights include an imposing, eight-armed Vishnu statue from the 6th century found at Phnom Da, and a staring Harihara, combining the attributes of Shiva and Vishnu, from Prasat Andet in Kompong Thom Province. The Angkor collection includes several striking statues of Shiva from the 9th, 10th and 11th centuries; a giant pair of wrestling monkeys (Koh Ker, 10th century); a beautiful 12th-century stele (stone) from Oddar Meanchey Province inscribed with scenes from the life of Shiva; and the sublime statue of a seated Jayavarman VII (r 1181–1219), his head bowed slightly in a meditative pose (Angkor Thom, late 12th century).

The museum also contains displays of pottery and bronzes dating from the pre-Angkorian periods of Funan and Chenla (4th to 9th centuries), the Indravarman period (9th and 10th centuries) and the classical Angkorian period (10th to 14th centuries), as well as more recent works, such as a beautiful wooden royal barge.

Note that visitors are not allowed to photograph the collection, only the central courtyard. English-, French- and Japanese-speaking guides are available for tours (US$6). A comprehensive booklet, *The New Guide to the National Museum* (US$10), is available at the front desk, while the smaller *Khmer Art in Stone* (US$2) covers some signature pieces.

★ **Tuol Sleng Genocide Museum** MUSEUM (សារមន្ទីរប្រល័យពូជសាសន៍; Map p54; www. tuolsleng.gov.kh; cnr Sts 113 & 350; adult/child US$5/3, guide US$6, audio tour US$3; ⊙8am-5pm) In 1975, Tuol Svay Prey High School was taken over by Pol Pot's security forces and turned into a prison known as Security

Greater Phnom Penh

Prison 21 (S-21); it soon became the largest centre of detention and torture in the country. S-21 has been turned into the Tuol Sleng museum, which serves as a testament to the crimes of the Khmer Rouge.

Between 1975 and 1978 more than 17,000 people held at S-21 were taken to the killing fields of Choeung Ek. Like the Nazis, the Khmer Rouge leaders were meticulous in keeping records of their barbarism. Each prisoner who passed through S-21 was photographed, sometimes before and after torture. The museum displays include room after room of harrowing B&W photographs; virtually all of the men, women and children pictured were later killed. You can tell which year a picture was taken by the style of number-board that appears on the prisoner's chest. Several foreigners from Australia, New Zealand and the USA were also held at S-21 before being murdered. It's worth hiring a guide, as they can tell you the stories behind some of the people in the photographs. A new audio tour is also available, and recommended for greater insight for visitors without a guide.

As the Khmer Rouge 'revolution' reached ever greater heights of insanity, it began devouring its own. Generations of torturers and executioners who worked here were in turn killed by those who took their places. During early 1977, when the party purges of Eastern Zone cadres were getting under way, S-21 claimed an average of 100 victims a day.

When the Vietnamese army liberated Phnom Penh in early 1979, there were only seven prisoners alive at S-21, all of whom had used their skills, such as painting or photography, to stay alive. Fourteen others had been tortured to death as Vietnamese forces were closing in on the city. Photographs of their gruesome deaths are on display in the rooms where their decomposing corpses were found. Their graves are nearby in the courtyard. Two of the survivors, Chum Mey and Bou Meng, are still alive, and often spend their time at S-21 promoting their first-hand accounts of their time in the prison.

A visit to Tuol Sleng is a profoundly depressing experience. The sheer ordinariness of the place makes it even more horrific: the suburban setting, the plain school buildings, the grassy playing area where children kick around balls juxtaposed with rusted beds, instruments of torture and wall after wall of disturbing portraits. It demonstrates the darkest side of the human spirit that lurks within us all. Tuol Sleng is not for the squeamish.

Behind many of the displays at Tuol Sleng is the **Documentation Center of Cambodia** (DC-Cam; Map p54; www.dccam.org; Sihanouk Blvd). DC-Cam was established in 1995 through Yale University's Cambodian Genocide Program to research and document the crimes of the Khmer Rouge. It became an independent organisation in 1997 and researchers have spent years translating confessions and paperwork from Tuol Sleng, mapping mass graves, and preserving evidence of Khmer Rouge crimes.

French-Cambodian director Rithy Panh's film *The Khmer Rouge Killing Machine* includes interviews with former prison guards, including chief interrogator Him Huy, and is shown daily at 9.30am. Another Khmer Rouge documentary, *Behind the Wall,* screens at 3.45pm daily.

Killing Fields of Choeung Ek   MEMORIAL

(វាលពិឃាតជើងឯក; admission incl audio tour US$6; ⊙7.30am-5.30pm) Between 1975 and 1978 about 17,000 men, women, children and infants who had been detained and tortured at S-21 were transported to the extermination camp of Choeung Ek. It is a peaceful place today, where visitors can learn of the horrors that unfolded here decades ago.

Admission to the Killing Fields includes an excellent audio tour, available in several languages.

The remains of 8985 people, many of whom were bound and blindfolded, were exhumed in 1980 from mass graves in this one-time longan orchard; 43 of the 129 communal graves here have been left untouched. Fragments of human bone and bits of cloth are scattered around the disinterred pits. More than 8000 skulls, arranged by sex and age, are visible behind the clear glass panels of the Memorial Stupa, which was erected in 1988.

The audio tour includes stories by those who survived the Khmer Rouge, plus a chilling account by Him Huy, a Choeung Ek guard and executioner, about some of the techniques they used to kill innocent and defenceless prisoners, including women and children. There's also a **museum** here with some interesting information on the Khmer Rouge leadership and the ongoing trial. A **memorial ceremony** is held annually at Choeung Ek on 9 May.

The site is well signposted in English about 7.5km south of the city limits. Figure on about US$10 for a *remork* (drivers may ask for more) for a half day. A shuttle-bus tour is available with Phnom Penh Hop On Hop Off (p88), which includes hotel pick-up from 8am in the morning or 1.30pm in the afternoon.

Wat Phnom   BUDDHIST TEMPLE

(វត្តភ្នំ; Map p60; Norodom Blvd; temple US$1, museum US$2; ⊙7am-6.30pm, museum 7am-6pm) Set on top of a 27m-high tree-covered knoll, Wat Phnom is on the only 'hill' in town. According to legend, the first pagoda on this site was erected in 1372 to house four statues of Buddha deposited here by the waters of the Mekong River and discovered by Lady Penh. Hence the city name Phnom Penh or 'hill of Penh'.

Royal Palace & Silver Pagoda

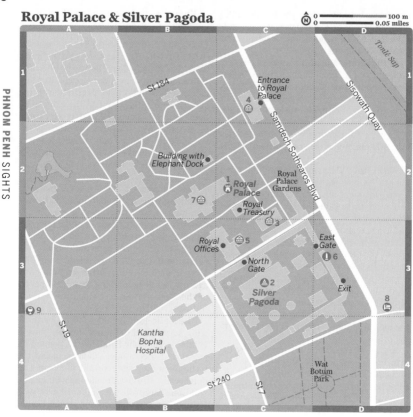

Royal Palace & Silver Pagoda

The main entrance to Wat Phnom is via the grand eastern staircase, which is guarded by lions and *naga* (mythical serpent) balustrades. Today, many people come here to pray for good luck and success in school exams or business affairs. When a wish is granted, the faithful return to deliver on the offering promised, such as a garland of jasmine flowers or a bunch of bananas (of which the spirits are said to be especially fond).

The *vihara* (temple sanctuary) was rebuilt in 1434, 1806, 1894 and 1926. West of the *vihara* is a huge stupa containing the ashes of King Ponhea Yat (r 1405–67). In a pavilion on the southern side of the passage between the *vihara* and the stupa is a statue of a smiling Lady Penh.

A bit to the north of and below the *vihara* is an eclectic shrine dedicated to the genie Preah Chau, who is especially revered by the Vietnamese. On either side of the entrance to the central altar are guardian spirits bearing iron bats. In the chamber to the right of the statue are drawings of Confucius, as well as two Chinese-style figures of the sages

Thang Cheng (on the right) and Thang Thay (on the left).

Down the hill from the *vihara,* in the northwest corner of the complex, is a **museum** with some old statues and historical artefacts, which you can definitely skip if you've been to the impressive National Museum.

Be aware that Wat Phnom can be a bit of a circus, with beggars, street urchins, women selling drinks and children selling birds in cages. You pay to set the bird free, but the birds are trained to return to their cage afterwards.

Independence Monument MONUMENT

(វិមានឯករាជ្យ; Map p54; cnr Norodom & Sihanouk Blvds) FREE Modelled on the central tower of Angkor Wat, Independence Monument was built in 1958 to commemorate the country's independence from France in 1953. It also serves as a memorial to Cambodia's war dead. Wreaths are laid here on national holidays.

Norodom Sihanouk Statue MEMORIAL

(រូបសំណាកព្រះបរមរតនកោដ្ឋ; Map p54; Sihanouk Blvd) In the park just east of Independence Monument is an impressive statue of the legendary former king/prime minister/statesman King Father Norodom Sihanouk, who died a national hero in 2012.

Wat Ounalom BUDDHIST TEMPLE

(វត្តឧណ្ណាលោម; Map p60; Samdech Sothearos Blvd; ⊙6am-6pm) FREE This wat is the headquarters of Cambodian Buddhism. It was founded in 1443 and comprises 44 structures. It received a battering during the Pol Pot era, but today the wat has come back to life. The head of the country's Buddhist brotherhood lives here, along with a large number of monks.

On the 2nd floor of the main building, to the left of the dais, is a statue of Huot Tat, fourth patriarch of Cambodian Buddhism, who was killed by Pol Pot. The statue, made in 1971 when the patriarch was 80 years old, was thrown into the Mekong by the Khmer Rouge to show that Buddhism was no longer the driving force in Cambodia. It was retrieved after 1979. To the right of the dais is a statue of a former patriarch of the Thummayuth sect, to which the royal family belongs.

Seek out the stairway to the left behind the dais. It leads up to the 3rd floor, where a glass case houses a small marble Buddha of Burmese origin that was broken into pieces by the Khmer Rouge and later reassembled. There are some nice views of the Mekong from up here.

Behind the main building is a stupa containing an eyebrow hair of Buddha with an inscription in Pali (an ancient Indian language) over the entrance.

Olympic Stadium LANDMARK

(ពហុកីឡដ្ឋានជាតិអូរំពិក; Map p54; Monireth Blvd; ⊙6am-10pm) FREE Known collectively as the National Sports Complex, the Olympic Stadium is a striking example of 1960s 'New Khmer' architecture and includes a sports arena and facilities for boxing, gymnastics, volleyball and other sports. Turn up after 5pm to see countless football matches, *pétanque* duels or badminton games. It's also a popular spot for sunrise or sunset mass musical aerobics.

French Embassy LANDMARK

(Map p44; 1 Monivong Blvd) Located at the northern end of Monivong Blvd, the French embassy played a significant role in the dramas that unfolded after the fall of Phnom Penh on 17 April 1975. About 800 foreigners and 600 Cambodians took refuge in the embassy. Within 48 hours, the Khmer Rouge informed the French vice-consul that they did not recognise diplomatic privileges – and if the Cambodians in the compound were not handed over, the lives of the foreigners inside would also be forfeited.

Cambodian women married to foreigners could stay; Cambodian men married to foreign women could not. Foreigners wept as servants, colleagues, friends, lovers and husbands were escorted out of the embassy gates. At the end of the month the foreigners were expelled from Cambodia by truck. Many of the Cambodians were never seen again. Today a high, whitewashed wall surrounds the massive complex, and the French have returned to Cambodia in a big way, promoting French language and culture in their former colony.

Wat Moha Montrei BUDDHIST TEMPLE

(វត្តមហាមន្ត្រី; Map p54; cnr Sihanouk Blvd & St 161) Situated close to the Olympic Stadium, Wat Moha Montrei was named in honour of one of King Monivong's ministers, Chakrue Ponn, who initiated the founding of the pagoda (*moha montrei* means 'the great minister'). The cement *vihara*, topped with a 35m-high tower, was completed in 1970. Between 1975 and 1979, it was used by the Khmer Rouge to store rice and corn.

Phnom Penh

Cambodia's capital casts its spell over all who enter. It might be the gleaming spires of the Royal Palace, or the graceful French architecture, a waft of lemongrass from a street stall, or the infectious buzz of the cafe-lined riverfront. Somehow, some way, Phnom Penh will grab you.

1. Royal Palace (p42)
The majestic King's Gate opens onto the Royal Palace.

2. Phnom Penh streets
Vendors still ply the streets with their wares.

3. Food markets (p73)
The markets offer a great insight into the myriad ingredients that make up Cambodian cuisine.

4. Throne Hall (p42)
The Throne Hall displays classic Khmer roofs and ornate gilding.

Check out the assorted Cambodian touches incorporated into the wall murals of the *vihara*, which tell the story of Buddha. The angels accompanying Buddha to heaven are dressed as classical Khmer dancers, while the assembled officials wear the white military uniforms of the Sihanouk period.

National Library
LANDMARK

(បណ្ណាល័យជាតិ, Bibliothèque Nationale; Map p60; St 92; ⊙8-11am & 2-5pm Mon-Fri) The National Library is in a graceful old building constructed in 1924, near Wat Phnom. During its rule, the Khmer Rouge turned the building into a stable and destroyed most of the books. Many were thrown out into the streets, where they were picked up by people, some of whom donated them back to the library after 1979; others used them as food wrappings. Today it houses, among other things, a time-worn collection of English and French titles.

Prayuvong Buddha Factories
BUDDHIST SITE

(សិប្បកម្មកសាងព្រះពុទ្ធរូប ព្រះយួវង្ស; Map p54; btwn St 308 & St 310) 🐾 In order to replace the countless Buddhas and ritual objects smashed by the Khmer Rouge, a whole neighbourhood of private workshops making cement Buddhas, *naga* and small stupas has grown up on the grounds of Wat Prayuvong. While the graceless cement figures painted in gaudy colours are hardly works of art compared with Angkorian sculpture, they are an effort by the Cambodian people to restore their Buddhist culture. The local neighbourhood around here is a fascinating warren of lanes.

Cambodia–Vietnam Friendship Monument
MONUMENT

(វិមានមិត្តភាពកម្ពុជា-វៀតណាម; Map p54; Wat Botum Park) The optimistically named Cambodia–Vietnam Friendship Monument was built to a Vietnamese (and rather communist) design in 1979. Concerts are often held in the park, which springs to life with aerobics, football and *takraw* (foot juggling with a rattan ball) enthusiasts after 5pm.

🏃 Activities

Backstreet Academy
EXPERIENCES

(www.backstreetacademy.com) A peer-to-peer social enterprise that matches visitors with local characters and unique experiences around Asia. In Phnom Penh, it offers kick-boxing classes, coconut and fruit carving, fishing from a houseboat, shadow-puppet classes and a whole lot more. Prices include pick-up from a designated hotel or guesthouse in town.

Kambol Kart Raceway
GO-KARTING

(✆012 232332; per 10min US$12) Kambol Kart Raceway is a professional circuit in a rural setting just outside of Phnom Penh. Prices include helmets and racing suits. It's about 2km off the road to Sihanoukville. Look for a hard-to-spot sign on the right, 8km beyond the airport; if you hit the toll booth, you've gone too far.

Aerobics

Every morning at the crack of dawn, and again at dusk, Cambodians gather in several pockets throughout the city to participate in quirky and colourful aerobics sessions. This quintessential Cambodian phenomenon sees a ringleader, equipped with boom box and microphone, whip protégés into shape with a mix of 1980s, Soviet-style calisthenics and *Thriller*-inspired line-dancing moves. It's favoured by middle-aged Khmer women, but you'll see both sexes and all ages participating, and tourists are more than welcome.

There are many places to join in the fun or just observe. Olympic Stadium (p49) is probably the best spot for the sheer volume of participants; several instructors compete for clients and the upper level of the grandstand becomes a cacophony of competing boom boxes.

The riverfront usually sees some action: the space opposite **Blue Pumpkin** (Map p60; ✆023-998153; www.bluepumpkin.asia; 245 Sisowath Quay; mains US$3-8; ⊙6am-11pm; ❊🎧) at the terminus of St 144 is a good bet. Another popular place that usually sees several groups in action is Wat Botum Park, along Samdech SotheAros Blvd.

Boat Cruises

Boat trips on the Tonlé Sap and Mekong Rivers are very popular with visitors. Sunset cruises are ideal, the burning sun sinking slowly behind the glistening spires of the Royal Palace. A slew of **cruising boats** (Map p44) are available for hire on the riverfront about 500m north of the tourist-boat dock. Just rock up and arrange one on the spot for around US$20 an hour, depending on negotiations and numbers. You can bring your own drinks or buy beer and soft drinks on the boat.

PHNOM PENH FOR CHILDREN

With chaotic traffic, a lack of green spaces and sights that are predominantly morbid, Phnom Penh would not seem like the most child-friendly city. Think again, as there are plenty of little gems to help you pass the time with your children in the capital. Plus, most children love a *remork-moto (tuk tuk)* ride.

Some children also love Buddhist temples – especially colourful temples such as **Wat Langka** (វត្តលង្កាព្រះកុសុមារាម; Map p54; cnr St 51 & Sihanouk Blvd) or **Wat Ounalom** (p49), and hill temples like **Wat Phnom** (p47) or, beyond town, Udong (p91). Shimmering gold Buddhas, shiny stupas, animal statues and the occasional monkey give children plenty of visual stimulation (hide little ones' eyes from potentially scary demons). The **Royal Palace** (p42) is similarly rich in Buddhist iconography.

Or consider renting bicycles and crossing the Mekong by ferry from the dock just north of the eastern end of Sihanouk Blvd. On the other side, smooth roads and trails lead 15km or so north to **Smango** (p56), a guesthouse with decent food and a refreshing swimming pool. The Mekong island of Koh Dach (p90) is also a great place to explore by bicycle with very little traffic and some good refreshment stops.

Phnom Penh has decent public play spaces, including a **playground** (Map p54; Samdech Sothearos Blvd) northwest of the Cambodia–Vietnam Friendship Memorial in Wat Botum Park, and another **playground** (Map p60; Wat Phnom) just south of Wat Phnom. Swimming pools are another popular option in a hot, hot city: many hotels with pools allow outside guests to swim for a fee or a minimum spend. **Kingdom Resort** (p56) is a great option for those willing to make a short excursion (6km) out of town; it has a huge pool and some slides.

Great for escaping the heat (or the rain), **Kids City** (Map p54; www.kidscityasia.com; Sihanouk Blvd; 1hr from US$5; ⊘8am-9.30pm) is a vast indoor play palace, with a world class Clip 'N' Climb climbing wall centre, an elaborate jungle gym, a science gallery and an ice rink. Younger children will enjoy **Monkey Business** (Map p54; St 370; child US$2-4, adult free; ⊘9am-7pm), which offers slides, ball ponds and a small swimming pool, as well as wi-fi and a cafe for adults. Many of the restaurants and cafes in town are also notably child-friendly.

The most interesting attraction is beyond the city limits and makes a good day trip: **Phnom Tamao Wildlife Rescue Centre** (p93), a rescue centre for Cambodia's incredible wildlife.

Public river cruises are another option. They leave every 30 minutes from 5pm to 7.30pm from the **tourist-boat dock** (Map p60; 93 Sisowath Quay) and last about 45 minutes (US$5 per head).

Koh Dach Boat Trips   BOATING
(Map p60; Sisowath Quay; per person US$10) Daily boat tours to Koh Dach depart at 8.30am, 9.30am and 1pm from the tourist-boat dock (minimum four people).

Kanika Boat Tour   BOATING
(Map p60; ☑089 848959; www.kanika-boat.com; sunset/dinner cruise US$8/22) The *Kanika* is a striking white catamaran that sails the waters of the Tonlé Sap and Mekong nightly (except Mondays). Choose from a sunset cruise (US$15 with free-flowing draught beer or tasting platters) at 5pm, or a longer dinner cruise from 7pm.

Cycling

It is easy enough to hire a bike and go it alone, although take some time to familiarise yourself with traffic conditions first. Koh Dach is a doable DIY trip, or venture across the Mekong River on a local ferry (1000r including bike), which departs from the riverfront just north of the eastern end of Sihanouk Blvd, and pick up bucolic back roads on the other side. Or opt for something more organised (with or without a guide). Vicious Cycle runs daily group tours to Udong or Koh Dach, departing before 8am.

Vicious Cycle   CYCLING
(Map p60; ☑012 430622; www.grasshopperadven tures.com; 23 St 144; road/mountain bike per day US$4/8; ♿) Plenty of excellent mountain and other bikes are available here. Kiddie seats can be attached to your mountain bike

South Phnom Penh

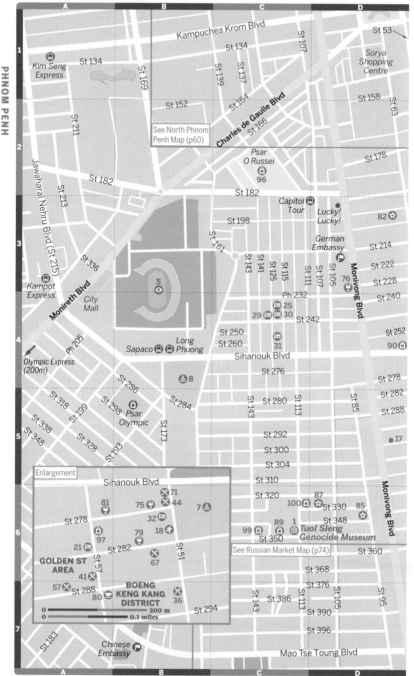

Kampuchea Krom Blvd

St 53

Sorya
Shopping
Centre

Kim Seng
Express

St 134

St 134

St 169

St 107

St 139

St 137

St 164

St 152

St 158

St 63

Charles de Gaulle Blvd

St 166

See North Phnom
Penh Map (p60)

St 211

St 178

Psar
O Russei
96

St 182

Jawaharal Nehru Blvd (St 215)

St 213

St 182

St 182

Capitol
Tour

Lucky!
Lucky!

82

St 336

St 198

German
Embassy

St 214

St 161

St 222

Kampot
Express

Monireth Blvd

City
Mall

5

St 143

St 141

St 125

St 115

St 111

St 107

St 105

76

St 228

Monivong Blvd

St 240

Ph 232

29 30

25

St 242

Olympic Express
(200m)

Ph 205

Sapaco Long
Phuong

St 250
St 260

31

Sihanouk Blvd

St 252

90

St 318

St 286

St 298

8

St 284

St 276

St 278

St 199

St 328

St 193

Psar
Olympic

St 173

St 143

St 280

St 113

St 282

St 85

St 288

St 338
St 348

St 292

St 300

St 304

17

Enlargement

Sihanouk Blvd

St 310

Monivong Blvd

St 278

81

75 44

71

7

St 320

100

87

85

St 330

St 348

St 282

97

79

32

18

89 1

99

Tuol Sleng
Genocide Museum

St 350

St 360

21

St 57

67

St 51

See Russian Market Map (p74)

St 368

GOLDEN ST
AREA

41

BOENG
KENG KANG
DISTRICT

36

St 376

St 143

St 386

St 113

St 105

St 95

57 St 288

80

St 294

St 390

0 ———— 200 m
0 ———— 0.1 miles

St 396

St 183

Chinese
Embassy

Mao Tse Toung Blvd

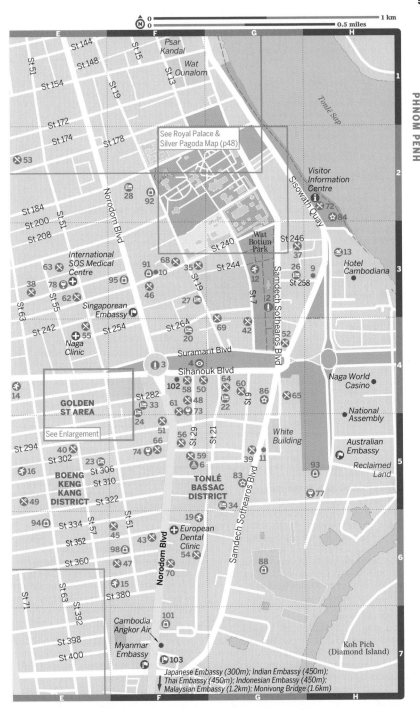

0   1 km
0   0.5 miles

St 144
St 148
St 15
Psar
Kandal
Wat
Ounalom
St 51
St 154
St 19
St 113

St 172
St 174
St 178

⊗ 53
See Royal Palace &
Silver Pagoda Map (p48)

Tonlé Sap

St 184
St 200
St 51
St 208

Norodom Blvd

🏨 28
🔒 92

Visitor
Information
Centre
ℹ️ 🔒 72
⭐ 84

International
SOS Medical
Centre
63 ⊗
95 🔒
91
🔒 10
68
35 ⊗
St 19
St 240
St 244
St 246
37
⊗ 13
Hotel
Cambodiana

Samdech Sothearos Blvd

Wat
Botum
Park

12
🔒 2
26
St 258
9

38 ⊗
78 🔒 ➕
62 ⊗
St 55
St 63
Singaporean
Embassy 🔒
46 ⊗
27 📠

➕ 55
Naga
Clinic
St 242
St 254
St 264
20
69 ⊗
42 ⊗
52 ⊗

Suramarit Blvd
4 ⊗
ℹ️ 3
Sihanouk Blvd
102 ⊗ 58 ⊗ 50 ⊗
61 ⊗ 48 ⊗
24 📠
33 📠
St 282
64 ⊗
60 ⊗
22 🏨
St 9
86 ⭐
⊗ 65
Naga World
Casino

🌍 14

**GOLDEN
ST AREA**
See Enlargement

51
66 ⊗
56 ⊗
St 29
St 21
National
Assembly

St 294
40 ⊗
St 302
23 📠
St 306
St 310
74 🔒 ⊗
59 ⊗
⚓ 6
White
Building
39 ⊗ 11

Australian
Embassy
93 🔒
Reclaimed
Land

🌍 16
**BOENG
KENG
KANG
DISTRICT** St 322

**TONLÉ
BASSAC
DISTRICT**
83 ⭐
34 📠

⊗ 49

🔒 77

94 🔒
St 334
St 57
St 51
45 ⊗
43 🔒
19 ⊗
➕ European
Dental
Clinic
54 ⊗
88 🔒

98 🔒
St 352
47 ⊗
St 360

Norodom Blvd

Samdech Sothearos Blvd

➕ 15
St 380
70 ⊗

St 71
St 63
St 392

St 398
St 400
101 🔒
Cambodia
Angkor Air
Myanmar
Embassy 🔒
🔒 103

Koh Pich
(Diamond Island)

Japanese Embassy (300m); Indian Embassy (450m);
Thai Embassy (450m); Indonesian Embassy (450m);
Malaysian Embassy (1.2km); Monivong Bridge (1.6km)

South Phnom Penh

for US$3. Vicious represents well-respected Grasshopper Adventures in Phnom Penh.

Fitness Centres & Swimming

The fanciest hotels in Phnom Penh will let you use their gyms and pools for a fee. A few of the boutique hotels will let you swim if you buy a few bucks' worth of food or cocktails. Keep in mind that the pools at most boutique hotels are pretty small, more for dipping and cooling off than for doing laps. Most other midrange boutiques charge US$5 for pool rights.

Himawari Hotel   SWIMMING
(Map p54; ☑023-214555; 313 Sisowath Quay; weekday/weekend US$7/8) The Himawari has one of the best hotel pools in town. It's located near the banks of the Mekong. Admission includes use of the gym.

Kingdom Resort   SWIMMING
(☑023-721514; www.thekingdomresort.net; off NH1; adult/child US$5/3) Kingdom Resort is a great option for those willing to make a short excursion (6km) out of town; it has a huge pool and some slides.

Smango   SWIMMING
(☑016-994555; www.smangohouse.com; pool US$5) On the other side of the Mekong River, smooth roads and trails lead 15km or so north to Smango, a guesthouse with decent food and a refreshing swimming pool. Best to check its website for exact directions.

The Place   GYM
(Map p54; ☑023-999799; 11 St 51; walk-in US$15; ☺6am-10pm) This is absolutely state of the art, with myriad machines, a big pool and a range of cardio classes.

Golf

If you can't survive without a swing, Phnom Penh has several 18-hole courses, but most of them lie about 30km or more out of town.

Grand Phnom Penh Golf Club GOLF
(☎023-690 0888; www.grandphnompenhgolf.com; Hanoi Rd; weekdays/weekends US$85/129, plus caddy & cart US$40) The most convenient of the 18-hole golf courses around the capital, this was designed by none other than Jack Nicklaus. Turn north off the Airport Rd and follow Hanoi Rd for 5km until you spot the imposing entrance on the right.

Massage & Spas

There are plenty of massage parlours in Phnom Penh, though some are purveying 'naughty' massages. However, there are also scores of legitimate massage centres and some superb spas for that pampering palace experience.

Bodia Spa SPA
(Map p60; ☎023-226199; www.bodia-spa.com; cnr Samdech Sothearos Blvd & St 178; massages from US$32; ◎10am-11pm) Arguably the best massages and spa treatments in town, and in a Zen-like setting just off the riverfront. All products are locally sourced and produced by the Bodia Nature team.

Bliss Spa SPA
(Map p54; ☎023-215754; www.blissspacambodia.com; 29 St 240; massages from US$23) One of the most established spas in town, set in a lovely old French house on popular St 240.

Nail Bar MASSAGE
(Map p60; www.mithsamlanh.org; Friends n' Stuff store, 215 St 13; 30/60min massages US$4/7;

GIVE BLOOD

Cambodia has a critical shortage of blood as there's a local stigma against donating blood and a high rate of thalassaemia. If you want to help, donate at the **National Blood Transfusion Centre** (Map p44; ☑ 023-217524; Khmer-Soviet Friendship Hospital, St 271; ⊗ 8am-5pm). It's perfectly safe and you get a T-shirt, although only 18 to 60 year olds can donate.

⊗ 11am-9pm) ✎ Provides cheap manicures, pedicures, foot massages, hand massages and nail painting, all to help Mith Samlanh train street children in a new vocation.

Daughters SPA
(Map p60; ☑ 077 657678; www.daughtersofcambodia.org; 321 Sisowath Quay; 1hr foot spa US$10; ⊗ 9am-5.30pm Mon-Sat) ✎ Hand and foot massages are administered by participants in this NGO's vocational training program for at-risk women. Shorter (15- to 30-minute) treatments are also available.

Seeing Hands Massage MASSAGE
(Map p60; ☑ 016 856188; 12 St 13; massages US$7; ⊗ 7am-10pm) ✎ The original Seeing Hands establishment, this place helps you ease those aches and pains and also helps blind masseurs stay self-sufficient. One of the best-value massages in the capital.

Meditation & Yoga

Yoga studios around town hold regular classes. Check their websites for schedules. Some offer discounts for multiple classes.

NaṭaRāj Yoga YOGA
(Map p54; ☑ 090 311341; www.yogacambodia.com; 52 St 302; classes from US$9) Popular yoga studio with a range of classes.

Yoga Phnom Penh YOGA
(Map p54; ☑ 012 739419; www.yogaphnompenh.com; 39 St 21; classes from US$7) Yoga classes available from 6am to 8pm daily, including weekends.

Running

Hash House Harriers RUNNING
(Map p60; www.p2h3.com; Phnom Penh Railway Station; ⊗ 2pm Sun) A good opportunity to meet local expatriates is via the Hash House Harriers, usually referred to simply as 'the Hash'. A run/walk takes place every Sunday.

Participants meet in front of Phnom Penh train station (p87) at 2pm. The fee of US$5 to US$8 includes refreshments – mainly a lot of beer – at the end.

⚲ Courses

Cambodia Cooking Class COOKING
(Map p54; ☑ 023-220953; www.frizz-restaurant.com; booking office 67 St 240; half-/full day US$15/23) Learn the art of Khmer cuisine through Frizz Restaurant on St 240. Classes are held on a breezy rooftop near the Russian embassy. Reserve one day ahead.

Pras Khan Chey Bokator School MARTIAL ARTS
(Map p60; ☑ 095 455555; www.bokatorcambodia.com; 10 St 109; ⊗ 8-10am & 6-8pm) Offers martial-arts lessons (per hour US$5) or full brown-belt courses (US$1500). Call ahead to ensure you get an English-speaking instructor.

Royal University of Phnom Penh LANGUAGE
(Map p44; ☑ 012 866826; www.rupp.edu.kh; Russian Blvd) The Institute of Foreign Languages at the Royal University of Phnom Penh offers some of the only official language courses available in Cambodia.

⚐ Tours

There are some interesting niche tours in and around Phnom Penh. If you want an organised city tour, most of the leading guesthouses and travel agencies can arrange one.

Khmer Architecture Tours CULTURAL
(www.ka-tours.org; tours US$10-55 (depending on numbers)) Those interested in the new-wave Khmer architecture from the Sangkum era (1953–70) should look no further. These two- to three-hour introductory tours take in some of the most prominent buildings in the city and take place on foot or by *cyclo* (bicycle rickshaw), starting at 8.30am two or three Sundays per month. The website also includes a DIY map of the most popular walking tour.

For more on this landmark architecture, pick up a copy of *Cultures of Independence* (2001) or *Building Cambodia: New Khmer Architecture 1953–70* (2006).

Cambodian Living Arts CULTURAL
(CLA; Map p54; ☑ 017 998570; www.cambodianlivingarts.org; 128 Samdech Sothearos Blvd) Cambodian Living Arts supports elder Cambodian musicians who train young Cambodians in traditional music, dance and other

forms. You can visit many of these classes through CLA's 'Living Arts Tours'. Among the most interesting is the **Pinpeat ensemble class** (10.45am to 12.15pm Monday to Friday) where students learn to play melodies that were used in the royal courts of Angkor to accompany ceremonies, dances and masked plays.

Cyclo Centre TOURS
(Map p60; ☑ 097 700 9762; www.cyclo.org.kh; 95 St 158; per hour/day from US$3/12) ✈ Dedicated to supporting *cyclo* drivers in Phnom Penh, these tours are a great way to see the sights. Themed trips such as pub crawls or cultural tours are also available.

Kingdom Brewery TOURS
(☑ 023-430180; 1748 NH5; tours US$15; ⊙ 1-5pm Mon-Sat) Tours include two drinks, and you don't even have to book ahead: just show up. It's exactly 1km north of the Japanese Bridge on NH5.

Village Quad Bike Trails QUAD BIKING
(☑ 099 952255; www.villagequadbiketrails.com; tours 90min/half-day/full day US$40/75/155) Offers quad biking in the countryside around Phnom Penh. The quads are automatic, and so are easy to handle for beginners (maximum two passengers per bike). Full-day tours take in Tonlé Bati and Phnom Tamao; despite its proximity to the capital, this is rural Cambodia and very beautiful. Longer trips and jeep tours are also available.

Follow signs to the Killing Fields of Choeung Ek; it's about 300m before the entrance. Call ahead as numbers are limited.

Dancing Roads TOURS
(☑ 012 822803; www.dancingroads.com) This operator offers motorbike tours around the capital and gentle tours further afield to the South Coast. Based in Phnom Penh, the driver-guides are fun and friendly.

✱✱ Festivals & Events

As the Cambodian capital and largest city in the country, Phnom Penh can be an interesting place to join in some local festivities. The city tends to empty out on big holidays like Khmer New Year and P'chum Ben, as residents return to their home provinces to visit families. However, the Water Festival (Bon Om Tuk) sees the opposite phenomenon as hundreds of thousands of rural residents flood the city to watch the boat races on the Tonlé Sap. The festival doesn't always go ahead and has been cancelled several times in the past decade.

🛏 Sleeping

Accommodation in Phnom Penh, as in the rest of the country, is great value no matter your budget, with quite literally hundreds of guesthouses and hotels to choose from. There are some great boutique hotels around the city if you want to treat yourself after an upcountry adventure.

🛏 North Central (Riverfront)

While the idea of resting up on the riverfront has obvious appeal, you'll find better value elsewhere. Also keep in mind that hotels along the river tend to be noisy, and most budget rooms are windowless or face away from the river. A few superb options exist at the top end, but worthwhile pickings are much slimmer in the budget and midrange categories.

Panorama Mekong Hostel HOSTEL $
(Map p60; ☑ 018 950 0400; www.facebook.com/panorama.mekong.hostel; 357 Sisowath Quay; dm US$3; ☎) There's good news and bad news here. The good news is this place has panoramic views of the Mekong and you can even look down on the iconic Foreign Correspondents' Club (FCC), something that is unique for a backpacker pad. The bad news is there is no lift and there are four flights of stairs. Get fit and enjoy the views!

Foreign Correspondents' Club BOUTIQUE HOTEL $$
(FCC; Map p60; ☑ 023-210142; www.fcccambodia.com; 363 Sisowath Quay; r incl breakfast US$40-90; ❄☎) This landmark location is a fine place to recapture the heady days of the war correspondents. The rooms are exquisitely finished in polished wood and include fine art, top-of-the-line furniture and vintage *Phnom Penh Post* covers on the wall. The deluxe rooms have breezy balconies with prime river views.

Renovations are planned during 2018.

Amanjaya Pancam Hotel BOUTIQUE HOTEL $$$
(Map p60; ☑ 023-214747; www.amanjaya-suites-phnom-penh.com; 1 St 154; r incl breakfast US$130-180; ❄@☎) Amanjaya boasts a superb riverfront location and spacious rooms finished with luxuriant dark-wood floors, elegant Khmer drapes and tropical furnishings. Luscious Le Moon bar is on the roof, trendy K West cafe at ground level.

North Phnom Penh

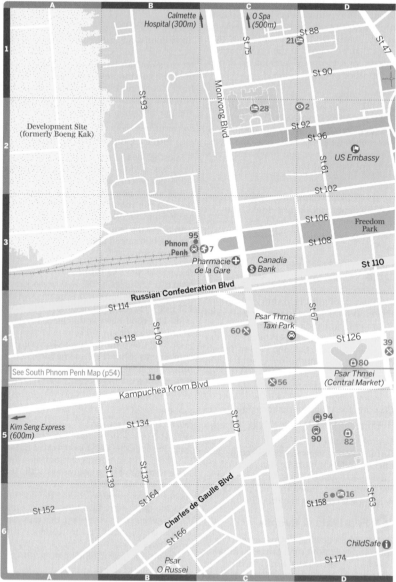

Calmette Hospital (300m)

O Spa (500m)

St 88
21

St 75

St 90

Development Site (formerly Boeng Kak)

St 93

Monivong Blvd

28

2

St 92

St 96

St 61

US Embassy

St 102

St 106

Freedom Park

St 108

95
Phnom Penh 7

Pharmacie de la Gare

Canadia Bank

St 110

Russian Confederation Blvd

St 114

St 118

St 109

Psar Thmei Taxi Park

St 67

60

St 126

39

80

See South Phnom Penh Map (p54)

11

Kampuchea Krom Blvd

56

Psar Thmei (Central Market)

Kim Seng Express (600m)

St 134

St 107

94

90

82

St 139

St 137

St 164

Charles de Gaulle Blvd

6 16

St 63

St 152

St 166

St 158

ChildSafe

Psar O Russei

St 174

North Central (Inland)

If you want to be near the riverfront but not pay riverfront prices, this area is a happy hunting ground. Be aware, though, that the blocks running west off the river from St 104 to about St 144 are gritty and have sleazy areas; a handful of delectable new boutique hotels point to the slow gentrification of this prime real estate. Meanwhile, St 172 between St 19 and St 13 has become Phnom Penh's most popular backpacker area.

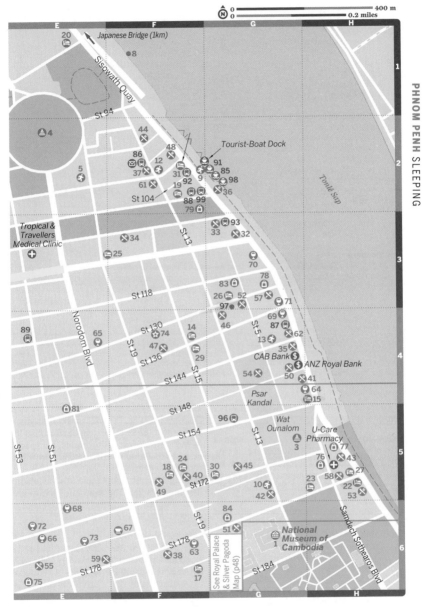

Japanese Bridge (1km)

Sisowath Quay

St 94

Tourist-Boat Dock

St 104

Tonle Sap

Tropical & Travellers Medical Clinic

St 118

St 13

Norodom Blvd

St 130

St 19

St 136

St 47

St 29

St 5

CAB Bank

ANZ Royal Bank

St 144

St 15

Psar Kandal

St 81

St 148

St 154

St 13

Wat Ounalom

U-Care Pharmacy

St 53

St 51

St 172

St 19

St 178

St 178

St 59

National Museum of Cambodia

See Royal Palace & Silver Pagoda Map (p48)

St 184

Samdech Sothearos Blvd

★**Eighty8 Backpackers**   HOSTEL $
(Map p60; ☎023-500 2440; www.88backpack ers.com; 98 St 88; dm US$6.40-8, r US$24-34; ❄@🛜⛱) A hostel with a swimming pool means party time, and this place hosts a big one on the first Friday of every month. The pool and the extensive villa are home to a variety of dorms and private rooms. The courtyard has a central bar with a pool table, and there are plenty of spots to lounge around the pool.

North Phnom Penh

◎ Top Sights

◎ Sights

◑ Activities, Courses & Tours

⬤ Sleeping

◯ Eating

The dorms come in air-con and fan varieties, plus there is a female dorm.

Blues Hostel
HOSTEL **$**

(Map p60; ☑010 302210; www.blueshostel.com; 149 St 19; dm US$3.50-4.50, r from US$10; ❄@☎) This impressive hostel opened its doors in the summer of 2017 and has some pretty attractive rates, even by hostel standards, and include private rooms with attached bathroom. Downstairs is a lively bar and a pool table where the occasional free beer is on offer to in-house guests.

DoDo Guesthouse
GUESTHOUSE **$**

(Map p60; ☑023-999912; http://dodoguesthouse. wordpress.com; 2B St 90; r US$15-25; ❄☎) An impressive little guesthouse north of Wat Phnom, the rooms here are clean, spacious and top value, and include bathrooms that are as big as some of the cell-like rooms in other places. Downstairs is a funky little cafe-bar.

11 Happy Backpacker
HOSTEL **$**

(Map p60; ☑088 777 7421; www.11happyback packers.com; 87-89 St 136; dm US$5, r US$8-18; ❄@☎) This is one of the original backpacker pads in Phnom Penh, with a sprawling rooftop bar-restaurant offering chairs for chilling out and a pool table. It's mellow by day, fun by night. The white-tiled rooms are clean and functional. The Flicks 2 cinema is conveniently located downstairs.

Happy House Zone
GUESTHOUSE **$**

(Map p60; ☑096 333 3288; http://the-happy-house-zone.hotel-phnompenh.com/en; 122 St 19; dm US$2-6, r US$10-24; ❄@☎) A popular backpacker spot on a strategic corner of Backpackersville, HHZ has dorms that are among the cheapest in town, starting at just a couple of bucks. The good range of rooms includes affordable twin and doubles, and 'family rooms' that are essentially four-bed dorms.

★ **Blue Lime** BOUTIQUE HOTEL $$
(Map p60; ☎023-222260; www.bluelime.asia; 42 St 19z; r incl breakfast US$63-99; ❈@🛜☀) The Blue Lime offers smart, minimalist rooms and a leafy pool area that invites relaxation. The pricier rooms have private plunge pools, four-poster beds and concrete love seats. The cheaper rooms upstairs in the main building are similarly appealing. No children.

Sun & Moon Urban Hotel DESIGN HOTEL $$
(Map p60; ☎023-961888; www.sunandmoonhotel.com.kh; 68 St 136; r US$69-129; @🛜☀) This is one of the most stylish high-rises in the Cambodian capital, offering designer rooms with geometric patterns on the walls and splashes of saffron in the furnishings. One of the most impressive features is the rooftop infinity pool with expansive views across the city and the attached Cloud 9 Sky Bar.

Sangkum BOUTIQUE HOTEL $$
(Map p44; ☎023-987775; www.thesangkum.com; 35A St 75; r US$55-85; ❈@🛜☀) Set in a 1960s villa to the north of Wat Phnom, the name pays homage to Cambodia's so-called Golden Years, under the rule of Sihanouk and his Sangkum political party. Rooms are decorated with a contemporary flourish and there's a small swimming pool for cooling off after exploring the city.

De Art Hotel BOUTIQUE HOTEL $$
(Map p60; ☎023-622 2298; www.dearthotel.com; 9-12 St 106; r US$30-70; ❈@🛜) Another boutique hotel that adds to a legion of chic sleeps in the city, De Art offers three-star comfort at two-star prices. Rooms are ultra-modern with some contemporary art adorning the walls, although the rooms can be noisy as the hotel is near bus company offices.

Monsoon Boutique Hotel BOUTIQUE HOTEL $$
(Map p60; ☎023-989856; www.monsoonhotel.com; 53-55 St 130; r incl breakfast US$30-45; ❈@🛜) Blink and you'll miss this little oasis on chaotic St 130. Hidden inside are attractive rooms with polished concrete walls and pleasing murals. It's a real deal considering

the sophistication of the design and the location close to the river.

Billabong
BOUTIQUE HOTEL **$$**
(Map p60; ☑023-223703; www.thebillabonghotel.com; 5 St 158; r incl breakfast US$18-70, dm US$5-8; ❋@🛜☀) Near Psar Thmei but an oasis of calm by comparison, the Billabong has stylish rooms surrounding an open courtyard with a large swimming pool in the middle. Aim for the ground-level pool-view rooms, which have private verandahs and more space compared with rooms at the back. The newer dorms make for some bargain boutique beds.

★Raffles Hotel Le Royal
HOTEL **$$$**
(Map p60; ☑023-981888; www.raffles.com/phnompenh; cnr Monivong Blvd & St 92; r from US$205; ❋@🛜☀) From the golden age of travel, this is one of Asia's grand old dames, in the illustrious company of the Oriental in Bangkok and Raffles in Singapore. This classic colonial-era property is Phnom Penh's leading address, with a heritage to match its service and style. Indulgent diversions include two swimming pools, a gym, a spa and lavish bars and restaurants.

Between 1970 and 1975 many famous journalists working in Phnom Penh stayed here. More recent celebrated guests have included Barack Obama and Angelina Jolie.

Plantation
BOUTIQUE HOTEL **$$$**
(Map p54; ☑023-215151; www.theplantation.asia; 28 St 184; r incl breakfast US$80-400; ❋@🛜☀) This is the largest and most ambitious hotel among the MAADS management group of properties. It ticks all the boxes with high ceilings, stylish fixtures and fittings, open-plan bathrooms and balconies. There are two swimming pools here and a beautiful courtyard reception that hosts regular art exhibitions.

Frangipani Royal Palace Hotel
BOUTIQUE HOTEL **$$$**
(Map p60; ☑023-223320; www.frangipanipalacehotel.com; 27 St 178; US$70-135; ❋@🛜☀) Frangipani is a homegrown chain of boutique hotels in Phnom Penh and Siem Reap; this is their flagship property overlooking the Royal Palace. Aim to live the high life and ask for a room on the upper floors. There's a rooftop swimming pool with a palace view and happy hours at the **skybar** from 5pm to 7.30pm.

La Maison D'Ambre
BOUTIQUE HOTEL **$$$**
(Map p60; ☑023-222780; www.lamaisondambre.com; 123 St 110; ste incl breakfast US$100-190; ❋@🛜) A designer hotel linked to Ambre, a leading house of couture, this place is fit for a fashion shoot. The ample themed suites feature stunning contemporary art, space-age lamps and designer kitchens. The psychedelic rooftop bar, the Fifth Element, has funky furniture and prime views of Wat Phnom, making it a great place for breakfast or a sundowner.

🛏 South Central (Norodom East)

The hotels in this zone are ideally positioned: they're located on or within walking distance of the river and are close to the Royal Palace. Cosy boutique hotels set around a pool are in abundance here. Walk-in backpackers can target St 258, which has a clutch of cheap guesthouses.

Number 9 Guesthouse
HOSTEL **$**
(Map p54; ☑023-984999; www.number9hotel.com; 7C St 258; r US$15-35; ❋🛜☀) The first of Phnom Penh's old-school backpacker pads to be transformed into a flashpacker hotel, Number 9 Guesthouse is still going strong thanks to great rates, a rooftop pool and a lively bar-restaurant with generous happy hours (4pm to 8pm). Worth a splash for backpackers who have been exploring rural Cambodia.

Lazy Gecko Guesthouse
GUESTHOUSE **$**
(Map p54; ☑078 786025; www.lazygecko.asia; 1D St 258; dm US$5, r with fan US$12, with air-con US$15; ❋🛜) Best known as a cafe, Lazy Gecko's rooms have recently been renovated with the addition of dorms. The air-con doubles have flat-screen TVs and plenty of space, while the fan rooms are on the small side. It's a great location amid the backpacker haunts of St 258.

Kabiki
BOUTIQUE HOTEL **$$**
(Map p54; ☑023-222290; www.thekabiki.com; 22 St 264; r incl breakfast US$55-120; ❋@🛜☀) The most family-friendly place in town, the Kabiki offers a large, lush garden and an inviting swimming pool with a kiddie pool. Family rooms include bunks and most rooms have a private garden terrace.

★Palace Gate Hotel
BOUTIQUE HOTEL **$$$**
(Map p48; ☑023-900011; www.palacegatepp.com; 44B Samdech Sothearos Blvd; r US$100-305;

❅ @ 🛜 🖾) New in 2017, the Palace Gate Hotel has an unrivalled location overlooking the walls of, well obviously, the Royal Palace and is very close to the riverfront. The hotel is built around an old French colonial villa and the majority of rooms are set in a modern building behind. All are beautifully appointed with contemporary furnishings.

★**Pavilion** BOUTIQUE HOTEL **$$$**
(Map p54; ☑023-222280; www.thepavilion.asia; 227 St 19; r incl breakfast US$73-107, apt US$120-150; ❅@🛜🖾) Housed in an elegant French villa, this immensely popular and atmospheric place kick-started Phnom Penh's boutique-hotel obsession. All rooms have inviting four-poster beds, stunning furniture, personal computers and iPod docks. Some of the newer rooms include a private plunge pool. Guests can use bamboo bikes for free. No children allowed.

🛏 South Central (BKK1 Area)

Popular among NGO workers and expats, the Boeng Keng Kang (BKK) and Tonlé Bassac districts, south of Independence Monument, comprise the flashpacker zone, with an expanding selection of fine midrange hotels to go with a wealth of trendy bars and restaurants (plus a few good hostels). Many of the hotels are centred on St 278, dubbed 'Golden St' because of the preponderance of hotels that feature 'Golden' in their name.

★**Mad Monkey** HOSTEL **$**
(Map p54; ☑023-987091; www.madmonkeyhostels.com; 26 St 302; dm US$5-7, r from US$18-25; ❅@🛜) This colourful and vibrant hostel is justifiably popular. The spacious dorms have air-con and sleep six to 20; the smaller ones have double-width bunk beds that can sleep two. The private rooms are swish for the price but lack TVs and, often, windows. The rooftop bar above quiet St 302 serves free beer on Mondays from 6pm to 8pm.

Top Banana Guesthouse HOSTEL **$**
(Map p54; ☑012 885572; www.topbananahostels.weebly.com; 9 St 278; dm from US$4, r US$12-16; ❅@🛜) The rooms are in good shape by hostel standards, and there are some dorms available, including a four-bed female dorm. The main draw is the strategic location overlooking Wat Langka and St 278, plus the open-air chill-out area. It can get noisy as the rooftop bar is raucous most nights. Book way ahead.

Mini Banana Guesthouse GUESTHOUSE **$**
(Map p54; ☑023-726854; www.mini-banana.asia; 136 St 51; dm US$6, r US$8-20; ❅🛜) It's almost a banana republic in this part of town, with three guesthouses playing on the name. Renovated dorms with sturdy bunks, comfortable rooms with fan or air-con and a lively little bar-restaurant make this one of the most likeable of the bunch.

★**Villa Langka** BOUTIQUE HOTEL **$$**
(Map p54; ☑023-726771; www.villalangka.com; 14 St 282; r incl breakfast US$55-125; ❅@🛜🖾) One of the first players in the poolside-boutique game, Villa Langka has long been a Phnom Penh favourite, even as the competition heats up. The rooms ooze postmodern panache, although there are big differences in size and style. The leafy pool area is perfect.

★**Rambutan Resort** BOUTIQUE HOTEL **$$**
(Map p74; ☑017 992240; www.rambutanresort.com; 29 St 71; r incl breakfast US$65-150; ❅🛜🖾) Sixties-groovy, gay-friendly and extremely well run, this striking villa once belonged to the US Embassy. The soaring original structure and a newer wing shade a boot-shaped swimming pool. Concrete floors set an industrial tone in the smart rooms, which are outfitted with top-quality furnishings.

Khmer Surin Boutique Guesthouse BOUTIQUE HOTEL **$$**
(Map p54; ☑012 731909; www.khmersurin.com.kh; 11A St 57; r incl breakfast US$40-65; ❅🛜) This guesthouse is attached to the long-running restaurant of the same name, set in a sumptuous villa. The 19 rooms come with flat-screen TVs, leafy balconies and antique furnishings, not to mention bathrooms that would put most four-star properties to shame.

You Khin Art House GUESTHOUSE **$$**
(Map p54; ☑061 828577; ykarthouse@gmail.com; St 830; r US$20-35; ❅🛜🖾) Tucked away down discreet St 830, this has the feel of a large private home and, tardis-like, is considerably bigger on the inside. The Franco-Khmer owners display their own artwork on the walls and the ample public spaces include a pool table and table tennis. 'Kitchen' rooms are suite-like, great value and a good choice for families.

Palm Tree Boutique Hotel BOUTIQUE HOTEL **$$**
(Map p74; ☑023-229933; www.palmtreeboutiquehotel.com; 7 St 398; r US$40-95; ❅@🛜🖾) This

boutique hotel is set in a spacious villa in Boeng Keng Kang (BKK). Rooms are finished with polished-wood floors and saffron silk furnishings. Best of all, the minibar is included in the rates, with some beers and soft drinks. Bicycles are also available for free.

La Rose Suites BOUTIQUE HOTEL **$$$**
(Map p54; ☑ 023-222254; www.larose.com.kh; 4B St 21; ste US$175-380; ✳@⛅✉) A stylish contemporary all-suite boutique hotel in lively little St 21, La Rose offers smart and spacious rooms, including some two-bedroom apartments for families. The elegant bathrooms include ample terrazzo bathtubs and rain showers.

🏠 South Central (Psar O Russei Area)

With the downfall of the Boeng Kak area, the zone south of Psar O Russei has emerged as a popular alternative for budget travellers. It's a mix of high-rise hotels and backpacker-oriented guesthouses.

Narin Guesthouse GUESTHOUSE **$**
(Map p54; ☑ 023-991955; 50 St 125; r with fan/aircon US$12/17; ✳@⛅) One of the stalwarts of the Phnom Penh guesthouse scene (we first stayed here back in 1995) run by a friendly family. Rooms are smart, bathrooms smarter still and the price is right. There is a super-relaxed, open-air restaurant-terrace where you can take some time out.

Smiley's Hotel HOTEL **$**
(Map p54; ☑ 012 365959; smileyhotel.pp@gmail. com; 37 St 125; s with fan US$6, d US$15-20; ✳@⛅) A migrant from Siem Reap, Smiley's is a huge seven-storey hotel with 40 spacious rooms that border on chic. The US$20 rooms have big flat-screen TVs. Includes a lift.

Tat Guesthouse GUESTHOUSE **$**
(Map p54; ☑ 012 921211; tatcambodia@yahoo.com; 52 St 125; s without bathroom US$4, r US$7-15; ✳@⛅) A super-friendly spot with a breezy rooftop hang-out that's perfect for chilling. The rooms aren't going to wow you but they are functional. For US$12 you get air-con. They also own nearby Tattoo Guesthouse (Map p54; ☑ 011 801000; 62A St 125; r US$5-10; ✳⛅), which has a great name and smarter rooms.

✖ Eating

For foodies, Phnom Penh is the real deal, boasting a superb selection of restaurants that showcase the best in Khmer cooking, as well as the greatest hits from world cuisines such as Chinese, Vietnamese, Thai, Indian, French, Italian, Spanish, Mexican and more. Visitors to Phnom Penh are spoilt for choice these days.

🍴 North Central (Riverfront)

18 Rik Reay BBQ BARBECUE **$**
(Map p60; ☑ 095 361818; 3 St 108; US$2-8; ⏱5pm-midnight) One of the best local barbecue restaurants near the riverfront, the Rik Reay is packed with locals every night, partly thanks to its convenient location near the Night Market, but more so it is a testament to the quality of its food. Choose from grilled beef, ribs, chicken, squid, shrimp and much more, all with signature dipping sauces.

Eric Kayser BAKERY **$**
(Map p60; ☑ 085 691333; http://maison-kayser-cambodia.asia; 277 Sisowath Quay; US$1-7; ⏱7am-10pm; ✳⛅) The flagship branch of this impressive French bakery chain in Phnom Penh, Eric Kayser offers designer breads, delectable pastries and a range of gourmand sandwiches. Set lunches are available with sandwich, pastry and drink for US$9 and weekend brunches are a popular draw.

Special Pho VIETNAMESE **$**
(Map p60; 11 St 178; mains US$2.50-4.50; ⏱8am-9pm) Boasting a great location near the riverfront for good pho – the noodle soup that keeps Vietnam driving forward – plus dirt-cheap fried rice and fried noodles.

Hummus House LEBANESE **$**
(Map p60; ☑ 092 483759; 95 Sisowath Quay; US$3-10; ⏱10.30am-11pm; ✳⛅) A popular Lebanese restaurant on the riverfront, Hummus House offers a bite from Beirut, including bargain chicken shawarma for US$3, a host of hummus dips and the full range of kefta and grills. Falafel balls include a three-cheese option with feta, mozzarella and cheddar.

¡Viva! MEXICAN **$**
(Map p60; 139 Sisowath Quay; dishes US$4-6; ⏱10am-11pm; ✳⛅) It doesn't look like much, but this riverfront place offers some bargain-basement dining and drinking, including a bucket of margarita for US$5. The Mexican is not the most authentic in town, but then nor are the prices.

★ Yi Sang Riverside
CHINESE **$$**

(Map p54; Sisowath Quay; mains US$3-20; ☻6am-11pm; ❄ ☎) The riverfront location is one of the few places in the city where you can dine right on the riverside, perfect for a relaxing sunset cocktail. The menu here includes a mix of well-presented Cambodian street flavours such as *naom bunchok* (rice noodles with curry), plus plenty of dim sum and some international flavours.

Metro
FUSION **$$**

(Map p60; ☏023-222275; 271 Sisowath Quay; small plates US$4-10, large plates US$8-26; ☻9.30am-1am; ❄ ☎) Metro is one of the hottest spots on the riverfront strip thanks to a striking design and an adventurous menu. Small plates are for sampling and include beef with red ants and tequila black-pepper prawns; large plates include steaks and honey-soy roasted chicken. It also does a mean eggs Benedict.

Pop Café
ITALIAN **$$**

(Map p60; ☏012 562892; 371 Sisowath Quay; mains US$6-12; ☻11am-2pm & 6-10pm; ❄) Owner Giorgio welcomes diners as if they are coming to his own home for dinner, making this a popular spot for authentic Italian cooking. Thin-crust pizzas, homemade pastas and tasty gnocchi – it could be Roma.

La Croisette
INTERNATIONAL **$$**

(Map p60; ☏023-220554; 241 Sisowath Quay; mains US$5-18; ☻7am-1am; ❄ ☎) The stylish La Croisette is a popular riverfront spot with homemade pasta and gnocchi, plus hearty steaks, lamb chops and even some Cambodian offerings.

Bopha Phnom Penh Restaurant
CAMBODIAN **$$**

(Map p60; ☏023-427209; www.bopha-phnom penh.com; Sisowath Quay; mains US$5-15; ☻6am-10.30pm; ☎) Also known as Titanic, it's right on the river and designed to impress, with Angkorian-style carvings and elegant wicker furniture. The menu is punctuated with exotic flavours – especially water buffalo – but there's a European menu for the less adventurous. Regular traditional music and dance performances take place here.

Limoncello
ITALIAN **$$**

(Map p60; No 14B St 264; pizzas US$5.50-8; ☻11.30am-2pm & 5.30-10pm; ❄ ☎) The pizza here is simply outstanding – some of the best in town – and it's got a plum riverfront setting to boot. Great desserts that can be washed down with an eponymous limoncello shot.

Happy Herb Pizza
PIZZA **$$**

(Map p60; ☏012 921915; 345 Sisowath Quay; medium pizzas US$6-9; ☻8am-11pm; ☎) Another Phnom Penh institution. No, happy doesn't mean it comes with free toppings, it means pizza à la ganja. The non-marijuana pizzas are also pretty good, but don't involve the free trip. It's a good place to sip a cheap beer and watch the riverfront action unfold.

Grand River
INTERNATIONAL **$$**

(Map p60; ☏023-220244; 357 Sisowath Quay; US$3-12; ☻7am-midnight; ☎) One of the more sophisticated riverfront restaurants, this is a great spot for watching the world go by. The menu includes moderately priced Cambodian and international dishes, plus a quaffable drinks selection.

Chinese House
FUSION **$$$**

(Map p44; ☏023-991514; 45 Sisowath Quay, cnr St 84; mains US$6-60; ☻11am-1am Mon-Thu, to 2am Fri & Sat, to midnight Sun; ☎) Housed in one of the city's true colonial-era masterpieces, Chinese House is worth a visit for the ambience alone. The menu promises contemporary Asian flavours such as black king fish with marinated squid, honey-mustard dressing and crispy baby potatoes, plus affordable East-meets-West tapas. Doubles as a chic cocktail bar downstairs, with weekday promotions, music events and a popular Sunday brunch.

✖ North Central (Inland)

Cam Cup Cafe
CAFE **$**

(Map p60; ☏093 771577; Main Post Office, St 13; US$2-5; ☻7am-9pm; ❄ ☎) This elegant little cafe is the perfect way to make the iconic main post office relevant once more for a new generation of travellers. It offers fresh brews, herbal teas and some of the best value Khmer dishes you will hope to find in this sort of setting.

Decoration includes old postage stamps and outmoded machinery from the bygone days of the postal system.

Museum Cafe
CAFE **$**

(Map p60; ☏023-722275; National Museum, St 178; US$2.50-6; ☻7am-8pm daily; ❄ ☎) Set in the spacious grounds of the National Museum, this is a cultured place for a cuppa, but the menu includes a good selection of well-priced Khmer classics and some international wraps

DON'T MISS

DINING FOR A CAUSE

There are several restaurants around town that are run by aid organisations to help fund their social programs in Cambodia. The proceeds of a hearty meal go towards helping Cambodia's recovery and allow restaurant staff to gain valuable work experience.

North Central

Daughters Cafe (Map p60; www.daughtersofcambodia.org; 321 Sisowath Quay; meals US$4-8; ☺9am-6pm Mon-Sat; ❋🖥) 🍴 This fantastic cafe on the top floor of the Daughters of Cambodia visitors centre features soups, smoothies, original coffee drinks, cupcakes and fusion-ish mains served by former victims of trafficking.

Dine in the Dark (DID; Map p60; ☎077 589458; www.didexperience.com; 126 St 19; set menu US$18; ☺6-11pm (last orders 9.30pm); ❋) 🍴 It's the Tea Garden by day, with a verdant hidden courtyard and speciality loose-leaf teas, but by night the lights go out and the upstairs is transformed into Dine in the Dark. A set menu of Khmer, Western or vegetarian dishes eaten in darkness with the help of a sight-impaired guide.

Friends (Map p60; ☎012 802072; www.tree-alliance.org; 215 St 13; tapas US$4-7, mains US$6-10; ☺11am-10.30pm; 🖥) 🍴 One of Phnom Penh's best-loved restaurants, with tasty tapas bites, heavenly smoothies and creative cocktails. It offers former street children a head start in the hospitality industry. Book ahead.

Romdeng (Map p60; ☎092 219565; www.tree-alliance.org; 74 St 174; mains US$5-9; ☺11am-9pm; 🖥) 🍴 Set in a gorgeous colonial villa, Romdeng specialises in Cambodian country fare, including a famous baked-fish *amok*, two-toned pomelo salad and tiger-prawn curry. Sample deep-fried tarantulas or stir-fried tree ants with beef and holy basil if you dare. Staffed by former street youths and their teachers.

Veiyo Tonlé (Map p60; 237 Sisowath Quay; mains US$3.50-6.50; ☺7am-11pm; 🖥) 🍴 Features mainly Khmer and Italian cuisine, including tasty pizzas. Proceeds go towards helping a local orphanage.

South Central

Cafe Yejj (Map p74; ☎092 600750; 170 St 450; mains US$3.50-6; ☺8am-9pm; ❋🖥📶) 🍴 An air-con escape from the Russian Market (walk upstairs), this bistro-style cafe uses organic ingredients to prepare pasta, salads and wraps, as well as a few more-ambitious dishes. Promotes fair trade and responsible employment.

Feel Good Cafe II (Map p54; ☎077 694702; www.feelgoodcoffee.com.kh; 11B St 29; dishes US$2-5; ☺7.30am-4.30pm) 🍴 One of the only cafes in town to roast and grind its own coffee, with responsibly sourced blends that are a fusion of Cambodian, Lao and Thai coffee beans.

Hagar (Map p54; ☎023-221501; www.hagarcatering.com; 44 St 310; lunch buffet US$7.50; ☺7am-2pm; ❋🖥) 🍴 Proceeds from the all-you-can-eat buffets here go towards assisting destitute or abused women. Usually Asian fusion or barbecue, except for the Tuesday lunchtime Italian buffet.

Jars of Clay (Map p74; 39B St 155; cakes US$1.50, mains US$3-5.50; ☺7.30am-9pm Mon-Sat; ❋🖥) 🍴 More than just a bakery, with authentic Khmer mains including their patented *lok lak* (a Cambodian beef dish), plus drinks and welcome air-con. Ten per cent of profits go to those in need.

Restore One Cafe (Map p74; ☎016 302727; 23 St 123; burgers US$5.75-6.50; ☺11am-9pm; ❋🖥) 🍴 Set in a handsome wooden house near the Russian Market. Choose from themed burgers such as American Oink or Rugged Cowboy, plus fish and chicken options, all with sauces and a side of fries. Support training and villages in extreme poverty.

and salads as well. Try lunch before or after browsing the museum or combine dinner with the excellent nightly traditional dance show.

Connecting Hands Cafe
INTERNATIONAL $

(Map p60; http://connectinghands.com.au; 42 St 178; US$2.50-7; ☉9am-6pm Mon-Sat, closed Sun; ✳☏) This smart little cafe on genteel St 178 is set up to assist victims of trafficking or abuse with vocational training as chefs, baristas and waitresses. The menu offers a good range of international faves and local specialities, from veggie burgers to beef *lok lak*, nicely rounded off with their signature turmeric crepes.

Sorya Food Court
ASIAN $

(Map p60; 11 St 63; 5000-10,000r; ☉9am-9pm; ✳) The top-floor food court is a sanitised, air-cooled way to experience a variety of local fare, with stalls serving a wide range of affordable Cambodian, Chinese, Vietnamese, Malaysian and Korean dishes. It works on a coupon system.

Noodle House
ASIAN $

(Map p60; ☏077 919110; 32A St 130; dishes US$3.50-5.50; ☉6am-10pm; ☏) Set in a lovingly restored French-era gem of a building, this place looks more expensive than it actually is. The menu is a regional tour of noodle soups with stops everywhere from Cambodian *kyteow* to Malaysian laksa.

Laughing Fatman
CAMBODIAN $

(Map p60; 63 St 172; mains US$2.50-6.50; ☉7am-midnight) A welcoming backpacker cafe with cheap food and big breakfasts. It was formerly called Oh My Buddha: 'New name, same body', joked the corpulent owner on our visit.

★Le Bouchon
RESTAURANT/WINE BAR $$

(Map p54; ☏077 881103; 82 St 174; mains $5-15; ☉11am-2pm & 4pm-midnight; ☏) Rehoused in a stunning French-colonial villa on St 174, Le Bouchon is now as much a classy restaurant as an elegant wine bar. The menu includes a braised lamb shank and some calorific homemade desserts. They also have a great selection of French wines by the glass, plus some of the more potent cocktails around town.

★Sam Doo Restaurant
CHINESE $$

(Map p60; ☏017 427688; 56-58 Kampuchea Krom Blvd; mains US$2.50-15; ☉7am-2am; ✳☏) Many Chinese Khmers swear that this upstairs eatery near Central Market has the best Middle Kingdom food in town. Choose from the signature Sam Doo fried rice, *trey chamhoy* (steamed fish with soy sauce and ginger), fresh seafood, hotpots and dim sum.

Sugar Palm
CAMBODIAN $$

(Map p60; ☏085 646373; www.thesugarpalm.com; 13 St 178; mains US$5-8; ☉11am-3pm & 6-10pm Mon-Sat) Set in an attractive French villa, the Sugar Palm is the place to sample traditional flavours infused with herbs and spices, including delicious *char kreung* (curried lemongrass) dishes. Owner Kethana showed celebrity chef Gordon Ramsay how to prepare *amok* (baked fish dish).

Le Saint Georges
FRENCH $$

(Map p60; ☏095 436541; 111 St 136; US$5-20; ☉6-10pm; ✳☏) Le Saint Georges specialises in the cuisine of southwest France, featuring a number of dishes that don't often turn up on other menus around town, including a signature *cassoulet* (chicken and sausage casserole) and a *confit de canard* made from whole fresh duck. A genuine dining experience thanks to the passionate host from Toulouse.

Sher-e-Punjab
INDIAN $$

(Map p60; ☏023-216360; 16 St 130; mains US$3-8; ☉11am-11pm; ☏) This is the top spot for a curry fix according to many members of Phnom Penh's Indian community. The tandoori dishes here are particularly good, as are the excellent-value prawn curries.

Dim Sum Emperors
CHINESE $$

(Map p60; ☏023-650 7452; 48 St 130; dim sum US$2-3, mains US$5-15; ☉7am-9pm; ✳☏) Wildly popular for both its dim sum and its powerful air-con, which comes as welcome relief after a shopping session at nearby Psar Thmei.

Khema La Poste
FRENCH $$

(Map p60; ☏015 841888; www.khema-restaurant.com; cnr Sts 13 & 98; US$5-15; ☉7am-10pm; ✳☏) This new French delicatessen restaurant is winning plaudits for its good-value French food, including boeuf bourguignon, Toulouse sausages and lamb shank. There are also competitively priced pastas and delicious desserts adding up to a great-value lunch in sophisticated surrounds.

Exchange
INTERNATIONAL $$

(Map p44; ☏023-992865; http://theexchange-cambodia.com; 28 St 47; US$5-15; ☉10am-midnight) One of the grandest old French houses in the city is home to this stylish bistro and bar. The menu takes diners on a global tour and includes some excellent sharing platters with Mediterranean and ocean themes, plus some top imported steaks.

Lone Star   TEX-MEX **$$**
(Map p60; 30 St 23; US$4.50-9; ⊙7am-11pm; 🔊)
Missing the US of A? You won't be after a
morning in here watching American foot-
ball via satellite and digging into the heaped
plates of meatloaf and Baja fish tacos. The
smoked pork ribs and the wings are both
among the best in town.

Van's Restaurant   FRENCH **$$$**
(Map p60; ☑023-722067; www.vans-restaurant.
com; 5 St 13; mains US$15-45; ⊙11.30am-2.30pm
& 5-10.30pm; ❄) Located in one of the city's
grandest buildings, the former Banque Indochine, Van's features old vault doors en route
to the refined dining room upstairs. Dishes
are presented with a decorative flourish;
menu highlights include langoustine ravioli, tender veal and boneless quail. Business
lunches include a glass of wine and a coffee.

Armand's The Bistro   FRENCH **$$$**
(Map p60; ☑092 305401; 33 St 108; meals US$12-
25; ⊙from 6pm Tue-Sun; ❄) The best steaks in
town are served in Cognac flambé-style by
the eponymous owner of this French bistro.
The meat is simply superb, but every item
on the chalkboard menu shines. Space is
tight, so this is one place to book ahead.

Le Broken Plate   JAPANESE **$$$**
(Map p60; ☑078 903335; 108 St 13; omakase
menu US$30, mains US$10-15; ⊙11.30am-2.30pm
& 6.30-10.30pm; ❄🔊) Canadian-Cambodian
chef Narith Plong delivers a Khmer twist to
the Japanese sushi and sashimi experience.
Sourcing only the freshest seasonal ingredients, he works his magic behind the bar
counter to create incredible *omakase* (chef's
choice) tasting menus. A la carte is also
available, including fresh oysters and Mekong lobster miso soup. Bookings essential.

Self-Catering

Thai Huot   SUPERMARKET **$**
(Map p60; 103 Monivong Blvd; ⊙7.30am-8.30pm)
This is the place for French travellers who
are missing home as it stocks many French
products, including Bonne Maman jam and
the city's best cheese selection. There are
several branches around the city.

🍴 South Central

★Boat Noodle Restaurant   THAI **$**
(Map p54; ☑012 774287; 57 Samdech Sothea-
ros Blvd; mains US$3-7; ⊙7am-9pm; 🔊) This
long-running Thai-Khmer restaurant has
some of the best-value regional dishes in

town. Choose from the contemporary but
traditionally decorated space at the front or
a traditional wooden house behind. There
are delicious noodle soups and lots of local
specialities ranging from fish cakes to spicy
curries.

★The Shop   CAFE **$**
(Map p54; ☑023-986964; 39 St 240; mains
US$3.50-6; ⊙7am-7pm, to 3pm Sun; 🔊🍴) If you
are craving the local deli back home, make
for this haven, which has a changing selection of sandwiches and salads with healthy
and creative ingredients such as wild lentils,
forest mushrooms and lamb. The pastries,
cakes and chocolates are delectable and well
worth the indulgence.

The Vegetarian   CAMBODIAN, VEGETARIAN **$**
(Map p54; 158 St 19; mains US$2-4; ⊙10.30am-
8.30pm Mon-Sat; 🍴) This is one of the
best-value spots in Phnom Penh as it doesn't
skimp on portions. Noodles and fried rice
are the specialities. The leafy setting in a
quiet nook off central Sihanouk Blvd is yet
another plus.

Sleuk Chhouk   CAMBODIAN **$$**
(Map p54; ☑012 979199; 165 St 51; mains US$3-
10; ⊙10.30am-3pm & 5-10pm; ❄🔊) This place
doesn't look like much from the street, but
venture inside for a dining experience that
includes a clay pot containing zesty frogs'
legs and quails' eggs in sugar palm and black
pepper, or a fish-egg soup. Or test your taste
buds with some stir-fried beef with red ants.

Kravanh   CAMBODIAN **$$**
(Map p54; ☑012 792088; 112 Samdech Sothearos
Blvd; mains US$3-8; ⊙11.30am-10pm; ❄🔊) A
stylish Khmer restaurant under the steward-
ship of a Franco-Khmer, the linen and decor
set this place apart from its neighbours. The
menu includes traditional salads, scented
soups and regional specialities.

Magnolia   VIETNAMESE **$$**
(Map p54; ☑012 529977; 55 St 51; mains US$3-
8; ⊙6am-10pm; ❄🔊) Set in a gracefully re-
stored old French villa, this place offers an
affordable lunchtime buffet, wafer-thin *ban
xeo* (Vietnamese savoury pancakes) and an
array of classics from Hanoi to Saigon. Great
value for those seeking an authentic Viet-
namese meal.

Ngon   HAWKER **$$**
(Map p54; ☑023-987151; www.ngonpnh.com; 60
Sihanouk Blvd; dishes US$3-9; ⊙6.30am-10pm;
🔊) A Cambodian outpost of the popular

Quan An Ngon in Saigon, this place brings street food to a sophisticated setting. The concept is simple: just wander around the hawkers with their wares and choose the tastiest looking dishes, although it's also fine to order straight from the menu.

Sonoma Oyster Bar SEAFOOD $$
(Map p54; ☑ 077 723911; 11 St 222; 6-oyster platters US$7.50-9; ⊙ 5-11pm; ❈ 🖥) The owner here sells premium imported oysters wholesale to top-end hotels and, luckily for us, sells them here to dine-in diners at bargain prices. A must for raw oyster lovers. Scallops and steaks are among other tempting options.

Enso Cafe CAFE $$
(Map p54; ☑ 078 626240; http://enso-cafe.com; 50B St 240; US$4-9.50; ⊙ 7am-8pm; 🖥🖊) A mod Australian cafe that started out with a top breakfast and brunch, and has moved on to include a dinner menu too. Brunch options include leek, Gruyère cheese and salmon tart and a hangover-tastic *chakchouka* (poached eggs in a tomato, pepper and onion sauce). The vegan menu includes shepherdless pie.

ARTillery CAFE $$
(Map p54; ☑ 078 985530; http://artillerycafe.com; St 240½; mains US$4-6; ⊙ 7.30am-9pm Tue-Sun, to 5pm Mon; 🖥🖊) Healthy salads, sandwiches, shakes and snacks like hummus and falafel are served in this creative space on an artsy alley off St 240, imaginatively named St 240½. The menu is mostly vegetarian, and pizza is among the offerings on its small raw-food menu. The daily specials are worth a sample.

Backyard Cafe VEGAN $$
(Map p54; ☑ 078 751715; www.backyardeats.com; 11B St 246; dishes US$3.50-4.30pm Mon, 7.30am-8pm Tue-Sun; ❈🖥🖊) A cool and contemporary superfoods cafe, this is the place to check the pulse(s) of the vegetarian dining scene in the capital. Raw foods include stuffed avocado and a vegan abundance bowl. The mouth-watering desserts are also vegan.

Black Bambu FUSION $$$
(Map p54; ☑ 023-966895; www.black-bambu.com; 29 St 228; US$3.50-21.50; ⊙ 8.30am-11pm Tue-Sun) 🖉 This contemporary space is home to the stylish Black Bambu, which works with the Cambodia Children's Fund to help train former dump children in the art of hospitality. The menu includes delicious sharing plates, such as homemade lamb-and-lemongrass sausages and black-pepper caramel pork belly.

🍴 Boeng Keng Kang & Tonle Bassac Area

Brown Coffee CAFE $
(Map p54; ☑ 023-217262; www.browncoffee.com. kh; cnr Sts 294 & 57; dishes US$2-5; ⊙ 7am-9pm; ❈🖥) The flagship outlet of a homegrown coffee chain that has outperformed all the expensive imports to produce some of the most refined spaces and best coffee in town. There are lots of branches around town as the company has set its sights on cracking Cambodia and, possibly, Asia.

Eleven One Kitchen CAMBODIAN $
(Map p54; ☑ 086 619111; 37 St 334; US$2.50-6.50; ⊙ 7am-9pm Mon-Thu, 7am-11pm Fri & Sat; 🖥) Eleven One Kitchen specialises in healthy Cambodian cuisine, using pesticide-free vegetables and no MSG in their flavoursome food. A standout dish is stir-fried chicken with mango and cashew nut. Set lunch options start from just US$3.50 and the menu includes some Western dishes to round things out.

Aeon Mall Food Court ASIAN $
(Map p54; 132 Samdech Sothearos Blvd; mains US$1-6; ⊙ 9am-10pm; ❈🖥) It may be surprising to venture into the country's swankiest mall to find cheap eats, but there are two food courts here covering the best of Asia and beyond. Downstairs is the more local option with noodle soups, fried rice and fresh sushi. Upstairs is the World Dining Food Court, with fancier furnishings and live music some evenings.

JoMa Bakery Cafe CAFE $
(Map p54; www.joma.biz; cnr Norodom Blvd & St 294; dishes US$2-6; ⊙ 8am-10pm; ❈🖥) Originating in Laos, JoMa Bakery Cafe has used a winning formula to expand rapidly in the Cambodian capital. Salads, soups and sandwiches in various combinations make up the menu, but the coffee, cakes and shakes are not to be missed.

Ramen & Gyoza Bar Masamune JAPANESE $
(Map p54; ☑ 012 734163; Bassac Lane, M47 St 308; mains US$2.50-10; ⊙ 11.30am-3pm & 5.30pm-midnight) At this hip Japanese ramen bar in the hipster Bassac Lane area of town, the ramen is lip-slurpingly good and comes in both dry and wet (soup) varieties. There are some great-value set lunches from US$7 to US$8. By night, it doubles as a bar and serves sake to a backdrop of live music.

Taste Budz　　　　　　　　INDIAN **$**
(Map p54; ☎ 092 961554; 13E St 282; mains US$3-6; ☺ 10am-2.30pm & 5-10pm; ❋) This pint-sized outfit with the curious moniker is one of the best of Phnom Penh's many Indian restaurants. The speciality is Kerala (South Indian) cuisine, including spicy *kedai* dishes, which are divine. Order *porotta* (flat bread) on the side and dig in with your hands.

Dosa Corner　　　　　　　INDIAN **$**
(Map p54; 5E St 51; mains US$1.50-5; ☺ 8.30am-2pm & 5-10pm) Fans of Indian dosas will be pleased to discover this place does just what it says on the label – namely, a generous variety of savoury pancakes from the south. Vegetarian thalis are a bargain at US$4.

★**Malis**　　　　　　　　CAMBODIAN **$$**
(Map p54; ☎ 023-221022; www.malis-restaurant.com; 136 Norodom Blvd; mains US$6-20; ☺ 7am-11pm; ❋ ☎) The leading Khmer restaurant in the Cambodian capital, Malis is a chic place to dine alfresco. The original menu includes beef in bamboo, goby with Kampot peppercorns, and traditional soups and salads. It's popular for a boutique breakfast: the breakfast sets are a good deal at US$3 to US$5. Book ahead for dinner.

★**Dashi**　　　　　　　　JAPANESE **$$**
(Map p54; ☎ 023-666 1602; www.dashi-kh.com; 2 St 352; US$7-15; ☺ 11.30am-2.30pm & 5-10pm Tue-Sun; ❋ ☎) Widely acknowledged to be the best Japanese restaurant in Phnom Penh by the growing Japanese community, Dashi offers one of the best set-lunch deals in the city with a selection of mains from US$7 to US$10 accompanied by an array of sides. Named in honour of the staple soup stock that helped shape a nation.

Java Café　　　　　　　　CAFE **$$**
(Map p54; ☎ 023-987420; www.javaarts.org; 56 Sihanouk Blvd; mains US$4-8; ☺ 7am-10pm; ❋ ☎) Consistently popular thanks to a breezy balcony, air-conditioned interior and a creative menu that includes crisp salads, delicious homemade sandwiches, burgers and excellent coffee from several continents. The upstairs doubles as an art gallery, the downstairs as a bakery.

Piccola Italia Da Luigi　　　　PIZZA **$$**
(Map p54; ☎ 017 323273; 36 St 308; pizzas US$5-10; ☺ 11am-2pm & 6-10pm; ☎) This is the place where it all began and it's hard to believe this was just a quiet residential street just

a few years ago. A bustling kerbside eatery just like you'd find in Italy, Luigi's certainly has a claim to making some of the best pizza in Phnom Penh. After dark, reservations are recommended.

Lost Room　　　　　　INTERNATIONAL **$$**
(Map p54; ☎ 078 700001; www.thelostroom.asia; 43 St 21; dishes US$4-12.50; ☺ 5pm-late Mon-Sat; ☎) Located in the back streets of Bassac district, look out for the symbolic key and you have found a hidden gem. The menu is all about small plates and sharing, so bring along some friends. Try the signature lamb tenderloin fillets or sea bass with goat-cheese tartare.

Mama Wong's　　　　CHINESE, FUSION **$$**
(Map p54; ☎ 097 850 8383; 41 St 308; mains US$3-8; ☺ 10am-10pm; ☎) This brings a contemporary touch to the Chinese dining scene in the city, serving up traditional noodle soups, steamed buns and congee, but with miniburgers, sliders and more that mix Asian and European flavours. Good value, good fun.

Bistrot Langka　　　　　　FRENCH **$$**
(Map p54; ☎ 010 740705; 132 Z13 St 51; US$6-15; ☺ 6-10pm daily; ❋ ☎) Located at the far end of this up-and-coming alley off St 51, Bistrot Langka offers fine French dining in a casual atmosphere at an affordable price. They specialise in the *sous vide* style of vacuum-packed cooking, which ensures tender meat and succulent fish. Tuna tataki and an original beef tartare are some standout moments.

Mexicano Restaurant　　　　MEXICAN **$$**
(Map p54; ☎ 096 861 2353; 29 St 288; US$4-9; ☺ noon-2.30pm & 6-11pm; ☎) One of the leading new wave of Mexican restaurants to open their doors in Phnom Penh, Mexicano offers some delicious tacos, including pulled pork or succulent river fish. Frozen margaritas and Corona beer complete the picture.

Sushi Bar　　　　　　　JAPANESE **$$**
(Map p54; ☎ 023-726438; 2D St 302; sushi sets from US$6; ☺ 11am-10pm; ❋ ☎) Purists will scoff at the low sushi prices, but it's always packed for a reason. Definitely one of the better places in town for quick-and-easy raw fish. Sit downstairs at the bar, outside on the patio or in private rooms upstairs.

Farm to Table　　　　　　　CAFE **$$**
(Map p54; ☎ 078 899722; 16 St 360; mains US$3.50-7; ☺ 8am-10pm; ☎ ✐) ✿ Farm to

GOING LOCAL

Khmer Barbecue & Soup Restaurants

After dark, Khmer eateries scattered across town illuminate their neon signs, calling locals in for fine fare and generous jugs of draught beer. Don't be shy – the food is great and the atmosphere lively.

The speciality at most of these places is grilled strips of meat or seafood, but they also serve fried noodles and rice, curries and other pan-fried faves, along with some veggie options.

Many of these places also offer *phnom pleung* (hill of fire), which amounts to cook-your-own meat over a personal barbecue. Another speciality is *soup chhnang dei* (cook-your-own soup in a clay pot), which is great fun if you go in a group. Other diners will often help with protocol, as it is important to cook things in the right order so as not to overcook half the ingredients and eat the rest raw.

Khmer barbecues are all over the place, so it won't be hard to find one. **Koh Pich**, east of hulking Naga World casino, has a cluster of well-reputed barbecues.

Sovanna II (Map p54; 2C St 21; mains US$2-8; ⊙6-11am & 3-11pm; 🐓) Sovanna II is always jumping with locals and a smattering of expats who have made this their barbecue of choice thanks to the huge menu and cheap local beer. It's also as good a place as any to sample the national breakfast, *bei sait chrouk* (pork and rice).

Psar Kabco Restaurant (Map p54; 📞012 702708; 5 St 9; dishes US$1.50-4; ⊙6am-9pm) Located opposite the very local Psar Kabco (Kabco Market), this is a great Cambodian-Chinese restaurant serving a panoply of street flavours, including noodle soups, point-and-eat curries and stews, and Khmer desserts.

Red Cow (Map p54; 126 Norodom Blvd; mains US$2.50-7; ⊙4-11pm) Grills up everything imaginable – eel, eggplant, frog, pig intestine, quail – and also offers curries and other traditional Khmer dishes.

Street Fare & Markets

Street fare is not quite as familiar or user-friendly here as in, say, Bangkok. But if you're a little adventurous and want to save boatloads of money, look no further. Breakfast is when the streetside eateries really get hopping, as many Cambodians eat out for breakfast. Look for filled seats and you can't go wrong.

Phnom Penh's many markets all have large central eating areas, where stalls serve up local faves like noodle soup and fried noodles. Most dishes cost a reasonable US$1 to US$2. The best market for eating is the **Russian Market** (p81), with an interior food zone that's easy to find and has a nice variety of Cambodian specialities; the large car park on the west side converts to seafood barbecues and more from around 4pm. **Psar Thmei** (p80) and **Psar O Russei** (p81) are other great choices. **Psar Kandal** (Map p60; btwn Sts 144 & 154), just off the riverfront, gets going a little later and is an early-evening option where Cambodians come for takeaway food.

If the markets are just too hot or claustrophobic for your taste, look out for the mobile street sellers carrying their wares on their shoulders or wheeling them around in small carts. Another popular all-day option is a row of **curry noodle stalls** (Map p54; St 7; mains US$1-2) opposite Wat Botum Park.

Table offers a lush garden laden with jackfruit trees, and with an old tractor for kids to clamber around on. It aims to promote organic farming methods in Cambodia and has a healthy menu of all-day breakfasts, salads, sandwiches and shakes. Live music from 6pm on Fridays.

Comme à la Maison FRENCH $$
(Map p54; 📞023-360801; www.commealamaison-delicatessen.com; 13 St 57; mains US$5-12; ⊙6am-10.30pm; 🐓) This attractive open-air restaurant under a thatched Balinese-style roof has an extensive menu of provincial French fare, plus pizza and pasta and enticing weekly specials. An on-site bakery makes this a good spot for delicious pastries.

Russian Market

Vego Salad Bar CAFE $$
(Map p54; ☎ 011 457711; 3 St 51; dishes US$4-7; ⊙7.30am-9pm; ✳🖥🖉) Vego attracts health nuts with its design-your-own salads and wraps. Choose your leaves, veggies, meat or dairy and condiments and you have a bespoke salad. Set combos are available with health drinks.

Aussie XL INTERNATIONAL $$
(Map p54; ☎ 023-301001; www.aussiexl.com; 205A St 51; mains US$7-14; ⊙9am-11pm) The name says it all: this is a place for serious stuffing. Supersized fish, lamb, chicken, steak and about every type of burger imaginable is available. Weekends sometimes see pigs roasted on spits. Also the place for Aussie sports on the telly.

Topaz FRENCH $$$
(Map p54; ☎ 023-221622; www.topaz-restaurant. com; 162 Norodom Blvd; dishes US$8-50; ⊙11am-2pm & 5.30-10.30pm; ✳🖥) One of Phnom Penh's original designer restaurants, Topaz is housed in an elegant villa with reflective pools and a walk-in wine cellar. The menu is classic Paris, including delicate Burgundy snails drizzled in garlic, and steak tartare for those with rare tastes.

Self Catering

Super Duper SUPERMARKET $
(Map p54; www.super-duper.biz; 3 Samdech Sothearos Blvd; ⊙24hr; ✳) Phnom Penh's only 24-hour supermarket, this could be handy if the midnight munchies strike. It has one of the best product ranges in town, as the owners import containers direct from the US and Australia.

✗ Russian Market Area

There is nothing better than an iced coffee or fresh fruit shake after surviving the scrum that is the Russian Market (p81). In the market's central food-stall area, look out for the

Russian Market

charismatic **Mr Bounnareth** (Map p74; Shop 547, Russian Market; ⏰7am-5pm), whose patented 'best iced coffee in Phnom Penh' has been living up to its name for more than three decades. Other stalls sell fried noodles and *banh chev* (meat or seafood and veggies wrapped inside a thin egg pancake and lettuce leaf) for US$1 to US$2.

The streets emanating east and south from the Russian Market are home to several stand-out restaurants and bars.

★**Vibe Cafe**   VEGAN $
(Map p74; ☏061 764937; www.vibecafeasia.com; 26A St 446; US$4.50-7; ⏰7.30am-9pm Tue-Sun, 7.30am-4.30pm Mon; ❄☎♨) Vibe Cafe sets itself out as the capital's first 100% vegan restaurant and creates original homemade superfood recipes in its laboratory-like kitchen. The signature Ritual Bowl is packed full of goodness including quinoa, beetroot, hummus and a whole lot more. It has innovative cleansing juices such as activated charcoal, coconut water, ginger, lemon and cayenne pepper. Detox!

Sesame Noodle Bar   NOODLES $
(Map p74; ☏089 750212; www.sesamenoodlebar.com; 9 St 460; mains US$2.50-5.75; ⏰11.30am-2.30pm & 5-9.30pm Tue-Sun; ☎) A Japanese-American duo is behind one of the Russian Market's longest-running little diners. Cold noodles arrive in vegetarian or

egg varieties and come heaped with an egg and carmelised pork or grilled tofu. Simply delicious.

Trattoria Bello   ITALIAN $
(Map p74; ☏096 341 0936; 17c St 460; medium pizzas US$3.25-8.80; ⏰noon-2.30pm & 5.30-10.30pm; ☎) Hidden away near the Russian Market, Bello turns out some of the most delicious pizzas in town at giveaway prices. The Japanese owner also offers pasta, gnocchi and *polpettine* (meatballs).

Sumatra   INDONESIAN $
(Map p74; 67 St 123; mains US$2.50-5; ⏰11am-8pm; ☎♨) The vegetarian dishes, which average around US$3, are fantastic value, although hearty eaters may want to order two. The spicy *balado* (tomato and chilli sauce) dishes are good. The restaurant recently relocated and dining is in a garden patio under a tin roof or an air-con interior.

★**Brooklyn Bistro**   INTERNATIONAL $$
(Map p74; ☏089 925926; 20 St 123; dishes US$3-17; ⏰11am-10pm; ❄☎) A stylish American diner, this is incredibly popular with Phnom Penh expats in the know. The 16in pizzas are the largest in town, plus there's a dedicated menu of wings, as well as great deli sandwiches and the best New York cheesecake we've tasted in this part of the world.

Buffalo Sister   SANDWICHES $$
(Map p74; ☏017 879403; 55D St 456; sandwiches from US$4.25; ⏰11am-7.30pm; ☎) The extensive sandwich list is written on a chalkboard on the walls of this self-described carvery. Dig into a roast pork with apple sauce sandwich or go healthy with a roast veggie or felafel wrap. Famous for its Sunday roast.

Drinking & Nightlife

Phnom Penh has some great bars and clubs, so it's definitely worth one big night out here. There are lots of late-night spots clustered around the intersection of Sts 51 and 172, appropriately nicknamed 'Area 51'. 'Golden St' (St 278) is also popular, and the riverfront has its share of bars as well. St 308 and Bassac Lane have emerged as the hipster area of town.

Bars

Happy hours are a big thing in Phnom Penh, so it pays to get started early, when even such storied watering holes as the Foreign Correspondents' Club and the Raffles offer two-for-one specials. Wednesday is 'Ladies' Night' at some of the smarter bars around town, with two-for-one deals all night or even free drinks.

Most bars are open until at least midnight, which is about the time that Phnom Penh's clubs swing into action.

There are now some good microbreweries around town turning out homegrown craft beer and these are well worth seeking out.

There are some great hostel bars in Phnom Penh, so keep these in mind if you want to meet other travellers on a big night out. Top Banana (p65) is one of the liveliest rooftop bars. OPr check out the rooftop bar at Mad Monkey (p65), in the same part of town. Eighty8 Backpackers (p61) has a 'first Friday of the month' party that sees the expat and backpacker worlds collide. Sundance Inn has two lively bars at its two locations on **St 172** (Map p60; ☑ 016 802090; www.sundancecambodia.com; 61 St 172; r US$26-40; ❋ @ ☎ ⛵) and the **riverside** (79 Sisowath Quay).

🍷 North Central (Riverfront)

★**FCC**   BAR

(Foreign Correspondents' Club; Map p60; 363 Sisowath Quay; ⊙ 6am-midnight; ☎) A Phnom Penh institution, the 'F' is housed in a colonial gem with great views and cool breezes. It's one of those must-see places in Cambodia. Happy hours are 5pm to 7pm and 10pm to midnight. If the main bar is too crowded, head up to the rooftop, which often sees live music at weekends. Renovations are scheduled during 2018. It also offers an excellent menu both day and night.

Oskar Bistro   BAR

(Map p60; www.oskar-bistro.com; 159 Sisowath Quay; ⊙ 5pm-2am; ☎) This upscale gastro-pub blends the bar and restaurant to perfection. Choose from creative cocktails and a huge wine list, while relaxing to the sound of subtle DJ beats. A top spot for a late-night feed, as the kitchen stays open until 11pm.

Chow   BAR

(Map p60; 277 Sisowath Quay; ⊙ 7am-11pm) The Quay hotel's swanky rooftop has river views, cooling breezes and happy hours (half-price off US$6 drinks) from 4pm to 8.30pm. The creative cocktail list includes zesty infusions such as ginger and lemongrass, plus a passion-fruit caipirinha.

Olala   BAR

(Map p60; ☑ 023-223193; 216 Sisowath Quay; ⊙ 7am-midnight; ☎) Probably the cheapest beer on the riverfront thanks to a generous happy hour that starts at 3pm and rumbles on until closing. US$1 bottles of local beer and a who's who of imported beers at bargain prices. A restaurant as much as a bar, it's a good place to watch the world go by.

Paddy Rice   IRISH PUB

(Map p60; 213 Sisowath Quay; ⊙ 24hr; ☎) A real jack of all trades with good pub grub, big screens for sports viewing, and occasional live music, plus Thursday is open-mic night. All this in a perfect riverside location.

🍷 North Central (Inland)

Elephant Bar   BAR

(Map p60; Raffles Hotel Le Royal, St 92; ⊙ noon-midnight; ☎) Few places are more atmospheric than this sophisticated bar at the Raffles. It has been drawing journalists, politicos, and the rich and famous for more than 80 years. Singapore slings and many more drinks are half-price during the generous happy hour (4pm to 9pm). The bar also boasts world class G and Ts.

Dusk Til Dawn   BAR

(Map p60; 46 St 172; ⊙ 5pm-late) Also known as Reggae Bar thanks to the laid-back beats, Dusk Til Dawn's rooftop setting makes it a great spot for a sundowner, but the party lasts well into the night. The bar is split over two levels, so continue upstairs if it's quiet. Ride the lift to the top floor in the tall building opposite Pontoon club.

Dodo Rhum House   BAR

(Map p60; 133 St 130; ⊙ 5pm-late) This French favourite specialises in homemade, flavoured rums infused with tropical fruits and spices. Also serves an excellent fish fillet and other tasty treats.

Blue Chili   GAY

(Map p60; 36 St 178; ⊙ 6pm-late; ☎) The owner of this long-running, gay-friendly bar stages his own drag show every Friday and Saturday at 10.30pm.

🍸 South Central

Hops Brewery   MICROBREWERY

(Map p54; ☑ 023-217039; www.hops-brewery.com; 17 St 228; ⊙ 11am-midnight; ☎) Hops is the latest microbrewery to claim a slice of the craft-beer action in Phnom Penh. German-run, it follows the 500-year-old purity law of brewing and tipples include pilsner Gold Angel, wheat beer Amber Witch and Hops IPA. There are some top pool tables and a spacious garden by day or night and a predominantly Mittel-Europa menu.

Eclipse
BAR

(Map p54; Phnom Penh Tower, 445 Monivong Blvd; ⊙5pm-2am) Located on the 24th floor, this open-air venue is the dry-season venue of choice for big breezes and bigger views. The menu includes cocktails, wine by the glass and beers, but you pay a premium for the dramatic location.

Boeng Keng Kang & Tonle Bassac Area

★Botanico Wine & Beer Garden
CRAFT BEER

(Map p54; ☑077 943135; www.facebook.com/botanicowineandbeergarden; 9B St 29; ⊙9am-10pm Mon-Sat; 🐾) Bringing US-style craft-brewing to Phnom Penh, this great little hideaway stocks Irish Red, IPA and other homebrewed beers. It is set in a verdant garden tucked down a winding alley. Monthly specials include yoga and beer, plus pork-knuckle nights.

★Score
BAR

(Map p54; ☑023-221357; www.scorekh.com; 5 St 282; ⊙8am-late; 🐾) With its cinema-sized screen and television banks on every wall, this cavernous bar is the best place to watch a big game. It's not just the usual footy and rugby, as almost all sports are catered for here. Several pool tables tempt those who would rather play than watch.

Zeppelin Bar
BAR

(Map p54; St 278; ⊙5pm-late) Who says vinyl is dead? It lives on here, thanks to the owner of this old-school rock bar spinning the turntables every night. The mainstay on the menu is '70s big rock. There is also a pool table. Zeppelin has a breezy upstairs location on popular 'Golden St'.

Che Culo
BAR

(Map p54; www.checulocambodia.com; 6B St 302; ⊙11am-late Mon-Sat; 🐾) A likeable little spot, this bar is all retro tiles and seated alcoves, making for an intimate atmosphere. Great cocktails are even greater during happy hours from 5pm to 7pm. A tapas-style menu is available day and night.

Duplex
BAR

(Map p54; 3 St 278; ⊙10am-2am; 🐾) A self-styled Belgian *taverne* with an extensive beer selection, it's also a cool contemporary space that hosts regular salsa and Latin evenings. Great cocktails and a good range of light meals are available. Upstairs it morphs into Club Love, a popular late-night spot for travellers and expats alike.

Le Boutier
COCKTAIL BAR

(Map p54; www.leboutier.com; 32 St 308; ⊙5pm-late Mon-Sat; 🐾) One of the coolest cocktail bars in Phnom Penh, Le Boutier has an original menu of concoctions that pay homage to Cambodia's golden era of the 1960s, including 'Sinn Sisamouth in the Second City' with bourbon, honey, averna, coffee and cinnamon. Golden hour kicks off at 5pm with discounted cocktails and two-for-one beers.

Battbong
BAR

(Map p54; ☑069 291643; St 288 Alley East; ⊙6pm-late; 🐾) A new speakeasy, Battbong is tricky to locate. Look out for the Coca-Cola machine at the end of the alley and locate the hidden button. Inside is a decadent beatnik-style bar with bottled beers, wine by the glass and some stiff drinks. Smoking is allowed, so the air can get hazy.

DON'T MISS

BASSAC LANE BARS

Bassac Lane is the moniker given to an alley that leads south off St 308. The brainchild of Kiwi brothers the Norbert-Munns, who have a flair for drinks and design, there are half a dozen or more hole-in-the-wall boozers in this eclectic spot. Choose from fusion wraps and burgers at the original **Meat & Drink** (Map p54; ☑089 666414; mains US$5-10; ⊙5pm-1am), tiny and intimate **Seibur** (Map p54; St 308; ⊙5pm-1am), the refined **Library** (Map p54; ⊙5pm-1am; 🐾), newcomer **Harry's Bar** (Map p54; ⊙5pm-1am) or custom-bike tribute bar, **Hangar 44** (Map p54; ⊙5pm-1am). There's even a gin palace, the tiny **Cicada Bar** (Map p54; ⊙5pm-1am). From out of nowhere, Bassac Lane has become the new Bohemian district of Phnom Penh and is well worth a visit.

Red Bar
BAR

(Map p54; cnr Sts 308 & 29; ☺5pm-1am; 🛜) A friendly little local bar in the popular St 308. The drinks here are so cheap that drinkers find themselves lingering long into the night...or maybe that's just us?

🍷 Russian Market Area

★Long After Dark
BAR

(Map p74; ☑093 768354; http://longafterdark cambodia.com; 86 St 450; ☺noon-midnight Sun-Thu, noon-2am Fri & Sat; 🛜) This place has kept visitors hanging around the Russian Market area long after dark thanks to a combination of rare single-malt whiskies, Cambodian craft beers and a vinyl collection that starts a-spinnin' at weekends. Brief happy hour at 5pm on Friday and some interesting whisky flights available with Highland or global themes. Cool and cosy all at once.

Alchemy GastroPub
MICROBREWERY

(Map p74; ☑023-620 3636; 36 St 123; ☺5pm-1.30am; 🛜) This is one of the capital's most stylish brew pubs, offering a selection of local and regional craft brews and some hioctane cocktails, with two-for-one offers on at least one cocktail every night. Weekend events include live music and there is an impressive menu to help ensure the drinking stays on track.

FLOWER DISEMPOWER

Anyone who spends a night or two on the town in Phnom Penh will soon be familiar with young girls and boys hovering around popular bars and restaurants to sell decorative flowers. The kids are incredibly sweet and most people succumb to their charms and buy a flower or two. All these late nights for young children might not be so bad if they were benefiting from their hard-earned cash, but usually they're not. Look down the road and there will be a driver of a *moto* (motorcycle taxi) with an ice bucket full of these flowers waiting to ferry the children to another popular spot. Yet again, the charms of children are exploited for the benefit of adults who should know better. Think twice before buying, as the child is unlikely to reap the reward.

Sundown Social Club
BAR

(Map p74; ☑016 936645; 86 St 440; ☺noon-11pm Tue-Sun; 🛜) Look at the Russian Market from a different angle from this funky rooftop bar on St 440. Head here for a sundowner including Club Tropicana–inspired cocktails, craft beers and a menu of innovative pub grub and bar snacks.

Cafes

Happy Damrei
CAFE

(Map p60; ☑010 227149; 1 St 174; ☺7.30am-11pm; 🛜) Formerly the Puzzle Chamber, this cool little cafe is the epicentre of board games in Phnom Penh and it has everything from classics such as Risk and Cluedo to contemporary offerings like Cards Against Humanity. US$3 per hour to play but heavily discounted for longer sessions. Food and drinks are available.

Starbucks Reserve
CAFE

(Map p54; ☑093 897784; 14 St 57; ☺6.30am-10pm; 🛜) This is no ordinary branch of Starbucks, but a flagship 'Reserve'. Make for the barista bar for small-batch coffees brewed in test tubes and served at your table at regular prices.

Nightclubs

For the low-down on club nights, check out Phnom Penh Underground (www.phnom-penh-underground.com), an online guide to the club scene in Cambodia's capital.

★Pontoon
CLUB

(Map p60; www.pontoonclub.com; 80 St 172; weekends US$3-5, weekdays free; ☺9.30pm-late; 🛜) After floating around from pier to pier for a few years (hence the name), the city's premier nightclub found a permanent home on terra firma. It draws top local DJs and occasional big foreign acts. Thursday is gay-friendly night, with a 1am lady-boy show. Adjacent Pontoon Pulse is more of a lounge-club, with electronica and ambient music.

Heart of Darkness
CLUB

(Map p60; 26 St 51; ☺8pm-late) This Phnom Penh institution with an alluring Angkor theme has evolved more into a nightclub than a bar over the years. It goes off every night of the week, attracting all – and we mean *all* – sorts. Everybody should stop in at least once just to bask in the aura and atmosphere of the place.

Vito
CLUB

(Map p48; 8 St 214; ⊗9pm-3am) A popular retro club spinning some older dance tunes, from the '90s to the '00s, and even back to the '80s. Popular with a slightly older crowd who want to have a conversation as well as a dance.

Epic
CLUB

(Map p54; ☎010 600608; www.epic.com.kh; 122b Tonlé Bassac; ⊗9pm-5am) The superclub comes to Phnom Penh with the emergence of Epic. This is a huge warehouse space but the decor and design is anything but 'warehouse' – this is aimed at Cambodia's rich young things.

Valentino's
GAY & LESBIAN

(Map p60; ☎093 839647; St 174; ⊗10.30-4am; ☎) Although other places have long been gay friendly, this is the first out-and-out gay club to open in Phnom Penh. It's a popular late-night spot thanks to a 10pm happy hour and a nightly show around midnight.

☆ Entertainment

For news on what's happening in town, *AsiaLife* is a free monthly with entertainment features and regular listings. The Friday edition of the *Phnom Penh Post* includes the '7 Days' supplement with listings information.

Cinema

★ Meta House
CINEMA

(Map p54; www.meta-house.com; 37 Samdech Sothearos Blvd; ⊗4pm-midnight Tue-Sun; ☎) This German-run cinema screens art-house films, documentaries and shorts from Cambodia and around the world most evenings at 4pm (admission free) and 7pm (admission varies). Films are sometimes followed by Q&As with those involved. Order German sausages, pizza-like 'flamecakes' and beer to supplement your viewing experience.

Major Cineplex
CINEMA

(Map p54; ☎023-901111; www.majorcineplex.com.kh; Aeon Mall, 132 Samdech Sothearos Blvd; US$3-15; ⊗9am-midnight) The smartest cinema in town, with seven screens, including a business-class-like VIP screen and a 4DX screen for interactive viewing (complete with moving seats and surprise effects).

Flicks
CINEMA

(Map p54; www.theflicks-cambodia.com; 39B St 95; tickets US$3.50; ☎) It shows at least two movies a day in an uber-comfortable air-conditioned screening room. You can watch both films on one ticket.

Bophana Centre
CINEMA

(Map p54; ☎023-992174; www.bophana.org; 64 St 200; ⊗8am-noon & 2-6pm Mon-Fri, 2-6pm Sat) **FREE** Established by Cambodian-French filmmaker Rithy Panh, this centre is an audiovisual resource for filmmakers and researchers. Visitors can explore its archive of old photographs and films and attend free film screenings held on on Saturdays at 4pm.

Classical Dance & Arts

★ Traditional Dance Show
PERFORMING ARTS

(Map p60; ☎017 998570; www.cambodianlivingarts.org; National Museum, St 178; adult/child from US$15/10; ⊗7pm daily Oct-Mar, Mon-Sat Jun-Aug, Mon, Wed, Fri & Sat Apr-May & Sep) ✏ The Traditional Dance Show is a series of must-see performances put on by Cambodian Living Arts (p58). There are three rotating shows, each lasting about an hour: *Shadow & Light* (Monday to Wednesday); *Grace & Grandeur* (Thursday and Saturday); and *Heaven & Earth* (Friday and Sunday). Set in the attractive grounds of the National Museum, there's also an optional dinner show (US$30, 5.30pm).

Sovanna Phum Arts Association
PERFORMING ARTS

(☎010 337552; 166 St 99, btwn Sts 484 & 498; adult/child US$5/3) ✏ Regular traditional shadow-puppet performances and occasional classical dance and traditional drum shows are held here at 7.30pm every Friday and Saturday night. Audience members are invited to try their hand at the shadow puppets after the 50-minute performance. Classes are available in the art of shadow puppetry, puppet making, classical and folk dance, and traditional Khmer musical instruments.

Apsara Arts Association
DANCE

(Map p44; ☎012 979335; www.apsara-art.org; 71 St 598; tickets US$6-7) ✏ Alternate performances of classical dance and folk dance are held most Saturdays at 7pm (call to confirm). Visitors are also welcome from 7.30am to 10.30am and from 2pm to 5pm Monday to Saturday to watch the students in training (suggested donation is US$3).

CAMBODIAN FIGHT CLUB

The whole world knows about *muay Thai* (Thai boxing) and the sport of kickboxing, but what is not so well known is that this contact sport probably originated in Cambodia. *Pradal serey* (literally 'free fighting') is Cambodia's very own version of kickboxing; you can see some fights in Phnom Penh. Popular Cambodian TV channel CTN hosts live bouts at 2pm on Friday, Saturday and Sunday out at its main studio on National Hwy 5, about 4km north of the Japanese Bridge. Entry is free and there is usually a rowdy local crowd surreptitiously betting on the fights. Most bouts are ended by a violent elbow move and there's a lot more ducking and diving than with other kickboxing genres.

An even older martial art is *bokator*, or *labokatao*, which some say dates back to the time of Angkor. It translates as 'pounding a lion' and was originally conceived for battle-field confrontations. Weapons include bamboo staffs and short sticks, as well as the *krama* (checked scarf) in certain situations. The **Pras Khan Chey Bokator School** (p58) in Phnom Penh offers lessons (US$5 per hour) or full brown-belt courses (US$1500). Call ahead to ensure you get an English-speaking instructor.

Chatomuk Theatre   THEATRE
(Map p54; Sisowath Quay) Check the flyer out front for information on performances at the landmark Chatomuk Theatre, located in the heart of Phnom Penh's popular riverfront. Officially, it has been turned into a government conference centre, but it regularly plays host to cultural performances.

Cambodia Living Arts Yike Class   OPERA
(Map p54; 65 Samdech Sothearos Blvd) ⏹ These daily traditional-opera classes for at-risk youth are run by master theatre performer Ieng Sithul from Cambodia Living Arts, and are open to tourists.

Amrita Performing Arts   PERFORMING ARTS
(Map p54; www.amritaperformingarts.org; 128 Samdech Sothearos Blvd) Amrita Performing Arts creates new stories with traditional Apsara dancers, and worked closely with CLA (p58) to organise the 'Season of Cambodia' in New York.

Live Music

Phnom Penh boasts a surprisingly active music scene, with several talented expat and mixed Khmer-expat bands. Check out Leng Pleng (www.lengpleng.com) for weekly live-music listings in Phnom Penh.

Showbox   LIVE MUSIC
(Map p54; 11 St 330; ⏱11am-1am; 🛜) This grungy music bar supports regular open-mic nights, as well as doubling up as a popular clubbing venue and occasional comedy club. Look out for cheap deals, including a rather generous free beer from 6.30pm to 7pm daily.

Doors   LIVE MUSIC
(Map p44; 18 St 84; ⏱7am-midnight; 🛜) Self-described as a 'music and tapas' bar, the Doors is a sophisticated place with a long bar, mouth-watering Spanish bites, expensive drinks, live jazz and more.

Sharky's   LIVE MUSIC
(Map p60; 126 St 130; ⏱5pm-late; 🛜) An old-school Phnom Penh hang-out long famous for billiards and babes, Sharky's has done a good job of redirecting its focus towards quality live music. Claims to be Indochina's longest-running rock-and-roll bar.

🛍 Shopping

There is some great shopping to be had in Phnom Penh, but don't forget to bargain in the markets or you'll have your 'head shaved' – local slang for being ripped off.

Markets & Malls

As well as the markets, there are now some shopping malls in Phnom Penh. While they are not quite as glamorous as the likes of the Siam Paragon in Bangkok, they are good places to browse (especially thanks to the air-conditioning) and offer some reliable food courts and restaurants, as well as retail therapy.

★ Psar Thmei   MARKET
(ផ្សារធំ, Central Market; Map p60; St 130; ⏱6.30am-5.30pm) A landmark building in the capital, the art-deco Psar Thmei (literally 'New Market') is often called the Central Market, a reference to its location and size. The huge domed hall resembles a Babylonian ziggurat and some claim it ranks as one of the 10 largest domes in the world.

The design allows for maximum ventilation, and even on a sweltering day the central hall is cool and airy. The market was recently renovated with French government assistance and is in good shape. The market has four wings filled with stalls selling gold and silver jewellery, antique coins, dodgy watches, clothing and other such items. For photographers, the fresh-food section affords many opportunities. For a local lunch, there are a host of food stalls located on the western side, which faces Monivong Blvd.

Psar Thmei is undoubtedly the best market for browsing. However, it has a reputation among Cambodians for overcharging on most products.

Russian Market   MARKET
(Psar Tuol Tom Pong; Map p74; St 155; ⊙ 6am-5pm) This sweltering bazaar is the one market all visitors should come to at least once during a trip to Phnom Penh. It is *the* place to shop for souvenirs and discounted name-brand clothing. We can't vouch for the authenticity of everything, but along with plenty of knock-offs you'll find genuine articles stitched in local factories.

You'll pay less than one-third of the price back home for brands like Banana Republic, Billabong, Calvin Klein, Colombia, Gap and Next. The Russian Market, so-called by foreigners because the predominantly Russian expat population shopped here in the 1980s, also has a large range of handicrafts and antiquities (many fake), including miniature Buddhas, woodcarvings, betel-nut boxes, silks, silver jewellery, musical instruments and so on. Bargain hard, as hundreds of tourists pass through here every day. There are some good food stalls in the Russian Market if you are feeling peckish.

Night Market   MARKET
(Psar Reatrey; Map p60; cnr St 108 & Sisowath Quay; ⊙ 5-11pm daily) A cooler, alfresco version of the Russian Market, this night market takes place every evening if it's not raining. Bargain vigorously, as prices can be on the high side. Interestingly, it's probably more popular with Khmers than foreigners.

Aeon Mall   MALL
(Map p54; www.aeonmallphnompenh.com; 132 Samdech Sothearos Blvd; ☎) The swankiest mall in Phnom Penh, this Japanese-run establishment has international boutiques,

several food courts and extensive dining outlets, plus a seven-screen multiplex cinema, ice skating and a bowling alley.

Jets Container Night Market   NIGHT MARKET
(Map p54; off National Assembly St; ⊙ 3-11pm) The first of a new wave of shipping-container night markets to open in Phnom Penh, it offers dining, drinking and shopping all in one compact space. It is very popular with young Cambodians, although the competing music from different venues ends up blending into a bit of a cacophony.

Psar O Russei   MARKET
(Map p54; St 182; ⊙ 6.30am-5.30pm) Much bigger than other noted markets in town, Psar O Russei sells foodstuffs, costume jewellery, imported toiletries, secondhand clothes and everything else you can imagine from hundreds of stalls. The market is housed in a huge labyrinth of a building that looks like a shopping mall from the outside.

Sorya Shopping Centre   MALL
(Map p60; cnr Sts 63 & 154; ⊙ 9am-9pm) Still a popular mall, this long-running place has a good range of shops, a food court, a cinema, a central location and superb views from the top-floor viewing gallery over the more traditional Psar Thmei.

Clothing, Textiles & Accessories
While the markets are best-known for international clothing from the local garment factories, a multiplying number of stores surrounding the Russian Market sell authentic brand-name gear, made locally and in neighbouring Vietnam. There are also several boutiques around town specialising in silk furnishings and stylish original clothing, as well as glam accessories. Many are conveniently located on St 240, Cambodia's answer to London's King's Rd.

★ Ambre   CLOTHING
(Map p60; ☎ 023-217935; www.romydaketh.net; 37 St 178; ⊙ 10am-6pm) Leading Cambodian fashion designer Romyda Keth has turned this striking French-era mansion into the perfect showcase for her stunning silk collection.

Bliss Boutique   CLOTHING, BEAUTY
(Map p54; 29 St 240; ⊙ 9am-9pm) Casual dresses, blouses and men's shirts made of wonderfully airy materials, plus pillows and scented creams and oils.

GOOD-CAUSE SHOPPING

There are a host of tasteful shops selling handicrafts and textiles to raise money for projects to assist disadvantaged Cambodians. These are a good place to spend some dollars, as it helps to put a little bit back into the country.

Artisans Angkor (Map p60; 12 St 13; ⊙9am-6pm) 🖉 Classy Phnom Penh branch of the venerable Siem Reap sculpture and silk specialist.

Cambodian Handicraft Association (CHA; Map p54; 1 St 350; ⊙8am-7pm) 🖉 Sells fine, handmade silk clothing, scarves, toys and bags produced by victims of land mines and polio.

Daughters of Cambodia (Map p60; www.daughtersofcambodia.org; 321 Sisowath Quay; ⊙9am-5.30pm Mon-Sat) 🖉 An NGO that runs a range of programs to train and assist former prostitutes and victims of sex trafficking. The clothes, bags and accessories here are made with ecofriendly cotton and natural dyes.

Mekong Blue (Map p60; http://mekongblue.com; 9 St 130; ⊙8am-6pm) 🖉 The Phnom Penh boutique for Stung Treng's best-known silk cooperative to empower women. Produces beautiful scarves and shawls, as well as jewellery.

Rajana (Map p74; www.rajanacrafts.org; 170 St 450; ⊙7am-6pm Mon-Sat, 10.30am-5pm Sun) 🖉 One of the best all-round handicraft stores, Rajana aims to promote fair wages and training. It has a beautiful selection of cards, some quirky metalware products, jewellery, bamboo crafts, lovely shirts, gorgeous wall hangings and more.

Rehab Craft (Map p54; 1 St 278; ⊙9am-9pm) 🖉 Sells carvings, weavings, wallets, jewellery and bags, all produced in the workshop by disabled artisans.

Sobbhana (Map p60; 23 St 144; ⊙8am-noon & 1-6pm) 🖉 A not-for-profit organisation training women in traditional weaving. Beautiful silks in a stylish boutique.

Tabitha (Map p54; 239 St 360; ⊙7am-6pm Mon-Sat) 🖉 A leading NGO shop with a good collection of silk bags, tableware, bedroom decorations and children's toys. Proceeds go towards rural community development.

Villageworks (Map p54; www.villageworks.biz; 118 St 113; ⊙8am-5pm Mon-Sat) 🖉 Opposite Tuol Sleng museum, this shop has the inevitable silk and bags, as well as coconut-shell utensils made by poor and disadvantaged artisans in Kompong Thom province.

Watthan Artisans (Map p54; www.wac.khmerproducts.com; 180 Norodom Blvd; ⊙8am-6.30pm) 🖉 At the entrance to Wat Than, selling silk and other products, including contemporary handbags, made by a cooperative of land-mine and polio victims. Also has on-site woodworking and weaving workshops.

Smateria FASHION & ACCESSORIES
(Map p54; 8 St 57; ⊙8am-9pm) Smateria does some clothing but the speciality is bags, including a line of quirky kids' backpacks, made from fishing net and other recycled materials.

Lost 'N' Found Vintage Shop CLOTHING
(Map p54; http://lostnfoundvintagestore.weebly.com; 321 St 63; ⊙9am-8pm) A vintage clothing store that hand-picks the best pieces from sources all over town. Predominantly women's clothing and accessories.

Couleurs d'Asie FASHION & ACCESSORIES
(Map p44; www.couleursdasie.net; 16A St 418; ⊙9.30am-6pm Mon, Wed, Fri & Sat) Great place for gift shopping, with lots of kids' clothes, silks, chunky jewellery, beautiful bags, knick-knacks and fragrant soaps, lotions, incense and oils.

Waterlily FASHION & ACCESSORIES
(Map p54; 37 St 240; ⊙10am-7pm Mon-Fri, 9am-5pm Sat) Strikingly original bags, jewellery, art and dolls, all made from recycled materials.

DAH Export CLOTHING, CHILDREN
(Map p54; 87 Sihanouk Blvd; ⊙9am-9pm) This is the biggest and best of the factory overrun outlets, with an impressive winter collection (North Face Gore-Tex ski jackets for US$99,

anyone?), plenty of kiddie clothing and a prominent location.

Tuol Sleng Shoes   SHOES
(Map p54; 136 St 143; ⊙7.30am-5pm) Scary name, but there's nothing scary about the price of these custom-fit, handmade shoes.

Art & Books
Plenty of shops sell locally produced paintings along St 178, opposite the Royal University of Fine Arts between Sts 13 and 19. With a new generation of artists coming up, the selection is much stronger than it once was. Lots of reproduction busts of famous Angkorian sculptures are available along this stretch, great for the mantelpiece back home. Make sure to bargain.

Theam's House   ARTS & CRAFTS
(Map p60; www.theamshouse.com; 47 St 178; ⊙8am-6pm) Renowned Siem Reap–based lacquerware designer Theam has opened a flagship gallery in the old Reyum premises. Both contemporary and classic.

Space Four Zero   MUSIC
(Map p60; https://spacefourzero.com; 40 St 118; ⊙10am-7pm) This funky pop-art gallery pays tribute to the lost artists of Cambodia's golden years, many of whom perished under the Khmer Rouge regime, in an original series of 'sticky fingers' art prints. It is also the unofficial HQ for the Cambodia Space Project, one of Cambodia's leading fusion bands, and rare vinyl is on sale.

Estampe   VINTAGE
(Map p54; 197A St 19; ⊙10am-7pm Mon-Sat) Reproduction images, posters, journals and more, plus original collectibles from old Indochine, including books, maps and postcards.

Monument Books   BOOKS
(Map p54; 111 Norodom Blvd; ⊙7am-8.30pm) The best-stocked bookshop in town, with almost every Cambodia-related book available and a superb maps-and-travel section.

D's Books   BOOKS
(Map p54; 79 St 240; ⊙9am-9pm) The largest chain of secondhand bookshops in the capital, with a good range of titles.

Bohr's Books   BOOKS
(Map p60; 5 Samdech Sothearos Blvd; ⊙9am-8pm) Secondhand bookshop near the riverfront with a great selection of novels and nonfiction.

ⓘ Information

DANGERS & ANNOYANCES
Phnom Penh is not as dangerous as people imagine, but it is important to take care.

➡ Armed robberies do sometimes occur, but statistically you would be very unlucky to be a victim. Should you become the victim, do not panic and do not struggle. Calmly raise your hands and let your attacker take what they want. *Do not* reach for your pockets, as the assailant may think you are reaching for a gun. Avoid carrying a bag at night.

➡ If you ride your own motorbike during the day, some police may try to fine you for the most trivial of offences. They will most likely demand US$5 and threaten to take you to the police station for an official US$20 fine if you do not pay. If you are patient and smile, you can usually get away with handing over a few dollars.

➡ The riverfront area of Phnom Penh attracts many beggars, as do Psar Thmei and the Russian Market. Generally, however, there is little in the way of push and shove. Watch out for fake monks from China or Taiwan begging as a scam. They usually have grey or brown robes instead of the saffron robes of Khmer monks.

➡ Flooding is a major problem in the wet season (June to October), and heavy downpours see some streets turn into canals for a few hours.

EMERGENCY
In the event of a medical emergency it may be necessary to be evacuated to Bangkok.

Ambulance	☑ 119 in emergency; 023-723840 in English
Fire	☑ 118 in emergency
Police	☑ 117 in emergency; 097 778 0002 in English

INTERNET
Pretty much all hotels, guesthouses, cafes and restaurants offer free wi-fi connections. Local SIM cards are widely available with cheap data packages, so if you are travelling with an unlocked mobile phone or tablet, sign up soon after arrival and stay connected.

Internet cafes are less common since the wi-fi explosion, but the main backpacker strips – St 258, St 278 and St 172 – have a few places. Most internet cafes are set up for Skype or similar services.

MEDIA
Listings Magazines *AsiaLife* is a monthly listings mag full of features targeted at Phnom Penh's expat community. Pick up a copy of the pocket-sized *Phnom Penh Pocket Guide* (www.cambodiapocketguide.com). The *Phnom Penh*

Visitors Guide (www.canbypublications.com) is brimming with useful information on the capital and beyond, plus detailed maps of the entire city.

Newspapers The *Phnom Penh Post* and the *Khmer Times* are widely available. They mix original local-news content with international stories pulled from wire services.

MEDICAL SERVICES

It is important to be aware of the difference between a clinic and a hospital in Phnom Penh. Clinics are good for most situations, but in a genuine emergency, it is best to go to a hospital.

Calmette Hospital (Map p44; ☑ 023-426948; www.calmette.gov.kh; 3 Monivong Blvd; ☺24hr) The best of the local hospitals, with the most comprehensive services and an intensive-care unit, but it really helps to go with a Khmer speaker.

European Dental Clinic (Map p54; ☑ 023-211363; www.eurodentalcambodia.com; 160A Norodom Blvd; ☺8am-noon & 2-7pm Mon-Fri, 8am-noon Sat) Has international-standard dental services and a good reputation.

International SOS Medical Centre (Map p54; ☑ 023-216911, 012 816911; www.international sos.com; 161 St 51; ☺8am-5.30pm Mon-Fri, 8am-noon Sat, emergency 24hr) Top clinic with a host of international doctors (and prices to match).

Naga Clinic (Map p54; ☑ 023-211300; www. nagaclinic.com; 11 St 254; ☺24hr) A reliable, French-run clinic.

Pharmacie de la Gare (Map p60; 81 Monivong Blvd; ☺7am-9pm) A pharmacy with English- and French-speaking consultants.

Royal Phnom Penh Hospital (Map p44; ☑ 023-991000; www.royalphnompenhhospital. com; 888 Russian Confederation Blvd; ☺24hr) International hospital affiliated with Bangkok Hospital. Boasts top facilities. Expensive.

Tropical & Travellers Medical Clinic (Map p60; ☑ 023-306802; www.travellersmedical-clinic.com; 88 St 108; ☺9.30-11.30am & 2.30-5pm Mon-Fri, to 11.30am Sat) Well-regarded

---

THE ABUSE OF INNOCENCE

The sexual abuse of children by foreign paedophiles is a serious problem in Cambodia. Paedophilia is a crime in Cambodia and several foreigners have served or are serving jail sentences. There is no such thing as an isolation unit for sex offenders in Cambodia. Countries such as Australia, France, Germany, the UK and the USA have also introduced much-needed legislation that sees nationals prosecuted in their home country for committing sex crimes abroad.

This child abuse is slowly but surely being combated, although in a country as poor as Cambodia, money can tempt people into selling babies for adoption and children for sex. The trafficking of innocent children has many shapes and forms, and the sex trade is just the thin end of the wedge. Poor parents have been known to rent out their children as beggars, labourers or sellers; many child prostitutes in Cambodia are Vietnamese and have been sold into the business by family back in Vietnam. Once in the trade, it is difficult to escape a life of violence and abuse. Drugs are also being used to keep children dependent on their pimps, with bosses giving out *yama* (a dirty methamphetamine) or heroin to dull their senses.

Paedophilia is not unique to Western societies and it is a big problem with Asian tourists as well. The problem is that some of the home governments don't treat it as seriously as some of their Western counterparts. Even more problematic is the domestic industry of virgin-buying in Cambodia, founded on the superstition that taking a girl's virginity will enhance one's power.

Visitors can do their bit by keeping an eye out for any suspicious behaviour. Don't ignore it – pass on any relevant information such as the name and nationality of the individual to the embassy concerned. To report abuse there is a Cambodian hotline (023-997919) and **ChildSafe** (Map p60; ☑ 023-986601; www.childsafe-cambodia.org; 71 St 174, Phnom Penh; ☺8am-5pm Mon-Fri) maintains confidential hotlines in Phnom Penh (012 311112), Siem Reap (017 358758), and Sihanoukville (012 478100). When booking into a hotel or jumping on transport, look out for the ChildSafe logo, as each establishment or driver who earns this logo is trained to identify and respond to child abuse. End Child Prostitution and Trafficking (www.ecpat.net) is a global network aimed at stopping child prostitution, child pornography and the trafficking of children for sexual purposes, and has affiliates in most Western countries.

WARNING: BAG SNATCHING

Bag snatching has become a real problem in Phnom Penh, with foreigners often targeted. Hot spots include the riverfront and busy areas around popular markets, but there is no real pattern; the speeding motorbike thieves, usually operating in pairs, can strike any time, any place. Countless expats and tourists have been injured falling off their bikes in the process of being robbed, and in 2007 a young French woman was killed after being dragged from a speeding *moto* (motorcycle taxi) into the path of a vehicle. Wear close-fitting bags (such as backpacks) that don't dangle from the body temptingly. Don't hang expensive cameras around the neck and keep things close to the body and out of sight, particularly when walking along the road, crossing the road or travelling by *remork-moto (tuk tuk)* or especially by *moto*. These people are real pros and only need one chance.

clinic, run by a British general practitioner for more than two decades.

U-Care Pharmacy (Map p60; 26 Samdech Sothearos Blvd; ⊙8am-10pm) International-style pharmacy with a convenient location near the river.

MONEY

There's little need to turn US dollars into riel, as greenbacks are universally accepted in the capital. You can change a wide variety of other currencies into dollars or riel in the jewellery stalls around Psar Thmei and the Russian Market. Many upmarket hotels offer 24-hour money-changing services, although this is usually reserved for their guests. Banks with ATMs and money-changing facilities are ubiquitous. Malls and supermarkets are good bets, and there are dozens of ATMs along the riverfront.

ANZ Royal Bank (Map p60; 265 Sisowath Quay; ⊙8.30am-4pm Mon-Fri, to noon Sat) ANZ has ATMs galore all over town, including at supermarkets and petrol stations, but there is a US$5 charge per transaction.

CAB Bank (Map p60; 263 Sisowath Quay; ⊙8am-9pm) Convenient hours and location, plus there's also a Western Union office here (one of several in the city).

Canadia Bank (Map p60; cnr St 110 & Monivong Blvd; ⊙8am-3.30pm Mon-Fri, to 11.30am Sat) Has ATMs around town, with a US$4 charge. Also offers free cash advances on MasterCard and Visa, and represents MoneyGram.

POST

Central Post Office (Map p60; St 13; ⊙8am-6pm) A landmark, it is housed in a French-colonial classic just east of Wat Phnom.

TOURIST INFORMATION

ChildSafe There's a centre here for tourists to learn about best behaviour relating to child begging, the dangers of orphanage tours, exploitation and other risks to children (see www.thinkchildsafe.org for tips). You can also look out for the ChildSafe logo on *remorks* and hotels: this network of people are trained to protect children in Cambodia.

Visitor Information Centre (Map p54; Sisowath Quay; ⊙8am-5pm Mon-Sat; 🛜) Located on the riverfront near the Chatomuk Theatre in the Yi Sang Riverside, it doesn't carry a whole lot of information. On the other hand, it does offer free internet access, free wi-fi, air-con and clean public toilets.

🛈 Getting There & Away

AIR

Many international air services operate to/from **Phnom Penh International Airport** (PNH; ☑023-862800; www.cambodia-airports.com). Domestically, there are now several airlines connecting Phnom Penh and Siem Reap. **Cambodia Angkor Air** (Map p54; ☑023-666 6786; www.cambodiaangkorair.com; 206A Norodom Blvd) flies five to six times daily to Siem Reap (from US$35 to US$110 one way, 30 minutes), while **Bassaka Air** (☑023-217613; www.bassakaair.com), **JC Airlines** (www.jcairline.com) and **Cambodia Bayon Airlines** (☑023-231555; www.bayonairlines.com) have at least one flight a day, from US$20 to US$75 one way. Healthy competition has really driven down prices recently, so it pays to book ahead for special promotions.

BOAT

Fast boats up the Tonlé Sap to Siem Reap and down the Mekong to Chau Doc in Vietnam operate from the tourist-boat dock (p53) at the eastern end of St 104. There are no public boat services up the Mekong to Kompong Cham and Kratie.

The fast boats to Siem Reap (US$35, five to six hours) aren't as popular as they used to be. When it costs from as little as US$6 for an air-conditioned bus or US$35 to be bundled on the roof of a boat, it's not hard to see why. It is better to save your boat experience for

ℹ GETTING TO VIETNAM: PHNOM PENH TO HO CHI MINH CITY

Getting to the border The original **Bavet/Moc Bai land crossing** between Vietnam and Cambodia has seen steady traffic for more than two decades. The easiest way to get to Ho Chi Minh City (HCMC; Saigon) is to catch an international bus (US$8 to US$13, seven hours) from Phnom Penh. There are several companies making this trip.

At the border Long lines entering either country are not uncommon, but otherwise it's straightforward provided you purchase a Vietnamese visa in advance (should you require one).

Moving on If you are not on the international bus, it's not hard to find onward transport to HCMC or elsewhere.

elsewhere in Cambodia. Several companies have daily services departing at 7am and usually take it in turns to make the run. The first stretch of the journey along the river is scenic, but once the boat hits the lake, the fun is over: it's a vast inland sea with not a village in sight. The boats to Siem Reap run from roughly August through March (water levels are too low at other times), but do not necessarily depart daily, so plan ahead.

BUS

All major towns in Cambodia are accessible by air-conditioned bus from Phnom Penh. Most buses leave from company offices, which are generally clustered around Psar Thmei or located near the corner of St 106 and Sisowath Quay. Buying tickets in advance is a good idea for peace of mind, although it's not always necessary.

Not all buses are created equal, or priced the same. Buses run by Capitol Tour and Phnom Penh Sorya are usually among the cheapest, while Giant Ibis and Mekong Express buses are better and pricier.

Most of the long-distance buses drop off and pick up in major towns along the way, such as Kompong Thom en route to Siem Reap, Pursat on the way to Battambang, or Kompong Cham en route to Kratie. However, full fare is usually charged anyway.

Express minivans are generally faster than buses on most routes, but some travellers prefer the size and space of a large bus.

To book bus tickets online, visit www.cambo ticket.com.

Capitol Tour (Map p54; ☎ 023-724104; 14 St 182; US$19) Cheap buses to popular destinations such as Siem Reap, Sihanoukville and Battambang.

ℹ GETTING TO VIETNAM: PHNOM PENH TO CHAU DOC

The most scenic way to end your travels in Cambodia is to sail the Mekong to Kaam Samnor (about 100km south-southeast of Phnom Penh), cross the border to Vinh Xuong in Vietnam, and proceed to Chau Doc overland or on the Tonlé Bassac River via a small channel. Chau Doc has onward land and river connections to points in the Mekong Delta and elsewhere in Vietnam.

Various companies do trips all the way through to Chau Doc using a single boat or some combination of bus and boat; prices vary according to speed and level of service. **Capitol Tour** (p86) departs Phnom Penh at 7.30am and involves a bus transfer; the trip is about six to seven hours. **Hang Chau** (Map p60; ☎ 088 878 7871; US$25) departs from the tourist-boat dock at 12.30pm and the entire journey is by boat; the more upmarket and slightly faster **Blue Cruiser** (Map p60; ☎ 023-633 3666; www.bluecruiser.com; US$35) departs at 1.30pm; **Victoria Chau Doc Hotel** (Map p60; www.victoriahotels.asia; US$95) also has a boat making several runs a week between Phnom Penh and its Victoria Chau Doc Hotel. These companies take about four hours, including a slow border check, and use a single boat to Chau Doc. Backpacker guesthouses and tour companies offer cheaper bus/boat combo trips. All boats depart from Phnom Penh's **tourist-boat dock** (p53).

Some nationalities require a Vietnam visa in advance and some do not require a visa. Check with the **Vietnamese Embassy** (Map p74; ☎ 023-726274; 436 Monivong Blvd, Phnom Penh) in Phnom Penh to see if you need a visa or not, as visas are not available on arrival. If arriving from Vietnam, Cambodia visas are available on arrival.

Giant Ibis (Map p60; ☑ 023-999333; www. giantibis.com; 3 St 106; 🛜) 'VIP' bus and express-van specialist. Big bus to Siem Reap has plenty of legroom and wi-fi. A portion of profits goes toward giant ibis conservation.

GST (Map p60; ☑ 023-218114; 13 St 142) Buses nationwide.

Long Phuong (Map p54; ☑ 097 311 0999; www.longphuongcambodia.com; 274 Sihanouk Blvd) Buses to Ho Chi Minh City.

Mekong Express (Map p60; ☑ 023-427518; www.catmekongexpress.com; Sisowath Quay) VIP buses to Ho Chi Minh City, plus Siem Reap and Sihanoukville.

Phnom Penh Sorya (Map p60; ☑ 023-210359; cnr Sts 217 & 67, Psar Thmei area) Bus services all over the country.

Sapaco (Map p54; ☑ 023-210300; www. sapacotourist.com; 309 Sihanouk Blvd) Buses to Ho Chi Minh City.

Virak Buntham (Map p60; ☑ 016-786270; 1 St 106) Night-bus specialist with services to Siem Reap, Sihanoukville and Koh Kong.

EXPRESS MINIVANS

Speedy express minivans (minibuses) with 12 to 14 seats serve popular destinations such as Siem Reap, Sihanoukville and Sen Monorom. These cut travel times significantly, but they tend to be cramped and often travel at very high speeds, so are not for the faint of heart. Several of the big bus companies also run vans, most famously Mekong Express. It's a good idea to book express vans in advance.

Cambodia Post (Map p60; ☑ 088 399 3555; www.cambodiapost.post; Main Post Office, St 13)

CTT Net (Map p60; ☑ 023-217217; 223 Sisowath Quay)

Golden Bayon Express (Map p60; ☑ 023-966968; 3 St 126)

Kampot Express (Map p54; ☑ 012 555123; 2 St 215)

Kim Seng Express (Map p54; ☑ 012 786000; 506 Kampuchea Krom Blvd)

Mey Hong Transport (☑ 023-637 2722)

Olympic Express (Map p44; ☑ 092 868782; 70 Monireth Blvd)

Neak Krorhorm (Map p60; ☑ 092 966669; 4 St 108)

Seila Angkor (Map p60; ☑ 077 888080; 43 St 154)

SHARE TAXI

Share taxis and local minibuses leave Phnom Penh for destinations all over the country. Taxis to Kampot, Kep and Takeo leave from **Psar Dang Kor** (Map p44; Mao Tse Toung Blvd), while packed local minibuses and taxis for most other places leave from the northwest corner of **Psar**

Thmei (Map p60). Vehicles for the Vietnam border leave from Chbah Ampeau taxi park, on the eastern side of Monivong Bridge in the south of town. You may have to wait awhile (possibly until the next day if you arrive in the afternoon) before your vehicle fills up, or pay for the vacant seats yourself.

TRAIN

Phnom Penh's train station is located at the western end of St 106 and St 108, in a grand old colonial-era building. Passenger train services returned to Cambodia in April 2016 with the inauguration of weekend trains from Phnom Penh to Kampot and Sihanoukville. **Royal Railways** (Map p60; ☑ 078-888583; http://royal-railway. com; St 106; ⊙ 8am-4.30pm Mon-Fri, 6am-noon Sat & Sun) runs trains in either direction, departing Phnom Penh or Sihanoukville at 7am on Saturday and Sunday. Phnom Penh to Sihanoukville is US$7 and takes about nine hours. Phnom Penh to Kampot is US$6 and takes about five hours. There are also evening services on Friday/Saturday/Sunday from Phnom Penh and a morning service from Sihanoukville to Phnom Penh on Monday at 7am.

❶ Getting Around

Being such a small city, Phnom Penh is quite easy to get around, although traffic is getting worse by the year and traffic jams are common around the morning and evening rush hour, particularly around the two main north–south boulevards, Monivong and Norodom.

GETTING TO/FROM THE AIRPORT

Phnom Penh International Airport is 7km west of central Phnom Penh, via Russian Confederation Blvd. Facilities include free wi-fi, a host of internationally recognisable cafes and restaurants and some decent handicraft outlets for last-minute purchases. There are also ATMs for US dollars withdrawals on arrival or departure.

When arriving by air at Phnom Penh International Airport, there is an official booth outside the airport arrivals area to arrange taxis to the centre for US$12; a *remork* costs a flat US$9. You can get a *remork* for US$5 to US$7 and a *moto* for about US$3 if you exit the airport and arrange one on the street.

The cheapest option to the city is the Bus No 3 (1500r) which has a stop right outside the airport and runs to the Night Market and riverfront. It can be slow with 20 or more stops along the way, but then so can taxis with all the traffic.

Heading to the airport from central Phnom Penh, a taxi/*remork*/*moto* will cost about US$10/6/3. The journey usually takes between 30 minutes and one hour depending on the

BUS DEPARTURES FROM PHNOM PENH

DESTINATION	DURATION (HR)	COST (US$)	COMPANIES	FREQUENCY
Ban Lung	11	12	PP Sorya	6.45am
Bangkok	12	18-23	Mekong Express, PP Sorya, Virak Buntham	1 daily
Battambang (day)	5-6	5-6	GST, PP Sorya	frequent
Battambang (night)	6	8-10	Virak Buntham	4 per night
Ho Chi Minh City	7	8-13	Capitol Tour, Long Phuong, Mekong Express, PP Sorya, Sapaco, Virak Buntham (night bus)	frequent
Kampot (direct)	3	5-6	Capitol Tour	2 daily
Kampot (via Kep)	4	6	PP Sorya	7.30am, 9.30am, 2.45pm
Kep	3	5	PP Sorya	7.30am, 9.30am, 2.45pm
Koh Kong	5½	7	Olympic Express, PP Sorya, Virak Buntham	2-3 daily (before noon)
Kompong Cham	3	5	PP Sorya; GST	hourly to 4pm
Kratie	6-8	8	PP Sorya	regularly in the morning
Poipet (day)	8	9-11	Capitol Tour, PP Sorya	frequently to noon
Poipet (night)	7	10-11	Virak Buntham	at least 1 daily
Preah Vihear City	7	10	GST, PP Sorya	morning only
Sen Monorom	8	9	Minivans only	regular
Siem Reap (day)	6	6-8	most companies	frequent
Siem Reap (VIP)	6	13-15	Giant Ibis, Mekong Express	regular
Siem Reap (night)	6	10	Virak Buntham	6pm, 8pm, 11pm, 12.30am
Sihanoukville	5½	5-6	Capitol Tour, GST, Mekong Express, PP Sorya, Virak Buntham	frequent
Stung Treng	9	10	PP Sorya	6.45am, 7.30am

traffic, but can take up to 90 minutes during rush hour.

BICYCLE

It's possible to hire bicycles at some of the guesthouses around town for about US$1 to US$2 a day, but take a look at the chaotic traffic conditions before venturing forth. Once you get used to the anarchy, it can be a fun way to get around. There are also shops that rent out road bicycles and mountain bikes.

BUS

Phnom Penh has a few local bus lines running north to south and east to west, but they are not widely used by visitors, as the routes are very limited. Most useful is Bus No 3 which links the city centre with the airport.

There is a popular sightseeing bus, the **Phnom Penh Hop On Hop Off** (☑ 016 745880; www.phnompenhhoponhopoff.com; 1/2 passengers US$15/25, excl entry fees), which connects leading sights around the city.

CAR & MOTORCYCLE

Exploring Phnom Penh and the surrounding areas on a motorbike is a very liberating experience if you are used to chaotic traffic conditions.

There are numerous motorbike-hire places around town. A 100cc Honda costs US$4 to US$7 per day and 250cc dirt bikes run from US$12 to US$30 per day. You'll have to leave your passport – a driver's licence or other form of ID isn't enough. Remember you usually get what you pay for when choosing a bike.

EXPRESS MINIVAN SERVICES FROM PHNOM PENH

DESTINATION	DURATION (HR)	PRICE (US$)	COMPANIES	FREQUENCY
Battambang	4½	10-12	Mekong Express, Golden Bayon	regular
Kampot	2	8-9	Giant Ibis, Kampot Express, Olympic Express	regular
Kep	2½	8	Olympic Express	7.15am, 1.30pm
Sen Monorom	5½	11	Kim Seng Express, Virak Buntham	regular
Siem Reap	5	10-12	Golden Bayon, Mekong Express, Mey Hong, Neak Krorhorm, Olympic Express, Seila Angkor, Virak Buntham	frequent
Sihanoukville	4	10-12	CTT Net, Giant Ibis, Golden Bayon, Mekong Express, Mey Hong	frequent

A Cambodia licence isn't a bad idea if you'll be doing extensive riding. Motorbike rental shops can get you one for about US$40. Otherwise you technically need an international licence to drive in Cambodia (although it is not unusual for police to take small bribes from drivers who don't have one). If you want to purchase insurance (available at motorbike rental shops for about US$22 per month), you'll need an international or Cambodian licence. Remember to lock your bike, as motorbike theft is common.

Car hire is available through travel agencies, guesthouses and hotels in Phnom Penh. Everything from cars (from US$30 per) to 4WDs (from US$60) are available for travelling around the city, but prices rise fast once you venture beyond.

Lucky! Lucky! (Map p54; ☏ 023-212788; 413 Monivong Blvd) Motorbikes are US$4 to US$7 per day, less for multiple days. Trail bikes from US$12.

Two Wheels Only (Map p74; ☏ 012-200513; www.twocambodia.com; 34L St 368) Has well-maintained bikes available to rent (motorbike/trail bike per day US$7/25).

Vannak Bikes Rental (Map p60; ☏ 012 220970; 46 St 130) Has high-performance trail bikes up to 600cc for US$15 to US$30 per day, and smaller motorbikes for US$5 to US$7.

CYCLO

Travelling by *cyclo* is a more relaxing way to see the sights in the centre of town, although they don't work well for long distances. For a day of sightseeing, expect to pay around US$10 – find one on your own or negotiate a tour through the **Cyclo Centre** (p59). For short, one-way jaunts costs similar to *moto* (motorcycle taxi) fares. You won't see many *cyclos* on the road late at night.

MOTO

In areas frequented by foreigners, *motodups* (*moto* drivers) generally speak English and sometimes a little French. Elsewhere around town it can be difficult to find anyone who understands where you want to go. Most short trips are about 2000r to 3000r, although if you want to get from one end of the city to the other, you have to pay US$1 or more. There are fewer *moto* drivers than in the past, as many have upgraded to *remorks*.

Cambodians never negotiate when taking rides (they just pay what they think is fair), but foreigners should always work out the price in advance, especially with *motodups* (*moto* drivers) who hang out in touristy areas like the riverside or outside luxury hotels. Likewise, night owls taking a *moto* home from popular drinking holes should definitely negotiate to avoid an expensive surprise.

The remaining *moto* drivers who wait outside the popular guesthouses and hotels have reasonable English and are able to act as guides for a daily rate of about US$10 and up, depending on the destinations.

REMORK-MOTO

Better known as *tuk tuks*, *remork-motos* are motorbikes with carriages and are the main way of getting around Phnom Penh for tourists. Average fares are about double those of *motos*: US$2 for short rides around the centre, US$3 and up for longer trips. *Remork* drivers will try to charge more for multiple passengers but don't let them – generally pay per ride not per person (although groups of four or more should pay an extra US$1 or so). Newer, partly electric-powered Indian-style auto-rickshaws are also now found on the streets of Phnom Penh. In theory, these are metered and exceptional value, but in practice tourists will need to negotiate similar fares to a *remork*.

SHARE TAXI CHARTERS FROM PHNOM PENH

DESTINATION	PRICE (US$)	DURATION (HR)
Battambang	55	4½
Kampot	35	3
Kep	40	3
Koh Kong	65	4½
Kompong Cham	35	2½
Kompong Thom	45	3
Kratie	50	5
Pursat	45	3
Siem Reap	70	5
Sihanoukville	50	4
Takeo	25	2
Vietnam border	50	3

TAXI

At 3000r per kilometre, taxis are cheap, but don't expect to flag one down on the street. Call **Global Meter Taxi** (☑ 011 311888), **Choice Taxi** (☑ 010 888010, 023-888023) or **Taxi Vantha** (☑ 012 855000) for a pick-up.

There are now several dedicated Phnom Penh taxi apps, although they are still very much in their infancy. Try Exnet or iTsumo. Uber has also recently launched in Cambodia.

AROUND PHNOM PENH

Exploring the sights around the capital will reward. The beautiful Mekong island of Koh Dach is the easiest trip to undertake and is best done by mountain bike or local transport. Udong, once the stupa-studded capital of Cambodia, is a half-day trip and can be combined with a visit to Kompong Chhnang.

The Angkorian temple of Tonlé Bati and the hilltop pagoda of Phnom Chisor are located near NH2 towards Takeo and can be combined with the excellent Phnom Tamao Wildlife Rescue Centre, where some behind-the-scenes tours get visitors closer to the animals.

Kirirom National Park, the closest protected area to Phnom Penh, en route to Sihanoukville, offers cool climes amid the pines.

Koh Dach

Known as 'Silk Island' by foreigners, Koh Dach (កោះដាច់) is actually a pair of islands lying in the Mekong River about 5km north-east of the Japanese Friendship Bridge. They make for an easy, half-day DIY excursion for those who want to experience the 'real Cambodia'. The hustle and bustle of Phnom Penh feels light years away here.

The name derives from the preponderance of silk weavers who inhabit the islands. When you arrive by ferry, you'll undoubtedly be approached by one or more smiling women who speak a bit of English and will invite you to their house to observe weavers in action and – they hope – buy a *krama* (checked scarf), sarongs or other silk items. If you are in the market for silk, you might follow them and have a look. Otherwise, feel free to smile back and politely decline their offer. You'll see plenty of weavers as you journey around the islands.

🛏 Sleeping & Eating

Most visitors to Koh Dach overnight in Phnom Penh for the stark contrast between urban and rural life. However, there are now a handful of homestays and guesthouses on Koh Dach where you can experience life with a local family. Conveniently, most of them are within walking distance of each other in the northern part of the island.

There are some food stalls and local restaurants located on Koh Dach but they are fairly rustic. The best restaurants are located at the guesthouses and homestays. Fresh fruit is available on the island, including coconut juice or sugar-cane juice, useful for an energy boost if you are pedalling on two wheels. The best option are the dry-season picnic stalls on the northern tip of the island.

★ **Bonnivoit**

Garden Homestay HOMESTAY $

(☎ 012 222583; www.homestay-cambodia.com; Koh Dach; dm US$12, r US$15-22, with air-con US$25; ▣ 🛜) The leading homestay on Koh Dach, Bonnivoit Garden is run by a German-(and English-) speaking tour guide who really understands what the guests want from the experience. Set in an extensive old wooden house, rooms come in a variety of shapes and sizes. The lush gardens include a large restaurant where day trippers can have a set meal for US$7.

Accommodation rates include a free bicycle for guests to explore the island.

Le Kroma Villa BOUTIQUE HOTEL $$

(☎ 012 933939; http://lekromavilla.com; Koh Dach; r US$35-75; ▣ 🛜 🏊) Boutique accommodation has come to Koh Dach in the shape of Le Kroma Villa, an attractive French-run establishment with its own swimming pool. Rooms are clean and contemporary and decorated with the ubiquitous *krama* (checked scarf) that gives the place its name. There is also a great little restaurant which serves some typical Khmer fare.

🛈 Getting There & Away

Remork drivers offer half-day tours to Koh Dach; US$20 should cover it (less if you just want to be dropped off at the ferry), but they have been known to charge as much as US$40. The daily boat tours, departing at 8.30am, 9.30am and 1pm from the tourist-boat dock, are another option (minimum four people). **Cambocruise** (☎ 092 290077; www.cambocruise.com; with lunch from US$24) offers a daily trip to Koh Dach at 12.30pm with lunch included, plus a free pick-up in town.

Otherwise, hire a mountain bike or motorbike and go it alone. Ferries cross the Mekong in three places and cost 500r per person, plus 500r per bike. The southernmost ferry crossing is the most convenient; it takes you to the larger, closer island. To get there, cross the Japanese Bridge and follow NH6 for 4km, then turn right just before the Medical Supply Pharmaceutical Enterprise. You immediately hit a small dirt road that parallels the Mekong. Turn left and follow it north for about 500m until you see the ferry crossing.

🛈 Getting Around

Over on the larger island, it is just a short cycle ride to a bridge that links the two islands. The smaller island (technically named Koh Okhna Tey, or Mekong Island) has better infrastructure, including a paved main road; the larger island is more rustic and remote feeling, especially as you venture north.

Udong

Udong (ឧដុង្គ, literally, 'victorious') served as the capital of Cambodia under several sovereigns between 1618 and 1866, during which time 'victorious' was an optimistic epithet, as Cambodia was in terminal decline. A number of kings, including King Norodom, were crowned here. The main attractions today are the twin humps of **Phnom Udong** (ភ្នំឧដុង្គ), which have several stupas on them. Both ends of the ridge have good views of the Cambodian countryside, dotted with innumerable sugar-palm trees.

The larger main ridge – the one you'll hit first if approaching from NH5 – is known as **Phnom Preah Reach Throap** (ភ្នំព្រះរាជទ្រព្យ; Hill of the Royal Fortune). It is so named because a 16th-century Khmer king is said to have hidden the national treasury here during a war with the Thais.

Phnom Udong really fills up with locals at weekends but is quiet during the week. Admission is free.

⊙ Sights

Ascending the main, monkey-lined north stairway from the parking area, the first structure you come to at the top of the ridge is a modern temple containing a relic of the Buddha, believed to be an eyebrow hair and fragments of teeth and bones. The relics were brazenly stolen in 2013 (though later recovered). Follow the path behind this stupa along the ridge and you'll come to a line of three large stupas. The first (northwesternmost) is **Damrei Sam Poan** (ចេតិយសាមពាន់), built by King Chey Chetha II (r 1618–26) to hold the ashes of his predecessor, King Soriyopor. The second stupa, **Ang Doung** (ចេតិយព្រះបាទអង្គឌួង), is decorated with coloured tiles; it was built in 1891 by King Norodom to house the ashes of his father, King Ang Duong (r 1845–59), although some say King Ang Duong was in fact buried next to the Silver Pagoda in Phnom Penh. The last stupa is **Mak Proum** (ចេតិយមុខព្រហ្ម), the final resting place of King Monivong (r 1927–41). Decorated with *garudas* (mythical half-man, half-bird creatures), floral designs and elephants, it has four faces on top.

Continuing along the path beyond Mak Proum, you'll pass a stone *vihara* (temple sanctuary) with a cement roof and a seated Buddha inside, then arrive at a clearing dotted by a gaggle of structures, including three small *vihara* and a stupa. The first *vihara* you come to is **Vihear Prak Neak**, its cracked walls topped with a tin roof. Inside is a seated Buddha who is guarded by a *naga* (*prak neak* means 'protected by a naga'). The second structure also has a seated Buddha inside. The third structure is **Vihear Preah Keo**, a cement-roofed structure that contains a statue of Preah Ko, the sacred bull; the original statue was carried away by the Thais long ago. Beyond this, near the stupa, red and black mountain lions guard the entrance to a modern brick-walled *vihara*.

Continue southeast along a lotus-flower-lined concrete path to the most impressive structure on Phnom Preah Reach Throap, **Vihear Preah Ath Roes** (វិហារព្រះអង្គអស់). The *vihara* and an enormous seated Buddha, dedicated in 1911 by King Sisowath, were blown up by the Khmer Rouge in 1977. The *vihara,* supported by eight enormous columns and topped by a soaring tin roof, has since been rebuilt, as has the 20m-high Buddha.

At the base of the main (northern) staircase leading up to Phnom Preah Reach Throap, near the restaurants, is a **memorial** (ទីលំនៅវិញ្ញាណក្ខន្ធដងដងគ្រោះសម្រាប់ខ្មែរក្រហម) to the victims of Pol Pot. It contains the bones of some of the people who were buried in approximately a hundred mass graves, each containing about a dozen bodies. Instruments of torture were unearthed along with the bones when a number of the pits were disinterred in 1981 and 1982. Just north of the memorial is a pavilion decorated with graphic murals depicting Khmer Rouge atrocities.

Southeast of Phnom Preah Reach Throap, the smaller ridge has two structures and several stupas on top. **Ta San Mosque** faces westward towards Mecca. Across the plains to the south of the mosque you can see **Phnom Vihear Leu**, a small hill on which a *vihara* stands between two white poles. To the right of the *vihara* is a building that was used as a prison under Pol Pot's rule. To the left of the *vihara* and below it is a pagoda known as **Arey Ka Sap** (អរិយកសិក្រ).

🛏 Sleeping & Eating

Cambodia Vipassana Dhura Buddhist Meditation Center MONASTERY $
(☑ contact Mr Um Sovann 016 883090; www.cambodiavipassanacenter.com; donation US$25) The

en suite guestrooms are fairly comfortable by monastic standards, albeit sans mattresses (wicker mats are as good as it gets). You'll be fed breakfast and lunch, but no dinner. There is no fixed price for a meditative retreat here, so donate according to your means; US$25 per day would be considered about average. Meditation sessions are free. There are scores of food stalls around the bustling main parking area at the base of the northern staircase.

🛈 Getting There & Away

Udong is 37km from the capital. Take a Phnom Penh Sorya bus bound for Kompong Chhnang (10,000r, one hour to Udong). It will drop you off at the access road to Phnom Udong, and from there it's 3km (4000r by *moto*). Other bus companies (p86) also make the trip to Udong. To return to Phnom Penh flag down a bus on NH5.

If going it alone, head north out of Phnom Penh on NH5 and turn left (south) at a prominent archway between the 36km and 37km markers.

A taxi for the day trip from Phnom Penh will cost around US$40. *Moto* drivers also run people to Udong for about US$15 or so for the day, but compared with the bus this isn't the most pleasant way to go, as the road is busy and dusty.

Tonlé Bati

Tonlé Bati is the collective name for a pair of old Angkorian-era temples, known as Ta Prohm and Yeay Peau, and a popular lakeside picnic area. It's worth a detour if you are on the way to Phnom Tamao and Phnom Chisor.

You can eat at one of many picnic restaurants here set on stilts over the water and hire an inner tube to float around the lake for 2000r. Just avoid Tonlé Bati at weekends, when it's mobbed with locals. Renting a motorbike or car from Phnom Penh is the easiest way to get here.

Ta Prohm HINDU TEMPLE
(តាព្រហ្ម; US$3, incl lake & temples) The laterite temple of Ta Prohm was built by King Jayavarman VII (r 1181–1219) on the site of a 6th-century Khmer shrine. The main sanctuary consists of five chambers, each containing a modern Buddha. The facades of the chambers contain intricate and well-preserved bas-reliefs. In the central chamber is a *linga* (phallic symbol) that shows signs of the destruction wrought by the Khmer Rouge.

Yeay Peau HINDU TEMPLE

(យាយ ពៅ; US$3, incl lake & temples) Yeay Peau temple, named after King Prohm's mother, is 150m north of Ta Prohm in the grounds of a modern pagoda.

Legend has it that Peau gave birth to a son, Prohm. When Prohm discovered his father was King Preah Ket Mealea, he set off to live with the king. After a few years, he returned to his mother but did not recognise her; taken by her beauty, he asked her to become his wife. He refused to believe Peau's protests that she was his mother. To put off his advances, she suggested a contest to avoid the impending marriage.

To read about the legend in full, see Phnom Psos (p276).

Phnom Tamao Wildlife Rescue Centre

This wonderful **wildlife sanctuary** (មជ្ឈ ឈមណ្ឌលសង្គ្រោះសត្វព្រៃភ្នំតាម៉ៅ; adult/child US$5/2; ⊘ 8am-5pm; 🅿) 🕊 for rescued animals is home to gibbons, sun bears, elephants, tigers, lions, deer, enormous pythons and a massive bird enclosure. They were all taken from poachers or abusive owners and receive care and shelter here as part of a sustainable breeding program. Wherever possible animals are released back into the wild once they have recovered.

The sanctuary occupies a vast site south of the capital and its animals are kept in excellent conditions by Southeast Asian standards, with plenty of room to roam in enclosures that have been improved and expanded over the years with help from Wildlife Alliance (www.wildlifealliance.org), Free the Bears (www.freethebears.org) and other international wildlife NGOs. Spread out as it is, it feels like a zoo crossed with a safari park.

The centre operates breeding and release programs for a number of globally threatened species, including pileated gibbons, smooth-coated otters and Siamese crocodiles and provides a safe home to other iconic species including tigers and the gentle giants – Asian elephants. The centre is home to the world's largest captive collection of Malayan sun bears and you'll also find a walk-through area with macaques, deer and a huge aviary.

Cambodia's wildlife is usually very difficult to spot, as larger mammals inhabit remote areas of the country, so Phnom Tamao is the perfect place to discover more about the incredible variety of animals in Cambodia. If you don't like zoos, you might not like this wildlife sanctuary, but remember that these animals have been rescued from traffickers and poachers and need a home. Visitors who come here will be doing their own small bit to help in the protection and survival of Cambodia's varied wildlife.

Both Wildlife Alliance and Free the Bears offer more-exclusive experiences at Phnom Tamao for fixed donations. Wildlife Alliance (p93) offers a behind-the-scenes tour, which includes access to feeding areas and the nursery area. Free the Bears has a 'Bear Care Tour', which allows guests to help out the on-site team for the day. These tours include transport from Phnom Penh. Otherwise, the easiest option is a rental motorbike or car from Phnom Penh in combination with Tonlé Bati or Phnom Chisor.

Wildlife Tours TOURS

(📱 095 970175; www.wildlifealliance.org; minimum donation US$150) Wildlife Alliance has created an exciting, full-day interactive tour to raise funds for Phnom Tamao Wildlife Rescue Centre. Donors get to interact with a variety of rescued animals, including elephants, macaques and gibbons, and get up close with tigers, crocodiles and what is possibly the world's only captive hairy-nosed otter. All proceeds go toward the rescue and care of wildlife at Phnom Tamao.

Tours include walks with elephants in the forest and you get to feed various baby animals in the sanctuary's nursery, which is normally off-limits to the public.

Free the Bears TOURS

(📱 092 434597; www.freethebears.org; per person US$70, groups of 5 or more per person US$50) Free the Bears operates a 'Bear Care' program to allow students and adults with a genuine interest in wildlife a better understanding of the Asian black bear and Malayan sun bear. Participants have no contact with the bears, but spend the day behind the scenes of the Phnom Tamao sanctuary learning the ins and outs of caring for the 130-plus bears being looked after here.

One- to 12-week volunteer positions are also available.

Betelnut Jeep Tours TOURS

(Map p54; 📱 012 619924; www.betelnuttours.com; 1D St 258; per person US$40) Betelnut Jeep Tours offers guided open-top jeep trips to Phnom Tamao Wildlife Rescue Centre from Tuesday to Saturday, departing at 9.45am from the Lazy Gecko Guesthouse (p64) in Phnom Penh. The price includes admission, lunch and a *krama* (checked scarf) to protect against the elements.

Phnom Chisor

A temple from the Angkorian era, **Phnom Chisor** (ភ្នំជីសូរ; US$2) is set upon a solitary hill in Takeo Province, offering superb views of the countryside. Try to get to Phnom Chisor early in the morning or late in the afternoon, as it is an uncomfortable climb in the heat of the midday sun. Phnom Chisor lies about 55km south of Phnom Penh.

The main temple stands on the eastern side of the hilltop. Constructed of laterite and brick with carved sandstone lintels, the complex is surrounded by the partially ruined walls of a 2.5m-wide gallery with windows. Inscriptions found here date from the 11th century, when this site was known as Suryagiri.

On the plain to the west of Phnom Chisor are the sanctuaries of **Sen Thmol** (just below Phnom Chisor), **Sen Ravang** and the former sacred pond of **Tonlé Om**. All three of these features form a straight line from Phnom Chisor in the direction of Angkor. During rituals held here 900 years ago, the king, his Brahmans and their entourage would climb a monumental 400 steps to Suryagiri from this direction.

If you haven't got the stamina for an overland adventure to Preah Vihear or Phnom Bayong (near Takeo), this is the next best thing for a temple with a view. Near the main temple is a modern Buddhist *vihara*, which is used by resident monks.

Renting a motorbike in Phnom Penh is one of the most enjoyable ways to get here in combination with Tonlé Bati or Phnom Tamao Wildlife Rescue Centre. Booking a share taxi is a comfortable option in the wet or hot seasons or you can take a Takeo-bound bus to the access road about 49km south of Phnom Penh and arrange a *moto* from there.

Kirirom National Park

You can really get away from it all at this lush, elevated **park** (ឧទ្យានជាតិគិរីរម្យ; US$5) 🏕 two hours' drive southwest of Phnom Penh. Winding trails lead through pine forests to cascading wet-season waterfalls and cliffs with amazing views of the Cardamom Mountains, and there's some great mountain biking to be done if you're feeling adventurous.

From NH4, it's 10km on a sealed road to a small village near the park entrance. From the village you have two choices: the left fork takes you 50m to the park entrance and then 17km up a fairly steep sealed road to the unstaffed **Kirirom Information Centre** inside the national park; the right fork takes you 10km along the perimeter of the park on a dirt road to **Chambok commune**, the site of an excellent **community-based ecotourism** (☏ 012 698529; mlup@online.com.kh; adult/child US$3/1) (CBET) program. These are two vastly different experiences, and they are nowhere near each other, so it's recommended to devote a day to each.

🏃 Activities

🏞 National Park

Up in the actual national park, you'll find myriad walking trails and dirt roads that lead to small wet-season waterfalls, lakes, wats and abandoned buildings, but you'll need a map or a guide to navigate them. There are some great trails for mountain bikers to follow through the pines, but you will need to plan your own routes as there are no official maps available.

Mr Mik (015 810271) is a park ranger and guide who can usually be found at the barbecue shacks near the busy main parking area, about 500m northeast of the information centre. For US$10 he can take you on a two-hour hike up to Phnom Dat Chivit (End of Life Mountain), where an abrupt cliff face offers an unbroken view of the Elephant Mountains and Cardamom Mountains to the west.

🏞 Chambok

The main attraction at the Chambok Community-Based Ecotourism (p94) site is a 4km hike to a series of three waterfalls (no guide required). The second waterfall has a swimming hole; the third one is an impressive 40m high. Bikes are available for US$1.50 but won't get you very far as the trail deteriorates fairly quickly. Other attractions include traditional ox-cart rides, a bat cave and guided nature walks (guides cost US$15 per day).

🛏 Sleeping & Eating

There are now two hotels located within the boundaries of Kirirom National Park, as well as cheaper homestays located near Chambok as part of the long-running community-tourism initiative.

Chambok Homestays HOMESTAY $
(☑ 012 938920; https://chambok.org/; per person US$4, home-cooked meals each US$3-4) Multiple homestays are available in Chambok commune as part of the CBET program.

Romantic Waterfall & Cafe GUESTHOUSE $
(☑ 012 733694; www.romantic-cafe.org; r from US$8; 🛜) About 1km south of Chambok commune, Romantic has a few basic rooms and a Khmer restaurant, but be sure to pre-order.

★vKirirom Pine Resort RESORT $$
(☑ 078 777384; www.vkirirom.com; camping US$20, r US$50-100, ste US$230; 🛇@🛜) A smart, Japanese-run resort, vKirirom has a dizzying array of rooms, including slightly surreal circular-pipe rooms, some impressively simple, open-plan Khmer cottages made of rattan, and luxurious bungalows with all the trimmings. There's an attractive open-plan restaurant here, which is the best lunch stop for day-trippers to the park.

Kirirom Mountain Lodge GUESTHOUSE $$
(☑ 092 490216; www.kirirom.asia; d weekday/weekends US$35/60, ste US$55/75; 🛇🛜) This long-running guesthouse has been given a much-needed makeover by the hotel group behind the Plantation in Phnom Penh. Rooms are simple but stylish and there's a good restaurant serving a mix of French, Moroccan and Asian flavours. With only six rooms you can rent the whole place for US$200 if you want to party amid the pines.

Kirirom Hillside Resort RESORT $$
(☑ 016 303888; www.kiriromresort.com; campsites US$15, bungalows US$50-80, ste from US$160; 🛇🛜🏊) Located beneath the park, this place has attractive Scandinavian-style bungalows, some with glorious balconies overlooking a small lake, dotting the sprawling grounds. There's a nice pool, a hit-or-miss restaurant, a zoo and even a plastic dinosaur park. Beware: advertised services like horseback riding, wi-fi and mountain-bike rental are rarely available.

ℹ Getting There & Away

Kirirom National Park is accessed from the village of Treng Trayern, which straddles NH4 87km southwest of Phnom Penh and 139km northeast of Sihanoukville. A taxi from either city is about US$60; or have a bus drop you off at the turnoff in Treng Trayern, where a *moto* will want US$5 per person to get you to the entrance (a bit more to Chambok commune, and still more to ascend into the national park itself). Travelling under your own steam is highly recommended.

Siem Reap

☑ 063 / POP 185,000 (TOWN) / AREA 10,299 SQ KM (PROVINCE)

Best Places to Eat

➡ Cuisine Wat Damnak (p117)

➡ Haven (p115)

➡ Marum (p115)

➡ Olive (p113)

➡ Flow (p116)

Best Places to Stay

➡ Phum Baitang (p112)

➡ Viroth's Hotel (p111)

➡ Onederz Hostel (p108)

➡ Mad Monkey (p109)

➡ Shinta Mani (p110)

Why Go?

The life-support system and gateway for the temples of Angkor, Siem Reap (*see*-em ree-*ep;* សៀមរាប) was always destined for great things. Visitors come here to see the temples, of course, but there is plenty to do in and around the city when you're templed out. Siem Reap has reinvented itself as the epicentre of chic Cambodia, with everything from backpacker party pads to hip hotels, world-class wining and dining across a range of cuisines, sumptuous spas, great shopping, local tours to suit both foodies and adventurers, and a creative cultural scene that includes Cambodia's leading contemporary circus.

Angkor is a place to be savoured, not rushed, and this is the base from which to plan your adventures. Still think three days at the temples is enough? Think again with Siem Reap on the doorstep.

When to Go
Siem Reap

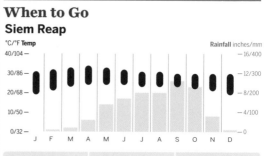

Nov–Mar Peak season gets very crowded. Look out for the Giant Puppet Parade in February.

Apr & May Can be shockingly hot, making exploring hard work and the countryside barren.

Jun–Oct Wet season; the town centre may be under water for several days in October.

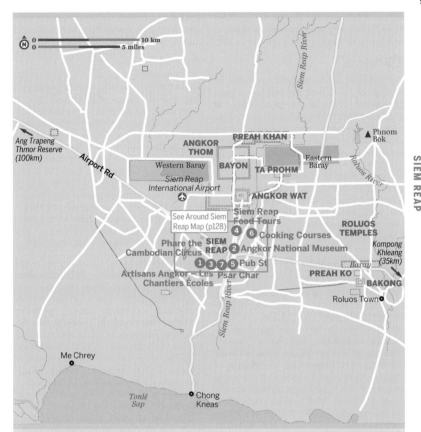

Siem Reap Highlights

1 Phare the Cambodian Circus (p119) Seeing a unique performance of the fabulous Cambodian Circus.

2 Angkor National Museum (p98) Discovering the Khmer civilisation and the majesty of Angkor.

3 Artisans Angkor – Les Chantiers Écoles (p98) Taking a tour of a school where students learn traditional artisanal skills

and browsing the attached shop.

4 Siem Reap Food Tours (p107) Getting an insider's view of Siem Reap culture and food on an epicurean adventure.

5 Pub St (p117) Diving into the drinking capital of Siem Reap after lining your stomach at nearby restaurants.

6 Cooking courses (p103) Learning the secrets of Khmer cuisine with a cooking course, the perfect way to impress friends back home.

7 Psar Chaa (p120) Browsing, bargaining and buying at Psar Chaa (Old Market) then following up with the Angkor Night Market.

History

Siem Reap was little more than a village when French explorers discovered Angkor in the 19th century. With the return of Angkor to Cambodian – or should that be French – control in 1907, Siem Reap began to grow, absorbing the first wave of tourists. The Grand Hotel d'Angkor opened its doors in 1932 and the temples of Angkor remained one of Asia's leading draws until the late 1960s, luring luminaries such as Charlie Chaplin and Jackie Kennedy. With the advent of war and the Khmer Rouge, Siem Reap entered a long slumber from which it only began to awaken in the mid-1990s.

◉ Sights

The sights in and around the town pale in comparison to Angkor, but they are a good diversion if you happen to get templed out after a few days. That said, some of the best sights are...yet more temples. The modern pagodas around Siem Reap offer an interesting contrast to the ancient sandstone structures of Angkor.

Outside town attractions include the up-and-coming Banteay Srei District and the stilted and floating villages of the Tonlé Sap lake, such as Kompong Khleang and Kompong Pluk. And don't forget to include a visit to the Angkor Centre for Conservation of Biodiversity out near Kbal Spean, one of the more remote Angkorian sites.

★ **Angkor National Museum**   MUSEUM
(សារមន្ទីរអង្គរ; Map p100; ☏ 063-966601; www.angkornationalmuseum.com; 968 Charles de Gaulle Blvd; adult/child under 1.2m US$12/6; ⏰ 8.30am-6pm, to 6.30pm Oct-Apr) Looming large on the road to Angkor is the Angkor National Museum, a state-of-the-art showpiece on the Khmer civilisation and the majesty of Angkor. Displays are themed by era, religion and royalty as visitors move through the impressive galleries. After a short presentation, visitors enter the Zen-like Gallery of a Thousand Buddhas, which has a fine collection of images. Other exhibits include the pre-Angkorian periods of Funan and Chenla; the great Khmer kings; Angkor Wat; Angkor Thom; and the inscriptions.

Exhibits include touch-screen videos, epic commentary and the chance to experience a panoramic sunrise at Angkor Wat, though there seems to be less sculpture on display here than in the National Museum in Phnom Penh.

Some of the standout pieces in the collection include a late 12th-/early-13th-century seated Buddha sheltered by a naga, a 7th-century standing Vishnu from Sambor Prei Kuk in Kompong Thom, and a stunning 10th-century lintel from the beautiful temple of Banteay Srei.

It is a very useful experience for first-time visitors, putting the story of Angkor and the Khmer empire in context before exploring the temples. As the museum is entirely air-conditioned, plan a visit during the middle of the day to avoid the sweltering midday temperatures at the temples of Angkor. Audio tours are available in a number of languages for US$5.

★ **Artisans Angkor –**
Les Chantiers Écoles   ARTS CENTRE
(អាទីសង់អង្គរ; Map p100; www.artisansdangkor.com; ⏰ 7.30am-6.30pm) 🌿 FREE Siem Reap is the epicentre of the drive to revitalise Cambodian traditional culture, which was dealt a harsh blow by the Khmer Rouge and the years of instability that followed its rule. Les Chantiers Écoles teaches wood- and stone-carving techniques, traditional silk painting, lacquerware and other artisan skills to impoverished young Cambodians. Free guided tours explaining traditional techniques are available daily from 7.30am to 6.30pm. Tucked down a side road, the school is well signposted from Sivatha St.

Angkor Silk Farm   FARM
(www.artisansdangkor.com; ⏰ 7.30am-5.30pm) 🌿 FREE Les Chantiers Écoles maintains the Angkor Silk Farm, which produces some of the best work in the country, including clothing, interior-design products and accessories. All stages of the production process can be seen here, from the cultivation of mulberry trees through the nurturing of silk worms to the dyeing and weaving of silk. Free tours are available daily. A free shuttle bus departs from Les Chantiers Écoles in Siem Reap at 9.30am and 1.30pm.

The farm is about 16km west of Siem Reap, just off the road to Sisophon in the village of Puok.

Wat Bo   BUDDHIST TEMPLE
(វត្តបូ; Map p100; Tep Vong St; ⏰ 6am-6pm) FREE This is one of the town's oldest temples and has a collection of well-preserved wall paintings from the late 19th century depicting the *Reamker,* Cambodia's interpretation of the *Ramayana.* The monks here regularly chant some time between 4.30pm and 6pm and this can be a spell-binding and spiritual moment if you happen to be visiting.

Preah Ang Chek
Preah Ang Chorm   BUDDHIST SHRINE
(ព្រះអង្គចេក ព្រះអង្គចម; Map p100; Royal Gardens; ⏰ 6am-10pm) FREE Located just west of the royal residence is the shrine of Preah Ang Chek Preah Ang Chorm. Said to represent two Angkorian princesses, these sacred statues were originally housed at the Preah Poan gallery in Angkor Wat, but were moved all over Siem Reap for their protection from

invaders, eventually settling here in 1990. Locals throng here to pray for luck, especially newly-weds, and it is an atmospheric place to visit around dusk, as the incense smoke swirls around.

Next to the shrine are the tall trees of the Royal Gardens, home to a resident colony of fruit bats or flying foxes that take off to feed on insects around dusk.

War Museum   MUSEUM
(សារមន្ទីរប្រវត្តិសាស្ត្រសង្គ្រាម; ☑097 457 8666; www.warmuseumcambodia.com; Kaksekam Village; admission incl guide US$5; ☺7am-5pm) The unique selling point here is that the museum encourages visitors to handle the old weapons, from an AK-47 right through to a rocket launcher. We're not sure what health and safety think about it, but it makes for a good photo op. Other war junk includes Soviet-era T-54 tanks and MiG-19 fighters. Former soldiers act as tour guides.

Apopo Visitor Centre   VISITOR CENTRE
(☑081 599 237; www.apopo.org; Koumai Rd; US$5; ☺8.30am-5.30pm Mon-Sat) ✏ Meet the hero rats that are helping to clear landmines in Cambodia. Apopo has trained the highly sensitive, almost-blind Gambian pouched rat to sniff explosives, which dramatically speeds up the detection of mines in the countryside. The visitor centre gives background on the work of Apopo, with a short video and the chance to meet the rats themselves.

Angkor Conservation   LANDMARK
(Map p106; Siem Reap River Rd West; US$5; ☺unofficially 8am-5pm) Angkor Conservation is a Ministry of Culture compound that houses more than 5000 statues, lingas (phallic symbols) and inscribed stelae, stored here to protect them from the wanton looting that has blighted hundreds of sites around Angkor. The finest statuary is hidden away inside Angkor Conservation's warehouses, meticulously numbered and catalogued. While it's not officially open to the public, it is sometimes possible to get a peek at the collection for a fee.

Cambolac   ARTS CENTRE
(កំពូលលក្ក៍; ☑088 355 6078; http://cambolac. com; Wat Polanka; ☺8-11.30am & 1-5pm Mon-Sat) **FREE** Cambodia has a long tradition of producing beautiful lacquerware, although the years of upheaval resulted in some of the skills being lost. Cambolac is a social enterprise helping to restore Cambodia's lacquer

tradition and create a new contemporary scene. You can tour the workshop to learn more about the perfectionist approach required to produce a piece. Most of the guides are hearing-impaired and a tour allows some great interaction and the opportunity to learn some basic sign language.

MGC Asian Traditional Textiles Museum   MUSEUM
(សារមន្ទីរវាយនភណ្ឌប្រពៃណីអាស៊ី អិម ជី ស៊ី; www.mgcatttmuseum.com; Rd 60; adult/child under 12 US$3/free; ☺8.30am-4pm, closed Tue) This museum showcases the best in Asian textiles from around the Mekong region, including Cambodia, Laos, Myanmar, Thailand and India. There are a variety of galleries showing the weaving process in each country and a mix of traditional and contemporary galleries showing different regional costumes past and present.

Senteurs d'Angkor Botanic Garden   GARDENS
(Airport Rd; ☺7.30am-5.30pm) The botanic garden of Senteurs d'Angkor (p121) is a sort of Willy Wonka's for the senses, where you can sample infused teas and speciality coffees in the on-site cafe. More a laboratory than a garden, they also make soaps, oils and perfumes here.

Wat Athvea   BUDDHIST TEMPLE
(វត្តអធ្វា; incl in Angkor admission 1/3/7 days US$37/62/72; ☺6am-6pm) South of the city centre, Wat Athvea is an attractive pagoda on the site of an ancient temple. The old temple is still in very good condition and sees far fewer visitors than the main temples in the Angkor area, making it a peaceful spot in the late afternoon.

Wat Preah Inkosei   BUDDHIST TEMPLE
(វត្តព្រះឥន្ទកោសីយ៍; Map p106; ☺6am-6pm) **FREE** This wat north of town is built on the site of an early Angkorian brick temple, which still stands today at the rear of the compound.

Wat Thmei   BUDDHIST TEMPLE
(វត្តថ្មី; ☺6am-6pm) **FREE** Wat Thmei has a small memorial stupa containing the skulls and bones of victims of the Khmer Rouge. It also has plenty of young monks eager to practise their English.

Angkor Panorama Museum   MUSEUM
(សារមន្ទីរសព្ទទស្សន៍អង្គរ; ☑063-766215; http://angkorpanoramamuseum.com; Rd 60; US$15; ☺9am-8pm) Donated by the North

Siem Reap

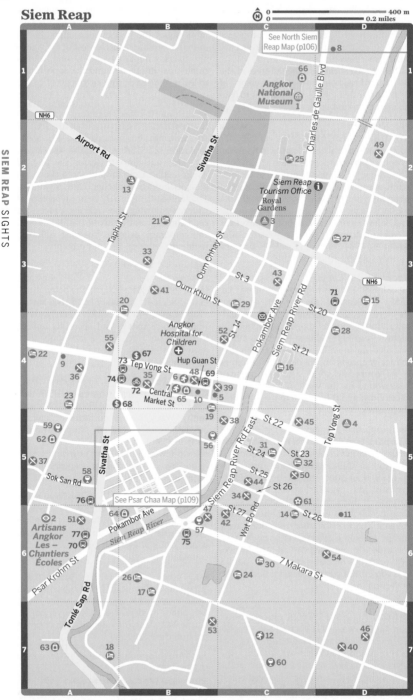

Siem Reap

Korean government, this stylish building conceals an incredible panoramic painting that is 13m high and 123m around. The detail is stunning with many of the figures such as the Buddhist monks extremely life-like. Apparently it took almost three years to complete, but this still doesn't really justify the entry fee.

TRAVEL WITH CHILDREN

Siem Reap is a great city for children thanks to the range of activities on offer beyond the temples. A temple visit may appeal to older children, particularly the Indiana Jones atmosphere found at Ta Prohm and Beng Mealea, the sheer size and scale of Angkor Wat, and the weird faces at the Bayon.

Other activities include boat trips on the Tonlé Sap to visit otherworldly villages, swimming at a hotel or resort, ziplining in the jungle, exploring the countryside on horseback or **quad bike** (☑ 012 893447; www.cambodiaquadbike.com; Sala Kamreuk Rd; 1hr/half day US$30/100), goofing around at the **Cambodian Cultural Village** (p102), playing minigolf at **Angkor Wat Putt** (p102), exploring the **Banteay Srei Butterfly Centre** (p127), or just enjoying the cafes and restaurants of Siem Reap at a leisurely pace. Icecream shops will be popular, while the local barbecue restaurants are always enjoyably interactive for older children.

Siem Reap is not necessarily that well geared up for travelling with infants and small children, but it's fine for parents willing to improvise. Dedicated baby-change facilities are rare, but many bathrooms are single sex, single cubicle. Child seats are not generally available unless requested through a travel agent. Supermarkets are well stocked with nappies (diapers), milk formula and more should you need supplies.

Cambodian Cultural Village CULTURAL CENTRE (ភូមិវប្បធម៌កម្ពុជា; ☑ 063-963836; www.cambodianculturalvillage.com; Airport Rd; adult/child under 1.1m US$9/free; ☺ 8am-7pm; ⓐ) It may be kitsch, it may be kooky, but it's very popular with Cambodians and provides a diversion for families travelling with children. This is the Cambodian Cultural Village, which tries to represent all of Cambodia in a whirlwind tour of re-created houses and villages. The visit begins with a wax museum and includes homes of the Cham, Chinese, Kreung and Khmer people, as well as miniature replicas of landmark buildings in Cambodia.

🏃 Activities

There is an incredible array of activities on offer in Siem Reap, ranging from predictable swimming pools, spa centres and golf courses right through to less predictable ziplining, horse riding, quad biking and an Angkor-themed minigolf course.

It's hot work clambering about the temples and there's no better way to wind down than with a dip in a swimming pool. You can pay by the day for use of the pool and/ or gym at most hotels; prices range from just US$5 at some of the midrange hotels to US$20 at the five-star palaces. More and more of the cheaper hotels and resorts are putting in pools and this can be a worthwhile splash for weary travellers. Locals like to swim in the waters of the Western Baray at the weekend.

The Great Escape CHALLENGE (☑ 063-506 9777; www.greatescapecambodia. com; C-39 Angkor Shopping Arcade, Airport Rd; per person US$18-25) Escape the room in 60 minutes using only your wits. That's the premise of The Great Escape, Siem Reap's answer to the Crystal Maze. Try the Warehouse of Jack Travis, an Angkor-themed mystery.

Helicopters Cambodia SCENIC FLIGHTS (Map p100; ☑ 012 814500; www.helicopterscambodia.com; 658 Hup Guan St) Part of Helicopters New Zealand, Helicopters Cambodia offers tourists flights around Angkor Wat (US$90) and the temples outside Angkor Thom (US$150), as well as more expensive flights to remote temples.

Helistar SCENIC FLIGHTS (www.helistarcambodia.com; NH6 West; Angkor Wat/Angkor Thom flights US$90/150) Offers scenic flights around Angkor Wat, the temples outside Angkor Thom and the Tonlé Sap lake.

Golf

Angkor Wat Putt GOLF (☑ 012 302330; www.angkorwatputt.com; Chreav District; adult/child US$5/4; ☺ 8am-8pm) Crazy golf to the Brits among us, this home-grown minigolf course contrasts with the big golf courses out of town. Navigate minitemples and creative obstacles for 14 holes and win a beer for a hole-in-one. Recently relocated to a more remote location, it is well worth seeking out.

Phokeethra Country Club
GOLF

(☎ 063-964600; www.phokeethraangkor.com; Dontro Village, near NH6; green fees US$100) This club hosts an annual tournament on the Asian tour and includes an ancient Angkor bridge amid its manicured fairways and greens.

Horse Riding

Happy Ranch
HORSE RIDING

(☎ 012 920002; www.thehappyranch.com; 1hr/half-day US$28/59) Forget the Wild West – try your hand at horse riding in the Wild East. Happy Ranch offers the chance to explore Siem Reap on horseback, taking in surrounding villages and secluded temples. This is a calm way to experience the countryside, far from the traffic and crowds.

Popular rides take in Wat Athvea, a modern pagoda with an ancient temple on its grounds, and Wat Chedi, a temple set on a flood plain near the Tonlé Sap lake. Riding lessons are available for children and beginners. Book direct for the best prices.

Massage & Spas

Foot massages are a big hit in Siem Reap – not surprising given all those steep stairways at the temples. There are half a dozen or more places offering a massage for about US$6 to US$8 an hour on the strip running northwest of Psar Chaa. Some are more authentic than others, so dip your toe in first before selling your sole.

For an alternative foot massage, brave the waters of Dr Fish: you dip your feet into a paddling pool full of cleaner fish, which nibble away at your dead skin. It's heaven for some, tickly as hell for others. The original is housed in the Angkor Night Market, but copycats have sprung up all over town, including a dozen or so tanks around Pub St and Psar Chaa.

★**Bodia Spa**
SPA

(Map p109; ☎ 063-761593; www.bodia-spa.com; Pithnou St; 1hr massage US$24-36; ⊙10am-midnight) Sophisticated spa near Psar Chaa offering a full range of scrubs, rubs and natural remedies, including its own line of herbal products.

Frangipani Spa
SPA

(Map p100; ☎ 063-964391; www.frangipanisiemreap.com; 615 Hup Guan St; ⊙10am-10pm) This delightful hideaway offers massages and a whole range of spa treatments.

Krousar Thmey
MASSAGE

(Map p106; www.krousar-thmey.org; Charles de Gaulle Blvd; 1hr massage US$7; ⊙9am-9pm) Massages here are performed by blind masseurs. In the same location is the free Tonlé Sap Exhibition, which includes a 'Seeing in the Dark' interactive exhibition exploring what it is like to be blind, guided by a vision-impaired student.

Quad Biking

Quad Adventure Cambodia
ADVENTURE SPORTS

(☎ 092-787216; www.quad-adventure-cambodia.com; Country Rd Laurent; sunset ride US$30, full day US$170) The original quad-bike operator in town. Rides around Siem Reap involve rice fields at sunset, pretty temples and back roads through traditional villages.

Siem Reap Quad Bike Adventure
ADVENTURE SPORTS

(Map p100; ☎ 012 324009; www.srquadbikingadventure.com; 169 Wat Bo Rd; 1hr US$30, with 1 child US$40) A locally owned ATV company with fully automatic quad bikes.

Yoga & Meditation

Peace Cafe Yoga
YOGA

(Map p106; ☎ 063-965210; www.peacecafeangkor.org; Siem Reap River Rd East; per session US$6) This popular community centre and cafe has daily morning and evening yoga sessions, including ashtanga and hatha sessions.

🥘 Courses

Cooking classes have really taken off in Siem Reap with a number of restaurants and

---

FIGHT CLUB

If the martial-arts action on the bas-reliefs of the Bayon inspires you to want to learn some of the moves, contact the **Angkor Fight Club** (☎ 095 839725; www.facebook.com/angkorfightclub; Bakheng Rd; private/group class US$15/5) for very reasonably priced kick-boxing or MMA classes with international instructors. There are also *bokator* classes, an ancient Khmer martial art that translates as 'strike like a lion', with Grand Master San Kimsean at his **Bokator Cambodia** (☎ 012 651845; http://sankimsean.com; Dragon Bridge, Sangkat Slokram) school, including residential courses to pass the belts.

Siem Reap

Siem Reap is known as the gateway to the temples of Angkor; however, there is much going on in and around town to warrant a visit on its own merit. Floating villages on the nearby Tonlé Sap, a superb selection of restaurants and bars, first-class shopping, first-rate cooking classes and a host of other activities as diverse as birdwatching and Vespa tours are all on offer.

ELISA BONOMINI/SHUTTERSTOCK ©

DEMAMIEL62/SHUTTERSTOCK ©

1. Kompong Pluk (p130)
Houses on stilts make up the floating village of Kompong Pluk.

2. Psar Chaa (p120)
The produce section at the Old Market is a lively place to visit.

3. Banteay Srei Butterfly Centre (p127)
The largest enclosed butterfly centre in Southeast Asia provides a sustainable living for locals.

4. Street food (p112)
Get your fried-noodle fix at Psar Chaa, where the food is cheap, tasty and filling.

JAROMIR CHALABALA/SHUTTERSTOCK ©

North Siem Reap ⊕

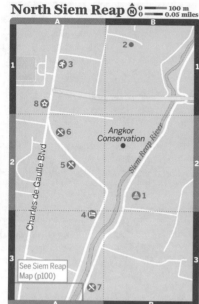

North Siem Reap

◉ Sights
1 Wat Preah Inkosei B2

⊕ Activities, Courses & Tours
2 Hidden Cambodia B1
3 Krousar Thmey A1
   Peace Cafe Yoga ....(see 7)
   Vegetarian Cooking Class............(see 7)

◎ Sleeping
4 HanumanAlaya Villa............................. A3

◉ Eating
5 Mahob.. A2
6 Mie Cafe... A2
7 Peace Cafe A3

◎ Entertainment
8 Beatocello A1

hotels, including many of the top-end places, now offering an introduction to the secrets of Cambodian cooking.

Le Tigre de Papier   COOKING
(Map p109; ✆012 265811; www.angkor-cooking-class-cambodia.com; Pub St; per person US$15) Classes include a visit to the market and the chance to prepare an *amok* degustation, a variation on the national dish. Daily classes are held at 10am, 1pm and 5pm.

Lily's Secret Garden
Cooking Class   COOKING
(✆016 353621; www.lilysecretgarden.com; off Sombai Rd; per person US$24; ⊗9am-1pm & 3-7pm) This immersive cooking class takes place in a traditional Cambodian house on the outskirts of Siem Reap. Morning and afternoon sessions end in a three-course lunch or dinner. The price includes pick-up and drop-off in town.

Vegetarian Cooking Class   COOKING
(Map p106; ✆092 177127; http://peacecafeangkor.org; Siem Reap River Rd East; per person US$20) A vegetarian cooking class with tofu *amok*, papaya salad and vegie spring rolls on the menu.

Khmer Ceramics Fine Arts Centre   ART
(សេរាម៉ិច; Map p100; ✆017 843014; www.khmerceramics.com; Charles de Gaulle Blvd; pottery course US$20; ⊗8am-8pm) ✎ Located on the road to the temples, this ceramics centre is dedicated to reviving the Khmer tradition of pottery, which was an intricate art during the time of Angkor. It's possible to visit and try your hand at the potter's wheel, and courses in traditional techniques, including pottery and ceramic painting, are available.

☞ Tours

Most visitors are in Siem Reap to tour the temples of Angkor, but not all operators are created equal. Be sure to ask around before booking. Nontemple tours include two-wheeled adventures on bicycles or motorbikes, as well as some foodie tours.

Beyond   TOURS
(Map p100; ✆063-969269; www.beyonduniqueescapes.com; 717 St 14, Kandal Village; ⊗7am-6pm) ✎ Responsible operator offering tours to Beng Mealea and Kompong Pluk, as well as cycling trips and cooking classes.

Indochine Exploration   TOURS
(www.indochineex.com) ✎ Me Chrey kayaking and remote temple tours.

Terre Cambodge   TOURS
(✆077 448255; www.terrecambodge.com) Francophone operator offering tours to remote sites around Angkor, bicycle tours, and boat trips on the Tonlé Sap lake.

Birding

★ Sam Veasna Center BIRDWATCHING

(SVC; Map p100; ☑ 063-963710; www.samveasna. org; St 26; per person from US$100) 🏃 Sam Veasna Center, in the Wat Bo area of Siem Reap, is the authority on birdwatching in Cambodia, with professionally trained English-speaking guides, powerful spotting scopes and a network of camps and bird hides scattered throughout north Cambodia. It uses ecotourism to provide an income for local communities in return for a ban on hunting and cutting down the forest.

Locally, SVC's most popular trip is to the spectacular Prek Toal Bird Sanctuary (p127) in the Tonlé Sap wetland area. It also runs trips to Ang Trapeng Thmor Reserve (p131), about 100km from Siem Reap, one of only a handful of places in the world where it's possible to see the extremely rare sarus crane. All tours include transport, entrance fees, guides, breakfast, lunch and water. New destinations opening up include Chung Kran Roi mountain in the Varin District, home to some rare forest birds.

Day trips include a visit to one of the local communities. Hotel pick-up is at around 6am and drop-off is by nightfall.

Osmose BIRDWATCHING

(☑ 063-765506; www.osmosetonlesap.net; per person in group of 5/2 US$95/165) Osmose runs organised day trips to see rare water birds in Prek Toal and visit one of the local communities. The price include transport, entrance fees, guides, breakfast, lunch and water, and binoculars are available on request. Hotel pick-up is at around 6am and drop-off is by nightfall. Overnight trips for serious enthusiasts can be arranged.

Prek Toal Tours & Travel TOURS

(☑ 077 797112; www.prektoal-tours.com; birdwatching per person in group of 5/2 US$65/128) Run by villagers from the floating village of Prek Toal, this outfit offers day or overnight trips with homestay accommodation to the fascinating floating village of Prek Toal. There's an option to visit the Prek Toal Bird Sanctuary.

Cycling

The beautiful countryside around Siem Reap is perfect for two-wheeled adventures. Specialist tour operators will get you on the back roads and away from tourist traffic.

★ KKO Bike Tours CYCLING

(Khmer for Khmer Organisation; Map p100; ☑ 093 903024; www.kko-cambodia.org; Taphul Rd; tours US$35-60) 🏃 Good-cause cycling and *moto* tours around the paths of Angkor or into the countryside beyond the Western Baray. Proceeds go towards the Khmer for Khmer Organisation, which supports education and vocational training.

PURE! Countryside Bicycle Tour CYCLING

(Map p100; ☑ 097 2356862; Hup Guan St; per person US$25-35) 🏃 Based out of the Sra May gift shop, this outfit organises half-day tours that take in local life around Siem Reap, including lunch with a local family. All proceeds go towards supporting Pure's educational and vocational-training projects. Book a few days ahead so they can notify the families.

Grasshopper Adventures CYCLING

(Map p100; ☑ 012 462165; www.grasshopper adventures.com; 586 St 26; per person from US$39; ⊙ 7am-8pm) Rides around the Siem Reap countryside, plus a dedicated temple tour on two wheels and a long-distance trip to Beng Mealea. Bicycle hire too.

Food

Cambodian food is now on the map and there are some cracking culinary tours to give you an insight into the food scene in Siem Reap. The night-time Vespa tours are a good option for those who want to combine a Vespa ride with a culinary adventure.

★ Siem Reap Food Tours FOOD & DRINK

(☑ 012 505542; www.siemreapfoodtours.com; per person US$75) Operated by an American food writer and an experienced Scottish chef with a penchant for stand-up comedy, these tours are a recipe for engaging food encounters. Choose from a morning tour that takes in local markets and the *naom banchok* noodle stalls of Preah Dak or an evening tour that takes in street stalls and local barbecue restaurants.

Motorbiking

Most Cambodians still use motorbikes to get around the countryside. 'When in Rome' also applies to 'When in Siem Reap', so consider taking a motorbike adventure deep into the countryside. There are also a couple of tours on modern Vespas. You can also customise a motorbike tour with any of the English-speaking *moto* drivers in Siem

SIEM REAP TOURS

Reap, which will work out a lot cheaper than taking an organised tour.

Cambodia Vespa Adventures   TOURS
(☑ 012 861610; www.vespaadventures-sr.com; P64 Borey Prem Prey; tours per person US$75-126) The modern Vespa is a cut above the average *moto* and is a comfortable way to explore the temples, learn about local life in the countryside or check out some street food after dark, all in the company of excellent and knowledgeable local guides.

Vespa Adventures   TOURS
(☑ 017 881384; http://vespaadventures.com/siem-reap-bike-tours; tours US$70-115) The original Vespa tour operator in Vietnam is now in Siem Reap offering a similar combination of countryside experiences and temple tours, and Siem Reap by night.

Khmer Ways   TOURS
(☑ 088 606 3374; www.khmerways.com; tours US$60-95) Live the dream with Khmer Ways...or at least ride the Honda Dream. Choose from a countryside tour, a longer ride to Beng Mealea or an adventure on the jungle roads of Phnom Kulen.

🛌 Sleeping

Siem Reap has the best range of accommodation in Cambodia. A vast number of family-run guesthouses (US$5 to US$20 per room) and a growing number of hostels cater for budget travellers. In the midrange, there's a dizzying array of good-value pool-equipped boutiques (US$30 to US$70) with something of a price war breaking out in low season. High-end options abound but don't always offer more than you'd get at the midrange.

Commission scams abound in Siem Reap, so keep your antennae up. Touts for budget guesthouses wait at the taxi park and at the airport. Even if you've not yet decided where to stay in Siem Reap, don't be surprised to see a noticeboard displaying your name, as most guesthouses in Phnom Penh either have partners up here or sell your name on to another guesthouse. This system usually involves a free ride into town. There's no obligation to stay at the guesthouse if you don't like the look of it, but the 'free lift' might suddenly cost a few dollars.

Most hotels will include a free transfer from the airport, bus station or boat dock if you ask, and breakfast is almost always included at the midrange end and up.

Many top-end hotels levy an additional 10% government tax, 2% tourist tax, and sometimes an extra 10% for service.

🏨 Psar Chaa Area

Psar Chaa is the liveliest part of town, brimming with restaurants, bars and boutiques. Staying here can be a lot of fun, but it's not the quietest area.

1920 Hotel   BOUTIQUE HOTEL **$$**
(Map p109; ☑ 063-969920; www.1920hotel.com; St 9; r US$45-77; ❄ @ 🛜) Set in a grand old building near Psar Chaa dating from, well, we'd hazard a guess at 1920, this is a thoughtfully presented budget boutique hotel with modernist touches in the rooms. The location is great for dining and drinking options in the gentrified alleys nearby.

Shadow of Angkor Residence   GUESTHOUSE **$$**
(Map p109; ☑ 063-964774; www.shadowangkorresidence.com; 353 Pokambor Ave; r US$31-48; ❄ @ 🛜 ⊠) In a grand old French-era building overlooking the river, this friendly place offers stylish air-conditioned rooms in a superb setting close to Psar Chaa. There is also an annexe across the river, which has a swimming pool.

Steung Siem Reap Hotel   HOTEL **$$**
(Map p109; ☑ 063-965167; www.steungsiemreap.com; near Psar Chaa; r incl breakfast from US$65; ❄ @ 🛜 ⊠) In keeping with the French colonial–era legacy around Psar Chaa, this hotel has high ceilings, louvre shutters and wrought-iron balconies. Three-star rooms feature smart wooden trim. The location is hard to beat if you want to be central.

🏨 Sivatha St Area

The area west of Sivatha St has good budget guesthouses and midrange boutique hotels. Off the southern end of Sivatha St is Sok San Rd, fast becoming Siem Reap's top traveller's mecca as high rents force many budget and midrange properties out of the centre.

★ Onederz Hostel   HOSTEL **$**
(Map p100; ☑ 063-963525; https://onederz.com; Angkor Night Market St; dm US$8.50-9.50, r US$26; ❄ @ 🛜 ⊠) Winner of several 'Hoscars' (Hostelworld's Oscars), this is one of the smartest hostels in Siem Reap. Facilities include a huge cafe-bar downstairs, which acts as a giant waiting room for all those

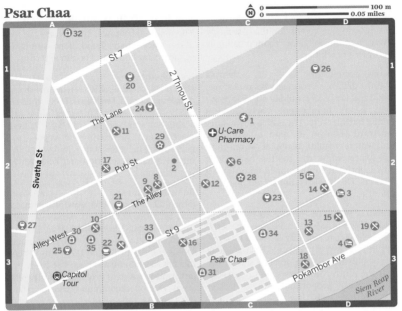

Psar Chaa

Psar Chaa

coming and going from Siem Reap. Dorms are a little pricey but don't forget this is because they include access to the rooftop swimming pool.

Mad Monkey HOSTEL $
(Map p100; www.madmonkeyhostels.com; Sivatha St; dm US$7-9, r US$16-26; ❄@🛜) The Siem Reap outpost of an expanding Monkey

business, this classic backpacker has deluxe dorms with air-con and extra-wide bunk beds, good-value rooms for those wanting privacy and the obligatory rooftop bar, only this one's a beach bar!

Funky Flashpacker HOSTEL $

(☎070 221524; www.funkyflashpacker.com; Funky Lane; dm US$5-8, r US$10-40; ❈@🖥🛋) Siem Reap's number-one party address among backpackers. The entire downstairs courtyard is taken up with a swimming pool where regular bouts of water polo take place, while the rooftop bar sizzles with inebriated youth hopped up on cheap shooters. Great hostel, but it's no place for quiet time.

Mulberry Boutique Hotel BOUTIQUE HOTEL $$

(Map p100; ☎063-621 2168; www.mulberry-boutiquehotel.com; Tep Vong St; r incl breakfast from US$66; ❈🖥🛋) Set amid lush gardens in a sophisticated villa down a side street near the centre, Mulberry scores points for its generously proportioned rooms decked out with love seats, Jacuzzi-like baths and balconies. The well-furnished suites, many with pool views, are a worthy splurge.

Memoire d'Angkor Boutique Hotel BOUTIQUE HOTEL $$

(Map p100; ☎063-766999; www.memoiredangkor. com; Sivatha St; r US$55-170; ❈@🖥🛋) Centrally located on the popular Sivatha St strip, this hotel pays homage to its Angkor heritage with some incredible pieces of local lacquerwork on display. Rooms are spacious, colourful and contemporary, and there's an inviting swimming pool in which to wind down after visiting the temples.

Sala Bai Hotel & Restaurant School HOTEL $$

(☎063-963329; www.salabai.com; Tonle Sap Rd, Wat Svay; r incl breakfast US$35-70; ⊘closed mid-Jul–mid-Oct; ❈@🖥) 🏊 In a rambling villa 1.5km south of Wat Dam Nak, on the eastern side of the river, this training-school hotel for disadvantaged youth features six spacious, minimalist rooms with brushed-concrete floors and boutique bathrooms. The deluxe rooms sleep three comfortably.

There's a fine training restaurant on-site. Some 1300 Sala Bai graduates are working in the hospitality industry across Siem Reap and other locales.

🏛 Riverfront & Royal Gardens

The smart end of town, this is where the royal residence is to be found, along with many of the luxury hotels and boutique resorts.

Ivy Guesthouse 2 GUESTHOUSE $

(Map p100; ☎012 800860; www.ivy-guesthouse. com; Psar Kandal St; r with fan US$6-8, with air-con US$15; ❈@🖥) An inviting guesthouse with a chill-out area and bar, the Ivy is a lively place to stay. The restaurant is as good as it gets among the guesthouses in town, with a huge vegetarian selection and US$1.25 'Tapas Fridays'.

Rosy Guesthouse GUESTHOUSE $

(Map p100; ☎063-965059; www.rosyguesthouse. com; Siem Reap River Rd East; d US$9, with bathroom & air-con US$16-35; ❈🖥) 🏊 A Brit-run establishment whose 13 value-for-money rooms come with TV and DVD, plus tasteful touches like silk furnishings. The lively pub downstairs has great grub and hosts regular events to support community causes, including a popular quiz night.

Raffles Grand Hotel d'Angkor HOTEL $$$

(Map p100; ☎063-963888; www.raffles.com; 1 Charles de Gaulle Blvd; r incl breakfast from US$220; ❈@🖥🛋) This historic hotel has been welcoming guests such as Charlie Chaplin, Charles de Gaulle, Jackie Kennedy and Bill Clinton since 1932. Ensconced in opulent surroundings, you can imagine what it was like to be a tourist in colonial days. Rooms include classic touches and a dizzying array of bathroom gifts.

Bemond La Résidence d'Angkor RESORT $$$

(Map p100; ☎063-963390; www.residencedangkor.com; Siem Reap River Rd East; r incl breakfast from US$300; ❈@🖥🛋) The original wood-finished rooms, among the most tasteful and inviting in town, come with verandahs or small gardens. The gorgeous swimming pool is perfect for laps. The newer wing is ultra-contemporary, as is the sumptuous Kong Kea Spa, but rates have shot up since the refurbishment.

Shinta Mani RESORT $$$

(Map p100; ☎063-761998; www.shintamani. com; Oum Khun St; r incl breakfast US$170-285; ❈@🖥🛋) 🏊 With a contemporary chic design by renowned architect Bill Bensley, Shinta Mani Shack features an inviting central pool, while Shinta Mani Angkor offers more exclusive rooms. Shinta Mani has won several international awards for responsible tourism practices and is regularly cited in leading hotel lists.

Wat Bo Rd Area

This up-and-coming area on the east bank of the Siem Reap River features socially responsible guesthouses as well as some hip boutique hotels. There is a great guesthouse ghetto in a backstreet running parallel to the northern end of Wat Bo Rd, which is a good option for browsers without a booking.

Siem Reap Hostel HOSTEL $
(Map p100; ☏063-964660; www.thesiemreaphostel.com; 10 Makara St; dm US$8-10, r incl breakfast US$30-45; ✳@🅿🏊) Angkor's original backpacker hostel is pretty slick. The dorms are well tended, while the rooms are definitely flashpacker and include breakfast. There is a lively bar-restaurant and a covered pool, plus a well-organised travel desk.

Seven Candles Guesthouse GUESTHOUSE $
(Map p100; ☏063-963380; www.sevencandlesguesthouse.com; 307 Wat Bo Rd; r US$20-38; ✳@🅿) 🖉 A good-cause guesthouse, Seven Candles uses profits to help a local foundation that seeks to promote education in rural communities. Rooms include hot water, TV and fridge, plus some decorative flourishes.

Babel Guesthouse GUESTHOUSE $
(Map p100; ☏063-965474; http://babel-siemreap. com; 738 Wat Bo Village; r incl breakfast US$22-32; ✳@🅿) 🖉 This Norwegian-run guesthouse set in a relaxing tropical garden offers service and presentation that are a cut above the nearby budget places. The Babel owners are keen supporters of responsible tourism.

Downtown Siem Reap Hostel HOSTEL $
(Map p100; ☏012 675881; www.downtownsiemreaphostel.hostel.com; Wat Dam Nak area; dm US$6-8, r US$12-18; ✳🅿🏊) The rates here are particularly inviting when you factor in the small pool in the garden. Chill out with aircon in the more expensive dorms or rooms. Outside visitors can use the pool with a US$6 spend on food and drink.

Soria Moria Hotel BOUTIQUE HOTEL $$
(Map p100; ☏063-964768; http://thesoriamoria.com; Wat Bo Rd; s US$45-65, d US$60-80; ✳@🅿🏊) 🖉 A hotel with a heart, promoting local causes to help the community, this boutique place has attractive rooms with smart bathroom fittings. There's a fusion

restaurant downstairs, sky hot tub upstairs and a swimming pool. Half the hotel was transferred to staff ownership in 2011, a visionary move.

Rambutan Resort RESORT $$
(Map p100; ☏063-766655; www.rambutans.info; Wat Dam Nak area; r incl breakfast US$60-80; ✳@🅿🏊) This atmospheric, gay-friendly resort is spread over two stunning villas, each with spacious and stylish rooms and an inviting courtyard swimming pool.

★**Viroth's Hotel** BOUTIQUE HOTEL $$$
(Map p100; ☏063-766107; www.viroth-hotel.com; St 24; r incl breakfast US$90-140; ✳@🅿🏊) Viroth's is an ultra-stylish, retro-chic property with 30 rooms fitted out with classy contemporary furnishings. Behind the impressive facade lies a 20m swimming pool, a gym and a spa. The original seven-bedroom hotel is still operating as Viroth's Villa.

Angkor Village BOUTIQUE HOTEL $$$
(Map p100; ☏063-963561; www.angkorvillage. com; St 26; r US$75-350; ✳@🅿🏊) The original boutique hotel in Siem Reap (when boutique was still an upmarket shopping experience to most), Angkor Village remains one of the most atmospheric places in temple town. Rooms are set in beautiful wooden bungalows around a stunning pond with a central restaurant. Sister hotel, Angkor Village Resort, is even more opulent.

Further Afield

Don't shy away from staying out of town, as some of the most memorable boutique hotels lie hidden beyond and are usually only a short *remork-moto (tuk tuk)* ride from the centre. Homestays are starting to take off around more distant temples like Banteay Srei, Bakong and Beng Mealea.

★**Green Home I** HOMESTAY $
(☏095 334460; www.thegreenhome.org; Chreav Commune; r with fan/air-con US$8/10; ✳🅿) Setting the standard for the homestay experience around Siem Reap, the Green Home is set up like a family guesthouse and offers beautiful garden views over the surrounding rice fields. Bathrooms are shared but meticulously clean and the downstairs rooms include air-con. Cooking classes are available, as well as village walks, farm visits and birding trips.

HI Siem Reap Deluxe
HOSTEL $

(Map p100; ☎063-765569; www.hisiemreap.com; 319 Siem Reap River Rd East; dm US$4-6, r US$15-30; ❄🖥📶📺) The official Hostelling International property in Siem Reap, the 'Deluxe' offers great services and facilities at rock-bottom prices. Dorm beds include two pillows and a reading light, while private rooms are definitely flashpacker. Throw in a rooftop pool and it's a steal.

Pavillon Indochine
BOUTIQUE HOTEL $$

(☎012 849681; www.pavillon-indochine.com; r US$60-140; ❄@📶📺) The Pavillon offers charming colonial-chic rooms set around a small swimming pool. The trim includes Asian antiques, billowing mosquito nets and a safe. Also included in the rates is a *remork* driver for the day to tour the temples, making it very good value.

Petit Villa Boutique
BOUTIQUE HOTEL $$

(Map p100; ☎063-764234; www.petitvilla.com; Wat Dam Nak area; r US$40-80; ❄@📶📺) Petit Villa is a blissful little boutique hideaway with a mellow retreat vibe in the suburbs of Wat Dam Nak. Rooms are spacious and include a balcony looking out over the central swimming pool and lush gardens. Cooking classes are available and there's a small spa.

★ Phum Baitang
RESORT $$$

(☎063-961111; www.zannierhotels.com; Neelka Way; villas US$500-725; ❄@📶📺) This beautiful resort feels like a boutique Cambodian village. Rooms are set in spacious, elegantly furnished wooden villas, some with private pools, and all connected by extensive wooden walkways over the rice fields. The decor is very designer driftwood. Angelina Jolie stayed here for three months while shooting *First They Killed My Father,* and it's not hard to see what attracted her to the place.

★ Sala Lodges
BOUTIQUE HOTEL $$$

(☎063-766699; www.salalodges.com; 498 Salakomroeuk; r US$230-510; ❄📶📺) An original concept, Sala Lodges offers 11 traditional Khmer houses that have been retro-fitted inside to bring them up to the standard of a rustic boutique hotel. Enter the resort and you'll think you have stumbled on an idyllic Cambodian village, but the pool and restaurant will soon confirm you have stumbled on a gem.

HanumanAlaya Villa
BOUTIQUE HOTEL $$$

(Map p106; ☎063-760582; www.hanumanalaya.com; Siem Reap River Rd West; r US$60-150; ❄@📶📺) A boutique hotel with traditional Cambodian stylings, HanumanAlaya Villa is set around a lush garden and pretty swimming pool. Rooms are decorated with antiques and handicrafts but include modern touches such as flat-screen TV, minibar and safe.

Sister hotel HanumanAlaya Boutique is nearby; on our last visit it was undergoing a renovation and expansion.

✗ Eating

Siem Reap's dining scene is something to savour, offering a superb selection of street food, Asian eateries and sophisticated international restaurants. The range encompasses something from every continent, with new temptations regularly opening up. Sample the subtleties of Khmer cuisine in town, or indulge in home comforts prior to – or after – hitting the remote provinces. Some of the very best restaurants also put something back into community projects or offer vocational training.

Tourist numbers mean many top restaurants are heaving during the high season. But with so many places to choose from, keep walking and you'll find somewhere more tranquil. Quite a lot of restaurants work with tour groups to some degree. If you prefer to avoid places with tour groups, stick to the Psar Chaa area and explore on foot.

Some budget guesthouses have good menus offering a selection of local dishes and Western meals. Several of the midrange hotels and all of the top-end places have restaurants, some of them excellent. Several hotels and restaurants around town feature dinner and a performance of classical dance.

✗ Psar Chaa & Pub St

Pub St may not seem to be the most relaxing dining area, particularly at night, but the criss-crossing alleys are wall-to-wall with good restaurants. Take a stroll and see what takes your fancy.

Psar Chaa and other markets are well stocked with fruit and fresh bread. Eating locally usually works out cheaper than self-catering, but some folks like to make up a picnic for longer days on the road.

Sister Srey Cafe
CAFE $

(Map p109; www.sistersreycafe.com; 200 Pokambor Ave; mains US$3-6; ⊙7am-6pm Tue-Sun; 🖥) Sister Srey, a funky and fun cafe on the riverfront near Psar Chaa, offers an ambitious breakfast menu, including eggs bene-delicious, that is perfect after a sunrise at the temples. Lunch is Western food with a creative twist, including burgers, wraps and salads.

Psar Chaa   CAMBODIAN $

(Map p109; mains US$1.50-4; ⏱7am-9pm) When it comes to cheap Khmer eats, Psar Chaa market has plenty of food stalls on the northwestern side, all with signs and menus in English. These are atmospheric places for a local meal at local-ish prices. Some dishes are on display, others are freshly wok-fried to order, but most are wholesome and filling.

Khmer Kitchen Restaurant   CAMBODIAN $

(Map p109; ☑012 763468; www.khmerkitchens. com; The Alley; mains US$2-5; ⏱11am-10pm; 🛜) Can't get no (culinary) satisfaction? Then follow in the footsteps of Sir Mick Jagger and try this popular place, which offers an affordable selection of Khmer and Thai favourites, including zesty curries. It expanded massively in 2017 and now covers a whole block of classic colonial-era buildings.

★**Le Malraux**   FRENCH $$

(Map p109; ☑012 332584; http://le-malraux-siem-reap.fr; mains US$5-15; ⏱10am-11pm; 🛜) Recently relocated to the network of alleys east of Psar Chaa, Le Malraux is one of the best French restaurants in Siem Reap. Eat or drink inside at the bar or alfresco in the street. Meals includes a superb *pavê* of *boeuf* and succulent fish.

Olive   FRENCH $$

(Map p109; ☑012 244196; www.facebook.com/ olivecuisinedesaison; off Siem Reap River Rd West; mains US$5-15; ⏱11am-10.30pm; ❋🛜) The crisp white linens and air-con beckon diners into this French restaurant hidden away down a side street near the Old Market. The menu includes a good range of Gallic classics, including rack of lamb and pork tenderloin. Save space for the desserts or a cheese platter.

Il Forno   ITALIAN $$

(Map p109; ☑063-763380; http://ilforno.restau-rant; The Lane; mains US$5-15; ⏱11am-11pm; 🛜) Aficionados of fine Italian cuisine will be delighted to know that there is, as the name suggests, a full-blown brick oven in this cosy little trattoria. The menu includes fresh antipasti, authentic pizzas and some home-cooked Italian dishes.

CRAVING ICE CREAM?

After a hot day exploring the temples, there's nothing quite like an ice-cream fix and Siem Reap delivers some superb surprises:

Gelato Lab (Map p109; www.facebook. com/gelatolabsiemreap; 109 Alley West; 1/2 scoops US$1.50/2.50; ⏱9am-11pm; 🛜) State-of-the-art equipment, all-natural ingredients and, most importantly, plenty of passion courtesy of the Italian owner add up to great ice cream

Blue Pumpkin (Map p109; www.blue pumpkin.asia; 2 Thnou St; mains US$3-8; ⏱6am-10pm; ❋🛜) Homemade ice cream in original tropical flavours from ginger to passionfruit.

The Glasshouse (Map p100; www. facebook.com/theglasshousedelipatisserie; Park Hyatt, Sivatha St; cones US$2; ⏱6am-10pm; 🛜) Velvety ice creams including white chocolate and tangy sorbets.

Swenson's Ice Cream (Map p109; Po-kambor Ave; cones US$1.25; ⏱9am-9pm) One of America's favourites has become one of Siem Reap's favourites. Located in the Angkor Trade Centre.

Cambodian BBQ   BARBECUE $$

(Map p109; www.restaurant-siemreap.com; The Alley; mains US$5-10; ⏱11am-11pm; 🛜) Crocodile, snake, ostrich and kangaroo meat add an exotic twist to the traditional *phnom pleung* (hill of fire) grills. Cambodian BBQ has spawned half a dozen or more copycats in the surrounding streets, many of which offer discount specials.

Cafe Central   INTERNATIONAL $$

(Map p109; ☑017 692997; www.facebook.com/ cafecentralsiemreap; Psar Chaa; meals US$4-9; ⏱7am-10pm; 🛜) Cafe Central occupies a handsome building overlooking Psar Chaa. The menu is East meets West, with marinated ribs, fish and chips, authentic pizzas plus some Cambodian faves like *amok* fish and vegetable curry. The coffee is highly regarded thanks to the La Marzocco coffee machine.

Red Piano   ASIAN, INTERNATIONAL $$

(Map p109; ☑063-963240; www.redpianocambo dia.com; Pub St; mains US$3-10; 🛜) Strikingly set in a restored colonial-era gem, Red Piano has a big balcony for watching the action unfold below. The menu has a reliable selection of Asian and international food, all at decent prices. Former celebrity guest Angelina Jolie has a cocktail named in her honour.

Le Tigre de Papier INTERNATIONAL $$
(Map p109; www.letigredepapier.com; Pub St; mains US$2-9; ⏱24hr; 🛜🖉) One of the best all-rounders in Siem Reap, the popular Paper Tiger serves up authentic Khmer food, great Italian dishes and a selection of favourites from most other corners of the globe. It conveniently offers frontage on both Pub St and the Alley; the latter is generally a lot quieter.

Chamkar VEGETARIAN $$
(Map p109; 📞 092 733150; The Alley; mains US$4-8; ⏱11am-10.30pm Mon-Sat, 5-10.30pm Sun; 🛜🖉) The name translates as 'farm' and the ingredients must be coming from a pretty impressive organic vegetable supplier given the creative dishes on the menu here. Asian flavours dominate and include dishes such as stuffed pumpkin and vegetable kebabs in black pepper sauce.

🍴 Sivatha St Area

⭐**Pot & Pan Restaurant** CAMBODIAN $
(Map p100; 📞 017 970780; www.thepotandpan restaurant.com; Stung Thmei Rd; meals US$2-5; ⏱10am-10pm; 🛜) One of the best-value Khmer restaurants in the downtown area, Pot & Pan specialises in well-presented, authentic dishes at affordable prices. The menu includes spicy soups and subtle salads and rice is beautifully served in a lotus leaf. Some of the cheapest pizzas in town are, somewhat surprisingly, also available here.

Bugs Cafe CAMBODIAN $
(Map p100; 📞 017-764560; www.bugs-cafe.com; Angkor Night Market St; dishes US$2-8; ⏱5-11pm; 🛜) Cambodians were onto insects long before the food scientists started bugging us about their merits. Choose from a veritable feast of crickets, water bugs, silk worms and spiders. Tarantula doughnuts, pan-fried scorpions, snakes – you won't forget this menu in a hurry.

Curry Walla INDIAN $
(Map p100; Sivatha St; mains US$2-6; ⏱10.30am-11pm) For good-value Indian food, this place is hard to beat. The *thalis* (set meals) are a bargain and the owner, long-time resident

Ranjit, knows his share of spicy specials from the subcontinent.

Burger Gourmand BURGERS $$
(Map p100; 📞 087 463640; www.facebook.com/burger.gourmand.siemreap; Sok San Rd; meals US$5-15; ⏱11am-3pm & 5-9.30pm Tue-Sun; 🖵🛜) This French-run burger joint really is gourmand, thanks to homemade buns and a list of patties that includes beef, pork, duck, chicken, fish and vegetarian. The toppings list is even more eclectic and includes such delicacies as foie gras. Set meals offer a good-value meal with drink and dessert.

Self-Catering
Angkor Market SUPERMARKET $
(Map p100; Sivatha St; ⏱8am-9pm) The best all-round supermarket in town, this place has a steady supply of international treats.

🍴 Kandal Village

Little Red Fox CAFE $
(Map p100; www.thelittleredfoxespresso.com; Hup Guan St; dishes US$2-8; ⏱7am-5pm Thu-Tue; 🖵) This foxy little cafe is incredibly popular with long-term residents in Siem Reap, who swear that the regionally sourced Feel Good coffee is the best in town. Add to that designer breakfasts, bagels, salads, creative juices and air-con and it's easy to while away some time here. The slick upstairs wing is popular with the laptop crowd.

The Hive Siem Reap CAFE $
(Map p100; www.facebook.com/thehive.siem reap; Psar Kandal St; dishes US$2-6; ⏱7am-6pm; 🖵🛜) This place has generated a real buzz among foreign residents in Siem Reap thanks to its creative coffees, jam-jar juices and healthy open sandwiches, such as smashed avocado or smoked salmon on rye. Try an espresso martini if you like your coffee with a kick.

⭐**Mamma Shop** ITALIAN $$
(Map p100; www.facebook.com/mammashop. italian.restaurant; Hup Guan St; mains US$5-9; ⏱11.30am-10.30pm Mon-Sat; 🖵🛜) A compact menu of terrific homemade pasta is the signature of this bright, friendly Italian corner bistro in the up-and-coming Kandal Village district. Add a selection of *piadina romagnola* (stuffed flatbread) pizza, a nice wine list and delicious desserts, and this place is highly recommended.

DON'T MISS

DINING FOR A CAUSE

There are some good restaurants in Siem Reap that support worthy causes or assist in the training of Cambodia's future hospitality staff with a subsidised ticket into the tourism industry. When you dine at the training places, it provides the trainees with a good opportunity to hone their skills with real customers.

Bloom Cafe (Map p100; www.bloomcakes.org; St 6; cupcakes US$1.50; ⊙10am-5pm Mon-Sat; 🛜) Cupcakes are elevated to an art form at this elegant cafe, with beautifully presented creations available in a rotating array of 48 flavours. Creative coffees, teas and juices are also on offer. Profits assist Cambodian women in vocational training.

Common Grounds (Map p100; www.commongroundscafes.org; 719 St 14; light meals US$3-5; ⊙7am-10pm; 🛜) This sophisticated international cafe, akin to Starbucks, has great coffee, homemade cakes, light bites, and free wi-fi and internet terminals. Offers free computer classes and English classes for Cambodians, and supports good causes.

Haven (Map p100; ☑078-342404; www.haven-cambodia.com; Chocolate Rd, Wat Dam Nak area; mains US$6-8; ⊙11.30am-2.30pm & 5.30-9.30pm Mon-Sat, closed Aug; 🛜) A culinary haven indeed. Dine here for the best of East meets West; the fish fillet with green mango is particularly zesty. Proceeds go towards helping young adult orphans make the step from institution to employment.

Joe to Go (Map p109; www.joetogo.org; St 9; mains US$2-5; ⊙7am-9.30pm) If you need coffee coursing through your veins to tackle the temples, then head here. Gourmet coffees, shakes and light bites, with proceeds supporting street children. Upstairs is a small boutique supporting the associated NGO, The Global Child.

Le Jardin des Délices (☑063-963673; www.ecolepauldubrule.org; Paul Dubrule Hotel & Tourism School, NH6; set lunch US$15; ⊙noon-2pm Tue-Fri; 🅰🛜) Enjoy Sofitel standards at an affordable price with a three-course lunch of Asian and Western food prepared by students training in the culinary arts. It also runs a 'Khmer Food Lovers' cooking class.

Marum (Map p100; ☑017 363284; www.marum-restaurant.org; Wat Polanka area; mains US$3.25-6.75; ⊙11am-10.30pm; 🛜🍴) Set in a delightful wooden house with a spacious garden, Marum serves up lots of vegetarian and seafood dishes, plus some mouthwatering desserts. Menu highlights include beef with red ants and chilli stir-fry, and mini crocodile burgers. Marum is part of the Tree Alliance group of training restaurants; the experience is a must.

New Leaf Book Cafe (Map p109; http://newleafeatery.com; near Psar Chaa; mains US$3-6; ⊙7.30am-10pm) The profits from this cafe and secondhand bookshop go towards supporting NGOs working in Siem Reap Province. The menu includes some home favourites, an Italian twist and some local Cambodian specials.

Sala Bai (p110) is a hospitality training school to help disadvantaged youth and the project includes a great restaurant serving Khmer and international set menus. Some 1300 Sala Bai graduates are working in the hospitality industry across Siem Reap and other locales.

Spoons Cafe (Map p100; ☑076 277 6667; www.spoonscambodia.org; Bamboo Rd; mains US$5.50-8; ⊙11.30am-10pm Tue-Sun; 🛜) This excellent contemporary-Cambodian restaurant supports local community EGBOK (Everything's Going to Be OK), which offers education, training and employment opportunities in the hospitality sector. The menu includes some original flavours such as *trey saba* (whole mackerel) with coconut-turmeric rice, tiger prawn curry and *tuk kroeung*, a pungent local fish-based broth. Original cocktails are shaken, not stirred.

Vibe Cafe   VEGAN **$$**
(Map p100; ☑069-937900; www.vibecafeasia.com; 715 Hup Guan St; ⊙7.30am-6pm; 🅰🛜🍴) This new vegan spot promises raw organically sourced superfood bowls and cleansing juices like the cashew, date, Himalayan salt, vanilla bean and Ayurvedic spices concoction. If that sounds too healthy for you after

partying on Pub St, try the excellent vegan desserts like raspberry cheesecake and chocolate-ganache truffle.

Village Cafe FRENCH **$$**
(Map p100; ☑092 305401; www.facebook.com/villagecafecambodia; 586 Tep Vong St; mains US$5-15; ☺5pm-late Mon-Sat; ✷🛜) The Village Cafe is a lively little bistro that has one of the longer bars in Siem Reap. Drop in for tapas, wholesome gastro-pub grub and a glass of wine or four to wash it all down. Regular DJ events at weekends draw a crowd.

✕ Riverfront & Royal Gardens

★Chanrey Tree CAMBODIAN **$$**
(Map p100; ☑063-767997; www.chanreytree.com; Pokambor Ave; mains US$5-12; ☺11am-2pm & 5.30-10pm; ✷🛜) Chantrey Tree is all about contemporary Khmer cuisine, combining a stylish setting with expressive presentation, while retaining the essentials of traditional Cambodian cooking. Try the eggplant with pork ribs or grilled stuffed frog.

FCC Angkor INTERNATIONAL **$$**
(Map p100; ☑063-760280; www.fcccambodia.com; Pokambor Ave; mains US$5-15; ☺7am-midnight; 🛜) This landmark building draws people in from the riverside thanks to a reflective pool, torchlit dining and a garden bar. Inside the colonial-chic atmosphere continues with lounge chairs and an open kitchen turning out a range of Asian and international food.

Siem Reap Brewpub INTERNATIONAL **$$**
(Map p100; ☑080 888555; www.siemreapbrewpub.asia; St 5; meals US$4-15; ☺11am-11pm) Designer dining meets designer brewing. Set in

***

KING'S ROAD

King's Road (Map p100; https://kingsroadangkor.com; Siem Reap River Rd East; ☺7am-midnight; 🛜) is an upmarket dining destination on the east bank of the Siem Reap River. You can browse the daily **Made in Cambodia** (p121) community market of craft stalls, then choose from about 10 restaurants set in beautiful traditional Cambodian wooden buildings. It hasn't been as successful as hoped, however, so it feels more like a market than dining destination. Dining choices include Cambodian, Asian, fusion and international.

***

an open-plan villa, the menu is international fusion, including everything from light bites and tapas to gourmet meals. The beer comes in several flavours, including blonde, golden, amber and dark, and a sampling platter is available.

✕ Wat Bo Rd Area

Banlle Vegetarian Restaurant VEGETARIAN **$**
(Map p100; www.banlle-vegetarian.com; St 26; dishes US$2-4; ☺11am-9.30pm Wed-Mon; 🛜✐) Set in a traditional wooden house with its own organic vegetable garden, this is a great place for a healthy bite. The menu offers a blend of international and Cambodian dishes, including a vegetable *amok* and zesty fruit and vegetable shakes.

Pages Cafe CAFE **$**
(Map p100; ☑092 966812; www.pages-siemreap.com; St 24; dishes US$2-6; ☺6am-10pm; 🛜) This hip little hideaway is no longer so hidden with popular Viroth's Hotel now opposite. Exposed brickwork and designer decor make it a good place to linger over the excellent breakfasts or tapas. On Saturday they offer an outdoor grill with wine and pool access. Rooms also available.

★Sugar Palm CAMBODIAN **$$**
(Map p100; www.thesugarpalm.com; St 27; mains US$5-9; ☺11.30am-3pm & 5.30-10.30pm Mon-Sat; 🛜) Recently relocated to the east bank, the Sugar Palm is a popular place to sample traditional flavours infused with herbs and spices, including delicious *char kreung* (curried lemongrass) dishes. Owner Kethana showed celebrity chef Gordon Ramsay how to prepare *amok*.

Flow FUSION **$$**
(Map p100; ☑012 655285; www.facebook.com/flowfoodandwine; St 26; dishes US$5-12; ☺5-11pm; ✷🛜) This chic, contemporary space is earning a local following for its creative cuisine that mixes the best of East and West. Starters include octopus carpaccio while mains include tender beef cheek and pan-fried sea bass. The wine list is extensive so go with the Flow!

Jungle Burger INTERNATIONAL **$$**
(Map p100; ☑098 293400; www.facebook.com/jungleburgersiemreap; St 26; burgers US$2.50-10; ☺11am-11pm; 🛜) There are more than 10 types of burger on offer here, including the huge Burg Kalifa burger, plus pizzas, foot-long subs and Kiwi comfort food such as homemade

pies thanks to the NZ owner. It doubles as a small sports bar with a popular pool table.

★ **Cuisine Wat Damnak** CAMBODIAN **$$$**
(Map p100; ☑077 347762; www.cuisinewatdam nak.com; Wat Dam Nak area; 5-/6-course menu US$24/28; ☉6.30-10.30pm Tue-Sat, last orders 9.30pm) Set in a traditional wooden house is this highly regarded restaurant from Siem Reap celeb chef Joannès Rivière. The menu delivers the ultimate contemporary Khmer dining experience. Seasonal set menus focus on market-fresh ingredients and change weekly; vegetarian options are available with advance notice.

Embassy CAMBODIAN **$$$**
(Map p100; ☑063-963840; www.restaurant-siemreap.com; King's Rd; set menus from US$27; ☉11am-11pm) Part of the King's Rd village, Embassy is all about Khmer gastronomy, offering an evolving menu that changes with the seasons. Under the supervision of the Kimsan twins, who studied with Michelin-starred chef Régis Marcon, this is Khmer cuisine prepared at its most creative.

Hashi JAPANESE **$$$**
(Map p100; www.thehashi.com; Wat Bo Rd; meals US$15-50; ☉11am-3pm & 6-11pm; ❀☏) A big, bright and boisterous sushi parlour. Navigate through the SUVs parked outside, waddle up to the fish-shaped sushi bar and order the likes of spicy tuna rolls, chirashi sushi bowls or, for the fish averse, wagyu beef tenderloin.

🍴 Further Afield

Road 60 Night Market MARKET **$**
(Rd 60; snacks US$1-4; ☉4-11pm) For a slice of local life, head to the Road 60 Night Market located on the side of the road near the main Angkor ticket checkpoint. Stallholders set up each night, and it's a great place to sample local Cambodian snacks, including the full range of deep-fried insects, barbecue dishes such as quail, and plenty of cheap beer.

Peace Cafe VEGETARIAN **$**
(Map p106; www.peacecafeangkor.org; Siem Reap River Rd East; mains US$2.50-4.50; ☉7am-9pm; ☑) ✔ This popular garden cafe serves affordable vegetarian meals, while healthy drinks include a tempting selection of vegetable juices. A focal point for community activities, it hosts twice-daily yoga sessions and twice-weekly Khmer classes and monk chanting.

★ **Mie Cafe** CAMBODIAN, INTERNATIONAL **$$**
(Map p106; ☑069 999096; www.miecafe-siem-reap.com; near Angkor Conservation; mains US$4-8; ☉11am-2pm & 5.30-10pm Wed-Mon) An impressive Cambodian eatery offering a fusion take on traditional flavours. It is set in a wooden house just off the road to Angkor and offers a gourmet set menu for US$24. Dishes include everything from succulent marinated pork ribs to squid-ink ravioli.

Mahob CAMBODIAN **$$**
(Map p106; ☑063-966986; www.mahobkhmer.com; near Angkor Conservation; dishes US$3.50-15; ☉11am-11pm) The Cambodian word for food is *mahob*, and at this restaurant it is delicious. Set in a traditional wooden house with a contemporary twist, they take the same approach to cuisine as they do to decor, serving up dishes such as caramelised pork shank with ginger and black pepper, or wok-fried local beef with red tree ants. Cooking classes available.

🍷 **Drinking & Nightlife**

The transformation from sleepy overgrown village to an international destination for the jet set has been dramatic and Siem Reap is now firmly on the nightlife map of Southeast Asia. For the morning after, there are lots of cafes and coffee shops, several of which operate as social enterprises to help local causes.

The heaving 'Pub St' area near Psar Chaa makes Siem Reap feel more like a beach town than a cultural capital. Pub St is closed to traffic every evening as food carts, drink carts and scores of party people take over. If this is you're thing, just stroll around and see what's happening. The action spills into the street as the night wears on.

Great spots running parallel to Pub St include the Alley, to the south, where the volume control is just a little lower, plus a series of smaller lanes to the north. Late night, the crowd wanders on to Wat Preah Prohm Roth St and, eventually, to Sok San Rd, where there are a number of 'late-night' bars – although 'early morning' might be more apt as they stay open until daybreak.

Most bars have happy hours, as do some of the fancier hotels. The FCC Angkor (p116) and Grand Hotel d'Angkor (p110) hotels both have legendary bars with happy hours.

Hostels bars are a big thing, drawing backpackers to guzzle shooters and play drinking games until the wee hours. The 'beach bar' at Mad Monkey (p109) is one of the best,

SIEM REAP DRINKING & NIGHTLIFE

although it closes before midnight. The no-holds-barred party at Funky Flashpacker (p110) near Sok San Rd, on the other hand, can go all night long. Several hostels also organise their own pub crawls which take in the most popular spots around Pub St.

★**Asana Wooden House**   BAR
(Map p109; www.asana-cambodia.com; The Lane; ⊙11am-late; 🛜) This is a traditional Cambodian countryside home dropped into the backstreets of Siem Reap, which makes for an atmospheric place to drink. Lounge on *kapok*-filled rice sacks while sipping a classic cocktail made with infused rice wine. Khmer cocktail classes (US$15 per person) with Sombai spirits are available.

★**Laundry Bar**   BAR
(Map p109; www.facebook.com/laundry.bar.3; St 9; ⊙4pm-late; 🛜) One of the most chilled, chic bars in town thanks to low lighting and discerning decor. This is the place to come for electronica and ambient sounds; it heaves on weekends or when guest DJs crank up the volume. Happy hour until 9pm.

★**Miss Wong**   BAR
(Map p109; www.misswong.net; The Lane; ⊙6pm-1am; 🛜) Miss Wong carries you back to chic 1920s Shanghai. The cocktails are a draw here, making it a cool place to while away

---

THE CAMBODIAN BEER-GARDEN EXPERIENCE

There are dozens of beer gardens around Siem Reap that cater to young Cambodians working in the tourism industry. These can be great places for a cheap beer and local snacks, as well as getting to know some Cambodians beyond your driver or guide. All serve up ice-cold beer, some in 3L beer towers complete with chiller. These beer gardens can be a bit laddish by Cambodian standards, so solo female travellers might want to hook up with a traveller crowd before venturing forth.

The best strip is just north of Airport Rd from the first set of traffic lights after Sivatha St, known locally as 'Cambodian Pub St'. Wander around this area to see where the locals are hanging out, although be warned that many have hostesses awaiting to greet drinkers and diners, which can feel a little awkward.

---

an evening, and there's a menu offering dim sum. Gay-friendly and extremely popular with the well-heeled expat crowd.

Soul Train Reggae Bar   BAR
(Map p109; www.facebook.com/soultrainreggaebar; 35 New St; ⊙5pm-late) One of the most lively late-night spots in town, this bar is tucked away down the side street that passes Wat Preah Prohm Roth, so hopefully the reggae beats are subtle enough not to disturb the monks. Great tunes, cheap drinks and a party atmosphere that is more chilled than Pub St.

Picasso   BAR
(Map p109; Alley West; ⊙5pm-late; 🛜) This tiny tapas bar in the Alley West area is a convivial spot for a bit of over-the-counter banter. With only a dozen or so stools, expect spillover into the street – especially once the cheap sangria, worldly wines and cheap Tiger bottles start flowing.

The Harbour   BAR
(www.theharboursiemreap.com; Stung Thmei St; ⊙10am-1am; 🛜) Shiver me timbers, this self-styled 'pirate tavern' is a loveable bar housed in an atmospheric wooden house in Stung Thmei. Upstairs are cocktails, booze aplenty and regular open mic, comedy and other events, downstairs is the famous Lex Roulor Tattoo Studio. Just make sure you don't get so drunk you wake up with an unplanned inking.

Beatnik Bar   BAR
(Map p109; www.facebook.com/beatniksiemreap; The Alley; ⊙9.30-1.30am; 🛜) A hip little bar on the corner of the Alley, it is just far enough away from Pub St not to be drowned out by the nightly battle of the bars. Cheap drinks, friendly staff and a convivial crowd add up to a great pit stop.

Score!   SPORTS BAR
(Map p100; www.scorekh.com; 12 Sok San Rd; ⊙8am-midnight Sun-Thu, to 2am Fri & Sat) Having expanded from Phnom Penh to Temple Town, Score commands the entrance to Sok San Rd, beckoning sports fans with an inviting open plan and ginormous two-storey screen.

Angkor What?   BAR
(Map p109; www.facebook.com/theangkorwhatbar; Pub St; ⊙5pm-late; 🛜) Siem Reap's original bar claims to have been promoting irresponsible drinking since 1998. The happy hour (to 9pm) lightens the mood for later when everyone's bouncing along to dance an-

thems, sometimes on the tables, sometimes under them.

X Bar
BAR

(Map p109; www.facebook.com/Xbar.Asia; Sivatha St; ⊙4pm-sunrise; ☎) One of *the* late-night spots in town, X Bar draws revellers for the witching hour when other places are closing up. Early-evening movies on the big screen, pool tables and even a skateboard pipe – take a breath test first!

The Republic
BAR

(Map p100; www.facebook.com/therepublicsiem reap; Sala Kamreuk Rd; ⊙3pm-1am; ☎) A new bar from the team at Siem Reap Food Coop, this is a great place for creative cocktails, weekend DJs or bands, and regular film screenings. The wooden house is the centrepiece of a landscaped garden and there is a pool table downstairs for hustlers.

Barcode
GAY

(Map p100; www.barcodesiemreap.com; Wat Preah Prohm Roth St; ⊙6pm-late; ☎) A superstylin' gay bar that's metrosexual friendly. The cocktails here are worth the stop, as is the regular drag show at 9.30pm. Happy hour runs from 5pm to 7pm daily.

Hard Rock Cafe
BAR

(Map p100; ☎063-963964; www.hardrock.com/cafes/angkor; King's Rd; ⊙11am-midnight; ☎) While you might not head to the Hard Rock Cafe in London or New York, it is well worth making the diversion across the bridge from the Old Market to catch the live band here. They bang out anthems from the 1960s to the '90s, ranging from the Rolling Stones to the Red Hot Chilli Peppers.

The menu is pretty standard Hard Rock and there is the obligatory gift shop on-site for the Hard Rock Angkor T-shirt you've secretly been craving.

Temple Container Pub Zone
BEER GARDEN

(www.facebook.com/templecontainerpubzone; Sok San Rd; ⊙5pm-late; ☎) The first container beer garden to open its doors in Siem Reap, it looks rather like a giant set of balancing blocks, with containers creatively connected on top of each other. Cheap beers, raucous noise levels and attached Hip Hop Nightclub where local bright young things go to dance.

Sombai
DISTILLERY

(Map p100; ☎095 810890; www.sombai.com; Angkor Night Market B; ⊙4-11pm) Is it drinking or is it shopping? A bit of both actually, as this booth at the Angkor Night Market sells beautiful hand-painted bottles of infused spirits and also offers free tastings from 6pm to 10pm. Choose from eight flavours including ginger and chilli or anise coffee.

☆ Entertainment

Several restaurants and hotels offer cultural performances during the evening, and for many visitors such shows offer the only opportunity to see Cambodian classical dance or traditional shadow puppetry. While they may be aimed at tourists and are nowhere near as sophisticated as a performance of the Royal Ballet in Phnom Penh, to the untrained eye they are nonetheless graceful and alluring. Prices usually include a buffet meal.

★ Phare the Cambodian Circus
CIRCUS

(☎015 499480; www.pharecircus.org; west end of Sok San Rd; adult/child US$18/10, premium seats US$38/18; ⊙8pm daily) Cambodia's answer to Cirque du Soleil, Phare the Cambodian Circus is so much more than a conventional circus, with an emphasis on performance art and a subtle yet striking social message behind each production. Cambodia's leading circus, theatre and performing arts organisation, Phare Ponleu Selpak opened its big top for nightly shows in 2013 and the results are a unique form of entertainment that should be considered unmissable when staying in Siem Reap.

Garavek
THEATRE

(Map p109; ☎078 938132; www.garavek.com; 2 Thnou St; US$7; ⊙shows 6.30pm & 8pm; ☎) Garavek is a traditional storytelling theatre that offers the chance to learn about everything from the mythical origins of the Khmer kingdom to folk tales and fables. Stories are told in English to a backdrop of traditional music. Each show lasts 45 minutes.

Beatocello
CLASSICAL MUSIC

(Map p106; www.beatocello.com; Charles de Gaulle Blvd; ⊙7.15pm Sat) 🎵 Better known as Dr Beat Richner, Beatocello performs cello compositions at Jayavarman VII Children's Hospital. Entry is free, but donations are welcome as they assist the hospital in offering free medical treatment to the children of Cambodia.

Apsara Theatre
DANCE

(Map p100; ☎063-963561; www.angkorvillage resort.asia/apsara-theatre; St 26; show US$27; ⊙7.30pm) The setting for this Cambodian classical-dance show is a striking wooden pavilion finished in the style of a wat. The

SIEM REAP ENTERTAINMENT

price includes dinner. It tends to be packed to the rafters with tour groups.

Temple Club DANCE
(Map p109; www.facebook.com/templeclubpub street; Pub St; ⏱ from 7.30pm; ☎) Temple Club stages a free traditional-dance show upstairs nightly, providing punters order some food and drink from the very reasonably priced menu.

🛍 Shopping

Siem Reap is a hub for handicrafts with stone and wood carvings, lacquerware, silk and cotton weaving and a whole lot more. Be sure to bargain at the markets, as overcharging is pretty common. Kandal Village is an up-and-coming shopping destination with boutiques, galleries, cafes and restaurants.

Much of what you see on sale in the markets of Siem Reap can also be purchased from children and vendors throughout the temple area. Some visitors get fed up with the endless sales pitches as they navigate the ancient wonders, while others enjoy the banter and a chance to interact with Cambodian people. It's often children out selling, and some visitors will argue that they should be at school instead. However, most do attend school at least half of the time, joining for morning or afternoon classes, alternating with siblings.

Cheap books on Angkor and Cambodia are hawked by kids around the temples and Pub St. Be aware that many are illegal photocopies and the print quality is poor.

★ **Angkor Night Market** MARKET
(Map p100; https://angkornightmarket.com; ⏱ 4pm-midnight) Siem Reap's original night market near Sivatha St has sprung countless copycats, but it remains the best and is well worth a browse. It's packed with stalls selling a variety of handicrafts, souvenirs and silks. In 'Night Market A' (to the south), you can catch live music at Island Bar, while adjacent 'Night Market B' has the Brick House bar.

You can also indulge in a Dr Fish massage or watch a 3D event movie (US$3) about the Khmer Rouge or the scourge of landmines.

★ **Theam's House** ART
(www.theamshouse.com; 25 Veal, Kokchak District; ⏱ 8am-7pm) After years spent helping Artisans Angkor (p98) revitalise Khmer handicrafts, Cambodian artist and designer Theam now operates his own studio of lacquer creations and artwork. Highly original,

it can be tricky to find, so make sure you find a driver who knows where it is. A beautiful and creative space.

★ **Samatoa** FASHION & ACCESSORIES
(www.samatoa.com; 11 Rd 63; ⏱ 9am-5pm Mon-Sat) Samatoa experiments in organic fibres, blending silk and cotton with lotus to create 'the most spiritual fabric in the world'. Plants like lotus and banana have natural fibres that create a softness and texture not found in pure silk or cotton. Order tailor-made clothes to measure or visit the lotus farm to learn about the process.

★ **trunkh.** GIFTS & SOUVENIRS
(Map p100; www.trunkh.com; Hup Guan St; ⏱ 10am-6pm) The owner here has a great eye for the quirky, stylish and original, including beautiful shirts, throw pillows, jewellery, poster art, and T's, plus some offbeat items such as genuine Cambodian water-buffalo bells.

Eric Raisina Couture House FASHION & ACCESSORIES
(☑ 063-963207; www.ericraisina.com; 75-81 Charles de Gaulle Blvd; ⏱ store 8am-7pm, workshop 8-11am & 1-5pm) Renowned designer Eric Raisina brings a unique cocktail of influences to his couture. Born in Madagascar, raised in France and resident in Cambodia, he offers a striking collection of clothing and accessories. Ask him for a free tour of the workshop upstairs if he's around. There are additional branches around town, including at FCC Angkor.

Psar Chaa MARKET
(Old Market; Map p109; ⏱ 6am-9pm) When it comes to shopping in town, Psar Chaa is well stocked with anything you may want, and lots that you don't. Silverware, silk, wood carvings, stone carvings, Buddhas, paintings, rubbings, notes and coins, T-shirts, table mats...the list goes on. There are bargains to be had if you haggle patiently and humorously.

Bear in mind, however, that much of the souvenir items are imports from Thailand and China and not actually produced in Cambodia. Avoid buying old stone carvings that vendors claim are from Angkor. Whether or not they are real, buying these artefacts serves only to encourage their plunder and they will usually be confiscated by customs.

T Galleria FASHION & ACCESSORIES
(Map p100; ☑ 063-962511; www.dfs.com/en/siemreap; 968 Charles de Gaulle Blvd; ⏱ 9am-10pm; ☎)

GOOD-CAUSE SHOPPING

Several shops support Cambodia's disabled and disenfranchised through their production process or their profits. The shop at Peace Cafe (p117) sells a range of products produced by other do-good brands.

AHA Fair Trade Village (☑078 341454; www.aha-kh.com; Rd 60, Trang Village; ⊗10am-7pm) For locally produced souvenirs (unlike much of the imported stuff that turns up in Psar Chaa) drop in on this handicraft market. It's a little out of the way, but there are more than 20 stalls selling a wide range of traditional items. There's a Khmer cultural show every second and fourth Saturday of the month, with extra stalls, traditional music and dancing.

Two-hour pottery classes are offered here through **Mordock Ceramics**, one of the stalls.

Artisans Angkor (Map p100; www.artisansdangkor.com; ⊗7.30am-6.30pm) On the premises of **Les Chantiers Écoles** (p98) is this beautiful shop, which sells everything from stone and wood reproductions of Angkorian-era statues to household furnishings. There's also a second shop opposite Angkor Wat in the Angkor Cafe building, and outlets at Phnom Penh and Siem Reap international airports.

All profits from sales go back into funding the school and bringing more young Cambodians into the training program, which is 20% owned by the artisans themselves.

IKTT (Institute for Khmer Traditional Textiles; Map p100; www.ikttearth.org; Tonlé Sap Rd; ⊗9am-5pm) This traditional wooden house is home to the Japanese-run Institute for Khmer Traditional Textiles, which sells fine *krama* (checked scarves), throws and more. They also operate a homestay out at their silk farm in Angkor Thom District.

Made in Cambodia (Map p100; www.facebook.com/madeincambodiamarket; Siem Reap River Rd East; ⊗noon-10pm) King's Road hosts the daily Made in Cambodia community market, bringing together many of the best local craftsfolk and creators in Siem Reap, many promoting good causes.

Rajana (Map p109; ☑063-964744; www.rajanacrafts.org; Sivatha St; ⊗8am-11pm Mon-Sat) Sells quirky wooden and metalwork objects, well-designed silver and brass-bullet jewellery, and handmade cards. Rajana promotes fair-trade employment opportunities for Cambodians.

Saomao (Map p109; ☑818130; www.facebook.com/saomaoenterprise; St 9; ⊗8.30am-10pm Mon-Sat) A social enterprise selling wonderful silver and other jewellery, some made from bomb casings and brass bullets. Also a wide variety of additional gifts, including coconut art, original *krama* and silks, pepper, and elegant runners and wall hangings.

Senteurs d'Angkor (Map p109; ☑063-964801; 2 Thnou St; ⊗7.30am-10.30pm) Opposite Psar Chaa, this shop has an eclectic collection of silk and carvings, as well as a superb range of traditional beauty products and spices, all made locally. The Kaya Spa is on-site. It targets rural poor and disadvantaged Cambodians for jobs and training, and sources local products from farmers.

Visit its **Botanic Garden** (p99) on Airport Rd, a sort of Willy Wonka's for the senses, where you can sample infused teas and speciality coffees.

Smateria (Map p109; www.smateria.com; Alley West; ⊗10am-10pm) Recycling rocks here with funky bags made from construction nets, plastic bags, motorbike seat covers and more. It's a fair-trade enterprise employing some disabled Cambodians.

Soieries du Mekong (Map p100; www.soieriesdumekong.com; 688 Hup Guan St; ⊗10am-7pm) Soieries du Mekong is the new Siem Reap gallery for the handwoven silk project based in remote Banteay Chhmar, which seeks to stem the tide of rural migration by creating employment opportunities in the village. Beautiful silk scarves and other delicate items are for sale.

Sra May (Map p100; 640 Hup Guan St; ⊗10am-6pm Mon-Sat) Sra May is a social enterprise that uses traditional local materials like palm leaves to create boxes and artworks. They also specialise in handwoven *krama*. This is also the drop-in office to book the PURE! Countryside Bicycle Tour (p107).

Located next to the Angkor National Museum, this is a flagship DFS duty-free shop that stocks everything from Paul Smith to Prada. It is extremely popular with Chinese visitors who flock here for discounted luxury items, but prices aren't really low compared with discount outlets back home.

Bambou Indochine   CLOTHING
(Map p109; www.bambouindochine.com; Alley West; ☺9am-10pm) Original clothing designs inspired by Indochina. A cut above the average souvenir T-shirts.

McDermott Gallery   ART
(Map p100; http://asiaphotos.net; FCC Angkor, Pokambor Ave; ☺10am-10pm) These are the famous sepia images you have seen of Angkor. Calendars, cards and striking images of the temples, plus regular exhibitions.

Monument Books   BOOKS
(Map p100; Pokambor Ave; ☺9am-9pm) Well-stocked bookstore near Psar Chaa, with an additional branch at the airport.

ℹ Orientation

Siem Reap is still a small town at heart and is easy enough to navigate. The centre is around Psar Chaa (Old Market) and nearby Pub St, but accommodation is spread throughout town. National Hwy 6 (NH6) cuts across the northern part of town, passing Psar Leu (Main Market) in the east of town and the Royal Residence and the Grand Hotel d'Angkor in the centre, and then heads to the airport and beyond to the Thai border. The Siem Reap River (Stung Siem Reap) flows north–south through the centre of town, and has enough bridges that you won't have to worry too much about being on the wrong side. Street numbering is haphazard to say the least, so take care when hunting down specific addresses.

Angkor Wat and Angkor Thom are only 6km and 8km north of town respectively.

ℹ Information

DANGERS & ANNOYANCES
Siem Reap is a pretty safe city, even at night, although it pays to stay in small groups if you are planning a drunken night out.
➟ If you rent a bike, don't keep your bag in the basket as it will be easy pickings for a drive-by snatch.
➟ Child vendors hawk souvenirs around the temples; have patience and give a thought to their circumstances.
➟ Out at the remote temple sites beyond Angkor, stick to clearly marked trails. There are still landmines at locations such as Phnom Kulen and Koh Ker.

There are a lot of commission scams in Siem Reap that involve certain guesthouses and small hotels paying *moto* and taxi drivers to deliver guests. Ways to avoid these scams include booking ahead via the internet and arranging a pick-up, or sticking with a partner guesthouse if you are coming from Phnom Penh. Alternatively, just go with the flow and negotiate with the hotel or guesthouse on arrival.

Watch out for the baby-milk-powder scam. A woman and baby approach asking for help to buy milk for the baby. Visitor agrees and gets asked to buy the most expensive brand in the nearby minimart. Transaction over, woman and baby then take the formula back to the shop and split the profit.

There are a lot of beggars around town and some visitors quickly develop beggar fatigue. However, try to remember that with no social-security network and no government support, life is pretty tough for the poorest of the poor in Cambodia. In the case of children, it is often better not to encourage begging, but if you are compelled to help, then offer food, as money usually ends up being passed on to someone else. These days the problem is less serious, as many former beggars have been retrained to sell books or postcards to tourists instead of simply begging.

EMERGENCY
Tourist Police (☎012 402424; Rd 60) Located at the main ticket checkpoint for the Angkor area, this is the place to lodge a complaint if you encounter any serious problems while in Siem Reap.

For medical emergencies, evacuation to Bangkok may be necessary.

Fire	☎012 784464
Hospital	☎063-761888
Tourist police	☎012 402424

INTERNET
Internet cafes are fast disappearing as most restaurants and bars offer reliable free wi-fi, though a few remain and prices are around US$0.50 per hour. Cheap internet-based telephone calls are also offered. Almost all guesthouses and hotels offer free internet access for guests, either via a terminal, wi-fi or both.

MEDICAL SERVICES
Siem Reap now has an international-standard hospital for emergencies. However, any serious complications will still require relocation to Bangkok.

Angkor Hospital for Children (AHC; Map p100; ☎063-963409; www.angkorhospital.

org; cnr Oum Chhay & Tep Vong Sts; ⊙24hr) This international-standard paediatric hospital is the place to take your children if they fall sick. They will also assist adults in an emergency for up to 24 hours. Donations accepted.

Royal Angkor International Hospital (☑063-761888; www.royalangkorhospital.com; Airport Rd) This international facility affiliated with the Bangkok Hospital is on the expensive side as it's used to dealing with insurance companies.

U-Care Pharmacy (Map p109; ☑063-965396; Pithnou St; ⊙8am-10pm) Smart pharmacy and shop similar to Boots in Thailand (and the UK). English spoken.

MONEY

For cash exchanges, markets (usually at jewellery stalls or dedicated money-changing stalls) are faster and less bureaucratic than the banks.

ABA Bank (Map p100; Tep Vong St; ⊙8.30am-3.30pm Mon-Fri, to 11.30am Sat) Withdrawals are limited to US$100 per transaction and there is a US$4 transaction fee per withdrawal.

ANZ Royal Bank (Map p100; Achar Mean St; ⊙8.30am-3.30pm Mon-Fri, to 11.30am Sat) Does credit-card advances. Several branches and many ATMs (US$5 per withdrawal) around town.

Canadia Bank (Map p100; Sivatha St; ⊙8.30am-3.30pm Mon-Fri, to 11.30am Sat) Offers credit-card cash advances (US$4) and changes travellers cheques in most major currencies at a 2% commission.

POST

Main Post Office (Map p100; Pokambor Ave; ⊙7am-5.30pm) Services are more reliable these days, but it doesn't hurt to see your stamps franked. Includes a branch of EMS express mail.

TOURIST INFORMATION

Check out *Siem Reap Pocket Guide* (www.cambodiapocketguide.com) for the low-down on restaurants, bars, shops and services, widely available in town. The *Siem Reap Angkor Visitors Guide* (www.canbypublications.com) is packed with listings and comes out quarterly.

ConCERT (www.concertcambodia.org) Works to build bridges between tourists and good-cause projects in the Siem Reap/Angkor area, with information offices at Sister Srey Cafe and New Leaf Book Cafe. It offers information on anything from ecotourism initiatives to volunteering opportunities.

Siem Reap Tourism Office (Map p100; ☑063-959600; Royal Gardens) A large new office is under construction in the Royal Gardens; it may become a useful stop in the future.

❶ Getting There & Away

AIR

All international flights arrive at the **Siem Reap International Airport** (☑063-962400; www.cambodia-airports.com), 7km west of the town centre. Facilities at the airport include cafes, restaurants, bookshops, international ATMs and money-changing services.

There are no direct flights between Cambodia and the West, so all visitors will end up transiting through an Asian hub such as Bangkok in Thailand; Vientiane, Luang Prabang and Pakse in Laos; Ho Chi Minh City (Saigon), Hanoi and Danang in Vietnam; Hong Kong; Kuala Lumpur in Malaysia; Beijing, Guangzhou, Kunming and Shanghai in China; Busan and Seoul in South Korea; Singapore; Taipei in Taiwan; and Manila in the Philippines.

Domestic links are currently limited to Phnom Penh and Sihanoukville. Airlines operating domestic flights include Bassaka Air (www.bassakaair.com), Cambodia Angkor Air (www.cambodiaangkorair.com), Cambodia Bayon Airlines (www.bayonairlines.com) and JC International Airlines (www.jcairlines.com). Demand for seats is high during peak season, so book as far in advance as possible.

BOAT

There are daily express boat services between Siem Reap and Phnom Penh (US$35, five to six hours) or Battambang (US$20, four to eight hours or more, depending on the season). The boat to Phnom Penh is rather overpriced these

TRANSPORT CONNECTIONS FROM SIEM REAP

DESTINATION	CAR & MOTORCYCLE	BUS	BOAT	AIR
Bangkok, Thailand	8hr	US$15-28, 10hr, frequent	N/A	US$50-150, 1hr, 8 daily
Battambang	3hr	US$5-8, 4hr, frequent	US$20, 6-8hr, 7am	N/A
Kompong Thom	2hr	US$5, 2hr, frequent	N/A	N/A
Phnom Penh	4-5hr	US$6-15, 5-6hr, frequent	US$35, 5hr, 7am	US$20-100, 30min, frequent
Poipet	3hr	US$5-8, 3hr, frequent	N/A	N/A

INTERNATIONAL BUSES TO BANGKOK

There are a few direct services to Bangkok that do not involve a change of bus at the border, but most require a change. There are some 'night' buses to Bangkok advertised, but these are pretty pointless given the Poipet border does not open until 7am!

Nattakan (p124) is the original and still one of the most reliable operators servicing Bangkok. It has direct buses to Bangkok (US$28, 7½ hours, 8am and 9am), which include fast-track immigration at the border – potentially a big advantage during peak periods to bypass long lines.

Any advertised services to Ho Chi Minh City or Pakse or the Four Thousand Islands in southern Laos invariably involve a time-consuming transfer or two. For Pakse, you're best off taking a minivan to Stung Treng and changing there – **Asia Van Transfer** (p124) can sort you out with this. Note that any advertised *bus* trip to Laos will invariably take a six-hour detour through Kompong Cham, with a possible overnight in Kratie. You've been warned.

days, given it is just as fast by road and so much cheaper. The Battambang trip is seriously scenic, but breakdowns are *very* common.

Boats from Siem Reap leave from the floating village of Chong Kneas near Phnom Krom, about 11km south of Siem Reap. The boats dock in different places at different times of the year; when the lake recedes in the dry season, both the port and floating village move with it. An all-weather road has improved access around the lake area, but the main road out to the lake takes a pummelling in the annual monsoon.

Most of the guesthouses in town sell boat tickets. Buying the ticket from a guesthouse usually includes a *moto* or minibus ride to the port. Otherwise, a *moto* out there costs about US$3, a *remork* about US$7 and a taxi about US$15.

BUS

All buses depart from the **bus station and taxi park**, which is 3km east of town and nearly 1km south of NH6. Tickets are available at guesthouses, hotels, bus offices, travel agencies and ticket kiosks. Some bus companies send a minibus around to pick up passengers at their place of lodging. Upon arrival in Siem Reap, be prepared for a rugby scrum of eager *moto* drivers when getting off the bus.

Bus companies in Siem Reap:

Asia Van Transfer (AVT; Map p100; ☏ 063-963853; www.asiavantransfer.com; Hup Guan St) A daily express minivan departs at 8am to Stung Treng (US$20, five hours) via Preah Vihear City, with onward services from Stung Treng to Don Det (Laos), Ban Lung and Kratie.

Capitol Tour (Map p109; ☏ 012 830170; www.capitoltourscambodia.com) Buses to destinations across Cambodia.

Giant Ibis (Map p100; ☏ 095 777809; www.giantibis.com) Has free wi-fi on board.

Golden Bayon Express (Map p100; ☏ 063-966968; https://bayonvip.com; Wat Bo Rd) Express minivan services to Phnom Penh.

Liang US Express (Map p100; ☏ 092 881183; Sivatha St) Has some direct buses to Kompong Cham.

Mekong Express (Map p100; ☏ 063-963662; https://catmekongexpress.com; 14 Sivatha St) Upmarket bus company with hostesses and drinks.

Nattakan (☏ 078 795333; www.nattakan-transport.com; Concrete Drain Rd) The first operator, and still one of the most reliable, to do direct trips to Bangkok (US$28, 7½ hours, 8am and 9am). It's out of the way so request a free pick-up.

Neak Krorhorm (Map p100; ☏ 063-964924; Siem Reap River Rd East) Direct buses to Bangkok (US$28, nine hours, 8am and 9am) with no change at the border.

Phnom Penh Sorya (Map p100; ☏ 096 766 6577; https://ppsoryatransport.com.kh; Sivatha St) Most extensive bus network in Cambodia.

Virak Buntham (Map p100; ☏ 017 790440; www.virakbuntham.com) The night-bus specialist to Phnom Penh and Sihanoukville.

Night buses are an option between Siem Reap and Phnom Penh, but leave as late as possible to avoid a middle-of-the-night arrival. Giant Ibis is the smartest operator servicing Phnom Penh (US$15, five hours), with four daytime and two overnight express services and free wi-fi on board.

Express minibus services to Phnom Penh (from US$10, four hours), such as those offered by **Mey Hong** (☏ 095 777933; www.meyhong.com; NH6), are popular as they can save considerable time compared with much slower buses. These services do have a reputation for speeding, however, and we strongly advise against using them at night. **Larryta Express**

BUS CONNECTIONS FROM SIEM REAP

DESTINATION	DURATION (HR)	PRICE	COMPANIES	FREQUENCY
Bangkok (direct)	9	US$15-28	Mekong Express, Nattakan, Neak Krohorm, Virak Buntham	morning only
Bangkok (with bus transfer)	10	US$10	Capitol Tour	8am
Battambang	3-4	US$4-6	Capitol Tour, Mekong Express, PP Sorya	frequent in the morning
Kompong Cham	5-6	US$6.50	Liang US Express	6.45am & 7.30am
Phnom Penh (bus)	6-7	US$6-15	Capitol Tour, Giant Ibis, Liang US Express, Mekong Express, PP Sorya, Virak Buntham (sleeper only)	frequent
Phnom Penh (minivan)	4-5	US$10-12	Capitol Tour, Golden Bayon Express, Larryta Express, Virak Buntham	frequent
Poipet	3	US$5-8	Capitol Tour	frequent in the morning
Preah Vihear City (via Kompong Thom)	5½	US$10	Liang US Express	2 daily
Sihanoukville	10-11	US$13-17	Capitol Tour, Virak Buntham	mostly night buses
Stung Treng	5	US$20	Asia Van Transfer	8am

(☑ 066 202020; http://larryta.com) runs smart Ford Transit minivans hourly to Phnom Penh throughout the day.

Many companies advertise trips to Sihanoukville. These almost all involve a change of bus in Phnom Penh. This can work out well if you're taking a night bus, as the stop in Phnom Penh can help towards a more reasonable hour of arrival, but if you're travelling to Sihanoukville by day be prepared for a long journey. The Virak Buntham sleeper buses to Sihanoukville do not usually involve a bus change, for what it's worth. Advertised services to Kep and Kampot are even less reliable, and may involve a huge detour and a second change of bus in Sihanoukville. Ask about the routing and timing when making a booking.

For Ratanakiri, take the Asia Van Transfer minivan across Preah Vihear Province to Stung Treng and change there. For Mondulkiri, change in Kompong Cham; Liang US Express advertises this trip, with the transfer, or Virak Buntham has a service via Phnom Penh. Be aware that you are not guaranteed a comfortable or efficient onward trip after your transfer: we've heard plenty of horror stories.

SHARE TAXI

The new road linking Siem Reap to Phnom Penh is in excellent shape and private cars can now do the journey in four hours, much of that on a divided four-lane highway. The roads west to Sisophon and north to Anlong Veng are also in great condition.

Share taxis and other vehicles operate along some of the main routes and these can be a little quicker than buses. Destinations include Phnom Penh (US$10, five hours), Kompong Thom (US$5, two hours), Sisophon (US$5, two hours) and Poipet (US$7, three hours). To get to the temple of Banteay Chhmar, head to Sisophon and arrange onward transport there (leave very early).

☉ Getting Around

GETTING TO/FROM THE AIRPORT

Siem Reap International Airport is 7km west of the city centre. Many hotels and guesthouses in Siem Reap offer a free airport pick-up service with advance bookings. Official taxis are available next to the terminal for US$9. A trip to the city centre on the back of a *moto* is US$3 or US$7 by *remork*.

BICYCLE

Some guesthouses around town hire out bicycles, as do a few shops around Psar Chaa, usually for US$1 to US$2 a day.

The **White Bicycles** (www.thewhitebicycles.org; per day US$2) project rents bikes through over 50 guesthouses and hotels in Siem Reap, with all proceeds going towards supporting local development projects around town. Imported mountain bikes are available from cycling tour operators for around US$8 to US$10 per day.

Another option are the wonderful **Green e-bikes** (Map p100; 095 700130; www.greene-bike.com; Central Market; per 24hr US$10; 7.30am-7pm), an environmentally sound compromise between bicycle and motorbike, with three charge points out at the temples and several more in the city. Several additional shops in the centre hire out electric bikes.

CAR & MOTORCYCLE

Most hotels and guesthouses can organise car hire for the day, with a going rate of US$30 and up. Upmarket hotels may charge more. Foreigners are technically forbidden to rent motorcycles in and around Siem Reap, but the rules have relaxed and motorbike hire is now widely available. You can now even rent self-drive *remorks* through **Angkor e-Tuk Hostel** (088 824 1919; Siem Reap River Rd East), which has a fleet of powerful, oversized electric *remorks* (per day US$24). You can easily drive these to outlying temples and back on a single charge.

MOTO

A *moto* (unmarked motorcycle taxi) with a driver will cost from US$10 per day depending on the destination. Far-flung temples will involve a higher fee. The average cost for a short trip within town is 2000r or so, and around US$1 or more to places strung out along the roads to Angkor or the airport. It is probably best to negotiate in advance as a lot of drivers have got into the habit of overcharging.

REMORK-MOTO

Remork-motos are sweet little motorcycles with carriages (commonly called *tuk tuks* around town), and are a nice way for couples to get about Siem Reap, although drivers like to inflate the prices. Trips around town start from US$2, but you'll need to pay more to the edge of town at night. Prices rise when you add three or more people.

AROUND SIEM REAP

Let's be honest, most people are in Siem Reap to explore the majestic temples of Angkor, rightly regarded as the most spectacular collection of temples on earth. But there is more to this province that the awe-inspiring remnants of the Khmer Empire. Beyond Temple Town are a handful of impressive attractions, including the otherworldly floating and stilted villages of the Tonlé Sap and some high-profile bird sanctuaries that are home to rare large water birds. The province is also emerging as an accessible place to

experience a local homestay and a slice of local life in a traditional village. Throw in a hatful of remote jungle temples and sacred mountains and it's best to extend your stay by a few days.

Banteay Srei District

Famous for its petite pink-coloured temple, there is more to Banteay Srei than its iconic Angkor sites, such as the 'River of a Thousand Lingas' at Kbal Spean and the 12th-century temple of Banteay Samré. New destinations and experiences, including homestays, village walks, ox-cart rides, fruit farms and handicraft workshops, are under development to encourage visitors to stay longer and explore further. It's a good area to explore on two wheels, either by motorbike from Siem Reap or by a bicycle rented via a local homestay.

⊙ Sights

While the temples of the Banteay Srei district are the main attraction, make sure you also check out the Angkor Centre for Conservation of Biodiversity when visiting the River of a Thousand Lingas at Kbal Spean (p170). Other activities include walks in the **Kbal Teuk Community Forest**, home to rare carnivorous pitcher plants.

★**Cambodia Landmine Museum**   MUSEUM
(សារមន្ទីរគ្រាប់មីនកម្ពុជា និងមូលនិធិសង្គ្រោះ; www.cambodialandminemuseum.org;   US$5; 7.30am-5pm) Established by DIY de-miner Aki Ra, this museum has eye-opening displays on the curse of landmines in Cambodia. The collection includes mines, mortars, guns and weaponry, and there is a mock minefield where visitors can attempt to locate the deactivated mines. Proceeds from the museum are ploughed into mine-awareness campaigns. The museum is about 25km from Siem Reap, near Banteay Srei.

Angkor Centre for Conservation of Biodiversity   WILDLIFE RESERVE
(ACCB, មជ្ឈមណ្ឌលអង្គរសម្រាប់ការអភិរក្សជីវចម្រុះ; 099 604017; www.accb-cambodia.org; donation US$3; tours 9am & 1pm Mon-Sat;) Conveniently located at the base of the trail to Kbal Spean is the Angkor Centre for Conservation of Biodiversity, which is committed to rescuing, rehabilitating and releasing threatened wildlife into the Cambodian forests. It also operates conservation breeding programs for selected threatened species

in an attempt to preserve them from extinction. Daily tours (in English) are available at 9am and 1pm (except Sunday), taking about 1½ hours.

Banteay Srei
Butterfly Centre   WILDLIFE RESERVE
(សួនមេអំបៅបន្ទាយស្រី; www.angkorbutterfly.com; adult/child US$5/2; ☺9am-5pm) 🏃 The Banteay Srei Butterfly Centre is one of the largest fully enclosed butterfly centres in Southeast Asia, with more than 30 species of Cambodian butterflies fluttering about. It is a good experience for children, as they can see the whole life cycle from egg to caterpillar to cocoon to butterfly.

The centre aims to provide a sustainable living for the rural poor and most of the butterflies are farmed around Phnom Kulen. It's about 7km before Banteay Srei temple on the left side of the road.

🛌 Sleeping

Tbeng Village Homestays   HOMESTAY $
(📞092 966047; Tbeng Village; house US$15) Tbeng is a pretty little village in the east of Banteay Srei where local schoolteacher Mr Khuon has set up a homestay project with around a dozen houses. Try and opt for a house with a tiled roof if you have the option, as it's cooler than corrugated metal. Mattresses and bedding are provided together with a mosquito net.

Village activities are on offer and local interaction is possible.

Bayon Smile Homestay   HOMESTAY $
(📞086 595402; sarouensean@gmail.com; Banteay Srei Village; s/d US$10/15) Run by the enthusiastic Mr Sarouen, this group of six spacious and attractive village homes is set just north of Banteay Srei temple. Guests sleep on mattresses under mosquito nets upstairs. Lots of activities are promoted here, including wood-carving, village tours, cycling and some more adventurous treks to remote sites such as Phnom Cheur and Phnom Hop.

Bong Thom Home Stay   HOMESTAY $$
(📞012 520092; www.thebongthomhomestay.com; r US$60-80; ☎) Very much a boutique homestay, Bong Thom offers some beautiful wooden houses in the countryside complete with four-poster beds and tasteful decor. Lots of activities are available including cooking classes, cycling and ox-cart rides. The restaurant here is well regarded and open to nonguests with an advance booking.

🍴 Eating

⭐**Naom Banchok Noodle Stalls** NOODLES $
(Preah Dak; noodles 4000r; ☺6am-6pm) Preah Dak village is renowned for its *naom banchok* (thick rice noodles) stalls, which hug the main road to Banteay Srei. These homemade noodles come with a mild fish broth or chicken curry, plus an assortment of vegetables and condiments.

Borey Sovann Restaurant   CAMBODIAN $
(meals US$3-6; ☺11am-6pm; ☎) The excellent Borey Sovann Restaurant, located near the entrance to Kbal Spean, is a great place to wind down before or after an ascent to the River of a Thousand Lingas. The menu includes a full range of Cambodian dishes, plus a smattering of Chinese, Thai and international options.

ℹ️ Information

For more on community-based tourism in Banteay Srei District, head to www.visitbanteaysrei.org.

ℹ️ Getting There & Away

Banteay Srei is about 32km northeast of Siem Reap on good roads. It should take about 45 minutes to reach by car or one hour by *remork*; agree to a price before setting off. As a rough guide, it will cost US$10/20/40 by *moto/remork*/car, but it really depends on the exact destinations on your itinerary.

Prek Toal Bird Sanctuary

Prek Toal is one of three biospheres on the Tonlé Sap lake, and this stunning **bird sanctuary** (ជម្រកសត្វស្លាបទឹកព្រែកទាល់; admission US$20; ☺6am-6pm) 🏃 makes it the most worthwhile and straightforward of the three to visit. It's an ornithologist's fantasy, with a significant number of rare breeds gathered in one small area, including the huge lesser and greater adjutant storks, the milky stork and the spot-billed pelican. Even the uninitiated will be impressed, as these birds have a huge wingspan and build enormous nests.

During the peak season (December to early February) visitors will find the concentration of birds like something out of a Hitchcock film. As water starts to dry up elsewhere, the birds congregate here. The birds remain beyond February but the sanctuary becomes virtually inaccessible due to low water levels. It is also possible to visit from September, but the bird numbers may

Around Siem Reap

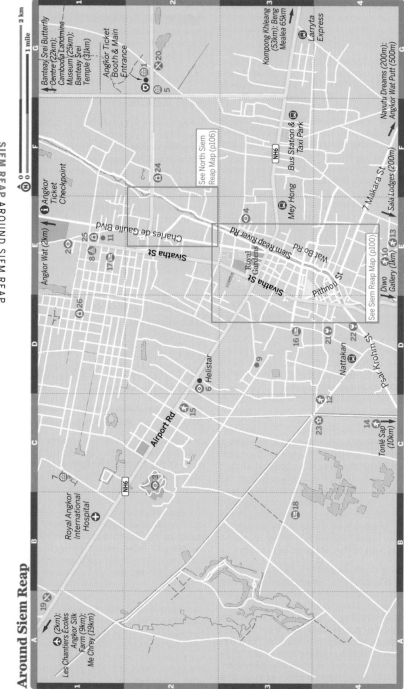

2 km
1 mile
0
0

Banteay Srei Butterfly
Centre (22km);
Cambodia Landmine
Museum (25km);
Banteay Srei
Temple (31km)

Angkor Ticket
Booth & Main
Entrance

Kompong Khleang
(53km); Beng
Mealea 65km

Larryta
Express

Navutu Dreams (200m);
Angkor Wat Putt (500m)

Bus Station &
Taxi Park

Mey Hong

NH6

7 Makara St

Sala Lodges (200m)

Angkor Ticket
Checkpoint

See North Siem
Reap Map (p106)

Charles de Gaulle Blvd

Sivatha St

Angkor Wat (2km)

Siem Reap River Rd

Wat Bo Rd

Royal
Gardens

Sivatha St

See Siem Reap Map (p100)

Diwo
Gallery (1km)

Pithnou St

Nattakan

Psar Krohm St

Airport Rd

NH6

Helistar

Royal Angkor
International
Hospital

(2km);
Les Chantiers Écoles
Angkor Silk
Farm (9km);
Me Chrey (19km)

Tonlé Sap
(10km)

Around Siem Reap

be lower. Serious twitchers know that the best time to see birds is early morning or late afternoon and this means an early start or an overnight at Prek Toal's environment office, where there is very basic accommodation (single/double bed US$15/20).

Several ecotourism companies in Siem Reap arrange trips out to Prek Toal including the Sam Veasna Center (p107), Osmose (p107) and Prek Toal Tours & Travel (p107), which is run by Prek Toal villagers. Tours include transport, entrance fees, guides, breakfast, lunch and water. Binoculars are available on request, plus the Sam Veasna Center has spotting scopes that they set up

at observation towers within the park. All three outfits can arrange overnight trips for serious enthusiasts. Day trips include a hotel pick-up at around 6am and a return by nightfall.

Getting to the sanctuary under your own steam requires you to take a 20-minute *moto* (US$3 or so) or taxi (US$15 one way) ride to the floating village of Chong Kneas (depending on the time of day, additional fees may have to be paid at the new port), and then a boat to the environment office (around US$55 return, one hour each way). From here, a small boat (US$30 including a park guide) will take you into the sanctuary, which is about one hour beyond. The park guides are equipped with booklets with the bird names in English, but they speak little English themselves, hence the advantage of visiting with a tour company that provides English-speaking guides.

Trips to the sanctuary also bring you up close and personal with the fascinating **floating village** of Prek Toal, a much more rewarding destination than over-touristed, scam-ridden Chong Kneas closer to Siem Reap. Part of your entrance to the sanctuary goes towards educating children and villagers about the importance of the birds and the unique flooded-forest environment.

Always bring sunscreen and head protection to Prek Toal, as it's a long day in boats and the sun can be relentless.

Floating Village of Chong Kneas

The famous floating village of **Chong Kneas** (ចុងឃ្នៀស) has become somewhat of a circus in recent years. Tour groups have taken over and there are countless scams to separate tourists from their money. In-the-know travellers opt for harder-to-reach but more memorable spots such as Kompong Khleang or Prek Toal.

For all its flaws, Chong Kneas is very scenic in the warm light of late afternoon and can be combined with a sunset from the nearby hilltop temple of Phnom Krom.

Avoid the crowds by asking your boat driver to take you down some back channels. Boat prices are fixed at US$20 per person, plus a US$3 entrance fee (although in practice it may be possible to pay just US$20 for the boat shared between several people). Your boat driver will invariably try and take you to an overpriced floating restaurant and

SIEM REAP FLOATING VILLAGE OF CHONG KNEAS

KHNAR PO HOMESTAYS

There are 12 **homestays** (☎ 061 947105; khnarpocommunity@gmail.com; Khnar Po Village; per person US$5) 🌿 in Khnar Po village and they have received support from a local tour operator to help improve standards. The community includes a best-practice 'model' homestay and the host families are known for the quality of their home-cooking (breakfast/meals US$3/6). Guests sleep on mattresses under a mosquito net. Activities include village walks and oxcart rides.

souvenir shop, but there is no obligation to buy anything.

One of the best ways to visit the floating village of Chong Kneas is to hook up with the **Tara Boat** (☎ 092 957765; www.taraboat. com; per person incl lunch/dinner US$29/36), which offers all-inclusive trips with a meal aboard its converted cargo boat. Prices include transfers, entry fees, local boats, a tour guide and a two-course meal.

Visitors to Chong Kneas should stop at the **Gecko Centre** (www.greengeckoproject.org; ⊙ 8.30am-5.30pm), an informative exhibition that is located en route to the floating village and helps to unlock the secrets of the Tonlé Sap. It has displays on flora and fauna of the area, as well as information on communities living around the lake.

To get to Chong Kneas from Siem Reap costs US$3 by *moto* each way (more if the driver waits), or US$15 or so by taxi. The trip takes 20 minutes. Alternatively rent a bicycle in town and just pedal out here, as it is a leisurely 11km through pretty villages and rice fields.

Visitors arriving by boat from Phnom Penh or Battambang get a sneak preview, as the floating village is near Phnom Krom, where the boat docks.

Kompong Pluk

The village of **Kompong Pluk** (ព្រលិចទឹកកំពង់ភ្លុក; boat trip per person US$20, community fee US$1) is a friendly, otherworldly place where houses are built on soaring stilts about 6m high. Nearby is a flooded forest, inundated every year when the lake rises to take the Mekong's overflow. As the lake drops, the petrified trees are revealed. Exploring this area by wooden dug-

out in the wet season is very atmospheric. Best visited from July to December, it is not worth the effort in the dry-season months of January to June.

Prices to visit have been fixed rather high, and when you add up all the separate costs, it may work out cheaper to sign up to a budget tour out of Siem Reap. If you are unlucky enough to come alone, you may be charged US$30, but have the option to link up with other independent travellers. There are a couple of basic homestays in Kompong Pluk and lots of good floating restaurants for lunch or a snack. There is also the incredible **Kompong Pluk Riverside Restaurant**, built on stilts over the flooded forest with an extensive wooden walkway passing through the treetops.

The most popular way to get here is via the small town of Roluos by a combination of road (about US$10/15/30 by *moto/ remork*/taxi) and then the boat. All said, the road-and-boat route will take up to two hours, but it depends on the season – sometimes it's more by road, sometimes more by boat. The new road brings the dry season access time to around one hour. Tara Boat (p130) also offers day trips here for US$60 per person. The other option is to come via the floating village of Chong Kneas, where a boat (1¼ hours, from US$55 return) can be arranged.

Me Chrey

One of the more recently 'discovered' floating villages, **Me Chrey** (មេជ្រៃ; boat trip per person from US$18, entrance fee US$1) lies midway between Siem Reap and Prek Toal. It is one of the smaller villages in the area but sees far fewer tourists than busy Chong Kneas. Arrange transport by road (*moto/ remork*/taxi around US$10/20/30) before switching to a boat to explore the area.

Me Chrey moves with the water level and is prettier during the wet season, when houses are anchored around an island pagoda. It is located to the south of Puok district, about 25km from Siem Reap on a pretty dirt road through lush rice fields if you are travelling between July and November.

Unique Kayak Cambodia   KAYAKING
(Map p100; ☎ 097 456 2000; http://unique kayakcambodia.com; half-day US$70-115, full day US$100-150) Unique Kayak Cambodia offers kayaking trips to explore the flooded forest

near Me Chrey and paddle around the village. The flooded forest is really beautiful and it's possible to spot some water birds. A half day is probably enough unless you are an Olympic rower. Tours include all car and boat transfers, so they work out reasonable if you have a group, and stop at the Artisans Angkor Silk Farm in Pouk District.

Kompong Khleang

One of the largest communities on the Tonlé Sap, Kompong Khleang (កំពង់ឃ្លាំង) is more of a town than the other villages, and comes complete with several ornate pagodas. Most of the houses here are built on towering stilts to allow for a dramatic change in water level. There is only a small floating community on the lake, but the stilted town is an interesting place to browse for an hour or two. Fewer tourists visit here compared with the floating villages closer to Siem Reap, so that might be a reason to visit in itself.

A boat trip around town and to the lake is US$26 for one person for a couple of hours, but drops to US$17.50 per person for a couple and less again for groups. The entrance fee is US$2.

There are a handful of homestays in Kompong Khleang for those who want to stay the night. All are set in imposing stilted houses and there's even a 'boutique' homestay available.

There are no real restaurants in Kompong Khleang, but several food stalls can cook up fresh fish and other dishes. Most homestays also provide meals for guests.

Kompong Khleang is about 50km from Siem Reap and not difficult to reach thanks to an all-weather road via the junction town of Dam Dek. The trip takes around an hour and costs about US$60 return by taxi; it's a longer ride by *remork-moto,* but should be around US$25 to US$30.

Ang Trapeng Thmor

The bird sancturay of **Ang Trapeng Thmor Reserve** (អាងត្រពាំងថ្ម; admission US$10) is one of only a handful of places in the world where it's possible to see the extremely rare sarus crane, as depicted on bas-reliefs at Bayon. Reputedly the tallest bird in the world, these grey-feathered birds have immensely long legs and striking red heads. Sam Veasna Center (p107) arranges birdwatching excursions (US$100 per person with a group of four) out here, which is probably the easiest way to undertake the trip.

The sanctuary is based around a reservoir created by forced labour during the Khmer Rouge regime, and facilities are very basic, but it is an incredibly beautiful place. Bring your own binoculars, as none are available.

The bird sanctuary is just across the border in the Phnom Srok region of Banteay Meanchey Province, about 100km from Siem Reap. To reach here, follow the road to Sisophon for about 72km before turning north at Prey Mon. It's 22km to the site, passing through some famous silk-weaving villages.

Temples of Angkor

Best Temples for Sunrise or Sunset

➡ Angkor Wat (p147)

➡ Phnom Bakheng (p156)

➡ Pre Rup (p160)

➡ Sra Srang (p160)

Best Temples for Film Buffs

➡ Angkor Wat (p147)

➡ Bayon (p155)

➡ Beng Mealea (p168)

➡ Angkor Thom East Gate (p154)

➡ Ta Prohm (p159)

Why Go?

Welcome to heaven on earth. Angkor (ប្រាសាទអង្គរ) is the earthly representation of Mt Meru, the Mt Olympus of the Hindu faith and the abode of ancient gods. The temples are the perfect fusion of creative ambition and spiritual devotion. The Cambodian 'god-kings' of old each strove to better their ancestors in size, scale and symmetry, culminating in the world's largest religious building, Angkor Wat.

The temples of Angkor are a source of inspiration and national pride to all Khmers as they struggle to rebuild their lives after the years of terror and trauma. Today, the temples are a point of pilgrimage for all Cambodians, and no traveller to the region will want to miss their extravagant beauty. Angkor is one of the world's foremost ancient sites, with the epic proportions of the Great Wall of China, the detail and intricacy of the Taj Mahal, and the symbolism and symmetry of the pyramids, all rolled into one.

Don't Miss

➡ Angkor Wat (p147) Watching the sun rise over the holiest of holies, Angkor Wat, the world's largest religious building.

➡ Bayon (p155) Contemplating the serenity and splendour of Bayon, its 216 enigmatic faces staring out into the jungle.

➡ Ta Prohm (p159) Witnessing nature reclaiming the stones at this mysterious ruin, the *Tomb Raider* temple.

➡ Banteay Srei (p167) Staring in wonder at the delicate carvings adorning Banteay Srei, the finest seen at Angkor.

➡ Kbal Spean (p170) Trekking deep into the jungle to discover the 'River of a Thousand Lingas'.

➡ Beng Mealea (p168) Exploring the tangled vines, crumbling corridors and jumbled sandstone blocks.

History

The Angkorian period spans more than 600 years from AD 802 to 1432. This incredible age saw the construction of the temples of Angkor and the consolidation of the Khmer empire's position as one of the great powers in Southeast Asia. This era encompassed periods of decline and revival, and wars with rival powers in Vietnam, Thailand and Myanmar.

The hundreds of temples surviving today are but the sacred skeleton of the vast political, religious and social centre of the ancient Khmer empire, a city that, at its zenith, boasted a population of one million when London was a small town of 50,000. The houses, public buildings and palaces of Angkor were constructed of wood – now long decayed – because the right to dwell in structures of brick or stone was reserved for the gods.

An Empire is Born

The Angkorian period began with the rule of Jayavarman II (r 802–50). He was the first to unify Cambodia's competing kingdoms before the birth of Angkor. His court was situated at various locations, including Phnom Kulen, 40km northeast of Angkor Wat, and Roluos (known then as Hariharalaya), 13km east of Siem Reap.

Jayavarman II proclaimed himself a *devaraja* (god-king), the earthly representative of the Hindu god Shiva, and built a 'temple-mountain' at Phnom Kulen, symbolising Shiva's dwelling place of Mt Meru, the holy mountain at the centre of the universe. This set a precedent that became a dominant feature of the Angkorian period and accounts for the staggering architectural productivity at this time.

Indravarman I (r 877–89) is believed to have been a usurper, and probably inherited the mantle of *devaraja* through conquest. He built a 6.5-sq-km *baray* (reservoir) at Roluos and established Preah Ko. The *baray* was the first stage of an irrigation system that created a hydraulic city, the ancient Khmers mastering the cycle of nature to water their lands. Form and function worked together in harmony, as the *baray* also had religious significance, representing the oceans surrounding Mt Meru. Indravarman's final work was Bakong, a pyramidal representation of Mt Meru.

Indravarman I's son Yasovarman I (r 889–910) looked further afield to celebrate his divinity and glory in a temple-mountain of his own. He first built Lolei on an artificial island in the *baray* established by his father, before beginning work on the Bakheng. Today this hill is known as Phnom Bakheng, a favoured spot for viewing the sunset over Angkor Wat. A raised highway was constructed to connect Phnom Bakheng with Roluos, 16km to the southeast, and a large *baray* was constructed to the east of Phnom Bakheng. Today it is known as the Eastern Baray but has entirely silted up. Yasovarman I also established the temple-mountains of Phnom Krom and Phnom Bok.

After the death of Yasovarman I, power briefly shifted from the Angkor region to Koh Ker, around 80km to the northeast, under another usurper king, Jayavarman IV (r 924–42). In AD 944 power returned again to Angkor under the leadership of Rajendravarman II (r 944–68), who built the Eastern Mebon and Pre Rup. The reign of his son Jayavarman V (r 968–1001) produced the temples Ta Keo and Banteay Srei, the latter built by a brahman rather than the king.

The Golden Age of Angkor

The temples that are now the highlight of a visit to Angkor – Angkor Wat and those in and around the walled city of Angkor Thom – were built during the golden age or classical period. While this period is marked by fits of remarkable productivity, it was also a time of turmoil, conquests and setbacks. The great city of Angkor Thom owes its existence to the fact that the old city of Angkor, which stood on the same site, was destroyed during the Cham invasion of 1177.

Suryavarman I (r 1002–49) was a usurper to the throne who rose to power through strategic alliances and military conquests. Although he adopted the Hindu cult of the god-king, he is thought to have come from a Mahayana Buddhist tradition and may even have sponsored the growth of Buddhism in Cambodia. Buddhist sculpture certainly became more commonplace in the Angkor region during his time.

Little physical evidence of Suryavarman I's reign remains at Angkor, but his military exploits brought much of central Thailand and southern-central Laos under the control of Angkor. His son Udayadityavarman II (r 1049–65) embarked on further military expeditions, extending the empire once more, and building Baphuon and the Western Mebon. Many major cities in the Mekong region were important Khmer settlements in the 11th and 12th centuries, including the Lao capital of Vientiane and the Thai city of Lopburi.

Temples of Angkor

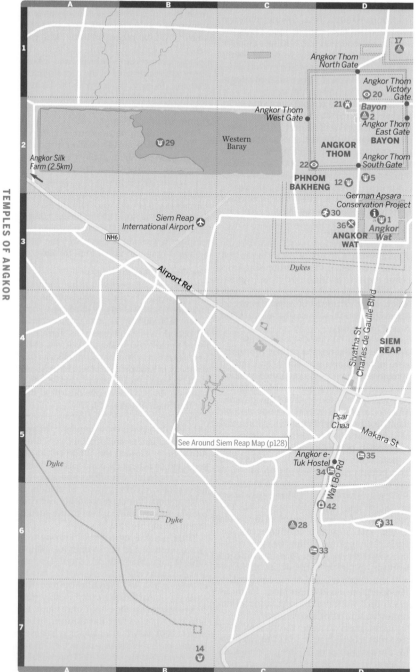

See Around Siem Reap Map (p128)

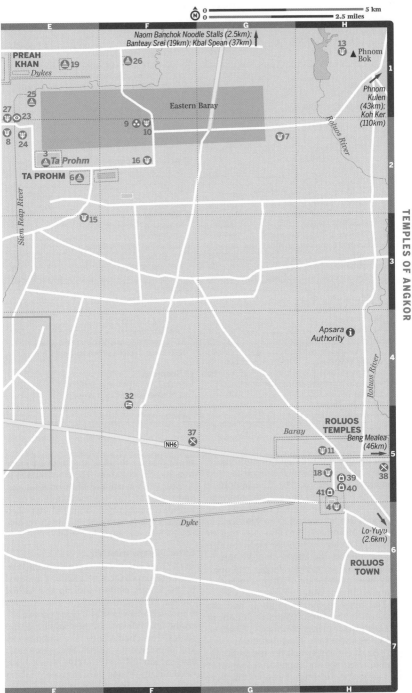

Temples of Angkor

TEMPLES OF ANGKOR HISTORY

From 1066 until the end of the century, Angkor was again divided as rival factions contested the throne. The first important monarch of this new era was Suryavarman II (r 1112–52), who unified Cambodia and extended Khmer influence to Malaya and Burma (Myanmar). He also set himself apart religiously from earlier kings through his devotion to the Hindu deity Vishnu, to whom he consecrated the largest and arguably most magnificent of all the Angkorian temples, Angkor Wat.

The reign of Suryavarman II and the construction of Angkor Wat signifies one of the high-water marks of Khmer civilisation. However, there were signs that decline was lurking. It is thought that the hydraulic system of reservoirs and canals that supported the agriculture of Angkor had by this time been pushed beyond its limits, and was slowly starting to silt up due to overpopulation and deforestation. The construction of Angkor Wat was a major strain on resources, and, on top of this, Suryavarman II led a disastrous campaign against the Dai Viet (Vietnamese) late in his reign, during the course of which he was killed in battle.

Enter Jayavarman VII

In 1177 the Chams of southern Vietnam, then the Kingdom of Champa and long annexed by the Khmer empire, rose up and sacked Angkor. This attack caught the Khmers completely unawares, as it came via sea, river and lake rather than the traditional land routes. The Chams burnt the wooden city and plundered its wealth. Four years later Jayavarman VII (r 1181–1219) struck back, emphatically driving the Chams out of Cambodia and reclaiming Angkor.

Jayavarman VII's reign has given scholars much to debate. It represents a radical departure from the reigns of his predecessors. For centuries the fount of royal divinity had reposed in the Hindu deity Shiva (and, occasionally, Vishnu). Jayavarman VII adopted Mahayana Buddhism and looked to Avalokiteshvara, the Bodhisattva of Compassion, for patronage during his reign. In doing so he may well have been converting to a religion that already enjoyed wide popular support among his subjects. It may also be that the destruction of Angkor was such a blow to royal divinity that a new religious foundation was thought to be needed.

During his reign, Jayavarman VII embarked on a dizzying array of temple projects that centred on Baphuon, which was the site of the capital city destroyed by the Chams. Angkor Thom, Jayavarman VII's new city, was surrounded by walls and a moat, which became another component of Angkor's complex irrigation system. The centrepiece of Angkor Thom was Bayon, the temple-mountain studded with faces that, along with Angkor Wat, is the most famous of Cambodia's temples. Other temples built during his reign include Ta Prohm, Banteay Kdei and Preah Khan. Further away, he rebuilt vast temple complexes, such as Banteay Chhmar and Preah Khan in Preah Vihear Province, making him by far the most prolific builder of Angkor's many kings.

Jayavarman VII also embarked on a major public-works program, building roads, schools and hospitals across the empire. Remains of many of these roads and their magnificent bridges can be seen across Cambodia. Spean Praptos at Kompong Kdei, 65km southeast of Siem Reap on National Hwy 6 (NH6), is the most famous, but there are many more lost in the forest on the old Angkorian road to the great Preah Khan, including the now accessible Spean Ta Ong, about 28km east of Beng Mealea near the village of Khvau.

After the death of Jayavarman VII around 1219, the Khmer empire went into decline. The state religion reverted to Hinduism for a century or more and outbreaks of iconoclasm saw Buddhist sculpture adorning the Hindu temples vandalised or altered. The Thais sacked Angkor in 1351, and again with devastating efficiency in 1431. The glorious Siamese capital of Ayuthaya, which enjoyed a golden age from the 14th to the 18th centuries, was in many ways a re-creation of the glories of Angkor from which the Thai

TEMPLE ADDICTS

The god-kings of Angkor were dedicated builders. Each king was expected to dedicate a temple to his patron god, most commonly Shiva or Vishnu, during the time of Angkor. Then there were the ancestors, including mother, father, and grandparents (both maternal and paternal), which meant another half dozen temples or more. Finally there was the mausoleum or king's temple, intended to deify the monarch and project his power, and each of these had to be bigger and better than one's predecessor. This accounts for the staggering architectural productivity of the Khmers at this time and the epic evolution of temple architecture.

conquerors drew inspiration. The Khmer court moved to Phnom Penh, only to return fleetingly to Angkor in the 16th century; in the meantime, it was abandoned to pilgrims, holy men and the elements.

Angkor Rediscovered

The French 'discovery' of Angkor in the 1860s made an international splash and created a great deal of outside interest in Cambodia. But 'discovery', with all the romance it implied, was something of a misnomer. When French explorer Henri Mouhot first stumbled across Angkor Wat on his Royal Geographic Society expedition, it included a wealthy, working monastery with monks and slaves. Moreover, Portuguese travellers in the 16th century encountered Angkor, referring to it as the Walled City. Diego do Couto produced an accurate description of Angkor in 1614, but it was not published until 1958. A 17th-century Japanese pilgrim drew a detailed plan of Angkor Wat, though he mistakenly recalled that he had seen it in India.

Still, it was the publication of *Voyage à Siam et dans le Cambodge* by Mouhot, posthumously released in 1868, that first brought Angkor to the public eye. Although the explorer himself made no such claims, by the 1870s he was being celebrated as the discoverer of the lost temple-city of Cambodia. In fact, a French missionary known as Charles-Emile Bouillevaux had visited Angkor 10 years before Mouhot and had published an account of his own findings. However, the Bouillevaux account was roundly ignored

TEMPLES OF ANGKOR HISTORY

Temples of Angkor

THREE-DAY EXPLORATION

The temple complex at Angkor is simply enormous and the superlatives don't do it justice. This is the site of the world's largest religious building, a multitude of temples and a vast, long-abandoned walled city that was arguably Southeast Asia's first metropolis, long before Bangkok and Singapore got in on the action.

Starting at the Roluos group of temples, one of the earliest capitals of Angkor, move on to the big circuit, which includes the Buddhist-Hindu fusion temple of ❶ **Preah Khan** and the ornate water temple of ❷ **Preah Neak Poan**.

On the second day downsize to the small circuit, starting with an early visit to ❸ **Ta Prohm**, before continuing to the temple pyramid of Ta Keo, the Buddhist monastery of Banteay Kdei and the immense royal bathing pond of ❹ **Sra Srang**.

Next venture further afield to Banteay Srei temple, the jewel in the crown of Angkorian art, and Beng Mealea, a remote jungle temple.

Saving the biggest and best until last, experience sunrise at ❺ **Angkor Wat** and stick around for breakfast in the temple to discover its amazing architecture without the crowds. In the afternoon, explore ❻ **Angkor Thom**, an immense complex that is home to the enigmatic ❼ **Bayon**.

Three days around Angkor? That's just for starters.

TOP TIPS

➡ To avoid the crowds, try dawn at Sra Srang, post-sunrise at Angkor Wat and lunchtime at Banteay Srei.

➡ Three-day passes can be used on non-consecutive days over the course of a week, but be sure to request this.

Bayon
The surreal state temple of legendary king Jayavarman VII, where 216 faces bear down on pilgrims, asserting religious and regal authority.

Terrace of the Leper King
Preah Palilay
Phimeanakas Temple
Tep Pranam
West Gate Angkor Thom
Baphuon Temple
Terrace of the Elephants
❼
South Gate Angkor Thom
Phnom Bakheng
Baksei Chamrong
❺

Angkor Wat
The world's largest religious building. Experience sunrise at the holiest of holies, then explore the beautiful bas-reliefs – devotion etched in stone.

Angkor Thom
The last great capital of the Khmer empire conceals a wealth of temples and its epic proportions would have inspired and terrified in equal measure.

Preah Khan
A fusion temple dedicated to Buddha, Brahma, Shiva and Vishnu; the immense corridors are like an unending hall of mirrors.

Preah Neak Poan
If Vegas ever adopts the Angkor theme, this will be the swimming pool; a petite tower set in a lake, surrounded by four smaller ponds.

North Gate, Angkor Thom

Preah Pithu

Thommanon Temple

Prasat Suor Prat

Victory Gate Angkor Thom

East Gate Angkor Thom

Chau Say Tevoda

Ta Keo Temple

Ta Nei Temple

Banteay Srei

Banteay Kdei Temple

Roluos, Beng Mealea

Prasat Kravan

Bat Chum Temple

Ta Prohm
Nicknamed the *Tomb Raider* temple; *Indiana Jones* would be equally apt. Nature has run riot, leaving iconic tree roots strangling the surviving stones.

Sra Srang
Once the royal bathing pond, this is the ablutions pool to beat all ablutions pools and makes a good stop for sunrise or sunset.

TOP 10 KINGS OF ANGKOR

A mind-numbing array of kings ruled the Khmer empire from the 9th to the 14th centuries AD. All of their names include the word 'varman', which means 'armour' or 'protector'. Forget the small fry and focus on the big fish in our Top 10:

Jayavarman II (r 802–50) Founder of the Khmer empire in AD 802.

Indravarman I (r 877–89) Builder of the first *baray* (reservoir), Preah Ko and Bakong.

Yasovarman I (r 889–910) Moved the capital to Angkor and built Lolei and Phnom Bakheng.

Jayavarman IV (r 924–42) Usurper king who moved the capital to Koh Ker.

Rajendravarman II (r 944–68) Builder of Eastern Mebon, Pre Rup and Phimeanakas.

Jayavarman V (r 968–1001) Oversaw construction of Ta Keo and Banteay Srei.

Suryavarman I (r 1002–49) Expanded the empire into much of Laos and Thailand.

Udayadityavarman II (r 1049–65) Builder of the pyramidal Baphuon and the Western Mebon.

Suryavarman II (r 1112–52) Legendary builder of Angkor Wat and Beng Mealea.

Jayavarman VII (r 1181–1219) The king of the god-kings, building Angkor Thom, Preah Khan and Ta Prohm.

and it was Mouhot's account, with its rich descriptions and tantalising pen-and-ink colour sketches of the temples, that turned the ruins into an international obsession.

Soon after Mouhot, other adventurers and explorers began to arrive. Scottish photographer John Thomson took the first photographs of the temples in 1866. He was the first Westerner to posit the idea that they were symbolic representations of the mythical Mt Meru. French architect Lucien Fournereau travelled to Angkor in 1887 and produced plans and meticulously executed cross-sections that were to stand as the best available until the 1960s.

From this time Angkor became the target of French-financed expeditions and, in 1901, the École Française d'Extrême-Orient (www.efeo.fr) began a long association with Angkor by funding an expedition to Bayon. In 1907 Angkor was returned to Cambodia, having been under Thai control for more than a century, and the EFEO took responsibility for clearing and restoring the whole site. In the same year, the first foreign tourists arrived in Angkor – an unprecedented 200 of them in three months. Angkor had been 'rescued' from the jungle and was assuming its place in the modern world.

Restoring Angkor

With the exception of Angkor Wat, which was restored for use as a Buddhist shrine in the 16th century by the Khmer royalty, the temples of Angkor were left to the jungle for many centuries. The majority of temples are made of sandstone, which tends to dissolve when in prolonged contact with dampness. Bat droppings took their toll, as did sporadic pilfering of sculptures and cut stones. At some monuments, such as Ta Prohm, the jungle had stealthily waged an all-out invasion, and plant life could only be removed at great risk to the structures it now supported in its web of roots.

Initial attempts to clear Angkor under the aegis of the École Française d'Extrême-Orient were fraught with technical difficulties and theoretical disputes. On a technical front, the jungle tended to grow back as soon as it was cleared; on a theoretical front, scholars debated the extent to which temples should be restored and whether later additions, such as Buddha images in Hindu temples, should be removed.

It was not until the 1920s that a solution was found, known as anastylosis. This was the method the Dutch had used to restore Borobudur in Java. Put simply, it was a way of reconstructing monuments using the original materials and in keeping with the original form of the structure. New materials were permitted only where the originals could not be found, and were to be used discreetly. An example of this method can be seen on the causeway leading to the entrance of Angkor Wat, as the right-hand side was originally restored by the French.

The first major restoration job was carried out on Banteay Srei in 1930. It was deemed such a success that many more extensive restoration projects were undertaken elsewhere around Angkor, culminating in the massive Angkor Wat restoration in the 1960s. Large cranes and earth-moving machines were brought in, and the operation was backed by a veritable army of surveying equipment.

The Khmer Rouge victory and Cambodia's subsequent slide into an intractable civil war resulted in far less damage to Angkor than many had assumed, as EFEO and Ministry of Culture teams had removed many of the statues from the temple sites for protection. Nevertheless, turmoil in Cambodia resulted in a long interruption of restoration work, allowing the jungle to resume its assault on the monuments. The illegal trade of *objets d'art* on the world art market has also been a major threat to Angkor, although it is the more remote sites that have been targeted recently. Angkor has been under the jurisdiction of the UN Educational Scientific and Cultural Organization (Unesco) since 1992 as a World Heritage Site, and international and local efforts continue to preserve and reconstruct the monuments. In a sign of real progress, Angkor was removed from Unesco's endangered list in 2003.

Many of Angkor's secrets remain to be discovered, as most of the work at the temples has concentrated on restoration efforts above ground rather than archaeological digs and surveys below. Underground is where the real story of Angkor and its

people lies – the inscriptions on the temples give us only a partial picture of the gods to whom each structure was dedicated, and the kings who built them.

To learn more about Unesco's activities at Angkor, visit http://whc.unesco.org. For a great online photographic resource on the temples of Angkor, look no further than www.angkor-ruins.com, a Japanese website with an English translation.

Architectural Styles

From the time of the earliest Angkorian monuments at Roluos, Khmer architecture was continually evolving, often from the rule of one king to the next. Archaeologists therefore divide the monuments of Angkor into nine periods, named after the foremost example of each period's architectural style.

The evolution of Khmer architecture was based on a central theme of the temple-mountain, preferably set on a real hill (but an artificial hill was allowed if there weren't any mountains to hand). The earlier a temple was constructed, the more closely it adheres to this fundamental idea. Essentially, the mountain was represented by a tower mounted on a tiered base. At the summit was the central sanctuary, usually with an open door to the east, and three false doors at the remaining cardinal points of the compass. For Indian Hindus, the Himalayas represent Mt Meru, the home of the gods, while the Khmer kings of old adopted Phnom Kulen as their symbolic Mt Meru.

TEMPLES OF ANGKOR ARCHITECTURAL STYLES

HIDDEN RICHES, POLITICAL GLITCHES

Angkor Conservation (p99) is a Ministry of Culture compound on the banks of the Siem Reap River, about 400m east of the Sofitel Phokheetra Royal Angkor Hotel. The compound houses more than 5000 statues, *lingas* (phallic symbols) and inscribed stelae, stored here to protect them from the wanton looting that has blighted hundreds of sites around Angkor. The finest statuary is hidden away inside Angkor Conservation's warehouses, meticulously numbered and catalogued. Unfortunately, without the right contacts, trying to get a peek at the statues is a lost cause. Some of the statuary is on public display in the **Angkor National Museum** (p98) in Siem Reap, but it is only a fraction of the collection.

Formerly housed at Angkor Conservation, but now going it alone in an impressive headquarters is **Apsara Authority** (Authority for Protection & Management of Angkor & the Region of Siem Reap; www.apsaraauthority.gov.kh; Prasat Bakong District; ☺8am-4pm Mon-Fri). This organisation is responsible for the research, protection and conservation of cultural heritage around Angkor, as well as urban planning in Siem Reap and tourism development in the region. Quite a mandate, quite a challenge, especially now that the government is taking such a keen interest in its work. Angkor is a money-spinner; it remains to be seen whether Apsara will put preservation before profits. It is a powerful authority that some have nicknamed the Ministry of Angkor.

LOCAL KNOWLEDGE

VISITOR CODE OF CONDUCT

While the temples of Angkor are not a million miles away from the beaches of Sihanoukville, it is important to remember that the temples of Angkor represent a sacred religious site to the Khmer people. Since the relocation of the ticket booth in 2016, the authorities have begun cracking down on inappropriate dress at the temples. Expect to be sent back to your guesthouse to change if you are wearing sleeveless tops, hot pants or short skirts. Local authorities have recently released visitor 'code of conduct' guidelines and a video to encourage dressing appropriately, as well as reminding tourists not to touch or sit on the ancient structures, to pay attention to restricted areas, and to be respectful of monks.

By the time of the Bakheng period, this layout was being embellished. The summit of the central tower was crowned with five 'peaks' – four at the points of the compass and one in the centre. Even Angkor Wat features this layout, though on a grandiose scale. Other features that came to be favoured include an entry tower and a causeway lined with *naga* (mythical serpent) balustrades leading up to the temple.

As the temples grew in ambition, the central tower became a less prominent feature, although it remained the focus of the temple. Later temples saw the central tower flanked by courtyards and richly decorated galleries. Smaller towers were placed on gates and on the corners of walls, their overall number often of religious or astrological significance.

These refinements and additions eventually culminated in Angkor Wat, which effectively showcases the evolution of Angkorian architecture. The architecture of the Bayon period breaks with tradition in temples such as Ta Prohm and Preah Khan. In these temples, the horizontal layout of the galleries, corridors and courtyards seems to completely eclipse the central tower.

The curious narrowness of the corridors and doorways in these structures can be explained by the fact that Angkorian architects never mastered the flying buttress to build a full arch. They engineered arches by laying blocks on top of each other, until they met at a central point; known as false arches, they can only support very short spans.

Most of the major sandstone blocks around Angkor include small circular holes. These originally held wooden stakes that were used to lift and position the stones during construction before being sawn off.

When to Go

→ Avoid the sweltering temperatures of March to May.

→ November to February is the best time of year to travel, but this is no secret, so it coincides with peak season. And peak season really is mountainous in this day and age, with more than two million visitors a year descending on Angkor.

→ The summer months of July and August can be a surprisingly rewarding time, as the landscape is emerald green, the moats overflowing with water, and the moss and lichen in bright contrast to the grey sandstone.

→ The Angkor Wat International Half Marathon takes place annually in December, including the option of bicycle rides for those not into running.

Itineraries

Back in the early days of tourism, the decision of what to see and in what order came down to a choice between two basic temple itineraries: the Small (Petit) Circuit and the Big (Grand) Circuit. It's difficult to imagine anyone following these to the letter any more, but in their time they were an essential component of the Angkor experience and were often undertaken on the back of an elephant.

Today, most budget and midrange travellers prefer to take in the temples at their own pace, and tend to use a combination of transport options, such as car, *remork*, bicycle or minivan. Plan a dawn-to-dusk itinerary with a long, leisurely lunch to avoid the heat of the midday sun. Alternatively, explore the temples through lunch, when it can be considerably quieter than during the peak morning and afternoon visit times. However, it will be hot as hell and the light is not conducive to photography.

Angkor in One Day

If you have only one day to visit Angkor, arrive at Angkor Wat (p147) in time for sunrise and then stick around to explore the mighty temple while it's quieter. From there continue to the tree roots of Ta Prohm (p159) before breaking for lunch. In the afternoon, explore the temples within the walled city of Angkor Thom (p153) and the beauty of the Bayon (p155) in the late-afternoon light.

Angkor in Two Days

A second day allows you to include some of the big hitters around Angkor. Spend the first morning visiting petite Banteay Srei (p167), with its fabulous carvings; stop at Banteay Samré (p170) on the return leg. In the afternoon, visit immense Preah Khan (p162), delicate Preah Neak Poan (p163) and the tree roots of Ta Som (p160), before taking in a sunset at Pre Rup (p160).

Three to Five Days

If you have three to five days to explore Angkor, it's possible to see most of the important sites. One approach is to see as much as possible on the first day or two and then spend the final days combining visits to other sites such as the Roluos temples (p165) and Banteay Kdei (p160). Better still is a gradual build-up to the most spectacular monuments. After all, if you see Angkor Wat (p147) on the first day, then a temple like Ta Keo (p161) just won't cut it. Another option is a chronological approach, starting with the earliest Angkorian temples and working steadily forwards in time to Angkor Thom (p153), taking stock of the evolution of Khmer architecture and artistry.

It is well worth making the trip to the 'River of a Thousand Lingas' at Kbal Spean (p170) for the chance to stretch your legs amid natural and human-made splendour, or the remote, vast and overgrown temple of Beng Mealea (p168). Both can be combined with Banteay Srei (p167) in one long day.

One Week

Those with the time to spend a week at Angkor will be richly rewarded. Not only is it possible to visit all the temples of the region, but a longer stay also allows for non-temple activities, such as relaxing by a pool, indulging in a spa treatment or shopping around Siem Reap. You may also want to throw in some of the more remote sites such as Koh Ker (p172), Prasat Preah Vihear (p262) or Banteay Chhmar (p256).

☞ Tours

Visitors who have only a day or two at this incredible site may prefer something organised locally. It is possible to link up with an official tour guide in Siem Reap, where a number of operators run tours ranging from simple day trips to cycling tours to excursions to more remote temple sites.

Khmer Angkor
Tour Guide Association   TOURS
(☎063-964347; www.khmerangkortourguide.com) The Khmer Angkor Tour Guide Association represents all of Angkor's authorised guides. English- or French-speaking guides can be booked for from US$30 per day; guides speaking other languages, such as Italian, German, Spanish, Japanese and Chinese, are available at a higher rate as there are fewer of them.

❶ Orientation

Heading north from Siem Reap, Angkor Wat is the first major temple, followed by the walled city of Angkor Thom. To the east and west of this city are two vast former reservoirs, which once helped to feed the huge population; the eastern reservoir is now completely dried up. Further east are temples including Ta Prohm, Banteay Kdei and Pre Rup. North of Angkor Thom is Preah Khan, and way beyond in the northeast, Banteay Srei, Kbal Spean, Phnom Kulen and Beng Mealea. To the southeast of Siem Reap is the early Angkorian Roluos group of temples.

❶ Information

ADMISSION FEES

Visitors have the choice of a one-day pass (US$37), a three-day pass (US$62) or a one-week pass (US$72). The three-day passes can be used over three non-consecutive days in a one-week period while one-week passes can be used on seven days over a month.

In 2016, the Angkor **ticket booth & main entrance** (Map p128; Rd 60; ⊙5am-6pm) moved to a new location out by the Siem Reap Convention Centre, about 2km east of the old checkpoint. It's part of a gleaming new complex that also includes the ambitious Angkor Panorama Museum. Tickets are not sold at the old ticket checkpoint.

Passes include a digital photo snapped at the entrance booth, so queues can be slow at peak times. Visitors entering after 5pm get a free sunset, as the ticket starts from the following day. The fee includes access to all the monuments in the Siem Reap area but not the sacred mountain of Phnom Kulen (US$20) or the remote complexes of Beng Mealea (US$5) and Koh Ker (US$10).

All the major temples now have uniformed staff to check the tickets, which has reduced the opportunity for scams. These days all roads

MOTIFS, SYMBOLS & CHARACTERS AROUND ANGKOR

The temples of Angkor are intricately carved with myths and legends, symbols and signs, and a cast of characters in the thousands. Deciphering them can be quite a challenge, so we've highlighted some of the most commonly seen around the majestic temples. For more help understanding the carvings of Angkor, pick up a copy of *Images of the Gods* by Vittorio Roveda.

Apsaras Heavenly nymphs or goddesses, also known as *devadas;* these beautiful female forms decorate the walls of many temples.

Asuras These devils feature extensively in representations of the Churning of the Ocean of Milk, such as at Angkor Wat.

Devas The 'good gods' in the creation myth of the Churning of the Ocean of Milk.

Flame The flame motif is found flanking steps and doorways and is intended to purify pilgrims as they enter the temple.

Garuda Vehicle of Vishnu; this half-man, half-bird creature features in some temples and was combined with his old enemy, the nagas to promote religious unity under Jayavarman VII.

Kala The temple guardian appointed by Shiva; he had such an appetite that he devoured his own body and appears only as a giant head above doorways. Also known as Rehu.

Linga A phallic symbol of fertility, lingas would have originally been located within the towers of most Hindu temples.

Lotus A symbol of purity, the lotus features extensively in the shape of towers, the shape of steps to entrances and in decoration.

Makara A giant sea serpent with a reticulated jaw; features on the corner of pediments, spewing forth a naga or some other creature.

Naga The multiheaded serpent, half-brother and enemy of garudas. Controls the rains and, therefore, the prosperity of the kingdom; seen on causeways, doorways and roofs. The seven-headed naga, a feature at many temples, represents the rainbow, which acts as a bridge between heaven and earth.

Nandi The mount of Shiva; there are several statues of Nandi dotted about the temples, although many have been damaged or stolen by looters.

Rishi A Hindu wise man or ascetic, also known as *essai;* these bearded characters are often seen sitting cross-legged at the base of pillars or flanking walls.

Vine Another symbol of purity, the vine graces doorways and lintels and is meant to help cleanse the visitor on their journey to this heaven on earth, the abode of the gods.

Yama God of death who presides over the underworld and passes judgement on whether people continue to heaven or hell.

Yoni Female fertility symbol that is combined with the linga to produce holy water infused with the essence of life.

into the central temples (including Angkor Wat, Angkor Thom and Ta Prohm) have checkpoints as well; foreigners who can't produce a pass will be turned away and asked to detour around the temples between 7am and 5pm. Visitors found inside any of the main temples without a ticket will be fined a whopping US$100.

USEFUL WEBSITES

Angkor – Unesco World Heritage Site
(http://whc.unesco.org/en/list/668) Information, images and videos on the world's top temples.

Angkor Ruins (www.angkor-ruins.com) For a great online photographic resource on the temples of Angkor, look no further than this Japanese website with an English version.

Lonely Planet (www.lonelyplanet.com/cambodia/temples-of-angkor) Destination information, bookings and more.

National Geographic (http://ngm.national geographic.com/2009/07/angkor/angkor-animation) Animated illustrations of life in the Khmer Empire.

ℹ Getting There & Around

Visitors heading to the temples of Angkor – in other words, pretty much everybody coming to Cambodia – need to consider the most suitable way to travel between the temples. The central temple area is just 8km from Siem Reap, and can be visited using anything from a car or motorcycle to a sturdy pair of walking shoes. For the independent traveller, there will be many alternatives to consider.

For the ultimate Angkor experience, try a pick-and-mix approach, with a *moto, remork-moto* or car for one day to cover the remote sites, a bicycle to experience the central temples, and an exploration on foot for a spot of peace and serenity.

Transport will be more expensive to remote temples such as Banteay Srei or Beng Mealea, due to extra fuel costs.

BICYCLE

Bicycle is a great way to get around the temples and they are used by most locals. There are few hills and the roads are good, so there's no need for much cycling experience. Moving about at a slower speed, you soon find that you take in more than from out of a car window or on the back of a speeding *moto*.

White Bicycles (p125) is supported by some guesthouses around Siem Reap, with proceeds from the hire fee going towards community projects. Many guesthouses and hotels in town rent bikes for around US$1 to US$2 per day.

Some rental places offer better mountain bikes, such as Trek or Giant, for US$7 to US$10 per day. Try Grasshopper Adventures (p107), which offers mountain bikes and helmets for US$8 per day. Electric bicycles hired out by Green e-bikes (p126) and others are also a very popular way to tour the temples.

When exploring by bicycle, always use a sturdy lock and leave it at a guarded parking area or with a stallholder outside each temple.

CAR & MOTORCYCLE

Car is a popular choice for getting about the temples. The obvious advantage is protection from the elements, be it heavy downpours or the punishing sun. Shared between several travellers, they can also be an economical way to explore. The downside is that visitors are a little more isolated from the sights, sounds and smells as they travel between temples. A car for the day around the central temples is US$25 to US$35 and can be arranged with hotels, guesthouses and agencies in Siem Reap. It costs more to outlying temples like Banteay Srei and Beng Mealea.

Motorcycle rental in Siem Reap was prohibited for more than a decade, but recently the rules seem to have been unofficially relaxed and a

ℹ WHERE TO STAY AROUND ANGKOR

For most people nearby Siem Reap is the base for exploring the temples of Angkor, with an incredible array of accommodation (p108) on offer from budget hostels to opulent hotels. There is no accommodation around Angkor as such, although there are some rustic options in the rural districts such Banteay Srei district (p126) for those seeking a local experience.

number of travellers are renting small motorbikes for around US$10 per day. When exploring by motorbike, leave it at a guarded parking area or with a stallholder outside each temple, otherwise it might be stolen.

ELEPHANT

Travelling by elephant was the traditional way to see the temples way back in the early days of tourism at Angkor, at the start of the 20th century. While you will see tourists taking an elephant ride between the south gate of Angkor Thom and the Bayon in the morning, or up to the summit of Phnom Bakheng for sunset, several elephant welfare organisations suggest it is detrimental to the health of these majestic creatures (see p301). Sambo, a female elephant, dropped dead outside the Bayon temple during a heatwave in April 2016. Lonely Planet does not endorse elephant riding in Cambodia.

HELICOPTER & HOT-AIR BALLOON

For those with a flexible budget, there are helicopter flights around Angkor Wat (US$90) and the temples outside Angkor Thom (US$150). **Helicopters Cambodia** (☑ 012 814500; www.helicopterscambodia.com) or **Helistar** (p102), which operate out of Siem Reap Airport, also offer expensive charters to remote temples such as Prasat Preah Vihear and Preah Khan.

Angkor Balloon (☑ 012 759698; per person US$15) offers a bird's-eye view of Angkor Wat. The balloon carries up to 30 people, is on a fixed line and rises 200m above the landscape. It doesn't drift across the temples like Balloons over Bagan, so it's best to manage expectations.

MINIVAN

Minivans are available from various hotels and travel agents around town. A 12-seat minivan costs from US$50 per day.

MOTO

Some independent travellers visit the temples by *moto* (unmarked motorcycle taxi). *Moto* drivers accost visitors from the moment they set

ℹ️ AVOIDING THE CROWDS

Angkor is well and truly on the tourist trail and it is only getting busier, with over two million visitors annually, but – with a little planning – it is still possible to escape the crowds. One important thing to remember, particularly when it comes to sunrise and sunset, is that places are popular for a reason, and it is worth going with the flow at least once.

It is received wisdom that as Angkor Wat faces west, one should be there for late afternoon, and in the case of the Bayon, which faces east, in the morning. Ta Prohm, most people seem to agree, can be visited in the middle of the day because of its umbrella of foliage. This is all well and good, but if you reverse the order, the temples will still look good – and you can avoid some of the crowds.

Only four temples are open at 5am for sunrise: Angkor Wat, Phnom Bakheng, Sra Srang and Pre Rup. The most popular place is Angkor Wat. Most tour groups head back to town for breakfast, so stick around and explore the temple while it's cool and quiet between 7am and 9am. Sra Srang is usually pretty quiet, and sunrise here can be spectacular thanks to reflections in the extensive waters. Phnom Bakheng could be an attractive option, because the sun comes up behind Angkor Wat and you are far from the madding crowd that gathers here at sunset, but there are now strict limitations on visitor numbers each day.

The hilltop temple of Phnom Bakheng is the definitive sunset spot. This was getting well out of control, with as many as 1000 tourists clambering around the small structure. However, new restrictions limit visitors to no more than 300 at any one time. It is generally better to check it out for sunrise or early morning and miss the crowds. Staying within the confines of Angkor Wat for sunset is a rewarding option, but it is quite busy at this time. Pre Rup is popular with some for an authentic rural sunset over the countryside, but this is also crowded these days. Better is the hilltop temple of Phnom Krom, which offers commanding views across Tonlé Sap lake, but involves a long drive back to town in the dark. The Western Baray takes in the sunset from the eastern end, across its vast waters, or from Western Mebon island, and is generally a quiet option.

When it comes to the most popular temples, the middle of the day is generally the quietest time. This is because the majority of the large tour groups head back to Siem Reap for lunch. It is also the hottest part of the day, which makes it tough going around relatively open temples such as Banteay Srei and the Bayon, but fine at well-covered temples such as Ta Prohm, Preah Khan and Beng Mealea, or even the bas-reliefs at Angkor Wat. The busiest times at Angkor Wat are from 6am to 7am and 3pm to 5pm; at the Bayon, from 8am to 10am; and at Banteay Srei, mid-morning and mid-afternoon. However, at other popular temples, such as Ta Prohm and Preah Khan, the crowds are harder to predict, and at most other temples in the Angkor region it's just a case of pot luck. If you pull up outside and see a car park full of tour buses, you may want to move on to somewhere quieter. The wonderful thing about Angkor is that there is always another temple to explore.

foot in Siem Reap, but they often end up being knowledgeable and friendly, and good companions for a tour around the temples. Prices start at around US$10 per day. They can drop you off and pick you up at allotted times and places, and even tell you a bit of background about the temples as you zip around. Many of the better drivers go on to become official tour guides, although most have upgraded their *motos* to *remorks* these days.

REMORK-MOTO

Remork-motos, motorcycles with twee little hooded carriages towed behind, are more commonly known as *tuk tuks.* They are a popular way to get around Angkor as fellow travellers can still talk to each other as they explore (unlike on the

back of a *moto*). They also offer some protection from the rain. Some *remork* drivers are very good companions for a tour of the temples. Prices run from US$15 to US$25 for the day, depending on the destination and number of passengers.

WALKING

From Siem Reap, it's easy enough to walk to Angkor Wat and the temples of Angkor Thom, and this is a great way to meet up with villagers in the area. Those who want to get away from the roads should try the peaceful walk along the walls of Angkor Thom. It is about 13km in total, and offers access to several small, remote temples and some bird life. One way to save more time at the temples is to negotiate a drop-off and pick-up by *moto* or *remork* at Angkor Thom and

GUIDE TO THE GUIDEBOOKS

Countless books on Angkor have been written over the years, with more and more new titles coming out, reflecting Angkor's rebirth as the world's top cultural hot spot. Here are just a few of the best:

A Guide to the Angkor Monuments (Maurice Glaize) The definitive 1944 guide, downloadable for free at www.theangkorguide.com.

A Passage Through Angkor (Mark Standen) One of the best photographic records of the temples.

A Pilgrimage to Angkor (Pierre Loti) One of the most beautifully written books on Angkor, based on the author's 1910 journey.

Ancient Angkor (Claude Jacques) Written by one of the foremost scholars on Angkor, this is a very readable guide to the temples, with photos by Michael Freeman.

Angkor: An Introduction to the Temples (Dawn Rooney) Probably the most popular contemporary guide.

Angkor – Heart of an Asian Empire (Bruno Dagens) The story of the 'discovery' of Angkor, complete with lavish illustrations.

Angkor: Millennium of Glory (various authors) A fascinating introduction to the history, culture, sculpture and religion of the Angkorian period.

Khmer Heritage in the Old Siamese Provinces of Cambodia (Etienne Aymonier) Aymonier journeyed through Cambodia in 1901 and visited many of the major temples.

The Angkor Guide (Andrew Booth; www.angkorguidebook.com) Excellent guide to the temples of Angkor with input from leading academics, beautiful overlay illustrations and profits helping to fund education in Siem Reap.

The Customs of Cambodia (Chou Ta-Kuan) The only eyewitness account of Angkor, by a Chinese emissary who spent a year at the Khmer capital in the late 13th century.

explore on foot. Another rewarding walk is from Ta Keo to Ta Nei through the forest, but the best all-round jungle hike is to the 'River of a Thousand Lingas' at Kbal Spean.

ANGKOR WAT

The traveller's first glimpse of **Angkor Wat** (អង្គរវត្ត; incl in Angkor admission 1/3/7 days US$37/62/72; ⊙5am-5.30pm), the ultimate expression of Khmer genius, is matched by only a few select spots on earth. Built by Suryavarman II (r 1112–52) and surrounded by a vast moat, the temple is one of the most inspired monuments ever conceived by the human mind.

Angkor Wat is the heart and soul of Cambodia: it is the national symbol, the epicentre of Khmer civilisation and a source of fierce national pride. It was never abandoned to the elements and has been in virtually continuous use since it was built.

Simply unique, it is a stunning blend of spirituality and symmetry, an enduring example of humanity's devotion to its gods. Relish the very first approach, as that

spine-tingling moment when you emerge on the inner causeway will rarely be felt again. It is the best-preserved temple at Angkor, and repeat visits are rewarded with previously unnoticed details.

Allow at least two hours on-site for a visit to Angkor Wat and plan a half day if you want to decipher the bas-reliefs with a tour guide and ascend to Bakan, the upper level, which is open to visitors on a timed ticketing system.

Symbolism

There is much about Angkor Wat that is unique among the temples of Angkor. The most significant fact is that the temple is oriented towards the west. Symbolically, west is the direction of death, which once led many scholars to conclude that Angkor Wat must have existed primarily as a tomb. This idea was supported by the fact that the magnificent bas-reliefs of the temple were designed to be viewed in an anticlockwise direction, a practice that has precedents in ancient Hindu funerary rites. Vishnu, however, is also

Angkor Wat

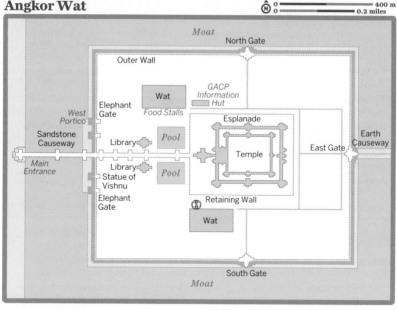

Moat

North Gate

Outer Wall

Wat

GACP Information Hut

West Portico

Elephant Gate

Food Stalls

Esplanade

Sandstone Causeway

Library

Pool

Temple

East Gate

Earth Causeway

Main Entrance

Library

Pool

Statue of Vishnu

Elephant Gate

Retaining Wall

Wat

South Gate

Moat

frequently associated with the west, and it is now commonly accepted that Angkor Wat most likely served both as a temple and as a mausoleum for Suryavarman II.

Visitors to Angkor Wat are struck by its imposing grandeur and, at close quarters, its fascinating decorative flourishes and extensive bas-reliefs. Holy men at the time of Angkor must have revelled in its multilayered levels of meaning in much the same way a contemporary literary scholar might delight in James Joyce's *Ulysses*.

Eleanor Mannikka explains in her book *Angkor Wat: Time, Space and Kingship* that the spatial dimensions of Angkor Wat parallel the lengths of the four ages (Yuga) of classical Hindu thought. Thus the visitor to Angkor Wat who walks the causeway to the main entrance and through the courtyards to the final main tower, which once contained a statue of Vishnu, is metaphorically travelling back to the first age of the creation of the universe.

Like the other temple-mountains of Angkor, Angkor Wat also replicates the spatial universe in miniature. The central tower is Mt Meru, with its surrounding smaller peaks, bounded in turn by continents (the lower courtyards) and the oceans (the moat). The seven-headed *naga* becomes a symbolic rainbow bridge for humanity to reach the abode of the gods.

While Suryavarman II may have planned Angkor Wat as his funerary temple or mausoleum, he was never buried there as he died in battle during a failed expedition to subdue the Dai Viet (Vietnamese).

Layout

Angkor Wat is surrounded by a 190m-wide moat, which forms a giant rectangle measuring 1.5km by 1.3km. From the west, a sandstone causeway crosses the moat. The sandstone blocks from which Angkor Wat was built were quarried more than 50km away (from the holy mountain of Phnom Kulen) and floated down the Siem Reap River on rafts. The logistics of such an operation are mind-blowing, consuming the labour of thousands – an unbelievable feat given the machinery we take for granted in contemporary construction projects. According to inscriptions, the construction of Angkor Wat involved 300,000 workers and 6000 elephants, yet it was still not fully completed.

The rectangular outer wall, which measures 1025m by 800m, has a gate on each side, but the main entrance, a 235m-wide porch richly decorated with carvings and sculptures, is on the western side. There is a statue of Vishnu, 3.25m in height and hewn from a single block of sandstone, located in the right-hand tower (it was originally housed in the central tower of the temple). Vishnu's eight arms hold a mace, a spear, a disc, a conch and other items. You may also see locks of hair lying about. These are offerings both from young people preparing to get married and from pilgrims giving thanks for their good fortune.

An avenue, 475m long and 9.5m wide and lined with *naga* balustrades, leads from the main entrance to the central temple, passing between two graceful libraries (restored by a Japanese team) and then two pools, the northern one a popular spot from which to watch the sun rise.

The central temple complex consists of three storeys, each made of laterite, which enclose a square surrounded by intricately interlinked galleries. The Gallery of a Thousand Buddhas (Preah Poan) used to house hundreds of Buddha images before the war, but many of these were removed or stolen, leaving just the handful we see today.

The corners of the second and third storeys are marked by towers, each topped with symbolic lotus-bud towers. The stairs to the upper level are immensely steep, because

reaching the kingdom of the gods was no easy task. Also known as Bakan, the upper level of Angkor Wat was closed to visitors for several years, but it is once again open (8am to 5pm daily, except religious holidays) to a limited number per day with a timed queuing system. This means it is once again possible to complete the pilgrimage with an ascent to the 55m summit: savour the cooling breeze, take in the extensive views and then find a quiet corner in which to contemplate the symmetry and symbolism of this Everest of temples. Clothing that covers to the elbows and knees is required to visit this upper level of Angkor Wat.

At the time of research, the western causeway was closed to visitors for an extensive renovation and access is via a floating pontoon, which has become something of a local tourist attraction in itself.

Bas-Reliefs

Stretching around the outside of the central temple complex is an 800m-long series of intricate and astonishing bas-reliefs. The majority were completed in the 12th century, but in the 16th century several new reliefs were added to unfinished panels.

Angkor Wat – Central Structure

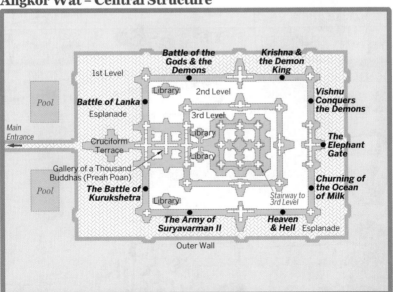

Temples of Angkor

Cambodia is the undisputed temple capital of Asia, and we're not just talking about the holiest of holies – the one and only Angkor Wat. Angkor is heaven on earth, but there are also temples dotted all over Siem Reap, the epicentre of the empire, that attest to the glories of Khmer civilisation.

STEPH PHOTOGRAPHIES/SHUTTERSTOCK ©

SIHASAKPRACHUM/SHUTTERSTOCK ©

1. Bayon (p155)

There are more than 210 faces of Cambodia's most celebrated king, Jayavarman VII, carved here.

2. Sra Srang (p160)

Only the stone base remains of the temple that once stood in this peaceful basin.

3. Ta Prohm (p159)

Jungle trees are entwined with temples at Angkor's most haunting ruin.

4. Banteay Srei (p167)

A Hindu temple with stunning stone carvings, known as the art gallery of Angkor.

LEVIN/SHUTTERSTOCK ©

THE APSARAS OF ANGKOR WAT

Angkor Wat is famous for its beguiling *apsaras* (heavenly nymphs). Almost 2000 *apsaras* are carved into the walls of Angkor Wat, each of them unique, and there are 37 different hairstyles for budding stylists to check out. Many of these exquisite *apsaras* have been damaged by centuries of bat droppings and urine, but they are now being restored by the **German Apsara Conservation Project** (GACP; www.gacp-angkor.de; ⊙ 7am-5pm). The organisation operates a small information booth in the northwestern corner of Angkor Wat, near the modern wat, where beautiful B&W postcards and images of Angkor are available.

The bas-reliefs at Angkor Wat were once sheltered by the cloister's wooden roof, which long ago rotted away except for one original beam in the western half of the north gallery. The other roofed sections are reconstructions.

Churning of the Ocean of Milk   BAS-RELIEF

The southern section of the east gallery is decorated by the most famous of the bas-relief scenes at Angkor Wat, the Churning of the Ocean of Milk. This brilliantly executed carving depicts 88 *asuras* on the left, and 92 *devas,* with crested helmets, churning up the sea to extract from it the elixir of immortality. The demons hold the head of the serpent Vasuki and the gods hold its tail. At the centre of the sea, Vasuki is coiled around Mt Mandala, which turns and churns up the water in the tug of war between the demons and the gods. Vishnu, incarnated as a huge turtle, lends his shell to serve as the base and pivot of Mt Mandala. Brahma, Shiva, Hanuman (the monkey god) and Lakshmi (the goddess of wealth and prosperity) all make appearances, while overhead a host of heavenly female spirits sing and dance in encouragement. Luckily for us, the gods won through, as the *apsaras* above were too much for the hot-blooded devils to take. Restoration work on this incredible panel by the World Monuments Fund (WMF) was completed in 2012.

The Army of Suryavarman II   BAS-RELIEF

The remarkable western section of the south gallery depicts a triumphal battle march of Suryavarman II's army. In the southwestern corner about 2m from the floor is Suryavar-man II on an elephant, wearing the royal tiara and armed with a battleaxe; he is shaded by 15 parasols and fanned by legions of servants.

Compare this image of the king with the image of Rama in the northern gallery and you'll notice an uncanny likeness that helped reinforce the aura of the god-king.

Further on is a procession of well-armed soldiers and officers on horseback; among them are bold and warlike chiefs on elephants. Just before the end of this panel is the rather disorderly Siamese mercenary army, with their long headdresses and ragged marching, at that time allied with the Khmers in their conflict with the Chams. The Khmer troops have square breastplates and are armed with spears; the Thais wear skirts and carry tridents.

The rectangular holes seen in the Army of Suryavarman II relief were created when, so the story goes, Thai soldiers removed pieces of the scene containing inscriptions that reportedly gave clues to the location of the golden treasures of Suryavarman II, later buried during the reign of Jayavarman VII.

The Battle of Kurukshetra   BAS-RELIEF

The southern portion of the west gallery depicts a battle scene from the Hindu *Mahabharata* epic, in which the Kauravas (coming from the north) and the Pandavas (coming from the south) advance upon each other, meeting in furious battle. Infantry are shown on the lowest tier, with officers on elephants, and chiefs on the second and third tiers.

Some of the more interesting details (from left to right): a dead chief lying on a pile of arrows, surrounded by his grieving parents and troops; a warrior on an elephant who, by putting down his weapon, has accepted defeat; and a mortally wounded officer, falling from his carriage into the arms of his soldiers. Over the centuries, some sections have been polished (by the millions of hands that fall upon them) to look like black marble. The portico at the southwestern corner is decorated with sculptures of characters from the *Ramayana*.

Heaven & Hell   BAS-RELIEF

The punishments and rewards of the 37 heavens and 32 hells are depicted in the eastern half of the south gallery. On the left, the upper and middle tiers show fine gentlemen and ladies proceeding towards 18-armed Yama (the judge of the dead) seated on a bull; below him are his assistants, Dharma and Sitragupta. On the lower tier, devils drag the wicked along the road to hell.

To Yama's right, the tableau is divided into two parts by a horizontal line of *garudas:* above, the elect dwell in beautiful mansions, served by women and attendants; below, the condemned suffer horrible tortures that might have inspired the Khmer Rouge. The ceiling in this section was restored by the French in the 1930s.

Battle of Lanka   BAS-RELIEF
The northern half of the west gallery shows scenes from the *Ramayana*. In the Battle of Lanka, Rama (on the shoulders of Hanuman), along with his army of monkeys, battles 10-headed, 20-armed Ravana, captor of Rama's beautiful wife Sita. Ravana rides a chariot drawn by monsters and commands an army of giants.

Battle of the Gods
& the Demons   BAS-RELIEF
The western section of the north gallery depicts the battle between the 21 gods of the Brahmanic pantheon and various demons. The gods are featured with their traditional attributes and mounts. Vishnu has four arms and is seated on a *garuda,* while Shiva rides a sacred goose.

Krishna & the Demon King   BAS-RELIEF
The eastern section of the north gallery shows Vishnu incarnated as Krishna riding a *garuda*. He confronts a burning walled city, the residence of Bana, the demon king. The *garuda* puts out the fire and Bana is captured. In the final scene Krishna kneels before Shiva and asks that Bana's life be spared.

Vishnu Conquers the Demons   BAS-RELIEF
The northern section of the east gallery shows a furious and desperate encounter between Vishnu, riding on a *garuda,* and innumerable devils. Needless to say, he slays all comers. This gallery was most likely completed in the 16th century, and the later carving is notably inferior to the original work from the 12th century.

The Elephant Gate   GATE
This gate, which has no stairway, was used by the king and others for mounting and dismounting elephants directly from the gallery. North of the gate is a Khmer inscription recording the erection of a nearby stupa in the 18th century.

✖ Eating

There is an extensive selection of restaurants lined up opposite the entrance to

Angkor Wat that includes several local eateries such as **Khmer Angkor Restaurant** (mains US$3-6; ⊘6am-6pm; 🔊) and **Angkor Reach Restaurant** (mains US$3-6; ⊘6am-6pm; 🔊). There is also a handy branch of **Blue Pumpkin** (www.bluepumpkin.asia; dishes US$2-8; ⊘7am-7pm; ❋🔊) turning out sandwiches, salads and ice creams, as well as divine fruit shakes, all to take away if required. Pricier **Chez Sophea** (✆012 858003; meals US$10-20; ⊘11am-10pm; 🔊) offers barbecued meat and fish, accompanied by a cracking homemade salad.

❶ Getting There & Away
There is a range of transport options from Siem Reap including *moto, remork-moto* and car. Cycling and walking are also possible.

ANGKOR THOM
It's hard to imagine any building bigger or more beautiful than Angkor Wat, but in Angkor Thom (Great City; អង្គរធំ) the sum of the parts add up to a greater whole. Set over 10 sq km, the aptly named last great capital of the Khmer empire took monumental to a whole new level.

Centred on Bayon, the surreal state temple of Jayavarman VII, Angkor Thom is enclosed by a formidable *jayagiri* (square wall) 8m high and 13km in length and encircled by a 100m-wide *jayasindhu* (moat) that would have stopped all but the hardiest invaders in their tracks. This architectural layout is an expression of Mt Meru surrounded by the oceans.

In the centre of the walled enclosure are the city's most important monuments, including Bayon, Baphuon, the Royal Enclosure, Phimeanakas and the Terrace of Elephants. Visitors should set aside a half-day to explore Angkor Thom in depth.

Angkor Thom was built in part as a reaction to the surprise sacking of Angkor by the Chams, after Jayavarman VII (r 1181–1219) decided that his empire would never again be vulnerable at home. At the city's height, it may have supported a population of one million people in the surrounding region.

The Gates of Angkor Thom
It is the gates that grab you first, flanked by a vast representation of the Churning of the Ocean of Milk, 54 demons and 54 gods

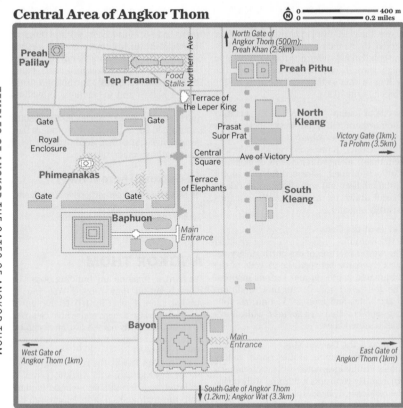

Central Area of Angkor Thom

0 — 400 m
0 — 0.2 miles

Preah Palilay

Tep Pranam

Food Stalls

Northern Ave

North Gate of Angkor Thom (500m); Preah Khan (2.5km)

Preah Pithu

Terrace of the Leper King

Prasat Suor Prat

North Kleang

Victory Gate (1km); Ta Prohm (3.5km)

Gate   Gate

Royal Enclosure

Central Square

Ave of Victory

Phimeanakas

Gate   Gate

Terrace of Elephants

South Kleang

Baphuon

Main Entrance

Bayon

Main Entrance

West Gate of Angkor Thom (1km)

East Gate of Angkor Thom (1km)

South Gate of Angkor Thom (1.2km); Angkor Wat (3.3km)

engaged in an epic tug of war on the causeway. Each gate towers above the visitor, the magnanimous faces of the Bodhisattva Avalokiteshvara staring out over the kingdom. Imagine being a peasant in the 13th century approaching the forbidding capital for the first time. It would have been an awe-inspiring, yet unsettling, experience to enter such a gateway and come face to face with the divine power of the god-kings.

The **south gate** is most popular with visitors, as it has been fully restored and many of the heads (mostly copies) remain in place. The gate is on the main road into Angkor Thom from Angkor Wat, and it gets very busy. More peaceful are the east and west gates, found at the end of dirt trails. The **east gate** was used as a location in *Lara Croft: Tomb Raider,* where the bad guys broke into the 'tomb' by pulling down a giant polystyrene *apsara.* The causeway at the **west gate** of Angkor Thom has completely

collapsed, leaving a jumble of ancient stones sticking out of the soil, like victims of a terrible historical pile-up.

Eating

There are no formal restaurants within the walls of Angkor Thom, but there are dozens of local noodle stalls just north of the Terrace of the Leper King that work well for a quick bite to eat.

Getting There & Away

If coming from Angkor Wat, you'll enter Angkor Thom through the south gate. From Ta Prohm, you'll enter through the Victory Gate on the eastern side. The immense north gate of Angkor Thom connects the walled city with Preah Khan and the temples of the Grand Circuit. The west gate leads to the Western Baray.

There is a range of transport options from Siem Reap including bicycle, *moto, remork-moto* and car.

Bayon

At the heart of Angkor Thom is the 12th-century **Bayon** (បាយ័ន; ⊘ 7.30am-5.30pm), the mesmerising, if slightly mind-bending, state temple of Jayavarman VII. It epitomises the creative genius and inflated ego of Cambodia's most celebrated king. Its 54 Gothic towers are decorated with 216 gargantuan smiling faces of Avalokiteshvara, and it is adorned with 1.2km of extraordinary bas-reliefs incorporating more than 11,000 figures.

The temple's eastward orientation leads most people to visit in the morning, but Bayon looks equally good in late afternoon.

Unique, even among its cherished contemporaries, the architectural audacity was a definitive political statement about the change from Hinduism to Mahayana Buddhism. Known as the 'face temple' thanks to its iconic visages, these huge heads glare down from every angle, exuding power and control with a hint of humanity. This was precisely the blend required to hold sway over such a vast empire, ensuring the disparate and far-flung population yielded to his magnanimous will. As you walk around, a dozen or more of the heads are visible at any one time, full face or in profile, sometimes level with your eyes, sometimes staring down from on high.

Though Bayon is now known to have been built by Jayavarman VII, for many years its origins were unknown. Shrouded in dense jungle, it also took researchers some time to realise that it stands in the exact centre of the city of Angkor Thom. There is still much mystery associated with Bayon – such as its exact function and symbolism – and this seems only appropriate for a monument whose signature is an enigmatic smiling face.

Unlike Angkor Wat, which looks impressive from all angles, Bayon looks rather like a glorified pile of rubble from a distance. It's only when you enter the temple and make your way up to the third level that its magic becomes apparent.

The basic structure of Bayon comprises a simple three levels, which correspond more or less to three distinct phases of building. This is because Jayavarman VII began construction of this temple at an advanced age, so he was never confident it would be completed. Each time one phase was completed, he moved on to the next. The first two levels are square and adorned with bas-reliefs. They lead up to a third, circular level, with the towers and their faces.

Some say that the Khmer empire was divided into 54 provinces at the time of Bayon's construction, hence the 54 pairs of

Bayon

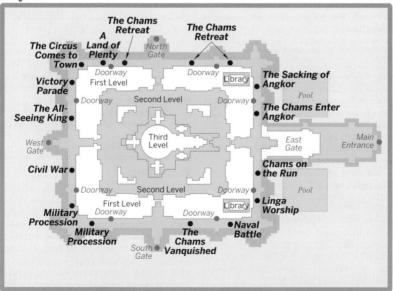

all-seeing eyes keeping watch on the kingdom's outlying subjects.

The famous carvings on the outer wall of the first level depict vivid scenes of everyday life in 12th-century Cambodia. The bas-reliefs on the second level do not have the epic proportions of those on the first level and tend to be fragmented. The reliefs described are those on the first level. The sequence assumes that you enter the Bayon from the east and view the reliefs in a clockwise direction.

Moving in a clockwise direction from just south of the east gate you'll encounter your first bas-relief, Chams on the Run, a three-level panorama. On the first tier, Khmer soldiers march off to battle – check out the elephants and the oxcarts, which are almost exactly like those still used in Cambodia today. The second tier depicts coffins being carried back from the battlefield. In the centre of the third tier, Jayavarman VII, shaded by parasols, is shown on horseback followed by legions of concubines (to the left).

Moving on, the first panel north of the southeastern corner, shows Hindus praying to a linga (phallic symbol). This image was probably originally a Buddha, later modified by a Hindu king.

The Naval Battle panel has some of the best-carved reliefs. The scenes depict a naval battle between the Khmers and the Chams (the latter with head coverings), and everyday life around the Tonlé Sap lake, where the battle was fought. Look for images of people picking lice from each other's hair, of hunters and, towards the western end of the panel, a woman giving birth.

In the Chams Vanquished, scenes from daily life are featured while the battle between the Khmers and the Chams takes place on the shore of Tonlé Sap lake, where the Chams are soundly thrashed. Scenes include two people playing chess, a cockfight and women selling fish in the market. The scenes of meals being prepared and served are in celebration of the Khmer victory.

The most western relief of the south gallery, depicting a military procession, is unfinished, as is the panel showing elephants being led down from the mountains. Brahmans have been chased up two trees by tigers.

The next panel depicts scenes that some scholars maintain is a civil war. Groups of people, some armed, confront each other, and the violence escalates until elephants and warriors join the melee.

Just north of the civil war panel, the fighting continues on a smaller scale in the All-Seeing King. An antelope is being swallowed by a gargantuan fish; among the smaller fish is a prawn, under which an inscription proclaims that the king will seek out those in hiding.

The next panel depicts a procession that includes the king (carrying a bow). Presumably it is a celebration of his victory.

At the western corner of the northern wall is a Khmer circus. A strongman holds three dwarfs, and a man on his back is spinning a wheel with his feet; above is a group of tightrope walkers. To the right of the circus, the royal court watches from a terrace, below which is a procession of animals. Some of the reliefs in this section remain unfinished.

In A Land of Plenty, two rivers – one next to the doorpost and the other a few metres to the right – are teeming with fish.

On the lowest level of the unfinished three-tiered Chams Defeat, the Cham armies are being defeated and expelled from the Khmer kingdom. The next panel depicts the Cham armies advancing, and the badly deteriorated panel shows the Chams (on the left) chasing the Khmers.

The Sacking of Angkor shows the war of 1177, when the Khmers were defeated by the Chams, and Angkor was pillaged. The wounded Khmer king is being lowered into the back of an elephant and a wounded Khmer general is being carried on a hammock suspended from a pole. Directly above, despairing Khmers are getting drunk. The Chams (on the right) are in hot pursuit of their vanquished enemy.

The next panel, the Chams Enter Angkor, depicts a meeting of the Khmer and Cham armies. Notice the flag bearers among the Cham troops (on the right). The Chams were defeated in the war, which ended in 1181, as depicted on the first panel in the sequence.

Baphuon

Some have called Baphuon (បាពួន; ⊙ 7.30am-5.30pm) the 'world's largest jigsaw puzzle'. Before the civil war the Baphuon was painstakingly taken apart piece-by-piece by a team of archaeologists, but their meticulous records were destroyed during the Khmer Rouge regime, leaving experts with 300,000 stones to put back into place. After years of excruciating research, this

TREKKING AROUND ANGKOR THOM

Spread over a vast area of the steamy tropical lowlands of Cambodia, the temples of Angkor aren't always the ideal candidates to tackle on foot. However, the area is blanketed in mature forest, offering plenty of shade, and following back roads into temples is the perfect way to leave the crowds behind.

Angkor Thom (p153) is the top trekking spot thanks to its manageable size and plenty of rewarding temples within its walls. Starting out at the spectacular south gate (p154), admire the immense representation of the Churning of the Ocean of Milk before bidding farewell to the masses and their motorised transport. Ascend the wall of this ancient city and then head west, enjoying views of the vast moat to the left and the thick jungle to the right. It is often possible to see forest birds along this route, as it is very peaceful. Reaching the southwestern corner, admire **Prasat Chrung**, one of four identical temples marking the corners of the city. Head down below to see the water outlet of **Run Ta Dev**. In its heyday this once powerful city was criss-crossed by canals.

Back on the gargantuan wall, continue to the west gate, looking out for a view to the immense Western Baray on your left. Descend at the west gate (p154) and admire the artistry of the central tower. Wander east along the path into the heart of Angkor Thom, but don't be diverted by the beauty of Bayon, as this is best saved until last. If you are with a tour guide you will have to travel this first and follow the designated running order, but independent travellers can plot their own course.

Veer north into Baphuon (p152) and wander to the back of what some have called the 'world's largest jigsaw puzzle'. Pass the small temple of Phimeanakas (p154) and the former royal palace compound, an area of towering trees, tumbling walls and atmospheric foliage. Continue further north to petite but pretty Preah Palilay (p158), overshadowed by an impressive cluster of kapok trees.

It's time to make for the mainstream with a walk through the Terrace of the Leper King (p157) and along the front of the royal viewing gallery, the Terrace of Elephants (p153). If there's time, you may want to zigzag east to visit the laterite towers of Prasat Suor Prat (p155) and the atmospheric Buddhist temple of Preah Pithu (p158). Otherwise, continue to the top billing of Bayon (p155): weird yet wonderful, this is one of the most enigmatic of the temples at Angkor. Take your time to decipher the bas-reliefs before venturing up to the legendary faces of the upper level.

temple has been partially restored. In the 16th century, the retaining wall on the western side of the second level was fashioned into a 60m reclining Buddha.

In its heyday, Baphuon would have been one of the most spectacular of Angkor's temples. Located 200m northwest of Bayon, it's a pyramidal representation of mythical Mt Meru. Construction probably began under Suryavarman I and was later completed by Udayadityavarman II. It marked the centre of the capital that existed before the construction of Angkor Thom.

The site is approached by a 200m elevated walkway made of sandstone, and the central structure is 43m high. Clamber under the elevated causeway for an incredible view of the hundreds of pillars supporting it.

It takes around one hour to fully explore Baphuon, although it is possible to have a faster visit if you skip the upper levels.

Terrace of the Leper King

The Terrace of the Leper King (ទីលានព្រះគម្លង់; ⊘7.30am-5.30pm) is just north of the Terrace of Elephants. Dating from the late 12th century, it is a 7m-high platform, on top of which stands a nude, though sexless, statue. The front retaining walls of the terrace are decorated with at least five tiers of meticulously executed carvings. On the southern side of the Terrace of the Leper King, there is access to a hidden terrace with exquisitely preserved carvings.

The aforementioned statue is yet another of Angkor's mysteries. The original of the statue is held at Phnom Penh's National Museum, and various theories have been advanced to explain its meaning. Legend has it that at least two of the Angkor kings had leprosy, and the statue may represent one of them. Another theory – a more likely explanation – is that the statue is of Yama, the god of death, and that the Terrace of the Leper King housed the royal crematorium.

The carved walls include seated *apsaras*, kings wearing pointed diadems, armed with short double-edged swords and accompanied by the court and princesses, the latter adorned with beautiful rows of pearls.

On the southern side of the Terrace of the Leper King (facing the Terrace of Elephants), there is access to the front wall of a hidden terrace that was covered up when the outer structure was built, a sort of terrace within a terrace. The four tiers of *apsaras* and other figures, including *nagas,* look as fresh as if they had been carved yesterday, thanks to being covered up for centuries. Some of the figures carry fearsome expressions. As you follow the inner wall of the Terrace of the Leper King, notice the increasingly rough chisel marks on the figures, an indication that this wall was never completed, like many of the temples at Angkor.

Terrace of Elephants

The 350m-long **Terrace of Elephants** (ទីលានដំរី; ⊙ 7.30am-5pm) was used as a giant viewing stand for public ceremonies and served as a base for the king's grand audience hall. Try to imagine the pomp and grandeur of the Khmer empire at its height, with infantry, cavalry, horse-drawn chariots and elephants parading across Central Square in a colourful procession. Looking on is the god-king, shaded by multi-tiered parasols and attended by mandarins and handmaidens bearing gold and silver utensils.

The Terrace of Elephants has five piers extending towards the Central Square – three in the centre and one at each end. The middle section of the retaining wall is decorated with life-size *garudas* and lions; towards either end are the two parts of the famous parade of elephants, complete with their Khmer mahouts.

Preah Palilay

Preah Palilay (ព្រះបាលិល័យ; ⊙ 7.30am-5.30pm) is located about 200m north of the Royal Enclosure's northern wall. It was erected during the rule of Jayavarman VII and originally housed a Buddha, which has long since vanished. There are several huge tree roots looming large over the central tower making for a memorable photo opportunity of a classic 'jungle temple'.

Royal Enclosure & Phimeanakas

Phimeanakas (ភិមានអាកាស; ⊙ 7.30am-5pm) stands close to the centre of a walled area that once housed the royal palace. There's very little left of the palace today except for two sandstone pools near the northern wall. Phimeanakas means 'Celestial Palace', and some scholars say that it was once topped by a golden spire. It is currently undergoing restoration and the upper level is off-limits to visitors.

Construction of the palace began under Rajendravarman II, although it was used by Jayavarman V and Udayadityavarman I. It was later added to and embellished by Jayavarman VII and his successors. The royal enclosure is fronted to the east by the Terrace of Elephants. The northwestern wall of the Royal Enclosure is very atmospheric, with immense trees and jungle vines cloaking the outer side, easily visible on a forest walk from Preah Palilay to Phimeanakas.

The temple is another pyramidal representation of Mt Meru, with three levels. Most of the decorative features are broken or have disappeared.

Preah Pithu

Preah Pithu (ព្រះពិធូ; ⊙ 7.30am-5.30pm), located across Northern Ave from Tep Pranam, is a group of 12th-century Hindu and Buddhist temples enclosed by a wall. It includes some beautifully decorated terraces and guardian animals in the form of elephants and lions. It sees few tourists so is a good place to explore at a leisurely pace, taking in the impressive jungle backdrop.

Kleangs & Prasat Suor Prat

Along the eastern side of Central Square are two groups of buildings, called **Kleangs** (ប្រាសាទឃ្លាំង និងប្រាសាទសួរព្រ័ត; ⊙ 7.30am-5pm). The North Kleang, dated from the period of Jayavarman V, and the South Kleang may at one time have been palaces. Along Central Square in front of the two Kleangs are 12 laterite towers – 10 in a row and two more at right angles facing the Ave of Victory – known as the Prasat Suor Prat, meaning 'Temple of the Tightrope Dancers'.

Archaeologists believe the towers, which form an honour guard, were constructed by

Jayavarman VII. It is likely that each one originally contained either a *linga* or a statue. It is said artists performed for the king on tightropes or rope bridges strung between these towers, hence the name.

According to 13th-century Chinese emissary Chou Ta-Kuan, the towers of Prasat Suor Prat were also used for public trials of sorts. During a dispute the two parties would be made to sit inside two towers, one party eventually succumbing to illness and proven guilty.

Tep Pranam

Tep Pranam (ទេពប្រណម្យ; ⊙ 7.30am-5.30pm), an 82m by 34m cruciform Buddhist terrace 150m east of Preah Palilay, was once the base of a pagoda. Nearby is a 4.5m-high Buddha, a reconstruction of the original. A group of Buddhist nuns lives in a wooden structure close by.

AROUND ANGKOR THOM

Small Circuit

The 17km Small Circuit begins at Angkor Wat and heads north to Phnom Bakheng, Baksei Chamkrong and Angkor Thom, including the city wall and gates, the Bayon, the Baphuon, the Royal Enclosure, Phimeanakas, Preah Palilay, the Terrace of the Leper King, the Terrace of Elephants, the Kleangs and Prasat Suor Prat. It exits from Angkor Thom via the Victory Gate in the eastern wall, and continues to Chau Say Tevoda, Thommanon, Spean Thmor and Ta Keo. It then heads northeast of the road to Ta Nei, turns south to Ta Prohm, continues east to Banteay Kdei and Sra Srang, and finally returns to Angkor Wat via Prasat Kravan.

Ta Prohm

The so-called 'Tomb Raider Temple', **Ta Prohm** (តាព្រហ្ម; ⊙ 7.30am-5.30pm) is cloaked in dappled shadow, its crumbling towers and walls locked in the slow muscular embrace of vast root systems. Undoubtedly the most atmospheric ruin at Angkor, Ta Prohm should be high on the hit list of every visitor. Its appeal lies in the fact that, unlike the other monuments of Angkor, it has been swallowed by the jungle, and looks very much the way most of the monuments

of Angkor appeared when European explorers first stumbled upon them.

Well, that's the theory, but in fact the jungle is pegged back and only the largest trees are left in place, making it manicured rather than raw like Beng Mealea. Still, a visit to Ta Prohm is a unique, other-worldly experience. There is a poetic cycle to this venerable ruin, with humanity first conquering nature to rapidly create, and nature once again conquering humanity to slowly destroy. If Angkor Wat is testimony to the genius of the ancient Khmers, Ta Prohm reminds us equally of the awesome fecundity and power of the jungle.

Built from 1186 and originally known as Rajavihara (Monastery of the King), Ta Prohm was a Buddhist temple dedicated to the mother of Jayavarman VII. It is one of the few temples in the Angkor region where an inscription provides information about the temple's dependents and inhabitants. Almost 80,000 people were required to maintain or attend at the temple, among them more than 2700 officials and 615 dancers.

Ta Prohm is a temple of towers, closed courtyards and narrow corridors. Many of the corridors are impassable, clogged with jumbled piles of delicately carved stone blocks dislodged by the roots of long-decayed trees. Bas-reliefs on bulging walls are carpeted with lichen, moss and creeping plants, and shrubs sprout from the roofs of monumental porches. Trees, hundreds of years old, tower overhead, their leaves filtering the sunlight and casting a greenish pall over the whole scene.

The most popular of the many strangulating root formations is the one on the inside of the easternmost *gopura* (entrance pavilion) of the central enclosure, nicknamed the Crocodile Tree. One of the most famous spots in Ta Prohm is the so-called 'Tomb Raider tree', where Angelina Jolie's Lara Croft picked a jasmine flower before falling through the earth into...Pinewood Studios.

It used to be possible to climb onto the damaged galleries, but this is now prohibited, to protect both temple and visitor. Many of these precariously balanced stones weigh a tonne or more and would do some serious damage if they came down. Ta Prohm is currently under stabilisation and restoration by an Indian team of archaeologists working with their Cambodian counterparts.

The temple is at its most impressive early in the day. Allow as much as two hours to

Ta Prohm

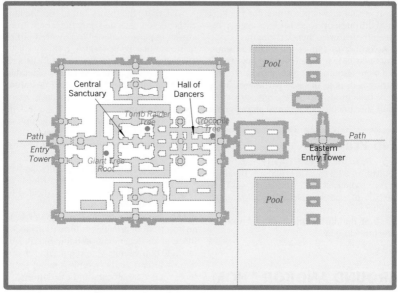

Pool

Central Sanctuary

Hall of Dancers

Tomb Raider Tree

Crocodile Tree

Path

Entry Tower

Giant Tree Root

Path

Eastern Entry Tower

Pool

visit, especially if you want to explore the maze-like corridors and iconic tree roots.

Banteay Kdei & Sra Srang

Banteay Kdei (បន្ទាយក្តីនិងស្រះស្រង់; ⊘ 7.30am-5.30pm), a massive Buddhist monastery from the latter part of the 12th century, is surrounded by four concentric walls. Each of its four entrances is decorated with *garudas,* which hold aloft one of Jayavarman VII's favourite themes: the four faces of Avalokiteshvara. East of Banteay Kdei is a vast pool of water, Sra Srang, measuring 800m by 400m, reserved as a bathing pool for the king and his consorts.

The outer wall of Banteay Kdei measures 500m by 700m. The inside of the central tower was never finished and much of the temple is in a ruinous state due to hasty construction. It is considerably less busy than nearby Ta Prohm and this alone can justify a visit.

A tiny island in the middle of Sra Srang once bore a wooden temple, of which only the stone base remains. This is a beautiful body of water from which to take in a quiet sunrise.

Allow about one hour to visit Banteay Kdei and admire the view over nearby Sra Srang. There are lots of good Cambodian restaurants lining the road along the north

side of Sra Srang and these make a good stop for lunch for those not planning to return to Siem Reap during the day.

Phnom Bakheng

Located around 400m south of Angkor Thom, the main attraction at **Phnom Bakheng** (ភ្នំបាខែង; ⊘ 5am-7pm) is the sunset view over Angkor Wat. For many years, the whole affair turned into a circus, with crowds of tourists ascending the slopes of the hill and jockeying for space. Numbers are now restricted to just 300 visitors at any one time, so get here early (4pm) to guarantee a sunset spot. The temple, built by Yasovarman I (r 889–910), has seven tiers, with seven levels.

Phnom Bakheng lays claim to being home to the first of the temple-mountains built in the vicinity of Angkor. Yasovarman I chose Phnom Bakheng over the Roluos area, where the earlier capital (and temple-mountains) had been located.

At the base are – or were – 44 towers. Each of the five tiers had 12 towers. The summit of the temple has four towers at the cardinal points of the compass as well as a central sanctuary. All of these numbers are of symbolic significance. The seven levels represent the seven Hindu heavens, while the total number of towers, excluding the central sanctuary, is 108, a particularly auspicious number and one that correlates to the lunar calendar.

Some prefer to visit in the early morning, when it's cool (and crowds are light), to climb the hill. That said, the sunset over the Western Baray is very impressive from here. Allow about two hours for the sunset experience.

To get a decent picture of Angkor Wat in the warm glow of the late-afternoon sun from the summit of Phnom Bakheng, you will need at least a 300mm lens, as the temple is 1.3km away.

Ta Keo

Ta Keo (តាកេវ; ⊙7.30am-5.30pm) is a stark, undecorated temple that undoubtedly would have been one of the finest of Angkor's structures, had it been finished. Built by Jayavarman V, it was dedicated to Shiva and was the first Angkorian monument built entirely of sandstone. The summit of the central tower, which is surrounded by four lower towers, is almost 50m high. The four towers at the corners of a square and a fifth tower in the centre is typical of many Angkorian temple-mountains.

No one is certain why work was never completed, but a likely cause may have been the death of Jayavarman V. Others contend that the hard sandstone was impossible to carve and that explains the lack of decoration. According to inscriptions, Ta Keo was struck by lightning during construction, which may have been a bad omen and led to its abandonment. Allow about 30 minutes to visit Ta Keo.

ON LOCATION WITH TOMB RAIDER

Several sequences for the film *Lara Croft: Tomb Raider* (2001), starring Angelina Jolie as Lara Croft, were shot around the temples of Angkor. The Cambodia shoot opened at Phnom Bakheng, with Lara looking through binoculars for the mysterious temple. The baddies were already trying to break in through the east gate of Angkor Thom by pulling down a giant (polystyrene!) *apsara*. Reunited with her custom Land Rover, Lara made a few laps around Bayon before discovering a back way into the temple from Ta Prohm. After battling a living statue and dodging Daniel Craig (aka 007) by diving off the waterfall at Phnom Kulen, she emerged in a floating market in front of Angkor Wat, as you do. She came ashore here before borrowing a mobile phone from a local monk and venturing into the Gallery of a Thousand Buddhas, where she was healed by the abbot.

Ta Nei

Ta Nei (តានៃ; ⊙7.30am-5.30pm), 800m north of Ta Keo, was built by Jayavarman VII (r 1181–1219). There is something of the spirit of Ta Prohm here, albeit on a lesser scale, with moss and tentacle-like roots covering many outer areas of this small temple. However, the number of visitors are also on a lesser scale, making it very atmospheric.

Phnom Bakheng

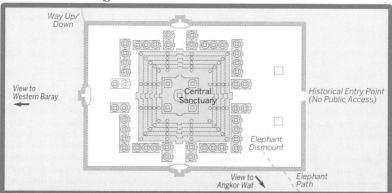

It can be accessed via a jungle road from Ta Keo through the forest, a guaranteed way to leave the crowds behind. Including the access, allow about one hour to visit Ta Nei.

Chau Say Tevoda

Just east of Angkor Thom's Victory Gate is **Chau Say Tevoda** (ចៅសាយទេវតា; ⊙7.30am-5.30pm). It was probably built during the second quarter of the 12th century, under the reign of Suryavarman II, and dedicated to Shiva and Vishnu. It has been renovated by the Chinese to bring it up to the condition of its twin temple, Thommanon.

Thommanon

Just north of Chau Say Tevoda, **Thommanon** (ធម្មនន្ទ; ⊙7.30am-5.30pm) borrows many features from Angkor Wat and was dedicated to Shiva and Vishnu. The small temple is in good condition thanks to extensive work undertaken by the EFEO in the 1960s. It is regularly used for high-end gala dinners by VIP visitors.

DON'T MISS

ANGKOR ZIPLINE

Angkor provides the ultimate backdrop for this zipline experience, although you won't actually see the temples while navigating the course. Formerly Flight of the Gibbon Angkor, the **Angkor Zipline** (☑096 999 9100; www.angkorzipline.com; short/full course US$60/100; ⊙6am-5pm) is located inside the Angkor protected area. The course includes 10 ziplines, 21 treetop platforms, four skybridges and an abseil finish. There is a panoramic rest stop halfway and highlights include a tandem line for couples.

Safety is a priority and high-flyers are permanently clipped to lines via karabiners, with clear English instruction throughout. There is also a conservation element to the project with a resident gibbon family living in the forest here. The price includes a minivan transfer to/from town, plus lunch before or after the zipline. It is located near Ta Nei temple, so those with a temple pass might want to build in a visit. You do not require a temple pass to enjoy the zipline experience.

Spean Thmor

Spean Thmor (ស្ពានថ្ម, Stone Bridge), of which an arch and several piers remain, is 200m east of Thommanon. Jayavarman VII constructed many roads with these immense stone bridges spanning watercourses. This is the only large bridge remaining in the immediate vicinity of Angkor. It vividly highlights how the water level has changed course over the centuries and may offer another clue to the collapse of Angkor's extensive irrigation system. Just north of Spean Thmor is a large water wheel.

There are more-spectacular examples of these ancient bridges elsewhere in Siem Reap Province, such as Spean Preah Tuos, with 19 arches, in Kompong Kdei on NH6 from Phnom Penh; and Spean Ta Ong, a 77m bridge with a beautiful *naga,* forgotten in the forest about 28km east of Beng Mealea.

Baksei Chamkrong

Located southwest of the south gate of Angkor Thom, **Baksei Chamkrong** (បក្សីចាំក្រុង; ⊙7.30am-5.30pm) is one of the few brick edifices in the immediate vicinity of Angkor. A well-proportioned though petite temple, it was once decorated with a covering of lime mortar. Like virtually all of the structures of Angkor, it opens to the east. In the early 10th century, Harshavarman I erected five statues in this temple: two of Shiva, one of Vishnu and two of Devi.

Big Circuit

The 26km Big Circuit is an extension of the Small Circuit: instead of exiting the walled city of Angkor Thom at the east gate, the Grand Circuit exits at the north gate and continues to Preah Khan and Preah Neak Poan, east to Ta Som, then south via the Eastern Mebon to Pre Rup. From there it heads west and then southwest on its return to Angkor Wat.

Preah Khan

The temple of **Preah Khan** (ប្រះខ័ន្ទ; Sacred Sword; ⊙7.30am-5.30pm) is one of the largest complexes at Angkor, a maze of vaulted corridors, fine carvings and lichen-clad stonework. It is a good counterpoint to Ta Prohm and generally sees slightly fewer visitors. Like Ta Prohm it is a place of towered enclosures and shoulder-hugging corridors. Unlike Ta Prohm, however, the temple of Preah

Preah Khan

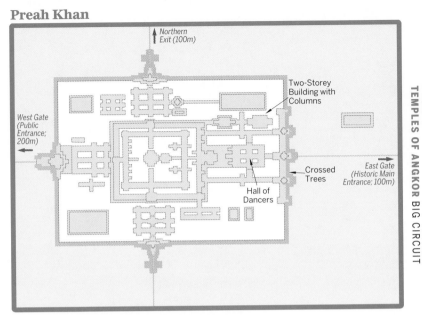

Khan is in a reasonable state of preservation thanks to the ongoing restoration efforts of the World Monuments Fund (WMF).

Preah Khan was built by Jayavarman VII and probably served as his temporary residence while Angkor Thom was being built. The central sanctuary of the temple was dedicated in AD 1191.

A large stone stela tells us much about Preah Khan's role as a centre for worship and learning. Originally located within the first eastern enclosure, this stela is now housed safely at Angkor Conservation (p99) in Siem Reap. The temple was dedicated to 515 divinities, and during the course of a year, 18 major festivals took place here, requiring a team of thousands just to maintain the place.

Preah Khan covers a very large area, but the temple itself is within a rectangular enclosing wall of around 700m by 800m. Four processional walkways approach the gates of the temple, and these are bordered by another stunning depiction of the Churning of the Ocean of Milk, as in the approach to Angkor Thom, although most of the heads have disappeared. From the central sanctuary, vaulted galleries extend in the cardinal directions. Many of the interior walls were once coated with plaster that was held in place by holes in the stone. Today many

delicate reliefs remain, including *rishi* and *apsara* carvings.

A genuine fusion temple, the eastern entrance is dedicated to Mahayana Buddhism with equal-sized doors, and the other cardinal directions dedicated to Shiva, Vishnu and Brahma with successively smaller doors, emphasising the unequal nature of Hinduism.

The main entrance to Preah Khan is in the east, but most tourists enter at the west gate near the main road, walk the length of the temple to the east gate before doubling back to the central sanctuary and exiting at the north gate. Approaching from the west, there is little clue to nature's genius, but on the outer retaining wall of the east gate is a pair of trees with monstrous roots embracing, one still reaching for the sky. There is also a curious Grecian-style two-storey structure in the temple grounds, the purpose of which is unknown, but it looks like an exile from Athens. Another option is to enter from the north and exit from the east. Given its vast size, it is sensible to set aside at least 1½ to two hours to explore this temple.

Preah Neak Poan

The Buddhist temple of **Preah Neak Poan** (ព្រះនាគព័ន្ធ, Temple of the Intertwined Nagas; ⊙7.30am-5.30pm) is a petite yet perfect

Preah Neak Poan

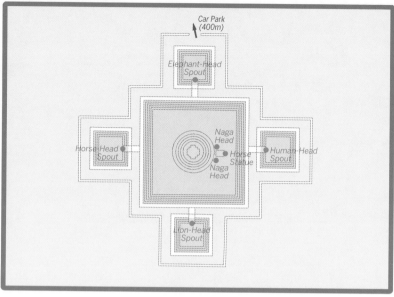

temple constructed by Jayavarman VII in the late 12th century. It has a large square pool surrounded by four smaller square pools. In the middle of the central pool is a circular 'island' encircled by the two *nagas* whose intertwined tails give the temple its name.

It's a safe bet that if an 'Encore Angkor' casino is eventually developed in Las Vegas or Macau, Preah Neak Poan will provide the blueprint for the ultimate swimming complex.

In the pool around the central island there were once four statues, but only one remains, reconstructed from the debris by the French archaeologists who cleared the site. The curious figure has the body of a horse supported by a tangle of human legs. It relates to a legend that Avalokiteshvara once saved a group of shipwrecked followers from an island of ghouls by transforming into a flying horse. A beautiful replica of this statue decorates the main roundabout at Siem Reap International Airport.

Water once flowed from the central pool into the four peripheral pools via ornamental spouts, which can still be seen in the pavilions at each axis of the pool. The spouts are in the form of an elephant's head, a horse's head, a lion's head and a human head. The pool was used for ritual purification rites.

Preah Neak Poan was once in the centre of a huge 3km-by-900m *baray* serving Preah Khan, known as Jayatataka, once again partially filled with water. Access is restricted to the edge of the complex via a wooden causeway, so a visit takes only 30 minutes.

Ta Som

Standing to the east of Preah Neak Poan, **Ta Som** (តាសោម; ☺ 7.30am-5.30pm) is one of the late-12th-century Buddhist temples of prolific builder Jayavarman VII. The most impressive feature at Ta Som is the huge tree completely overwhelming the eastern *gopura,* which provides one of the most popular photo opportunities in the Angkor area.

Eastern Baray & Eastern Mebon

Eastern Mebon (☺ 7.30am-5.30pm) is a Hindu temple, erected by Rajendravarman II, would once have been situated on an islet in the centre of the Eastern Baray (p160), but it is now very much on dry land. Its temple-mountain form is topped off by a quintet of towers. The elaborate brick shrines are dotted with neatly arranged holes, which attached the original plasterwork. The base of the temple is guarded at its corners by perfectly carved stone figures of elephants.

The Eastern Mebon is flanked by earthen ramps, a clue that this temple was never finished and a good visual guide to how the temples were constructed.

The enormous one-time reservoir known as the Eastern Baray was excavated by Yasovarman I, who marked its four corners with stelae. This basin, now entirely dried up, was the most important of the public works of Yasodharapura, Yasovarman I's capital, and is 7km by 1.8km. It was originally fed by the Siem Reap River.

Pre Rup

Built by Rajendravarman II, **Pre Rup** (ប្រែរូប; ⊙ 5am-7pm) is about 1km south of the Eastern Mebon and is a popular spot for sunset. The temple consists of a pyramid-shaped temple-mountain with the uppermost of the three tiers carrying five lotus towers. Pre Rup means 'Turning the Body' and refers to a traditional method of cremation in which a corpse's outline is traced in the cinders: this suggests that the temple may have served as an early royal crematorium.

The brick sanctuaries here were once decorated with a plaster coating, fragments of which remain on the southwestern tower; there are some amazingly detailed lintel carvings here. Several of the outermost eastern towers are perilously close to collapse and are propped up by an army of wooden supports.

Pre Rup is one of the most popular sunset spots around Angkor, as the view over the surrounding rice fields of the Eastern Baray is beautiful. It gets pretty crowded.

Prasat Kravan

Uninspiring from the outside, the interior brick carvings concealed within its towers are the hidden treasure of **Prasat Kravan** (ប្រាសាទក្រវ៉ាន់; ⊙ 7.30am-5.30pm). The five brick towers, arranged in a north–south line and oriented to the east, were built for Hindu worship in AD 921. The structure is unusual in that it was not constructed by royalty; this accounts for its slightly distant location, away from the other temples. Prasat Kravan is just south of the road between Angkor Wat and Banteay Kdei.

Prasat Kravan was partially restored in 1968, returning the brick carvings to their former glory. The images of Vishnu in the largest central tower show the eight-armed deity on the back wall, taking the three gigantic steps with which he reclaimed the world

THE LONG STRIDER

One of Vishnu's best-loved incarnations was when he appeared as the dwarf Vamana, and proceeded to reclaim the world from the evil demon king Bali. The dwarf politely asked the demon king for a comfortable patch of ground upon which to meditate, saying that the patch need only be big enough so that he could easily walk across it in three paces. The demon agreed, only to see the dwarf swell into a mighty giant who strode across the universe in three enormous steps. From this legend, depicted at Prasat Kravan, Vishnu is sometimes known as the 'long strider'.

on the left wall; and riding a *garuda* on the right wall. The northernmost tower displays bas-reliefs of Vishnu's consort, Lakshmi.

ROLUOS TEMPLES

The monuments of Roluos (រលួស), which served as Indravarman I's capital, Hariharalaya, are among the earliest large, permanent temples built by the Khmers and mark the dawn of Khmer classical art. Before the construction of Bakong temple, generally only lighter (and less durable) construction materials such as brick were employed. As well as the imposing pyramid temple of Bakong, the Roluos group also includes Preah Ko and Lolei.

Plan a half-day visit together with the stilted village of Kompong Pluk or allow three hours or so to explore the three temples and nearby handicraft projects.

◉ Sights

Bakong   HINDU TEMPLE
(បាគង; ⊙ 7.30am-5.30pm) Bakong is the largest and most interesting of the Roluos group of temples. Built and dedicated to Shiva by Indravarman I, it's a representation of Mt Meru, and it served as the city's central temple. The east-facing complex consists of a five-tier central pyramid of sandstone, 60m square at the base, flanked by eight towers of brick and sandstone, and by other minor sanctuaries. A number of the lower towers are still partly covered by their original plasterwork.

The complex is enclosed by three concentric walls and a moat. There are well-preserved statues of stone elephants on each corner of the first three levels of the central temple. There are 12 stupas – three to each side – on the third tier. The sanctuary on the fifth level of Bakong temple was a later addition during the reign of Suryavarman II, in the style of Angkor Wat's central tower. There is an active Buddhist monastery here, dating back a century or more, which has recently been restored.

Preah Ko   HINDU TEMPLE

([ព្រះគោ]; ⊙7.30am-5.30pm) Preah Ko was erected by Indravarman I in the late 9th century and dedicated to Shiva. In AD 880 the temple was also dedicated to his deified ancestors; the front towers relate to male ancestors or gods, the rear towers to female ancestors or goddesses. Lions guard the steps up to the temple. Preah Ko (Sacred Ox) features three *nandis* (sacred oxen), all of whom look like a few steaks have been sliced off over the years.

The six *prasat* (stone halls), aligned in two rows and decorated with carved sandstone and plaster reliefs, face east; the central tower of the front row is a great deal larger than the other towers. Some of the best surviving examples of plasterwork in Angkor can be seen here, restored by the German Apsara Conservation Project (p152). There are elaborate inscriptions in the ancient Hindu language of Sanskrit on the doorposts of each tower.

Lolei   HINDU TEMPLE

(លលៃ; ⊙7.30am-5.30pm) The four brick towers of Lolei, an almost exact replica of the towers of Preah Ko (although in much worse shape), were built on an islet in the centre of a large reservoir – now rice fields – by Yasovarman I, the founder of the first city at Angkor. The sandstone carvings in the niches of the temples are worth a look and there are Sanskrit inscriptions on the doorposts.

According to one of the inscriptions, the four towers were dedicated by Yasovarman I to his mother, his father and his maternal grandparents on 12 July 893.

🛏 Sleeping & Eating

The vast majority of travellers who visit the Roluos temples stay in Siem Reap, although there are some homestays and a boutique hotel located in Prasat Bakong District.

Lom Lam Homestay   HOMESTAY $$

(☑012 656662; http://lomlameco.weebly.com; s/d/tr US$40/45/50; 🖎) This traditional village homestay has support from a Japanese benefactor ensuring that comfort and quality are a cut above the average homestay around Siem Reap. Set in the downstairs of a large Cambodian house, the furnishing and bedding are more like that of an upscale guesthouse than homestay. Airport transfers and Angkor activities such as a *tuk tuk* tour and a village experience are included.

Angkor Rural
Boutique Hotel   BOUTIQUE HOTEL $$$

(☑012 817616; www.angkorruralboutique.com; Chrey Thom Village; r US$130-180; ❋🖎🛏) This charming boutique hotel offers a slice of the countryside in comfort. Rooms are in traditional houses set around a lush garden with a small swimming pool and natural pond. Furnishings are elegant and in keeping with the surrounds. The owner is involved in community tourism initiatives in the district, including recycled jewellery and offering oxcart rides. Airport transfers are included.

Natural Vegetable Food Place   CAMBODIAN $

(☑012 674670; meals US$3-7; ⊙9am-9pm) Set amid extensive farmland on the road between Siem Reap and Roluos, this restaurant specialises in organic vegetables grown in its

---

GOOD-CAUSE SHOPPING AROUND ROLUOS

Several good-cause initiatives have sprung up around the Roluos area. Look out for **Prolung Khmer** (www.prolungkhmer.blogspot.com; ⊙8am-5pm) 🖉 on the road between Preah Ko and Bakong. It's a weaving centre producing stylish cotton *krama* (checked scarves), set up as a training collaboration between Cambodia and Japan.

Right opposite Preah Ko is the **Khmer Group Art of Weaving** (⊙7am-5pm), turning out silk and cotton scarves on traditional looms. Also here is **Dy Proeung Master Sculptor** (donations accepted; ⊙6am-6pm), who has created scale replicas of Preah Ko, Bakong and Lolei, plus Angkor Wat, Preah Vihear and Banteay Srei for good measure.

Not far from here on NH67 is the **Lo-Yuyu** (www.loyuyuceramics.com; ⊙8am-6pm) ceramics workshop, producing traditional Angkorian-style pottery.

very own gardens. Fish and meat dishes are also available, but all come with a variety of freshly grown vegetables such as okra, long bean and cucumber with a pungent *prahoc ktis* dip (fermented fish and herbs).

Stoeng Trorcheak Restaurant CAMBODIAN $$
(☏012 717815; meals US$3-12; ☺7am-10pm; ✳☎) The shady gardens at this sprawling restaurant are by the Roluos River are a good place to cool off during the heat of the day. The extensive menu includes Cambodian classics, Chinese favourites, Thai tasters and some international appearances. Many of the tables are set underneath pretty thatched pavilions but some indoor air-con dining is available.

❶ Getting There & Away

The temples can be found 13km east of Siem Reap along NH6 near the modern-day town of Roluos. A half-day trip from Siem Reap to the Roluos temples by *remork-moto* costs about US$20, or you can add the temples to an existing *remork* tour of the main temples around Siem Reap for an extra US$5 or so (US$20 to US$25 total for the day). You can also reach the temples easily enough on your own by bicycle or electric bike.

BEYOND ANGKOR

Banteay Srei

Considered by many to be the jewel in the crown of Angkorian art, **Banteay Srei** (បន្ទាយស្រី; incl in Angkor admission 1/3/7 days US$37/62/72; ☺7.30am-5.30pm) is cut from stone of a pinkish hue and includes some of the finest stone carving anywhere on earth. Begun in AD 967, it is one of the smallest sites at Angkor, but what it lacks in size it makes up for in stature. The art gallery of Angkor, Banteay Srei, a Hindu temple dedicated to Shiva, is wonderfully well preserved and many of its carvings are three-dimensional.

Banteay Srei means 'Citadel of the Women', and it is said that it must have been built by a woman, as the elaborate carvings are supposedly too fine for the hand of a man.

Banteay Srei is one of the few temples around Angkor to be commissioned not by a king but by a brahman, who may have been a tutor to Jayavarman V. The temple is square and has entrances at the east and west, with the east approached by a causeway. Of interest are the lavishly decorated libraries and the three central towers, which are decorated with male and female divinities and beautiful filigree relief work.

Classic carvings at Banteay Srei include delicate women with lotus flowers in hand and traditional skirts clearly visible, as well as breathtaking re-creations of scenes from the epic *Ramayana* adorning the library pediments (carved inlays above a lintel). However, the sum of the parts is no greater than the whole – almost every inch of these interior buildings is covered in decoration. Standing watch over such perfect creations are the mythical guardians, all of which are copies of originals stored in the National Museum.

Banteay Srei was the first major temple restoration undertaken by the EFEO in 1930 using the anastylosis method. The project, as evidenced today, was a major success and soon led to other larger projects such as the restoration of Bayon. Banteay Srei is also the first to have been given a full makeover in terms of facilities, with a large car park, a designated dining and shopping area, clear visitor information and a state-of-the-art exhibition on the history of the temple and its restoration. There is also a small *baray* behind the temple where local boat trips (US$7 per boat) are possible through the lotus pond.

When Banteay Srei was first rediscovered, it was assumed to be from the 13th or 14th centuries, as it was thought that the refined carving must have come at the end of the Angkor period. It was later dated to AD 967, from inscriptions found at the site.

Banteay Srei is about 32km northeast of Siem Reap and 21km northeast of Bayon. It is well signposted and the road is surfaced all the way, so a trip from Siem Reap should take about 45 minutes by car or one hour by *remork. Moto* and *remork* drivers will want a bit of extra cash to come out here, so agree on a sum first. You can eat at one of several small restaurants, complete with ornate wood furnishings cut from Cambodia's forests, near the entrance to the temple.

There's plenty to do in Banteay Srei District as well as several homestays should you wish to stay and explore the area. It is possible to combine a visit to Banteay Srei as part of a long day trip to the River of a Thousand Lingas at Kbal Spean and Beng Mealea. A half-day itinerary might include Banteay Srei, the Cambodia Landmine Museum and Banteay Samre. It takes 45 minutes to explore Banteay Srei temple, but allow 1½ hours to visit the information centre and explore the area.

Beng Mealea

A spectacular sight to behold, **Beng Mealea** (បឹងមាលា; US$5; ⊙7.30am-5.30pm), located about 68km northeast of Siem Reap, is one of the most mysterious temples at Angkor, as nature has well and truly run riot. Exploring this titanic of temples, built to the same floor plan as Angkor Wat, is the ultimate Indiana Jones experience. Built in the 12th century under Suryavarman II, Beng Mealea is enclosed by a massive moat measuring 1.2km by 900m.

The temple used to be utterly consumed by jungle, but some of the dense foliage has been cut back and cleaned up in recent years. Entering from the south, visitors wend their way over piles of finely chiselled sandstone blocks, through long, dark chambers and between hanging vines. The central tower has completely collapsed, but hidden away among the rubble and foliage are several impressive carvings, as well as a well-preserved library in the northeastern quadrant. The temple is a special place and it is worth taking the time to explore it thoroughly. The large wooden walkway to and

around the centre was originally constructed for the filming of Jean-Jacques Annaud's *Two Brothers* (2004), set in 1920s French Indochina and starring two tiger cubs.

Beng Mealea has a large *baray* to the east and some atmospheric satellite temples such as Prasat Chrey. Apsara Authority (p141) has plans to reflood the ancient *baray*, as they did earlier with Jayatataka (Northern Baray), surrounding Neak Poan temple.

There are several stop-and-dip food stalls (dishes US$2 to US$4) opposite the temple entrance. Run by friendly, English-speaking Sreymom, the **Sreymom Beng Mealea Homestay** (☑087 555229; Beng Mealea Village; r incl meals US$25) is just a short walk away from the jungle temple of Beng Mealea. The overnight rates include all home-cooked meals. It is also possible to pre-arrange lunch here, even if you don't stay overnight.

It costs US$5 to visit Beng Mealea and there are additional small charges for transport, so make sure you work out in advance with the driver or guide who is paying for these.

Beng Mealea is at the centre of an ancient Angkorian road connecting Angkor Thom and Preah Khan (Prasat Bakan) in Preah Vihear Province, now evocatively numbered route 66. A small Angkorian bridge just west of Chau Srei Vibol temple is the only

Beng Mealea

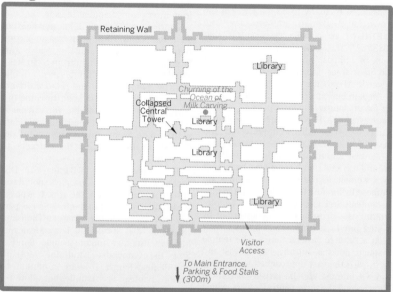

Retaining Wall

Library

Churning of the Ocean of Milk Carving

Collapsed Central Tower

Library

Library

Library

Visitor Access

To Main Entrance, Parking & Food Stalls (300m)

remaining trace of the old Angkorian road between Beng Mealea and Angkor Thom; between Beng Mealea and Preah Khan there are at least 10 bridges abandoned in the forest. This is a way for extreme adventurers to get to Preah Khan temple, but do not undertake this journey lightly.

Otherwise, a more direct and leisurely route, Beng Mealea is about 40km east of Bayon (as the crow flies) and 6.5km southeast of Phnom Kulen. By road it is about 68km (one hour by car, longer by *moto* or *remork-moto*) from Siem Reap. The shortest route is via the junction town of Dam Dek, located on NH6 about 37km from Siem Reap in the direction of Phnom Penh. Turn north immediately after the market and continue on this road for 31km. The entrance to the temple lies just beyond the left-hand turn to Koh Ker. Allow a half day to visit, including the journey time from Siem Reap or combine it with Koh Ker in a long day trip best undertaken by car or 4WD.

Phnom Kulen

Considered by Khmers to be the most sacred mountain in Cambodia, **Phnom Kulen** (ភ្នំគូលែន; www.adfkulen.org; US$20; ☉ 6-11am to ascend, noon-5pm to descend) is a popular place of pilgrimage on weekends and during festivals. It played a significant role in the history of the Khmer empire, as it was from here in AD 802 that Jayavarman II proclaimed himself a *devaraja* (god-king), giving birth to the Cambodian kingdom. Attractions include a giant reclining Buddha, hundreds of lingas carved in the riverbed, an impressive waterfall and some remote temples.

From the entrance a sealed road winds its way through some spectacular jungle scenery, emerging on the plateau after a 12km ascent. The road eventually splits: the left fork leads to the picnic spot, waterfall and ruins of a 9th-century temple; the right fork continues over a bridge (you'll find the riverbed carvings around here) to the base of Wat Preah Ang Thom, which sits at the summit of the mountain and houses the large reclining Buddha carved into the sandstone boulder upon which it is built. This is the focal point of a pilgrimage for Khmer people, so it is important to take off your shoes and any head covering before climbing the stairs to the sanctuary. These days the views from the 487m peak are partially obstructed by foliage run amok.

The waterfall is an attractive spot and was featured in *Lara Croft: Tomb Raider*. However, it could be much more beautiful were it not for all the litter left here by families picnicking at the weekend. Near the top of the waterfall is a jungle-clad temple known as Prasat Krau Romeas, dating from the 9th century.

There are plenty of other Angkorian sites on Phnom Kulen, including as many as 20 minor temples around the plateau, the most important of which is Prasat Rong Chen, the first pyramid or temple-mountain to be constructed in the Angkor area. Most impressive of all are the giant stone animals or guardians of the mountain, known as Sra Damrei (Elephant Pond). These are quite difficult to reach, particularly during the wet season. The few people who make it, however, are rewarded with a life-size replica of a stone elephant – a full 4m long and 3m tall – and smaller statues of lions, a frog and a cow. These were constructed on the southern face of the mountain and from here there are spectacular views across the plains below. Getting to Sra Damrei requires taking a *moto* from Wat Preah Ang Thom for about 12km on very rough trails. Don't try to

THE LOST CITY OF MAHENDRAPARVATA

Phnom Kulen hit the headlines in 2013 thanks to the 'discovery' of a lost city known in Angkorian times as Mahendraparvata. Using jungle-piercing LIDAR radar technology, the structures of a more extensive archaeological site have been unveiled beneath the jungle canopy. However, it wasn't quite as dramatic a discovery as initially reported, as Phnom Kulen had long been known as an important archaeological site. The LIDAR research confirmed the size and scale of the ancient city, complete with canals and *barays*, in the same way NASA satellite imagery had helped identify the size and scale of the greater Angkor hydraulic water system more than a decade earlier. Some new temples and features were identified beneath the jungle, but remain remote and inaccessible due to terrain and the possibility of land mines. An additional LIDAR survey of the entire Kulen plateau was conducted in 2015.

find it on your own; expect to pay the *moto* driver about US$10 for a two-hour trip to explore this area and carry plenty of water.

Other impressive sites that could be included in an adventurous day trip around Phnom Kulen include the ancient rock carvings of Poeung Tbal, an atmospheric site of enormous boulders, and the partially restored temple of Damrei Krap. Add these to the mix and it will cost more like US$15 to explore for three hours or more.

Phnom Kulen is a huge plateau around 50km from Siem Reap and about 15km from Banteay Srei. To get here on the toll road, take the well-signposted right fork just before Banteay Srei village and go straight ahead at the crossroads. Just before the road starts to climb the mountain, there is a barrier and it is here that the admisson charge is levied. It is only possible to go up Phnom Kulen before 11am and only possible to come down after midday, to avoid vehicles meeting on the narrow road. There are plenty of small restaurants and food stalls located around the parking area at the base of Wat Preah Ang Thom.

Moto drivers are likely to want about US$20 or more to bring you out here, and rented cars will hit passengers with a surcharge, more than double the going rate for Angkor; forget coming by *remork-moto* as the hill climb is just too tough. With the long journey here, it is best to plan on spending the best part of a day exploring, although it can be combined with either Banteay Srei or Beng Mealea.

Kbal Spean

A spectacularly carved riverbed, **Kbal Spean** (ក្បាលស្ពាន, River of a Thousand Lingas; incl in Angkor admission 1/3/7 days US$37/62/72; ⊙7.30am-5.30pm) is set deep in the jungle to the northeast of Angkor. More commonly referred to in English as the 'River of a Thousand Lingas', the name actually means 'bridgehead', a reference to the natural rock bridge here. Lingas (phallic symbols) have been elaborately carved into the riverbed, and images of Hindu deities are dotted about the area. It was 'discovered' in 1969, when ethnologist Jean Boulbet was shown the area by a hermit.

It is a 2km uphill walk to the carvings, along a pretty path that winds its way up into the jungle, passing by some interesting boulder formations along the way. Carry plenty of water up the hill, as there is none available beyond the parking area. The path eventually splits to the waterfall or the river carvings. There is an impressive carving of Vishnu on the upper section of the river, followed by a series of carvings at the bridgehead itself, some of which were hacked off in the past few years, but have since been replaced by excellent replicas. This area is now roped off to protect the carvings from further damage.

Following the river down, there are several more impressive carvings of Vishnu, and Shiva with his consort Uma, and further downstream hundreds of *lingas* appear on the riverbed. At the top of the waterfall are many animal images, including a cow and a frog, and a path winds around the boulders to a wooden staircase leading down to the base of the falls. Visitors between January and June will be disappointed to see very little water here. The best time to visit is between July and December. When exploring Kbal Spean it is best to start with the river carvings and work back down to the waterfall to cool off. From the car park, the visit takes about two hours including the walk, nearer three hours with a natural shower or a picnic. A day trip here can be combined with Angkor Centre for Conservation of Biodiversity (p126), Banteay Srei temple and the Cambodia Landmine Museum (p126).

Kbal Spean is about 50km northeast of Siem Reap or about 18km beyond the temple of Banteay Srei. The road is in great shape, as it forms part of the main road north to Anlong Veng and the Thai border, so it takes just one hour or so from town. There are food stalls at the bottom of the hill that can cook up fried rice or a noodle soup, or the fancier, excellent Borey Sovann Restaurant (p127), located near the entrance.

Moto drivers will no doubt want a bit of extra money to take you here; figure US$15 or so for the day, including a trip to Banteay Srei. Likewise, *remork-moto* drivers will probably up the price to US$25 or so. A surcharge is also levied to come out here by car. Admission to Kbal Spean is included in the general Angkor pass; the last entry to the site is at 3.30pm.

Banteay Samré

Dating from the same period as Angkor Wat, **Banteay Samré** (បន្ទាយសំរែ; ⊙7.30am-5.30pm) was built by Suryavarman II. The temple is in a fairly healthy state of preservation due to some extensive renovation work, although its isolation has resulted in some looting during the past few decades. The area consists of a central temple with four wings, preceded by a hall and also accompanied by two libraries, the southern one remarkably well preserved.

The whole ensemble is enclosed by two large concentric walls around what would have been the unique feature of an inner moat, now dry.

Banteay Samré is 400m east of the Eastern Baray. A visit here can be combined with a trip to Banteay Srei and/or Phnom Bok.

Chau Srei Vibol

This petite hilltop temple (ចៅស្រីវិបុល; ⊙7.30am-5.30pm) is actually part of a larger complex that spanned the entire hill. It is relatively under-visited compared with more centrally located temples, making it an atmospheric option for sunset. The central sanctuary is in a ruined state but is nicely complemented by the construction of an early 20th century wat nearby.

Surrounding the base of the hill are laterite walls, each with a small entrance hall in reasonable condition, outlining the dimensions of what was once a significant temple. To get here, turn east off the Bakong to Anlong Veng highway at a point about 8km north of NH6, or 5km south of Phnom Bok. There is a small sign (easy to miss) that marks the turn. Locals are friendly and helpful should you find yourself lost.

Phnom Bok

One of three temple-mountains built by Yasovarman I in the late 9th or early 10th century, Phnom Bok (ភ្នំបូក; ⊙7.30am-5.30pm) is a peaceful but remote location (about 25km from Siem Reap) that sees few visitors. The small temple is in reasonable shape, but it is the views of Phnom Kulen to the north and the plains of Angkor to the south from this 212m hill that make it worth the trip.

The remains of a 5m *linga* are visible at the opposite end of the hill and it's believed there were similar *linga* at Phnom Bakheng and Phnom Krom.

There is a long, winding trail snaking up the hill at Phnom Bok, which takes about 20 minutes to climb, plus a faster cement staircase, but the latter is fairly exposed. Avoid the heat in the middle of the day and carry plenty of water, which can be purchased locally.

Phnom Bok is clearly visible from the road to Banteay Srei. It is accessed by continuing east on the road to Banteay Samré for another 6km. It is possible to loop back to Siem Reap via the temples of Roluos by heading south instead of west on the return journey, and gain some rewarding glimpses of the countryside. Unfortunately, it is not a sensible place for sunrise or sunset, as it would require a long journey in the dark.

Phnom Krom

The temple of Phnom Krom (ភ្នំក្រោម; incl in Angkor admission 1/3/7 days US$37/62/72; ⊙7.30am-5.30pm), 12km south of Siem Reap on a hill overlooking Tonlé Sap lake, dates from the reign of Yasovarman I in the late 9th or early 10th century. The name means 'Lower Hill' and is a reference to its geographic location in relation to its sister temples of Phnom Bakheng and Phnom Bok. Phnom Krom remains one of the more tranquil spots from which to view the sunset, complete with an active wat.

The three towers, dedicated (from north to south) to Vishnu, Shiva and Brahma, are in a ruined state. It is necessary to have an Angkor pass to visit the temple at the summit of Phnom Krom, so don't come all the way out here without one, as the guards won't allow you access to the summit of the hill. If coming here by *moto* or car, try to get the driver to take you to the summit, as it is a long, hot climb otherwise. Consider a half-day visit in tandem with exploring the floating village of Chong Kneas.

LINGER AMONG THE LINGAS

Fertility symbols are prominent around the temples of Angkor. The *linga* is a phallic symbol and would have originally been located within the towers of most Hindu temples. It sits inside a *yoni*, the female fertility symbol, combining to produce holy water, charged with the sexual energy of creation. Brahmans poured the water over the *linga* and it drained through the *yoni* and out of the temples through elaborate gutters to anoint the pilgrims outside.

Western Baray & Western Mebon

The Western Baray, measuring an incredible 8km by 2.3km, was excavated by hand to provide water for the intensive cultivation of lands around Angkor. These enormous *barays* weren't dug out, but had huge dykes built up around the edges. In the centre of the Western Baray is the ruin of the Western Mebon temple, where the giant bronze statue of Vishnu, now in the National Museum in Phnom Penh, was found. The Western Mebon is accessible by boat.

The Western Baray is the main local swimming pool around Siem Reap. There is a small beach of sorts at the western extreme, complete with picnic huts and inner tubes for rent, which attracts plenty of Khmers at weekends.

REMOTE ANGKORIAN SITES

Koh Ker

Abandoned to the forests of the north, **Koh Ker** (កោះកេរ្តិ៍; US$10; ◷7.30am-5.30pm), capital of the Angkorian empire from AD 928 to AD 944, is within day-trip distance of Siem Reap. Most visitors start at Prasat Krahom where impressive stone carvings grace lintels, doorposts and slender window columns. The principal monument is Mayan-looking Prasat Thom, a 55m-wide, 40m-high sandstone-faced pyramid whose seven tiers offer spectacular views across the forest. Koh Ker is 127km northeast of Siem Reap.

LANDMINE ALERT!

Many of the Koh Ker temples were mined during the war, but by 2008 most had been cleared: de-mining teams reported removing from the area a total of 1382 mines and 1,447,212 pieces of exploded and unexploded ordnance. However, considering what's at stake, it's best to err on the side of caution. Do not stray from previously trodden paths or wander off into the forest, as there may be landmines within a few hundred metres of the temples.

Long one of Cambodia's most remote and inaccessible temple complexes, the opening of a toll road from Dam Dek (via Beng Mealea) put Koh Ker (pronounced ko-kayer) within striking distance of Siem Reap. To really appreciate the temples – the ensemble has 42 major structures in an area that measures 9km by 4km – it's recommended to overnight nearby.

Prasat Krahom (Red Temple; ◷7.30am-5.30pm), the second-largest structure at Koh Ker, is so named for the red bricks from which it is constructed. Sadly, none of the carved lions for which this temple was once known remain, though there's still plenty to see, with stone archways and galleries leaning hither and thither. A *naga*-flanked causeway and a series of sanctuaries, libraries and gates lead past trees and vegetation-covered ponds. Just west of Prasat Krahom, at the far western end of a half-fallen colonnade, are the remains (most of the head) of a statue of Nandin.

The principal monument at Koh Ker is **Prasat Thom** (Prasat Kompeng; ◷7.30am-5.30pm). The staircase to the top is open to a limited number of visitors and the views are spectacular if you can stomach the heights. Some 40 inscriptions, dating from 932 to 1010, have been found here.

South of this central group is a 1185m-by-548m *baray* known as the **Rahal**. It is fed by the Sen River, which supplied water to irrigate the land in this arid area.

Some of the largest Shiva *linga* in Cambodia can still be seen in four temples about 1km northeast of Prasat Thom. The largest is found in Prasat Thneng, while **Prasat Leung** (◷7.30am-5.30pm) is similarly well endowed.

Among the many other temples that are found around Koh Ker, **Prasat Bram** (◷7.30am-5.30pm) is a real highlight. It consists of a collection of brick towers, at least two of which have been completely smothered by voracious strangler figs; the probing roots cut through the brickwork like liquid mercury.

Koh Ker is one of the least-studied temple areas from the Angkorian period and no restoration work was ever undertaken here. Louis Delaporte visited in 1880 during his extensive investigations into Angkorian temples. It was surveyed in 1921 by the great Henri Parmentier for an article in the *Bulletin de l'École d'Extrême Orient*. Archaeological surveys were also carried out by Cam-

Koh Ker

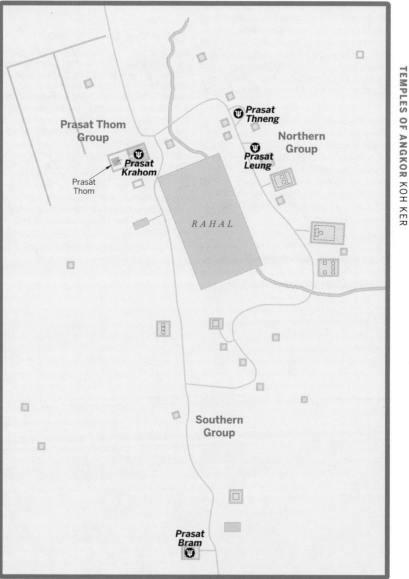

bodian teams in the 1950s and '60s, but all records vanished during the destruction of the 1970s, helping to preserve this complex as something of an enigma.

Several of the most impressive pieces in the National Museum (p43) in Phnom Penh come from Koh Ker, including the huge *garuda* (mythical half-man, half-bird creature) that greets visitors in the entrance hall and a unique carving depicting a pair of wrestling monkey-kings.

🛏 Sleeping & Eating

There are no places to stay in the immediate vicinity of Koh Ker's temples, but there are a couple of guesthouses within 10km.

Near the main temple of Prasat Thom there are a few small food stalls (open during daylight hours) run by the wives of the heritage police stationed here. The nearby village of Srayong (10km) also has a few eateries.

Mom Morokod Koh Ker
Guesthouse   GUESTHOUSE **$**

(☑ 078 365656; r US$12) About 200m south of the Koh Ker toll plaza, 8km south of Prasat Krahom, this quiet guesthouse has 11 clean, spacious rooms with elaborately carved wooden doors and bathrooms. There's no restaurant on-site, but the host family can cook up meals on request.

Ponloeu Preah Chan
Guesthouse   GUESTHOUSE **$**

(☑ 012 489058; Srayong; r US$5) Located in the village of Srayong, this friendly, family-run guesthouse has 14 rooms with bare walls, mosquito nets and barely enough space for a double bed. Toilets and showers are out back.

ℹ Getting There & Away

Koh Ker is 127km northeast of Siem Reap (two hours by car) and 72km west of Tbeng Meanchey (1½ hours). The toll road from Dam Dek, paved only as far as the Preah Vihear Province line, passes by Beng Mealea, 61km southwest of Koh Ker; one-day excursions from Siem Reap often visit both temple complexes. Admission fees are collected at the toll barrier near Beng Mealea if travelling from Siem Reap.

From Siem Reap, hiring a private car for a day trip to Koh Ker costs about US$80. There's no public transport to Koh Ker, although a few minibuses (10,000r) link Srayong, 10km south of Prasat Krahom, with Siem Reap. It might also be possible to take one of the shared taxis that link Siem Reap with Tbeng Meanchey and get off at Srayong.

South Coast

POP 2 MILLION

Best Places to Eat

➡ Twenty Three Bistro (p218)

➡ Crab Market (p227)

➡ Happy Beach (p179)

➡ Stung Takeo (p229)

➡ May's Kitchen (p212)

Best Places to Stay

➡ Four Rivers Floating Lodge (p182)

➡ Green House (p216)

➡ Veranda Natural Resort (p226)

➡ Huba-Huba (p209)

➡ Nomads Land (p212)

Why Go?

Cambodia's South Coast (ឆ្នេរខាងត្បូង) provides the antidote to temple-hopping tick lists. The beaches draw most folk here, but stick around and you'll see this region is more than its sandy bits.

The Koh Kong Conservation Corridor's emerald-green vistas offer trekking potential that is only now being tapped into, providing a host of nature-filled adventures. Down south, travellers can dig into history, admiring Kampot's preserved architecture, then dig into plates piled with crab in Kep, before exploring the surrounding countryside, patchworked with rice fields and studded with caves.

Just here to answer the call of the beach? While brash Sihanoukville isn't everyone's cup of tea, the islands offshore have something for everyone, from die-hard partiers to those seeking sun-kissed solitude. Pick your beach, sprawl on the sand, make friends with your hammock. There's a reason many visitors never leave.

When to Go
Sihanoukville

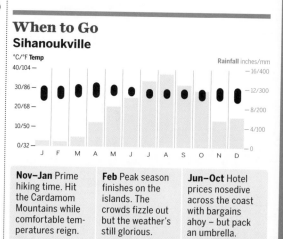

Nov–Jan Prime hiking time. Hit the Cardamom Mountains while comfortable temperatures reign.

Feb Peak season finishes on the islands. The crowds fizzle out but the weather's still glorious.

Jun–Oct Hotel prices nosedive across the coast with bargains ahoy – but pack an umbrella.

South Coast Highlights

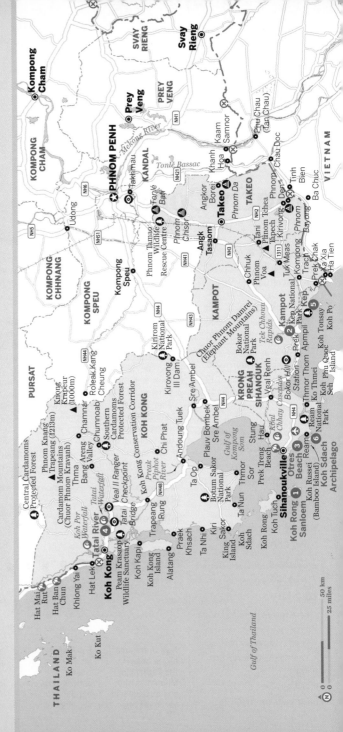

1 Koh Rong Sanloem (p207) Basking on the photogenic white sands of Saracen Bay or Sunset Beach.

2 Kampot (p212) Ambling the alleys of Cambodia's best-preserved old town, then heading out for river and cave adventures in the countryside.

3 Otres Beach (p186) Topping-up your tan and downing cocktails on the sands of Sihanoukville's southern stretch.

4 Tatai River (p181) Long-boating to secluded riverside accommodations, then trekking or kayaking the nearby waterfall.

5 Kep (p223) Feasting on the famous Kampot pepper crab then working off the calories in Kep National Park.

6 Koh Sdach Archipelago (p211) Adventuring your way to lesser-explored islands, and peeking in on the undersea life that thrives around them.

0 50 km
0 25 miles

ℹ Getting There & Away

Depending on your destination, getting to and from the South Coast isn't always straightforward, particularly in the low season. So while it may be easy enough to hop a bus to Sihanoukville, Kampot or Koh Kong, the far-flung islands and Central Cardamoms destinations often require a combination of *moto* (motorcycle taxi), taxis, boats, bicycles and your own two feet.

Taking the train, which runs between Phnom Penh, Takeo, Kampot and Sihanoukville is good fun, and a lovely, if sluggish, way to see the countryside. And flying into or out of the Sihanoukville Airport can be a time-saver, if you don't mind spending a few extra dollars.

KOH KONG CITY

🎵 035 / POP 36,053

Sleepy Koh Kong (ក្រុងកោះកុង) was once Cambodia's Wild West with its isolated frontier economy dominated by smuggling, prostitution and gambling. Although remnants of its less-salubrious past still cling on, today this low-slung town is striding towards respectability as ecotourists, aiming to explore the Cardamom Mountains and coastline, shoo away the sleaze.

These days motorboats from Koh Kong can whisk you to rushing waterfalls, secluded, sandy coves and Venice-like fishing villages on stilts. The city's still-dusty sprawl of streets sits on the banks of the Koh Poi River, which spills into the Gulf of Thailand a few kilometres south of the centre.

◎ Sights

Koh Kong's main appeal is as a launching pad for adventures in and around the Cardamom Mountains and the Koh Kong Conservation Corridor, but there are a few diversions around town as well. If you want to take a dip, the pool at Oasis Bungalow Resort is open to non-guests (US$4) from 9am to 6pm.

Sun-worshippers will discover additional beaches further north on the Gulf of Thailand near the Thai border.

Peam Krasaop
Wildlife Sanctuary   NATURE RESERVE
(ជម្រកសត្វព្រៃបឹងក្រពើយ៉ាក នៅពាមក្រសោប; 5000r; ⏰ 6am-6pm) Anchored to alluvial islands – some no larger than a house – this 260-sq-km sanctuary's magnificent mangroves protect the coast from erosion, offer vital breeding and feeding grounds for fish, shrimp and shellfish, and are home to myriad birds.

Koh Kong City

To experience the delicate mangrove ecosystem, try the 600m-long concrete mangrove walk, which runs above the briny waters to a 15m observation tower. The entrance is 5.5km southeast of Koh Kong. A *moto/remork-moto (tuk-tuk)* ride costs US$5/10 return.

Although the main raised walkway is made from concrete blocks, there are various wooden paths that shoot off from the main trail. Travellers with little ones in tow should keep a vigilant eye on children as the walkway (particularly on the wooden sections) is not maintained well. If you're lucky, you'll come across cavorting monkeys with a fondness for fizzy drinks.

You can also hire a motorboat to take you through the sanctuary; wooden boats are available for hire from the dock at the sanctuary entrance (short tours US$5, long tours US$10), but a better plan is to head into the park's interior on a boat tour out of Koh Kong.

On a boat tour you'll have a chance to visit **fishing hamlets** where residents use spindly traps to catch fish, which they keep alive till market time in partly submerged nets attached to floating wooden frames. Further out, on some of the more remote mangrove islands, you pass isolated little beaches where you can land and lounge alongside ambling hermit crabs.

Much of Peam Krasaop is on the prestigious **Ramsar List of Wetlands of International Importance** (www.ramsar.org). The area, which is part of the Koh Kong Conservation Corridor, is all the more valuable from an ecological standpoint because similar forests in Thailand have been trashed by short-sighted development. Today Peam Krasaop's habitats and fisheries are threatened by the large-scale dredging of sand for Singapore.

Koh Yor Beach   BEACH
(ឆ្នេរកោះយ៉ នៅប៉ាក់ខ្លង) This long wind-swept beach is on the far (western) side of the peninsula that forms the west bank of Koh Poi River opposite Koh Kong City. Although it's not the world's prettiest beach, it offers good shell-collecting and you're nearly guaranteed to have it to yourself. To get there, cross the toll bridge that spans the river north of the town centre and go left at the roundabout 1.5km beyond the tollbooth. The beach is about 6km from the turn-off.

Wat Neang Kok   BUDDHIST TEMPLE
(វត្តនាងកុក) This rocky promontory on the right (western) bank of Koh Poi River is decorated with life-size statues demonstrating the violent punishments that await sinners in the Buddhist hell. This graphic tableau belongs to Wat Neang Kok, a Buddhist temple. To get there, cross the bridge, turn right

600m past the tollbooth (a *moto* ride costs 1400r), and proceed 150m beyond the temple to the statues.

☞ Tours

Boat tours are an excellent way to view Koh Kong's many coastal attractions. Many companies run group tours from the **boat dock** (cnr St 1 & St 9) to Koh Kong Island, taking in some of the mangroves of Peam Krasaop Wildlife Sanctuary (full day per person including lunch and snorkelling equipment from US$21, or overnight for US$55). Overnight trips involve beach camping or a homestay on the island. There's a good chance of spotting Irrawaddy river dolphins early in the morning on these trips. Note that trips to Koh Kong Island don't take place in the rainy season (June to September) because of strong onshore (southwesterly) breezes, although half-day excursions to Peam Krasaop are possible year-round.

Most operators offer overland trips in the Cardamom Mountains as well as boat tours.

Neptune Adventure (p181) is a well-established ecotourism operator based on the Tatai River, offering highly recommended jungle treks as well as multi-activity adventures combining trekking, kayaking and boating.

Ritthy Koh Kong
Eco Adventure Tours   ADVENTURE
(☏ 012 707719; www.kohkongecoadventure.com; St 1; ☉8am-9pm) A one-stop shop for all your tour needs in Koh Kong, this is the longest-running ecotourism operator in town. Ritthy's excursions include excellent Koh Kong Island boat tours, birdwatching, and multi-day jungle trekking and camping in the Areng Valley within the Koh Kong Conservation Corridor. Check the website for pricing.

🛌 Sleeping

Koh Kong is a popular holiday destination for Khmer families; hotels fill up and raise their rates during Cambodian holidays. If staying in town doesn't appeal, check out Tatai River (18km east), with its handful of fabulous eco-accommodation options. Peam Krasaop also has a newly revamped resort that's unique and stunning for its location on stilts within the mangrove forest.

Ritthy's Retreat   GUESTHOUSE $
(☏ 097 555 2789; ritthy.info@gmail.com; St 1; dm US$4, r US$6-15; ❄☎) Long-time tour operator Ritthy has opened a welcoming guesthouse and restaurant on the riverfront.

It features spacious en-suite dorms with double-wide beds and a nice variety of roomy doubles. The fancier air-con rooms upstairs have semi-private balconies with river views, while the downstairs bar-restaurant, with a pool table, is a top hang-out.

Koh Kong City Hotel   HOTEL $
(☑ 035-936777; St 1; r US$15-20; ❄ @ 🛜) Ludicrous value for what you get: each squeaky-clean room includes a huge bathroom, two double beds, 50 TV channels, a full complement of toiletries, free water and – in the US$20 rooms – a river view. Friendly staff top off the experience.

Paddy's Bamboo Guesthouse   HOSTEL $
(☑ 015 533223; ppkohkong@gmail.com; dm without/with fan US$2/3; r US$5-10; ❄ 🛜) Paddy's targets backpackers with basic rooms, a bustling bar with pool table, and a balcony for chilling out. Shoot for the wood-floored, fan-cooled rooms upstairs over the cramped dorms and the musty concrete air-con rooms at the back.

Paddy is a good source of travel info and can arrange boat tours and other excursions.

⭐**Oasis Bungalow Resort**   BUNGALOW $$
(☑ 092 228342; http://oasisresort.netkhmer.com; d/tr US$35/40; ❄ 🛜 🏊) Surrounded by lush forest, 2km north of Koh Kong centre, Oasis really lives up to its name. Five large, airy bungalows set around a gorgeous infinity pool with views of the Cardamom Mountains provide a tranquil base in which to chill out and reset your travel batteries. To get here, follow the blue signs from Acleda Bank.

Mangrove Sanctuary Resort   BUNGALOW $$
(☑ 097 244 5196; bungalows US$50-140) Once a bit of an eyesore, this place has been revamped by a new owner to blend more seamlessly with the surrounding habitat, and the result is a unique and enchanting stay within a mangrove forest. Fifteen charming white bungalows with thatched roofs perch on stilts among the trees, and at night, fireflies light up the place.

✖ Eating & Drinking

Koh Kong's dining scene is surprisingly appealing, with local restaurants that are cheap, authentic and delicious. There are also food stalls in the southeast corner of the market, **Psar Leu** (St 3; mains from US$1.50; ☺ 8am-11pm), and riverfront food carts sell noodles and cans of beer for a few thousand riel, doubling up as sunset drinking spots.

⭐**Happy Beach**   CAMBODIAN $
(☑ 097 744 4454; mains US$2-5; ☺ 24hr) Northeast of town, this place offers a unique slice of Cambodian life with seaside, covered decks on stilts where families and friends laze about with their shoes off, taking down heaping portions of Khmer food served off a wooden block on the ground.

Crab Shack   SEAFOOD $
(☑ 081 447093; Koh Yor Beach; mains US$4-8; ☺ hours vary) A family-run place over the bridge on Koh Yor Beach, this spot is known for perfect sunsets and heaping portions of fried crab with pepper (on request). If Crab Shack isn't open, the neighbouring restaurant also serves delicious crab and coconut water in little beach huts strung with hammocks.

Café Laurent   INTERNATIONAL $$
(☑ 088 829 0410; St 1; mains US$4-15; ☺ 10.30am-9.30pm Wed-Mon; 🛜) This chic waterfront cafe and restaurant offers atmospheric dining in over-water pavilions where you can sit back and watch the sunset while feasting on refined Western and Khmer cuisine. As well as French-accented steaks and a decent pasta menu, there's a huge range of fresh seafood and Asian classics, all served with fine-dining panache.

Wild Life Café   INTERNATIONAL $$
(St 1; mains US$3.50-7.50; ☺ 6am-10pm) Formerly called Seta's Ice Cream and still known for its desserts, this place also features scrumptious French-influenced seafood dishes such as bouillabaisse, pizza and baguettes along with a full range of Asian specials, with breakfast (US$1.50 to $4.50) thrown in for good measure. The friendly and knowledgeable owner speaks excellent English.

Paddy's Bamboo Pub   BAR
The US$1 beers and pool table at this sociable hostel pub occasionally draw a crowd, though don't waste your time coming out here in the low season. There's a menu of home-grown comfort flavours (mains US$2 to US$4).

ℹ Information

Thai baht are widely used so there's no urgent need to change baht into dollars or riel. To do so, use one of the many mobile-phone shops around Psar Leu.

Acleda Bank (St 3; ☺ 8am-3.30pm Mon-Fri, to 11.30am Sat, ATM 24hr)

Canadia Bank (St 1; ☉8am-3.30pm Mon-Fri, to 11.30am Sat, ATM 24hr)

Ritthy Koh Kong Eco Adventure Tours and guesthouses are the best places to get the local low-down.

In a medical emergency, evacuation to Thailand via the Cham Yeam–Hat Lek border crossing is possible 24 hours a day. In Thailand there's a hospital in Trat, 92km from the border.

ⓘ Getting There & Away

Koh Kong City is on NH48, 220km northwest of Sihanoukville, 290km west of Phnom Penh and 8km southeast of the Thai border. It's linked to the Thai border by a surfaced road that begins on the other side of the 1.9km toll bridge over the Koh Poi River.

BUS

The three main bus companies in town are **Olympic Transport** (☏011 363678; St 3), **Rith Mony** (☏012 640344; St 3) and **Virak Buntham** (☏089 998760; St 3). Most buses drop passengers at Koh Kong's **bus station** (St 12), on the northeast edge of town, where *moto* and *remork* drivers await, eager to overcharge tourists. Don't pay more than US$1/2 for the three-minute *moto/remork* ride into the centre. Departures are from the company offices in town.

Destinations include the following:

Bangkok Virak Buntham and Rith Mony serve Bangkok via Ko Chang (US$15 to US$18, including ferry to the island), with a change to a minivan at the border.

Phnom Penh Served by all three companies via both bus and minivan; the last trip each day is at around 1.30pm.

Sihanoukville Virak Buntham runs a direct bus at 8am and Olympic Transport has a direct minibus at 1.15pm; other trips to Sihanoukville, as well as to Kampot and Kep, involve a bus transfer.

Note that all three bus companies claim to offer night buses between Siem Reap and Koh Kong, but these require a long detour and bus change in Sihanoukville, leaving many a backpacker justifiably annoyed.

TAXI

From the **taxi lot** (St 12) next to the bus station, shared taxis head to Phnom Penh (US$11, five hours) and occasionally to Sihanoukville (US$10, four hours) and Andoung Tuek (US$5, two hours). As with anywhere, the best chance for a ride is in the morning. Guesthouses can set you up with a private taxi to Phnom Penh (US$55) or Sihanoukville (US$50).

Hiring a taxi to or from the Thai border costs about US$12 (bridge toll included), while a *moto/remork* will cost about US$3/8.

ⓘ Getting Around

Short *moto* rides within the centre are 2000r; *remork* rides are double that, but overcharging is common.

Motorbike hire is available from most guesthouses, as well as Ritthy Koh Kong Eco Adventure Tours. Ritthy Koh also rents out bicycles for half (US$1) and full days (US$2). **99 Guesthouse** (☏035-660 0999; 99guesthouse@gmail.com) rents them for US$1.50 a day and Paddy's Bamboo Guesthouse offers them free to guests.

KOH KONG CONSERVATION CORRIDOR

Stretching along both sides of NH48 from Koh Kong to the Gulf of Kompong Som (the bay northwest of Sihanoukville), the Koh Kong Conservation Corridor encompasses many of Cambodia's most outstanding natural sites, including the southern reaches of the fabled Cardamom Mountains, an area of breathtaking beauty and astonishing biodiversity, and the jungle-flanked Tatai River, with its myriad eco-adventures and fairytale accommodations.

The southern stretch of the corridor contains Botum Sakor National Park, which has been infringed upon by a multi-billion-dollar tourism development. Trail-bikers and

BUSES FROM KOH KONG CITY

DESTINATION	FARE	DURATION	FREQUENCY	COMPANY	TYPE
Bangkok	US$20-22	8hr	3 daily	Rith Mony, Virak Buntham	bus/minivan
Phnom Penh	US$8-12	6-5hr	10 daily	Olympic Transport, Rith Mony, Virak Buntham	bus/minivan
Sihanoukville	US$8-10	4½-5hr	8am	Olympic Transport, Virak Buntham	bus/minibus

---

ℹ GETTING TO THAILAND: KOH KONG TO TRAT

Getting to the border The **Cham Yeam/Hat Lek border crossing** (open 6am to 10pm), between Cambodia's Koh Kong and Trat in Thailand, links the beaches of Cambodia and Thailand. Leaving Cambodia, take a taxi (US$10 plus toll), *remork* (US$8), *moto* (US$3) or minibus (US$15 for nine people) from Koh Kong across the toll bridge to the border. Once in Thailand, catch a minibus to Trat, from where there are regular buses to Bangkok.

At the border Departing Cambodia via the Hat Lek border is pretty straightforward. Coming in the other direction and arriving in Cambodia, be aware that the Cham Yeam border is notorious for visa overcharging; these days you'll usually pay US$35.

Moving on From the Hat Lek border, take a silver minibus straight to Trat (120B, running every 40 minutes from 7.10am to 5.10pm). From here the company Cherdchai runs regular buses to Bangkok's Ekami bus terminal (230B, five hours). Buses depart hourly from 6am until 11.30pm. Anyone heading to the nearby island of Koh Chang can arrange onward transport in Trat.

Coming into Cambodia, note that you'll get a better deal on all transport from the border to Koh Kong if you pay in dollars not baht.

---

intrepid *moto* riders can still bypass the highway, though, taking a rugged road on the eastern coast to a scenic fishing village.

Tatai River & Waterfall

The Phun Daung (Tatai) Bridge, about 18km east of Koh Kong on NH48, is your gateway to jungle living. The main sight here is the waterfall.

However, the real attraction of the Tatai River is its isolated setting with dense forest plunging down to the riverbank. Spending a few days here, either exploring the lush and tranquil natural environment or swinging in a hammock while contemplating river life, is a pure get-away-from-it-all experience that offers extra kudos for sustainability.

◉ Sights

Tatai Waterfall   WATERFALL
(ទឹកធ្លាក់តាតៃ; US$1) Tatai Waterfall is a thundering set of rapids during the wet season, plunging over a 4m rock shelf. Water levels drop in the dry season, but you can swim year-round in the surrounding refreshing pools. The water is fairly pure as it comes down from the isolated high Cardamom Mountains. Access to the waterfall is by car or motorbike. The clearly marked turn-off is on NH48 about 15km southeast of Koh Kong, or 2.8km northwest of the Tatai Bridge.

From the highway it's about 2km to the falls along a rough access road. There's a

stream crossing about halfway – at the height of the wet season you may have to cross it on foot and walk the last kilometre. From Koh Kong, a half-day *moto/remork* excursion to Tatai Waterfall costs US$10/15 return, or less to go one way to the bridge.

☞ Tours

Neptune Adventure   ECOTOUR
(📱088 777 0576; www.neptuneadventure-cambodia.com; Tatai River) 🖉 This well-established ecotourism operator is based at Neptune River Bungalows on the Tatai River and offers highly recommended jungle treks as well as multi-activity adventures combining trekking, kayaking and boating. Day tours range from US$10 to US$25 per person.

🛏 Sleeping & Eating

The resorts all have their own restaurants and there are local eateries along the highway near the bridge.

Neptune River Bungalows   ECOLODGE **$$**
(📱088 777 0576; http://neptuneadventure-cambodia.com; Tatai River; bungalows incl breakfast US$35-50) 🖉 Want to play Robinson Crusoe? You're in the right place. Thomas (ecotour operator of long-running Neptune Adventure) has created a jungle getaway with bags of rustic charm. The four stilted bungalows, made of all natural materials, are set amid fruit trees. Meals (US$3 to $7), using produce from the on-site gardens, are usually eaten communally, adding to the homely vibe.

★ **Four Rivers Floating Lodge**   RESORT **$$$**
(☑097 643032, 097 758 9676; www.ecolodges.
asia; Tatai River; d incl breakfast US$279; ☎)
Glamping with extra wow-factor. The 12
canvas tent-villas here float on a pontoon
on a branch of the Tatai River estuary 6km
downriver from Tatai Bridge. The lavish
use of wicker and rich dark wood provides
a colonial-cool ambience, topped off by the
most sumptuous bathrooms you'll see under
canvas anywhere. Boat transfers to/from
Tatai Bridge are included (20 minutes).

Rainbow Lodge   ECOLODGE **$$$**
(☑012 160 2585; www.rainbowlodgecam
bodia.com; Tatai River; s/d/f incl all meals
US$75/95/135; ☎) 🗭 A slice of jungle-chic,
Rainbow Lodge proves being sustainable
doesn't mean having to sacrifice creature
comforts. Powered by solar panels and bio-
fuel, the bungalows here are set back from
the river. They are reached by elevated
walkways hugged by foliage and centred on
a sleek open-air lounge with an impressive
bar.

❶ Getting There & Away

All buses travelling to or from Koh Kong pass
through Tatai. If heading to one of the resorts,
ask the driver to let you off at the bridge and
arrange onward transport through your resort.

A *moto/remork* trip from Koh Kong to the
bridge will cost about US$7/10 return.

Koh Kong Island

Cambodia's largest island, Koh Kong
(កោះកុង) towers over seas so crystal-clear
you can make out individual grains of sand
in a couple of metres of water. A strong military presence on the island means access is
tightly controlled. You must visit on a guided boat tour out of Koh Kong or Tatai. These
cost US$21 per person, including lunch and
snorkelling equipment, or US$55 for over-
night trips with beach camping or homestay
accommodation. The island is only accessible from October to May.

During the June to September rainy season, strong onshore (southwesterly) breezes
make access impossible. It's forbidden to explore the island's thickly forested interior at
any time of year.

The island has seven beaches, all of
them along the western coast. Several of
the beaches – lined with coconut palms and
lush vegetation, just as you'd expect in a

tropical paradise – are at the mouths of little
streams. At the sixth beach from the north,
a narrow channel leads to a hidden lagoon.

Unfortunately the beaches are becoming
increasingly polluted as irresponsible tour
operators fail to properly dispose of waste.
Hopefully the situation can be reversed,
as the island is a real gem. Rampant sand
fleas are also notoriously bad during certain
times of the year.

On Koh Kong Island's eastern side, half
a dozen forested hills – the highest towering 407m above the sea – drop steeply to
the mangrove-lined coast. The Venice-like
fishing village of Alatang, with its stilted
houses and colourful fishing boats, is on the
southeast coast facing the northwest corner
of Botum Sakor National Park.

Central Cardamoms Protected Forest

The Central Cardamoms Protected Forest
(ឧទ្យានជាតិដូវភ្នំក្រវាញកណ្ដាល, CCPF) encompasses three of Southeast Asia's most
threatened ecosystems: lowland evergreen
forests, riparian forests and wetlands. The
rangers and military police who protect this
vast 4013 sq km area from illegal hunting
and logging are based at a few ranger stations, including one in Thma Bang.

The nearby Areng Valley, some of whose
inhabitants belong to the Khmer Daeum
minority community, is home to Asian elephants and the dragonfish (Asian arowana),
which is almost extinct in the wild. It also
has the world's second-largest population
of critically endangered wild Siamese crocodiles. These toothy critters can grow up to
3.5m long, but don't eat people, preferring
to dine on fish, snakes, frogs and small
mammals.

🏃 Activities

Mostly covered with dense rainforest,
Thma Bang is perfect for birdwatching
or hiking to a waterfall with a local guide
(rangers can help you find one). A new
community-based ecotourism project
(☑035-675 6444, 092 720925; ccheb@conserva
tion.org) is also set to launch here.

From December to May the truly intrepid
can take an eight-day trek from Thma Bang
north to Kravanh, or from Chamnar (linked
to Thma Bang by road) over the mountains
to Kravanh, a five- or six-day affair.

An easier, year-round option is the three- or four-day hike from Chumnoab, east of Thma Bang, eastwards to Roleak Kang Cheung, linked to Kompong Speu by road. Between the two is Knong Krapeur (1000m), set amid high-elevation grassland and pines. Inhabited five centuries ago, the area is known for its giant ceramic funeral jars, still filled with human bones.

There's no reservation system in Thma Bang; just show up and arrange trekking and accommodation on the spot. Or if you're based in Koh Kong, you can book an overnight excursion here with Ritthy Koh Kong Eco Adventure Tours (p178).

🛏 Sleeping & Eating

Here you'll find two basic **guesthouses** (per person US$5) – one run by the rangers, the other by the local community – each with a couple of rooms and a dorm, and with electricity from 6pm to 9pm. Meals can be prepared for US$2. Bring warm clothes, as the temperature can drop as low as 10°C.

❶ Getting There & Away

The southern reaches of the Central Cardamoms Protected Forest are easiest to reach from the south. The road to Thma Bang from NH48 has been widened and it now takes only about an hour to drive from Koh Kong. Turn off NH48 about 10km east of the Tatai River bridge at the Veal II (Veal Pii) ranger checkpoint.

Thma Bang is linked to Chi Phat by a difficult trail that can be handled by motorbike, but just barely and only in the dry season. We don't recommend it. Only attempt it in a large group of experienced bikers who can help navigate bikes over the more difficult river crossings and dried-out waterfall beds.

An improved road (though still much easier to navigate in the dry season), goes north from Koh Kong through the Cardamoms to Pursat, Pailin and Battambang, passing by remote mountain towns such as Veal Veng, Osoam (where there's an excellent ecotourism project) and Pramoay (the main town in the Phnom Samkos Wildlife Sanctuary). Near Koh Kong, the turn-off is on the old road to Phnom Penh past the airport, a few hundred metres beyond the army base.

Going south, share taxis link Pursat with Pramoay, Osoam and Koh Kong during the dry season. In the wet season, it may still be possible to hire a *moto* for the long trip from Pramoay to Koh Kong, depending on local road conditions and seasonal rainfall. Heading north from Koh Kong, share taxis are rare on this route.

The CCPF's northern sections are most easily accessible from Pursat.

Botum Sakor National Park

Occupying almost the entirety of the 35km-wide peninsula northwest across the Gulf of Kompong Som from Sihanoukville, this 1834-sq-km national park, encircled by mangroves and beaches, is home to a

A CAMBODIA TREASURE

The Cardamoms cover 20,000 sq km of southwestern Cambodia. Their remote peaks – up to 1800m high – and 18 major waterways are home to at least 59 globally threatened animal species including tigers, Asian elephants, bears, Siamese crocodiles, pangolins and eight species of tortoise and turtle.

Containing the second-largest virgin rainforest on mainland Southeast Asia, the Cardamoms are one of only two sites in the region where unbroken forests still connect mountain summits with the sea (the other is in Myanmar). Some highland areas receive up to 5m of rain a year. Conservationists hope the Cardamoms will someday be declared a Unesco World Heritage Forest.

While forests and coastlines elsewhere in Southeast Asia were being ravaged by developers and well-connected logging companies, the Cardamom Mountains and the adjacent mangrove forests were protected by their sheer remoteness and also by Cambodia's long civil war. As a result, much of the area is still in pretty good shape. The potential for ecotourism is huge – akin, some say, to that of Kenya's game reserves or Costa Rica's national parks.

The next few years will be critical in determining the future of the Cardamom Mountains. NGOs such as Conservation International (www.conservation.org), Fauna & Flora International (www.fauna-flora.org) and Wildlife Alliance (www.wildlifealliance.org), along with teams of armed enforcement rangers, are working to help protect the area's 16 distinct ecosystems from loggers and poachers. Ecotourism, too, can play a role by providing local people with sustainable alternatives to logging and poaching.

profusion of wildlife, including elephants, deer, leopards and sun bears.

Alas, a US$3.5 billion tourism project is developing the western third of the park into resort-cities, leaving the eastern third of the peninsula as the only viable area to visit. Boats can be hired in Andoung Tuek.

Chi Phat

Once notorious for land-grabbing, illegal logging and poaching, the river village of Chi Phat (population 630 families) is now home to a popular community-based eco-tourism project (CBET) launched by Wildlife Alliance (www.wildlifealliance.org) in 2002 to transform the Southern Cardamoms Protected Forest (1443 sq km), into a source of jobs and income for local people.

Chi Phat offers travellers an opportunity to explore the Cardamoms ecosystems while contributing to their conservation and providing an alternative livelihood to the former poachers who now act as the landscape's protectors and guides. Accommodation is in basic homestays and guesthouses, and there's a menu of activities on offer, from birdwatching kayak trips to combo hike-and-mountain-bike expeditions.

Note that the village only has electricity in the morning between 5am and 9am, and in the evening from 6pm to 9pm, so bring a torch (flashlight).

WILDLIFE ALLIANCE RELEASE STATION TOURS

Wildlife Alliance (☑ 095 970175; www.wildlifereleasecambodia.com; 1-night stay adult/child US$120/50, 2-night stay US$200/75) 🖉 operates tours to its release station (about 45 minutes from Chi Phat), where animals such as sun bears, binturongs and a great many hornbills are released into the wild after being rescued from illegal trafficking. Accommodation, food and activities – jungle trekking, wildlife tracking, and river swims – are included. Advance bookings essential.

Transport (by motorbike) is provided from either Andoung Tuek or Chi Phat, and it's one thrilling ride through forests, over streams and across grasslands.

🏃 Activities & Tours

All activities in Chi Phat are controlled through **CBET Community Visitor Centre** (☑ 035-675 6444, 092 720925; www.chi-phat.org; Chi Phat; ⊙ 7am-7pm; 🛜) 🖉, a two-minute walk from the river pier. Some guests report excellent experiences, though management can be a bit disorganised. Note that there's not a lot of English spoken.

All tours must be booked at the visitor centre by 5pm the day before. Head straight there when you arrive to meet the guides and other guests returning from treks. This is the time to get information about activities and the condition of the trails, and learn how the local community is now a force to protect the forests it once plundered.

Prices for tours range from US$25 to US$35 per person including lunch, transport and equipment. All-inclusive multi-day trips cost a bit more per day. Prices include a contribution to the community conservation fund. Most tours require guides, many of whom once worked as poachers and loggers.

As well as the many trekking, boating and mountain-biking activities on offer, you can also hire kayaks to explore the river by yourself. Khmer cooking classes are the latest addition to the local menu of activities.

Wildlife Alliance operate tours to its release station (p184) (about 45 minutes from Chi Phat), where animals such as sun bears and binturongs are released into the wild after being rescued from illegal trafficking. Advance bookings are essential.

Treks

CBET treks (per person per day US$25 to US$35) range from one to seven days, with shorter trips exploring the bat caves, waterfalls, mountain communities and mysterious burial-jar sites in the nearby surroundings.

On overnight trips you either sleep in hammocks or at one of five campsites set up by Wildlife Alliance, equipped with eco-toilets, field kitchens and comfortable hammocks with mosquito-proof nets. Wildlife-spotting isn't guaranteed but there are usually plenty of opportunities to shoot (with a camera) monkeys and hornbills. Although the guides wear flip-flops, it's recommended to bring walking shoes for the treks. Also, bring bug spray.

Boat Tours

CBET's sunrise birdwatching boat trips and sunset stargazing cruises (per person US$12 to US$35) are a great way to experience the languid beauty of the Preak Piphot River. The former involves a 1½-hour longtail boat ride before jumping in a traditional stand-up-rowing boat (with rower) and silently paddling along the placid Proat River, an unlogged tributary.

Silver langurs, long-tailed macaques, greater hornbills and other rainforest creatures can often be seen along the banks of the Proat River. Gibbons are hard to spot, but can often be heard calling to each other through the forest canopy.

Mountain Biking

CBET's one- to two-day mountain-biking tours (per person per day US$20 to US$25) follow trails to waterholes, burial-jar sites, waterfalls and rural communities in the surrounding forest. Overnight trips use hammocks (with mosquito nets) for sleeping. If you want to explore the countryside around Chi Phat village solo, you can also hire mountain bikes at the CBET visitor centre.

🛏 Sleeping

There's not a huge difference between the guesthouses and the homestays, some in town, others out amongst the orchards. All rooms are clean and commodious, and come with fans, mosquito nets, cotton sheets, foam mattresses, towel and free bottled water. Book ahead or when you arrive at the CBET visitor centre. The bungalows are more private but the one we stayed in lacked proper electrical outlets and was pretty buggy.

CBET Homestays HOMESTAY $
(r US$4) 🍃 Many of Chi Phat's 15 homestays are in wooden, stilted Khmer houses that offer a glimpse into rural life. Rooms are all cosy and simple, and bathrooms are shared with the family. Some homestays have squat toilets and traditional shower facilities (a rainwater cistern with a plastic bucket). Dinner (US$3) can be provided.

CBET Guesthouses GUESTHOUSE $
(r with shared/private bathroom US$5/7) 🍃 Chi Phat's CBET project operates 18 family-run guesthouses that provide small, clean rooms. While some only have shared bathrooms, others come with en-suite facilities. You can specify your preference when booking at the CBET visitor centre. All guesthouses are connected to the village's electricity grid, which operates mornings and evenings only.

CBET Bungalows BUNGALOW $
(www.chi-phat.org; bungalows US$15-30) 🍃 Chi Phat's assorted bungalow options provide a greater degree of privacy than the village's guesthouse and homestay accommodation. The bungalows are built from natural materials and come with en-suite bathrooms and balconies. They have electricity in the mornings and evenings, but don't expect proper outlets. Do expect insects and be sure to use the mosquito net.

🍴 Eating

Aside from the Visitor Centre Restaurant, several food stalls on the main strip between the river pier and the visitor centre sell simple local food for about US$2 a dish. Soft drinks and beer are available in local stores.

Visitor Centre Restaurant CAMBODIAN $
(breakfasts US$2.50, mains US$3.50; ⊙8am-9pm; 🍴) 🍃 The best restaurant in town is located at the visitor centre. Everybody enjoys the same selection of three dishes for lunch, and three dishes for dinner, and the menu changes daily. Vegetarians are catered for and packed lunches are available. All of the food is sourced locally, and much is locally grown or raised.

ℹ Information

Chi Phat has no bank or ATM, but it does have a credit-card machine. Bring a decent amount of cash just in case, though.

For information on all activities, tours, accommodation and getting to Chi Phat, visit the CBET Community Visitor Centre, which also offers bookings by email.

ℹ Getting There & Away

Chi Phat is on the scenic Preak Piphot River, 21km upriver from Andoung Tuek, which is on NH48, 98km from Koh Kong. All buses travelling between Koh Kong and Phnom Penh or Sihanoukville pass through here.

Arriving in Andoung Tuek, buses usually stop outside Kim Chhoun Guesthouse (the restaurant with blue pillars), where the management work in conjunction with CBET to help organise onward transport to Chi Phat. This is the place to organise a *moto* or ask about the CBET boat if you haven't already booked through the CBET website (www.chi-phat.org).

CBET's longtail boat (US$30), which makes the two-hour trip from Andoung Tuek when reserved in advance, is the most atmospheric way to get to Chi Phat. It's best to book at least 48 hours in advance through the CBET website.

The latest the boat can pick you up at Andoung Tuek is 4.30pm. The CBET community works only with local boatmen who have been trained in safety standards and whose boats have been remodelled to offer tourists a degree of comfort. The CBET-sanctioned boats have life jackets and carry a spare engine. If you miss the CBET boat, you can usually hire a local to take you upstream to Chi Phat for US$30 for up to five people.

A *moto* is faster (45 minutes) and costs US$7 for the 17km trip. A CBET-partnered *moto* that supplies passenger helmets can be booked in advance through the CBET site, although this is also easily organised upon arrival in Andoung Tuek. *Moto* drivers drop passengers off across the river from Chi Phat and a tiny raft-ferry (1000r) takes passengers to the village itself.

Travelling from Chi Phat, a boat or *moto* can be booked the night before to return to Andoung Tuek in the morning, in time to catch onward buses. The CBET office can also book bus tickets.

If you have your own transport, the road to Chi Phat is unsurfaced but in pretty good shape. Follow the telephone lines and use the car ferry to cross the river. Motorbikers can use the smaller raft-ferry, located 100m to the left of the main ferry.

SIHANOUKVILLE

📄 034 / POP 91,000

Sure, Sihanoukville (ក្រុងព្រះសីហនុ) would never win first prize in a pretty-town competition, and much of it is now dominated by casinos and tacky commercial centres. But despite the rapid and mostly unwanted development, it has remained the jumping-off point for the best of Cambodia's white-sand beaches and castaway-cool southern islands. The Serendipity Beach area is a decompression chamber for backpackers, who flock here to rest up between travels and party through the night.

Away from the hustle south of town is relaxed Otres Beach, where cheap bungalow joints and bohemian-flavoured guesthouses are now neighbours with rather swish boutique resorts. Although much of the beachfront will likely be cleared for large-scale development in the future, for now the mellow scene still allows for lazy days of sunbathing and whirlwind nights of bar-hopping.

👁 Sights

Wat Leu   BUDDHIST TEMPLE
(វត្តលើ, Wat Chhnothean; Map p187; Wat Leu Rd) Spectacular views of almost the entire city and gorgeous sunset panoramas await at Wat Leu, situated on a peaceful, forested hilltop 1.5km northwest of the city centre.

From the city centre, a *moto* ride due north up the hill costs 6000r, but drivers will likely want US$2. *Remork* drivers have to take the long way around and ask US$5.

Kbal Chhay Cascades   WATERFALL
(ទឹកធ្លាក់ក្បាលឆាយ; US$1, picnicking platforms per day 5000r) Thanks to their appearance in *Pos Keng Kong* (*The Giant Snake*; 2000), one of the most successful Cambodian films of the post-civil-war era, these cascades on the Prek Toeuk Sap River draw numerous domestic tourists. Hence all the picnicking platforms, drink stands and food stalls.

To get here from Sihanoukville, head east along NH4 for 5.5km from the Cambrew junction, then, at the sign, head north along a wide dirt road for 8km. By *moto/remork* a return trip costs US$7/15.

👁 Beaches

Sihanoukville's beaches each have a wildly different character, offering something for just about everyone. For a more isolated sandy strip, the beaches of Ream National Park (p200) are only a short ride away.

⭐ Otres Beach   BEACH
(ឆ្នេរអូរត្រេះ; Map p194) Past the southern end of Ochheuteal Beach, beyond the **Phnom Som Nak Sdach** (Hill of the King's Palace) headland, lies stunning Otres Beach, a seemingly infinite strip of casuarinas that gives southern Thailand a run for its money. Although no longer the empty stretch of sand it once was, Otres has cleaner water and is more relaxed than anything in Sihanoukville proper, and is lengthy enough that finding a patch to call your own is not a challenge... just walk south.

Long eyed-up by large-scale developers, Otres has so far managed to shun major construction work, and DIY development has blossomed with dozens of small-scale independent resorts and beach-bungalow places in the area, including a handful of upmarket boutique hotels. Otres is split into three distinct sections: **Otres 1** (Map p194) is the first and busiest stretch, while about 2km south is quieter **Otres 2** (Map p194), separated by a slated resort development currently known as 'Long Beach'. Inland lies laid-back **Otres Village**, an up-and-coming estuary area.

Otres Beach is about 5km south of the Serendipity area. It's a US$2 *moto* ride (re-

Sihanoukville

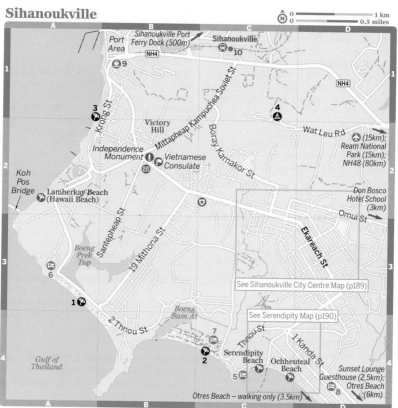

Sihanoukville

◎ Sights
1 Independence Beach A3
2 Sokha Beach C4
3 Victory Beach A1
4 Wat Leu C1

⊖ Sleeping
5 Cloud 9 ....C4
6 Dara Independence Beach
   Resort A3
7 Sokha Beach Resort C4
8 Tamarind D4

ℹ Transport
9 GTVC Speedboat B1
10 Train Ticket Counter C1

mork US$5) to get here (more at night). If going it alone, follow the road southeast along the beach and skirt the hill by heading inland on the inviting tarmac. From the city centre, you can take Omui St from Psar Leu east out of town for 5km.

Serendipity Beach BEACH
(ឆ្នេរសិរិន ឌីភីធី; Map p190) The rocky strip at the northwestern end of Ochheuteal Beach is known as Serendipity Beach. It has a some r e s o r t bar-restaurants where waves lap a few metres from the tables, providing a romantic backdrop.

Sokha Beach BEACH
(ឆ្នេរសុខា; Map p187) Midway between Independence and Serendipity Beaches lies Sihanoukville's prettiest stretch of sand, 1.5km-long Sokha Beach. Its fine, silicon-like sand squeaks loudly underfoot. The tiny eastern end of Sokha Beach is open to the public and is rarely crowded. The rest is part of the exclusive **Sokha Beach Resort** (Map p187; ☏ 034-935999; www.sokhahotels.com; Thnou St; r/ste from US$171/210; ❋ @ 🛜 ☀). Tourists are welcome to enjoy the sand near the resort

DRESS CODE

One annoyance for locals is under-dressed foreigners wandering about town. Cambodia is not Thailand; Khmers are generally more conservative than their neighbours. Just look at the Cambodians frolicking in the sea – most are fully dressed.

Wearing bikinis on the beach is fine, but strolling around the streets in a swimsuit is considered disrespectful. Female travellers should note that top-less or nude bathing is a definite no-no.

but are expected to buy something to drink or eat. You might even duck into the resort to use the pool (US$5).

Ochheuteal Beach   BEACH

(ឆ្នេរអូរឈើទាល; Map p190) This 4km-long beach is by far Sihanoukville's most popular. The rocky strip at the northwestern end is a happy, easy-going travellers' hang-out known as Serendipity Beach. East of the pier, a string of beach-bars rim the white sand. This is a good place for happy hour, but during the day becomes packed with vendors and beggars.

Escape the mayhem by walking 2km to 3km down to the much cleaner southern section of the beach. The character of Ochheuteal will change dramatically if local authorities implement a plan to evict all beachfront businesses, with any new development required to occur at least 50m from the shoreline. Plans also call for high-end resorts to be built at the isolated southern end.

Victory Beach   BEACH

(ឆ្នេរជ័យជំនះ; Map p187) Not the best beach in town due to the looming backdrop of the Sihanoukville Port development, which has closed off part of Victory Beach. But the part that remains open offers some hotels, nicer seafood restaurants and a couple of casinos. Up from the beach, Victory Hill has emerged recently as a nighttime hot spot, with a street of bars frequented by sports fans and hostess-bar enthusiasts.

Independence Beach   BEACH

(ឆ្នេរឯករាជ្យ, 7-Chann Beach; Map p187) Northwest of Sokha Beach, much of Independence Beach (also known as 7-Chann Beach) has been taken over by a gargantuan new property development, but a 500m swath is open

to the public and features about a dozen restaurants and bars.

🏃 Activities

Sala Santepheap   MASSAGE

(Map p189; off 7 Makara St, Starfish Bakery; per hr US$6-10; ⊙7am-6pm) 🦯 Visually impaired or physically disabled therapists trained by the Starfish Project perform Khmer, Thai, oil, foot and Indian head massages in the Starfish Bakery garden. Profits go towards social projects.

Seeing Hands Massage 3   MASSAGE

(Map p189; ☑034-679 2555; 95 Ekareach St; per hr US$6; ⊙8am-9pm) 🦯 Some of the blind masseurs who work here speak English.

Diving & Watersports

Scuba Nation   DIVING

(Map p190; ☑012 604680; www.divecambodia.com; Serendipity Beach Rd; 2-dive package US$85, PADI Open Water Diver course US$445; ⊙9am-8pm) The longest-running dive operator in Sihanoukville, Scuba Nation is a PADI five-star IDC (instructor development centre) with a comfortable boat for day and live-aboard trips.

Dive Shop   DIVING

(Map p190; ☑034-933664, 097 723 2626; www.diveshopcambodia.com; Serendipity Beach Rd; PADI Discover Scuba course US$95, 2-dive package US$80; ⊙7am-9pm) A PADI five-star dive centre offering full gamut of PADI courses, as well as fun dives, out of its bases at Sunset Beach (high season) and Saracen Bay (low season) on Koh Rong Sanloem. Also runs snorkelling tours.

EcoSea Dive   DIVING

(Map p190; ☑016 953610; www.ecoseadive.com; Serendipity Beach Rd; 2-dive package US$90; ⊙7am-8pm) Offers both PADI and SSI courses and has competitively priced fun-dive rates. Has an island base at its resort near M'Pai Bay on Koh Rong Sanloem. EcoSea has its own accommodations on the island as well, Koh Rong Sanloem Villas (r US$30 to US$40, dorm US$5).

Otres Sailing Club   BOATING

(Map p194; ☑087 891778; per hr kayak/paddleboard rental from US$6; ⊙7.30am-midnight) Rents paddleboards, kayaks and large catamarans. Those with the know-how can sail to nearby islands and even do self-guided overnight trips.

Sihanoukville City Centre

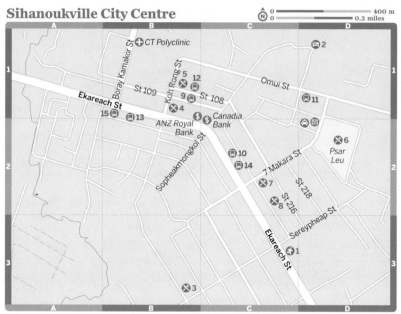

N 0 — 400 m
0 — 0.2 miles

Sihanoukville City Centre

Activities, Courses & Tours
Sala Santepheap .... (see 8)
1 Seeing Hands Massage 3 ....C3

Sleeping
2 Don Bosco Guesthouse......................... D1

Eating
3 Cabbage Restaurant..............................B3
4 Espresso Kampuchea...........................B1
5 Gelato Italiano..B1
6 Psar Leu..D2
7 Samudera Supermarket C2
8 Starfish Bakery & Cafe C2

Shopping
Starfish..(see 8)

Transport
9 Bus Station B1
10 Capitol Tour..C2
11 Mekong Express D1
12 Olympic Express.....................................B1
13 Phnom Penh Sorya.................................B1
14 Rith Mony...C2
15 Virak Buntham B1

SOUTH COAST SIHANOUKVILLE

🎓 Courses

Don Bosco Hotel
Khmer Cooking Course   COOKING
(☏016 919834; www.donboscohotelschool.com/
cooking; Ou Phram St, Don Bosco Hotel School; per
person US$30) ✎ The cooking classes here pro-
vide a great opportunity to learn some Khmer
culinary skills. They include a slap-up three-
course lunch (which you've helped create), as
well as a tour of the hotel school. Classes run
from 8.30am to 1.30pm every weekday and
start with a market trip, but guests can also
join at 10am after the market (for US$5 less).

Classes support the worthy Don Bosco
Hotel School, a well-run operation that helps
underprivileged young Cambodians learn
practical skills in the hospitality industry.

☞ Tours

Popular **day tours** go to some islands such
as Koh Rong, Koh Rong Sanloem or Koh Ta
Kiev, and to Ream National Park (per person
US$20).

You can also **hire a boat** and make your
own way to nearer islands such as Koh Ta
Kiev (US$50) or Koh Russei (US$40), while
a space on a shared boat to the same islands

Serendipity

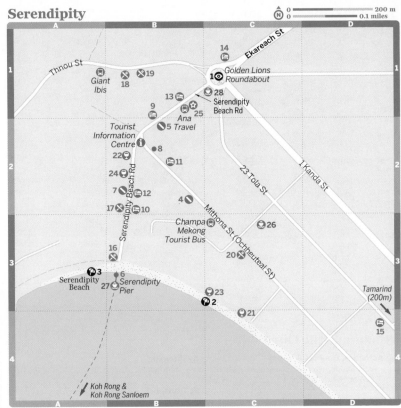

will only cost US$5; on Otres Beach, where prices are cheaper than Ochheuteal Beach, head to either **Sam's Bar** (Map p194; ☺7am-1am) or SeaGarden to arrange a boat.

Booze cruises offer backpackers the chance to spend the day on-board getting sloshed under the sun. Be aware that accidents have occurred (including one boat sinking due to overloading passengers) and there are rarely enough life jackets to go around. Check out the boat operator thoroughly before signing up.

Suntours   BOATING
(☏096 379 4133; per adult/child US$25/12.50; ☺departs at 10am, back at 5pm) Suntours offers island cruises aboard a motor yacht, with day trips to Koh Rong Sanloam that get rave reviews. Trips include snacks, buffet lunch, coffee and tea, as well as snorkelling, kayaking and fishing equipment. Pickup points vary.

Party Boat   BOATING
(Map p190; ☏034-666 6106; Serendipity Beach Pier; per person US$25) The daily cruise (9.30am to 5pm) to Koh Rong Sanloem includes snacks, lunch, snorkelling and a free drink. This outfit also runs return transport to Koh Rong Island's full-moon parties, leaving Sihanoukville at 5pm and returning around 8am.

Stray Dogs of Asia   ADVENTURE
(Map p190; ☏017 810125; www.straydogasia.com; Mithona St; tour US$120; ☺9am-6pm) Runs all-day countryside dirt-bike tours that take in some of the natural attractions around Sihanoukville.

Liberty Ranch   HORSE RIDING
(Map p194; ☏016 339774; www.horseback-cambodia.com; Otres Village; 1/2/3hr trail ride US$25/45/65; ☺7-11am & 2-6pm) A horseback tour is a great way to discover the tranquil countryside around Sihanoukville. Total be-

Serendipity

ginners can opt for trails along Otres Beach and explore the small villages nearby, while more advanced riders can venture on longer tours that head further out towards the hills.

🛏 Sleeping

Location, location, location; each Sihanoukville district has its own distinct character and attracts a different type of clientele. We quote prices for the high season (approximately November to March). Rates drop between June and October, especially on Serendipity and Otres Beaches, but can skyrocket on Khmer holidays at some establishments.

Serendipity Area

The main backpacker hang-out is Serendipity Beach Rd which runs up the hill from Serendipity Beach, connecting to Ekareach St at the **Golden Lions Roundabout** (Map p190; Ekareach St). A string of wallet-friendly crash pads and guesthouses meander all the way up the street. Decent midrange options can be found on the roads running southeast from here.

Late-night noise from the nearby clubs affects most of the accommodations around here, while the din lessens substantially in the hotels slightly further east. Light sleepers may want to bunk elsewhere.

★ **Chochi Garden** GUESTHOUSE $
(Map p190; ☎ 096 274 7674; www.facebook.com/ Chochi-Garden-Guest-House-944887078922026; Serendipity Beach Rd; r with fan/air-con US$15/25; ❄ 🛜) Run by a friendly expat couple, this boutique backpacker pad is the closest Serendipity gets to a tranquil oasis right in the heart of the action. Out front is a cool bar-restaurant while simple rooms, some with palm-thatch roofs and pretty painted window-grills, are in a plant-filled garden strewn with comfy seating areas.

Onederz Hostel HOSTEL $
(Map p190; ☎ 096 339 0005; onestophostelsshv@ gmail.com; Golden Lions Roundabout; dm US$8; ❄ @ 🛜 ≋) The six- and eight-bed dorms here are decked out in lashings of white-on-white and centred on a wall-to-ceiling glassed courtyard with a small pool, proving slick styling doesn't have to cost the earth. The 68 beds have individual reading lamps and luggage lock-boxes, and all dorms are air-conditioned. One quibble is that the bottom bunks are basically on the floor.

Big Easy HOSTEL $
(Map p190; ☎ 081 943930; Serendipity Beach Rd; dm US$4, r US$8-10; 🛜) This classic backpacker joint offers accommodation, comfort food and a lively rock bar, all rolled into one. The dorms are basic but have some amenities: AC, hot water, privacy curtains and plentiful

power outlets. Still, you'll most likely spend your time in the bar. There's a great vibe with occasional live music, live English Premier League games and beer pong.

Happy-hour specials go from 5pm to 11pm and the hostel runs a famous pub crawl on Fridays.

Monkey Republic
HOSTEL $

(Map p190; ☑ 012 490290; www.monkeyrepublic. info; Serendipity Beach Rd; dm US$6, r with fan US$15-22, with air-con US$18-30; ❋ @ 🛜 ☒) Self-proclaimed 'backpacker central', Monkey Republic rose from the ashes in 2013 following a dramatic fire (no casualties). It offers decent dorms and plain, affordable rooms in a building fronted by a yellow French colonial facade. The bar-restaurant constantly heaves with young travellers.

★ Ropanha Boutique Hotel
BOUTIQUE HOTEL $$

(Map p190; ☑ 012 556654; www.ropanha-boutique hotel.com; 23 Tola St; r incl breakfast US$45-55; ❋ 🛜 ☒) The pick of the pack when it comes to affordable atmosphere in the Serendipity area. Set around a lush courtyard garden and pool, Ropanha's rooms include flatscreen TVs and accompanying DVD players, plus rain showers in the bathrooms. Deluxe rooms have pool views but all have lashings of white and are exceptionally well cared for.

Sunset Lounge Guesthouse
RESORT $$

(Map p194; ☑ 097 734 0486; www.sunset lounge-guesthouse.com; South Ochheuteal; r US$35, bungalows US$54; ❋ 🛜) Way down at the windswept far-south end of Ochheuteal Beach, this secluded boutique-quality resort suits those for whom Otres Beach is too busy. With thick mattresses, dreamy shaded balconies, appealing bathrooms and a well-reputed restaurant, this is one of the top values in town. The bungalows are worth the small splurge.

It's much quicker to walk to Otres Beach from here (10 minutes) than to central Ochheuteal (30 minutes).

Cloud 9
BUNGALOW $$

(Map p187; ☑ 098 215166; www.cloud9bungalows. com; Serendipity Beach; d/tr from US$50/60; 🛜) The westernmost hotel on Serendipity Beach is a fine choice, and not just because it's furthest removed from the club noise. Cloud 9 has a cosy tropical bar perched over the shore, and we really like its range of rustic, Khmer-style wooden bungalows with fans and ocean-view balconies.

Holiday Villa Nataya
HOTEL $$

(Map p190; ☑ 034-935061; www.holidayvillahotels. com; Serendipity Beach Rd; r incl breakfast from $55; ❋ 🛜 ☒) Set around a somewhat bizarre interior courtyard pool, the rooms here are tranquil cocoons above the din of Serendipity Beach Rd, with luscious beds, huge flatscreen TVs, attractive art and an appealing slate-grey colour scheme. It's worth paying extra to get one of the ocean-view rooms with balconies.

Coolabah Resort
HOTEL $$

(Map p190; ☑ 017 678218; www.coolabah-hotel. com; 14 Mithona St; r US$42-80; ❋ @ 🛜 ☒) Kudos to Coolabah for having the most on-the-ball staff in the Serendipity area. Rooms are classically styled in soothing neutrals with smart art and contemporary bathrooms, and come in a variety of sizes including family options. The bar here is one of Serendipity's more relaxed places to sit down with a beer.

🛏 City Centre & Around

The shabby city centre, spread out along and north of Ekareach St, is preferred by some long-termers because it's cheap, removed from the traveller scene and near the buses. Most banks and businesses are here too, as is Sihanoukville's main market.

Victory Hill (also known as 'The Hill') is a backpacker haven up the hill from Victory Beach. The main drag is fairly sleazy, though, and far removed from its original hippytrippy vibe. Still, some long-running budget guesthouses remain here and are good value.

Independence Beach and Sokha Beach both have high-end resorts occupying their prime beach real estate.

Don Bosco Guesthouse
GUESTHOUSE $

(Map p189; ☑ 087 919834; www.donboscoguest house.com; r US$10-18) This large, concrete yellow structure, once a brothel, now contains a charming guesthouse where Cambodian students practise hospitality skills they learned over at the Don Bosco Hotel School. The resulting service is adorable and excellent. Rooms are spacious, with lovely checkered tile flooring, comfy beds and spotless en-suite bathrooms.

Tamarind
BOUTIQUE HOTEL $$

(Map p187; ☑ 097 5002429; www.the-tamarind. com; 23 Tola St; d/tr incl breakfast US$60/80; 🛜 ☒) Finally Sihanoukville has a poolside boutique hotel to rival those in Siem Reap and Phnom Penh. The amply sized rooms push all the right buttons, with private balconies, clean white walls, large flat-screen TVs and just the right mix of smart furniture. A lush garden and small pool lend the place an intimate vibe.

Don Bosco Hotel School HOTEL **$$**
(☑016 919834; www.donboscohotelschool.com; Ou Phram St; s US$25, d US$30-55; ※ ⚡ ❄) ◢
This excellent training hotel offers disadvantaged youngsters a helping hand into the hospitality industry. Rooms are great value with three-star trim throughout. Facilities include a pool, a gym and an Italian restaurant. The location isn't great but the experience more than compensates. It's signposted from Omui St when travelling out of the city centre on the road to Otres Beach.

**Dara Independence
Beach Resort** HOTEL **$$$**
(Map p187; ☑034-934300; www.independence hotel.net; 2 Thnou St; d/ste from US$130/160; ※ @ ⚡ ❄) Originally opened in 1963, this striking seven-storey hotel still has the jet-set feel of Sihanoukville's movie-star heyday. Following years of neglect it was reopened in 2007 and features fresh, contemporary rooms with sea panoramas or views of the landscaped gardens, and a few bungalows overlooking the water. Ride the elevator to the private beach.

There's a free shuttle that runs downtown throughout the day and evening.

🛏 Otres

Groovy little Otres is Sihanoukville's laid-back beach colony with a cluster of bungalows, guesthouses and stylish boutique resorts running along the sand. The beach is split into two sections, separated by a 2.5km section of empty sand. Otres 1 has most of the accommodation while quieter Otres 2, further south, is home to the boutique resorts.

Just inland is Otres Village with a selection of relaxed places nestled on a river estuary. Otres Beach has long been slated for development; if that happens, many of the backpacker places would be forced to move off the beach, with Otres Village being an obvious relocation option.

★ Wish You Were Here HOSTEL **$**
(Map p194; ☑097 241 5884; Otres 1; dm from US$6, r without bathroom US$12-16, r with bathroom US$20; ⚡) This rickety wooden building is one of the hippest hang-outs in Otres. Rooms are simple but the upstairs balcony

and sunset deck encourage serious sloth-time, while the bar-restaurant downstairs has a great vibe thanks to chilled-out tunes and friendly staff.

Even if you're not staying here, stop in to have a drink or sample the Aussie meat pies (US$4.50 to US$7) or the quesadillas (US$3 to US$4.50).

Otres Orchid BUNGALOW **$**
(Map p194; ☑034-633 8484; www.otresor chid.com; Otres 1; bungalows with fan/air-con US$20/35; ※ ⚡) Cracking value, the Orchid offers simple bungalows at sensible prices in a garden setting a hop, skip and jump to the beach. The fan-only bungalows have more character than the air-con options and come with hammock-strung balconies.

Footprints HOSTEL **$**
(Map p194; ☑097 262 1598; footprintotres@gmail. com; dm US$5, bungalows US$25) This homey, two-story hostel in Otres Beach is a charmer. Rooms are fan-cooled and sprawled around a garden and restaurant just a few steps from the beach.

Jumanji Hostel HOSTEL **$**
(Map p194; ☑096 490 2711; Otres Village; dm US$3-6, r US$10-20) This hostel and sports bar opened in Otres Village in 2017 and quickly began drawing nighttime action, particularly on Mondays, with live sports and bar games. It offers a variety of accommodations at different price points (with bathrooms and without, with air-conditioning and without).

SeaGarden BUNGALOW **$**
(Map p194; ☑096 253 8131; www.facebook.com/ seagarden.otres; Otres 1; dm US$6, r US$15-20; ⚡) Look no further for a cheap bungalow right on the sand. SeaGarden offers basic huts, and rooms in a stilted building, both on the beach. While everything is neat as a pin, the 13-bed dorm, with individual fans, plugs and attractive wood-framed beds, stands out.

★ Mama Clare's BUNGALOW **$$**
(Map p194; ☑097 690 2914; www.mamaclares.com; Otres Village; bungalows US$20-30; ⚡) Peaceful downtime is on the cards at this homely place on Otres' riverbank. The wood-and-thatch stilted bungalows are a rustic retreat from the world and vegetarian dinners (US$4 to US$5, high season only) are eaten communally. Guests can use the kitchen in the low season.

Kayak rental is available and you can paddle to Otres Beach from here when the water is up. Book ahead so Mama is ready for you.

Otres Beach

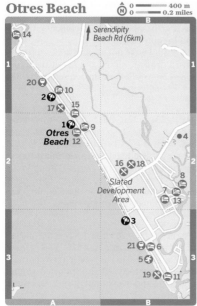

N 0 — 400 m
0 — 0.2 miles

Serendipity
Beach Rd (6km)

Papa Pippo BUNGALOW **$$**
(Map p194; ☑010 359725; www.papapippo.com;
Otres 1; bungalows US$30-40) Sandy-toed bliss
is at hand in these cosy, and rather classy,
beachfront bungalows. Glass doors make
the most of the sea views while the interiors,
with painted-wood walls and tiled floors,
add a touch of individual style.

Mushroom Point BUNGALOW **$$**
(Map p194; ☑097 712 4635; mushroompoint.
otres@gmail.com; Otres 1; bungalows US$25-30;
☜) The lobby in the shape of a mushroom
wins the award for most creative in Cambodia. Even those averse to communal living
will be content in their mosquito-net-draped
pods, good for two. Quirky 'shroom-shaped
bungalows are beautifully conceived with
hammocks outside for lounging. The beach
annex has more bungalows and a bar.

Sok Sabay BOUTIQUE HOTEL **$$**
(Map p194; ☑016 406080; www.facebook.com/
Sok-Sabay-Resort-634629623345356; Otres Vil-
lage; r US$50; ❄☜☵) Escape from the world
in style at this new poolside boutique, which
ups the ante for accommodation in Otres
Village. The rooms have inlaid-bamboo walls
and balconies strewn with well-cushioned
furniture. The restaurant overlooks the

village lake and shares an owner with top
Otres Beach eatery Chez Paou.

Secret Garden RESORT **$$$**
(Map p194; ☑097 649 5131; www.secretgardenotres.
com; Otres 2; bungalows incl breakfast from US$109;
❄☜☵) Otres' first upmarket boutique resort
is still one of its best. Cute bungalows, set
amid a manicured garden with swimming
pool and attached kiddie pool, have bright
and breezy decor, while sun-lounging heaven
is available at the delicious beachside bar-
restaurant across the road.

Tamu BOUTIQUE HOTEL **$$$**
(Map p194; ☑088 901 7451; www.tamucambodia.
com; Otres 2; r incl breakfast US$115-185; ❋ ⛄ ⛑)
This ultra-contemporary boutique hotel offers
a range of simple, yet chic rooms set around
a courtyard pool. Bag a pool-front room for a
Balinese-style alfresco bathroom. There's also
a hip beachside restaurant open to all.

Ren RESORT **$$$**
(Map p194; ☑066 292526; www.ren-resort.com;
Otres 2; r incl breakfast US$90-160; ❋ ⛄ ⛑) Ren
has gone for super-slick minimalism with a
nod to mid-century modern in its 24 stylish
rooms set around an inviting pool and surrounded by lush foliage. Three rooms have
rather sumptuous outdoor bathrooms, while
others have balconies that flow right into
the pool – great for those who fancy a swim
as soon as they wake up.

✗ Eating
If you've had your fill of noodles for awhile,
Sihanoukville's globe-trotting mash-up menus should hit the right spot. The Serendipity
area has the most dining choice, but the gritty
commercial centre also holds a few culinary
surprises, as well as cheap eats around the
main market, **Psar Leu** (Map p189; 7 Makara St;
mains from US$1; ⏱7am-9pm). Otres is your best
bet for atmospheric meals on the beach.

✗ Serendipity & Ochheuteal
For ambience, check out the over-the-water
resort restaurants at Serendipity Beach. Two
blocks inland, Tola St was once developing
into a restaurant zone, but many of its best
spots are being replaced with casinos.

★**Sandan** CAMBODIAN **$$**
(Map p190; ☑034-452 4000; 2 Thnou St; mains
US$4-10; ⏱11.30am-11pm; ⛄⛲) ✐ Loose-
ly modelled on the beloved Phnom Penh
institution Romdeng (p68), this superb
restaurant is an extension of the vocational-
training programmes for at-risk Cambodi-
ans run by local NGO M'lop Tapang. The
menu features creative Cambodian cuisine
targeted at a slightly upmarket clientele.
The place is brimming with potted plants
and hosts occasional cultural shows.

★**Manoha** FRENCH **$$**
(Map p190; ☑034-657 2666; www.facebook.com/
pg/restaurant.manoha; mains from US$5; ⏱24hr)
At this charming but modest-looking place
on Serendipity Rd, the French and Khmer

menu is enormous – with 130 dishes, to be
exact. And whether it's a sandwich, a salad,
an omelette, some frogs' legs or even barra-
cuda carpaccio you're after, this place will
nail it. And it's always open.

Sushi Bar Shin JAPANESE **$$**
(☑069 588117; Serendipity Beach Rd; sushi platters
from US$9.50; ⏱11.30am-10pm) Formerly located
in Otres, and now on the main drag in Seren-
dipity, Shin is still all about freshly prepared
sushi, with just tempura and a few other al-
ternatives on the menu. A contemporary Japa-
nese interior rounds out the experience.

Taj Mahal INDIAN **$$**
(Map p190; 23 Mithana St; curries US$3-10; ⏱8am-
11pm; ⛄) British expats rave about the food
here. Selecting bespoke dishes can add up to
an expensive spread, so the thalis (set meals,
US$4 to US$7) are a particularly good deal.

✗ City Centre & Around
Starfish Bakery & Cafe CAFE **$**
(Map p189; ☑012 952011; www.starfishcambo-
dia.org; off 7 Makara St; sandwiches US$3.50-
4.75; ⏱7am-5.30pm; ⛄⛲) ✐ This relaxing,
NGO-run garden cafe specialises in filling
Western breakfasts, baked cakes and tarts,
and healthy, innovative sandwiches heavy
on Mexican and Middle Eastern flavours.
Sitting down for coffee here on the shady
terrace is a peaceful reprieve from Sihanoukville's hustle. Income goes to sustainable development projects.

Espresso Kampuchea CAFE **$**
(Map p189; Boray Kamakor St; mains US$2-4;
⏱8am-10pm) Serious caffeine aficionados
should definitely make the trip down a nondescript side street in Sihanoukville centre
to get to Espresso Kampuchea. The owner,
Sophal, personally sources her coffee from
Thailand and serves up excellent double-shot
cappuccinos and espresso. There's a small
menu of baguettes, fried noodles and other
breakfasts – and draught beer for US$0.75.

Dao of Life VEGAN **$**
(Map p190; Serendipity Beach Rd; mains US$3.50-
6; ⏱8am-10pm; ⛄⛲) ✐ Draped with Chinese lanterns and awash with recycled
furniture, Dao dishes up creative and tasty
vegan meals. Its veggie burger (made from
sweet potato and kidney beans) is particularly good, or tuck into other healthy options
such as crispy cumin-and-coriander falafel.

Cabbage Restaurant CAMBODIAN $
(Chamka Spai; Map p189; mains 8000-15,000r; ◎11am-10pm) Known to locals as Chamka Spai, this restaurant gets rave reviews for its seafood and spicy seasonings. An authentic Khmer dining experience. A sign in English on Sereypheap St points the way, but look out for nearby, imposter restaurants with the same name.

Gelato Italiano ICE CREAM $
(Map p189; St 109; mains US$2-5, gelatos US$1; ◎7.30am-9pm; ✷🛜) ✐ Run by students from Don Bosco Hotel School, this cafe specialises in gelato (Italian-style ice cream) but offers so much more, including coffee drinks, pizza and full-blown Asian fusion meals in a bright, airy space. Wonderful value.

Marco Polo ITALIAN $$
(Map p190; ✆092 920866; Thnou St; mains US$3-8; ◎noon-10pm; 🛜) Some of the best Italian food for miles around is created by the Italian owner and chef of Marco Polo. The pasta dishes are perfectly al dente and the thin-crust pizzas emerging from the wood-fired oven are divine.

Self-Catering

Samudera Supermarket SUPERMARKET $
(Map p189; 7 Makara St; ◎6.30am-9pm) Selection of fruit, veggies and imported food brands, including European cheeses and wine.

🍴 Otres

Otres City Restaurant CAMBODIAN $
(Map p194; ✆016 208797; Otres Village; mains US$3.50; ◎7am-10pm; ✐) A local spot in Otres Village serving Khmer and Western grub, with a lip-smackin' scallop, pepper and potato dish that'll set you back a whole US$3.50. Lots of veggie options, too.

Bob's Bar BAGELS $
(Map p194; Otres Village; bagels from US$2; ◎hours vary) This is the morning spot for fresh-from-the-oven bagels and deliciously potent Bloody Marys. In the evening it's a pretty fun cocktail bar, too.

★Chez Paou INTERNATIONAL $$
(Map p194; Otres 1; mains US$5-22; ◎8am-11pm; 🛜) This is fine dining Otres style: right on the beach. The menu contains a good selection of steaks, pasta and burgers, but it's the Khmer specials (order in advance) – stingray cooked on embers with fresh Kampot pepper, prawns flambéed in pastis, and crabs

cooked two different ways – that make this place really stand out.

★Amareina ITALIAN $$
(Map p194; ✆070 900306; pizzas US$6-8) This Italian restaurant and guesthouse has quickly gained a reputation for the best party pool in town, which is free for non-guests as well, and its pizzas and pastas are divine. There's also a small but decent selection of wine and the best carpaccio in Otres Beach.

Papa Pippo ITALIAN $$
(Map p194; Otres 1; mains US$5-7; ◎9am-9.30pm; 🛜) Located on the beachfront, Papa Pippo brings Italian flair to Otres. Its home-made pasta is some of the best on the coast and there are plenty of regional specialities from Emilia-Romagna (where the owners hail from) on the menu. The pizza oven stays fired up well past the official closing time, often 'til the wee hours.

Secret Garden Restaurant SEAFOOD $$
(Map p194; ✆097 649 5131; www.secretgarden-notres.com/bar-and-restaurant; Otres 2; mains US$7-8.50; ◎7am-10pm; 🛜✐) ✐ Across from the eponymous hotel, this seaside, open-air restaurant is easily the top place to eat in Otres 2, and a great spot for sundowners as well. The chef specialises in fresh seafood but has range, from Western to Asian to vegetarian to gluten-free, drawing from an on-site garden and what's fresh in the market.

🍷 Drinking & Nightlife

There's no shortage of venues in which to quaff locally brewed Angkor Beer, on draught for as little as US$0.25.

Serendipity Beach Rd hotels have lively bars; Big Easy (p191) hosts a Friday pub crawl, and the beach-shack bars on Ochheuteal Beach are a scene, albeit a sleazy one.

A few long-standing regular bars remain amid Victory Hill's trashy hostess bars.

Maybe Later BAR
(Map p190; Serendipity Beach Rd; ◎11am-11pm) This popular little Mexican taco restaurant that doubles as a bar serves top-notch margaritas and some refined tequilas for those who prefer sips to shots. It's a civilised escape from the beachside party scene.

Martini Bar BAR
(Map p190; ◎8.30am-11.30pm) The classiest joint on Ochheuteal Beach is also the friendliest, and its yummy Italian dishes and de-

cent wine list regularly seduce the expat crowd. We just wish they'd keep the reds at room temp.

Last Hippie Standing BAR
(Otres Corner; Map p194; ☑ 097 579 5329; Otres 1; ⊙ 24hr) The first place you'll see when you enter the Otres area and, often, the last place you'll have been seen on particularly rowdy nights. DJs play dance and trance music 'til the wee hours and the owners offer basic, US$10 accommodations to guests who decide they never want to leave.

La Rhumerie BAR
(Map p190; Serendipity Beach Rd; ⊙ 9am-2am) Pull up a bar stool at La Rhumerie for salsa music and yummy rum infused with ingredients such as Kampot pepper, ginger and coffee. The rum selection hails from 17 countries and pairs well with many of the food items on the menu, including BBQ. Not a rum fan? The bar also whips up mean cocktails, such as a spicy mango margarita.

JJ's Playground BAR
(Map p190; Ochheuteal Beach; ⊙ 6pm-6am) The go-to spot for those seeking late-night debauchery. The scene here is pretty much summed up by JJ's slogan: 'let's get wasted'. Expect shots, loud techno music, a fire show or two, and a lot of chaos. And don't say we didn't warn you about the toilets.

☆ Entertainment

Otres Market LIVE MUSIC
(Map p194; www.facebook.com/otres.market; Otres Village; ⊙ 5pm-late Sat) Located on Otres Village's estuary, this wooden shack, known as 'the barn', turns into a live-music venue every Saturday during high season. Vendors set up food and craft stalls while DJs and bands take to the stage from around 8pm. Look out for special events – in the past the venue has hosted top local bands such as Cambodian Space Project.

Cosmos CINEMA
(Map p194; ☑ 096 668 9413; per person per hour US$2) On the second storey of a building next to Otres Market, this cinema offers air-conditioned rooms, surround sound and watching parties for various popular TV shows and movies.

Top Cat Cinema CINEMA
(Map p190; ☑ 012 790630; Serendipity Beach Rd; tickets US$4; ⊙ 11am-6am) Shows films on a 5m-by-3m high-definition screen (for groups

of at least six) or on large flat-screen TVs (for smaller groups). Has cosy chairs and powerful air-con. Also has seven private rooms with air-con and access to the cinema's network of movies.

🔒 Shopping

Starfish ARTS & CRAFTS
(Map p189; ☑ 012 952011; www.starfishcambodia. org; off 7 Makara St; ⊙ 7am-5.30pm) 🖉 Beside the bakery and cafe (p195) of the same name; it sells silks and other gifts produced by good-cause NGO the Handicraft People.

Tapang ARTS & CRAFTS
(Map p194; www.mloptapang.org; Otres 2; ⊙ 11am-9pm) 🖉 Run by a local NGO that works with at-risk children, this shop sells good-quality bags, scarves and T-shirts made by street kids (and their families) so that they can attend school instead of peddling on the beach. Tapang has another outlet at Sandan restaurant.

ℹ Information

Sihanoukville's banks – all with ATMs – are in the city centre along Ekareach St. There are plentiful standalone ATMs along Serendipity Beach Rd and a couple on Otres 1 at Otres Beach.

ANZ Royal Bank (Map p189; 215 Ekareach St; ⊙ 8am-4pm Mon-Fri, to 11.30am Sat, ATM 24hr)

Canadia Bank (Map p189; 197 Ekareach St; ⊙ 8am-3.30pm Mon-Fri, to 11.30am Sat, ATM 24hr)

Most guesthouses and hotels offer free wi-fi, as do the majority of cafes, restaurants and bars. There are also a few shops on Serendipity Beach Rd and on Ekareach St that have public internet terminals.

Tourist Information Centre (Map p190; ☑ 016 635599; Serendipidity Rd; ⊙ 9am-11.30am & 2-5pm Mon-Sat)

Vietnamese Consulate (Map p187; ☑ 034-934039; 310 Ekareach St; ⊙ 8am-noon & 2-4pm Mon-Sat) Exceedingly speedy at issuing tourist visas.

DANGERS & ANNOYANCES

Theft is a problem on the beaches (especially Ochheuteal Beach) so leave valuables in your room. It's often children who do the deed, sometimes in conjunction with adults. Arriving in a team, one or more will distract you while another lifts whatever valuables are lying on your towel. Or they'll strike when you're out swimming.

You'll likely encounter a steady stream of beggars, many of them children or amputees, on Ochheuteal Beach. NGO M'lop Tapang, which exists to improve the welfare of street kids,

ℹ️ ARRIVING IN SIHANOUKVILLE

Bus Station Most bus departures leave from the company terminals on Ekareach St and arrive at the **bus station** (Map p189; St 109) in the city centre. Most bus companies will include free pickup from the Serendipity area or Victory Hill. Otherwise figure on about US$3/1.50 for *remork/moto* from the bus station to the Serendipity area.

Sihanoukville International Airport A taxi to/from the airport into town costs about US$20, and there's a shuttle bus for US$6. Figure US$5 one way for a *moto*; US$10 for a *remork*.

Train Station From the train station a *remork* will cost US$1 to US$2 for Victory, US$2 to US$3 for downtown, US$3 to US$4 to Ochheuteal and US$5 to US$6 for Otres.

advises to never give money or food to children begging.

As in Phnom Penh, drive-by bag snatchings occasionally happen and are especially dangerous when you're riding a *moto*. Hold your shoulder bags tightly in front of you, especially at night. The road between Otres and Sihanoukville is considered especially risky after dark, so arrange a *remork* or *moto* via your guesthouse if staying in this area, and not just a ride with a random stranger in town.

At night, travellers (especially women) should avoid walking alone along dark, isolated beaches and roads.

The currents off Ochheuteal can be deceptively strong, especially during the wet season.

ℹ️ Getting There & Away

National Hwy 4 (NH4), which links Sihanoukville to Phnom Penh (230km), is in okay condition, but because of heavy truck traffic and the prevalence of high-speed overtaking on blind corners, this is one of Cambodia's most dangerous highways; it's doubly dicey around dusk and at night.

It's both faster and safer to drive via Kampot (105km) along NH3, which is in excellent condition. NH48 to Koh Kong (220km) and the Thailand border (230km) is also in good shape.

AIR

Sihanoukville International Airport (☎ 012-333524; www.cambodia-airports.com) is 15km east of town, just off NH4. Cambodia Bayon Airlines, **Cambodia Angkor Air** (☎ in Phnom Penh 023 666 6786; www.cambodiaaangkorair.com), Sky Angkor Airlines and JC International all fly to Siem Reap several times per week. Flights to Phnom Penh tend to be on-again, off-again – check at your time of travel whether they are operating.

Internationally, Cambodia Angkor Air offers flights to and from Ho Chi Minh City five days a week. Lucky Air has flights twice a week to and from Kunming, China. Air Asia has flights to and from Kuala Lumpur four times a week.

Note that schedules change often and without notice.

BOAT

Sihanoukville is the gateway to Cambodia's southern islands, with various companies operating speedboats between Sihanoukville and various stops on Koh Rong and Koh Rong Sanloem.

The oldest and most reliable is **Speed Ferry Cambodia** (Map p190; www.speedferrycambodia.com; Serendipity Beach Rd, Koh Rong Dive Centre), which sells return tickets for around US$20 (varying based on season and competition). You must confirm your trip back a full day in advance to book your seat. These boats leave from **Serendipity Pier** (Map p190; weather permitting) and tickets can be purchased online in advance. Speed Ferry Cambodia offers sailings from Sihanoukville to Koh Rong Sanloem's Saracen Bay and M'Pai Bay, then Koh Rong's Koh Tuch, at 9am, 11.30am and 3pm. There's also a slow boat at 9.30am. Return trips from both islands are at 10am, 12.30pm and 4pm.

Island Speed Ferry Cambodia (TBC; Map p190; ☎ 015 811711; www.islandspeedboatcambodia.com; Serendipity Pier) has two sea vessels: one is a new 150-seat air-conditioned boat, and the other is older and worse. The trip takes between 45 and 60 minutes depending on which stop is yours, and boats go to and from Serendipity Pier, weather permitting. Ticket price is around US$20, varying based on season and competition. These ferries depart Sihanoukville for Saracen Bay, M'Pai Bay and Koh Rong (Koh Tuch) at 9am, noon and 3pm. They return from Koh Rong at 10.30am, 1.30pm and 4.30pm (with stops at M'Pai Bay and Saracen Bay).

Two newer companies service both islands with smaller speedboats that can carry 25 to 50 passengers: **Buva Sea** (Map p190; ☎ 098 888950; www.buvasea.com; Serendipity Pier) and **GTVC Speedboat** (Map p187; ☎ 017 338821; www.gtvcspeedboat.com; Old Port). Buva Sea also advertises twice-daily trips to Long Beach (Sok San Beach), Nature Beach and Coconut Beach on Koh Rong. GTVC has four boats a day connecting Sihanoukvlle to the islands in either direction that cost US$12, but note that these depart from Sihanoukville Port, which is 7km north of the Serendipity area.

Finally, **Angkor Speed Ferry** (Map p190; ☎ 010 647766; St 501) is the newest and fanciest of the larger ferries, launching in late 2016 as as a first-class catamaran service to Koh Rong, Koh Rong Sanloem and Long Set Beach. Tickets are US$20; departures from Sihanoukville's Serendipidity pier are at 8.30am, noon and 2.30pm, with return trip times varying depending on where you are.

Hopping between the two islands (with any of the speedboats) costs an additional US$5. The companies are all prone to cancelling trips or reversing loops without notice. The smaller speedboats are quicker (about 30 minutes to each island) but somehow manage to run late almost as often as the larger ones, particularly Buva Sea.

A cheaper option to Koh Rong and Koh Rong Sanloem is the cargo 'slow boat' from the New Royal Pier at the ferry dock at Sihanoukville Port (US$5 each way). Life jackets aren't guaranteed on these, and they take hours. Best to avoid them.

Tickets for boats can be purchased from most guesthouses and travel agencies, or booked online via www.bookmebus.com. Transport to more remote resorts and beaches on Koh Rong and Koh Rong Sanloem is by day-trip boats or on private boats owned by resorts.

BUS
All of the major bus companies have frequent connections to Phnom Penh from early morning until at least 2pm. Capitol Tour and Rith Mony are the cheapest. Giant Ibis runs a more expensive 'deluxe' minibus, complete with hostess and wi-fi, four times a day.

Bookings made through hotels and travel agencies incur a commission. Most travel agents only work with two or three bus companies, so ask around if you need to leave at a different time than what's being offered.

Companies include the following:
Ana Travel (Map p190; ☎ 034-933929; Serendipity Beach Rd; ⊙ 8.30am-8.30pm)
Capitol Tour (Map p189; ☎ 034-934042; 169 Ekareach St)
Champa Mekong Tourist Bus (Map p190; ☎ 069 698282; Mithona St)
Giant Ibis (Map p190; ☎ 023 999333; www.giantibis.com; Thnou St)
Mekong Express (Map p189; ☎ 010 833329; Omui St)
Olympic Express (Map p189; ☎ 015 540240; St 109)
Phnom Penh Sorya (Map p189; ☎ 034-933888; 236 Ekareach St)
Rith Mony (Map p189; ☎ 081 785858; Ekareach St)
Virak Buntham (Map p189; ☎ 016 754358; Ekareach St)

SHARE TAXI
Cramped share taxis (US$5 per person or US$45 per car) and minibuses (15,000r) to Phnom Penh depart from the bus station until about 8pm. Avoid the minibuses if you value things like comfort and your life. Hotels can

BUSES FROM SIHANOUKVILLE

DESTINATION	FARE	DURATION	FREQUENCY	COMPANY
Bangkok	US$25-28	12-14hr	7am, 8.15am, 8.45am, 9am, 9.15am, 7pm	Rith Mony, Virak Buntham (night)
Battambang	US$11-17	10-12hr	8 daily	Capitol Tour, Rith Mony, Virak Buntham (night)
Ha Tien, Vietnam	US$13-25	3½hr	several until 1.30pm	Ana Travel, Champa Mekong, Kampot Tours & Travel, Mekong Express
Kampot (minivan)	US$5-6	2hr	several daily	Ana Travel, Champa Mekong, Kampot Tours & Travel
Kep (minivan)	US$7-8	2¼hr	several daily	Ana Travel, Champa Mekong
Koh Kong	US$8-10	4½hr	3 or 4 daily	Olympic Express, Virak Buntham
Phnom Penh	US$5-12	4-5hr	frequent	Capitol Tour, Phnom Penh Sorya, Rith Mony
Phnom Penh (minivan)	US$10-12	4hr	frequent 7.30am-7pm	Giant Ibis, Mekong Express, Virak Buntham
Siem Reap	US$12-17	12hr	6 daily	Rith Mony, Virak Buntham (night)

TRANSPORT COMMISSIONS

Many guesthouses pay US$2 to *moto* drivers who bring them customers from the bus station, train station or airport. But some places pay drivers far higher sums – US$4 or even US$5 – to send custom their way, so if you've just arrived, getting your *moto* guy to take you where *you* want may turn into a battle of wills. If your chosen accommodation is one that won't pay up, don't be surprised to hear that it's 'closed', has contaminated water or is 'full of prostitutes'.

arrange taxis to Phnom Penh for US$50 to US$60 (about four hours). Share taxis to Kampot (US$5, 1½ hours) leave mornings only from a **taxi park** (Map p189; 7 Makara St) opposite Psar Leu.

This taxi park and the bus station are good places to look for share taxis to Koh Kong or the Thai border. If nobody's sharing, expect to pay US$60 for Koh Kong and US$45 to US$60 to the Thai border.

TRAIN

Royal Railways (p87) operates trains from the **train station** (Map p187; Pher St) to Phnom Penh (US$7, nine hours) via Kampot (US$6, five hours) at 7am on Friday, Saturday, Sunday and Monday.

❶ Getting Around

Sihanoukville's *moto* drivers are notorious for aggressively hassling passers-by and, more than anywhere else in Cambodia, shamelessly trying to overcharge, so haggle hard (with a smile) over the price before setting out.

A *moto* should cost about US$1 from the centre to Serendipity, Ochheuteal and Victory Beaches; a *remork* ride around US$2. A *remork* from Serendipity to Victory Hill/Beach should cost US$3, but drivers ask US$5 for this trip.

Motorbikes can be rented from many guesthouses for US$4 to US$7 a day. The police sometimes 'crack down' on foreign drivers. Common violations: no driver's licence, no helmet, no wing mirrors and, everybody's favourite, driving with the lights on during the day.

Hiring a *moto* (including the driver) for the day costs US$10 plus petrol; a *remork* is about US$20 a day.

Bicycles can be hired from many guesthouses for about US$2 a day.

Ream National Park

Just 15km east of Sihanoukville, Ream National Park (ឧទ្យានជាតិរាម) offers trekking opportunities in primary forest, invigorating boat trips through coastal mangroves and long stretches of unspoilt beach. This is an easy escape for those looking to ditch the crowds of Sihanoukville.

The park is home to breeding populations of several regionally and globally endangered birds of prey, including the Brahminy kite, grey-headed fish eagle and white-bellied sea eagle: look for them soaring over Prek Toeuk Sap Estuary. Endangered birds that feed on the mudflats include the lesser adjutant, milky stork and painted stork.

Despite its protected status, Ream is gravely endangered by planned tourism development, especially along its coastline. By visiting, you can demonstrate that the park, in its natural state, is not only priceless to humanity but also a valuable economic resource.

◎ Sights & Activities

🏖 Beaches

The coastline of Ream National Park is lined with isolated beaches that you'll generally have all to yourself. To get to the main beach, **Ream Beach**, drive south from the park headquarters and Sihanoukville Airport for about 9km along a surfaced road until you get to Ream Naval Base. Jog left around the base and follow the dirt roads to Ream Beach.

East of Ream Beach is a series of long white beaches lined with casuarina trees. To reach these, you can either walk or drive along a dirt road that roughly parallels the shoreline.

Much further east is the park's finest beach, **Koh Sampoach Beach**, which is also nicknamed the 'Chinese beach' as Chinese developers have the concession for this area. A major new road has been cut through the park to provide easy access to Koh Sampoach Beach, though it was closed at the time of research. Take an immediate left-hand turn off the Ream National Park road when leaving NH4. If you pass the airport entrance, you've gone too far. Follow the road for about 12km and you will eventually arrive at a small beachside restaurant on Koh Sampoach Beach.

Boat Trips

Popular ranger-led boat trips head through the mangrove channels of the **Prek Toeuk Sap Estuary**. These leave from the Prek Toeuk Sap ranger station, which is located about 3km east of **Ream National Park Headquarters** (☑016 328882; NH4; ☺7-11.30am & 2-5pm) next to a major bridge on NH4 – the rangers at headquarters will help you get there and arrange for a boat to be waiting.

From the Prek Toeuk Sap ranger station it's a two-hour boat ride (US$35 return for one to five people).

Ream National Park's territory includes two islands with some fine snorkelling, Koh Thmei (p202) and – just off Vietnam's Phu Quoc Island – **Koh Seh**, which is best accessed from Koh Thmei. Much easier to access than either of those is Koh Ta Kiev (p201), which is just offshore from Ream Beach. You can easily kayak to Koh Ta Kiev from Ream Beach, and guesthouses around the Naval Base rent out kayaks, though all were closed at the time of research and whether they'd reopen was uncertain.

Jungle Walks

Jungle walks led by rangers – most, but not all, speak some English – are easy to arrange at the park headquarters. Hiking unaccompanied is not allowed. Guided two-hour walks in the forest behind the headquarters cost US$8 per person.

🛏 Sleeping & Eating

You'll find a few food stalls around Ream Beach, plus a smattering of guesthouses for sit-down dining.

★**Monkey Maya**   BUNGALOW **$$**
(☑078 760853; www.monkeymayaream.com; dm US$8, bungalows US$45; 🖥) Among the pioneers on Koh Rong, the Monkey Republic group is once again a few steps ahead of the pack with this secluded gem on the fringes of Ream National Park. Choose from solid, en-suite ocean-view bungalows, rustic family jungle bungalows or a stilted all-wood 16-bed dorm further up the hill. Also has a great bar – a Monkey Republic trademark.

To get here, follow dirt roads east from Ream Beach proper (near the Naval Base) for 5km or so. Or take a *remork* from Monkey Republic in Sihanoukville (US$6) or Otres Beach (US$5).

ℹ Getting There & Away

Ream National Park is a breeze to get to – just follow NH4 east from Sihanoukville to the airport turn-off, which is 15km from the Cambrew brewery at the junction of NH4 and Wat Leu Rd. Go right and drive 500m to the park headquarters, or continue straight (south) 9km to the Naval Base and, beyond, Ream Beach.

A return trip to Ream Beach from Sihanoukville by *moto* should cost US$7 to US$15; a *remork* US$15 to US$20. The price depends on how well the driver speaks English and how long you stay.

Sihanoukville travel agencies offer day trips to Ream National Park for about US$20 per person, including a boat ride, a jungle walk and lunch.

THE SOUTHERN ISLANDS

Cambodia's southern islands are the tropical Shangri-La many travellers have been seeking – as yet untouched by the mega-resorts that have sprouted across southern Thailand. Many of the islands have been tagged for major development by well-connected foreign investors, but the big boys have been slow to press go, paving the way for DIY development to move in with rustic bungalow resorts.

That's not to say that all small-scale development is fine. Koh Rong, in particular, has changed dramatically in the past couple of years due to unchecked construction in the Koh Tuch area. But for the most part, Cambodia's islands are still paradise the way you imagined it: endless crescents of powdered-sugary-soft sand, hammocks swaying in the breeze, photogenic fishing villages on stilts, technicolour sunsets and the patter of raindrops on thatch as you slumber. It seems too good to last, so enjoy it while it does.

Koh Ta Kiev

If your beach-break perfection is about logging off and slothing out, this little island off Ream National Park ticks all the right boxes. Despite the fact that much of the island has been leased to a Chinese property company – and a proper road has recently been sliced through the jungle interior, signalling major development may not be far off – for the moment the southern tip of Koh Ta Kiev (កោះតាកៀវ) still has budget-friendly, basic digs with serious chill-out factor.

There were once beach-bungalow accommodations along **Long Beach**, a white-sand beach on the island's west side, but those are currently abandoned. Various tracks branch off from here through the forest for those who want to explore.

Sleeping & Eating

There's no wi-fi on Koh Ta Kiev, electricity is limited (bring a torch/flashlight) and most places only have rudimentary shared bathrooms (bucket showers and squat toilets). The best sleeping option is actually a closely kept secret, and we swore we'd leave it at that. You'll find it if you try.

The lodgings are the main option for food, with a handful of beach vendors around selling the occasionally odd snack (fried frogs on a stick, anyone?).

Last Point   BUNGALOW $
($\boxtimes$ 088 502 6930; www.lastpointisland.com; hammocks US$2, dm US$6, bungalows US$15-30) The Last Point sits in splendid isolation on a sandy stretch of Koh Ta Kiev's south coast; a 40-minute walk from the bungalows on the island's western shoreline. There's a variety of small, sweet palm-thatch bungalows where you can play out your Robinson Crusoe dreams, as well as a breezy open-air dorm just steps from the sand.

Ten103 Treehouse Bay   BUNGALOW $
($\boxtimes$ 097 943 7587; www.ten103-cambodia.com; hammocks US$5, dm US$7, huts with shared bathroom US$20-25, with private bathroom US$35; $\odot$ Oct-May) Unplug, unwind, de-stress – Ten103 is a beachfront backpacker bolthole that dishes up simple beach living the way it used to be. Stilted open-air 'treehouse' huts have sea views, while the open-air dorm and palm-thatch hammock shelters provide even more basic back-to-nature options.

ⓘ Getting There & Away

Resorts have their own boats, and will connect you with a return trip for around US$13.

Koh Ta Kiev sometimes appears on island-hopping itineraries out of Otres Beach in Sihanoukville, along with Koh Russei and some smaller uninhabited islands in the area. Day trips run from US$12 to US$15.

Koh Russei

Less than an hour by boat from Sihanoukville, tiny Koh Russei has been cleared of all accommodations by Alila Hotels, which is building a five-star resort on the is-

land. Day trips out of Sihanoukville still stop offshore to snorkel.

Koh Thmei

The large island of **Koh Thmei** (កោះថ្មី) is part of Ream National Park. It was once slated for a major development, including a bridge to the mainland, but as projects elsewhere have taken priority, this bird-laden island has remained miraculously pristine. There's only one resort on the island, expat-managed **Koh Thmei Resort** ($\boxtimes$ 097 737 0400; www.koh-thmei-resort.com; bungalows US$45, f US$70) 🍃.

Koh Thmei Resort has excellent Khmer meals (US$6); other than that there is little choice aside from what you can catch yourself. The resort is a one-hour boat ride from the mainland fishing village of Koh Kchhang, and can arrange a six-passenger boat for US$8.50 per person (or you can negotiate in the village). The resort can also arrange pickups from Sihanoukville.

To get to Koh Kchhang, make your way to Bat Kokir (Ou Chamnar), on NH4 about 12km east of Sihanoukville airport, then hire a *moto* (US$2) to take you 10km to the resort pier. All buses heading to or from Sihanoukville pass by Bat Kokir.

Koh Rong

Koh Rong (កោះរ៉ុង) was once little more than a jungle-clad wilderness rimmed by swaths of sugary-white sand, with a few beach-hut resorts speckling the shore around tiny Koh Tuch village. Today the Koh Tuch village street-strip that leads out from the pier is a bottleneck of back-to-back backpacker crash pads, restaurants and hole-in-the-wall bars blasting competing music. You'll either love it or hate it, but for young travellers who descend off the ferry in droves, Koh Rong (particularly Koh Tuch Beach) is a vital stop on any Southeast Asia party itinerary.

It's still possible to escape the mayhem, though. The further you walk away from the village, the more sedate it gets. The evening frog chorus overpowers the drifting bass from the late-night raves, phosphorescence shimmers in the sea and the island's natural charms, of head-turning beaches backed by lush forest interior, are clear to see.

◎ Sights

Long Beach BEACH
(Sok San Beach) On the back (west) side of the island is Koh Rong's finest beach, a 7km stretch of drop-dead-gorgeous white sand, dubbed Long Beach (also called Sok San Beach after the fishing village at its northern end). Longtail boats head here from Koh Tuch pier, depositing sun-seekers on the sand for a day of sunbathing and swimming. You can also walk here via a fairly rough trail through the jungle from Koh Tuch Beach (about 1½ hours).

Long Set Beach BEACH
(4km Beach) Past the Koh Tuch Beach headland (near Treehouse Bungalows) is Long Set Beach, where you can walk at least another hour along the sand and encounter little more than hermit crabs. A clutch of small bungalow resorts is moving in but it's still very peaceful. Round the headland at the east end of Long Set Beach and you'll find hidden Vietnamese Beach, and beyond that, Nature Beach and Coconut Beach (p203), which unfortunately draw crowds of island-hopping boats from Sihanoukville.

Coconut Beach BEACH
(ឆ្នេរដូង) At the easternmost point of the island, this jungle-clad, white-sand cove saw its first guesthouse and tent camp (Coconutbeach Bungalows) open in 2015, and a few other accommodations and a pier popped up shortly after. The still-dreamy escape is accessible via car and motorbike, as long as the road isn't too wet, and there's one speedboat company that delivers guests a couple of times a day. Sadly, island-hopping boats from Sihanoukville sometimes invade the quietude during prime sunbathing hours.

The walk from Koh Tuch to Coconut Beach takes under two hours.

Koh Tuch Beach BEACH
The wide sweep of Koh Tuch Beach extends for about 1km northeast from Koh Tuch village pier and gets lovelier the further out you go. Walk towards the headland (near Treehouse Bungalows) for white sand and a more mellow scene.

Police Beach BEACH
(ឆ្នេរប៉ូលិស) Named because the island's police station is located here, Police Beach hosts wild all-night parties on Wednesdays and Saturdays, and during full moons.

ISLAND KNOW-HOW

➡ There are no banks or ATMs on any of the islands. Bring enough cash.

➡ Don't forget to pack insect repellent. The sand flies can be ferocious.

➡ It's not a bad idea to come equipped with a decent topical antiseptic. Insect bites can quickly turn into tropical ulcers if scratched.

➡ A torch (flashlight) is also useful.

➡ When leaving, if you have an onward transport connection booked from Sihanoukville, don't take the last possible ferry/boat. Sailing times can be delayed or cancelled at short notice due to sea conditions.

⚡ Activities

Longtail **boat day trips** to Long Beach (with snorkelling, fishing and swimming thrown in) are the main Koh Rong activity. Pretty much every place in Koh Tuch village organises them for about US$10 per person. For US$20 you can stay out longer and add an evening excursion to see bioluminescence.

It's also viable to walk one to two hours from Koh Tuch to Long Beach via a rigorous jungle track, but be aware that it involves scrambling and is definitely not flip-flops territory. Don't do this at night or alone.

For an adventurous day out packed full of scenery, it's possible to organise a boat to **Sangker village** on the island's east coast (US$30), then hire a *moto* driver to whiz you around the island. Adventure Adam is a popular tour guide.

There's good **snorkelling** around the island and resorts rent out gear for about US$5 per day. The best snorkelling around Koh Tuch is in the cove in front of Treehouse Bungalows.

Several places hire **sea kayaks** for about US$5 per hour for a single kayak (US$8 for a tandem). From Koh Tuch Beach, it's a 30-minute paddle out to Pagoda Island, an idyllic islet topped by a wat, just offshore.

★ **Adventure Adam** BOATING
(☑ 010 354002; www.facebook.com/AdventureAdamTours; Koh Rong) ✍ If lazing about by day and partying all night on Koh Rong seems like a missed opportunity to, you know, actually experience the island, consider booking a trip with Adventure Adam. His day and

Koh Rong

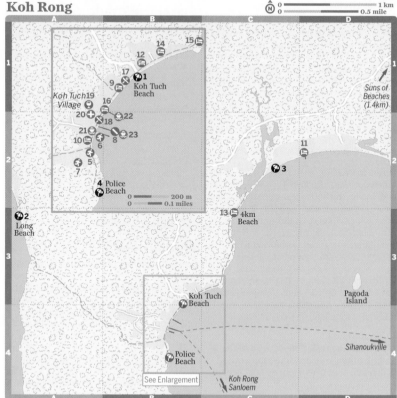

overnight tours around Koh Rong include stops at fishing villages, remote beaches and deep jungle and earn high marks for cultural immersion and adventure.

High Point
Rope Adventure ADVENTURE SPORTS
(☏ 016 839993; www.high-point.asia; Koh Tuch village; per person US$35; ⊗ 9am-6pm) A collection of ziplines, swing bridges and walking cables takes thrill-seekers on an adrenaline-packed, 400m-long journey through the forest canopy, not far from Koh Tuch. Your ticket gets you unlimited access to the course for the entire day. From April to October, tickets are US$5 cheaper.

Koh Rong Dive Centre
DIVING
(☏ 096 560 7362; www.kohrongdivecenter.com; Koh Rong pier; ⊗ 9am-6pm) Koh Rong's main dive centre organises trips in the waters around Koh Rong, Koh Rong Sanloem and a few other islands nearby. Also offers boat

trips to other islands, snorkelling excursions and diving courses.

Friends of Koh Rong
VOLUNTEERING
(☏ 096 552 0416; www.friendsofkohrong.org; Local pier, Koh Tuch village) 🖉 This grassroots NGO takes on qualified teachers to volunteer with its education programmes. Volunteer opportunities in community development and local health projects are also available, and travellers can get involved in the group's regular beach clean-ups.

🛏 Sleeping

During high season (particularly December and January), Koh Rong's accommodation fills up fast. If you're nervous about turning up on the island without a bed, it's worthwhile to book a place for the first night and, once here, check out the rest of the hostel scene. Travellers with no bed for the night during busy periods usually end up renting a hammock.

Koh Rong

◉ Sights

✚ Activities, Courses & Tours

⊜ Sleeping

✖ Eating

⊜ Drinking & Nightlife

ⓘ Information

ⓘ Transport

If you want to hang out with fellow travellers, hit a late-night rave and crash out on the sand during the day, Koh Tuch Beach is the spot. Nearly all accommodation in Koh Tuch has 24-hour electricity, wi-fi, mosquito nets and fans. Air-con and hot water are rarities. The situation gets mellower as you walk north along Koh Tuch Beach, where a string of wonderful flashpacker resorts awaits.

Those looking for a more relaxed vibe would be wise to pick a bungalow-resort well away from Koh Tuch village. Options include Long Set Beach, which is directly north of Koh Tuch Beach, Long Beach on the west side of the island and the newest spot, Coconut Beach. Away from Koh Tuch electricity gets more sporadic.

★**Nest** HOSTEL **$**
(dm US$10; ❄🛜) On the southern end of Long Set Beach is this new flashpacker crash pad, and it's a step up from anything you'll find in Koh Tuch. The well-designed dorms feature private bunks divided by walls and curtains, and the restaurant has a stunner of an open-air, oceanfront terrace with delicious Khmer battered chicken, veggie wraps and sweet-potato chips.

Suns of Beaches GUESTHOUSE **$**
(📱010 550355; Vietnamese Beach; dm US$5, r US$10-20) On a glorious private beach a little north of Long Set Beach, this newer expat-owned hostel is for shoestringers who are into serious chilling. The huge and airy fan-cooled dorms are things of beauty, while a well-stocked bar means you won't go thirsty. Hammocks are everywhere and the beach is just wow. This is backpacker bliss.

There's an excellent restaurant with some ingredients sourced from the guesthouse's garden. It's a loooong (about 5km) beach walk from Koh Tuch, or you can take the thrice-daily (twice-daily in low season) boat shuttle from Monkey Island.

Vagabonds HOSTEL **$**
(📱096 568 6298; www.vagabondskohrong.com; Koh Tuch; dm/r US$4/8) Firstly, you don't come here for the facilities. Rooms and dorms (with lockers) are bare-bones, with shared bathrooms, though made cheery by colourful murals. Vagabonds' following is instead due to its friendly staff and the fun vibe of the lively bar downstairs, at which guests are entitled to one free drink per day.

Bong's Guesthouse GUESTHOUSE **$**
(📱070 260065; www.bongsguesthouse.com; Koh Tuch; dm incl breakfast US$6-8, r with private/shared bathroom US$20/15; 🛜) The well-looked-after wooden rooms at Bong's (above the bar of the same name) are a great deal if you want to stay in the centre of the action. Stays include free water refills, tea and coffee, and it's happy hour all day, meaning US$0.75 draught beer, US$2 house mixers and two-for-one cocktails. There's live music a few times a week.

Paradise Bungalows BUNGALOW **$$**
(📱092 548883; www.paradise-bungalows.com; Koh Tuch Beach; bungalows US$35-100; 🛜) The delightfully rustic bungalows here come in all shapes and sizes, and climb up a hill amid rambling jungle foliage. The US$35 rooms are way up the slope while more expensive

SOUTH COAST KOH RONG

options are practically lapped by waves at high tide. The loungey restaurant, with its soaring palm-leaf panel roof and shoreline panorama, is a real highlight.

Long Set Resort RESORT $$

(☑ 034 477 8888; www.longsetresort.com; d US$78; ❋ �) In the middle of the eponymous beach, Long Set Resort is by far Koh Rong's classiest digs – with hot water, mini-fridges, air-con, bathrobes and spa tubs – which makes it sort of comical that arriving guests must cross a waist-deep tributary or be dropped by boat in knee-deep ocean. The exquisite grounds, ginormous pool and comfy beds are worth it, though.

Coconutbeach Bungalows TENTED CAMP $$

(☑ 077 766333, 010 351248; www.coconutbeach bungalows.com; Coconut Beach; tents US$15, r $10-25, bungalows US$50-60;) A serene spot on the island's northwestern shores, surrounded by cerulean water and powdery white sand, and the owners go above and beyond for guests. The semi-private rooms have shared bathrooms. Those who prefer more comfortable digs should opt for the bungalows up the hill, but the tents atop platforms near the ocean will please more adventurous types.

Treehouse Bungalows BUNGALOW $$

(☑ 015 755594; www.treehouse-bungalows.com; Koh Tuch Beach; bungalows US$30-55, treehouses US$70-75;) Nestled on a secluded cove about a 15-minute beach walk from Koh Tuch pier, Treehouse has more than a touch of the fairy tale about it. The glass-doored bungalows have balconies strung with seashells, high-raised bungalow 'treehouses' have prime vistas, and the restaurant (specialising in wood-fired pizza) is set beside a natural reservoir with an organic garden out back.

Monkey Island BUNGALOW $$

(☑ 081 830992; www.monkeyisland-kohrong. com; Koh Tuch Beach; dm from US$5, bungalows US$25-40;) Linked to the popular Monkey Republic in Sihanoukville, Monkey Island's action revolves around its bamboo-and-thatch bar, which is always jam-packed with backpackers. Some of the basic bungalows can fit up to five people at a squeeze and come with hammocks on the porches; the cheapest ones share bathrooms.

✖ Eating

The midrange resorts towards the eastern end of Koh Tuch Beach have the best food; Paradise Bungalows and the Nest are particularly recommended. Otherwise there is plenty of choice closer to the piers.

Koh Lanta INTERNATIONAL $

(Koh Tuch; mains US$3-6; ⊙ 24hr) Named after the famous French version of *Survivor*, which is filmed on Koh Rong, this place offers some of the best pizzas on the island.

Rising Sun VEGETARIAN $

(Koh Tuch Beach; mains US$3-4; ⊙ 8am-10pm;) Occupying a central position on Koh Tuch Beach, Rising Sun attracts herbivores by serving vegan and vegetarian meals with a Middle Eastern flair, such as couscous salads and falafel wraps. Has a nice earthy vibe and also rents out kayaks and stand-up paddleboards for US$5 per hour, along with rooms from US$10.

Red Onion TURKISH $$

(mains US$3-8.50; ⊙ 8am-11pm) It's almost unheard of to find a restaurant on Koh Rong that doesn't double as a guesthouse (and a bar, and a tour-booking place...), but Red Onion is an exception to that rule. Offering a mix of Turkish kebabs, burgers, salads and steaks, this place earns high marks from travellers. Also, the service is super-friendly.

❂ Drinking & Nightlife

Hostels Bong's and Vagabonds are both great places to relax with a beer. Koh Rong's famous parties take place on Wednesdays and Saturdays on Police Beach, just south of Koh Tuch village, with additional parties added for full moons and other special occasions. Lately, these parties have been kept more tame in an effort to rescue the island's reputation.

Sky Bar BAR

(Koh Tuch; ⊙ 8am-midnight) Koh Rong's first cocktail bar is perched way up on the hill overlooking the pier. The views and drink specials make this a great happy-hour option, with the action usually continuing until well into the evening. Also has a few solid-wood bungalows (from US$30) with murals on the walls and fantastic balconies for those who don't mind the noise.

Dragon Den Pub PUB

(Koh Tuch; ⊙ 9am-late) In addition to a convivial atmosphere nourished by proprietor Jay, the Dragon Den serves excellent craft beer from Sihanoukville's Five Men Microbrewery. There are rooms (from US$10) upstairs if stumbling somewhere else seems too hard.

ℹ Information

Bring all the cash you think you'll need with you as there are no banks or ATMs on Koh Rong, or any of the other southern islands. If you do run out of money, Vagabonds, Bong's and **Green Ocean** (☑ 010 850079; Koh Tuch village) offer money-lending services for a 10% fee.

Emergency Services Centre (☑ whatsapp 1-912-663-1640; Koh Tuch Beach; ⊘ walk-in 9.30am-4pm, emergency 24hr) is the best medical facility on Koh Rong.

DANGERS & ANNOYANCES

Theft can be a problem on Koh Rong. Use lock-boxes if supplied in dorms, or leave valuables in your accommodation's safe.

In 2013 an American woman was murdered while hiking the jungle trail to Long Beach, and in 2015 there was an attempted attack on a Japanese tourist. Travellers – both male and female – should buddy up when walking in more isolated areas of the island, and on the beach late at night.

Koh Rong's full-tilt surge into tourism is not without problems that threaten the pristine environment that attracted travellers here in the first place. Many hastily knocked-up hostels and bars on Koh Tuch Beach don't have proper septic systems, with waste running directly into the sea, and the sand nearest the village can become strewn with trash. Apparently, business owners are working on getting septic tanks and cleaning up the beach.

ℹ Getting There & Away

Several companies – including **Island Speed Ferry Cambodia** (TBC Speed Boat; ☑ 069 811711; www.islandspeedboatcambodia.com), **Speed Ferry Cambodia** (www.speedferrycambodia.com), **Buva Sea** (☑ 015 888970; www.buvasea.com) and **GTVC Speedboat** (www.gtvcspeedboat.com) – operate ferries and catamarans that transport people from Koh

Rong Sanloem's Saracen Bay and M'Pai Bay to Koh Rong and Sihanoukville. Note that schedule changes, unpredictable delays and cancellations are common, meaning you'll need to check up on the details of your ferry directly with the company.

Tickets cost around US$20 return between Koh Rong and Sihanoukville. Hopping to Koh Rong Sanloem costs US$5.

Tickets for boats can be purchased from most guesthouses and travel agencies, or booked online via www.bookmebus.com. Transport to more remote resorts and beaches on Koh Rong is by day-trip boats or on private boats owned by resorts.

Koh Rong Sanloem

This horseshoe-shaped, 10km-long island is many peoples' vision of tropical bliss. The most popular destination on Koh Rong Sanloem (កោះរ៉ុងសន្លឹម) is Saracen Bay – a crescent-shaped sweep of white sand on the island's east coast. If that's not isolated enough, the beaches on the island's western side (reached by walking trail or private boat) are home to just a few secluded resorts and tent camps, where the cares of the world seem a million miles away.

Those looking for an alternative island experience can head to the village of M'Pai Bay at the island's northern tip. There's no photogenic white sands here (the beach is a grainy-yellow hue), and a growth spurt in the town has meant lots of construction noise. But a clutch of budget guesthouses offer a proper local vibe that will suit the more intrepid.

⊙ Sights & Activities

From Saracen Bay it's an easy 25-minute walk to Lazy Beach, and a 45-minute hike (sneakers

---

SIHANOUKVILLE FERRY TIPS

A few things to keep in mind about the ferry system between Sihanoukville and its islands:

➡ During low season, some of the advertised ferries simply don't run, so be sure to check with a person who works for the company in advance.

➡ Sometimes ferries do not go direct, and this can mean transfer times to and from the islands can be quite lengthy. There's not much you can do about this; just try to relax and enjoy the scenery, and be extremely conservative in your estimates of when you'll arrive anywhere.

➡ All companies ask that tickets are stamped in advance (some say day before, others three hours before). In high season this is particularly important, because a large number of people are transferring and seat availability often becomes an issue. In low season this is not as crucial, but sometimes the smaller ferries still fill up.

Koh Rong Sanloem

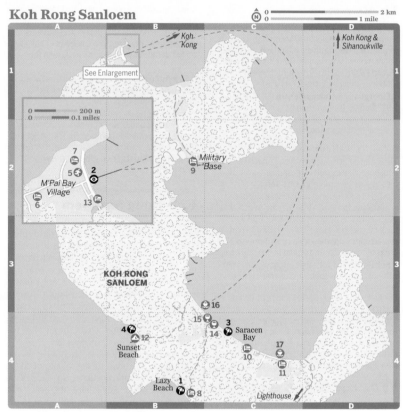

necessary) to Sunset Beach. Several resorts rent kayaks (US$10) and most can arrange snorkelling excursions, while Cambodian Diving Group and Dive Shop (p188) offer scuba trips around the island and beyond.

There's also a harder trail (about 1½ hours) to the lighthouse on a hill overlooking the ocean at the island's extreme southern tip, which is also a prime nesting spot for sea eagles. Be aware that there are soldiers stationed at the lighthouse and they may ask you for a tip (US$1 is usually fine).

Saracen Bay
BEACH

(ឆ្នេរសារាសិន) Koh Rong Sanloem's most popular destination is Saracen Bay – a crescent-shaped 2.5km-long sweep of white sand on the island's east coast, lined by two dozen or so resorts backed by lush jungle. If you're not staying on the island, the party boats out of Sihanoukville call in here for a couple of hours of drinking and beach play.

Lazy Beach
BEACH

Koh Rong Sanloem's best strip of sand is Lazy Beach, home to the Lazy Beach Resort. Non-guests will need to buy a drink or meal at the resort restaurant to stay and admire the sand. It's an easy 25-minute stroll (flip-flops are okay) across the island from Saracen Bay.

Sunset Beach
BEACH

This idyllic swath of sand is home to just a few resorts that are all quite lovely. It's a 45-minute hike (sneakers necessary) here from Saracen Bay, or in high season a boat brings guests over from Sihanoukville.

M'Pai Bay
BAY

(ឆ្នេរម្ពៃ) This northern stretch of yellowish sand appeals to backpackers looking for something a bit more chill (but not more pricey) than Koh Rong. The town seems to have figured that out and made a mad dash to throw up additional infrastructure. Call

Koh Rong Sanloem

it the next Koh Rong, only better-integrated with the community and a bit more eco-friendly (so far).

Cambodian Diving Group   DIVING
(☑ 096 224 5474; www.facebook.com/cambodian diving; M'Pai Bay; 2-dive package US$80) ⚐ This M'Pai Bay-based outfit has expert knowledge of the surrounding underwater world that only comes from years of experience diving here. Offers excellent one-day dive packages, various PADI courses (including Discover Scuba for US$95 and the three-day Open Water Diver for US$380) and longer three-day exploration dive trips for experienced divers. Also involved in local marine-conservation efforts.

The group runs Save Cambodian Marine Life and also the guesthouse **Big Moon** (☑ 096 245474; www.bigmooncambodia.com; r US$12.50, bungalows US$25-50) ⚐.

Save Cambodian Marine Life   VOLUNTEERING
(☑ 096 224 5474; www.savecambodianmarinelife. com; M'Pai Bay; 1-week volunteer package US$295) ⚐ This NGO works to protect the local reefs surrounding Koh Rong Sanloem with ongoing projects including maintaining a coral nursery, organising reef clean-up dives, producing natural sunscreen and more. Volunteer packages include diving, shared accommodation and all meals.

🛏 Sleeping

Saracen Bay is the most developed beach with close to two dozen resorts spread out along its 2.5km-long sands. Most of Koh Rong Sanloem's resorts have 24-hour electricity. For more secluded digs on beaches that feel a bit more natural, head to either Lazy Beach or Sunset Beach.

The chilled-out hostels of M'Pai Bay are attractive for backpackers.

Most places offer healthily discounted rates for bungalows during June to October.

Dragonfly Guesthouse   HOSTEL $
(☑ 069 493914; dm US$7, r US$15, bungalows US$25) This chilled-out spot in M'Pai Bay operates at a languid pace, with a scenic check-in area and papasan chairs overlooking the frothy sea. Accommodations are airy and clean, and restaurant and bar are beloved for wine and cheeseboards. Live music and movie nights are hosted frequently.

The Drift   GUESTHOUSE $
(☑ 015 865388; www.facebook.com/thedriftsam loem; M'Pai Bay; dm/r US$8/15) On the south end of M'Pai Bay, the Drift has spick-and-span dorms and a couple of private rooms in a cute wooden house on the sand. There's a good social vibe with home-cooked meals (US$3) often eaten communally.

★ **Huba-Huba**   HOSTEL $$
(☑ 088 554 5619; www.huba-huba-cambodia.com; Sunset Beach; dm US$7-8, bungalows US$30-60) Perched on secluded Sunset Beach and flanked by the jungle, this small collection of thatched-roof bungalows and glistening hardwood common spaces looks like an island fantasy land. During high season, a beach restaurant with a bar constructed from the bow of a boat serves up cold beers, wine, cocktails and BBQ, and everybody goes snorkelling on a nearby reef.

★ **Mad Monkey Island Resort**   HOSTEL $$
(☑ 016 762654; www.madmonkeyhostels.com; dm US$9-10, bungalows US$40; 🕾) The latest

addition to the Mad Monkey hostel empire wins big with its secluded private cove and beaches to the north of Saracen Bay. Dorms of varying size and private bungalows are oceanfront, simple and fan-cooled, and the atmosphere is laid-back and convivial. A big, open-air bar and restaurant overlooks the sea, where people laze about in hammocks all day.

Paradise Villas BUNGALOW $$
(📳 096 954 8599; www.paradise-bungalows.com; Saracen Bay; bungalows US$35-100) The sister resort of long-running favourite Paradise Bungalows on Koh Rong, this version follows a similar script: smart, solid-wood bungalows (in big and small sizes) with thick mattresses, sea-facing balconies and rain showers, and a beautifully designed restaurant mixing Asian fusion with hearty European dishes (mashed potatoes and gravy, anyone?). Electricity is available from 6pm to 6am.

Lazy Beach RESORT $$
(📳 016 214211; www.lazybeachcambodia.com; bungalows US$65) Alone on the southwest coast of Koh Rong Sanloem, this idyllic getaway fronts one of the most stunning beaches you'll find anywhere. The 20 bungalows have balconies and hammocks outside, and spiffy stone-floor bathrooms and double beds inside. The combined restaurant and common area is stocked with books and board games, making the resort a good fit for families.

Sleeping Trees TENTED CAMP $$
(📳 071 773 6403; www.sleeping-trees.com; Sunset Beach; tree tents US$19, teepees US$29, bungalows US$49) With unique accommodations such as tree tents and teepees sprawled around a common area housing a restaurant, bar and pool table, this expat-owned beach retreat will make you feel like an incredibly fortunate castaway. There aren't many frills, but what more do you need than a tent strung in the trees when you're waking up on a far-flung, jungle-covered beach?

Easy Tiger GUESTHOUSE $$
(📳 096 864 4392, 096 532 6150; www.easytigerbungalows.com; M'Pai Bay; dm US$7.50, bungalows from US$30) This friendly guesthouse in M'Pai Bay village has plenty of homespun appeal, thanks to its helpful owners, winning restaurant and communal feel. The main building houses simple dorms and small private rooms; out back, sturdy basic bungalows with large verandas for those seeking more privacy. At the time of research, a 25-bed dorm and rooftop bar were in the works.

Moonlight Resort RESORT $$$
(📳 034-666 6106; www.moon-light-resort.com; Saracen Bay; r from US$80; ☎) Staying at this place will make you feel like a one cool alien. The white, dome-shaped bungalows look like mysterious igloos stolen from the moon, but they are sumptuous, air-conditioned and immaculate. The restaurant likewise sits beneath a giant blue dome with shimmery-looking panels. There's also a couple of pools and a late-night cocktail bar.

Pipes Resort RESORT $$$
(📳 069 945678; http://thepipes-resort.com; Saracen Bey; from US$80; ☎) As Saracen Bay crowds up with bungalows and resorts, newcomers are distinguishing themselves with unique architecture. At the Pipes Resort, that means recycled cylindrical (and a few square-shaped) concrete accommodations featuring king-sized beds and floor-to-ceiling windows facing the sea. It caters to honeymooners. The tasty restaurant serves Khmer, Chinese, Vietnamese and Western dishes family-style.

🍴 Eating & Drinking

There are no stand-alone restaurants in Saracen Bay or on Lazy or Sunset Beaches, but all the resorts have attached restaurants, and there's quite a good selection of food on offer.

Koh Rong Sanloem is tame compared with Koh Rong, but you can find some action. Mad Monkey Island Resort is full-moon party central, while there's usually something cracking at Octopussy and Tree Bar.

On Sunset Beach, Sleeping Trees and Huba-Huba both have fantastic bars, and M'Pai Bay's Dragonfly Guesthouse is the place to relax with wine and a cheeseboard.

Fishing Hook INTERNATIONAL $
(M'Pai Bay; mains US$1.25; ☺8am-9pm) Some of the finest food on Koh Rong Sanloem is being served up at a food stall near M'Pai Bay pier. The menu waltzes from Khmer-influenced curries to chilli onion rings to more global offerings. Keep an eye out for a bigger and better Fishing Hook up the hill from Dragonfly Guesthouse.

Tree Bar BAR
(Saracen Bay; ☺10am-late; ☎) Travellers regularly perch at this locally owned tiki bar until late into the night, playing drinking games and sizing up who might be interested in a skinny-dip in the plankton. There's also a sign for free Khmer lessons here.

Octopussy Beach Bar BAR
(☑ 010 817801; www.facebook.com/Octopussy-Bar-Cambodia-1679470585650019; Saracen Bay; ☺ 8am-midnight) This bamboo beach bar under a cone-shaped, thatched roof is centrally located on Saracen Bay just in front of its parent resort, Royal Retreat. Shots and cold beers, along with tackily named cocktails, flow steadily throughout the day, and gush into the night.

❶ Getting There & Away

Several companies operate ferries and catamarans that transport people from Koh Rong Sanloem's Saracen Bay and M'Pai Bay to Koh Rong and Sihanoukville, including **Island Speed Ferry Cambodia** (TBC; ☑ 093 811711; www.islandspeedferry.com), **Speed Ferry Cambodia** (http://speedferrycambodia.com), **Buva Sea** (☑ 015 888970; www.buvasea.com) and **GTVC Speedboat** (www.gtvcspeedboat.com).

Note that schedule changes, unpredictable delays and cancellations are common, meaning you'll need to check up on the details of your ferry directly with the company.

Tickets cost around US$20 return between Koh Rong Sanloem and Sihanoukville. Hopping to Koh Rong costs US$5.

Tickets for boats can be purchased from most guesthouses and travel agencies, or booked online via www.bookmebus.com. Transport to more remote resorts and beaches on Koh Rong Sanloem is by day-trip boats or on private boats owned by resorts.

Koh Sdach Archipelago

Just off the southwest tip of Botum Sakor National Park, the Koh Sdach Archipelago (ប្រជុំកោះស្ដេច) is a modest grouping of 12 small islands, most of them uninhabited. Basing yourself at one of the two islands with accommodation – Koh Sdach (King Island) or Koh Totang – you can spend a day or two exploring the other islands, some of which have utterly isolated beaches and good snorkelling and scuba diving. Koh Sdach has 24-hour electricity.

The area has changed markedly as a huge Chinese 'resort city' has taken over the nearby mainland, once known for pristine beaches backed by virgin forest. Years in the making, the project includes an 18-hole golf course, though much of the plan had yet to unfold during our last visit.

Fortunately, the islands appear to be largely excluded from the development, and existing accommodations are far enough

from the mainland that the commotion is out of earshot and eyesight.

❖ Sights & Activities

Koh Sdach has the only village of any size in the entire archipelago and is thoroughly off the tourist trail with the small local economy based entirely around fishing.

Most island-hopping tours target **Koh Ampil**, which is a cluster of three tiny islands surrounding a spit of sand, and the long white beaches on either side of **Koh Smach**.

When conditions are right, these islands have some of the best diving in the country, with colourful, abundant corals and awe-inspiring creatures such as cuttlefish, nudibranchs, sea horses and bamboo sharks. Octopuses Garden Diving Centre offers trips to all the best spots.

Octopuses Garden Diving Centre DIVING
(☑ 086 412432; www.octopuscambodia.com; Koh Sdach; ☺ half-day (2-tank) dive incl lunch US$85, Open Water Diver course US$400) Run by a knowledgeable, entertaining expat couple, this boutique dive shop on Koh Sdach offers excellent underwater experiences around the archipelago. Octopuses also has laid-back waterfront digs on the nature-y, north-eastern tip of the island including a dorm (US$15) and private tree-house bungalow (US$35). Delicious meals are communal (breakfast included; dinners US$7) and the schedule is oriented around dive trips.

🛏 Sleeping & Eating

Koh Sdach has a few guesthouses and there's a single resort on almost-uninhabited Koh Totang.

The resorts are the best option for food, otherwise there are local eateries in the main village of Koh Sdach, the best of which is May's Kitchen. If you are invited by a local to eat fresh fish, accept.

Mean Chey Guesthouse GUESTHOUSE $
(☑ 011 979797; Koh Sdach; r from US$15) This simple guesthouse with 15 powder-blue concrete cottages is close to the main fishing village on the northwest side of Koh Sdach. The structures are low on charm, but the view certainly isn't.

Yvone Guesthouse GUESTHOUSE $$
(☑ 012 450925; Koh Sdach; huts from US$15) These six wooden huts are basic and small, each with only a fan and a bed, but they are as oceanfront as you can get. Lovely covered

terraces feature hammocks and fantastic island views, and the on-site Yvonne restaurant serves tasty French and Khmer food.

★ Nomads Land

RESORT $$$

(☑011 916171; www.nomadslandcambodia. com; Koh Totang; bungalows s/d incl meals from US$60/90; ☺Nov-Aug) 🌿 It's hard to imagine a more relaxed place than Nomads, the greenest resort in the islands with five funky bungalows powered by solar panels and rainwater collected for drinking. It sits on a white beach on Koh Totang and is the sole accommodation on this island speck, a 15-minute ride from the mainland's Poi Yopon village on the resort's boat.

★ May's Kitchen

CAMBODIAN $

(☑093 561847, 011 308561; mains US$1.50-5; ☺hours vary) A great local restaurant uphill from town, on the left just before the pier. May shops at the market each morning and bases her Khmer and Thai dishes on what's available, often including pepper-and-garlic pork and crab. To guarantee a meal, stop by in the morning to let May know what you fancy for dinner. Ask about cooking classes too.

🛈 Getting There & Away

Getting to the Koh Sdach Archipelago can be rather convoluted. The easiest, but most expensive, way is to hire a car from Koh Kong (US$60), Sihanoukville (US$75) or Phnom Penh (US$85) and travel overland along a new highway to Poi Yopon village on the mainland opposite Koh Sdach. The partially surfaced highway was built for the Chinese resort and cuts right through Botum Sakor National Park.

Another, cheaper option is to take a public bus or share taxi travelling NH48 and get off at the cafe near the turn-off for the Chinese highway, 6km west of Andoung Tuek. From here you can either get a local minibus (US$7.50, two hours, mornings only) or moto (US$15 to US$20, depending on your negotiating skills) to take you to Poi Yopon. It's a blazing-fast, hour-plus moto ride – not for the faint-hearted.

Hiring an outboard from Poi Yopon to Koh Sdach costs about 10,000r. Nomads Land resort has its own private boat, which can pick you up, and can also can organise taxis to Poi Yopon. The trip to either island takes 10 to 15 minutes.

KAMPOT PROVINCE

Kampot Province (ខេត្តកំពត) has emerged as one of Cambodia's most alluring destinations thanks to a hard-to-beat combination of easy-going seaside towns and lush countryside riddled with honeycombed limestone caves.

The province is renowned for producing some of the world's finest pepper. Durian-haters be warned: it is also Cambodia's main producer of this odoriferous fruit.

Kampot

☑033 / POP 39,500

It's not hard to see why travellers become entranced with Kampot (កំពត). This riverside town, with streets rimmed by dilapidated shophouse architecture, has a dreamy quality; as if someone pressed the snooze button a few years back and the entire town

---

DIVING IN CAMBODIA

Cambodia might not be as famous for diving as neighbouring Thailand, but heading below the water's surface here still offers up some serious highlights. Though fish stocks may indeed be lower than in other Asian dive destinations (a consequence of years of irresponsible fishing practices, now being reversed by marine conservation organisations), the waters surrounding the southern islands off Sihanoukville are famed for their biodiverse, multicoloured corals and unique array of tiny sea creatures.

The best of Cambodia's diving is among the fringing reefs of Koh Rong Sanloem and **Koh Koun**, which are home to a mind-boggling collection of weird and wacky nudibranchs, starfish and seahorses. Commonly spotted fish include angelfish, damselfish and scorpionfish. Further afield, the island of Koh Sdach is a great base for exploring nearby reefs where cuttlefish and massive cobias are often spotted, and the islands of **Koh Tang** and **Koh Prins** are famous for bamboo sharks, bluespotted ribbontail rays, wrasse and batfish. Whale sharks have also been sighted by divers here.

Three of the area's most experienced dive operators, who know the best dive sites for macro life, are **Cambodian Diving Group** (p209), **Scuba Nation** (p188) and **Dive Shop** (p188). A newer addition with a great set-up on Koh Sdach is **Octopuses Garden Diving Centre**. (p211)

forgot to wake up. The Kompong Bay River – more accurately an estuary – rises and falls with the moons, serving as both attractive backdrop and water-sports playground for those staying in the boutique resorts and backpacker retreats that line its banks upstream from the town proper.

Eclipsed as a port when Sihanoukville was founded in 1959, Kampot also makes an excellent base for exploring Bokor National Park, the neighbouring seaside town of Kep, and the superb cave-temples and verdant countryside of the surrounding area. A growing expat community is contributing to new cultural developments and more culinary variety.

⊙ Sights

Kampot is more about ambience than actual sights and the most enjoyable activity is strolling or cycling through the central old town district where lanes are lined with crumbling shophouses, many built in the mid-20th century by the town's then-vibrant Chinese merchant population. The best streets, a couple of which have been well-restored in recent years, are between the triangle delineated by the central **Durian Roundabout**, the post office and the old French bridge.

Kampot Provincial Museum MUSEUM
(សារមន្ទីរខេត្តកំពត; www.kampotmuseum.org; River Rd; US$2; ⊙3-6pm Tue-Thu, 8-11am & 3-6pm Sat & Sun) This tiny museum, inside the finely preserved French colonial-era Old Governor's Mansion, traces the history of Kampot and the outlying area. The artefacts, photos and text (in Khmer, French and English) are informative and neatly displayed, including a series of oversized panels explaining the province's historic milestones. There's also a significant amount of student-created material.

Kampot Traditional Music School CULTURAL CENTRE
(☑010 223325; www.kcdi-cambodia.org; St 724; ⊙2-5pm Mon & Tue, 5-7pm Fri) **FREE** During set hours, visitors are welcome to observe traditional music and dance training sessions and/or performances at this school that teaches children who are orphaned or have disabilities. Donations are very welcome.

Tek Chhouu Rapids RIVER
(ទឹកឈូ; Tek Chhouu Rd; US$1) Popular with locals, these modest rapids at the end of Tek Chhouu Rd northwest of Kampot are surrounded by food stalls and picnicking platforms. A *remork* here from Kampot costs around US$5. There's also a spa on the water called Tada Bokor, and it is said (by the owner) that the water has therapeutic qualities.

🏃 Activities

Kampot is fast carving out a niche as a base for adventure sports. Climbing and water sports on the Kampong Bay River are the main attractions. Battambang's Butterfly Tours (p243) now runs bicycle tours in Kampot.

Be extremely careful swimming in the Kampong Bay River; tourists have drowned in the unpredictable currents. If you're not a strong swimmer, don't go in.

Love the River BOATING
(☑016 627410; per person US$15-19) Offers longtail boat charters and cruises from the Green House along the river, with stops for beach swimming and exploring a durian plantation. Captain Bjorn earns high marks for local knowledge and foresight (he brings fresh fruit and cold beer to go with the sunset).

Climbodia CLIMBING
(☑070 255210; www.climbodia.com; St 710; half day US$35-40, full day US$80; ⊙3-8pm Tue-Sun, from 5pm Mon) Cambodia's first outdoor rock-climbing outfit offers highly recommended half-day and full-day programmes of climbing, abseiling and caving amid the limestone formations of Phnom Kbal Romeas, 5km south of Kampot. Cabled routes (via ferratas) have been established across some of the cliffs and the programme offerings cater for both complete novices and the more experienced.

SUP Asia WATER SPORTS
(☑093 980550; www.supasia.org; Old Market; 2½hr tour US$25, half-day tour US$55; ⊙open daily, closed Sep) SUP (stand-up paddleboarding) has come to Kampot in a big way; this company offers it as an alternative form of touring the river. Daily tours depart at 8.30am, 2.30pm and 3.30pm, taking in the riverbank sights of the local area (with a SUP lesson beforehand). There's also a two-day (18km) trip that traverses the Kampong Bay River to the sea.

Kampot Cruiser SCENIC DRIVE
(☑010 796919; St 730; from US$35) The most fabulous way to roll up to a pepper plantation, Bokor Hill Station or any given salt field, fishing village or far-flung cave is in the Kampot Cruiser, a baby-blue 1991 Toyota Camry

modified to look like a *remork,* with open-air seating and oriental decor in the back. Up to six people fit comfortably.

Golden Hands Massage MASSAGE
(☑ 017 855200; St 724; 1hr masssage US$5, with oil US$7; ⊙ 10am-11pm) Best massage in town, according to locals, and cheap to boot. Springing for the lemongrass-scented oil is a great idea.

🎓 Courses

Khmer Roots Cafe COOKING
(☑ 088 356 8016; www.khmerrootscafe.com; off NH33; US$20; ⊙ 10am-4pm) More than just a cooking class, Khmer Roots Cafe is a slice of Cambodian rural life set amid owner Soklim's shady trees and organic vegetable gardens about an hour east of Kampot. Classes usually involve preparing two dishes (including gathering the ingredients), eating lunch and having the opportunity to explore the tranquil countryside by bicycle afterwards.

The cafe is a small, family-run business in quite a remote area, making it necessary to book a day in advance. Adventuresome guests can also stay overnight in (provided) hammocks and have a campfire by the river. Or there are lovely bungalows for US$35/50 s/d per night, breakfast included.

👣 Tours

Everybody and their grandmother wants to sell you a tour in Kampot. The main day trips are to Bokor Hill Station (US$13 to US$18) which also includes a sunset cruise. There are also countryside tours that usually include Phnom Chhnork cave, the nearby salt fields, a pepper farm and the Kep crab market (US$12 to US$14).

Alternatively, you can hire a *remork* driver and cobble together your own tour of the caves, Kep and surrounding countryside. Depending on locations, a half/full-day tour costs about US$15/25, but if you want an English-speaking driver or the Kampot Cruiser, it'll be more like US$35.

Sunset cruises (US$5 with one drink) are also extremely popular, and include stops to see fireflies, which are most visible at the new moon and around sunset.

Bart the Boatman BOATING
(☑ 092 174280; 2-person tour US$40) Known simply as Bart the Boatman, this expat runs original private boat tours along the small tributaries of the Kampong Bay River. His backwater tour is highly recommended by travellers.

Sok Lim Tours TOURS
(☑ 010 796919, 012 796919; www.soklimtours.com; St 730; ⊙ 8am-7pm) Kampot's longest-running tour outfit is well-regarded and organises all the usual day tours and river cruises. For private countryside tours there are good English-speaking *remork* driver-guides who understand the process and history behind Kampot pepper. If there's no one in the actual office, check the neighbouring **Jack's Place** (St 730; mains US$2.50-6; ⊙ 6.30am-10.30pm; 🖥☑) restaurant.

Captain Chim's BOATING
(☑ 012 321043; St 724, Captain Chim's Guesthouse; sunset boat trip per person US$5) A sunset cruise with firefly-watching on a traditional boat, including a cold beer, is one of Captain Chim's popular excursions. Also on offer are fishing trips for US$11 including lunch, and bicycle hire (US$2 per day).

🛏 Sleeping

Inside or outside of town, there are accommodations for every budget, from the US$2.50 dorm bed to the US$100-plus boutique-hotel room.

🛏 In Town

Options in the town proper include several cheap hostels and some gorgeous boutique properties in renovated old shophouses.

Monkey Republic Kampot HOSTEL $
(☑ 012 848390; monkeyrepublickampot@gmail.com; St 730; dm with air-con US$5-7, r with fan US$8-12; 🌀🖥) This 100-bed backpacker mecca in a restored villa features Kampot's nicest dorm rooms. Choose from large dorms in the main building, or brand-new, six-bed 'pods' in the neighbouring house. Think individual lockers, privacy curtains and charging stations. There's an upstairs hammock lounge, while French tiles and big booths add character to the lively bar downstairs.

Baraca GUESTHOUSE $
(☑ 011 290434; www.baraca.org; St 726; d US$12-16, f US$20; 🖥) Just off the river, Baraca has bags of old-world charm, with high ceilings and original tilework floors in its four airy rooms. There's no hot water, but it's popular nonetheless, so book ahead. Great tapas restaurant and a gin bar, too.

Blue Buddha Hotel HOTEL $
(☑ 017 843550; www.bluebuddhahotel.com; 1 St 730; d/tr/f US$24/26/38; 🌀🖥) Raising the bar

for budget digs in Kampot, Blue Buddha has exceptionally helpful owners and spacious, minimalist-style rooms with comfortable beds, cable TV, minibars and big modern bathrooms. Guests also benefit from a swag of discounts at businesses around town, and free bike hire.

Pepper Guesthouse GUESTHOUSE $
(☑ 017 822626; guesthousepepper@yahoo.com; St 730; dm US$3, r with fan US$10, bungalows US$25; ❄ 🛜) We're fans of this homely, locally run guesthouse in a slightly creaky mid-century villa. Fan-only rooms have bags of character with beautiful old wood floors (room 101 is the best), while out in the front garden are two nicer bungalows with rain showers and tasteful decor. Hot water costs US$5 extra, and bicycle (US$1) and motorbike (US$4) hire are available.

Magic Sponge GUESTHOUSE $
(☑ 017 946428; www.magicspongekampot.com; St 730; dm US$6, d with fan US$15-23, with air-con US$23-28; ❄ 🛜) This popular backpacker place has a rooftop dorm with impressive through-breezes, personalised fans and reading lights. Good-value private rooms are exceptionally well-cared-for and bright. Downstairs is a movie lounge and a lively bar-restaurant with happy hour from noon to 8pm and well-regarded Indian food. There's even minigolf in the garden.

★**Rikitikitavi** BOUTIQUE HOTEL $$
(☑ 012 235102; www.rikitikitavi-kampot.com; River Rd; r incl breakfast US$53, f from US$70; ❄ 🛜) One of Cambodia's best-run boutique hotels, Rikitikitavi's rooms are a lesson in subtle luxury, fusing Asian-inspired decor with modern creature comforts. Ceilings are graced with stunning beams, and palm panels and beautiful artwork adorn the walls. Plus you get swish contemporary bathrooms and mod-con amenities such as flat-screen TV, DVD player, fridge and kettle. Service is sublime. Highly recommended.

The Columns BOUTIQUE HOTEL $$
(☑ 092 128300; www.the-columns.com; St 728; r incl breakfast US$45-59, ste US$75; ❄ 🛜) Set in a row of thoughtfully restored shophouses near the riverfront, this boutique hotel blends classic and modern with minimalist rooms featuring a touch of mid-century furniture, iPhone docking stations, flat-screen TVs and slick modern bathrooms. Downstairs is Green's, an inviting cafe with a lovely old tilework floor and a menu of healthy salads and shakes.

Makk Hotel BOUTIQUE HOTEL $$
(☑ 081 375375; www.makkhotel.com; Riverside Rd; r US$45-65; 🛜) This riverside hotel offers comfortable and stylish rooms along with a rooftop bar and its killer sunset views. The service is superior as well; during our visit a staff member was filling a suite with flower petals for a couple's honeymoon. Free bikes too!

Mea Culpa GUESTHOUSE $$
(☑ 012 504769; www.meaculpakampot.com; St 729; r US$25-30; ❄ 🛜) This modern villa has 11 rooms with plenty of homely appeal, while the location, south of the centre, guarantees a relaxed, peaceful vibe. The garden restaurant here (open 7am-9.30pm) spins the best pizza in town, straight from a wood-fired oven.

🏊 On the River

Most of the out-of-town places on the river aren't *that* far out of town – usually just a 10-minute *remork* ride from the centre. They all have over-water pavilions or docks to facilitate swimming, and most offer some sort of kayak or other watercraft rental.

Arcadia Backpackers & Water Park HOSTEL $
(☑ 097 519 7902; www.arcadiabackpackers.com; Tek Chhouu Rd; dm US$7-10, r US$20; 🛜) One of Kampot's great backpacker party scenes, riverside Arcadia offers a wide range of accommodations, from large, mixed dorms by the bar to quiet, private doubles by the water. All beds come with mosquito nets and free entry to the water park, which includes a Russian swing, a 50m water slide, a climbing wall, a diving platform and a zipline.

Those who only wish to visit the water park can do so for US$7. There are plans to introduce a wakeboarding feature.

Naga House HOSTEL $
(☑ 012 289916; nagahousekampot@gmail.com; Tek Chhouu Rd; dm US$4, bungalows US$9-14; 🛜) This classic backpacker hang-out offers basic ground-level and stilted thatched bungalows (all with shared bathrooms) amid lush foliage, and coveted four- and eight-bed dorms in the main house on the river. There's an attractive and extremely social bar-restaurant that often rocks into the night, especially on Saturdays when it hosts DJ sets.

High Tide Kampot HOSTEL $
(☑ 096 416 9345; www.facebook.com/hightidekampot; dm US$3-4, bungalows US$10-15, with shared bathroom US$6-7; 🛜) This chill spot

Kampot

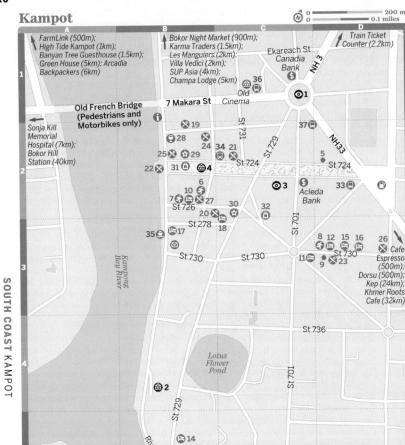

N 0   200 m
0   0.1 miles

FarmLink (500m);
High Tide Kampot (1km);
Banyan Tree Guesthouse (1.5km);
Green House (5km); Arcadia
Backpackers (6km)

Bokor Night Market (900m);
Karma Traders (1.5km);
Les Manguiers (2km);
Villa Vedici (2km);
SUP Asia (4km);
Champa Lodge (5km)

Train Ticket
Counter (2.2km)

Ekareach St
Canadia
Bank

NH 3

Old
Cinema

7 Makara St

Old French Bridge
(Pedestrians and
Motorbikes only)

Sonja Kill
Memorial
Hospital (7km);
Bokor Hill
Station (40km)

NH33

St 731

St 729

St 724

St 724

Acleda
Bank

St 726

St 278

Kampong
Bay River

St 730

St 730

St 701

St 730

Cafe
Espresso
(500m);
Dorsu (500m);
Kep (24km);
Khmer Roots
Cafe (32km)

St 736

Lotus
Flower
Pond

St 701

St 729

River Rd

SOUTH COAST KAMPOT

on the river caters to long-term backpackers who enjoy grabbing a cold one from the bamboo bar, then relaxing in hammocks and papasan chairs, listening to trance and electronic music. Rooms are wood huts with thatched roofs, all perched on stilts; the nicer accommodations offer porches slung with hammocks.

Banyan Tree Guesthouse HOSTEL **$**
(☑ 078 665094; www.banyantreekampot.com; Tek Chhouu Rd; dm US$3, r US$6-12; ☎) Boat sports by day, booze by night, and plenty of downtime in between on the sublime riverside

chill-out deck. Choose from a 20-bed dorm, simple rooms above the bar or pleasing rattan bungalows out back. Fridays are party nights with live music from top local band Kampot Playboys or visiting Phnom Penh acts. This is no place for light sleepers.

★ **Green House** BUNGALOW **$$**
(☑ 088 886 3071; www.greenhousekampot.com; Tek Chhouu Rd; bungalows US$25-35; ☎) This gorgeously conceived riverfront pad is all about tranquillity, with the best of its palm-thatch bungalows and colourful wooden cottages (with balconies) right on the riv-

Kampot

◎ Sights
1 Durian Roundabout	C1
2 Kampot Provincial Museum	B4
3 Kampot Traditional Music School	C2
4 Old Market	B2

◈ Activities, Courses & Tours
5 Captain Chim's	D2
6 Climbodia	B2
7 Golden Hands Massage	B2
8 Kampot Cruiser	D3
9 Sok Lim Tours	D3
SUP Asia	(see 4)

⊜ Sleeping
10 Baraca	B2
11 Blue Buddha Hotel	C3
12 Magic Sponge	D3
13 Makk Hotel	B5
14 Mea Culpa	B5
15 Monkey Republic Kampot	D3
16 Pepper Guesthouse	D3
17 Rikitikitavi	B3
18 The Columns	C3

⊗ Eating
19 Ciao	B2
20 Ellie's	B2
21 Epic Arts Café	C2
22 Fishmarket	B2
23 Jack's Place	D3
24 Jetzt Kampot	B2
Rikitikitavi	(see 17)
25 Rusty Keyhole	B2
26 Thai Fire	D3
27 Twenty Three Bistro	B2

◉ Drinking & Nightlife
Moi Tiet	(see 4)
28 Nelly's Bar	B2
Sharpen the Axe	(see 4)

✪ Entertainment
29 Ecran	B2
30 KAMA	C2

⊜ Shopping
31 Kepler's Kampot Books	B2
32 Tiny Kampot Pillows	C2

⊕ Transport
33 Capitol Tours	D2
34 Champa Mekong Tourist Bus	C2
35 Crab Shuttle	B3
36 Giant Ibis	C1
37 Kampot Express	C2
Phnom Penh Sorya	(see 33)

SOUTH COAST KAMPOT

erbank. The historic teak-wood main building, which houses the restaurant, was once home to the legendary Phnom Penh bar 'Snowy's' (aka 'Maxine's'), transported lock, stock, and barrel here in 2011. No children under age 12.

Sabay Beach BUNGALOW $$
(☏031-417 9304; www.sabaybeach.com; Village Ordnung Chimern; dm US$6, bungalows from US$45; ☏) Those who make it all the way to Sabay Beach will be handsomely rewarded for their ambition. From the palm-tree-flanked boardwalk and the dreamy bungalows to the darling open-air restaurant and the impeccable service, this unpretentious resort is nonetheless one of the finest stays in the region.

Sabay also has its own swath of sandy beach on the river, and the abundant fruit trees provide the ingredients for delicious smoothies.

Les Manguiers RESORT $$
(☏092 330050; www.mangokampot.com; Kompong Bay River east bank; r with shared bathroom US$14-26, bungalows US$39-67; @☏) This rambling garden complex has canoes and bikes for rent, badminton, table tennis and a children's playground. You can jump into the river from one of four over-water gazebos. Accommodation ranges from large, bright simple rooms to stilted wooden bungalows, all with fan and cold water. Meals are served with a limited number of options at a fixed price.

Champa Lodge BUNGALOW $$
(☏092 525835; www.champalodge.com; Kompong Kreang; bungalows US$38-60; ☏) Set on a bend in the river amid traditional Cambodian countryside scenes, Champa is a rural hideaway with arty rooms in several traditional Khmer wooden houses, all with verandas for slothing out and admiring the bucolic views. Kayak and bike hire is available if you can drag yourself away. The restaurant-bar includes a great selection of Belgian beers.

✖ Eating

With everything from sushi to handmade pasta to tapas, Kampot is a culinary capital full of international influences and plenty of Khmer goodness as well. Local street-food eateries on Old Bridge Rd between the bridge and the Durian Roundabout are great places to grab fried noodles, soups and Khmer desserts such as sticky rice with coconut sauce.

Many of Kampot's guesthouses are worthy of a meal. Mea Culpa has wood-fired pizzas, Magic Sponge has good Indian food, or enjoy a meal on the water at one of the out-of-town riverside places – Green House is particularly good.

★ Thai Fire THAI $
(☑ 081 364559; www.facebook.com/ThaiFireKampot; Guesthouse Rd; mains US$4.50-5; ☺ noon-10.30pm Mon-Sat) Guests here are in the capable hands of Nalee, a culinary genius from Laos who taught herself to cook in Thailand and opened this restaurant with her husband Rhett, who handles non-cooking details. Don't miss the excellent whole fried fish, enormous and Thai-style, with crispy skin, delicate flakes and chili, lemongrass and cashews galore. Just dig in.

★ Ciao ITALIAN $
(St 722; mains US$2.75-4; ☺ from 6pm) Kampot's most beloved Western street-food vendor is an Italian who cooks delicious pizzas one at a time in a modified dustbin out of this ramshackle space on Kampot's street-food row. The pizzas take awhile but are *sooo* worth it. Also serves home-made gnocchi and pasta.

Cafe Espresso CAFE $
(NH33; mains US$4-6; ☺ 8.30am-4pm Tue-Fri, 9am-4.30pm Sat & Sun; ☎ ⁄) It's worth the trip to this cafe on the outskirts of town. The owners are real foodies and offer a global menu that traipses from vegetarian quesadillas to Brazilian-style pork sandwiches with some especially tempting breakfast options. But it is caffeine-cravers who will really be buzzing, thanks to the regionally grown coffee blends, roasted daily on-site.

Jetzt Kampot BURGERS $
(☑ 015 572380; www.facebook.com/pg/jetztkampot; burgers US$5; ☺ 5.30-10pm) Easily the best burgers in Kampot, with new toppings and flavour combinations being invented each week. 'The cricket', for example, comes with cream cheese, jalapeños, spring onions and tomatoes. The place also offers dorms with hot showers (US$5) and at check-in everybody gets a free draught beer.

Ellie's CAFE $
(☑ 096 309 2300; St 726; mains US$3-5; ☺ 8am-4pm Wed-Mon; ☎ ⁄) Eggs Benedict, French toast, English muffins – Ellie's whips up some of the most scrumptious breakfasts in town for travellers pining for a taste of home. The cakes and original sandwich fillings, such as pumpkin, or spinach and feta, make for a tasty lunch too. Also sells vintage clothing, original flip-flops, bags and more.

Epic Arts Café CAFE $
(www.epicarts.org.uk; St 724; mains US$2-4; ☺ 7am-4pm; ☎) ⁄ A great place for breakfast, home-made cakes, infused tea and light lunches, this mellow eatery is staffed by young people who are deaf or have a disability. Profits fund arts workshops for Cambodians with disabilities and there's an upstairs shop that sells art, bags, jewellery, stuffed toys and the like.

★ Twenty Three Bistro INTERNATIONAL $$
(☑ 088 697 9731; 23 East St; mains US$4.50-10; ☺ 11am-10pm; ☎) Hot damn, there's now a twice-baked cheddar soufflé in Kampot, and this is the place that loses money making it for you. We're not sure how the owners manage it, but this seems to be haute cuisine on clearance, from expats with hefty experience in world-class restaurants and a range of European cuisines. Their cocktails slay, too.

Fishmarket FUSION $$
(☑ 012 728884; River Rd; mains US$6-15; ☺ 11am-10.30pm Mon-Fri, from 7.30am Sat & Sun) The signature eatery of Kampot's up-and-coming dining scene lives in a restored art-deco masterpiece on the banks of the Kompong Bay River. Plop down in the breezy open-air dining area and dig into green-tea-smoked duck, a spicy beef salad or local favourites such as peppercorn crab and *amok*.

Rikitikitavi INTERNATIONAL $$
(www.rikitikitavi-kampot.com; River Rd; mains US$5-8; ☺ 7am-10pm; ☎ ⁄) Named after the mongoose in Rudyard Kipling's *The Jungle Book,* this riverfront terrace is all about the ambience. It's also known for its Kampot pepper chicken, burritos, slow-cooked curry and salads. Happy hour from 5pm to 7pm brings two-for-one cheer on all cocktails. This is the best place in town to kick back and enjoy a sundowner.

Rusty Keyhole INTERNATIONAL $$
(☑ 095 212485; River Rd; ribs US$5-10; ☺ 8am-11.30pm Nov-May, 11am-11pm Jun-Oct; ☎) This popular riverfront bar-restaurant turns out a global menu of comfort food and Khmer home cooking. Most people are here for its famous ribs; order in advance, but beware of the enormous, extra-large portions. Three more Rusty restaurants have opened in the last few years, with varying ownership.

🍷 Drinking & Nightlife

Sharpen the Axe COCKTAIL BAR
(📞096 358 4401; Old Market St; ⊙7pm-3am) Kampot's first high-end craft-cocktail bar is set in charming gardens and revered for its vast list of spirits and innovative concoctions. Our favourite is the spicy Palomasia, with Absolute vodka, home-made holy basil & Kampot pepper syrup, and lemon, lime and pomelo.

Moi Tiet BAR
(Old Market) This artsy little enclave in the **Old Market** (Riverfront Rd) specialises in 'brews and tattoos' according to its signage, but also does things like home-brewed ginger beer and tasty French dishes. It's beloved most for its garden setting, intriguing patrons and delicious cocktails.

Nelly's Bar BAR
(📞016 861849; River Rd; ⊙3pm-late) Occupying a street corner under a bougainvillea tree outside a beautiful colonial building, Nelly's is a fine place to throw back a few drinks, with groovy tunes and a nice mix of travellers and colourful Kampot expats. The high season occasionally sees acoustic acts set up on the sidewalk, and the bar offers bungalow accommodation for US$10 per night.

⭐ Entertainment

Karma Traders LIVE MUSIC
(📞016 556504; www.karmatraderskampot.com) Reserve Tuesday nights for a visit to Karma Traders' rooftop bar, where there's live music, US$2 tacos (try the Coca-Cola pulled pork) and two-for-one well drinks if you can beat the bartender in rock, paper, scissors. There's also a ping-pong room, a cinema, a mini-basketball court, a slackline and more toys at the popular hostel downstairs from the bar.

KAMA ARTS CENTRE
(Kampot Arts & Music Association; 📞096 255 5393; St 726; ⊙8am-7.30pm; 📶) Owned by Julien Poulson, a founding member of acclaimed band Cambodian Space Project, KAMA is part boho cafe, part art space. It spins tunes from an eclectic vinyl collection, plays movies occasionally and hosts creative events. Pop in for a beer, or the dish of the day, and check out what's happening while you're in town. Hours can be unpredictable.

Ecran CINEMA
(📞093 249411; St 724; per movie US$2.50; ⊙closed Tue) Ecran (French for screen) is a little movie-cafe offering big-screen films and a private room for movie-watching. Cambodian-related movies such as *The Killing Fields*, *The Missing Picture* and *Enemies of the People* screen most days at 4pm, with various cult classics and other films screened at 7.30pm daily. Drinks and popcorn available.

🛍 Shopping

Bokor Night Market MARKET
(parking 1000r; ⊙4-10pm) With about 100 stands offering things such as jewellery, karaoke, fried ice cream, sneakers and well, everything else, this nightlife experience and shopping mecca on Kampot's market circuit has loads of potential, if not many customers. The riverside setting is pleasant and family-friendly, a stage welcomes regular concerts and the aroma of tasty street food wafts on the breeze.

Dorsu CLOTHING
(📞012 960225; www.dorsu.org; NH33; ⊙8am-5pm) Sharing a contemporary factory space on the outskirts of town with Cafe Espresso (p218), Dorsu sells a range of high-quality wardrobe staples, all designed and produced locally by a small team. There's also a Dorsu branch near the Old Market, on 724 St, that's open 10am to 7pm.

FarmLink FOOD
(📞033-690 2354; www.farmlink-cambodia.com; ⊙7.30-11.30am & 1.30-4.30pm Mon-Fri) In Kampot you can purchase pouches of peerless pepper at the FarmLink boutique, one of the pioneers of geographical-indication pepper production (see p222). You can see pepper being dried in the garden out front and visitors can observe the pepper-sorting room. It's just over the New Bridge; take the first right and look for it on the left.

Tiny Kampot Pillows HANDICRAFTS, CLOTHING
(📞097 766 6094; www.tinykampotpillows.com; 2000 Roundabout; ⊙10am-7pm) This textile shop sells, well, lots of tiny pillows made from handwoven silk, plus plenty of other accessories from clothing to bags.

Kepler's Kampot Books BOOKS
(St 724; ⊙7.30am-9pm) This is the place for secondhand books in Kampot, with a good selection of English-language titles.

ℹ Information

Acleda Bank (St 724; ⊙7.30am-4pm Mon-Fri, to 11.30am Sat, ATM 24hr)
Canadia Bank (Durian Roundabout; ⊙8am-3.30pm Mon-Fri, to 11.30am Sat, ATM 24hr)

There's a strip of copy shops with internet access southwest of the Durian Roundabout on 7 Makara St. Wi-fi is free at most guesthouses, cafes and restaurants.

Tourist Information Centre (☑ 097 899 5593; lonelyguide@gmail.com; River Rd; ☺7am-5pm) Led by the knowledgeable Mr Pov, Kampot's tourist office doles out free advice, sells tours and can arrange transport to area attractions such as caves, falls and Kompong Trach.

The free and often hilarious *Kampot Survival Guide* (www.kampotsurvivalguide.com) takes a tongue-in-cheek look at local expat life. There's also the free *Coastal* guide to Kampot and Kep, with heaps of info on local businesses.

Getting There & Away

Kampot, on NH3, is 148km southwest of Phnom Penh, 105km east of Sihanoukville.

BOAT

An atmospheric way to get to Kep is on the **Crab Shuttle** (☑ 088 829 6644; crabshuttle@gmail. com; ☺ weather-dependent) boat (one-way/return US$10/13.50, 2½ hours), which departs at 9am and returns at 3pm for sunset views. Rabbit Island (Koh Tonsay) drop-offs and pickups are possible for an extra few dollars, with a boat transfer at Kep's Rabbit Island Pier.

BUS

If heading to Phnom Penh, be aware that a couple of the bus companies, including **Phnom Penh Sorya** (NH33), go via Kep, which adds at least an hour to the trip. You're better off with the direct buses run by **Capitol Tours** (☑ 092 665001; NH33) (twice daily) or 'luxury' bus company **Giant Ibis** (☑ 095 666809; www.giantibis.com; 7 Makara St) (8.30am and 2.45pm). Even quicker are the direct minivan services to Phnom Penh run by **Kampot Express** (☑ 078 555123; NH33), with daily departures at 8am, 11am and 1pm.

Champa Mekong Tourist Bus (☑ 087 630036; St 724) has five minivan departures daily to Sihanoukville and twice-daily departures to Ha Tien, Ho Chi Minh City, Phnom Penh and Bangkok.

Several bus companies stop in Kep (US$3, 30 minutes) en route to Ha Tien or Phnom Penh, or you can take a *remork* (US$10, 45 minutes) or *moto* (US$6).

Guesthouses and tour agencies can arrange tickets and pickups, although they'll usually take a commission.

TRAIN

The rehabilitated train is a slow but scenic option to Phnom Penh (US$6, five hours) and Sihanoukville (US$5, four hours). Departures take place on Friday, Saturday, Sunday and Monday, at varying times; check the schedule at **www.royal-railway.com**.

Kampot's **ticket counter** (☑ 099 222566, 078 888582) is open 8am to 4pm Wednesday to Monday; it's best to purchase tickets a few days in advance.

Getting Around

A *moto* ride in town costs around 2000r (*remork* US$1). Sometimes the driver will ask for more if it's a holiday, you're a big group, it's raining or you take a ride longer than a few minutes.

Bicycles (US$2 per day) and motorbikes (about US$5 per day) can be rented from many guesthouses around town.

Around Kampot

The limestone hills east of Kampot towards Kep are littered with caves. Phnom Chhnork, surrounded by blazingly green countryside, is a real gem and can easily be visited in an afternoon along with Phnom Sorsia.

BUSES FROM KAMPOT

DESTINATION	FARE	DURATION	FREQUENCY	COMPANY	TYPE
Bangkok	US$32	12hr	2 daily	Champa Mekong	minivan
Ha Tien, Vietnam	US$8	1½ hrs	2 daily	Champa Mekong	minivan
Ho Chi Minh City	US$18	9 hrs	2 daily	Champa Mekong	minivan
Phnom Penh	US$5-9	2¾-3¼ hrs	9 daily	Capitol Tours, Champa Mekong, Giant Ibis, Kampot Express	bus/minivan
Sihanoukville	US$5	2 hrs	5 daily	Champa Mekong	minivan

★ La Plantation
FARM

(☎ 017 842505; www.kampotpepper.com; guided tours US$18-20; ⊙ 9am-6pm) 🌿 FREE This sprawling, lovely organic pepper farm offers guided walks in French, English and Khmer, explaining how several varieties of pepper are grown, harvested and processed. The farm also grows fruits, chillis, herbs and peanuts, and there's a restaurant and shop where you can buy pepper at steep prices. (The money helps pay for children's English classes at local schools.)

A *remork* trip out to the farm with an English-speaking driver costs around US$20, and brings guests past salt flats and a 'secret lake'. Shorter tours are free; longer guided walks include a BBQ lunch and cost US$18.

Phnom Chhnork
CAVE

(ភ្នំឈ្នក; US$1; ⊙ 7am-6pm) Phnom Chhnork is a short walk through a quilt of rice paddies from Wat Ang Sdok, where a monk collects the entry fee and a gaggle of friendly local kids offer their services as guides. From the bottom, a 203-step staircase leads up the hillside and down into a cavern as graceful as a Gothic cathedral. The view from up top is especially magical in the late afternoon, as is the walk to and from the wat.

Inside the cave you'll be greeted by a stalactite elephant, with a second elephant outlined on the flat cliff face to the right. Tiny chirping bats live up near two natural chimneys that soar towards the blue sky, partly blocked by foliage of an impossibly green hue.

Within the **main chamber** stands a remarkable 7th-century (Funan-era) **brick temple**, dedicated to Shiva. The temple's brickwork is in superb condition thanks to the protection afforded by the cave. Poke your head inside and check out the ancient stalactite that serves as a *linga* (phallic symbol). A slippery passage, flooded in the rainy season, leads through the hill.

To get to Phnom Chhnork turn left off NH33 about 5.5km east of Kampot. Look for the sign to 'Climbodia'. From the turn-off it's 6km to the cave on a bumpy road. A return *moto* ride from Kampot costs about US$6 (*remork* US$10).

Phnom Sorsia
CAVE

(ភ្នំសរសៀរ, Phnom Sia; ⊙ 7am-5pm) FREE Phnom Sorsia is home to several natural caves. From the parking area, a stairway leads up the hillside to a gaudy modern **temple**. From there, steps lead left up to

Rung Damrey Saa (White Elephant Cave). A slippery, sloping staircase (where one false step will send you into the abyss) leads down and then up and then out through a hole in the other side. Exit the cave and follow the right-hand path which leads back to the temple.

To see the **Bat Cave**, take the steps leading to the right from the temple. Inside the cave, countless bats flutter and chirp overhead, flying out to the forest and back through a narrow natural chimney. Locals once used bamboo poles to hunt the creatures by swatting them out of the air, but tourists didn't like it, and now police do frequent checks to ensure the bats are not being killed. The circuit ends near a hilltop stupa with impressive views.

Local kids will attempt to serve as guides here. Let them lead you with a torch and don't forget to give a dollar or two at the end. The turn-off to Phnom Sorsia is on NH33, 13.5km southeast of Kampot and 1.3km northwest of the White Horse Roundabout near Kep. Look for a sign reading 'Phnom Sorsia Resort' – from there a dirt road leads about 1km northeast through the rice fields.

Bokor Hill Station

The once-abandoned French retreat of Bokor Hill Station (កស្តានីយភ្នំបូកគោ), inside the 1581-sq-km Bokor National Park, is famed for its refreshingly cool climate and creepy derelict buildings that had their heyday during the 1920s and 1930s. On cold, foggy days it can get pretty spooky up here as mists drop visibility to nothing and the wind keens through abandoned buildings. Appropriate, then, that the foggy showdown that ends the Matt Dillon crime thriller *City of Ghosts* (2002) was filmed here.

These days the hill station is becoming more famous for the Thansur Bokor Highland Resort, the ugly modern casino that blights the summit. It's part of a huge development project that includes a golf course (or, given the mist, a spot-the-ball competition?) and numerous holiday villas on sale at speculative prices.

History

In the early 1920s the French, ever eager to escape the lowland heat, established a hill station atop Phnom Bokor (1080m), known for its dramatic vistas of the coastal plain one vertical kilometre below.

KAMPOT PEPPER

Before Cambodia's civil war, no Paris restaurant worth its salt would have been without pepper from Kampot Province, but the country's pepper farms were all but destroyed by the Khmer Rouge, who believed in growing rice, not spice.

Today, thanks to a group of eco-entrepreneurs and foodies who are passionate about pepper, Kampot-grown peppercorns are making a comeback.

Kampot pepper is grown on family farms that dot Phnom Voar and nearby valleys northwest of Kompong Trach, where the unique climate and the farmers' fidelity to labour-intensive growing techniques produce particularly pungent peppercorns. In fact, Kampot pepper is so extraordinary that it is Cambodia's first-ever product to receive a 'geographical indication' (GI), just like French cheeses.

Peppercorns are picked from February to May. Black pepper is plucked from the trees when the corns are starting to turn yellow and turns black during sun-drying; red pepper is picked when the fruit is completely mature; and mild white pepper is soaked in water to remove the husks. September to February is the season for green pepper, whose sprigs have to be eaten almost immediately after harvesting – the **crab market restaurants** (p227) of Kep are among the best places to experience its gentle freshness.

A packet of pepper from **FarmLink** (p219) boutique in Kampot, **La Plantation** (p221) organic pepper farm or **Sothy's Pepper Farm** (🗷 088-951 3505; www.mykampot pepper.asia; Phnom Vour, off NH33; ⊗ 9am-5pm) **FREE** near Kep makes an excellent souvenir or gift: the corns are lightweight and unbreakable, and if stored properly – that is, *not* ground! – will stay fresh for years.

The hill station was twice abandoned to the howling winds: first when Vietnamese and Khmer Issarak (Free Khmer) forces overran it in the late 1940s while fighting for independence from France, and again in 1972, when the Lon Nol regime left it to the Khmer Rouge forces that were steadily taking over the countryside. Because of its commanding position, the site was strategically important to all sides during the civil war and was one location the Vietnamese really had to fight for during their 1979 invasion. For several months, the Khmer Rouge held out in the Catholic church here while the Vietnamese shot at them from Bokor Palace, 500m away.

◉ Sights

Bokor National Park NATIONAL PARK
(ឧទ្យានជាតិបូកគោ, Preah Monivong National Park; motorbike/car 2000/10,000r) Bokor's moist evergreen forests – with dry dipterocarp and mixed deciduous forests in the north – shelter a wide variety of rare and threatened animals, including the Indian elephant, leopard, Asiatic black bear, Malayan sun bear, pileated gibbon, pig-tailed macaque, slow loris, red muntjac deer, pangolin, yellow-throated martin, small Asian mongoose and various species of civet, porcupine, squirrel and bat.

Trekking trips here used to be very popular, but recent development within the park has scuppered hiking opportunities.

More than 300 species of bird, including several types of hornbill, also live here. Don't expect to see much wildlife, though – most of the animals are nocturnal and survive by staying in more remote parts of the park. Long kept off the tourist map due to Khmer Rouge activity, Bokor today is still threatened by poaching, illegal logging and development. The summit of Phnom Bokor, once home only to the abandoned buildings of Bokor hill station, is now part of a multi-million-dollar tourism development that includes the ugly Thansur Bokor Highland Resort casino, while in the southeast the Kamchay hydropower project has flooded a small section of the park.

Popokvil Falls WATERFALL
(ទឹកធ្លាក់ពពកវិល; 2000r) From the Thansur Bokor Highland Resort, the road heads north for several kilometres to two-tiered Popokvil Falls, which are impressive from July to October, but dry up outside of the rainy season. The hike to the falls is an hour or two, and don't even think of wearing flip-flops.

Bokor Palace Hotel HISTORIC BUILDING
(ដំណាក់បូកគោ) **FREE** Opened in 1925, this once-grand hotel was a chief playground for hobnobbing French officials. As you wander

through the building, you'll need your imagination to envisage the lavish interiors that adorned the opulent ballroom and guestrooms as today the hotel is a vast, empty shell with just scraps of original floor tilework still hanging on.

Catholic Church
CHURCH

FREE The squat belfry of the Romanesque Catholic church still holds aloft its cross, and fragments of glass brick cling to the corners of the nave windows; one side window holds the barest outline of a rusty crucifix. It's easy to imagine a small crowd of French colonials in formal dress assembled here for Sunday Mass. The subdividing walls inside were built by the Khmer Rouge. A bit up the hill, a sheer drop overlooks rainforest.

Wat Sampov Pram
BUDDHIST TEMPLE

(វត្តសំពៅព្រាំ) In the rare absence of fog, lichen-caked Wat Sampov Pram (Five Boats Wat) offers tremendous views over the jungle to the coastline below, including Vietnam's Phu Quoc Island. Wild monkeys like to hang out around the wat.

🛏 Sleeping & Eating

Bokor is best visited on a day trip from Kampot, as the bizarre and monolithic Thansur Bokor Highland Resort casino is currently the only place to stay. Its parent company, Sokha Hotels, had two more hotels under construction on the mountaintop at the time of research.

Tours up here inevitably include a packed lunch; otherwise bring your own or eat at the casino, which offers a Thai buffet.

❶ Getting There & Away

You can either visit the hill station on one of the numerous day trips organised in Kampot or rent a motorbike and travel under your own steam. The road up here is newer and constructed by the Thansur Bokor Highland Resort, so it's in excellent condition.

KEP

🎵 036 / POP 35,000

Founded as a seaside retreat for the French elite in 1908 and a favoured haunt of Cambodian high-rollers during the 1960s, sleepy Kep (កែប, Krong Kep, also spelled Kaeb) is drawing tourists back with seafood, sunsets and hikes in butterfly-filled Kep National Park. Its impressive range of boutique hotels squarely targets a more cultured beach crowd than the party-happy guesthouses of Sihanoukville and the islands.

Some find Kep a bit soulless because it lacks a centre, not to mention a long sandy shoreline. Others revel in its torpid pace, content to relax at their resort, nibble on peppery crab at the famed crab market and poke around the mildewed shells of modernist villas, which still give the town a sort of post-apocalyptic feel.

◎ Sights

Scattered throughout Kep are the blackened husks of handsome mid-20th-century villas that speak of happier, more carefree times before the Khmer Rouge evacuated the town. All built according to the precepts of the modernist style, with clean lines and little adornment, they keep alive the memory of Kep's short and sweet heyday. Today many are covered in graffiti and shelter squatters (and, some say, ghosts). A few have been renovated and turned into fancy boutique hotels. Don't get your hopes up about buying one, as they were all snapped up for a song in the mid-1990s by well-connected speculators.

★ Kep National Park
NATIONAL PARK

(ឧទ្យានជាតិកែប; 4000r) The interior of Kep peninsula is occupied by Kep National Park, where an 8km circuit, navigable by foot and mountain bike, winds through thick forest passing by wats and viewpoints. Quirky yellow signs point the way and show trailheads to off-shooting walking paths that lead into the park's interior. The 'Stairway to Heaven' trail is particularly worthwhile, leading up the hill to a pagoda, a nunnery and the Sunset Rock viewpoint. The main park entrance is behind Veranda Natural Resort.

Koh Tonsay
ISLAND

(កោះទន្សាយ, Rabbit Island) If you like the rustic beachcomber lifestyle, Koh Tonsay's 250m-long main beach is for you, but come now as the island is tagged for development. The beach is one of the nicest of any of the Kep-area islands but don't expect sparkling white sand. This one has shorefront flotsam, chickens and wandering cows. Restaurant-shacks and rudimentary bungalows (from US$7 per night) rim the sand. Boats to Rabbit Island (30 minutes) leave from Rabbit Island pier at 9am and 1pm.

Return trips from Kep are at 3pm in the rainy season, 4pm in the dry season. Return

Kep

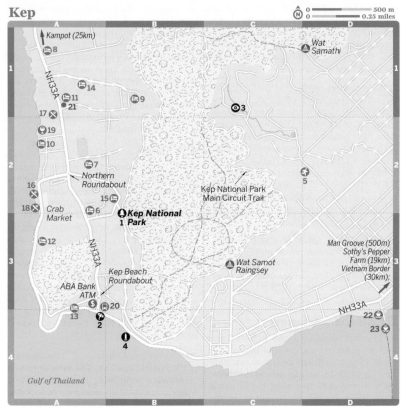

tickets cost US$8. Kep guesthouses can arrange boat tickets or you can head to the **Koh Tonsay Boat Ticket Office** at the pier. Private boats to the island can be arranged at the pier and cost US$25 return for up to six people. Rabbit Island is so named because locals say it resembles a rabbit – an example of what too much local brew can do to your imagination.

Other Kep-area islands include **Koh Pos** (Snake Island; about 30 minutes beyond Rabbit Island), which has a deserted beach and fine snorkelling but no overnight accommodation. Getting out there costs about US$50 for an all-day trip by 10-person boat. There's also small, beachless **Koh Svay** (Mango Island), whose summit offers nice views.

Kep Butterfly Garden   FARM
(កសិដ្ឋានមេអំបៅកែប; Jasmine Valley Trail, Kep National Park; US$1, guided tour US$2; ⊙7am-5pm) **FREE** This small and beautifully kept flower-filled garden is home to myriad butterflies.

You can cycle or motorbike here, or hike here from the Kep National Park trail by taking the off-shooting 'Connection Path' track.

Beaches
Most of Kep's beaches are too shallow and rocky to make for good swimming. It is possible to swim off the beach or the jetty at the Sailing Club, but the water is particularly shallow here.

The beach at Koh Tonsay (Rabbit Island) is a popular excursion. Buy your tickets at the Koh Tonsay Boat Ticket Office at the Rabbit Island pier.

Kep Beach   BEACH
(ឆ្នេរកែប) This handkerchief-sized strip of sand is Kep's only proper beach. In the prewar period, powder-white sand was trucked in from other beaches and this practice began again in 2013, ensuring the beach is now in better shape than it has been for years. It's still somewhat pebbly and can get packed

Kep

on weekends. The eastern end of the shaded promenade along the beach is marked by **Sela Cham P'dey**, a statue depicting a nude fisherman's wife awaiting her husband's return.

🏃 Activities & Tours

Kep makes a good base for visiting Sothy's Pepper Farm and La Plantation, along with several delightful cave temples including Wat Kiri Sela near Kompong Trach and Phnom Chhnork and Phnom Sorsia on the road to Kampot. The best way to see the sights is to hire one of the many English-speaking *remork* drivers in town (about US$20 to $US30 per day) and tailor your own countryside tour.

Kep Sailing Club   WATER SPORTS
(☑078 333685; www.knaibangchatt.com/the-sailing-club; Knai Bang Chatt; ⊗8am-5pm) Open to all, the newly expanded sailing club and activity centre at the hotel Knai Bang Chatt hires out sea kayaks (US$8 per hour), Hobie Cats (from US$20 per hour), paddleboards (US$8 per hour) and Optimists (US$10 per hour). The latter are small boats for children, for whom sailing lessons are available.

Mountain bikes are also available at US$12 per day, as well as guided kayak tours to the mangroves (US$40 per person) and sunset cruises in high season (US$25 per person).

Magic Tree   CLIMBING
(☑097 958 1414; www.maxdiscoverycambodia. wordpress.com; adult/child US$15/12) Max Discovery Cambodia organises a range of events and leisure and team-building activities around Kep, and the Magic Tree is an alternative experience for families. Explore the interior of a huge old ficus tree in Kep National Park with safety ropes and instruction.

Ranch de la Plantation   HORSE RIDING
(☑097 847 4960; www.facebook.com/kep.plantation; 1/2hr ride US$20/35; ⊗8am-6pm) Horse rides are available through the lower reaches of Kep National Park and into the countryside around town. There's a horse for every skill level here, and beginners can opt to simply trot around the corral (US$15).

Marine Conservation Cambodia   VOLUNTEERING
(☑016 715444; www.marineconservationcambodia. org; Koh Seh) 🏊 Based on the island of Koh Seh (18km from Kep), Marine Conservation Cambodia works to preserve the marine environment around Kep and combat the destruction caused to sea life by illegal fishing. Volunteers can get hands-on practice, getting involved with patrols to spot illegal fishing, as well as learning about marine conservation and helping with research projects.

🛏 Sleeping

Kep meanders along the shoreline for a good 5km, with resorts and guesthouses speckled along the length of the main road and perched on the dirt tracks that wander up the hills leading to Kep National Park. Prices at the classiest places can feel at bit inflated, but there are plenty of good midrange options.

Botanica Guesthouse
BUNGALOW $

(☑097 899 8614; www.kep-botanica.com; NH33A; r with fan/air-con US$22/29; ❄️🛜🏊) A little way from the action (if Kep can be said to have any action), Botanica offers exceptional value for money with attractive bungalows boasting contemporary bathrooms. There's a well-shaded pool and guests can use free bicycles to pedal into town. Renovations have only improved what was already a good thing.

Bird of Paradise
BUNGALOW $

(☑090 880413; www.birdofparadisebungalows. com; bungalows incl breakfast with fan/air-con from US$14/20; ❄️🛜) Set in a relaxed, peaceful garden, Bird of Paradise offers stupendous value and is well-located just uphill from the main road, within walking distance of the crab market. Simple but sweet wooden bungalows, with hammocks strung from the porch, are delightfully rustic, while the aircon concrete cottages are more spacious.

Bacoma
BUNGALOW $

(☑088 411 2424; www.bacoma.weebly.com; NH33A; r US$15-30; 🛜) Cheap and cheerful *rondavels* (circular dwellings with conical thatched roofs) in the garden all have mosquito nets and fan, with sparkling-clean shared bathrooms. There are also roomy bungalows and traditional Khmer houses with private bathrooms, and the owner is a super-nice guy.

★ Tara Lodge
GUESTHOUSE $$

(☑097 623 6167; www.taralodge-kep.com; d incl breakfast US$50-60, f US$75; ❄️🛜🏊) The hugely friendly Tara Lodge gets a big tick from us for its split-level bungalows with wide verandahs and all the mod-cons, secreted within a verdant garden of palms and flowers, and set around a glistening pool. This is a secluded spot for some serious downtime. The upstairs terrace-restaurant serves excellent Khmer and French food and has views to Bokor.

Kep Lodge
BUNGALOW $$

(☑092 435330; bungalows from US$33; 🛜🏊) An atmospheric place with bungalows tucked into the jungle with breathtaking mountain and ocean views, a saltwater infinity pool and free bicycles, making it a fantastic deal. Some guests complain of inconsistent service and elusive wi-fi and hot water.

Saravoan Hotel
BOUTIQUE HOTEL $$

(☑036-639 3909; r US$45-55; ❄️🛜🏊) Classic Kep contemporary minimalist design is the hallmark of Saravoan. The spacious rooms come with polished concrete floors, stonewall detailing and floor-to-ceiling glass doors that open out onto arguably the best sea-view balconies in town, although they are susceptible to street noise. The terrace pool is just the place to cool off after exploring Kep National Park.

Le Flamboyant Resort
RESORT $$

(☑017 491010; www.leflamboyant-resort.com; NH33A; d incl breakfast from US$75; ❄️🛜🏊) Although less flamboyant than the name would suggest, this attractive, large garden property (complete with lawn-mowing horse) has a boutique-resort feel. Cottage-style bungalows have blue accents and wood detailing, and open out onto dinky verandas. There are two swimming pools, a small spa hut and a good restaurant onsite. Expect some street noise during busy weekends.

★ Veranda Natural Resort
RESORT $$$

(☑012 888619; www.veranda-resort.asia; Kep Hillside Rd; r incl breakfast from US$110; ❄️🛜🏊) The unique hillside bungalows here are built of wood, bamboo and stone, and are connected by a maze of stilted walkways, making this a thoroughly memorable spot for a romantic getaway. Check out several rooms because the size and shape vary wildly. There are a couple of pools, the food is excellent and views from the restaurant pavilion are stunning.

Le Ponton Hotel
BOUTIQUE HOTEL $$$

(☑017 780061; www.ponton-hotel.com; bungalows incl breakfast from US$80; ❄️🛜🏊) This hotel radiates an effortless beach-holiday vibe with its colourful lounging areas and very attractive pool area. Bungalow-style rooms with little balconies are simple but chic, and are set within a wonderful tropical garden of blooming flowers and well-tended trees. It's strolling distance to both the crab market and Kep Beach.

Knai Bang Chatt
BOUTIQUE HOTEL $$$

(☑078 888556; www.knaibangchatt.com; s/d incl breakfast from US$188/319; ❄️@🛜🏊) Kep's first stab at a design hotel occupies a cluster of 1960s waterfront villas, with rooms out of the pages of a slick magazine. On the seafront, with only a sliver of beach but a lovely infinity pool right before the ocean. Free yoga in the morning and in-room bathtubs, but for this price, we would've expected flawless wi-fi.

✖ Eating

Deli's Kep
DELI $

(☑ 088 470 7952; NH33A; sandwiches US$3.50-4; ⊙ 7am-7pm) This new gourmet food store is earning high praise for its *coppa, lomo,* saucisson and other imported meats, along with top-notch pepper (100g for US$5 to US$8), coffee and craft booze. Grab a sandwich on the way to a pepper farm, or plop down for a relaxing meal in the airy, modern space.

★ Crab Market
MARKET $$

(1kg crab from 40,000r) Eating at the crab market – a row of wooden waterfront restaurants by a wet fish market – is a quintessential Kep experience. Fresh crabs fried with Kampot pepper are a taste sensation. You can dine at one of the restaurants or buy crab and have your guesthouse prepare it.

There are lots of great places to choose from at the crab market, so keep an eye on where the Khmer crowd are eating.

Strand
INTERNATIONAL $$

(☑ 078 333686; Knai Bang Chatt; buffet breakfasts US$12, lunch and dinner mains from US$8; ⊙ 7am-10pm) The best breakfast in town is at the hotel Knai Bang Chatt, with an array of Khmer and Western morning favourites, fresh salad, pastries, à la carte eggs and more. The restaurant can also arrange special 'floating dinners' at a secluded, candlelit table out on a dock over the sea.

La Baraka
INTERNATIONAL $$

(☑ 097 461 2543; Crab Market; mains US$6-10; ⊙ 9.30am-10pm, bar later Nov-Feb; 🕾) A breath of fresh air from the other crab-market restaurants' identical menus, La Baraka serves up a mix of European and Asian flavours with bags of seafood dishes such as swordfish carpaccio. For non-fish-lovers there's also great pizza and pasta. The terrace, over the waves, is sunset cocktail perfection.

Kep Sur Mer
FUSION $$

(Democrat; Crab Market; mains US$5-10; ⊙ 11am-10.30pm; 🕾) Kep Sur Mer (more widely known as the Democrat) is part of a wave of slightly more upscale eateries that are gradually moving in on the crab-market scene. The crab cakes and crab *amok* (a baked seafood dish) are winners, and epitomise the more refined cuisine. Great drinks (half-price at happy hour, 5pm to 7pm).

🍷 Drinking & Nightlife

★ Sailing Club
COCKTAIL BAR

(mains US$7-12.50; ⊙ 10am-10pm; 🕾) With a small beach, a breezy wooden bar and a wooden jetty poking out into the sea, this is one of Cambodia's top sundowner spots. The Asian fusion food is excellent and you can get your crab fix here too. There's now an outdoor cocktail lounge and a vastly expanded seafront terrace.

Man Groove
BAR

(☑ 097 916 1553; ⊙ 6pm-late Wed-Mon) Seemingly the only proper bar in Kep, with lots of beer options (including US$0.75 draughts) and cocktails. Also has a few seafront bungalows for US$10 a night.

ℹ Information

There's no bank in Kep but there are a couple of ATMs. One is the **ABA Bank ATM** (⊙ 24hr) near Kep Beach.

Nearly all hotels and many restaurants have free wi-fi.

ℹ Getting There & Away

Kep is 25km from Kampot and 41km from the Prek Chak–Xa Xia border crossing to Vietnam.

Buses stop at Kep Beach in front of a line of travel agencies and minivan offices. You can purchase tickets here or from most guesthouses.

Phnom Penh Sorya buses depart a few times daily (7.45am, 9.30am, 1.30pm) for Phnom

BUSES FROM KEP

DESTINATION	FARE	DURATION	FREQUENCY	COMPANY	TYPE
Ha Tien	US$7-8	45min	4 daily	Anny Tours, Champa Tourist Bus	minivan
Phnom Penh	US$5-8	3-4hr	7 daily	Anny Tours, Phnom Penh Sorya, Vibol Transport	bus/minivan
Sihanoukville	US$7	2½hr	5-6 daily	Anny Tours, Champa Tourist Bus	minivan

<table>
<tr><td>① GETTING TO VIETNAM: KEP TO HA TIEN</td></tr>
</table>

Getting to the border The **Prek Chak/Xa Xia border crossing** (in theory open 6am to 6pm) has become a popular option for linking Kampot and Kep with Ha Tien, and then onwards to either the popular Vietnamese island of Phu Quoc, or to Ho Chi Minh City.

The easiest way to get to Prek Chak and on to Ha Tien is to catch a minivan from Sihanoukville (US$12, 3½ hours), Kampot (US$8, 1½ hours), or Kep (US$7, 45 minutes). Anny Tours and Champa Tourist Bus run this service with no change of vehicles at the border.

A more flexible alternative from Phnom Penh or Kampot is to take any bus to Kompong Trach, then a *moto* (about US$3) for 15km, on a good road, to the border.

In Kep, guesthouses can arrange a *moto* (US$8, 45 minutes), *remork* (US$12, one hour) or taxi (US$20, 30 minutes). Rates and times are almost double from Kampot. Private vehicles take a new road that cuts south to the border 10km west of Kompong Trach.

At the border Vietnam grants 15-day visas on arrival for nationals of several European and Asian countries. Other nationalities, and anyone staying longer than 15 days, must purchase a visa in advance.

At Prek Chak, a *moto* driver will ask US$5 to take you to the Vietnamese border post 300m past the Cambodian one, and then all the way to Ha Tien (15 minutes, 7km). You'll save money walking across no-man's land and picking up a *moto* on the other side for US$2 to US$3.

Moving on Travellers bound for Phu Quoc should arrive in Ha Tien no later than 12.30pm to secure a ticket on the 1pm ferry (230,000d or about US$11, 1½ hours). Extreme early risers may be able to make it to Ha Tien in time to catch the 8am ferry. The morning minivans from Cambodia to Ha Tien arrive before the 1pm boat departs.

Penh, as do **Vibol Transport** (Kep Beach Rd) buses and **Anny Tours** (☑ 096 764 6666; Kep Beach Rd; ☺ 6am-9pm) minivans. A private taxi to the capital costs US$40 to US$45.

Anny Tours and **Champa Tourist Bus** (☑ 088 727 7277; Kep Beach Rd; ☺ 6.30am-8pm) send minivans over the border to Ha Tien in Vietnam twice daily. Going the other way, the same companies serve Sihanoukville two or three times daily, with a van change in Kampot, and also serve Koh Kong with several van transfers.

For Kampot, take a *remork* (US$10, 45 minutes), the sunset Crab Shuttle boat trip (US$10, 2½ hours, 4pm) or any eastbound bus or minivan. There are very few *moto* drivers in town.

Motorbike rental is US$5 with **Diamond and Moon Moto Rental** (☑ 097 864 5062; diamondandmoon@gmail.com; scooter rental per day US$5); guesthouses and travel agencies also rent them.

Around Kep

The Buddhist temple **Wat Kiri Sela** (វត្តគិរីសីលា; US$1; ☺ 7am-6pm) sits at the foot of Phnom Kompong Trach, a dramatic karst formation riddled with more than 100 caverns and passageways. From the wat, an underground passage leads to a fishbowl-like formation, surrounded by vine-draped cliffs and open to the sky. Various stalactite-laden caves shelter reclining Buddhas and Buddhist shrines. The closest town is Kompong Trach. From here, take the dirt road opposite the old Acleda Bank, on NH33 in the town centre, for 2km.

Kompong Trach is 28km northeast of Kep on NH33, making it an easy day trip from both Kep and Kampot. At the wat, friendly local kids with torches (flashlights) are keen to put their evening-school English to use by serving as guides. Tip them if you use them.

TAKEO

☑ 032 / POP 40,000

There's not much happening at all in the languid, lakeside provincial capital of Takeo (តាកែវ), but it makes a good base from which to take a motorboat ride to the pre-Angkorian temples of Angkor Borei and Phnom Da and experience river life. Since few visitors make it out to this impoverished rural province, you'll likely have these temples, among Cambodia's most ancient and fascinating, virtually to yourself. The main attraction in Takeo town is eating freshwater lobster on the waterfront (rainy season only).

A 7th-century Chenla (pre-Angkorian) temple at Phnom Bayong and the nearby Kirivong Waterfall can be reached on day trips from Takeo, while further-flung temples in the Takeo Province such as Tonlé Bati and Phnom Chisor are usually visited as day trips from Phnom Penh.

Although it's nothing compared to Kampot, some attractive French-era shophouses, slowly slouching into genteel decay, line the streets around the **Psar Nat** (St 10; ⊘6am-8pm) market. The building housing Psar Nat itself is a concrete monstrosity built after the overthrow of the Khmer Rouge.

A pleasant stroll via a 150m-long, railings-free bridge takes you to **Ta Mok's House** (ផ្ទះតាម៉ុក, FREE), the house of Takeo Province's most notorious native son, Ta Mok – aka 'The Butcher' – the Khmer Rouge commander of the Southwestern Zone, where he presided over horrific atrocities. The house is now occupied by a university, but you can wander around the grounds.

🛏 Sleeping & Eating

Meas Family Homestay HOMESTAY $
(☑016 781415, 011 687554; http://cambodianhomestay.com; Angk Tasaom District; adult/child incl all meals US$18/13; @ 🗑) This popular and friendly family homestay has 12 rooms in a spacious compound located just off the road between Angk Tasaom and Takeo. It's a gorgeous place to ride a bike around the rice paddies, and the homestay provides complimentary wheels. Rates also include some delicious home-cooked Khmer food and cooking classes are available. While staying here, it's also possible to volunteer to teach English at the local school.

Daunkeo Guesthouse GUESTHOUSE $
(☑032-210303; www.daunkeo.com; St 9; s/d with fan US$6/8, r with air-con US$15; ❋🗑) The smartest guesthouse in Takeo, Daunkeo is spread over three modern villas. Spotlessly clean, air-con rooms include satellite TV and hot-water showers, though the service leaves something to be desired and the wi-fi is unreliable. Don't spring for the US$25 VIP room; it's small and not particularly special.

★**Stung Takeo** CAMBODIAN $
(☑032-665 4111; St 9; mains US$3-5; ⊘7am-9pm) Perched over the seasonal lake, this is easily Takeo's best restaurant for both food and ambience. The seafood-heavy menu is full of traditional local flavour, such as squid and Kampot pepper. This is also the place to come for remarkably good – and affordable – freshwater lobster (otherwise known as crayfish). The season for these toothsome creatures is approximately August to November.

Delikes INTERNATIONAL $
(☑081 402020; St 10; mains US$2-5; ⊘6am-8pm; 🗑) This small place serves excellent

---

WORTH A TRIP

ANGKOR BOREI & PHNOM DA

Takeo itself offers few attractions, but is a jumping-off point for visiting two fabulous sights: the archaeological museum **Angkor Borei** (សារមន្ទីរបុរាណវិទ្យាអង្គរបុរី; ☑012 201638; US$1; ⊘8am-4.30pm) and the temple-topped hills of **Phnom Da** (ប្រាសាទភ្នំដា; US$2).

Angkor Borei was known as Vyadhapura when it served as the 8th-century capital of 'water Chenla', as Takeo Province was called in Chinese annals (no doubt a reference to the extensive annual floods that still blanket much of the area). It was also an important centre during the earlier Funan period (1st to 6th centuries), when Indian religion and culture were carried to the Mekong Delta by traders, artisans and priests from India, as the great maritime trade route between India and China passed by the Mekong Delta. The earliest datable Khmer inscription (AD 611) was discovered here and hints of this past greatness can be found in the 5.7km moated wall that still surrounds this impoverished riverine townlet.

The 45-minute open-air motorboat ride to reach Angkor Borei and Phnom Da from Takeo, along Canal No 15, dug in the 1880s, is one of the best opportunities you'll have in Cambodia to see rural riverside living. There aren't accommodations or formal restaurants here, though, so you'll want to bring water and a snack from Takeo.

Hiring a **boat** from Takeo's dock costs around US$35 return for up to four people. The canal leading out to Angkor Borei is clearly delineated in the dry season but surrounded by flooded rice fields the rest of the year. In the rainy season the water can get rough in the afternoon, so it's a good idea to head out early. When the water levels are too low you will have to travel by *moto* (motorcycle taxi) for the 10-minute ride between Angkor Borei and Phnom Da (US$5 return).

Angkor Borei can also be reached year-round via a circuitous land route from the north.

ℹ GETTING TO VIETNAM: TAKEO TO CHAU DOC

Getting to the border The remote and seldom-used **Phnom Den/Tinh Bien border crossing** (open 7am to 6pm) between Cambodia and Vietnam lies about 50km south-east of Takeo town in Cambodia and offers connections to Chau Doc. Most travellers prefer the Mekong crossing at Kaam Samnor or the newer Prek Chak crossing near Ha Tien to the south. Take a share taxi (10,000r), a chartered taxi (US$25) or a *moto* (US$10) from Takeo to the border (48km).

At the border Several nationalities can get 15-day Vietnam visas on arrival; everyone else needs to arrange one in advance. Coming into Cambodia from Vietnam, note that e-visas are not accepted for entry here.

Moving on Travellers are at the mercy of Vietnamese *xe om (moto)* drivers and taxis for the 30km journey from the border to Chau Doc. Prepare for some tough negotiations. Expect to pay US$10 to US$12.50 for a *moto*, and US$20 for a taxi.

Asian breakfasts, tasty fresh spring rolls and salads, and a range of pizzas. The green-mango-and-dried-shrimp salad makes for a light but flavourful lunch.

ℹ Information

Canadia Bank (NH2; ⊘8am-3.30pm Mon-Fri, to 11.30am Sat, ATM 24hr)

Takeo Tourism (☑032-931323; ⊘7.30-11am & 2-5pm Mon-Fri, 7.30-11am Sat & Sun) May be able to arrange an English-speaking guide (US$15 to US$20) to the temples.

ℹ Getting There & Away

Takeo is on NH2, 77km south of Phnom Penh, 40km north of Kirivong and 48km north of the Phnom Den–Tinh Bien border crossing to Vietnam.

At the time of research, no bus company serves Takeo. To get to Phnom Penh direct, take a shared taxi (US$5 per seat, US$25 for the whole taxi) from a lot in front of the transit hub **Psar Thmei** (NH2, Central Market). For a more roundabout journey, hop on a nine-seater *remork* (2000r) from Psar Thmei, a *remork* (US$4) from Psar Thmei or the hospital, or a *moto* (US$3) wherever you spot one, and head to Angk Tasaom, the chaotic transport junction 13km west of Takeo on NH3. Here you can flag down both northbound buses to Phnom Penh and southbound buses to Kampot and Kep.

Private taxis will make the 45-minute trip down to Kirivong for US$20, or you can hire a *moto* for US$10. To get to the Phnom Den–Tinh Bien border crossing to Vietnam, go to Kirivong and switch to a *moto* (US$2) for the final 8km, or continue to the border in the taxi for an extra US$10.

Coming from the border, you may have to ask the Cambodian border officials to call a *moto* or taxi to pick you up.

Trains service Takeo on Friday, Saturday, Sunday and Monday, connecting it with Phnom Penh, Kampot and Sihanouville. Tickets cost from US$4 to US$7 and should be purchased at the **train station** (☑099 222566; ⊘8am-4pm Wed-Mon) a few days in advance. To view the schedule, visit www.royal-railway.com.

ℹ Getting Around

You can rent a *moto* for around US$5 per day.

Around Takeo

Affording breathtaking views of Vietnam's pancake-flat Mekong Delta, the cliff-ringed summit of **Phnom Bayong** (ភ្នំបាយ័ង; US$5) is graced by a 7th-century Chenla temple built to celebrate a victory over Funan. The *linga* (phallic symbol) originally in the inner chamber is now in Paris' Musée Guimet, but a number of flora- and fauna-themed bas-relief panels can still be seen, for example on the lintels of the three false doorways, and carved into the brickwork.

The sweltering climb up to the temple takes about an hour (bring plenty of water), or you can hire a *moto* in Kirivong to take you up in less than 30 minutes (US$5). It's a pretty treacherous path.

Phnom Bayong is about 3km west of the northern edge of Kirivong; the turn-off is marked by a painted panel depicting the temple.

Gentle **Kirivong Waterfall** (Chruos Phaok Waterfall) is reached by a 1.5km access road that begins about 1km south of Kirivong (and 40km south of Takeo). Market stalls here sell the area's most famous products: topaz and quartz, either cut like gems or carved into tiny Buddhas and nagas (mythical serpent-beings). It's a popular destination for locals on a day out and travellers visiting Phnom Bayong. From Takeo, a *moto* to Kirivong costs about US$10 (US$15 return).

Northwestern Cambodia

POP 4 MILLION

Best Places to Eat

➡ Apsara Restaurant (p265)

➡ Kompong Thom Restaurant (p269)

➡ Jaan Bai (p247)

➡ Coconut Lyly (p243)

Best Places to Stay

➡ Kompong Luong Homestays (p238)

➡ La Villa (p244)

➡ BeTreed Adventures (p269)

➡ Maisons Wat Kor (p245)

➡ Sambor Village Hotel (p268)

Why Go?

Looking for temples without the tourist hordes? The remote temples of Northwestern Cambodia are a world apart. While hilltop Prasat Preah Vihear is the big hitter, the other temple complexes – wrapped in vines and half-swallowed by jungle – are all fabulous to explore.

In the region's heart is Tonlé Sap, one of the world's most fish-rich lakes and a birder's paradise. Boat trips from Kompong Chhnang and Krakor (near Pursat) to the rickety floating villages that cluster along this important waterway allow you to dip your toes in lake life.

When forays into the region's far-flung corners are complete, the Northwest has one more surprise up its sleeve. Laid-back Battambang, with its colonial architecture and burgeoning arts scene, is the main city here. There's a wealth of brilliant sights all within day-tripping distance of town – making it a worthy pit stop when all the hard travelling is done.

When to Go
Battambang

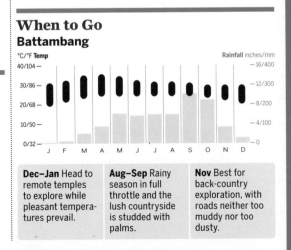

Dec–Jan Head to remote temples to explore while pleasant temperatures prevail.

Aug–Sep Rainy season in full throttle and the lush countryside is studded with palms.

Nov Best for back-country exploration, with roads neither too muddy nor too dusty.

Northwestern Cambodia Highlights

1 Battambang (p239) Chilling around the city's colonial charms and venturing to verdant countryside and hilltop temples.

2 Prasat Preah Vihear (p262) Soaking up the stupendous vistas from atop this dramatic mountain perch.

3 Sambor Prei Kuk (p269) Exploring the pre-Angkorian brick temples of Cambodia's third Unesco World Heritage Site.

4 Osoam (p238) Finding the true Cambodia in this rural mountain community, a jumping-off point for trekking and dirt-biking journeys to spot wild elephants and Siamese crocodiles.

5 Kompong Luong (p237) Gliding on a paddle-boat through the watery thoroughfares of this floating village.

6 Banteay Chhmar (p256) Admiring the intricate bas-reliefs at this massive 12th-century temple complex.

7 Preah Khan of Kompong Svay (p265) Following a lonely road to stand in awe of this temple's mighty, jungle-encroached *gopura* (entrance pavilion).

KOMPONG CHHNANG

🎵 026 / POP 45,000

Kompong Chhnang Province (ខេត្តកំពង់ឆ្នាំង) is a relatively wealthy province, thanks to its proximity to the capital and its fishing and agricultural industries and abundant water resources. While nothing much may be happening in the province's sleepy capital city of Kompong Chhnang (Clay Pot Port), the bustling dock on the Tonlé Sap River is the jumping-off point for serene boat rides to two floating villages. Skimming through the watery streets in a tiny wooden paddle-boat as the late-afternoon sun sends a shimmer over the river is a gorgeous way to end a day.

Outside of town you'll find a lush landscape of yellow-green rice fields. Here, in the tiny hamlets where cows slumber beside curvaceous hay bales, the area's distinctive pottery is crafted underneath stilted homes, providing another reason to linger.

◉ Sights

★ Floating Villages   VILLAGE

Much less visited than other floating villages, the Tonlé Sap River hamlets of **Phoum Kandal** (ភូមិកណ្ដាល) and **Chong Kos** (ចុងកោះ) are a colourful vision of brightly painted wooden houses, with tiny terraces strung with hammocks, all built on rickety DIY pontoons. To fully explore the villages, hire a wooden boat (with captain) at Kompong Chhnang dock (US$10 per hour, up to three people) to paddle you through these fully buoyant towns, complete with shops, satellite TV – check out the ingenious bamboo electricity poles! – and mobile vegetable vendors.

A one-hour boat ride will allow you to see one village; with 1½ or two hours, you have enough time to visit both. Hiring a paddle-boat allows you to glide within the maze of watery streets to glimpse how village life functions when everything floats.

Phoum Kandal (directly southeast of the boat dock) is an ethnic Vietnamese village, while Chong Kos (to the north) is Khmer.

Ondong Rossey   VILLAGE

(អណ្ដូងរូស្សី) The quiet village of Ondong Rossey, where the area's famous red pottery is made under every stilted house, is a delightful 7km ride west of town through serene rice fields dotted with sugar palms, many with bamboo ladders running up the trunk. The unpainted pots, decorated with etched or appliqué designs, are either turned with a foot-spun wheel (for small

Kompong Chhnang

🛏 Sleeping
1 Chanthea Borint Hotel A3
2 Sovann Phum Hotel B3

🍴 Eating
3 Heng Chamreun Bakery A1
4 Psar Leu B1
5 Soksan Restaurant A2

pieces) or banged into shape with a heavy wooden spatula (for large ones).

The golden-hued mud piled up in the yards is quarried at nearby Phnom Krang Dai Meas and pounded into fine clay before being shaped and fired; only at the last stage does it acquire a pinkish hue. Pieces can be purchased at the **Pottery Development Center**, although you'll get better deals buying directly from the potters at their houses.

Phnom Santuk   VIEWPOINT

(ភ្នំសន្ទុក) Phnom Santuk, a rocky hillock behind **Wat Santuk**, is a few kilometres southwest of Kompong Chhnang. The boulder-strewn summit affords fine views of the countryside, including Tonlé Sap lake, 20km to the north.

🛏 Sleeping & Eating

Sovann Phum Hotel   HOTEL $
(☎ 026-989333; sovannphumkpchotel@yahoo.com;
NH5; r with fan/air-con from US$8/15; ❄ @ ☎)
A step up from most Kompong Chhnang
options in cleanliness and style, this is a
popular spot for the NGO crowd. It has 30
good-sized rooms with modern bathrooms
and plenty of light, plus a decent restaurant.
Book ahead.

Chanthea Borint Hotel   GUESTHOUSE $
(☎ 012 762988, 026-988622; cbrint@yahoo.com;
Prison St; r with fan/air-con US$8/15; ❄ ☎) Set
in a shady garden, this 30-room family pad
offers the most charming and friendly accommodation in town. The rooms are small
but tidy and well cared for. The restaurant
serves breakfast only.

Soksan Restaurant   CAMBODIAN $
(NH5; mains US$2-2.50; ☺ 6am-8pm) It may
lack English signage, but there's an English
menu at this restaurant next to Kompong
Chhnang's taxi park. It specialises in fried
everything, and soups – or be adventurous
and order the porcupinefish with omelette.

Psar Leu   MARKET $
(☺ 7am-6pm) Kompong Chhnang's central
market has plenty of cheap and cheerful
food stalls and is a bustling hub of local life.

Heng Chamreun Bakery   BAKERY $
(NH5; baked goods 2000-5000r; ☺ 8am-9pm)
Part of a renowned chain, this glistening
bakery sells good sandwiches, rice cakes and
other snacks ideal for the road.

ℹ Information

Remork-moto (tuk tuk) driver Channy (077
357361) and his cousin Kosal (092 471816) are
highly informative about Kompong Chhnang.
They hang out near the taxi park when not with
customers.
Acleda Bank (NH5; ☺ 7.30am-4pm Mon-Fri, to
11am Sat, ATM 24hr)
Canadia Bank (NH5; ☺ 8am-3.30pm Mon-Fri,
to 11.30am Sat, ATM 24hr)

ℹ Getting There & Away

Kompong Chhnang is 91km north of Phnom
Penh, 93km southeast of Pursat and 198km
southeast of Battambang.
   You can buy tickets for Rith Mony and several
other companies at the **bus stand** (NH5), a
vendor-cart with bus company signage in front.
You can also flag down buses on the NH5 at the
Acleda Bank corner.

Buses south to Phnom Penh (20,000r, 2½
hours), and north to Pursat (20,000r, two hours)
and Battambang (24,000r, five hours), pull
through town hourly throughout the day.
   The fastest way to get to Phnom Penh is by
share taxi (20,000r, two hours). Vehicles wait at
the central taxi park. Share taxis do not generally serve destinations to the northwest, such as
Battambang.

ℹ Getting Around

A several-hour *remork* tour taking in the pottery
villages and Phnom Santuk costs around US$10.
A *moto* (motorcycle taxi) should be about US$5.
A *moto/remork* to the port is US$1/2 one way.
   Chanthea Borint Hotel rents out bicycles
(US$2 for the day).

PURSAT

☎ 052 / POP 38,000

Pursat Province (ខេត្តពោធិ៍សាត់), Cambodia's fourth-largest, stretches from the remote forests of Phnom Samkos, on the Thai
border, eastwards to the fishing villages and
marshes of Tonlé Sap lake. Famed for its oranges, it encompasses the northern reaches
of the Cardamom Mountains, linked with
the town of Pursat by disreputable roads.
   You know you've hit Pursat town when
huge marble monument shops begin to rim
the roadside – if you're in the market for a
life-size statue of a rearing horse, you're in
the right place. This dusty provincial capital, known for its carvers, is no beauty but it
makes a good base for a day-trip to the floating village of Kompong Luong or an expedition into the wilds of the Central Cardamoms.

⊙ Sights

Bunrany Hun Sen
Development Center   ARTS CENTRE
(☎ 052-951606; St 109; ☺ 7-11am & 2-5pm Mon-Fri,
to 11am Sat) Bunrany Hun Sen teaches cloth
and mat weaving, sewing, marble carving
and other artisanal skills to young people,
and sells the items they make from a large
shop on the premises. There are some real
bargains here on beautiful *krama* (checked
scarves) and baskets. Travellers are welcome
to visit classes.

Koh Sampovmeas   PARK
(កោះសំពៅមាស, Golden Ship Island) This
bizarre island-park, built in the shape of
a ship, is Pursat's place to see and be seen
around sunset. Young locals drop by for

NORTHWESTERN CAMBODIA PURSAT

Pursat

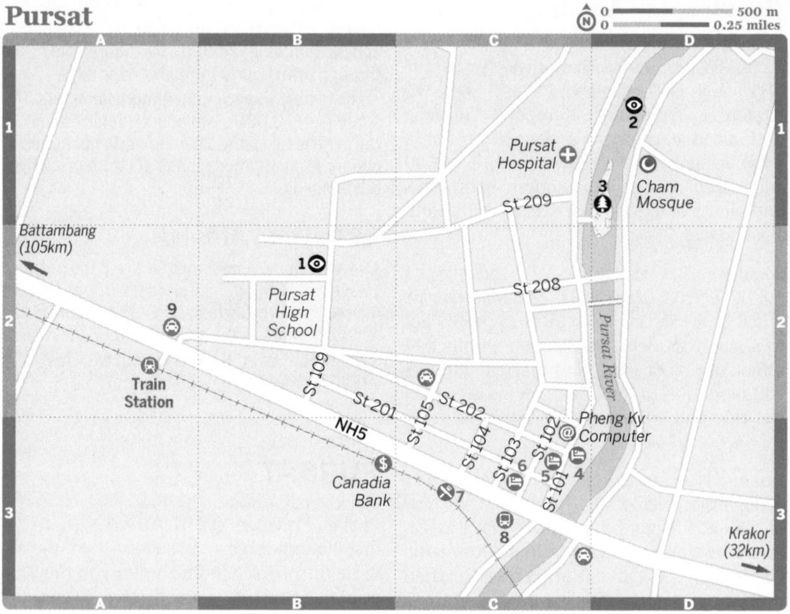

Pursat

Sights
1 Bunrany Hun Sen Development Center B2
2 Khmer Rouge–Era Dam D1
3 Koh Sampovmeas D1

Sleeping
4 KM Hotel C3
5 Phnom Pech Hotel C3
6 Thansour Thmey Hotel C3

Eating
7 Lam Siv Eng Restaurant C3
Reak Smey Angkor Restaurant .... (see 5)

Transport
8 Phnom Penh Sorya C3
Rith Mony .... (see 8)
9 Taxis to Battambang A2

aerobics (classes from 5pm) or a game of badminton, while power-walkers pound the circuit between the manicured lawns and Khmer-style pavilions.

Khmer Rouge–Era Dam DAM
This dam, built during the Khmer Rouge era, is now a popular local fishing and bathing spot.

Sleeping & Eating

★ **Thansour Thmey Hotel** HOTEL $
(☎012 962395; thansourthmey@gmail.com; St 102; r with fan/air-con US$7/15;) If you've always wanted to sleep in an intricately carved bed, now is your chance. Rooms are tidy and the restaurant, which serves Khmer and Chinese dishes (mains 8000r to 16,000r), is one of the best in Pursat.

KM Hotel HOTEL $
(☎052-952168; St 101; r incl breakfast from US$23, deluxe US$45;) This 146-room hotel is ridiculously good value, with plush rooms hosting flat-screen TVs and beds that guarantee a contented sleep. The bathrooms offer old shower heads and warm rather than hot water, but we're not complaining because outside you'll find two big swimming pools.

There's also a good restaurant where the included breakfast and other meals are served from 6am to 9pm.

Reak Smey Angkor Restaurant CAMBODIAN $
(St 101; mains 4000-8000r; 6am-9pm) Popular with Khmer tour groups, this family-run restaurant dishes up an extensive menu of local favourites, with plenty of noodle soups and fried-rice options. There's also a small menu of omelettes and Western breakfast plates.

CENTRAL CARDAMOMS PROTECTED FOREST

Rangers in the Central Cardamoms Protected Forest, who are supported by Conservation International (www.conservation.org), operate out of three stations in the north that are rarely visited. Even so, rangers and military policemen based there play a crucial role in defending the territory, particularly at the **Kravanh ranger station** deep in the jungle south of Pursat.

The most valuable contraband at the front-line **Rovieng ranger station** is aromatic *mreah prew* (sassafras, or safrole) oil, extracted from the roots of the endangered *Cinnamomum parthenoxylon* tree. One tonne of wood produces just 30L of the oil, which has a delightful, sandalwood-like scent. Local people use it in traditional medicine, but it's safrole oil's use as the precursor in the production of the drug MDMA that has caused the most illegal logging of this tree species.

A few kilometres from Rovieng (and 53km southwest of Pursat) are the **L'Bak Kamronh Rapids**, which attract Khmers on holidays. About 25km west of Rovieng, in Pramoay Commune, the old-growth **Chhrok Preal Forest** can also be visited (though it rarely is).

To prearrange a guide, homestay or guesthouse near the Kravanh or Rovieng ranger station, try contacting forestry official **Peov Somanak** (peovsomanak@gmail.com; 017 464663) for advice. At the time of research, he was starting a program that would allow travellers to trek with rangers on patrol.

Lam Siv Eng Restaurant   CHINESE **$**
(☑ 012 826948; www.facebook.com/pages/Lam-Siv-Eng-Restaurant-Pursat; NH5; mains US$2.50-5) This popular Chinese place fills up particularly at breakfast, when Vietnamese iced coffee and noodle soups fly out of the kitchen.

ℹ Information

Staff members at **Phnom Pech Hotel** (☑ 052-951515; St 101) are helpful if you need information on getting around the province, including to more remote bits such as the Cardamoms.
Canadia Bank (NH5; ⊙ 8am-3.30pm Mon-Fri, to 11.30am Sat, ATM 24hr)
Pheng Ky Computer (St 101; per hr 2000r; ⊙ 6am-7pm) Offers internet access.

ℹ Getting There & Away

Pursat is 105km southeast of Battambang and 185km northwest of Phnom Penh along NH5.

Buses, including those of **Rith Mony** (NH5), pass through Pursat virtually all day long, shuttling southeast to Kompong Chhnang and Phnom Penh (20,000r, four hours) hourly; and north to Battambang (15,000r, 1½ hours), hourly from around 11am onwards. **Phnom Penh Sorya** (NH5) offers direct trips to Kompong Cham (35,000r, six hours, 11.30am) and Siem Reap (32,000r, five hours, 7.15am and 2.30pm).

Share taxis serve Phnom Penh (24,000r, three hours) from NH5 just east of the bridge. Share taxis to Battambang (20,000r, 1½ hours) depart from NH5 on the western edge of town.

Pick-ups and share taxis to the remote Cardamoms outpost of Osoam (40,000r, 3¼ hours) and Pramoay (Veal Veng; 30,000r, three hours) via Kravanh (one hour) and Rovieng (two hours) leave from next to the old market, Psar Chaa.

ℹ Getting Around

Phnom Pech Hotel rents out bicycles (US$3 per day) and can try to set you up with a motorbike (US$10), which means finding a local to rent you his or hers.

Moto/remork drivers in town charge US$10/15 for a round-trip to Kompong Luong.

Kompong Luong

POP 10,000

Kompong Luong (កំពង់ហ្លួង) has all the amenities you might expect to find in an oversized fishing village – except that here everything floats on water. The result is a charming if slightly ramshackle Venice without the dry land. The cafes, shops, chicken coops, fish ponds, ice-making factory, petrol station and karaoke bars are kept from sinking by boat hulls, barrels or bunches of bamboo – as are the pagodas, the blue-roofed church and the colourful houses. In the dry season, when water levels drop and Tonlé Sap lake shrinks, the entire aquapolis is towed, boat by boat, a few kilometres north.

The population of this fascinating and picturesque village is partly Vietnamese, so – reflecting their ambiguous status in Cambodian society – you may find the welcome here slightly more subdued than in most rural Cambodian towns, at least from the adults. Children delight in waving hello.

The way to explore Kompong Luong is, naturally, by boat. The official tourist rate to charter a wooden motorboat (complete with life jackets) at Kompong Luong boat landing is US$13 per hour for one to six passengers, US$20 for seven to 10, and US$2 per person for 11 or more.

The tours aren't particularly informative, as few captains speak much English, but gliding through the town and simply observing daily life makes this worthwhile. Tours include a crocodile-feeding attraction for US$1 extra.

Homestay hosts can also provide boats for village exploring.

Kompong Luong has three **homestays** (per person US$4-6) available with local families. The stays, while rustic, offer a glimpse into everyday life on the water. Meals are available for US$2. You can book a homestay when you arrive at the boat landing.

ℹ Getting There & Around

The jumping-off point for Kompong Luong is the town of Krakor, 32km east of Pursat. From Krakor to the boat landing, where tours begin, it's 1.5km to 6km, depending on the time of year. You can get a ride on a *moto* for 2000r to 5000r.

Note that a boat ride to or from the Kompong Luong homestays will set you back US$5 (each way). If you book a tour, the boat will drop you off at the homestay for no additional charge.

Northern Cardamom Mountains

◉ Sights & Activities

**Phnom Aural
Wildlife Sanctuary**   WILDLIFE RESERVE
The 2538-sq-km sanctuary boasts the country's highest peak, Phnom Aural (1813m), and is just east of the Central Cardamoms Protected Forest. Unfortunately the area is being destroyed from the south and the east by corrupt land speculation and rampant illegal logging, but the long-standing and reputable DutchCo Trekking Cambodia runs three-day trips to the region. Phnom Aural can be done in a day but most do it in two or three.

**Phnom Samkos
Wildlife Sanctuary**   ANIMAL SANCTUARY
Sandwiched between the Central Cardamoms Protected Forest and the Thai frontier, the Phnom Samkos Wildlife Sanctuary (3338

sq km) is well and truly out in the sticks. It is threatened by timber laundering and agricultural concessions, but wildlife still abounds.

Boasting Cambodia's second-highest peak, **Phnom Samkos** (1717m), the sanctuary's main town is Pramoay (Veal Veng), 125km west of Pursat. This remote little outpost has three guesthouses (rooms US$5). Local *moto* drivers can take visitors to nearby ethnic-minority villages.

**Crocodile Protection
Sanctuary**   ANIMAL SANCTUARY
Some 13km south of Osoam village lies this protected crocodile habit, where about 40 to 60 Siamese crocodiles reside. Visitors have the best chance of spotting the mostly fish-eating (never human-eating) reptiles from December to May, but the area has other attractions, too: namely a spirit house built by the Choung indigenous group, and wildlife such as hornbills and banteng.

☞ Tours

**★Osoam Cardamom
Community Centre**   TOURS
(☑016 309075, 089 899895; http://osoamccc. weebly.com) In the isolated settlement of Osoam, this excellent community centre organises hiking, dirt-bike and boat trips in the surrounding countryside, as well as day trips and overnights to Phnom Samkos, where elephants can be spotted. The property has seven well-kept rooms (US$6) along with connections to simple guesthouses and homestays (single/double US$5/6) nearby.

Electricity is limited and showers come from buckets, but this is about as close to real Cambodia as you can get. Mr. Lim, the enigmatic, self-made Cambodian who runs the place, is becoming a legend among travellers.

Jungle Cross   ADVENTURE
(☑097 9257000, 015 601633; www.junglecross. com; dirt-bike rental per day US$28) Fantastic, expat-run dirt-bike and 4WD operation based deep in the Cardamoms. The knowledgeable and entertaining owner also leads trekking tours to more remote parts, with transport by 4WD to the start point. The office is at Osoam Cardamom Community Centre.

DutchCo Trekking Cambodia   TREKKING
(☑097 6792714; www.trekkingcambodia.com) Offers three-day treks in the Phnom Aural Wildlife Sanctuary, with a jumping-off point at Kompong Speu and stays in dorms and bungalows in the rural village of Voar Sar.

🛏 Sleeping & Eating

There aren't many overnight options in the Northern Cardamoms apart from the Osoam Cardamom Community Centre and a few basic guesthouses within the larger towns.

There are some simple restaurants scattered about, but your best bet is the spicy and authentic Khmer cuisine prepared at the community centre.

ℹ Getting There & Away

Roads and bridges in the area have been upgraded to service a new hydro-dam in Osoam, and you can now get into the park at any time of the year. Areas in and near the CCPF are still being demined, so stay on roads and well-trodden trails.

From Psar Chaa in Pursat, share taxis and pick-ups serve Kravanh (one hour), Rovieng (two hours) and Pramoay (three hours) year-round. From Pramoay, the track south to Osoam is in rougher shape. It's passable by *moto* year-round, but taxis can't handle it during the height of the wet season. The road south from Osoam to Koh Kong is much better and can accommodate taxis year-round. In the dry season you can go from Pursat all the way to Koh Kong by share taxi.

You can also get to Pramoay via a dirt road (no public transport) from Samlaut in Pailin Province.

Phnom Aural Wildlife Sanctuary is best accessed from Kompong Speu, 45km west of Phnom Penh.

BATTAMBANG PROVINCE

Battambang Province (ខេត្តបាត់ដំបង; Bat Dambong) is said by proud locals to produce Cambodia's finest rice, sweetest coconuts and tastiest oranges (don't bring this up in Pursat). It has a long border with Thailand and a short stretch of the Tonlé Sap shoreline.

Battambang has passed from Cambodia to Thailand and back again several times over the past few centuries. Thailand ruled the area from 1794 to 1907 and again during WWII (1941 to 1946), when the Thais cut a deal with the Japanese and the Vichy French.

Battambang

🎵 053 / POP 147,000

There's something about Battambang (បាត់ដំបង) that visitors just love. Forget the fact that there's really not all that much to do in the city proper: the colonial architecture teetering into genteel disrepair, the riverside setting, the laid-back cafes – they all make up for it. It's the perfect blend of relatively urban modernity and small-town friendliness.

Outside the city's confines, meanwhile, timeless hilltop temples and bucolic villages await. Not to mention the most scenic river trip in the country, which links Battambang with Siem Reap.

That Cambodia's best-known circus (the magnificent Phare Ponleu Selpak) is here is no coincidence: the city has an enduring tradition of producing many of Cambodia's best-loved singers, actors and artists.

◉ Sights

Much of Battambang's charm lies in its early-20th-century architecture, a mix of vernacular shophouses and French colonial construction that makes up the historic core of the city. Some of the finest colonial buildings are dotted along the waterfront (St 1), especially just south of Psar Nath, itself an architectural monument, albeit a modernist one.

Wat Kor Village   VILLAGE
(ភូមិវត្តគរ) About 2km south of central Battambang, the village of Wat Kor is centred around the **temple** of the same name. It's a great place to wander, especially late in the afternoon when the opposite (east) bank of the Sangker River is bathed in amber tones by the sinking sun. Picturesque bridges span the river, the spires of Wat Kor glow bright platinum and Khmer village life is on full display.

About 1.5km beyond Wat Kor, you'll encounter a cluster of Khmer **heritage houses** that the village is known for. Built of now-rare hardwoods almost a century ago and surrounded by orchard gardens, they have wide verandahs and exude the ambience of another era.

Two of the approximately 20 heritage houses in the Wat Kor area are open to visitors: **Mrs Bun Roeung's Ancient House** (🎫 017 818419; www.facebook.com/mrsbunshouse; suggested donation US$1) and neighbouring **Khor Sang House** (🎫 092 467264; suggested donation US$1). The owner of each will give you a short tour in French or English. They have floors worn lustrous by a century of bare feet and are decorated with old furniture and family photos.

Mrs. Bun Roeung's Ancient House was built in 1920 by a local lawyer. The owners recently turned the rear section of the house

Battambang

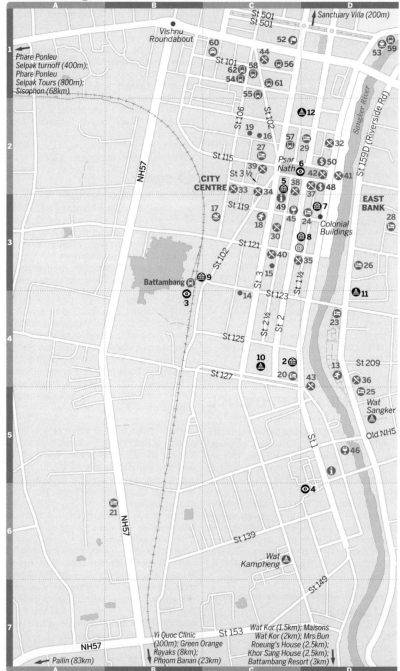

St 501
St 501

Sanctuary Villa (200m)

Vishnu
Roundabout

52

60
St 101

53 59

Phare Ponleu
Selpak turnoff (400m);
Phare Ponleu
Selpak Tours (800m);
Sisophon (68km)

44
58 56
62
54 61

55

12

St 106

St 102

19
16

57
29

32

27

St 115

50

39
St 3½

Psar
Nath 6

42

41

CITY
CENTRE

33 34

5
38 37

48

EAST
BANK

28

17

St 119

49
45 24

7

18

8

Colonial
Buildings

30

26

St 121

40
35

Battambang 9

15

St 102

14

11

St 123

St 3

St 125

23

St 2½
St 2

10 2

13

St 209

20

36

St 127

43

25

Wat
Sangker

St 1

46

i

St 1

4

St 139

21

NH57

Wat
Kampheng

St 149

St 153

Wat Kor (1.5km); Maisons
Wat Kor (2km); Mrs Bun
Roeung's House (2.5km);
Khor Sang House (2.5km);
Battambang Resort (3km)

Yi Quoc Clinic
(100m); Green Orange
Kayaks (8km);
Phnom Banan (23km)

NH57

Pailin (83km)

Sangker River

St 159D (Riverside Rd)

NORTHWESTERN CAMBODIA BATTAMBANG

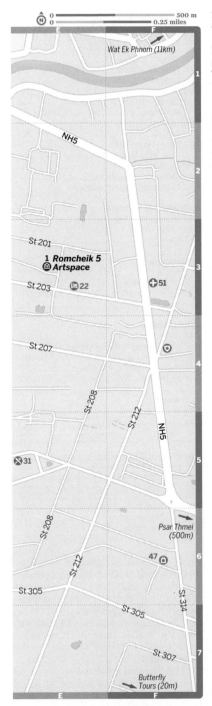

into homestay accommodation – a unique option for architecture and history fans.

Khor Sang House was built in 1907 by the French-speaking owner's grandfather, who served as a secretary to the province's last Thai governor. The rear section dates from 1890.

Battambang Museum MUSEUM
(សារមន្ទីរខេត្តបាត់ដំបង; ☑ 012 238320; St 1; US$1; ⊘8-11am & 2-5.30pm) This small and rather dusty museum displays a trove of fine Angkorian lintels and statuary from all over Battambang Province, including pieces from Prasat Banan and Sneng. Signs are in Khmer, English and French.

A museum enlargement and renovation project was under way during our last visit.

Governor's Residence NOTABLE BUILDING
(off St 139) The two-storey Governor's Residence, with its balconies and wooden shutters, is a handsome legacy of the early 1900s. The interior is closed but it should be possible to stroll the grounds. It was designed by an Italian architect for the last Thai governor, who departed in 1907.

Train Station HISTORIC BUILDING
(St 102) Here at Battambang's disused train station, the time on the stopped clock is always 8.02. Just along the tracks to the south, you can explore a treasure trove of derelict **French-era repair sheds**, warehouses and rolling stock. Note that this area is potentially unsafe and best visited in a group.

Wats

Battambang's Buddhist temples survived the Khmer Rouge period relatively unscathed thanks to a local commander who ignored orders from on high. Some of the best are **Wat Phiphétaram** (St 4), **Wat Damrey Sar** (វត្តដំរីស, White Elephant Pagoda; St 127) and **Wat Kandal** (វត្តកណ្ដាល; Riverside Rd).

🏃 Activities

Heritage Walking Trail WALKING
(www.ka-tours.org) Phnom Penh–based Khmer Architecture Tours (p58) is highly regarded for its specialist tours in and around the capital and has collaborated with Battambang Municipality to create heritage walks in Battambang's historic centre. The walks concentrate both on the French period and on the modernist architecture of the '60s. The company's website has two downloadable PDFs including a colour map and numbered

Battambang

highlights. The maps are also available in the free *Faceguide* pamphlet handed out at Bric-à-Brac (p247) and a few other places around town. This is a great way to spend half a day exploring the city. Those with less time can rent a bicycle and run the combined routes in just an hour or so.

Green Orange Kayaks   KAYAKING
(☑012 207957; www.fedacambodia.org; Ksach Poy; half-day US$12) 🛶 Kayaks can be rented from Green Orange Kayaks, part of the Friends Economic Development Association (FEDA), a local NGO which runs a community centre in Ksach Poy village, 8km south of Battambang. Half-day, self-guided kayaking trips begin at Ksach Poy's Green Orange Cafe. From there you paddle back to the city along the Sangker River. A FEDA student guide (US$5) is optional. Booking ahead is recommended.

FEDA also runs a guesthouse, the **Green Orange Village Bungalows** (☑012 207957; www.fedacambodia.org; Ksach Poy; r from US$25).

Delux Villa SWIMMING
(☑ 077 336373; www.deluxvilla.com; St 4) Whereas most Battambang poolside hotels are outside the centre, Delux Villa is just a five-minute walk away. Nonguests can use the pool for US$3.

**Khmer New Generation
Organization** VOLUNTEERING
(☑ 092 790597; www.kngocambodia.org; Bospo village) 🏊 This local NGO is always looking for volunteer teachers to help out with its English-language teaching program. Commitments of one month or longer are preferred.

Aerobics Classes HEALTH & FITNESS
(St 159D; per person 1000r) Head to Battambang's east bank to see the locals burning off the rice carbs doing aerobics, from about 6am to 7am and 5pm to 7pm daily. Just five minutes of working out should be enough to teach you some numbers in Khmer.

**Hope of Blind
Seeing Hand Massage** MASSAGE
(☑ 089 782663; St 119; per hour US$7; ⊘ 8am-10pm) 🏊 Trained blind masseurs offer soothing work-overs in an air-conditioned space.

🍽 Courses

Coconut Lyly COOKING
(☑ 016 399339; St 111; per person US$10) These classes are run by Chef Lyly, a graduate from Siem Reap's Paul Dubrule Cooking School. Three-hour classes (start times 9am and 3.30pm) include a visit to Psar Nath market, preparing four typical Khmer dishes (recipe book included) and then eating your handiwork afterwards. The excellent restaurant here is open from 9am to 10pm.

Nary Kitchen COOKING
(☑ 012 763950; www.narykitchen.com; St 111; half-day course US$10) This popular cooking class includes a visit to the local market, a four-course menu and a keepsake recipe book. Courses start at 9am and 3.30pm, lasting about three hours, plus time to eat your creations. If you're more interested in eating than cooking, Nary's restaurant is open from 8am to 10pm.

**Australian Centres
for Development** LANGUAGE
(☑ 053-677 7772; www.acdcambodia.weebly.com; St 123) 🏊 Offers well-regarded Khmer language classes, with one-to-one lessons available as well as regular weekly classes.

👉 Tours

Butterfly Tours CYCLING
(☑ 086 959569; www.butterflytours.asia; St 309; half-/full-day from US$17/38; ⊘ departs 7.30am & 1.30pm) Begun by a group of local university students, Butterfly's bicycle tours are focused on landscapes and sights or traditional life in the local area. The traditional-livelihoods tour gets rave reviews from visitors, and the company also runs tours in Kampot and Siem Reap.

Soksabike CYCLING
(☑ 012 542019; www.soksabike.com; St 1½; half-day US$23-27, full-day US$34-40; ⊘ departs 7.30am) 🏊 Soksabike is a social enterprise aiming to connect visitors with the Cambodian countryside and its people. The half- and full-day trips cover 25km and 40km respectively, and include stops at family-run industries such as rice-paper making and the prahoc factory, as well as a visit to a local home. Tour prices depend on group size.

It's associated with Kinyei cafe a few doors to the north.

L'Atelier Architecture Tours WALKING
(☑ 096 537 9599; www.facebook.com/LAtelier Cambodia; St 2½; per person US$6-15; ⊘ 4pm) These city architecture tours, bicycle tours and *remork* adventures get high marks from travellers.

L'Atelier also has a small and comfy dorm, well placed in the centre of Battambang.

Phare Ponleu Selpak Tours CULTURAL
(☑ 077 554413; https://phareps.org; US$5; ⊘ 9.30am, 10.30am, 2.30pm & 3.30pm Mon-Fri) 🏊 Guests are welcome to take a guided tour of the Phare complex during the day and observe circus, dance, music, drawing and graphic-arts classes. This is definitely US$5 well-spent, and if you buy a circus ticket as well, the cost drops to US$3.

Battambang Bike CYCLING
(☑ 095 578878; www.thebattambangbike.com; St 2½; tours half-/full-day US$18/38; ⊘ 7am-7pm) Leads a variety of bike tours, including a half-day city tour and a half-day cycle trip to Phnom Sampeau (p250). It also runs free Saturday fun-rides and rents out both city and mountain bikes (US$2 to $5 per day). Can do bike repairs also.

🛏 Sleeping

Most of Battambang's budget options are clustered close to the central Psar Nath market, while midrange and luxury accommodation tends to be either on the east bank or out of the centre (both locations require short *remork* or *moto* rides to get to the tourist belt in the old quarter). South of town near Wat Kor village are some dreamy, away-from-it-all stays (this is where Brangelina used to hang out).

City Centre

★ **Angkor Comfort Hotel** HOTEL $
(☑ 077 306410; www.angkorcomforthotel.com; St 1; r with air-con US$15-25; ✴ 🛜) Offering serious bang for your buck, the Angkor's huge rooms are sparkling clean and come with midrange amenities on a backpacker budget. White linens on the beds, flat-screen TVs, enough powerpoints to charge all your devices at once, and modern bathrooms with walk-in showers all feature.

Seng Hout Hotel HOTEL $
(☑ 012 530327; www.senghouthotel.com; St 2; r with fan US$10-15, with air-con US$15-35; ✴ 🛜 ⬛) Known for its on-the-ball staff who are quick to help with traveller queries, the Seng Hout has a variety of nicely decorated rooms. Some can be a bit poky, so check out a few before deciding. The open-air rooftop space is a key drawcard, and the third-floor pool has great views as well.

Ganesha Family Guesthouse GUESTHOUSE $
(☑ 092 135570; www.ganeshaguesthouse.com; St 1½; dm US$4.50, r US$11-25; 🛜) The best of Battambang's cheapies, Ganesha has a light-filled dorm with double-wide beds, and small private rooms with bamboo furniture and tiled bathrooms (cold water only). Downstairs is a funky cafe with a pool table.

Royal Hotel HOTEL $
(☑ 016 912034; www.royalhotelbattambang.com; St 115; s/d with fan US$7/10, r with air-con from US$15; ✴ @ 🛜) An old-timer on the Battambang scene, the Royal is deservedly popular. Some rooms may be faded but the air-con rooms are decently sized and come with fridge and TV. Staff here are some of the most clued-up in town, and there's a new bar and Jacuzzi tub on the rooftop.

Au Cabaret Vert BOUTIQUE HOTEL $$
(☑ 053-656 2000; www.aucabaretvert.com; NH57; r incl breakfast from US$75; ✴ 🛜 ⬛) Contemporary meets colonial at this pretty resort, a short *remork* ride southwest of the centre. Rooms are stylish and include flat-screen TV and rain shower. The swimming pool is a natural, self-cleaning pond surrounded by lush gardens, and the French-influenced food is top-notch.

Sanctuary Villa BOUTIQUE HOTEL $$
(☑ 097 216 7168; thesanctuaryvillabattambang@ gmail.com; off St Tea Cham Rath; r incl breakfast US$60-75; ✴ @ 🛜 ⬛) This intimate, luxurious and recently renovated boutique has 16 attractive villas furnished with traditional woods, tasteful silks and throw rugs – but the out-of-the-way location won't be for everybody. From the White Horse roundabout on NH5 go 500m north and take a right.

East Bank

★ **Here Be Dragons** HOSTEL $
(☑ 089 264895; www.herebedragonsbattambang. com; St 159D; fan/air-con dm US$4/6, r from US$12/15; ✴ 🛜) A funky fun bar, leafy front garden for relaxing and free beer on arrival make Here Be Dragons a top backpacker base. Six- and eight-bed dorms come with lock-boxes, while sunny private rooms are cheerfully decked out with brightly coloured bedding. The quiet location next to the riverside park on the east bank is a bonus.

★ **La Villa** BOUTIQUE HOTEL $$
(☑ 053-730151; St 159D; r incl breakfast from US$70; ✴ @ 🛜 ⬛) For a taste of colonial life, try this French-era villa renovated in vintage 1930s style. It's one of the most romantic boutique hotels in Cambodia. Gauzy mosquito nets drape over four-poster beds, original tilework graces the floors and art-deco features adorn every corner, creating an old-world ambience that can't be beaten.

Classy Hotel & Spa HOTEL $$
(☑ 053-952555; www.classyhotelspa.com; r US$50; ✴ 🛜 ⬛) This popular monolith on the east bank of the Sangker River is a gem particularly for its amenities, which nonguests can also enjoy. It has an excellent spa (go for a cheap, hour-long Khmer massage followed by a soak in the hot tub), a rooftop bar with stunning city views and a refreshing pool that's popular with the international crowd.

Sangker Villa Guest House BOUTIQUE HOTEL $$
(☑ 097 764 0017; www.sangkervilla.com; off St 203; r incl breakfast US$45-55; ✴ 🛜 ⬛) Sangker Villa may lack the pizazz of Battambang's fancier poolside boutiques, but it beats them hands-

RURAL LIFE ON THE ROAD TO WAT EK PHNOM

The rural lanes that squiggle out from Battambang are brimming with paddy-field panoramas and tiny villages where traditional crafts and produce are made. The roads leading to Wat Ek Phnom temple are particularly rewarding to explore and make for a great half-day circuit, soaking up a mix of historic sights and village life. Some highlights:

Wat Somrong Knong (វត្តសំរោងក្នុង) Built in the 19th century on the site of a pre-Angkorian temple complex, this wat was used by the Khmer Rouge as a prison and it's believed that around 10,000 people were executed here. The complex today houses the gorgeous main pagoda and a mishmash of ancient ruins, glittery modern structures and memorials to those who perished here.

Prahoc Factory Here visitors can see the bustling local industry behind Cambodian *prahoc* (fermented fish paste), and the photogenic bamboo trays of fish drying in the sun along the roadside.

Pheam Ek (ពាមឯក) The industry of the village of Pheam Ek is making rice paper for spring rolls. All along the road, in family workshops, you'll see rice paste being steamed and then placed on a bamboo frame for drying in the sun.

Wat Ek Phnom (វត្តឯកភ្នំ; US$2) Hidden behind a colourful modern pagoda and a gargantuan Buddha statue is this atmospheric, partly collapsed 11th-century temple measuring 52m by 49m and surrounded by the remains of a laterite wall and an ancient *baray* (reservoir). A lintel showing the Churning of the Ocean of Milk can be seen above the eastern entrance to the central temple, whose upper flanks hold some fine bas-reliefs.

down on price. Out back the small pool and bar provide tranquil retreats, while the bright, simply decorated rooms come with contemporary bathrooms.

★**Bambu Hotel** HOTEL $$$
(☏012 731405, 053-953900; www.bambuhotel.com; St 203; r incl breakfast from US$90; ❖@🛜🏊) Bambu's spacious rooms are designed in a Franco-Khmer motif with gorgeous tiling, stone-inlaid bathrooms and exquisite furniture. The fusion restaurant is one of the best in town and the poolside bar invites lingering. Above all else, though, it's Bambu's gracious staff that set it in a category above Battambang's other boutique offerings. Book ahead – it's extremely popular.

🛏 Beyond the Centre

★**Maisons Wat Kor** BOUTIQUE HOTEL $$$
(☏098 555377; www.maisonswatkor.com; Wat Kor Village; r US$100-110; ❖🛜🏊) About 2km south of central Battambang, Maisons Wat Kor is a secluded sanctuary of 10 rooms in traditional-style Khmer houses. Rooms are light-filled, spacious and come with contemporary bathrooms, and the saltwater swimming pool surrounded by lush foliage provides plenty of opportunity for chill-out time. The delightful, open-air restaurant offers a set menu for US$10, and nonguests are welcome.

In 2016, Angelina Jolie and Brad Pitt stayed here, and photographs of the visit are prominently displayed. As you might guess, the service is excellent.

Battambang Resort RESORT $$$
(☏012 510100; www.battambangresort.com; Wat Kor Village; r US$75-95; ❖🏊) Down a dirt road from laid-back Wat Kor village, Battambang Resort is a place to unwind in style. Surroundings include ponds of lily pads, tropical gardens and rice fields, while the interior common spaces are replete with Cambodian art and cultural artefacts and slung with hammocks. Service is top-notch, and the fine restaurant draws many ingredients from an on-site garden.

There's a free shuttle to town, but many guests prefer to just relax around the saltwater pool.

🍴 Eating

The heart of Battambang's culinary scene is its neighbouring Cambodian cooking schools, Coconut Lyly and Nary Kitchen, which double as restaurants. There's a fine selection of international restaurants, in and out of town; La Villa and Maisons Wat Kor are our favourites.

For street food, there are three night markets. The original **night market** (snacks & mains 2000-8000r; ⏱4-9pm) is at the northeast corner of **Psar Nath** (St 1; ⊙6am-late) and dishes up barbecued chicken, fish and pork. The **new night market** (St 1; mains 4000-8000r; ⊙6pm-midnight) is across the road along the riverfront, and is more of a sit-down affair. There's another **riverside night market** (St 1; mains 4000-8000r; ⊙3pm-midnight), across from the Battambang Museum.

🍴 City Centre

★**Lonely Tree Cafe**   CAFE $
(www.thelonelytreecafe.com; St 121; mains US$4-5.50; ⊙10am-10pm; 🛜) 🍴 Upstairs from the shop of the same name, this uber-cosy cafe serves Spanish tapas-style dishes and a few Khmer options under a soaring, bamboo-inlaid ceiling. Its mascot is an actual tree on the road to Siem Reap. Proceeds support cultural preservation and people with disabilities, among other causes.

About the World   INTERNATIONAL $
(☑086 920476; St 2½; mains US$2.50-4; ⊙8am-10pm Mon-Sat; 🍴) Travellers love this cosy spot for its relaxed ambiance and tasty vegetarian options, including the recommended Spanish omelette and tofu burger. Those who sit indoors, where art and photography festoon the walls, do so barefoot and perched atop floor pillows. The home-brewed jackfruit rice wine (US$1) is deliciously potent.

Kinyei   CAFE $
(www.kinyei.org; 1 St 1½; coffee US$1.50-2.50, mains US$2.75-5.25; ⊙7am-4pm; 🛜) 🍴 Besides having the best coffee in town (national barista champs have been crowned here), teensy-weensy Kinyei does surprisingly good Mexican food, veggie burgers, energy salads and some of the best breakfasts in town. Aussies will appreciate the long blacks and flat whites among the coffee selection.

Jewel in the Lotus   CAFE $
(☑092 260158; St 2½; mains US$3.50-6; ⊙8am-5pm; 🛜🍴) In a beautifully renovated shop-house, this funky street-level cafe serves Middle Eastern–inspired vegetarian and vegan snacks plus some specials on a chalkboard. The cold drinks include unique ingredients such as Himalayan pink salt or apple-cider vinegar, with homemade herbal tinctures for flavouring.

Green Mango Café & Bakery   BAKERY $
(☑017 315450; St 159D; dishes US$2.50-5; ⊙7am-8.30pm; ❄🛜) Much more than just a bakery, Green Mango serves salads, sandwiches

and delicious appetizers like hummus and black-bean nachos to complement its coffee and tea list. It has crisp air-con and wi-fi for those looking to hang out awhile.

It's a social enterprise, too, helping poor women from the countryside find work.

Buffalo Alley   FUSION $
(☑069 723312; St 1½; small plates US$1.50-3, mains US$3-4; ⊙2.30-11pm; 🛜🍴) A friendly place run by local students, serving burgers and a bevvy of delicious tapas, including strong vegetarian options. The chatty owners are happy to teach you some Khmer, and the spontaneous karaoke sessions upstairs are a riot.

Vegetarian Foods Restaurant   VEGETARIAN $
(St 102; mains 1500-3000r; ⊙6.30am-2pm; 🍴) This hole-in-the-wall eatery serves some of the most delicious vegetarian dishes in Cambodia, including rice soup, homemade soy milk and dumplings for just 1000r. Tremendous value.

Chinese Noodle Dumpling   NOODLES $
(Lan Chov Khorko Miteanh; ☑092 589639; 145 St 2; mains 4000-6000r; ⊙9am-9pm) The Chinese chef at this Battambang institution does bargain dumplings and serves fresh noodles a dozen or more ways, including with pork or duck soup.

Flavours of India   INDIAN $
(☑053-731553; http://flavorsofindia.webs.com; St 121; mains US$3.50-5; ⊙9.30am-11pm; 🛜🍴) This Battambang outpost of a popular Phnom Penh Indian restaurant opened after some curry-craving expats ordered takeaway all the way from the capital (290km to the southeast). Opt for the *thalis* (US$5 to US$7) for an excellent-value meal.

Cafe HOC   FUSION $
(☑012 591210; cnr Sts 106 & 117; mains US$3-4; ⊙8am-2pm & 5-10pm; 🛜) This social enterprise has a cute picture menu with a compact list of Khmer and Japanese favourites, but it's best known for its all-you-can-eat Western/Khmer breakfast – for just US$3! Wicker furniture and a wall-mounted chalkboard specials menu liven up the bland space on a busy street corner.

The cafe supports Hope of Children, a local orphanage.

La Casa   ITALIAN $$
(St 115; mains US$5-10; ⊙11am-2.30pm & 5-10pm Tue-Sun) La Casa serves the best thin-crust pizza in Battambang, as well as excellent

pasta dishes and salads, out of an attractive space near the bus offices.

★ **Jaan Bai** FUSION $$
(☎ 078 263144; www.cambodianchildrenstrust.org/projects/social-enterprise/jaan-bai; cnr Sts 1½ & 2; small plates US$3, mains US$4-10; ⊙ 11am-9pm; 🛜🍴) 🍴 Jaan Bai ('rice bowl' in Khmer) is Battambang's foodie treat, with a sleekly minimalist interior offset by beautiful French-Khmer tilework lining the wall. The menu likewise is successfully bold. Order a few of the small plates to experience the range of flavours, or go all-out with the tasting menu: seven plates plus wine for US$15 per person (minimum two people).

You're eating for a good cause. Jaan Bai trains and employs vulnerable youth through the Cambodia Children's Trust (www.cambodianchildrenstrust.org).

Cafe Eden CAFE $$
(☎ 053-731525; www.cafeedencambodia.com/main; St 1; mains US$4-7; ⊙ 7.30am-9pm Wed-Mon; ❄🛜) 🍴 This American-run social enterprise offers a relaxed space for a hearty breakfast or an afternoon coffee. The compact lunch-and-dinner menu is Asian-fusion style, with burgers, Mexi flaves, the best chips in town and superior jam-jar shakes, all amid blissful air-con.

🍴 **East Bank**

Battambang BBQ & Buffet BARBECUE $
(☎ 096-303 3833; Old NH5; buffet 26,000r; ⊙ 5-10pm) Offering an all-inclusive tabletop barbecue and serve-yourself buffet, this place is unbelievably popular with local Khmers and domestic tourists. Exceptional value.

★ **La Villa** INTERNATIONAL $$
(☎ 053-730151; St 159D; mains US$5-15; ⊙ 11am-3pm & 6-9.30pm; ❄🛜) Battambang's most atmospheric dinner option dishes up delectable Khmer, Vietnamese, French and Italian dishes, plus wines from around the world. Specialities include a tender fish fillet in lemon sauce. Sit inside under the glass atrium or bask in the colonial glow of the courtyard outside, and start with the local ice tea.

🍷 **Drinking & Nightlife**

Here Be Dragons BAR
(St 159D; ⊙ 7am-midnight; 🛜) Before there was the popular Dragons hostel, there was this popular bar. The watering hole hasn't forgotten its roots, and frequently rumbles till late

with a mix of backpackers and expats. There's a Wednesday pub quiz, informal ping-pong tourneys and a Saturday afternoon BBQ.

River BAR
(☎ 012 781687; St 1; ⊙ 6am-11pm) Locals flock here during the evening for the riverfront breezes and for the football and movies this place blasts out on its outdoor screen.

Libations Bar BAR
(☎ 077 531562; 112 St 2; ⊙ 5-9pm; 🛜) Downstairs in the Bric-à-Brac hotel, this classy street-side bar caters to a relatively refined crowd with creative cocktails, craft beer, and wine and champagne by the glass. The chatty owners are a great source of information on the area. Upstairs are three arty, designed rooms.

☆ **Entertainment**

★ **Phare Ponleu Selpak** CIRCUS
(☎ 077 554413; www.phareps.org; adult/child US$14/7) Battambang's signature attraction is the internationally acclaimed circus (cirque nouveau) of this multi-arts centre for Cambodian children. Although it also runs shows in Siem Reap, it's worth timing your visit to Battambang to watch this amazing spectacle where it began. Shows are held two to four nights per week, depending on the season (check the website), and kick off at 7pm.

Phare, as it's known to locals, does a ton of stuff – contrary to popular belief, it is not just a circus. It trains musicians, visual artists and performing artists as well. Many of the artists you'll bump into around town, such as Ke of Choco l'art Café fame, lived and studied at Phare. Guests are welcome to take a guided tour of the Phare complex during the day and observe circus, dance, music, drawing and graphic-arts classes.

Tickets are sold at the door from 6pm and at many retailers around town. To get here from the Vishnu Roundabout on NH5, head west for 900m, then turn right and continue another 600m.

🛍 **Shopping**

Lonely Tree Shop ARTS & CRAFTS
(☎ 053-953123; 56 St 2½; ⊙ 10am-10pm) 🍴 Fine silk bags, chunky jewellery, fashionable shirts and skirts: definitely not your run-of-the-mill charity gift shop.

Bric-à-Brac HOMEWARES
(☎ 077 531549; www.bric-a-brac.asia; 112 St 2; ⊙ 9am-9pm) This swish store, downstairs in the bijou hotel of the same name, sells

BATTAMBANG'S EMERGING ART SCENE

Before the Khmer Rouge era, Battambang had a long history as the nation's hub for art and culture. Today, a new generation of artists is building on this heritage and Battambang is regaining its reputation as Cambodia's cultural capital. A clutch of galleries, shops and funky bars have set up in recent years – many of them on St 2½, creating an informal arts district right in the heart of town. Check out the local scene at the following spots:

Jewel in the Lotus (p246) The cafe doubles as a shop and features an upstairs gallery, with paintings, prints, vintage items, unique postcards, souvenirs, underground comics, literature, clothing and jewellery. The owner couple, Darren Swallow and Khchao Touch, know the Battambang art scene well, and Touch is a top artist in her own right.

Make Maek Art Space (☑ 092 985365; 66 St 2½; suggested donation US$2) This gallery and workshop displays the works of a rotation of local artists, including paintings and photographs, in a beautifully renovated space above the Battambang Traveller Shop.

Romcheik 5 Artspace (ទីសិល្បៈរំចេក៥; ☑ 089 373683; St 201A; US$2.50; ⏱ 2-7pm) This impressive space has a permanent collection upstairs displaying the edgy, contemporary works of its four founders, who in their youth were expelled from Thailand and forced to work as child labourers, before being rescued by an NGO and encouraged to express themselves through art.

Sangker Gallery (វិចិត្រសាលនៃលំហាសិល្បៈសង្កែ; ☑ 087 298086; St 1½; ⏱ 9.30am-noon & 2-6pm Mon-Fri) This little, two-storey art space runs regular exhibitions by local artists. The gallery also runs a new city art tour from 2pm to 6pm. Cost depends on the number of participants, starting at US$25 per person for two people, and the tour must be booked at least one day in advance.

Choco l'art Café (☑ 010 661617; St 117; mains US$1.50-5; ⏱ 8am-11pm; ☎) Run with gusto by local painter Ke and his partner, Soline, this inviting gallery-cafe sees foreigners and locals alike gather to drink and eat Soline's wonderful bread, pastries and breakfast crêpes. Occasional open-mic nights, live painting sessions and musical performances.

Tep Kao Sol (ទេពកោសល្យ; ☑ 017 982992; St 2; ⏱ hours vary) This is the gallery space of local artist Loeum Lorn, who's known for creating works out of melting coloured ice and then photographing them. It's open sporadically, so just stop by and hope for the best.

HUMAN Gallery (☑ 096 730 0590; www.josebaetxebarria.com/human-gallery; St 1½; ⏱ 10am-2pm & 4-9pm Mon-Sat) Joseba Etxebarria travelled 37,000 kilometeres through 29 countries on a bicycle, and took some pictures of people while he was at it. The results are stunningly displayed in this gallery, which includes portraits, postcards and books that can only be purchased here.

handmade *passementrie* (trimmings), textiles, antiques and accessories. It also produces some of the world's finest tassels for export.

Rachana Handicrafts FASHION & ACCESSORIES (off St 314; ⏱ 8am-5pm) 🌿 This tiny, NGO-run sewing workshop on the outskirts of town trains disadvantaged women and sells purses, stuffed toys, *krama* (checked scarves) and cotton and silk accessories.

ℹ️ Information

For information on what's happening in town, look out for copies of the free, biannual *Battambang Buzz* magazine, and the handy *Battambang Traveller* (www.battambangtraveler.com), which comes out four times a year.

Informative and hip, **Battambang Traveller Shop** (☑ 092 955744; Street 2½; ⏱ 9am-7pm) does transport and tour bookings, rents out *motos* and sells interesting local handicrafts and clothing. A decent city map is distributed by the otherwise moribund **tourist office** (☑ 012 534177; www.battambangtourism.org; St 1; ⏱ 7.30-11.30am & 2-5.30pm Mon-Fri).

Free wi-fi access is the norm at hotels and most cafes and restaurants. **World Tel Internet** (St 2; per hour 2000r; ⏱ 8am-5pm) has internet access and copying services.

ANZ Royal Bank (St 1; ⏱ 8am-4pm Mon-Fri, ATM 24hr)

Canadia Bank (Psar Nath; ⊘8am-3.30pm Mon-Fri, to 11.30am Sat, ATM 24hr)

Handa Medical Centre (☑095 520654; https://thehandafoundation.org/programs/medical-center; NH5; ⊘emergency 24hr) Has two ambulances and usually a European doctor or two in residence.

Yi Quoc Clinic (☑053-953163, 012 530171; off NH57; ⊘24hr) The best clinic in town.

Vietnamese Consulate (☑097 332 1188, 053-952894; St 3; ⊘8.30-11am & 2-5pm Mon-Fri) Issues visas in a day.

ⓘ Getting There & Away

Battambang is 290km northwest of Phnom Penh along NH5 and 80km northeast of Pailin along NH57 (formerly NH10).

BOAT

The riverboat to Siem Reap (US$20, 7am daily) squeezes through narrow waterways and passes protected wetlands, taking from five hours in the wet season to nine or more hours at the height of the dry season. Cambodia's most memorable boat trip, it's operated on alternate days by **Angkor Express** (☑012 601287) and **Chann Na** (☑012 354344), which have informal offices on the docks at the eastern end of St 501, where the boats leave from. Buy tickets in advance.

In the dry season, passengers are driven to a navigable section of the river. The best seats are away from the noisy motor. It may be possible to alight at the Prek Toal Bird Sanctuary (p127) and then be picked up there the next day for US$5 extra. Be aware that these boats, while scenic, are not always popular with local communities along the way, as the wake has caused small boats to capsize and fishing nets are regularly snagged. Copious travellers also complain of overcrowding and safety issues – there are rarely enough life jackets to go around.

BUS

Some buses now arrive and depart from Battambang's new **bus station** (NH5), 2km west of the centre. Companies offer free shuttles for departing passengers, but arriving passengers will have to pay for a *remork* (US$3) into town. However, most companies still use their company offices, which are clustered in the centre just south of the intersection of NH5 and St 4.

To Phnom Penh, if you're pinching pennies, **Capitol Tour** (☑012 810055; St 102) generally has the lowest prices, followed by **Phnom Penh Sorya** (☑092 181804; St 106). For a quicker journey to the capital, many companies run express minivan services (US$8 to US$12, 4½ hours), including **Cambotra Express** (☑017 866286; St 106), Capitol Tour, **Golden Bayon Express** (☑070 968966; St 101), **Mekong Express** (☑088 576 7668; St 3) and **Virak Buntham** (St 106).

Virak Buntham runs full-recline-sleeper night buses to Phnom Penh, but be aware that these, like all night buses to Phnom Penh, arrive at an ungodly hour.

The Mekong Express minibus is the most comfortable way to Siem Reap (US$7, 3½ hours, 8am and 2pm), while Golden Bayon Express runs a speedy minivan service (US$10, three hours, four daily).

Most buses to Bangkok involve a change at the border – usually to a minibus on the Thai side.

Rith Mony (☑092 888847; St 1)

TSS Transport (☑011 892121; St 102)

BUSES FROM BATTAMBANG

DESTINATION	DURATION	COST	FREQUENCY	COMPANIES
Bangkok, Thailand	9hr	US$15-16	7.45am, 8.30am, 10.30am, 11.30am, noon	Mekong Express, PP Sorya, Virak Buntham, Capitol
Ho Chi Minh City, Vietnam	10-11hr	US$26	7.30am	Mekong Express
Kompong Cham	8hr	US$9	9am	Rith Mony
Pailin	1¼hr	US$4	1pm, 3pm	Rith Mony
Phnom Penh (day)	4½-7hr	US$5-12	frequent	All companies
Phnom Penh (night)	5-6hr	US$6-15	many departures, 10pm to midnight	Capitol, Mekong Express, TSS, Virak Buntham
Poipet	2¼hr	US$4	regular to 4pm	Capitol, PP Sorya, Rith Mony, TSS
Siem Reap	3-4hr	US$4-10	regular to 3pm	Capitol, Golden Bayon Express, Mekong Express, PP Sorya, Rith Mony

TAXI

At the **taxi station** (cnr Sts 101 & 110), share taxis to Phnom Penh (40,000r per person, 4½ hours) and Pursat (20,000r, two hours) leave from the southeast corner. Also here you'll find share taxis to Poipet (20,000r, 1¾ hours), Sisophon (16,000r, 1¼ hours) and Siem Reap (26,000r, three hours). Share taxis to Pailin (20,000, two hours) and the Psar Pruhm-Ban Pakard border leave from the corner of St 101 and St 4.

Prices are based on six-passenger occupancy; for the price of a whole taxi, multiply the per-passenger fare by six.

ⓘ Getting Around

English- and French-speaking *remork* drivers are commonplace in Battambang, and all are eager to whisk you around on day trips. A half-day trip out of town to a single sight such as Phnom Sampeau might cost US$12, while a full-day trip taking in three sights costs US$16 to US$20, depending on your haggling skills. A *moto* costs about half that.

A *moto* ride in town costs around 2000r, while a *remork* ride starts from US$1.50.

Gecko Moto (☑ 089 924260; St 1; ⊙ 8am-10pm) and the Royal Hotel rent out motorbikes for US$6 to US$8 per day. Bicycles can be rented at the Royal Hotel, Soksabike, Battambang Bike and several guesthouses for about US$2 per day.

Around Battambang

The countryside around Battambang is dotted with old temples and other worthwhile sights. Heading south, Prasat Banan and Phnom Sampeau can be combined for a good half-day trip by *moto* or *remork*. Moving north, a half-day excursion can take in Wat Ek Phnom, Wat Somrong Knong and a few other sites.

Combined admission to Phnom Sampeau, Prasat Banan and Wat Ek Phnom costs US$3 (if you purchase a ticket at Prasat Banan, it's valid all day long at the other two, although at the time of research there was talk of discontinuing this deal).

A detailed guidebook on many sites in the area is *Around Battambang* (US$10) by Ray Zepp, which has details on temples, wats and excursions in the Battambang and Pailin areas. Proceeds go to monks and nuns working to raise HIV/AIDS awareness and to help AIDS orphans.

Phnom Sampeau

This fabled **limestone outcrop** (ភ្នំសំពៅ; US$1) 12km southwest of Battambang along NH57 (towards Pailin) is known for its gorgeous views and mesmerising display of bats, which pour out of a massive cave in its cliff face. Access to the summit is via a cement road or – if you're in need of a workout – a steep staircase. The road is too steep for *remorks*. *Moto* drivers hang out near the base of the hill and can whisk you up and back for US$4.

About halfway up to the summit, a road leads under a gate and 250m up to the **Killing Caves of Phnom Sampeau**, now a place of pilgrimage. A staircase, flanked by greenery, leads into a cavern, where a golden reclining Buddha lies peacefully next to a glass-walled memorial filled with bones and skulls – the remains of some of the people bludgeoned to death by Khmer Rouge cadres and then thrown through the skylight above. Next to the base of the stairway is the old memorial, a rusty cage made of chicken wire and cyclone fencing and partly filled with human bones.

On the summit, several viewpoints can be discovered amid a **complex of temples**. As you descend from the summit's **golden stupa**, dating from 1964, turn left under the gate decorated with a **bas-relief** of Eiy Sei (an elderly Buddha). A deep **canyon**, its vertical sides cloaked in greenery, descends 144 steps through a natural arch to a 'lost world' of stalactites, creeping vines and bats; two Angkorian warriors stand guard.

Near the westernmost of the two antennas at the summit, two government **artillery pieces**, one with markings in Russian, the other in German, are still deployed. Near the base of the western antenna, jockey for position with other tourists on the **sunset lookout pavilion**. Looking west you'll spy Phnom Krapeu (Crocodile Mountain), a one-time Khmer Rouge stronghold.

If you visit on your own, a local guide may try to escort you around the sites and give you some history. Phors is a good guide who works for donations, with US$3 being appropriate for an hour-long tour.

Back down at the hill base, people gather at dusk (around 5.30pm) to witness a thick column of bats pouring from a cave high up on the north side of the cliff face. The display lasts a good 30 minutes as millions of bats head out in a looping line to their feeding grounds near Tonlé Sap. Note that there are lots of monkeys at this site; be careful with your food, as hungry monkeys have been known to become aggressive.

Prasat Banan

It's a 358-stone-step climb up Phnom Banan to reach **Prasat Banan** (ប្រាសាទភ្នំបាណន់; US$3; ☉6am-sunset), but the incredible views across surrounding countryside from the top are worth it. Udayadityavarman II, son of Suryavarman I, built Prasat Banan in the 11th century; some locals claim the five-tower layout here was the inspiration for Angkor Wat, although this seems optimistic. There are impressive carved lintels above the doorways to each of the towers and bas-reliefs on the upper parts of the central tower.

From the temple, a narrow stone staircase leads south down the hill to three caves, which can be visited with a local guide.

Prasat Banan is located 23km south of Battambang.

Prasat Phnom Banon Winery

Midway between Battambang and Prasat Banan, in an area known for its production of chilli peppers (harvested from October to January), is Cambodia's only winery. **Prasat Phnom Banon Winery** (កន្លែងផលិតស្រាភ្នំបាណន់; ☎012 665238; Bot Sala Village; wine tasting US$2.50, bottles US$15-25; ☉8am-8pm) grows Shiraz grapes to make reds. It tastes unlike most wine you've ever encountered, but is actually quite earthy and complex.

Officially recognised by Cambodia's Ministry of Industry, Mines & Energy, Banon wines belong to that exclusive club of wineries whose vintages improve significantly with the addition of ice cubes. Also made here is Banon brandy, which has a heavenly bouquet and a taste that has been compared to turpentine. Sampling takes place in an attractive garden pavilion.

The winery is 10km south of Battambang and 8km north of Prasat Banan.

Kamping Puoy

Also known as the Killing Dam, **Kamping Puoy** (កំពីងពួយ) was one of the many grandiose Khmer Rouge projects intended to recreate the sophisticated irrigation networks that helped Cambodia wax mighty under the kings of Angkor. As many as 10,000 Cambodians are thought to have perished during its construction, worked to death under the shadow of executions, malnutrition and disease.

There's little to see but people come to picnic, and to take row boats (10,000r for two hours) out on the water.

These days, thanks to the dam, the Kamping Puoy area is one of the few parts of Cambodia to produce two rice crops a year.

Kamping Puoy is 27km west of Battambang (go via NH5 and follow the irrigation canal). It's easy to combine a visit here with a stop at Phnom Sampeau.

Sneng

This town, located on NH57 20km southwest of Battambang towards Pailin, is home to two small yet interesting temples. **Prasat Yeay Ten** (ប្រាសាទយាយទែន; NH57), dedicated to Shiva, dates from the end of the 10th century and, although in a ruinous state, has above its doorways three delicately carved lintels that somehow survived the ravages of time and war; the eastern one depicts the Churning of the Ocean of Milk. The temple is situated on the east side of the highway, so close to the road that it resembles an ancient Angkorian tollbooth.

SAMLAUT

The northernmost tip of the Cardamom Mountains – home to elephants, gibbons, pangolins, hornbills and many other endangered creatures – covers the southern half of Pailin Province (pretty much everything south of NH57). Known as the **Samlaut Multiple Use Area** (600 sq km), this expanse of forested mountains is contiguous with two Thai parks (Namtok Klong Kaew National Park and Khlong Kreua Wai Wildlife Sanctuary), with which it is joined as a transboundary **Peace Park**. Countless landmines make the area too dangerous for trekking, but there is a durian plantation and some waterfalls to which Memoria Palace (p253) runs tours.

Samlaut is administered and patrolled with help from the **Maddox Jolie-Pitt Foundation**, named after the Cambodian-born adopted son of its founder and president, the American actress Angelina Jolie.

Behind Prasat Yeay Ten is a contemporary wat; tucked away at the back of the wat compound are three **brick sanctuaries** (off NH57) that have some beautifully preserved carvings around the entrances.

PAILIN

055 / POP 35,000

Apart from shopping for gemstones and visiting a particularly colourful hilltop temple, the remote Wild West town of Pailin (ប៉ៃលិន) has little to recommend it. That said, the forested Cardamom foothills surrounding the city are beautiful. Just don't wander into them by yourself – or you may literally be walking into a minefield.

◉ Sights

Phnom Keu Waterfall   WATERFALL
(ភ្នំកែវ, Blue Mountain Waterfall; motorbike/car 3000/10,000r) Phnom Keu is the most accessible of the numerous waterfalls dropping out of the Cardamoms south of Pailin, and has water year-round. To get here, turn right off NH57 1.5km east of Wat Phnom Yat (p252), then proceed 5km on a rough road (which gets dodgy in the rainy season). From the entrance, cross the small river via the dirt road and walk about 3km to the falls.

The area's other waterfalls are more difficult to access due to being at their most impressive during the rainy season, when the roads are often impassable. Getting to the more remote falls is risky because of the lingering presence of landmines.

Wat Phnom Yat   BUDDHIST TEMPLE
(វត្តភ្នំយ៉ាត; off NH57) From NH57, stairs lead through a garish gate up to Wat Phnom Yat, a psychedelic temple centred on an ancient po (sacred fig) tree. A 27m Buddha looms over the top of the staircase, while a path leads up to the colourful temple and the large golden stupas at the top of the hill.

Along the path a life-sized cement tableau shows naked sinners and their punishments: being heaved into a cauldron (the impious), de-tongued (liars) and forced to climb a spiny tree (adulterers). Medieval European triptychs don't portray a hell that is nearly so scary. The sunrises and sunsets at the top are usually nice enough to take your mind off the fire and brimstone.

Pailin

Pailin

◉ **Sights**
1 Independence Monument................... B2
2 Psar Pailin..A1
3 Wat Khaong Kang................................. B3
4 Wat Phnom Yat...................................... B3

🛏 **Sleeping**
5 Pailin Ruby Guesthouse A1

Wat Khaong Kang   BUDDHIST TEMPLE
(វត្តកោងកង) At the base of Phnom Yat hill, an impressive gate dating to 1968 leads to Wat Khaong Kang, an important centre for Buddhist teaching before the Khmer Rouge madness. The exterior wall is decorated with a long bas-relief of the Churning of the Ocean of Milk. At time of research the interior couldn't be viewed due to restoration work, but that could be finished by the time you visit.

🛏 Sleeping & Eating

Bamboo Guesthouse   GUESTHOUSE $
(012 405818; r US$12-30; ❄ ⚞ ⚟) Bamboo is an oasis of calm on Pailin's northwestern outskirts, with 27 comfortable bungalows. The restaurant serves excellent Khmer and Thai food (mains US$4 to US$8) in outdoor pavilions, and the pool is free for guests, US$4

Getting to the border The laid-back **Psar Pruhm/Ban Pakard border crossing** (6.30am to 8pm) is 102km southwest of Battambang and 18km northwest of Pailin via good sealed roads.

First get to Pailin from Battambang. In Pailin, patient travellers might get a share taxi (6000r) to the border. If nothing is going, take a *moto* (US$5) or private taxi (US$10).

At the border Formalities are straightforward and quick on both sides. Immigration officials usually quote US$35 for Cambodian tourist visas here. Ignore all offers from touts on the Thai side to help with visas.

Moving on On the Thai side, you can avoid being overcharged for transport to Chanthaburi (150B, 1½ hours, 10am, 11am, 6.30pm) by hopping on a *moto* (50B) to the nearby *sŏrngtăaou* (pick-up truck) station. From Chanthaburi's bus station there are frequent buses to Bangkok (200B, four hours).

for outsiders. From the market head west on NH57 for 2km, turn right and proceed 800m.

Pailin Ruby Guesthouse GUESTHOUSE $
(☑ 016 477933; NH57; s with fan US$6-8, d with fan US$8-11, s with air-con US$11, d with air-con US$13-16; ❄ 🗢) A good-value place in the centre, with 63 clean, spacious rooms. It's worth paying for the air-con options as they have natural light.

★**Memoria Palace** RESORT $$
(☑ 015 430014; www.memoriapalace.com; hut US$45, bungalow US$55-80; ❄ 🗢 ⊠) Located 5km west of Pailin, this resort has humongous bungalows with boutique touches and great views, and a 20m-long hilltop swimming pool. There's also three fan-only, palm-thatch huts. The restaurant (mains US$5 to US$10) is Pailin's best; breakfast is included. To get here, go straight where the highway bends sharply to the right 500m beyond the turnoff to Bamboo Guesthouse.

ℹ Information

Puthi Cheat, an English-speaking staff member of the Memoria Palace hotel, is about the only useful source of information in Pailin. He can put together tours that take in gem mines, farms and waterfalls, among other attractions.
Canadia Bank (NH57; ⊙8am-3.30pm Mon-Fri, to 11.30am Sat, ATM 24hr)

ℹ Getting There & Away

Highway NH57 (sometimes still called Highway 10), a sealed highway, originates about 6km west of Pailin and runs north to Poipet along the Thai border, making for a straightforward journey by bus, car or motorbike.
Rith Mony (NH57) has morning buses that originate in Psar Pruhm at the Thai border

around 7.30am, pick up passengers in Pailin around 8am, and continue to Phnom Penh (38,000r, eight hours) via Battambang (15,000r, 1½ hours).

Share taxis to Battambang (20,000r, one hour) leave from the taxi stand opposite Psar Pailin on NH57.

A rough track goes from Treng District, about 25km east of Pailin, southward through the Cardamom Mountains to Koh Kong via Samlaut and Pramoay.

POIPET

☑ 054 / POP 89,500
Long the armpit of Cambodia, notorious for its squalor, scams and sleaze, Poipet (ប៉ោយប៉ែត, pronounced 'poi-*peh*' in Khmer) has recently splurged on a facelift and no longer looks like the post-apocalyptic place it once was. Thanks mainly to the patronage of neighbouring Thais, whose own country bans gambling, its casino resorts – with

ⓘ GETTING TO THAILAND: POIPET TO ARANYA PRATHET

Getting to the border By far the busiest crossing between Cambodia and Thailand, the **Poipet/Aranya Prathet border crossing** (6am to 10pm in theory, 6.30am to 7.30pm in practice) is the route most people take when travelling between Bangkok and Siem Reap. It has earned a bad reputation over the years, with scams galore to help tourists part with their money, especially coming in from Thailand.

Frequent buses and share taxis run from Siem Reap and Battambang to Poipet. Don't get off the bus until you reach the big roundabout adjacent to the border post. Buying a ticket all the way to Bangkok can expedite things and save you the hassle of finding onward transport on the Thai side. There are now several bus companies that offer through-buses from Siem Reap to Mo Chit (p124) bus station in Bangkok.

At the border Be prepared to wait in sweltering immigration lines on both sides – waits of two or more hours are not uncommon, especially in the high season. Show up early in the morning to avoid the crowds, but be aware that rarely does anybody get across before 6.30am. You can pay a special 'VIP fee' (aka a bribe) of 200B on either side to skip the lines, but beware of scams and realise that you are contributing to longer wait times for everybody else. There is no departure tax to leave Cambodia despite what Cambodian border officials might tell you. Entering Thailand, most nationalities are issued 15-day visa waivers free of charge.

Coming in from Thailand, under no circumstances should you deal with any 'Cambodian' immigration officials who might approach you on the Thai side – this is a scam. Entering Cambodia, the official tourist visa fee is US$30, but it's common to be charged $35. If you don't mind waiting around, you can usually get the official rate if you politely hold firm. Procuring an e-visa (US$37) before travel won't save you any money but will lower your stress levels.

Moving on Minibuses wait just over the border on the Thai side to whisk you to Bangkok's Victory Monument (230B, four hours, every 30 minutes from 6.30am to 4.30pm). Or make your way 7km to Aranya Prathet by *tuk tuk* (100B) or *sŏrngtǎaou* (pick-up truck; 15B), from where there are regular buses to Bangkok's Mo Chit and Eastern station between 5am and 3pm (229B, five to six hours). Make sure your *tuk tuk* driver takes you to the main bus station in Aranya Prathet for your 100B, not to the smaller station about 1km from the border (a common scam). The 6.40am and the 1.55pm trains (six hours) are other options to Bangkok.

names like Tropicana and Grand Diamond City – are turning the town into Cambodia's little Las Vegas. However, beyond the border zone it's still a chaotic, trash-strewn strip mall sprinkled with dodgy massage parlours. The Khmers' gentle side is little in evidence, but don't worry, the rest of the country does not carry on like this.

Poipet extends southeast from the border (the filthy O Chrou stream) for a few kilometres along NH5.

ⓘ Information

The faster you get used to making quick conversions between Cambodian riel, US dollars and Thai baht, all of which are in use here, the easier it'll be. A good rule of thumb is 4000r = US$1 = 30B.

Don't change money at the places suggested by touts, no matter how official they look. In fact, there's no need to change money at all, as baht work just fine here.

Canadia Bank (NH5; ◷ 8am-3.30pm Mon-Fri, to 11.30am Sat, ATM 24hr) is about 1km east of the border roundabout.

ⓘ Getting There & Away

It's worth mastering the transport tricks of this scam-ridden border to save both hassle and money.

Poipet has two bus stations: the Poipet Tourist Passenger International Terminal, situated 9km east of town in the middle of nowhere, and the main bus station, which is at the main market, one block north of Canadia Bank off NH5. Unless you don't mind overpaying or are desperate for convenience, avoid the international tourist terminal. Unfortunately this is easier said than done, as upon exiting immigration you'll be herded toward a 'free' tourist shuttle to this terminal, where onward buses depart to Phnom Penh (US$15, eight hours), Siem Reap (US$9, 2½ hours) and Battambang (US$10, 2½ hours). Share/private taxis to Siem Reap from the international terminal cost an inflated US$12/48.

Instead, stay solo and walk or take a *moto* (2000r) for 1km along NH5 to the bus company offices near Canadia Bank, or to the main bus station nearby. Bus fares here are on average around US$5 less than at the international tourist terminal.

Unfortunately, the vast majority of buses depart in the morning (before 10.30am). If you can't get a bus, just take a share taxi – these also depart from NH5 around Canadia Bank – onward to Siem Reap (seat/whole taxi US$7.50/30), Battambang (seat/whole taxi US$7.50/30) or Phnom Penh (seat/whole taxi US$20/80). Don't take the taxis that hang out near the roundabout by the border – these charge tourists much more.

The many bus companies here include Capitol Tour, Phnom Penh Sorya, Kampuchea Angkor Express and Rith Mony. Several companies offer trips to Bangkok (US$10, five hours) until about 1pm.

All roads leading out of Poipet are sealed and in fine condition.

ℹ Getting Around

Moto drivers wait at the big roundabout adjacent to the border post to whisk you around the town proper – pay 2000r for a short ride (though they may try to charge you US$1).

SISOPHON

📞 054 / POP 61,600

Sisophon (សិសុផុន) is strategically situated at northwest Cambodia's great crossroads, the intersection of NH5 and NH6. This dusty transit hub doesn't have much going for it, but it's the nearest town to use as a base for exploring the Angkorian temples of Banteay Chhmar. Confusingly, it's also known as Svay, Svay Sisophon, Srei Sophon and Banteay Meanchey.

NH6 (from Siem Reap and Phnom Penh) intersects NH5 (from Battambang and Phnom Penh) at the western tip of the triangular town centre.

ℹ Information

Canadia Bank (🕐8am-3.30pm Mon-Fri, to 11.30am Sat, ATM 24hr)

ℹ Getting There & Away

Sisophon is 45km east of Poipet, 105km west of Siem Reap and 68km northwest of Battambang. Most long-haul buses stop around the bus area,

spread through the centre of town. Capitol Tour, Rith Mony and Phnom Penh Sorya each have four or five buses per day south to Battambang (15,000r, two hours) and Phnom Penh (US$8, eight hours). Capital Tour and PP Sorya also have a couple of buses to Poipet. A few morning buses from Poipet come through en route to Siem Reap (15,000r, two hours). **Mean Chey Express** (📞090 922111; NH6) also runs comfortable minivans to Phnom Penh (US$8, 6½ hours).

From the taxi park, near the bus station, share taxis serve Poipet (12,000r, 40 minutes), Siem Reap (20,000r, 1½ hours), Battambang (16,000r, 1½ hours) and Phnom Penh (US$10, six hours); a private taxi to Siem Reap costs about US$25. There are also share taxis to Samraong via Kralanh for the O Smach border crossing (25,000r, three hours).

Share taxis to other northbound destinations, including Banteay Chhmar (p257), depart from **Psar Thmei** (St 1).

BANTEAY CHHMAR

Far from the madding crowds, Banteay Chhmar is an impressive temple complex that offers the atmosphere of the Angkor of old before the advent of mass tourism. It was constructed by Cambodia's most prolific builder, Jayavarman VII (r 1181–1219), on the site of a 9th-century temple. The Global Heritage Fund (www.globalheritagefund.org) is assisting with conservation efforts here, and it is now a top candidate for Unesco World Heritage Site status.

Next to the ruins, Banteay Chhmar village is part of a worthwhile community-based tourism (CBT) scheme offering homestays, activities and guides for temple tours to assist with community development in the area. All activities can be booked through the **CBT Office** (Community-Based Tourism Office; ☑ 012 435660, 097-516 5533; www.visitban teaychhmar.org; NH56).

◉ Sights

The Banteay Chhmar temple complex consists of the impressive main temple and nine satellite temples in the immediate vicinity.

The satellite temples, many hidden deep in the jungle and with Bayon-style faces of their own, are all in a ruinous state and some are accessible only if you chop through the undergrowth. Along with Prasat Ta Prohm, they include include Prasat Samnang Tasok, Prasat Mebon, Prasat Prom Muk Buon, Prasat Yeay Choun, Prasat Pranang Ta Sok and Prasat Chen Chiem Trey. The latter, which vaguely translates as 'Fish Farm Temple', is about 1km north of the main temple and has been all but consumed by trees. To explore these lesser-seen temples, hire a guide from the CBT Office for US$10.

★ Banteay Chhmar   BUDDHIST TEMPLE
(បន្ទាយឆ្មារ; US$5; ⊙ 8am-6pm) Beautiful, peaceful and covered in astonishingly intricate bas-reliefs, Banteay Chhmar is one of the most impressive temple complexes beyond the Angkor area. About a two-hour drive from Siem Reap, these remote ruins are also the site of a superb community-based homestay and tourism program. If you're looking for an opportunity to delve into Cambodian rural life and spend some quality time amid a temple complex far from the crowds, you could hardly find a more perfect spot.

Banteay Chhmar and its nine satellite temples were constructed by Cambodia's most prolific builder, Jayavarman VII (r 1181–1219), on the site of a 9th-century temple. The main temple housed one of the largest and most impressive Buddhist monasteries of the Angkorian period, and was originally enclosed by a 9km-long wall. Now atmospherically encroached upon by forest, it features several towers bearing enigmatic, Bayon-style four-faced Avalokiteshvara (Buddhist deities) with their mysterious and iconic smiles. The temple is also renowned for its 2000 sq metres of intricate carvings

that depict war victories and scenes from daily life.

The artistic highlight are the bas-reliefs of multi-armed Avalokiteshvaras, unique to Banteay Chhmar, on the exterior of the southern section of the temple's western ramparts. Unfortunately, several of these were dismantled and trucked into Thailand in a brazen act of looting in 1998; of the original eight figures, only two – one with 22 arms, the other with 32 – remain in situ, but they still evoke the dazzling, intricate artistry involved in creating these carvings. The segments of the looted bas-reliefs that were intercepted by the Thais are now on display in Phnom Penh's National Museum of Cambodia.

The nine satellite temples, many hidden deep in the jungle and with Bayon-style faces of their own, are well worth exploring for serious tomb-raider types. Guides booked through the CBT Office can show you the way. The easiest to find is **Prasat Ta Prohm** (ប្រាសាទតាព្រហ្ម) `FREE`, hidden in the bush just 200m south of the main temple's southern wall, its single crumbling tower bearing a well-preserved four-faced Avalokiteshvara.

The Global Heritage Fund (www.globalheritagefund.org) is assisting with conservation efforts here, and a wonderful community-based tourism (CBT) scheme gives visitors incentive to stay another day. The scheme includes fantastic homestays, activities and guides for temple tours, all encouraging community development and booked through the CBT Office. Activities include ox-cart rides and traditional music shows, and they can arrange trips to outlying temples by local transport. The office is opposite and just south of the Banteay Chhmar main (eastern) entrance.

Banteay Chhmar can easily be done as a day trip with private transport out of Siem Reap. Shared taxis from Sisophon, 61km south of the temple along the sealed NH56, usually only go as far as Thmor Puok, although a few continue on to Banteay Chhmar (15,000r, one hour) and Samraong. A *moto* from Sisophon to Banteay Chhmar will cost US$15 to US$20 return, a taxi US$50 to US$60 return.

Banteay Top   BUDDHIST TEMPLE
(បន្ទាយទ័ព) `FREE` Banteay Top (Fortress of the Army) may be small, but its impressively tall, damaged towers are highly photogenic. Constructed around the same time as Banteay Chhmar, it may be a tribute to the army

of Jayavarman VII, which confirmed Khmer dominance over the region by comprehensively defeating the Chams.

To get here from Banteay Chhmar, head towards Sisophon along NH56 for 7km, take the left-hand turn through the red ornamental gate and head east down the track for 5km.

🛏 Sleeping & Eating

CBT Homestay Program HOMESTAY **$**
(☏012 435660, 097-516 5533; www.visitbanteay chhmar.org; r US$7) 🌿 Thanks to the homestay project run by the CBT (Community-Based Tourism) Office, it's possible to stay in Banteay Chhmar and three nearby hamlets. Rooms are in private homes and come with mosquito nets, fans that run when there's 24-hour electricity, and downstairs bathrooms. Part of the income goes into a community development fund. Book at least one day in advance.

If you're with a group of seven or more, book at least a month ahead.

CBT Meal at the Temple CAMBODIAN **$**
(per person US$4) For those interested in a particularly atmospheric meal, the CBT Office (p256) can set up lunch or dinner in the main temple at Banteay Chhmar. There's an additional charge of US$10 to US$20 for the set-up, dependent on the size of your group.

Banteay Chhmar Restaurant CAMBODIAN **$**
(☏031-247 5353; NH56; mains US$1-4; ☺6am-2pm) Near the temple's eastern entrance, this rustic restaurant is the only place to dine without pre-ordering. It serves really tasty Khmer food.

🛍 Shopping

Soieries du Mékong ARTS & CRAFTS
(Mekong Silk Mill; www.soieriesdumekong.com; NH56; ☺7.30am-noon & 1.30-5pm Mon-Fri) It is possible to see silk being woven and to purchase top-quality silk products destined for the French market at Soieries du Mékong, 150m south of where NH56 from Sisophon meets the *baray* (the reservoir surrounding the temple). It's affiliated with the French NGO Enfants du Mékong (www.enfants dumekong.com).

ⓘ Information

The main road through town runs west to east, south of the *baray*, and then takes a 90-degree turn north just after it. The market and taxi park

---

> **LANDMINE ALERT!**
> ....
> Banteay Meanchey and Oddar Meanchey are among the most heavily landmined provinces in Cambodia. Do *not*, under any circumstances, stray from previously trodden paths. If you've got your own wheels, travel only on roads or trails regularly used by locals.

are at the turn; a few hundred metres north is the temple's main (eastern) entrance.

The CBT Office is the main source of local information as well as the place to book tours, activities and homestays.

ⓘ Getting There & Away

Banteay Chhmar is 61km north of Sisophon and about 50km southwest of Samraong along the smoothly paved NH56. Most people visit on a long day trip from Siem Reap, which is about a two-hour drive in private transport.

From Sisophon's Psar Thmei share taxi stand (1km north of NH6), most northbound share taxis go only as far as Thmor Puok, although a few continue on to Banteay Chhmar (20,000r, one hour) and Samraong. A *moto* from Sisophon to Banteay Chhmar will cost US$15 to US$20 return, a taxi US$50 to US$60 return.

ANLONG VENG

☏065 / POP 46,464

For almost a decade this was the ultimate Khmer Rouge stronghold, home to notorious leaders of Democratic Kampuchea, including Pol Pot, Nuon Chea, Khieu Samphan and Ta Mok. Anlong Veng (អន្លង់វែង) fell to government forces in April 1998 and about the same time Pol Pot died mysteriously nearby. Soon after, Prime Minister Hun Sen ordered that the NH67 road be bulldozed through the jungle, to ensure the population didn't have second thoughts about ending the war.

Today Anlong Veng is a poor, dusty town with little going for it, and unprecedented flooding in 2017 didn't help. However, the nearby Choam–Chong Sa-Ngam border crossing connects Cambodia with an isolated part of Thailand, and for those with an interest in contemporary Cambodian history, the area's Khmer Rouge sites will have appeal. Most of the local residents, and virtually the entire political leadership

DANGREK MOUNTAINS

For years the world wondered where Pol Pot and his cronies were hiding out: the answer was right here in the densely forested Dangrek Mountains, close enough to Thailand that they could flee across the border if government forces drew nigh. North of Anlong Veng, hidden in these hills near the Thai frontier, are a number of key Khmer Rouge sites.

About 2km before the border, the road splits to avoid a house-sized boulder. A group of **statues** (NH67) hewn entirely from the boulder by the Khmer Rouge can be seen, and have been preserved as a shrine. The statues depict a woman carrying bundles of bamboo sticks on her head and two uniformed Khmer Rouge soldiers (the latter were decapitated by government forces).

Just after you arrive in the bustling border village of Choam, look for a sign for the **cremation site of Pol Pot** (US$2) on the east side of NH67 (it's 50m south of and opposite the Sangam Casino entrance). Pol Pot's ashes lie under a rusted corrugated iron roof surrounded by rows of partly buried glass bottles. The Khmer Rouge leader was hastily burned here in 1998 on a pile of rubbish and old tyres – a fittingly inglorious end, some say, given the suffering he inflicted on millions of Cambodians.

Bizarre as it may sound, Pol Pot is remembered with affection by some locals, and people sometimes stop by to light incense. According to neighbours, every last bone fragment has been snatched from the ashes by visitors in search of good-luck charms. Pol Pot's spirit, like that of his deputy Ta Mok, is said to give out winning lottery numbers.

The **Choam–Chong Sa-Ngam border crossing** is a few hundred metres north of here, near a ramshackle **smugglers' market**. From behind the smugglers' market, a dirt road with potholes the size of parachutes – navigable only by 4WD vehicles and motorbikes (and not navigable at all in the depth of the wet season) – heads east, parallel to the Dangrek escarpment. Domestic tourists head 700m along this road to reach **Peuy Ta Mok** (ពើយតាម៉ុក, Ta Mok's Cliff) (Ta Mok's Cliff) for spectacular views of Cambodia's northern plains.

About 4km east along the dirt track after Peuy Ta Mok (when the trail forks at the water-lily lake, take the left-hand track) you'll arrive at **Pol Pot's house**. Surrounded by a cinder-block wall, the jungle hideout has been comprehensively looted, though you can still see a low brick building whose courtyard hides an underground bunker. This narrow part of the track is navigable only by motorbike.

Much more difficult to get to is **Khieu Samphan's house**, buried in the jungle on the bank of a stream about 5km east of Pol Pot's house.

and upper class, are ex–Khmer Rouge or descendants.

◎ Sights

The main sights in Anlong Veng are locations once associated with Ta Mok (Uncle Mok, aka Brother Number Five). To his former supporters, many of whom still live in Anlong Veng, he was harsh but fair, a benevolent builder of orphanages and schools, and a leader who kept order, in stark contrast to the anarchic atmosphere that prevailed once government forces took over. But to most Cambodians, Pol Pot's military enforcer – responsible for thousands of deaths in successive purges during the terrible years of Democratic Kampuchea – was best known as 'the Butcher'. Arrested in 1999, he died in July 2006 in a Phnom Penh hospital, awaiting trial for genocide and crimes against humanity.

Ta Mok's House   HISTORIC SITE
(ផ្ទះតាម៉ុក; suggested donation for caretaker US$1) On a peaceful lakeside site, Ta Mok's house is a spartan structure with a bunker in the basement, five childish wall murals downstairs (one of Angkor Wat, four of Prasat Preah Vihear) and three more murals upstairs, including an idyllic wildlife scene. About the only furnishings that weren't looted are the floor tiles.

To get here, head north from the bridge on NH67 for 600m, turn right (signposted for the house) and continue 200m past the so-called Tourism Information hut.

Ta Mok's Lake   LAKE
(បឹងតាម៉ុក) Swampy Ta Mok's Lake was created on Brother Number Five's orders, but the water killed all the trees; their skeletons are a fitting monument to the devastation he and his movement left behind. In the

middle of the lake is a small brick structure – an outhouse, and all that remains of
Pol Pot's residence in Anlong Veng.

Ta Mok's Grave   MONUMENT

(ផ្នូរសពតាម៉ុក; US$2) Ta Mok's Angkorian-
style mausoleum was built by a rich grand-
son in 2009. The cement tomb of the Khmer
Rouge military enforcer bears no name or
inscription. Locals come here to light incense and, in a bizarre local tradition, hope
his spirit grants them a winning lottery
number.

To get here, head north from the bridge
on NH67 for about 7½km to Tumnup Leu
village, where a signposted right turn brings
you 200m to a fork. Take the left fork and
proceed another 200m to the mausoleum.
It's on the grounds of a modest pagoda;
take a hard right (south) as you enter the
grounds to find the grave.

🛏 Sleeping & Eating

North of the roundabout are a few restaurants, while south of the roundabout blazing
braziers barbecue chicken, fish and eggs on
skewers at the lively **night market**.

★ Bot Uddom Guesthouse   GUESTHOUSE $

(☑011 500507; r with fan/air-con from
US$6.50/15; ❄️🌐) The best option in An-
long Veng, this place offers spotless rooms
with massive hardwood beds. An annexe
looks out on Ta Mok's Lake (well, swamp),
and the kind owner Tola speaks excellent
English. He can help arrange tours of the
nearby sights and mountain camping trips
in the dry season.

The guesthouse is a few hundred metres
east of the Dove of Peace roundabout on the
road to Preah Vihear.

Monorom Guesthouse   HOTEL $

(☑065-690 0468; NH67; r with fan/air-con
US$7.50/15; ❄️🌐) The air-con rooms here
are nondescript, but it's central, clean and
everything works. Fan-only rooms are a bit
dreary. It's 200m north of the main roundabout. No English spoken.

Monorom Restaurant   CAMBODIAN $

(mains 8000-16,000r; ⏱5am-9pm) Attached to
the hotel of the same name, Monorom dishes up a small but tasty selection of typical
fried vegetable and meat dishes and breakfast noodle soups. It's pretty much the only
place in town with an English menu.

Som O   THAI $

(NH67; mains 4000-8000r) This new, open-air
Thai place is a hit, with excellent noodle
soups, rice dishes and iced coffee. Picture
menus posted above the kitchen are helpful
and surprisingly accurate.

ℹ️ Information

Acleda Bank (⏱7.30am-4pm Mon-Fri, to 11am
Sat, ATM 24hr)

ℹ️ Getting There & Away

Anlong Veng is 124km north of Siem Reap along
the nicely sealed NH67, and about 76km west of
Sra Em, the turnoff for Prasat Preah Vihear.

The bus depots are on NH67, just north of the
roundabout, while share taxis gather on NH67
just southwest of the roundabout.

Share taxis to Siem Reap (20,000r, 1½ hours)
and Sra Em (20,000r, two hours) are most frequent in the morning. A private taxi to Sra Em
costs US$30.

Rith Mony (☑092 511911; NH67) and **Liang
US Express** (☑092 881175; NH67) have
early-morning bus services to Phnom Penh
(US$6 to US$7.50, seven hours) via Siem Reap
(US$5, three hours) at 7am and 8am.

ℹ️ GETTING TO THAILAND: ANLONG VENG TO PHUSING

Getting to the border The remote **Choam/Chong Sa-Ngam border crossing** connects Anlong Veng in Oddar Meanchey Province with Thailand's Si Saket Province, and
is open from 7am to 8pm. A *moto* from Anlong Veng to the border crossing, 16km away,
costs US$3 or US$4 (more like US$5 in the reverse direction). This road is sealed and in
good condition. The crossing is right next to the smugglers' market.

At the border Formalities are straightforward, but note that if you are coming in from
Thailand, e-visas are not accepted here. Cambodian visas on arrival are usually charged
at US$35.

Moving on Once in Thailand, it should be possible to find a *sörngtǎaou* to Phusing, and
from there a bus to Khu Khan or Si Saket. Another option is the casino buses, which
leave hourly to/from Khu Khan (30 minutes) and Phusing.

ℹ Getting Around

The town's focal point is the Dove of Peace Roundabout at the junction of NH67 and the new highway east to Preah Vihear. About 600m north of this monument (a gift from Hun Sen), the NH67 crosses a bridge and continues 16km to the Thai border.

A *moto* circuit to the Thai border and back, via Ta Mok's house and grave, costs about US$8. To explore the sights along the Dangrek Mountain track as well, expect to pay around US$20 for a three-to-four-hour circuit.

PREAH VIHEAR PROVINCE

Vast, remote and hardly touched by tourism, Preah Vihear Province (ខេត្តព្រះវិហារ) is home to three of Cambodia's most impressive Angkorian legacies. Stunningly perched on a promontory high in the Dangrek Mountains, Prasat Preah Vihear became Cambodia's second Unesco World Heritage Site in 2008, sparking an armed stand-off with Thailand. Further south are the lonely, jungle-engulfed temples of Preah Khan – totally isolated and imbued with secret-world atmosphere. More accessible is 10th-century capital Koh Ker (p172),

LANDMINE ALERT!

Until as recently as 1998, landmines were used by the Khmer Rouge to defend Prasat Preah Vihear against government forces. During the past decade, de-mining organisations made real headway in clearing the site of these enemies within. However, the advent of a border conflict with Thailand led to this area being heavily militarised once again. Both sides denied laying new landmines during the armed stand-off between Cambodia and Thailand from 2008 to 2011, but rumours persist, as several Thai and Cambodian soldiers were killed by mines in the vicinity of the temple. So do *not*, under any circumstances, stray from marked paths around Prasat Preah Vihear.

The rest of the province is heavily landmined, too, especially around Choam Ksant. Those with their own transport should travel only on roads or trails regularly used by locals.

which is within day-tripping distance of Siem Reap.

Preah Vihear Province is genuine 'outback' Cambodia and remains desperately poor – partly because many areas were under Khmer Rouge control until 1998, and partly because until recently its transport infrastructure was in a catastrophic state. The needs of the Cambodian army in its confrontation with Thailand have expedited dramatic road upgrades in the province, making travel more straightforward, although public transport is still in short supply on some routes.

Preah Vihear City

🕿 064 / POP 25,000

Preah Vihear City, still commonly known by its old name, Tbeng Meanchey (ត្បូងមានជ័យ), is a sleepy provincial capital where dogs lounging in the middle of the street are only occasionally jolted awake by passing vehicles. There's very little to see or do here, but the town is useful as a base for journeys to Prasat Preah Vihear, Preah Khan and Koh Ker. Note that a closer base for Prasat Preah Vihear is Sra Em, only 30km south of the temple.

With the smooth highway running 130km east to Thala Boravit and the bridge over the Mekong to Stung Treng, Preah Vihear City and the province's remote temples are a good stopoff for travellers heading east, between the temples of Angkor and Stung Treng, Ratanakiri and Champasak Province in southern Laos.

🛏 Sleeping

Home Vattanak Guesthouse   HOTEL $
(🕿 064-636 3000; St A14; r from US$15; ❄ @ 🛜)
The 27 well-maintained rooms at this sparkling-clean hotel include wonderful beds, decent bathrooms and luxuries such as flat-screen TVs. Its central but quiet location, tucked down a quiet side street, is an extra bonus.

Lyhout Guesthouse   HOTEL $
(🕿 012 737116; www.lyhoutguesthouse.blog spot.com; Koh Ker St; r US$15-35; ❄ 🛜) The smart rooms here have wooden desks and white bedspreads adorned with handsome bed-runners. Upgrade to VIP status for an ornate Khmer-carving headboard on the bed, and a fridge and kettle in your room.

Heng Heng Guesthouse — HOTEL $

(☏ 012 900992; Mlou Prey St; r with fan/air-con from US$7/12; ❄ ☎) Rooms at this pink concrete monstrosity are rather timeworn but nonetheless a good deal. Grab a room on the top floor for its sweeping public balcony (alas, with no furniture).

★ Green Palace Hotel — BOUTIQUE HOTEL $$

(☏ 064-210757; Koh Ker St; s/d/ste incl breakfast US$47/54/67; ❄ ☎) This classy new spot raises the bar in Preah Vihear City with its glistening marble columns and crystal chandeliers in the lobby, contemporary furnishings in the oversized suites and silky bathrobes in the closets. A 7th-floor sky bar was under construction at the time of research, with pastoral and mountain views for miles. There's also a good breakfast-buffet restaurant.

✗ Eating

Phnom Tbaeng Restaurant — CAMBODIAN $

(Mlou Prey St; mains 12,000-20,000r; ⊙ 6am-10pm) This open-air restaurant is one of the few places in town with an English menu. Dishes include prawn soup, *tom yam* (a hot-and-sour Thai soup), noodle soups and steamed fish – as well as more-adventurous options such as fried eel and pig's intestines.

Psar Kompong Pranak — MARKET $

(Koh Ker St; mains 2000-4000r) The northern side of Psar Kompong Pranak is home to plenty of food stalls hawking Khmer-style baguettes, grilled chicken and simple rice and noodle dishes.

🛍 Shopping

Weaves of Cambodia — ARTS & CRAFTS

(☏ 092 346415; www.weavescambodia.com; St A22; ⊙ 7-11am & 1-5pm Mon-Fri, to 11am Sat) Originally established by the Vietnam Veterans of America Foundation, Weaves of Cambodia, known locally as Chum Ka Mo, is a silk-weaving centre that provides work and rehabilitation for landmine and polio victims, widows and orphans. Handloomed silk scarves (US$30 to US$40) and sarongs (US$70) cost half what you'll pay in Phnom Penh.

It is now part of the silk empire of Vientiane-based American textile designer Carol Cassidy.

ⓘ Information

Canadia Bank (☏ 023 868222; ⊙ 8am-3.30pm Mon-Fri, to 11.30am Sat, ATM 24hr)

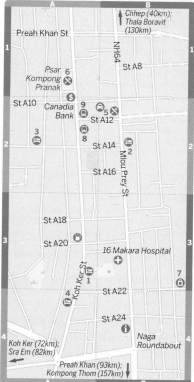

Tourist Office (☏ 088 885 9366, 097 997 9698; Mlou Prey St; ⊙ 7.30-11am & 2-5pm Mon-Fri) The with-it, English-speaking Mr Thin is the man in charge here. He and his colleague Mr Heng, an expert on temples, can guide you to Preah Khan and a few lesser-known temples in the province.

ℹ Getting There & Away

Preah Vihear City is 133km north of Kompong Thom, 82km south of Sra Em, 72km east of Koh Ker and 185km northeast of Siem Reap. These roads are all in good shape.

GST Transport (☑ 088 800 8002; Koh Ker St), **TSS Transport Co** (☑ 088 252 5264; Koh Ker St) and several more companies have 7am buses to Phnom Penh (US$5, seven hours). Both also offer later services. All buses travel via Kompong Thom (15,000r, two hours). For Siem Reap, transfer in Kompong Thom.

Asia Van Transfer (p124) has daily express minivan that passes through Preah Vihear City on its way to Stung Treng, Don Det (Laos), Ban Lung and Kratie.

Share taxis leave from the **taxi station** (St A10) and go to Kompong Thom (20,000r, 1½ hours), Siem Reap (25,000r, 2½ hours), Sra Em (20,000r, one hour), Stung Treng (20,000r, one hour) and Choam Ksant (20,000r, two hours).

Private taxis can be hired at the taxi station to Siem Reap (US$70), Prasat Preah Vihear (one-way/return US$60/80), and Preah Khan (US$80 return).

Prasat Preah Vihear

Cambodia's most dramatically situated Angkorian monument, this 800m-long **temple** (ប្រាសាទព្រះវិហារ; adult/child US$10/free; ⏱ tickets 7.30am-4.30pm, temple to 5.30pm) is perched atop an escarpment in the Dangrek Mountains (elevation 625m) – with breathtaking views of lowland Cambodia, 550m below, stretching as far as the eye can see. In July 2008, Prasat Preah Vihear was declared Cambodia's second Unesco World Heritage Site (after the Angkor Archaeological Complex in Siem Reap).

Cambodia and Thailand have been sparring over ownership of Prasat Preah Vihear for centuries, with tensions flaring up most recently from 2008 to 2011. There is still a large military presence in and around the temple – ostensibly for security, though it might make some visitors uncomfortable, and money or cigarettes are occasionally requested by soldiers. Always check the latest security situation when in Siem Reap or Phnom Penh, before making the long overland journey here.

The temple is laid out along a north–south processional axis with five cruciform *gopura* (entrance pavilions), decorated with exqui-

site carvings, separated by esplanades up to 275m long. From the parking area, walk up the hill to toppled and crumbling Gopura V at the north end of the temple complex. From here, the grey-sandstone Monumental Stairway leads down to the Thai border.

Walking south up the slope from Gopura V, the next pavilion you get to is Gopura IV. On the pediment above the southern door, look for an early rendition of the Churning of the Ocean of Milk, a theme later depicted awesomely at Angkor Wat. Keep climbing through Gopura III and II until finally you reach Gopura I. Here the galleries, with their inward-looking windows, are in a remark-

Prasat Preah Vihear

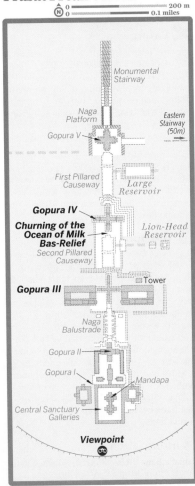

ably good state of repair, but the Central Sanctuary is just a pile of rubble. Outside, the cliff affords stupendous views of Cambodia's northern plains, with the holy mountain of Phnom Kulen (487m) looming in the distance. This is a fantastic spot for a picnic.

History
An important place of pilgrimage for millennia, the temple was built by a succession of seven Khmer monarchs, beginning with Yasovarman I (r 889–910) and ending with Suryavarman II (r 1112–1152). Like other temple-mountains from this period, it was designed to represent Mt Meru and was dedicated to the Hindu deity Shiva.

For generations, Prasat Preah Vihear (called Khao Phra Wiharn by the Thais) has been a source of tension between Cambodia and Thailand. This area was ruled by Thailand for several centuries, but returned to Cambodia during the French protectorate, under the treaty of 1907. In 1959 the Thai military seized the temple from Cambodia; then–Prime Minister Sihanouk took the dispute to the International Court of Justice in the Hague, gaining worldwide recognition of Cambodian sovereignty in a 1962 ruling.

The next time Prasat Preah Vihear made international news was in 1979, when the Thai military pushed more than 40,000 Cambodian refugees across the border in one of the worst cases of forced repatriation in UN history. The area was mined and many – perhaps several hundred – refugees died from injuries, starvation and disease before the occupying Vietnamese army could cut a safe passage and escort them on the long walk south to Kompong Thom.

Prasat Preah Vihear hit the headlines again in May 1998, when the Khmer Rouge regrouped here after the fall of Anlong Veng and staged a last stand that soon turned into a final surrender. The temple was heavily landmined during these final battles and de-mining was ongoing up until the outbreak of the conflict with Thailand in 2008. Re-mining seems to be the greater threat right now, with both sides accusing the other of using landmines.

When Prasat Preah Vihear was declared a Unesco World Heritage Site in 2008, the Thai government, which claims 4.6 sq km of territory right around the temple (some Thai nationalists even claim the temple itself), initially supported the Unesco nomination. However, the temple soon became a pawn in Thailand's chaotic domestic politics. Within a week, Thai troops crossed into Cambodian territory, sparking an armed confrontation that has taken the lives of several dozen soldiers and some civilians on both sides. The Cambodian market at the bottom of the Monumental Stairway,

---

ℹ ACCESSING PRASAT PREAH VIHEAR

➡ Driving in from Sra Em, your first stop is the **information centre** (⊙7am-4.30pm) in the village of Kor Muy (23km north from Sra Em). This is where you pay for entry, secure an English-speaking guide if you want one (US$15), and arrange transport via *moto* (US$5 return) or 4WD (US$25 return, maximum six passengers) up the 6.5km temple access road.

➡ Bring your passport with you when visiting Prasat Preah Vihear. You may be asked for your passport number when buying your ticket.

➡ The first 5km of the access road are gradual enough, but the final 1.5km is extremely steep. Nervous passengers might consider walking this last bit, especially if it's wet, but be sure to don appropriate footwear for slippery conditions. Private vehicles are allowed up this road, but you'll need a motorbike or 4WD. Parking a motorbike/car at the bottom costs 2000/3000r and at the top costs 2000/5000r.

➡ Another option is to walk up the Eastern Staircase – look for signs to the 'Ancient Staircase' on the road from Sra Em before you get to the information centre in Kor Muy. It's around 2000 steps.

➡ It used to be possible to get to Prasat Preah Vihear from Thailand, where paved roads from Kantharalak led almost up to the Monumental Stairway. However, due to the long stand-off between Thailand and Cambodia, access from the Thai side has been forbidden since mid-2008. Of course, that could change, so check the situation on the ground.

TMATBOEY: ON THE TRAIL OF THE GIANT IBIS

Cambodia's remote northern plains, the largest remaining block of deciduous diptero-carp forest, seasonal wetlands and grasslands in Southeast Asia, have been described as Southeast Asia's answer to Africa's savannahs. Covering much of northwestern Preah Vihear Province, they are one of the last places on earth where you can see Cambodia's national bird, the critically endangered **giant ibis**.

Other rare species that can be spotted here include the woolly-necked stork, white-rumped falcon, green peafowl, Alexandrine parakeet, grey-headed fish eagle and no fewer than 16 species of woodpecker, as well as owls and raptors. Birds are easiest to see from January to April.

In a last-ditch effort to ensure the survival of the giant ibis, protect the only confirmed breeding sites of the **white-shouldered ibis** and save the habitat of other globally endangered species, including the sarus crane and the greater adjutant, the **Wildlife Conservation Society** (www.wcs.org) set up a pioneering community-ecotourism project here.

Situated in the isolated village of Tmatboey inside the **Kulen Promtep Wildlife Sanctuary** (តំបន់អភិរក្សត្វលៃនព្រៃហូរទេព; www.samveasna.org) ✐, the initiative provides local villagers with education, income and a concrete incentive to do everything possible to protect the ibis. All visitors make a donation to the village conservation fund to help with maintenance and improvements to the project.

Tmatboey village lies about 5km off the smooth highway that links Preah Vihear City and Sra Em. The turnoff is 46km southeast of Sra Em and 39km northwest of Preah Vihear. The village is accessible year-round. To arrange a four-day, three-night visit contact the Siem Reap–based Sam Veasna Center (p361). Visitors sleep in wooden bungalows with bathrooms and solar hot water.

For those wanting to explore an even more remote corner of Cambodia, the Kulen Promtep Wildlife Sanctuary's newest birding site is based at the tiny outpost village of **Prey Veng** – about 60km from Tmatboey (as the giant ibis flies). Here the WCS and SVC aim to replicate the success of Tmatboey to ensure conservation of this habitat. Over 150 bird species have been spotted here, including the giant ibis, greater adjutant and white-winged duck.

As well as birding, Prey Veng offers great opportunities for **hiking** through the open dry forest to a hilltop Angkorian temple. Prey Veng's community-managed guesthouses provide simple accommodation.

Trips to both Tmatboey and Prey Veng can include visits to Beng Mealea, Koh Ker and Prasat Preah Vihear en route and are often combined with visits to Veal Krous Vulture Feeding Station (p265). Contact SVC for tour pricing details.

which used to be home to some guesthouses, burned down during an exchange of fire in April 2009. In 2011, exchanges heated up once more and long-range shells were fired into civilian territory by both sides.

In July 2011, the International Court of Justice ruled that both sides should withdraw troops from the area to establish a demilitarised zone. Then in November 2013, the ICJ confirmed its 1959 ruling that the temple belongs to Cambodia, although it declined to define the official borderline, leaving sovereignty of some lands around the temple open to dispute. The border dispute has died down in recent years and all was peaceful during the last research period, but tensions could reignite any time.

🛏 Sleeping & Eating

All accommodation in the area is in Sra Em, the bustling junction town 30km south of the temple. There's plenty of basic budget accommodation about 1km west of the centre along the highway to Anlong Veng.

There are basic eateries near the entrance to the temple, just off the parking area. They serve authentic Khmer food and a few have English menus. Choice is limited in Sra Em, though there are local eateries and BBQ shacks off the main roundabout.

Sok San Guesthouse GUESTHOUSE **$**
(✆ 097 715 3839; s/d with fan US$8/10, with air-con from US$13/15; ❄ 🛜) Sok San has a variety of dimly lit rooms and a restaurant with decent Thai and Cambodian food. Cheaper rooms

are small and windowless. Air-con options come with mismatched furniture and windows (which look out onto the corridor). It's 1km west of Sra Em centre.

★ Preah Vihear
Boutique Hotel   BOUTIQUE HOTEL $$$
(✆ 088 346 0501; www.preahvihearhotels.com; Oknha Franna St, Sra Em; r incl breakfast US$35-100; ❄ ⓪ ⓪) A slick boutique hotel in the unlikely setting of Sra Em, the PVBH is looking to coax higher-end temple goers from Siem Reap to stay a night. With lush bedding and a shimmering 20m outdoor pool to cool off in, it has a pretty good case. It's about 1km out of town on the road to Prasat Preah Vihear.

The simple but air-conditioned US$35 rooms off the parking lot are ostensibly for drivers and tour guides, but work just fine for flashpackers who don't want to pay full whack for their boutique experience.

★ Apsara Restaurant   CAMBODIAN $$
(✆ 088 346 0501; www.preahvihearhotels.com; Oknha Franna St, Sra Em; mains US$5-7; ⊙ 6.30am-10pm; ⓪) Up a grand staircase at Preah Vihear Boutique Hotel, this atmospheric, open-air restaurant offers striking views of surrounding greenery and the hotel pool, along with tasty Khmer cuisine. The *amok* (baked) chicken and fish dishes, which arrive in a bath of coconut curry, are sensational.

❶ Information

Acleda Bank (⊙ 7.30am-3.30pm Mon-Fri, to 11.30am Sat, ATM 24hr)

❶ Getting There & Away

Do not confuse Prasat Preah Vihear with Preah Vihear City (Tbeng Meanchey), which lies some 110km southeast. Most buses advertising trips to 'Preah Vihear' are headed to the city, not the temple. Prasat Preah Vihear is near Sra Em, which is 80km from Anlong Veng and 200km from Siem Reap along good paved roads.

With a private car you can get to Prasat Preah Vihear in about 2½ hours from Siem Reap. The day tour usually takes in Koh Ker and/or Beng Mealea and/or Banteay Srei en route and costs US$100 to US$150.

It makes much more sense to break up the long trip with a night in Sra Em, which is 23km from Kor Muy, where the temple information office is, and 30km from the temple proper. From Sra Em's central roundabout, take a *moto* to Kor Muy (US$10 to US$15 return – your driver will wait for you), from where an official park-supplied *moto* will take you up to the temple

(US$5 return). There is no public transport from Sra Em to Kor Muy.

From the roundabout in Sra Em, share taxis go to Siem Reap (US$10, 2½ hours), Phnom Penh (US$12.50, six hours), Preah Vihear City (US$5, one hour) and Anlong Veng (US$5, one hour). Departures to all destinations besides Siem Reap are in the morning only.

Liang US Express runs a 7.30am bus from the Sra Em roundabout to Phnom Penh (US$7.50, 10 hours) via Preah Vihear City and Kompong Thom. **Rith Mony** (✆ 092 511811) also has a 7.30am bus to Phnom Penh (US$10, 10 hours).

Preah Khan of Kompong Svay (Prasat Bakan)

For tantalising lost-world ambience, this remote **temple complex** (ប្រាសាទព្រះខាន់; US$5) about 90km south of Preah Vihear City can't be beaten. Covering almost 5 sq km, Preah Khan of Kompong Svay (not to be confused with the similarly gargantuan Preah Khan temple at Angkor) is the largest temple enclosure constructed during the Angkorian period – quite a feat when you consider the competition. Wrapped by vines and trees, and thanks to its back-of-beyond location, the site is astonishingly peaceful and you'll very likely be the only visitor.

> **OFF THE BEATEN TRACK**
>
> ### VEAL KROUS VULTURE FEEDING STATION
>
> In order to save three critically endangered species – the white-rumped, slender-billed and red-headed vultures – the Wildlife Conservation Society (www.wcs.org) set up the **Veal Krous Vulture Feeding Station** (ស្ថានីយ៍ដាក់ចំណីក្អែក វាលក្រូស) – a 'vulture restaurant' in the village of Dongphlet, northeast of Chhep on the edge of the Preah Vihear Protected Forest. A cow carcass is put out in a field, and visitors waiting in a nearby bird hide watch as these incredibly rare vultures move in to devour the carrion.
>
> Visits are offered by Siem Reap–based Sam Veasna Center (p361).
>
> Trips here involve an overnight at a WCS forest safari camp. Access to the site is year-round, but try to give SVC at least a week's notice to assure your spot.

Traditionally, Preah Khan has been the toughest of Preah Vihear Province's remote temples to reach, but upgraded provincial highways and a new dirt road to the temple have improved things dramatically. Locals say there are no landmines in the vicinity of Preah Khan, but stick to the marked paths just to be on the safe side.

Preah Khan's history is shrouded in mystery, but it was long an important religious site, and some structures here date back to the 9th century. Both Suryavarman II, builder of Angkor Wat, and Jayavarman VII lived here at various times during their lives, suggesting Preah Khan was something of a second city in the Angkorian empire. Originally dedicated to Hindu deities, Preah Khan was reconsecrated to Mahayana Buddhist worship during a monumental reconstruction in the late 12th and early 13th centuries.

As recently as the mid-1990s, the main temple was thought to be in reasonable shape, but at some point in the second half of the decade, looters arrived seeking buried statues under each *prang* (temple tower). Assaulted with pneumatic drills and mechanical diggers, the ancient temple never stood a chance – many of the towers simply collapsed in on themselves, leaving the mess we see today. Once again, a temple that had survived so much couldn't stand the onslaught of the 20th century and its all-consuming appetite.

Among the many carvings found at Preah Khan – or recovered from looters – was the bust of Jayavarman, now in Phnom Penh's National Museum and widely copied as a souvenir for tourists. The body of the statue was discovered in the 1990s by locals who alerted authorities, making it possible for a joyous reunion of head and body in 2000.

Most locals refer to Preah Khan of Kompong Svay as Prasat Bakan; scholars officially refer to it as Bakan Svay Rolay, combining the local name for the temple and the district name.

◎ Sights

Preah Khan includes the main temple as well as several satellite temples, most notably Prasat Damrei, Prasat Preah Thkol and Prasat Preah Stung. You'll pass these on the way to the main temple. From Prasat Preah Stung at the western end of Preah Khan's *baray*, an access road leads to the magnificently well-preserved eastern *gopura* of the main temple. The US$5 entry fee gains you admission to all temples.

★ **Preah Khan Main Temple** BUDDHIST TEMPLE
(ប្រាសាទព្រះខាន់, Prasat Bakan) The main temple is surrounded by a (now dry) moat similar to the one around Angkor Thom. Once through the grand gateway, the trail meanders past a *dharmasala* (pilgrim's rest house) and through another crumbling pavilion to the central temple area of half-toppled *prang* (temple towers), entangled with trees and overgrown by forest.

Despite all the damage by looters in the 1990s and and more recent problems with theft, this crumbling temple, half lost to the jungle, is a remarkable site with some well-preserved bas-reliefs.

Prasat Preah Stung BUDDHIST TEMPLE
(ប្រាសាទព្រះស្ទឹង, Prasat Muk Buon) About 2km west of Preah Khan's *baray* stands Prasat Preah Stung (known to locals as Prasat Muk Buon or Temple of the Four Faces). It's particularly memorable because its central tower (held up by bamboo scaffolding) is adorned with four enigmatic, Bayon-style faces of Avalokiteshvara.

Prasat Preah Thkol BUDDHIST TEMPLE
(ប្រាសាទព្រះថ្កោល) On the western shore of Preah Khan's *baray* is Prasat Preah Thkol (known as Mebon), an island temple similar in style to the Western Mebon at Angkor.

Prasat Damrei BUDDHIST TEMPLE
(ប្រាសាទដំរី) Prasat Damrei (Elephant Temple) lies at the eastern end of a 3km-long *baray* and is the first temple on the Preah Khan access road. On the summit of this small pyramid temple, two of the original exquisitely carved elephants can still be seen; two others are at Phnom Penh's National Museum (p43) and the Musée Guimet in Paris.

🛏 Sleeping & Eating

For a fantastic, ecologically responsible lodging option in the area, head for BeTreed Adventures (p269) and its delicious vegetarian meals. There are also a couple of guesthouses in surrounding towns, but nothing fancy. There are no eating options around Preah Khan so bring your own food – this is a great picnic spot.

ℹ️ Information

The nearest banks are in Preah Vihear City or Kompong Thom.

ℹ️ Getting There & Away

Upgraded provincial highways and a new dirt road to the temple mean that you can now visit Preah Khan year-round, although it's still easiest in the dry season. There's no public transport, so you'll need to drive yourself or hire a *moto* or a taxi in Preah Vihear City or Kompong Thom, or in Siem Reap for an extra-long day trip.

To get there on your own, turn west off smooth NH62 in Svay Pak, about 60km south of Preah Vihear City and 75km north of Kompong Thom. From here an all-season dirt road (substantially pitted with potholes) takes you to Ta Seng, about 30km from the highway and just 4km from the temple. These last 4km are in good shape.

Coming from Siem Reap there are other options for hardcore trail bikers. The most straightforward route is to take NH6 to Stoeng and then head north. You can also take NH6 to Kompong Kdei, head north to Khvau and then ride east on a difficult stretch of NH66 (see below).

An amazing alternative is to approach from Beng Mealea along the ancient Angkor road (Cambodia's own Route 66 – NH66). You'll cross about 10 splendid Angkorian *naga* (mythical serpent-like being) bridges, including the remarkable 77m-long Spean Ta Ong, 7km west of Khvau. The road from Beng Mealea to Khvau is now in fine condition. However, it deteriorates rapidly after Khvau. The 23km from Khvau to Ta Seng are impassable in the rainy season.

Only experienced bikers should attempt these alternative routes on rental motorbikes, as conditions range from difficult to extremely tough from every side – and you could end up lost.

KOMPONG THOM PROVINCE

For those not wanting to rush between Phnom Penh and Siem Reap, Kompong Thom Province (ខេត្តកំពង់ធំ) makes a rewarding stopover, thanks to several intriguing sights spread across the countryside surrounding provincial capital Kompong Thom.

The most impressive sight is Sambor Prei Kuk, a collection of ancient, octagonal forest temples that were originally part of Isanapura, the capital of the Chenla Empire that flourished in the late 6th and 7th centuries. In 2017, the temples became Cambodia's third Unesco World Heritage Site.

Kompong Thom

📞 062 / POP 68,000

The friendly, bustling town of Kompong Thom (កំពង់ធំ) rims the NH6 with the lazy curves of the Stung Sen River winding through the centre. The town may be sparse on attractions, but it's a prime launching pad for exploring nearby sights. Both the serene, tree-entwined temples of Sambor Prei Kuk, named a Unesco World Heritage Site in 2017, and the colourful wats of Phnom Santuk are easy half-day trips, while boutique accommodation and decent eating options make Kompong Thom an excellent base for a long day trip to Preah Khan of Kompong Svay.

⊙ Sights & Activities

Sambor Village Hotel offers a variety of river cruises, including a sunset cruise and a longer journey to the boat pagodas of Trey Leak village.

Kompong Thom Museum MUSEUM
(NH6; ⊙8am-5pm) FREE This seriously bijou museum (it's one room and a small outdoor gallery) actually packs a pretty good punch with statuary and stelae from local sites, including a fine selection of beautiful pieces from Sambor Prei Kuk. It's well worth a look on your way back from the site itself.

French Governor's Residence HISTORIC BUILDING
(Stung Sen St) About 500m west of Kompong Thom bridge is the dilapidated old French governor's residence (no entry), chiefly interesting as being next to three old mahogany trees that hold an extraordinary sight: hundreds of large bats (in Khmer, *chreoun*), with 40cm wingspans. They spend their days suspended upside-down like winged fruit, fanning themselves with their wings to keep cool. Head here around dusk (from about 5.30pm or 6pm) to see them fly off in search of food.

Im Sokhom Travel Agency HISTORY
(📞012 691527; St 3) Runs guided tours, including cycling trips to Sambor Prei Kuk, and can arrange transport by *moto* to Sambor Prei Kuk (US$10) or Phnom Santuk and Santuk Silk Farm (US$8).

🛏️ Sleeping

Vimean Sovann Guesthouse HOTEL $
(📞078 220333; St 7; s/d with fan US$6/7, with air-con US$12/14; ❄️🛜) It may not look like much from the outside, but hiding inside

Kompong Thom

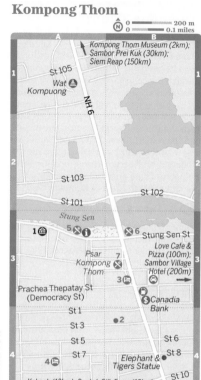

Kompong Thom Museum (2km);
Sambor Prei Kuk (30km);
Siem Reap (150km)

ble rooms (with two beds), which come with private balcony.

Arunras Hotel
HOTEL $

(☎062-961294; NH6; s/d with fan US$5/8, d with air-con US$15; ❄⊗) Dominating Kompong Thom's accommodation scene, this central establishment has 58 good-value rooms with Chinese-style decoration and on-the-ball staff. The popular restaurant downstairs dishes up tasty Khmer fare. They also operate the 53-room **Arunras Guesthouse** (☎012 865935; NH6; s/d with fan US$6/8, with air-con US$10/13; ❄⊗) next door.

Extra bonus for the lazy traveller: buses through town stop literally right outside the door.

★ Sambor Village Hotel
BOUTIQUE HOTEL $$

(☎062-961391; www.samborvillage.asia; Prachea Thepatay St; r/ste incl breakfast US$50/60; ❄@⊗⊠) This French-owned place brings boutique to Kompong Thom. Spacious, bungalow-style rooms with four-poster beds and chic bathrooms are set amid a tranquil and verdant garden with an inviting pool under the shade of a mango tree. The upstairs terrace restaurant has international cuisine and impressive hardwood flooring. Free use of mountain bikes. Located riverside, about 700m east of NH6.

Glorious Hotel & Spa
BUSINESS HOTEL $$

(☎062-210366; www.glorioushotel.asia; NR6; r US$30-45; ❄⊗⊠) This chic new business hotel just a few kilometres south of Kompong Thom is the perfect place to clean the grit out of your nails and get a massage after a dusty *moto* journey to nearby attractions. There's an enormous pool, relaxing spa and sparkling rooms, and staff members are warm and professional. The restaurant serves tasty Khmer and international cuisine.

✗ Eating

Dana Café
CAFE $

(☎011 920972; Stung Sen St; mains US$2.50-4.50; ⊗7am-8pm; ⊗) Dana serves really good cold coffee, Italian sodas and heaping Asian fried-rice breakfast plates. It also houses Kompong Thom's 'tourist information centre', which is a shelf of helpful brochures.

Psar Kompong Thom
CAMBODIAN $

(NH6; mains 2000-4000r; ⊗4pm-2am) Sit on a plastic chair at a neon-lit table outside Kompong Thom's main market and dig into chicken rice soup, chicken curry noodles and Khmer-style baguettes.

are the smartest budget rooms in town, all with fresh paint, modern bathroom fixtures and cute wall art. Opt for the spacious dou-

A NIGHT IN THE TREES

If the long, bumpy journey to remote Preah Khan seems tame, consider booking the treehouse at the even-more-secluded **BeTreed Adventures** (☑ 078 960420, 012 765136; http://betreed.com; Phnom Tnout, Ta Bos Village; bungalows US$60, treehouse US$40; ☎) ☞. Started in 2015 by a couple of conservation-minded expats, this place is Cambodia at its wildest – the driveway alone takes guests through four different forest ecosystems. In the rainy season, be ready to ditch the car, wade through belly-button-high water and jump on a *moto*.

Well constructed from reclaimed wood and powered with solar panels, the digs include two comfy bungalows on stilts and a 10m-high treehouse. The 7000-hectare property also includes a zipline attraction that whisks guests over a massive ravine with stunning forest and mountain views, in addition to hikes for days, one with a stop at an ancient temple.

While adventure may be in abundance here, it isn't actually the point. The proprietors Ben and Sharyn, along with their two young daughters, have made this their home in an effort to preserve the area's natural splendour, and all the long-tailed macaques, pileated gibbons, slow lorises and other wildlife that come with it. Ben's eight camera traps have recorded species including Asiatic wild dogs, sambar deer and banteng (endangered wild cattle), though all too often the animals are limping due to injuries from snare traps. Cambodia's environment minister recently visited and agreed that the property should become a wildlife preserve, which would help stop loggers and poachers from destroying it.

Sharyn's mostly vegetarian cooking (US$15 per day) alone is worth the trip. It's US$10 for a guide, and there's also a US$15-per-person fee for community development and preservation. Be sure to book as early as possible and call for detailed directions. Note that the trails out here are easily flooded during the wet season, making access challenging.

★ **Kompong Thom**
Restaurant   CAMBODIAN **$$**
(NH6; mains US$3-8; ⊙7am-10pm; ☎☑) With delightful waiters and a pocket-sized terrace overlooking the river, this restaurant is also Kompong Thom's most adventurous. Unique concoctions featuring Kampot pepper, water buffalo and stir-fried eel feature on the menu of Khmer classics, which come in generous portions.

Love Cafe & Pizza   INTERNATIONAL **$$**
(☑017 916219; Democrat St; mains US$2.50-8.75; ⊙2pm-9pm Mon-Sat; ☎) If you're in the mood for comfort food, this bamboo-walled place is a real gem. The big menu of pizzas and burgers is a winner, as is its fantastic selection of ice cream. The restaurant recently moved to this location and added Khmer dishes.

❶ Information

Canadia Bank (NH6; ⊙8am-3.30pm Mon-Fri, to 11.30am Sat, ATM 24hr)
Tourist Information Office (☑011 920972; Stung Sen St; ⊙7am-8pm) Within Dana Café, this is basically a shelf with some helpful tourist brochures and a pamphlet on Kompong Thom sights.

❶ Getting There & Away

Kompong Thom is 165km north of Phnom Penh, 147km southeast of Siem Reap and 157km south of Preah Vihear City.

Dozens of buses travelling between Phnom Penh (US$5, 3½ hours) and Siem Reap (US$5, 2½ hours) pass through Kompong Thom. They drop off passengers right in front of the Arunras Hotel (p268), which is also where you flag down a bus when you're leaving town.

Share taxis are the fastest way to Phnom Penh (25,000r, three hours) and Siem Reap (25,000r, 2½ hours). Heading north to Preah Vihear City, share taxis cost US$5 and take two hours. Most taxi services depart from the taxi park, one block east of the Tela Gas Station on NH6; taxis to Phnom Penh depart from the Tela Gas Station.

❶ Getting Around

Im Sokhom Travel Agency (p267) rents out bicycles (US$1 per day) and motorbikes (US$5 per day).

Around Kompong Thom

Sambor Prei Kuk

Cambodia's most impressive group of pre-Angkorian monuments, **Sambor Prei Kuk** (សំបូរប្រៃគុក; www.samborpreikuk.com;

US$10; ⏱6am-6pm) encompasses more than 100 mainly brick temples huddled in the forest, among them some of the oldest structures in the country. To the delight of Cambodians, the attraction recently became the country's third Unesco World Heritage Site.

Originally called Isanapura, the site served as the capital of Upper Chenla during the reign of the early 7th-century King Isanavarman, and was an important learning centre during the Angkorian era. In the early 1970s, Sambor Prei Kuk was bombed by US aircraft in support of the Lon Nol government's doomed fight against the Khmer Rouge. Some of the craters, ominously close to the temples, can still be seen. The area's last landmines were cleared in 2008.

An easy 40-minute drive from Kompong Thom, the area has a serene and soothing atmosphere, with the sandy trails between temples looping through shady forest.

◎ Sights

The main temple area consists of three complexes, each enclosed by the remains of two concentric walls. Their basic layout – a central tower surrounded by shrines, ponds and gates – may have served as an inspiration for the architects of Angkor five centuries later. Many of the original statues are now in the National Museum (p43) in Phnom Penh.

It's well worth hiring a guide through community-based tourism organisation Isanborei (p270) to show you around (half-/full-day US$6/10). Guides are usually found

KAKAOH CARVING VILLAGE

The village of Kakaoh straddles the NH6 about 13km south of Kompong Thom and 2km north of the Phnom Santuk entrance. It is famous for its stonemasons, who fashion giant Buddha statues, decorative lions and other traditional Khmer figures with hand tools and a practised eye. It's fascinating to watch the figures, which range in height from 15cm to over 5m, slowly emerge from slabs of stone. Statues range wildly in price – from US$20 for a statuette to US$3500 (not including excess baggage charges) for a 2.5m-high Buddha carved from a single block of the highest-quality stone. The statues are often donated to wats by wealthy Khmers.

hanging around the old entrance near Prasat Sambor.

Prasat Yeai Poeun   HINDU TEMPLE

(ប្រាសាទយាយពើន, Prasat Yeay Peau) Prasat Yeai Poeun is arguably the most atmospheric of Sambor Prei Kuk's three temple groups, as it feels lost in the forest. The eastern gateway is being both held up and torn asunder by an ancient tree, the bricks interwoven with the tree's extensive, probing roots. A truly massive tree shades the western gate.

Prasat Sambor   HINDU TEMPLE

(ប្រាសាទសំបូរ) The principal temple group, Prasat Sambor (7th and 10th centuries) is dedicated to Gambhireshvara, one of Shiva's many incarnations (the other groups are dedicated to Shiva himself). Several of Prasat Sambor's towers retain brick carvings in fairly good condition, and there is a series of large *yoni* (female fertility symbols) around the central tower.

Prasat Tor   HINDU TEMPLE

(ប្រាសាទតោ, Lion Temple) The largest of the Sambor Prei Kuk temple complexes, Prasat Tor boasts excellent examples of Chenla carving in the form of two large, elaborately coiffed stone lions. It also has a fine, rectangular pond, Srah Neang Pov.

🏃 Activities

Isanborei   COOKING

(📱017 936112; www.samborpreikuk.com) 📶 This organisation works hard to encourage visitors to Sambor Prei Kuk to stay another day. Besides running a community-based homestay program (dorm/double US$4/6), Isanborei offers cooking courses, rents out bicycles (US$2 per day) and organises oxcart rides.

🛏 Sleeping & Eating

Isanborei runs a great homestay program to encourage visitors to Sambor Prei Kuk to stay another day.

You'll find plenty of restaurants (mains US$2 to US$4) serving local fare around the handicrafts market near the temple entrance.

🔒 Shopping

By the ticket office near the bridge, about 500m from the main ruins, is a giant handicrafts market with *kramas* (checked scarves), baskets and other products made by local villagers.

ℹ Information

Isanborei is a good source of information on the area.

ℹ Getting There & Away

To get here from Kompong Thom, follow NH6 north for 5km before continuing straight on NH62 towards Preah Vihear (the paved road to Siem Reap veers left). After 11km turn right at the laterite sign, and continue for 14km on a new sealed road to the new temple entrance and parking area, which is about 500m from the Prasat Sambor temple group.

Isanborei operates a stable of *remorks* to whisk you safely to/from Kompong Thom (US$15 one way). Call for a pick-up if you're in Kompong Thom. Otherwise, a round-trip *moto* ride out here from Kompong Thom (under an hour each way) should cost US$10.

Phnom Santuk

Its forest-surrounded summit adorned with Buddha images and a series of pagodas, the holy temple mountain (207m) of **Phnom Santuk** (ភ្នំ សន្តុក; US$2), 15km south of Kompong Thom, is a popular site of Buddhist pilgrimage. To reach the top, huff up 809 stairs – with the upper staircase home to troops of animated macaques – or wimp out and take the paved 2.5km road. Santuk hosts an extraordinary ensemble of colourful wats and stupas, a kaleidoscopic mishmash of old and new Buddhist statuary and monuments.

Near the main white-walled pagoda is pyramid-shaped **Prasat Tuch**, which features an intricately carved sandstone exterior. Just beneath the southern side of the summit, there are a number of **reclining Buddhas**; several are modern incarnations cast in cement, while others were carved into the living rock in centuries past. Phnom Santuk has an active wat and the local monks are always interested in receiving foreign tourists.

Boulders located just below the summit afford panoramic views south towards Tonlé Sap. For travellers spending the night in Kompong Thom, Phnom Santuk is a good place from which to catch a magnificent sunset over the rice fields, although this means descending in the dark (bring a torch).

To get here from Kompong Thom, turn left (east) off NH6 at the well-marked sign at about the 149km marker. It's around 2km from the highway to the base of the temple stairs. From Kompong Thom, a return trip by *moto* costs about US$8, and a *remork* about US$10.

Santuk Silk Farm

Santuk Silk Farm (កសិដ្ឋានសូត្រ សន្ទុក; ☑ 012 906604; ☉ 7am-5pm) **FREE** is one of the few places in Cambodia where you can see the entire process of silk production, starting with the seven-week life cycle of the silkworm. The farm employs 18 locals, mostly women, as artisan weavers; you can watch them weave scarves (US$20 to US$35) and other items.

The entrance is 200m north of the Phnom Santuk entrance, on the opposite (west) side of NH6.

Silkworms are delicate creatures that feed only on mulberry leaves and have to be protected from predators such as geckos, ants and mosquitoes. Although most of the raw silk used here comes from China and Vietnam, the local worms produce 'Khmer golden silk', so-called because of its lush golden hue.

The farm is run by Navin, the widow of an American Vietnam War veteran who once ran the place with her. If possible, call ahead before your visit so she can put the scarves out. Groups of five or more can pre-order an excellent home-cooked meal.

Bronze Lake

Popular with Khmer families, **Bronze Lake** (មេឃាយដ្ឋានបឹងសំរិទ្ធិ; ☑ 078 666308; adult/child 10,000/5000r; ☉ 9am-5pm) is a lakefront water park that feels a little run-down but is nevertheless interesting to visit, as much for the water slides and ziplines as to watch how locals behave on an authentically Cambodian weekend getaway. There's a sort of fancy restaurant on site, and some bungalows surrounding the lake that can be rented by the night.

Prasat Kuha Nokor

Prasat Kuha Nokor (ប្រាសាទកុហានគរ; US$2), an 11th-century temple constructed during the reign of Suryavarman I, is in extremely good condition thanks to a lengthy renovation before the civil war. It is on the grounds of a modern wat and is an easy-enough stop for those with their own transport. The temple is signposted from NH6 about 70km southeast of Kompong Thom and 22km north of Skuon; it's 2km from the main road. From NH6, you can get a *moto* to the temple.

Eastern Cambodia

POP 6.5 MILLION / AREA 68,472 SQ KM

Best Places to Eat & Drink

➡ Green Carrot (p293)

➡ Oromis Restaurant (p303)

➡ Smile Restaurant (p277)

➡ The Hangout (p303)

➡ Tokae Restaurant (p283)

Best Places to Stay

➡ Tree Top Ecolodge (p291)

➡ Terres Rouges Lodge (p292)

➡ Koh Trong Community Homestay I (p281)

➡ Mayura Hill Hotel & Resort (p302)

➡ Nature Lodge (p300)

Why Go?

Home to diverse landscapes and peoples, the 'Wild East' shatters the illusion that Cambodia is all paddy fields and sugar palms. There are plenty of those in the lowland provinces, but in the northeast they yield to the mountains of Mondulkiri and Ratanakiri Provinces, where ecotourism is playing a major role in the effort to save dwindling forests from the twin ravages of illegal logging and land concessions.

Rare forest elephants and vocal primates are found in the northeast, and endangered freshwater Irrawaddy dolphins can be seen year-round near Kratie and Stung Treng. Thundering waterfalls, crater lakes and meandering rivers characterise the landscape, and trekking, biking, kayaking, ziplining and ethical elephant interactions are all taking off. The rolling hills and lush forests also provide a home to many ethnic minority groups, known collectively as Khmer Leu (Upper Khmer) or *chunchiet* (ethnic minorities).

When to Go
Kratie

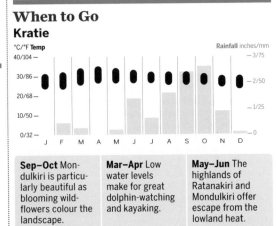

Sep–Oct Mondulkiri is particularly beautiful as blooming wildflowers colour the landscape.

Mar–Apr Low water levels make for great dolphin-watching and kayaking.

May–Jun The highlands of Ratanakiri and Mondulkiri offer escape from the lowland heat.

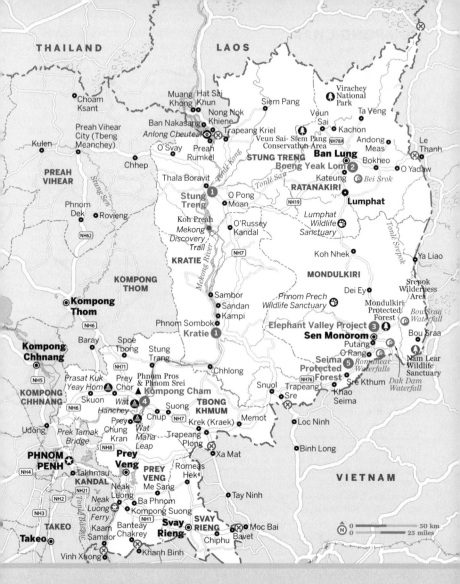

Eastern Cambodia Highlights

1 Irrawaddy dolphins
(p281) Kayaking with rare
freshwater Mekong Irrawaddy
dolphins near Kratie and
Stung Treng.

2 Boeng Yeak Lom (p288)
Diving into the crystal-clear
waters of this crater lake in
Ratanakiri.

3 Elephant Valley Project
(p297) Walking with elephants
in their element.

4 Kompong Cham (p274)
Soaking up the charms of
this relaxing city, gateway
to historic temples, lush
countryside and friendly
locals.

5 Seima Protected Forest
(p302) Spotting black-
shanked doucs and gibbons in
Mondulkiri's wildlife treasure
trove.

KOMPONG CHAM

🎵 042 / POP 125,000

Kompong Cham (កំពង់ចាម) is a peaceful provincial capital spread along the banks of the Mekong. It was an important trading post during the French period, the legacy of which is evident as you wander through the streets of crumbling yet classic buildings. Nearby attractions include several Angkorian temples, as well as some atmospheric riverbank rides for cyclists and motorbikers. The town offers an accessible slice of the real Cambodia: a land of picturesque villages, pretty wats and fishing communities.

Long considered Cambodia's third city after Phnom Penh and Battambang, Kompong Cham has lately been somewhat left in the dust by the fast-growing tourist towns of Siem Reap and Sihanoukville. However, Kompong Cham remains a travel hub and acts as the stepping stone to eastern Cambodia.

Kompong Cham used to be the most heavily populated province in Cambodia, but was divided in two, giving birth to Tbong Khmum Province.

⊙ Sights

There's still a fair-sized population of Cham Muslims in the area (hence the name 'Kompong Cham'). One Cham village is on the left (east) bank of the Mekong north of the French lighthouse; its big, silver-domed mosque is clearly visible from the right bank. Another one is south of the bridge just beyond **Wat Day Doh**, a Buddhist temple which is worth a detour if visiting Koh Paen via the bamboo bridge.

Wat Nokor Bachey, Phnom Pros and Phnom Srei have a combined entrance ticket: US$3 gets you into all three.

Wat Maha Leap   BUDDHIST TEMPLE

(វត្តមហាលាភ) Sacred Wat Maha Leap southeast of town is one of the last remaining wooden pagodas left in the country. More than a century old, this beautiful pagoda was only spared devastation by the Khmer Rouge because they converted it into a hospital. The wide black columns supporting the structure are complete tree trunks, resplendent in gilded patterns. The Khmer Rouge painted over the designs to match their austere philosophies, but monks later stripped it back to its original glory.

Many of the Khmers who were put to work in the surrounding fields perished here; 500 bodies were thrown into graves on site, now camouflaged by a tranquil garden.

The journey to Wat Maha Leap is best done by boat from Kompong Cham. Follow the Mekong downstream for a short distance before peeling off on a sublime tributary known as Small River, which affords awesome glimpses of rural Cambodian life. A guided trip on a 40HP outboard (US$50 round-trip, including stops in nearby weaving villages) gets there in less than an hour each way. Outboards can be found at the boat dock.

Small River is navigable only from July to December; at other times, travel overland. It's pretty difficult to find on your own without some knowledge of Khmer, as there are lots of small turns along the way, so hire a *moto* (motorcycle taxi; US$10 per return trip including a stop in Prey Chung Kran, one hour each way). It's 20km by river and almost twice that by road.

Wat Hanchey   BUDDHIST TEMPLE

(វត្តហាន់ជ័យ) Wat Hanchey is a hilltop pagoda 20km north of Kompong Cham that was an important centre of worship during the Chenla period when, as today, it offered some of the best Mekong views in Cambodia. The foundations of several 8th-century structures, some of them destroyed by American bombs, are scattered around the compound, along with a clutch of bizarre fruit and animal statues. The smooth trip out here takes about 30 minutes from Kompong Cham on a motorbike.

The highlight is a remarkable Chenla-era brick sanctuary with well-preserved inscriptions in ancient Sanskrit on the door frame. A hole in the roof lets in a lone shaft of light. The sanctuary sits in front of a large, contemporary wat. During the time of the Chenla empire, this may have been an important transit stop on journeys between the ancient cities of Thala Boravit (near Stung Treng to the north) and Angkor Borei (near Takeo to the south).

Cycling out here through the pretty riverbank villages is a good way to pass half a day.

Koh Paen   ISLAND

(កោះប៉ែន) For a supremely relaxing bicycle ride, it's hard to beat Koh Paen, a rural island in the Mekong River, connected to the southern reaches of Kompong Cham town by an elaborate **bamboo bridge** (foreigner US$1) in the dry season or a local ferry (with/without bicycle 1500/1000r) in the wet season.

Kompong Cham

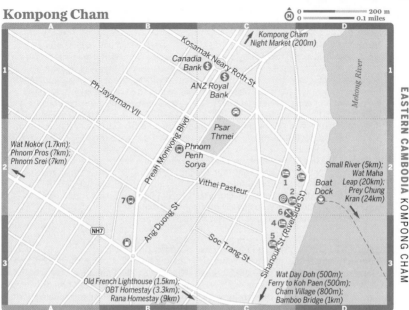

Kompong Cham

🛏 Sleeping
1 Daly Hotel	C2
2 LBN Asian Hotel	C2
3 Monorom 2 VIP Hotel	D2
4 Moon River Guesthouse	C3
5 Tmor Da Guesthouse	C3

✖ Eating
Destiny Coffee House	(see 6)
Lazy Mekong Daze	(see 5)
6 Mekong Crossing	C2
Smile Restaurant	(see 3)

ⓘ Transport
7 Liang US Express	B2

The bamboo bridge is an attraction in itself, built entirely by hand each year and looking from afar like it is made of matchsticks. However, its future is in doubt as a new concrete bridge has just opened to traffic.

The island offers a slice of rural local life, with fruit and vegetable farms and traditional wooden houses. During the dry season, several sandbars – the closest thing to a beach in this part of Cambodia – appear around the island.

Bicycles can be hired from some local guesthouses.

Wat Nokor Bachey   BUDDHIST TEMPLE

(វត្តនគរបាជ័យ; US$2) The original fusion temple, Wat Nokor is a modern Theravada Buddhist pagoda squeezed into the walls of a 12th-century Mahayana Buddhist shrine of sandstone and laterite. It's located down a pretty dirt road just off the highway to Phnom Penh, about 2.5km west of the centre.

It's a kitschy kind of place; many of the older building's archways have been incorporated into the new building as shrines for worship. On weekdays there are only a few monks in the complex and it's peaceful to wander among the alcoves and their hidden shrines. The entry price includes admission to Phnom Pros and Phnom Srei, both just outside town.

Old French Lighthouse   HISTORIC BUILDING

(ប៉មបាវាំងចាស់) Looming over the Mekong River opposite town is an old French lighthouse. For years it was an abandoned shell, but it's been renovated and features an incredibly steep and precarious staircase (more like a series of ladders). Don't attempt the climb if you're scared of heights. There are great views across the Mekong from the summit, especially at sunset.

Chup Rubber Plantation Factory   FACTORY

(រោងចក្រផលិតជ័រកៅស៊ូជប់; US$1) Kompong Cham was the heartland of the

WORTH A TRIP

PHNOM PROS & PHNOM SREI

Man Hill' and 'Woman Hill' are the subjects of local legends with many variations, one of which describes a child taken away at infancy only to return a powerful man who falls in love with his own mother. Disbelieving her protestations, he demands her hand in marriage. Desperate to avoid this disaster, the mother cunningly devises a deal: a competition between her team of women and his team of men to build the highest hill by dawn. If the women win, she won't have to marry him. As they toil into the night, the women build a huge fire, with flames reaching high into the sky. The men, mistaking this for sunrise, lay down their tools – and the impending marriage is foiled. Locals love to relay this tale, each adding their own details as the story unfolds. Admission to the hills is US$3 and includes entry to Wat Nokor Bac.

Phnom Srei has fine views of the countryside during the wet season and a very stroke-able statue of Nandin (a sacred bull that was Shiva's mount). Phnom Pros is a good place for a cold drink among the inquisitive monkeys that populate the shady trees. The area between the two hills was once a killing field; a small, gilded brick stupa on the right as you walk from Man Hill to Woman Hill houses a pile of skulls.

The hills are about 7km out of town on the road to Phnom Penh.

Cambodian rubber industry and plantations still stretch across the province. Some of the largest plantations can be visited. Using an extended scraping instrument, workers graze the trunks until the sap appears, which they let drip into the open coconut shells on the ground. At Chup Rubber Plantation, about 15km east of Kompong Cham, you can observe harvesting in action.

👁 Prey Chung Kran

Kompong Cham is famous for high-quality silk. The tiny village of Prey Chung Kran is set on the banks of the river and nearly every household has a weaving loom. Under the cool shade provided by their stilted homes, weavers work deftly to produce *krama* (checked scarves) that are fashionable and traditional. The most interesting thing to watch is the dyeing process, as the typical diamond-and-dot tessellations are formed at this stage. Prey Chung Kran is about 4km from Wat Maha Leap. There are additional weavers all along the road between Wat Maha Leap and Prey Chung Kran.

🏃 Activities

Aerobics takes place on the riverfront near the bridge at dusk if you want to get down with the locals.

Consider hiring an outboard at the **boat dock** opposite the Mekong Hotel and heading upstream for about 30 minutes to a clutch of idyllic Mekong islands where you'll encounter a slice of rustic rural life. It costs about US$40. Get the timing right and turn it into a sunset cruise.

Cheung Kok Village   ECOTOUR
Cheung Kok village, opposite the entrance to Phnom Pros, is home to a local ecotourism initiative, run by the NGO **Amica** (www.amica-web.org), aimed at introducing visitors to rural life in Kompong Cham. Villagers teach visitors about harvesting rice, sugar palm and other crops. There is also a small shop in the village selling local handicraft products.

🛌 Sleeping

Most visitors prefer to stay on the riverfront for a view over the Mekong, but keep in mind that there is an early morning soundtrack, including boat horns and the muezzin's call from the Cham mosque across the river.

⭐**Moon River Guesthouse**   GUESTHOUSE $
(☎ 016 788973; moonrivermekong@gmail.com; Sihanouk St; r with fan US$7-15, with air-con US$12-25; ❊ ⊚) The best of the riverfront guesthouses, Moon River is a great all-rounder with smart, spacious rooms, including some triples. Downstairs is a popular restaurant-bar (mains US$2 to US$4) that serves hearty breakfasts and draws a crowd by night.

Mekong Bamboo Hut Guesthouse   HOSTEL $
(☎ 015 905620; mekongbamboohut@gmail.com; Koh Paen; hammock US$3; ⊚) This French-run riverside guesthouse has the feel of a hippy commune and is a great place to get away from it all if the pace of life is too fast back on the mainland. Accommodation is very basic with hammocks strung across bamboo pavilions with mosquito nets, but it certainly has a chilled vibe. It has a little restaurant on site.

Tmor Da Guesthouse HOTEL $

(☎042-941951; Sihanouk St; r US$15-30; ❄ ☜) This smart new place is really more of a hotel than a guesthouse, offering stylish and tasteful rooms with a contemporary wood trim. Don't be put off by the low ceiling of the mezzanine lobby, as the rooms are really very spacious once you are inside.

Daly Hotel HOTEL $

(☎042-666 6631; www.dalyhotel.net; d/tw US$18/20, ste US$40; ❄ ☜) A contemporary hotel just one block from the river, the Daly is one of the better Khmer-style high-rise hotels in town. Rooms are large and bright with wall-mounted flat-screen TVs, spick-and-span bathrooms and luscious linens.

Monorom 2 VIP Hotel HOTEL $

(☎092 777102; www.monoromviphotel.com; Sihanouk St; r US$15-50; ❄ @ ☜) One of the smarter options on the riverfront; rooms include heavy wood furnishings and inviting bathtubs. The lavish suites have private balconies grandstanding the Mekong and large bathrooms loaded with toiletries. The cheapest rooms are, however, windowless.

OBT Homestay HOMESTAY $

(☎017 319194; p_sophal@yahoo.com; volunteer/ tourist incl 2 meals US$5/10) The Organization for Basic Training accepts volunteers to teach English to local kids, but ordinary travellers looking to spend a few days going local in a Khmer village are also welcome. Tours by ox-cart, horse or boat along the Mekong are available. It's in Chiro village, on the east bank of the Mekong, a few kilometres north of the French lighthouse.

LBN Asian Hotel HOTEL $$

(☎092 665228; www.lbnasian.com; Sihanouk Blvd; r US$30-110; ❄ ☜ ☷) This high-rise hotel is a sign that the times they are a changing in Kompong Cham. The rooms are excellent value given the 4-star standard and include everything from flat-screen TVs to rain showers. Non-guests can venture up to the Sky Bar on the 11th floor which offers expansive views over the Mekong River and has some happy hour promotions.

Rana Homestay HOMESTAY $$

(☎012 686240; http://rana-ruralhomestay-cam bodia.webs.com; per person US$25) Located in the countryside beyond Kompong Cham, this homestay offers an insight into electricity-free life in rural Cambodia. The price includes all meals and tours of the local area. There's a two-night minimum stay, a two-person minimum and advance booking is required.

✖ Eating

There's little reason to stray beyond the atmospheric restaurants on the riverfront, which include a couple of international eateries and a highly regarded local restaurant.

★ Smile Restaurant CAMBODIAN $

(www.bsda-cambodia.org; Sihanouk St; mains US$3-5; ☉6.30am-10pm; ☜) ✎ Run by the Buddhism and Society Development Association (BSDA), this handsome nonprofit restaurant is a huge hit with the NGO crowd for its big breakfasts and authentic Khmer cuisine, such as *char k'dau* (stir-fry with lemongrass, hot basil and peanuts) and black-pepper squid. Western dishes are on the menu as well, and it sells BSDA-made *krama* (checked scarves) and trinkets.

Destiny Coffee House CAFE $

(☎017 860775; 12 Vithei Pasteur St; mains US$3-5; ☉7am-5pm Mon-Sat; ☜ ☷ ✎) This stylish cafe has relaxing sofas and a contemporary look. The international menu includes delicious hummus with dips, lip-smacking home-made cakes, breakfast burritos, salads and wraps.

Lazy Mekong Daze INTERNATIONAL $

(Sihanouk St; mains US$3-5.50; ☉7.30am-last customer; ☜) One of the go-to places to gather after dark thanks to a mellow atmosphere, a pool table and a big screen for sports and movies. The menu includes a range of Khmer, Thai and French food, plus the best pizzas in town, chilli con carne and tempting ice creams.

Mekong Crossing INTERNATIONAL $

(2 Vithei Pasteur St; mains US$2-5; ☉6am-10pm; ☜) Occupying a prime corner on the riverfront, this old favourite serves an enticing mix of Khmer curries and Western favourites, such as big burgers and tasty sandwiches. Doubles as a popular bar by night and offers a dozen rooms upstairs (fan/air-con room US$7/12).

Kompong Cham Night Market MARKET $

(Preah Bat Ang Chan St; US$1-3; ☉4-10pm daily) This is not a tourist night market in the conventional sense, but more a market by night for locals to browse stalls and snack out. It's a good place to sample inexpensive Cambodian food and there are plenty of

ℹ GETTING TO VIETNAM: KOMPONG CHAM TO TAY NINH

Getting to the border The Trapeang Plong/Xa Mat border crossing (7am to 5pm) has become increasingly popular for those travelling between northeast Cambodia and Ho Chi Minh City. From Kompong Cham take anything heading east on NH7 toward Snuol, and get off at the roundabout in Krek (Kraek), on NH7, 55km east-southeast of Kompong Cham. From there, it's 13km south by *moto* (motorcycle taxi; US$3) along NH72 to snoozy Trapeang Plong.

At the border This border is a breeze: just have your Vietnamese visa ready should you require one.

Moving on On the Vietnamese side, motorbikes and taxis go to Tay Ninh, 45km to the south – but be prepared to negotiate a lot harder than in Cambodia.

drinks stalls selling fresh fruit shakes and ice-cold beers.

ℹ Information

ANZ Royal Bank (Preah Monivong Blvd; ⊘ 8.30am-4pm Mon-Fri, ATM 24hr) Has an ATM.

Canadia Bank (Preah Monivong Blvd; ⊘ 8am-3.30pm Mon-Fri, 8-11.30am Sat, ATM 24hr) ATM plus cash advances on credit cards.

Lazy Mekong Daze (p277) Hands out a decent map that highlights the major sights in and around Kompong Cham.

Mekong Internet (Vithei Pasteur St; per hour 1500r; ⊘ 6.30am-10pm) Among a cluster of internet cafes on Vithei Pasteur St.

ℹ Getting There & Away

Phnom Penh is 120km southwest of Kompong Cham. If you are heading north to Kratie or beyond, arrange transport via the sealed road to Chhlong rather than taking a huge detour east to Snuol on NH7.

Besides buses, share taxis (15,000r) and overcrowded local minibuses (10,000r) do the dash to Phnom Penh from the **taxi park**

(Preah Bat Ketmealea St) near the New Market (Psar Thmei). The trip takes two hours or more depending on traffic in the capital. Express minivans are another option to the capital (US$6, two hours); arrange these through your guesthouse.

Morning share taxis and minibuses to Kratie (US$5, two hours) and Stung Treng (US$10, four hours) depart when full from the **Caltex station** (NH7) at the main roundabout, and there are morning minibuses from the taxi park as well.

BUS

Several bus companies offer services connecting Kompong Cham to Phnom Penh, Kratie, Stung Treng and Mondulkiri. The **Phnom Penh Sorya** (☑ 092 181810; www.phnompenhsorya. com; Preah Monivong Blvd) bus to Ban Lung does not stop in town, so it is necessary to wait for it out on the NH7 highway.

ℹ Getting Around

Kompong Cham has a surplus of *moto* (motorcycle taxi) and *remork-moto* (tuk tuk) drivers who speak great English and can guide you around the sites. If you sip a drink overlooking the Mekong, one of them will find you before too long. Mr Vannat is the veteran of the group

BUSES FROM KOMPONG CHAM

DESTINATION	PRICE (US$)	DURATION (HR)	COMPANIES	FREQUENCY
Ban Lung	10	7	PP Sorya	10am
Battambang	7.50	7½	Liang US Express, PP Sorya	7.30am & 8.30am
Kratie via Snuol	4.50	4	PP Sorya	10.30am & 12.30pm
Phnom Penh	4-5	3	Liang US Express, PP Sorya	hourly till 6pm
Sen Monorom	9	6	Minivans only	A few in morning
Siem Reap	6.50	6	Liang US Express	7.30am & 8.30am
Stung Treng via Snuol	6.50	6	PP Sorya	10am

and has a 4WD for hire (he also speaks French; contact him on 012 995890 or vannat_kom pongcham@yahoo.com). Figure on US$10 to US$15 per day for a *moto* and US$15 to US$20 for a *remork* (slightly more if including Wat Maha Leap in your plans). Round-trip *remork* journeys to Wat Hanchey or Phnom Pros and Phnom Srei are a negotiable US$10.

Most guesthouses and restaurants on the riverfront rent motorbikes (US$3 to US$5 per day) and bicycles (US$1 per day), including **Lazy Mekong Daze** (p277).

KRATIE

072 / POP 45,000

A supremely mellow riverside town, Kratie (ក្រចេះ, pronounced kra-*cheh*) has an expansive riverfront and some of the best Mekong sunsets in Cambodia. It is the most popular place in the country to see Irrawaddy dolphins, which live in the Mekong River in ever-diminishing numbers. There is a rich legacy of French-era architecture, as it was spared the wartime bombing that destroyed so many other provincial centres.

Many visitors are drawn to the rare freshwater Irrawaddy dolphins found in Kampi, about 15km north of the provincial capital, but the town itself is a little charmer and makes a good base from which to explore the surrounding countryside.

As a travel hub Kratie is the natural place to break the journey when travelling overland between Phnom Penh and Ratanakiri or the 4000 Islands area in southern Laos.

◉ Sights

The main draw here is the chance to spot the elusive Irrawaddy dolphin north of town in Kampi, as well as the scenic Mekong island of Koh Trong, located just across the river from Kratie.

Located 35km north of Kratie, Sambor is home to a turtle conservation centre and the largest wat in Cambodia.

Phnom Sombok　　　　BUDDHIST TEMPLE
(ភ្នំសំបុក; ⊙6am-6pm) FREE Phnom Sombok is a small hill with an active wat, located on the road from Kratie to Kampi. The hill offers the best views across the Mekong on this stretch of the river and a visit here can easily be combined with a trip to see the dolphins for an extra couple of dollars.

Kratie

Wat Sorsor Moi Roi　　　　BUDDHIST TEMPLE
(វត្តសសរមួយរយ, Hundred Columns Temple; Sambor) FREE Located 35km north of Kratie in the village of Sambor, Wat Sorsor Moi Roi is thought to be the largest wat in Cambodia, complete with 108 columns. It was constructed on the site of a 19th-century wooden temple, a few pillars of which are still located at the back of the compound. The Mekong Turtle Conservation Centre is located within the temple grounds.

KRAMA CHAMELEON

The colourful chequered scarf known as the *krama* is almost universally worn by rural Khmers and is still quite popular in the cities. The scarves are made from cotton or silk, and the most famous silk *kramas* come from Kompong Cham and Takeo Provinces.

Kramas have a multitude of uses. They are primarily used to protect Cambodians from the sun, the dust and the wind, and it is for this reason many tourists end up investing in one during a visit. However, they are also slung around the waist as mini-sarongs, used as towels for drying the body, knotted at the neck as decorations, tied across the shoulders as baby carriers, placed upon chairs or beds as pillow covers, used to tow broken-down motorbikes and stuffed inside motorbike tyres in the event of remote punctures – the list goes on.

Kramas are sold in markets throughout Cambodia and are an essential purchase for travellers using motorbikes or bicycles or taking boat services. They have become very much a symbol of Cambodia: for many Khmers, wearing one is an affirmation of their identity.

Sambor was the site of a thriving pre-Angkorian city during the time of Sambor Prei Kuk and the Chenla empire. Not a stone of this remains in the modern town of Sambor. To get here, follow the road north from Kampi to Sandan, before veering left along a reasonable 10km stretch of road.

**Mekong Turtle
Conservation Centre**   WILDLIFE RESERVE
(មជ្ឈមណ្ឌលអភិរក្សអណ្តើកកន្ថាយមេគង្គ; ☏ 012 712071; www.mekongturtle.com; Sambor; adult/child US$4/2; ⊗ 8.30am-4.30pm) This wildlife conservation centre is located within the temple grounds of Wat Sorsor Moi Roi in Sambor, about 35km north of Kratie. Established by Conservation International (www.conservation.org), it is home to several species of turtle, including the rare Cantor's giant softshell, which was only rediscovered along this stretch of the Mekong in 2007. One of the largest freshwater turtles, it can grow to nearly 2m in length. Hatchlings are nurtured here for 10 months before being released in the wild.

Tourists can participate in the release on select weeks, usually in September and May or June. Check the website for the exact dates.

Wat Roka Kandal   BUDDHIST TEMPLE
(វត្តរកាកណ្ដាល; Rue Preah Suramarit; 2000r) About 2km south of Kratie on the road to Chhlong is this beautiful little temple dating from the 19th century, one of the oldest in the region. To see the beautifully restored interior, ask around for someone with the key. Even if you can't get in, the shaded grounds, adjacent to some lovely traditional wooden houses, are worth a wander.

Chhlong   VILLAGE
(ឆ្លូង) Chhlong is a somnolent riverside town 31km south of Kratie. The main attraction is the old governor's residence, a gorgeous, yellow-and-white French colonial mansion near the river. Once a top-end boutique hotel, it is scheduled to reopen its doors sometime in 2018. Architecture buffs might also drop in at the House of a Hundred Pillars (1884), about 500m north of Le Relais. According to the house's owner, the Khmer Rouge removed many of the pillars, so only 56 remain.

A few more decrepit French colonial buildings line the river. Chhlong is worth a wander if you are driving through with your own transport, but is probably not worth a special trip from Kratie. Keen cyclists might like to follow the old river road between Kratie and Chhlong, as it passes through some traditional Cham minority villages along the way.

🏃 Activities

Riding a bike along the banks of the Mekong River is always rewarding. Other activities include kayaking and boat trips.

★ **Sorya Kayaking Adventures**   KAYAKING
(☏ 090 241148; www.soryakayaking.com; Rue Preah Suramarit; US$24-52, depending on numbers; ⊗ 7am-9pm) Sorya has a fleet of seven tandem kayaks and runs memorable half-day trips on the Mekong north of Kratie (November to June only), or on the Te River to the south (August to October). The Mekong trips pass through secluded sandbar beaches and areas of beautiful flooded forest to bring you close to the dolphins – without the engine noise.

The Te River trips are arguably more scenic, but you don't get to see the dolphins as part of the experience.

🜲 Tours

CRDTours TOURS
(Cambodia Rural Discovery Tours; ☎ 099 834353; www.crdtours.org; St 3; ⊙8am-noon & 2-5.30pm) 🏍 Run by the Cambodian Rural Development team, this company focuses on sustainable tours along the Mekong Discovery Trail (p284). Homestays, volunteer opportunities and various excursions are available on the Mekong island of Koh Pdao, 20km north of Kampi. The typical price is US$38 to US$60 per day, including all meals and tours.

Tours and homestays on Koh Preah (near Stung Treng) and Koh Trong are also possible. Mountain-bike tours from Kratie to Koh Pdao are another option.

CRDT can also organise boat trips from Stung Treng to Kratie, sleeping in remote river villages along the way (US$130 to US$300 per person, depending on numbers), or doing it in one day (about five hours).

Cambodian Pride Tours TOURS
(☎ 088 836 4758; http://cambodianpridetours. com) Local tours operated by experienced, Kratie-born guide Sithy, who is keen to promote real-life experiences in his community, such as visiting family members and learning about farming methods.

🛏 Sleeping

Kratie offers a good selection of guesthouses and hotels, many with river views. For something even more relaxed than Kratie, consider staying directly on the island of Koh Trong, where homestays and boutique accommodation await.

★Le Tonlé
Tourism Training Center GUESTHOUSE $
(☎ 072-210505; www.letonle.org; St 3; r without bathroom US$10-20; ❀🌐) 🏍 CRDT runs this fantastic budget guesthouse in a beautiful wooden house in the centre. With silk pillows and bed runners, agreeable art and photos, wood floors and a great hang-out area, it puts plenty of care into the design. Rooms are somewhat dark but share boutique-quality bathrooms. It doubles as a training centre for at-risk locals.

There's a great restaurant (open 7.30am to 9.30pm) downstairs with delicious food prepared by program trainees. There are a few equally appealing rooms across the street above the main CRDTours office.

★Koh Trong
Community Homestay I HOMESTAY $
(Koh Trong; mattress per person US$4, room US$8) Set in an old wooden house, offering two proper bedrooms and fancy-pants bathrooms

---

DON'T MISS

DOLPHIN WATCHING AROUND KRATIE

The freshwater Irrawaddy dolphin (*trey pisaut* in Khmer) is an endangered species throughout Asia, with shrinking numbers inhabiting stretches of the Mekong in Cambodia and Laos, and isolated pockets in Bangladesh and Myanmar. The blue-grey cetaceans grow to 2.75m long and are recognisable by their bulging foreheads and small dorsal fins. They can live in fresh or salt water, although they are seldom seen in the sea. For more on this rare creature, see www.worldwildlife.org/species/irrawaddy-dolphin.

Before the civil war, locals say, Cambodia was home to as many as 1000 dolphins. However, during the Pol Pot regime, many were hunted for their oils, and their numbers continue to plummet even as drastic protection measures have been put in place, including a ban on fishing and commercial motorised boat traffic on much of the Mekong between Kratie and Stung Treng. The dolphins continue to die off at an alarming rate, and experts now estimate that there are only around 80 Irrawaddy dolphins left in the Mekong between Kratie and the Lao border.

The best place to see them is at Kampi, about 15km north of Kratie, on the road to Sambor. A *moto/remork* (motorcycle taxi/*tuk tuk*) should be around US$7/10 return, depending on how long the driver has to wait. Motorboats shuttle visitors out to the middle of the river to view the dolphins at close quarters. It costs US$9 per person for one to two persons and US$7 per person for groups of three to four (children are US$4). Encourage the boat driver to use the engine as little as possible once near the dolphins, as the noise is sure to disturb them. **Sorya Kayaking Adventures** runs excellent half-day trips to see the dolphins by kayak, passing through remote flooded forest and sandbars. It is also possible to see the river dolphins near the Lao border in Stung Treng Province.

(that is, thrones not squats). It's located about 2km north of the ferry dock near Rajabori Villas. Ride your bike, take a *moto* (motorcycle taxi; US$1) or ride an ox-cart.

Balcony Guesthouse
GUESTHOUSE $
(☏016 604036; www.balconyguesthouse.net; Rue Preah Suramarit; dm US$5, r US$5-15; ✳@⑳) This long-running backpacker place has a few tasteful private rooms, a four-bed dorm, a popular bar overlooking the Mekong and a huge balcony on the 3rd floor for prime river views. The bar has a gigantic snooker table, which is a lot harder to master than a standard pool table.

U-Hong II Guesthouse
GUESTHOUSE $
(☏085 885168; 119 St 10; r US$4-13; ✳@⑳) A lively little shoes-off guesthouse between the market and the riverfront. There are eight rooms here, plus 11 more in a nearby annex, some with air-con. There is a buzzing bar-restaurant that boasts the most extensive cocktail list in town.

Silver Dolphin Guesthouse
HOSTEL $
(☏012 999810; silver.dolphinbooking@yahoo.com; 48 Rue Preah Suramarit; dm US$2-3, r US$6-14; ✳@⑳) This backpacker hostel is a cheap deal. The en-suite US$3 dorm is up top next to the rooftop bar (a fine place for sunset), while the US$2 dorm is roomier but at the back. Even the cheapest doubles have a TV, bathroom and some furniture. Owner Pech speaks English and French.

River Dophin Hotel
HOTEL $$
(☏072-210570; www.riverdolphinhotel.com; r US$5-55; ✳@⑳⑳) Stranded somewhat inland from the riverfront action, it is nonetheless a deservedly popular place thanks to a high level of comfort and service (for Kratie) and one of the town's only swimming pools. They run the full gamut of rooms from fan-cooled cupboards to genuinely boutique beds. Add US$5 for breakfast. Non-guests can use the pool for US$3 per day.

Mekong Dolphin Hotel
HOTEL $$
(☏072-666 6666; www.mekongdolphinhotel.com; Rue Preah Suramarit; r US$15-50; ✳⑳) Looming large on the riverfront, this concrete high-rise is the fanciest in town, offering slick river-view rooms for US$35 and suites for your inner VIP at US$50. There's even a small gym and sauna (if Kratie isn't hot enough for you already). The cheaper rooms at the back are a huge step down in quality.

Arun Mekong
GUESTHOUSE $$
(☏017 663014; www.arunmekong.wordpress.com; Koh Trong; r with/without bathroom from US$27/22) A nice mix of tastefully furnished rooms and bungalows in a lovely setting at the north tip of idyllic Koh Trong. Electricity runs only from 6pm to 11pm, however, which means hot nights at certain times of the year.

Rajabori Villas
BOUTIQUE HOTEL $$$
(☏012 770150; www.rajabori-kratie.com; Koh Trong; r incl breakfast US$65-150; ✳✳⑳) A boutique lodge with a swimming pool and large dark-wood bungalows finished in inspired French-Khmer style, this is the best accommodation in the Kratie region by some margin. It's located at the northern tip of Koh Trong and includes a swimming pool.

They will pick you up for free from the ferry pier, or a private boat from Kratie costs about US$6.

✖ Eating & Drinking

When in Kratie, keep an eye out for two famous specialities, sold on the riverfront and elsewhere: *krolan* (sticky rice, beans and coconut milk steamed inside a bamboo tube) and *nehm* (tangy raw, spiced river fish wrapped in banana leaves).

WORTH A TRIP

KOH TRONG: AN ISLAND IN THE MEKONG

Lying just across the water from Kratie is the island of Koh Trong (កោះត្រង់), an almighty 6km-long sandbar in the middle of the river. Cross here by boat and enjoy a slice of rural island life. Attractions include an old **stupa** and a small **floating village**, as well as the chance to encounter one of the rare **Mekong mud turtles** who inhabit the western shore. There are homestays and boutique hotels here for those that want to linger longer.

Catch the little ferry (with/without bicycle 2000r/1000r, 10 minutes, last trip 6pm) from the **boat dock** in Kratie. From the ferry landing on Koh Trong, a *moto* costs US$1.50 to the north tip where most of the accommodation is. A private boat to the resorts costs about US$6. Bicycle rental is available on the island near the ferry landing for US$1, or do the loop around the island on a *moto* (US$2.50).

> **ⓘ GETTING TO VIETNAM: KRATIE TO BINH LONG**
>
> **Getting to the border** The **Trapeang Sre/Loc Ninh border crossing** (7am to 5pm) is useful for those trying to get straight to Vietnam from Kratie or points north. First get to the bustling junction town of Snuol by bus, share taxi or minibus from Sen Monorom, Kratie or Kompong Cham. In Snuol catch a *moto* (motorcycle taxi; US$5) for the 18km trip southeastward along smooth NH74.
>
> **At the border** You'll need a prearranged visa to enter Vietnam should your nationality require it, and US$30 for a visa-on-arrival to enter Cambodia.
>
> **Moving on** On the Vietnamese side, the nearest town is Binh Long, 40km to the south. Motorbikes and taxis await at the border.

Kratie is not known for nightlife, although people often linger in the riverfront restaurants until 11pm or so. Otherwise your best bet for drinking and late-night camaraderie are hostels such as Balcony Guesthouse or Silver Dolphin.

Le Tonlé Tourism Training Center (p281) has a very well-regarded restaurant. The south end of the *psar* (market) turns into a carnival of barbecue stands hawking meat-on-a-stick by night.

★**Tokae Restaurant**   CAMBODIAN $
(☑097 297 2118; St 10; mains US$2-4; ☺6am-11pm; 🛜) Look out for Cambodia's largest *tokae* (gecko) on the wall and you've found this excellent little eatery. The menu offers a good mix of cheap Cambodian food such as curries and *amok* (a baked fish dish), plus equally affordable Western breakfasts and comfort food.

Pete's Pizza Pasta & Cafe   INTERNATIONAL $
(☑090 241148; www.petescafekratie.com; Rue Preah Suramarit; US$1-5; ☺7am-9pm daily; 🛜) Get your home fix of pizza, pasta, toasties and salads at this internationally run riverfront cafe; it is also the base for Sorya Kayaking Adventures. The menu includes homemade bakery items such as pumpkin bread, muffins and cookies. By night it doubles as a small sports bar with a flat-screen television and will stay open later for big games.

Red Sun Falling   INTERNATIONAL $
(Rue Preah Suramarit; mains US$2-4; ☺7am-10pm; 🛜) One of the liveliest spots in town, the long-running Red Sun has a relaxed cafe ambience, a good riverfront location, used books for sale and a good selection of Asian and Western meals.

Jasmine Boat Restaurant   INTERNATIONAL $$
(☑096 331 1998; Rue Preah Suramarit; mains US$4-22; ☺7am-10pm; 🛜) Occupying a prime location overlooking Kratie's busy ferry dock, this is the only place on the riverbank in town. The boat-shaped restaurant has a mixed menu of affordable Khmer specials and pricey international cuts of meat. It really shines at sunset but is a good perch any time of day.

ⓘ Information

U-Hong II and Silver Dolphin guesthouses have public internet access.

Canadia Bank (Rue Preah Suramarit; ☺8.30am-3.30pm Mon-Fri, ATM 24hr) ATM offering cash withdrawals, plus currency exchange.

ⓘ Getting There & Away

Kratie is 250km northeast of Phnom Penh (via the Chhlong road) and 141km south of Stung Treng.

Phnom Penh Sorya (☑081 908005; Rue Preah Suramarit) operates three buses per day to Phnom Penh (US$8, seven hours) along the slow route (via Snuol). Express minivans get to Phnom Penh in four hours via Chhlong (US$9, about six daily), and usually offer transfers onward to Sihanoukville.

Sorya's daily bus to Siem Reap (US$11, nine hours) involves a change in Suong. There's also an express minivan to Siem Reap (US$11, six hours, 7am). Share taxis (US$10) head to Phnom Penh between 6am and 8am, with possible additional departures after lunch.

For Ban Lung, the Sorya (US$8, five hours, around 12.30pm) bus passes through from Phnom Penh. A few local minibuses also serve Ban Lung from the **taxi park** (Rue Preah Sihanouk). Sorya has a 2.30pm bus to Stung Treng (US$5, 2½ hours), and there's also a 7am minibus. There's a 7.30am minibus to Preah Vihear City (Tbeng Meanchey; US$15, five hours). To get to Laos, you must transfer in Stung Treng and Kratie guesthouses can arrange this.

For Sen Monorom, take a local minibus from the taxi park (30,000r, four hours, two or three early-morning departures) or head to Snuol and change.

MEKONG DISCOVERY TRAIL

It's well worth spending a couple of days exploring the various bike rides and activities on offer along the Mekong Discovery Trail, an initiative to open up stretches of the Mekong River around Stung Treng and Kratie to community-based tourism. Once managed by the government with foreign development assistance, its trails and routes are now being kept alive by private tour companies, such as **Cambodia Mekong Trail** in Stung Treng and CRDTours in Kratie.

It's a worthy project, as it intends to provide fishing communities an alternative income in order to protect the Irrawaddy dolphin and other rare species on this stretch of river.

There's a great booklet with routes and maps outlining excursions around Kratie and Stung Treng, but you'll be hard-pressed to secure your own copy; ask tour operators if you can photograph theirs. The routes can be tackled by bicycle or motorbike. They range in length from a few hours to several days, with optional overnights in village homestays. Routes criss-cross the Mekong frequently by ferry and traverse several Mekong islands, including Koh Trong.

ℹ️ Getting Around

Most guesthouses can arrange bicycle (from US$1) and motorbike (from US$5) hire. An English-speaking *moto* (motorcycle taxi) will set you back US$10 to US$15 per day, and a *remork* about US$20 to US$25, depending on the destinations.

STUNG TRENG

📞 074 / POP 35,000

Located on the Tonlé San near its confluence with the Mekong, Stung Treng (ស្ទឹងត្រែង) is a quiet town with limited appeal, but sees a lot of transit traffic heading north to Laos, south to Kratie, east to Ratanakiri and west to Siem Reap. Just north of the town centre, a major bridge across the San leads north to the Lao border, while an important newer bridge traverses the Mekong south of town connecting Stung Treng to Preah Vihear and Siem Reap.

Loaded with largely untapped tourist potential, Stung Treng could benefit from the increased traffic if people stuck around. The main attractions are near the Lao border, where you can kayak out to a pod of Irrawaddy dolphins then continue downstream along a pretty stretch of the Mekong dotted with flooded forest. Further north, thundering rapids cascade over the border, a spectacular sight that's a continuation of the huge Khone Falls.

🔵 Sights & Activities

Dolphin-watching and kayaking trips near the Lao border are the main draw, and can be arranged by tour companies out of Stung Treng.

Mekong Blue   ARTS CENTRE

(មេគង្គប្លូ; 📞 012 622096; www.mekongblue.com; 🕐 7.30-11.30am & 2-5pm Mon-Sat) 🌿 Part of the Stung Treng Women's Development Centre, Mekong Blue is a silk-weaving centre on the outskirts of Stung Treng. Mekong Blue specialises in exquisite silk products for sale and export. At this centre it is possible to observe the dyers and weavers, most of whom come from vulnerable or impoverished backgrounds. The centre is located about 4km east of the centre on the riverside road that continues under the bridge.

There is a small showroom on-site with a selection of silk for sale, plus a cafe. However, it only serves cold drinks unless you book a meal in advance.

Thala Boravit   BUDDHIST TEMPLE

(ថាឡាបរិវត្ត) This crumbling temple is across the Mekong from Stung Treng. Thala Boravit was an important Chenla-period trading town on the river route connecting Champasak and the sacred temple of Wat Phu with the ancient cities of Sambor Prei Kuk (Isanapura) and Angkor Borei. For all its past glories, there is very little to see today.

👉 Tours

Cambodia Mekong Trail   ADVENTURE

(Xplore-Asia; 📞 011 433836; www.cambodia mekongtrail.com) Doles out brochures, booklets and advice, and tailors one- to several-day cycling-and-kayak combo tours along the Mekong Discovery Trail, including kayaking with the dolphins around Preah Rumkel with an overnight homestay. Rents out kayaks (US$10 per day), motorbikes (US$10 per day) and sturdy Trek mountain bikes (US$5 per day). Multiday rides possible with a mountain-bike drop-off in Kratie.

Mlup Baitong TOURS
(ម្លុប់បៃតង; ☑ in Phnom Penh 012 413857; www.mlup-baitong.org) This NGO runs the Preah Rumkel ecotourism project.

🛏 Sleeping

Most people prefer to stay on the riverfront in Stung Treng, that is assuming they choose to spend a night here at all.

4 Rivers Hotel HOTEL $
(☑ 070 507822; www.fourrivershotel.com; US$15-30; ✳@🛜) In no way affiliated with the floating 4 Rivers in Koh Kong, this is most definitely located on dry land overlooking the Tonlé San and Mekong River. Rooms feature a contemporary trim and it is worth paying a little extra for the river-view rooms.

Mekong Bird Lodge BUNGALOW $
(☑ 074-690 0885; ankgorlu@gmail.com; r US$15-45; ✳🛜) This self-styled ecolodge sits on a bluff overlooking a peaceful Mekong eddy north of town. Set in lush tropical gardens, it has undergone renovation and expansion. Sturdy wood bungalows have balconies with sunset views, plus there are now large family bungalows with air-con. To get here, turn left at the sign 4km north of the Tonlé San bridge.

There are also a couple of rustic restaurants on site which have excellent verandah views over the Mekong River.

Riverside Guesthouse GUESTHOUSE $
(☑ 012-257207; kimtysou@gmail.com; r with fan/air-con US$6/12; @🛜) Overlooking the riverfront area, the Riverside has long been a popular travellers' hub. Rooms are basic, but then so are the prices. It's a good spot for travel information and there's a bar-restaurant downstairs.

Golden River Hotel HOTEL $$
(☑ 074-690 0029; www.goldenriverhotel.com; r US$15-35; ✳@🛜) The best all-rounder in town, the Golden River has 50 well-appointed rooms complete with hot-water bathrooms, fridges and TVs. Rooms at the front are a few dollars more thanks to panoramic views of the Tonlé San.

🍴 Eating

On the riverside promenade west of the ferry dock, street-side vendors peddle cold beer and noodle soup until late in the evening.

Stung Treng

❂ Activities, Courses & Tours
1 Cambodia Mekong Trail B1

🛏 Sleeping
2 Golden River Hotel B1
3 Riverside Guesthouse B1

🍴 Eating
4 Diniya Restaurant B1
5 Ponika's Palace B1

❶ Transport
6 Asia Van Transfer................................B1

Ponika's Palace INTERNATIONAL $
(☑ 012 919441; mains US$2-5; ⊘6am-10pm) Need a break from *laab* (a spicy salad with chicken, pork or fish) after Laos? Burgers, pizza and English breakfasts grace the menu, along with Indian food and wonderful Khmer curries. Affable owner Ponika speaks English and cold beer is available to slake a thirst.

Diniya Restaurant BREAKFAST $
(☑ 012 963664; US$1-3; ⊘6am-6pm; 🛜) This local restaurant, located one block back from the Tonlé San, is a devoutly popular place for breakfast, turning out steaming bowls of *kyteow* (noodle soup), *bobor* (rice porridge) and other staples.

❶ Information

Canadia Bank (⊘8.30am-3.30pm Mon-Fri, ATM 24hr) Has an international ATM.

Rany Neh Internet (per hour 4000r; ⊙7am-8pm)

Riverside Guesthouse specialises in getting people to/from Laos, Siem Reap or just about anywhere else. Also runs boat tours to the Lao border, with a trip to see the resident dolphin pod (US$100/120 for two/four people). English-speaking guides offer motorbike tours around the province.

ⓘ Getting There & Away

NH7 north to the Lao border and south to Kratie is in reasonable shape these days.

Express minivans with guesthouse pick-ups as early as 4am are the quickest way to Phnom Penh (US$10 to US$13, seven hours). Book through Riverside Guesthouse or Ponika's Palace.

Phnom Penh Sorya (☑092 181805) has a 6.30am bus to Phnom Penh (US$12, 10 hours) via Kratie (US$5, 2½ hours) and Kompong Cham (US$8, seven hours). Additionally, local minibuses to Kratie depart regularly until 2pm from the market area.

There is a comfortable tourist van to Ban Lung (US$6, two hours, 8am and 1pm), with additional morning trips in cramped local minibuses from the market (US$5, three hours).

The new highway west from Thala Boravit to Preah Vihear via Chhep is in great shape. **Asia Van Transfer** (☑in Siem Reap 063-963853; www.asiavantransfer.com; Riverside Guesthouse) has an express minibus to Siem Reap at 2pm daily (US$20, five hours), with a stop in Preah Vihear City (Tbeng Meanchey; US$12, three hours).

For Laos, minivans head over the border at noon and 2pm, serving Don Det and Pakse.

ⓘ Getting Around

Riverside Guesthouse rents out motorbikes (from US$5), while both Riverside and Ponika's Palace have bicycles for hire (US$1 to US$2).

AROUND STUNG TRENG

In addition to the homestay program (p287) at Preah Rumkel, there are worthwhile community-based tourism initiatives, including homestays, in O'Russey Kandal, about 28km south of Stung Treng, and in Koh Preah, about 15km south of Stung Treng. Both programs have a slew of tours and activities on offer and there are volunteer opportunities as well. Contact CRDTours in Kratie for more information on these. Cambodia Mekong Trail can also help organise homestay-based itineraries.

Preah Rumkel

The small village of Preah Rumkel (ព្រះរំកិល) is emerging as a hotbed of ecotourism thanks to an established homestay program and its proximity to the Anlong Cheuteal Irrawaddy dolphin pool near the Lao border. With this

---

ⓘ GETTING TO LAOS: TRAPEANG KRIEL TO NONG NOK KHIENE

Getting to the border The remote **Trapeang Kriel/Nong Nok Khiene border** (open 6am to 6pm), 65km north of Stung Treng, is a popular crossing point on the Indochina overland circuit. For many years, there was a separate river crossing here, but that's no longer open. There are also no longer any through buses between Phnom Penh and Pakse. You'll need to get yourself to Stung Treng, from where there are at least two minivans per day (at noon and 2pm) that run across the border and onward to the 4000 Islands and Pakse. The only other option to the border is a private taxi (around US$35 to US$40) or *moto* (motorcycle taxi; around US$15) from Stung Treng.

At the border Both Lao and Cambodian visas are available on arrival. Entering Laos, it costs US$35 to US$42 for a visa, depending on nationality, plus a US$2 fee (dubbed either an 'overtime' or a 'processing' fee, depending on when you cross) upon both entry and exit.

Entering Cambodia, they jack up the price of a visa to US$35 from the normal US$30. The extra US$5 is called 'tea money', as the border guards have been stationed at such a remote crossing. In addition, the Cambodians sometimes charge US$1 for a cursory medical inspection upon arrival in the country, and levy a US$2 processing fee upon exit. These fees might be waived if you protest, but don't protest for too long or your vehicle may leave without you.

Moving on There's virtually zero traffic on either side of the border. If you're dropped at the border, expect to pay 150,000/50,000 kip (US$12/4) for a taxi/*săhm-lór* (Lao *tuk-tuk*) heading north to Ban Nakasang (for Don Det).

stretch of the Mekong River recognised by the Ramsar List of Wetlands of International Importance (www.ramsar.org), dozens of islands, a rich array of bird life, and various rapids and waterfalls cascading down from Laos, this is one of the mother river's wildest and most beautiful stretches.

The half-dozen frolicking dolphins in the Anlong Cheuteal pool (known as Boong Pa Gooang in Laos) can easily be sighted from shore in Preah Rumkel. There's a US$2 per person charge to see the dolphins.

Excursions out of Preah Rumkel include a hike up a nearby mountain and a boat/hiking trip to view the rampaging Mekong rapids cascading down from Laos. The rapids are an awesome display of nature's force, especially in the wet season.

Mlup Baitong runs Preah Rumkel's community-based homestay (☑097 503 9836, 081 993693; pcstmlup@gmail.com; per person US$3) program with about 10 families participating in the program.

Meals at Preah Rumkel are available through your homestay for around US$3 to US4 per person. If you're visiting on a day trip, your tour company will arrange for villagers to prepare your lunch.

Hire a longtail boat in O'Svay or, closer to the Laos border, Anlong Morakot, to explore the area and view the dolphins at Anlong Cheuteal. Boats cost a negotiable US$25 round-trip to Preah Rumkel and the dolphin pool. Add US$10 if you want to continue upstream to the rapids. Anlong Morakot is only 4km from the border so travellers coming in from Laos could get there in about 10 minutes on the back of a *moto* (motorcycle taxi; about US$2). Be sure to arrange onward transport to Stung Treng – either at the border or in advance through Cambodia Mekong Trail or Riverside Guesthouse in Stung Treng. These companies can also prearrange your *moto* and boat ride from the border to Preah Rumkel. A taxi to Stung Treng from this area costs about US$45.

Better yet, through Cambodia Mekong Trail you can kayak with the dolphins and then paddle downstream to O'Svay, or through bird-rich flooded forests all the way to Stung Treng. A full-day kayak excursion south of O'Svay costs US$65 per person; add US$20 per person to include the boat trip upstream to the dolphin pool and the Mekong rapids.

Siem Pang

A relatively prosperous town that stretches for about 6km along the Tonlé Kong, Siem Pang (សៀមប៉ាង) is a good place to observe rural life or just relax by the riverside in a remote outpost. It acts as the western gateway to Virachey National Park (p294) and is renowned for its rich wildlife. Rare giant ibis and white-shouldered ibis roost around here. You can arrange a park permit (preferably well in advance) and find a guide through Theany Guesthouse.

BirdLife International (☑097 974 5966, in Phnom Penh 023-993631; www.birdlife.org) runs a 'vulture restaurant' (feeding station) that attracts all three species of critically endangered vultures found in Cambodia. It's set up for research rather than tourism, but if you time your visit for the twice-monthly 'feed', which involves killing a water buffalo or cow and leaving it in a field near an observation hideout, you may get a chance to spot the vultures. Or you can up the ante with US$300 to organise a private feed.

There is only one decent guesthouse in Siem Pang. Theany Guesthouse (☑077 257773; r US$7.50-10) offers simple rooms in a traditional wooden house. Upstairs rooms are cheaper, but there is a decent breeze blowing through the verandah.

There are lots of local food stalls clustered along the riverfront, including barbecue meat stands by night. Leang Ay Restaurant (US$1-3; ⊙6am-9pm) is the only substantial place in town, located in an attractive wooden house perched over the river.

Regular morning and occasional afternoon vans make the trip from Stung Treng to Siem Pang (US$5, 2½ hours). From Stung Treng, drive 50km north on NH7, turn right, and proceed another 52km on an unsealed road. There are no longer any public boats along the Tonlé Kong to/from Stung Treng.

A ferry takes passengers (1000r) and motorbikes (2500r) across the river, where the tough trail to Veun Sai in Ratanakiri starts. Theany Guesthouse offers one-way motorbike rentals for this ride (US$70, including the cost of returning the motorbike to Siem Pang). However, much of this trail is sand and not for the novice rider. It is better tackled on a 250cc dirt bike by experienced riders, as it is essentially the last remaining stretch of the infamous 'Death Highway'.

RATANAKIRI PROVINCE

POP 195,000

Popular Ratanakiri Province (ខេត្តរតនគិរី) is a diverse region of outstanding natural beauty that provides a remote home for a mosaic of peoples – Jarai, Tompuon, Brau and Kreung minorities, plus Lao.

Adrenalin activities abound. Swim in clear volcanic lakes, shower under waterfalls, or trek in the vast Virachey National Park. Tourism is set to take off, provided the lowland politicians and generals don't plunder the place first. Hopefully someone will wake up and smell the coffee – there's plenty of that as well – before it's too late.

Roads in Ratanakiri are not as impressive as the sights. In the dry season, prepare to do battle with the dust of 'red-earth Ratanakiri', which will leave you with orange skin and ginger hair. The roads look like a papaya shake during the wet season. The ideal time to explore is November, after the rains have stopped and before the dusty season begins.

Ban Lung

📞 075 / POP 45,000

Affectionately known as *dey krahorm* ('red earth') after its old dust-fuelled, rust-coloured affliction, Ban Lung (បានលុង) provides a popular base for a range of Ratanakiri romps. These days the roads are mostly surfaced and the bustling town lacks the backwater charm of Sen Monorom in Mondulkiri, but with attractions such as Boeng Yeak Lom just a short hop away, there is little room for complaint. Many of the minorities from the surrounding villages come to Ban Lung to buy and sell at the market.

◎ Sights & Activities

There are no real sights in the centre of town. The big draws on the outskirts are Boeng Yeak Lom and several waterfalls.

Overnight treks with nights spent in minority villages around Ban Lung or camping are popular, as are multiday hikes in Virachey National Park. For wildlife spotting, check out Cambodian Gibbon Ecotours (p290). Elephant rides are offered near Ka Tieng Waterfall, but are not recommended due to concerns about the well-being of the animals. Save your elephant experience for walking with the herd (p297) in Mondulkiri.

Keep in mind that trekking in Virachey National Park is the exclusive domain of Virachey National Park Eco-Tourism Information Centre (p293). Private tour operators also offer multiday treks, but these only go as far as the park's buffer zone. There's little forest left standing outside the park boundary, so be careful that you're not being taken for a loop – literally – around and around in the same small patch of forest.

Despite being shut out from the park, private tour companies can still design creative treks that take in minority villages and scenic spots around the province.

★ **Boeng Yeak Lom**   LAKE

(បឹងយក្សល្អម; US$2) At the heart of the protected area of Boeng Yeak Lom is a beautiful, emerald-hued crater lake set amid the vivid greens of the towering jungle. It is one of the most peaceful, beautiful locations Cambodia has to offer and the water is extremely clear. Several wooden piers are dotted around the perimeter, making it perfect for swimming. A small Cultural and Environmental Centre has a modest display on ethnic minorities in the province and hires out life jackets for children.

The lake is believed to have been formed 700,000 years ago; some believe it must have been formed by a meteor strike as the circle is so perfect. The indigenous minority people in the area have long considered Boeng Yeak Lom a sacred place and their legends talk of mysterious creatures that inhabit the waters, but don't let that put you off swimming.

The local Tompuon minority has a 25-year lease to manage the lake through to 2021, and proceeds from the entry fee go towards improving life in the nearby villages. However, developers, backed by local politicians, have long been clamouring for the sacred lands around the lake. One can only hope they are kept at bay and that Boeng Yeak Lom is preserved in all of its pristine glory.

To get to Boeng Yeak Lom from Ban Lung's central roundabout, head east toward Vietnam for 3km, turn right at the prominent minorities statue and proceed 2km or so. *Motos* (motorcycle taxis) charge about US$5 return (more if you make them wait), while *remorks* have been known to charge about US$10 return. It takes about an hour to reach the lake on foot from Ban Lung.

Waterfalls

Tucked amid the sprawling cashew and rubber plantations just west of Ban Lung are three waterfalls worth visiting: Chaa Ong

Ban Lung

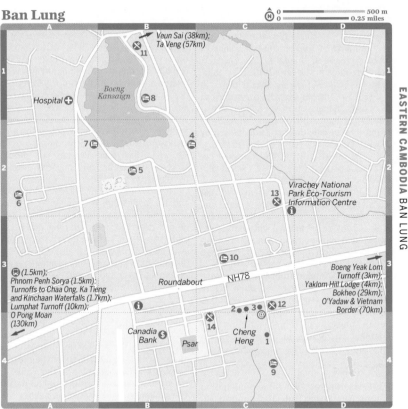

Ban Lung

Activities, Courses & Tours
1	DutchCo Trekking Cambodia	C4
2	Highland Tours	C3
3	Parrot Tours	C3

Sleeping
4	Banlung Balcony	B2
5	Flashpacker Pad	B2
6	Nature House Ecolodge	A2
7	Ratanakiri Boutique Hotel	A2
8	Terres Rouges Lodge	B1
9	Tree Top Ecolodge	C4
10	Yeak Loam Hotel	C3

Eating
	Cafe Alee	(see 1)
11	Coconut Shake Restaurant	B1
	Everest	(see 2)
12	Green Carrot	C3
	Pteas Bay Khmer	(see 7)
13	Rith Any Banh Chav	C2
14	Ta Nam	C4

(ចាអុីង; 2000r), **Ka Tieng** (ការទៀង; 3000r) and **Kinchaan** (កាចាញ, Kachanh; 2000r). All are within a 20-minute *moto* (motorcycle taxi) ride of town, and visits to all three are usually included in tour companies' half- and full-day excursions. The turn-offs to all three waterfalls are 200m west of the new bus station, just beyond a Lina petrol station. Turn right (north) for Chaa-Ong, left for the other two. There's signage but it's barely visible.

You can access all three falls year-round, although they dry up from January to May. Think twice about driving yourself on a motorbike in the rainy season, as the red-clay access roads are extremely slippery when wet and you're almost guaranteed to wipe out. *Motos* (return US$6 for one waterfall, or US$10 for all three) and *remork;* US$10/20 for one/three waterfalls) can get you here safely.

◉ Lumphat & Bei Srok

The former provincial capital of Lumphat, on the banks of Tonlé Srepok, is a shadow of its former self thanks to sustained US bombing raids in the early 1970s. The Tonlé Srepok is believed to be the river depicted in the seminal antiwar film *Apocalypse Now*, in which Martin Sheen's Captain Benjamin Willard goes upriver into Cambodia in search of renegade Colonel Kurtz, played by Marlon Brando.

Bei Srok (បីស្រុក; Tuk Chrouu Bram-pul; 2000r) is a popular waterfall with seven gentle tiers. It's about 20km east of Lumphat. You can also get here on a rough road that leads south/southwest from Boeng Yeak Lom. Many Ban Lung tour companies offer Bei Srok as a day tour combined with some abandoned gem mines nearby and bomb-crater spotting around Lumphat. Access is difficult to impossible in the rainy season.

To get to Lumphat from Ban Lung, take the road to Stung Treng for 10km before heading south. The 35km journey takes about 45 minutes. Pick-ups to the taxi park in Ban Lung leave early in the morning from Lumphat and return in the afternoon on most days.

☞ Tours

Day tours usually take in some combination of waterfalls, Boeng Yeak Lom, minority villages, gem mines and jungle walks. Figure on US$45 to $50 per person per day for a couple (less for bigger groups).

Bespectacled Khieng is an indigenous Tompuon guide who runs unique one- to two-night trips in some fairly well-preserved jungle around Lumphat, with overnight stays in minority villages. His tours are cheap and he seems genuinely interested in seeing money go to Tompuon communities and guides, so tip him well. He also has an impressive hand-drawn map of Ratanakiri province. Khieng can often be found around Boeng Yeak Lom, or you can contact him by phone on 097 923 0923 or email at khamphaykhieng@yahoo.com.

Several of the accommodations in town – Flashpacker Pad (Sophat Tours), Tree Top Ecolodge (Smiling Tours) and Terres Rouges Lodge (who can provide French-speaking guides) – are also good at arranging guided tours and treks, as are the dedicated tour companies.

Cambodian Gibbon Ecotours   WILDLIFE
(☑097 752 9960; www.cambodiangibbons.wordpress.com; tours from US$100) Spend the night in the jungle, then rise well before dawn to spend time with semi-habituated northern buff-cheeked gibbons at this community-based ecotourism project (CBET) set up by Conservation International (CI; www.conservation.org) just outside the border of Virachey National Park, north of Veun Sai. The high-season-only tours cost US$100 to US$200 per person for a one-night/two-day tour, depending on group size and which tour company you choose. Most companies in Ban Lung can arrange these trips on behalf of CI.

This species was only discovered in 2010 and the population here is believed to be one of the largest in the world at about 500 groups. Hearing their haunting dawn call and seeing them swing through the canopy is memorable. These tours also offer the opportunity to experience dense jungle, open savannah, rivers and waterfalls, and to visit Kavet and Lao villages.

CI has an exclusive arrangement with the village near the gibbon site to run these tours within the Veun Sai–Siem Pang Conservation Area (VSSPCA). You stay at least one night in the jungle sleeping in hammocks or in a community-based homestay. The fee includes entrance to the VSSPCA, guide, homestays and camps, and all meals. The gibbon viewing season runs from November to mid-June – it's too wet at other times – and the visits are limited to six people at a time. For an organised tour to the area with transportation, try **Gibbon Spotting Cambodia** (☑063-966355; www.gibbonspottingcambodia.com) 🏃.

DutchCo Trekking Cambodia   TOURS
(☑097 679 2714; www.trekkingcambodia.com) One of the most experienced trekking operators in the province, run by – wait for it – a friendly Dutchman. Runs four- to five-day treks north of Veun Sai through Kavet villages and community forests, and one- to two-day trips around Kalai (south of Veun Sai), among many other tours.

Highland Tours   TOURS
(☑097 658 3841; highland.tour@yahoo.com) Kimi and Horng are husband-and-wife graduates of Le Tonlé Tourism Training Center in Stung Treng, who have moved to the highlands to run a range of tours, including fun day trips and a multiday tour between Veun Sai and Ta Veng that combines trekking with

floating down the Tonlé San on a bamboo raft. Horng is one of the only female guides in Ratanakiri.

Parrot Tours TOURS
(📞 097 403 5884; www.jungletrek.blogspot.com) Parrot runs a range of overnight treks in the forests north of Itub, home to throngs of gibbons. Sitha Nan is a national-park-trained guide with expert local knowledge.

🛏 Sleeping

Accommodation in Ratanakiri is terrific value, even by Cambodia standards. If the best places are booked out, several bog-standard high-rise hotels near the market have rooms in the US$10 to US$20 range, but none are worth writing home about.

★ Tree Top Ecolodge BUNGALOW $
(📞 012 490333; www.treetop-ecolodge.com; d US$7, cottage with cold/hot water US$12/15; 🖥) This is one of the best places to stay in Cambodia's 'wild east', with oodles of atmosphere. 'Mr T's' place boasts rough-hewn walkways leading to huge bungalows featuring mosquito nets, thatch roofs and hammock-strewn verandahs with verdant valley vistas. Like the bungalows, the restaurant is fashioned from hardwood and dangles over a lush ravine.

Up-to-date travel advice is plentiful, especially for those who are Laos bound.

Banlung Balcony GUESTHOUSE $
(📞 097 809 7036; www.balconyguesthouse.net; Boeng Kansaign; dm US$2, r US$5-20; @🖥) Under super-friendly French management, this long-standing backpackers has upped its game with a tip-top renovation of both the atmospheric main house and the enviably placed bar and restaurant, which features sunset views over the lake. The upstairs rooms, all polished wood and high ceilings, are borderline boutique, only at budget prices.

The cheapest rooms share bathrooms and there's a huge public balcony.

Flashpacker Pad HOTEL $
(📞 093 785259; flashpackerpad@gmail.com; Boeng Kansaign; r US$8-15; 🌬🖥) Quite literally a flashpacker pad, the rooms here have a touch of class, with flat-screen TVs and indigenous-made runners on white bedspreads. Go for a room with a view for misty mornings on the lake. Owner Sophat is a great source of info and runs a tour company.

LUMKUT LAKE & BOKHEO

Lumkut (បឹងលំកុដ) is a large crater lake hemmed in by dense forest on all sides, similar to the more illustrious and accessible Boeng Yeak Lom. To get to the lake turn south off the highway to O'Yadaw about 33km east of Ban Lung. The lake is 15km south along a rough road. Access is difficult in the rainy season, so most visitors opt for the convenience of Boeng Yeak Lom.

On the way to the lake you can stop off in **Bokheo** (បរកែវ), the current hotspot for gem mining, 29km east of Ban Lung. Locals dig a large pit in the ground and then tunnel horizontally in their search for amethyst and zircon. The mines tend to move around so ask around where to find them.

That gem mining is big business in the province is hardly surprising given that Ratanakiri means 'hill of the precious stones'. Just don't get suckered into a dream deal, as gem scams here are as old as the hills themselves.

Nature House Ecolodge GUESTHOUSE $
(📞 088 204 5888; r US$10-20; 🖥) Hidden away in the remote northwest corner of town, this place is worth seeking out for its expansive yet inexpensive rooms. Cheaper rooms are in the main building, which includes a small restaurant, while higher-priced rooms are in striking wooden bungalows in the garden.

Yaklom Hill Lodge LODGE $
(📞 011 725881; www.yaklom.com; s/d/tr US$10/15/20; 🖥) 🍃 Ratanakiri's only authentic ecolodge, staffed by ethnic Tompuon, is set amid lush forest near Boeng Yeak Lom, 5km east of Ban Lung's central roundabout. It will appeal to those who like nature. The all-wood bungalows are atmospheric but can get damp. A generator enables hot showers and light from 6pm to 9pm.

Hiking trails lead to the lake and beyond. Breakfast is included in the low season.

★ Ratanakiri Paradise Hotel HOTEL $$
(📞 016 300239; www.ratanakiriparadise.com; US$29-69; 🌬🖥🏊) A new ecolodge located to the south of Boeng Yeak Lom, the Ratanakiri Paradise Hotel is fast earning a name for itself as a great place to stay. Rooms are set in bungalows amid the lush, landscaped gardens and include a couple of two-bedroom

RESPONSIBLE TREKKING AROUND RATANAKIRI

Overnight treks in the forests of Ratanakiri are very popular these days. Diehard trampers spend up to eight days sleeping in replica US Army hammocks and checking out some of the country's last virgin forest in and around Virachey National Park.

Where possible, we recommend using indigenous guides for organised treks and other excursions around Ban Lung. They speak the local dialects and can secure permission to visit cemeteries that are off-limits to Khmer guides.

Unfortunately, with a few notable exceptions, the level of English among indigenous guides tends to be limited. If you need a more fluent English guide, we suggest hiring both an English-speaking Khmer guide and a minority guide, if it's within your budget.

A loose association of Tompuon guides is based at Boeng Yeak Lom – they can take you on an exclusive tour of several Tompuon villages around Boeng Yeak Lom. They have neither a phone number nor an email so you'll just have to show up. You can observe weavers and basket-makers in action, learn about animist traditions and eat a traditional indigenous meal of bamboo-steamed fish, fresh vegetables, 'minority' rice and, of course, rice wine.

Among private tour companies, only Yaklom Hill Lodge (p291) employs a full-time indigenous (Tompuon) guide, but you'll need to request him. Virachey National Park also employs some indigenous guides and uses minority porters, while the tour companies we recommend can all hire indigenous guides on request.

units for families. There is an infinity swimming pool with views over the garden.

There is also a spa with an unusually wide selection of rubs and scrubs, given the hotel's remote location.

★ **Terres Rouges Lodge**　BOUTIQUE HOTEL $$
(☏ 012 770650; www.ratanakiri-lodge.com; Boeng Kansaign; r/ste incl breakfast from US$55/80; ❄@🛜🏊) Even as the competition kicks in, Terres Rouges remains one of the most atmospheric places to stay in provincial Cambodia. The standard rooms are finished in classy colonial style, with beautiful Cambodian furniture, tribal artefacts and a long common verandah. The suites consist of spacious Balinese-style bungalows with open-plan bathrooms, set in the gorgeous garden.

If you're travelling with kids or looking for a little more comfort in Ban Lung, this option is a no-brainer.

Ratanakiri Boutique Hotel　HOTEL $$
(☏ 070 565750;　www.ratanakiri-boutiquehotel.com; incl breakfast standard/lakeview r US$29/39, ste US$69; ❄🛜🏊) This smart hotel with panoramic lake views offers spry service for this remote corner of the country. With inlaid-stone bathroom walls and indigenous bed runners, the Khmer-inspired design is eye-catching, but you're mainly staying here for the combination of lake-view balconies and generous mod-cons.

Ratanak Resort　BOUTIQUE HOTEL $$
(☏ 092 244114; www.ratanakresort.com; r US$39-100; ❄@🛜🏊) Located a few kilometres out of town on a bluff near Boeng Yeak Lom, Ratanak is a stylish, all-wooden resort with accommodation in upmarket bungalows. Rooms include four-poster beds with billowing drapes and useful extras for the dapper adventurer, such as a bathrobe and hair dryer. The small infinity pool here is open to non-guests for US$5.

Yeak Loam Hotel　HOTEL $$
(☏ 075-974975; www.yeakloamhotel.com; r US$20-99; ❄@🛜🏊) Looming large over downtown Ban Lung, this hotel offers 70 contemporary rooms with 40-inch smart TVs and inviting bathrooms. Only VIP rooms costing US$79 and up include breakfast. The hotel has an illuminated sky bar which draws a local crowd on weekend nights.

🍴 Eating & Drinking

Among the guesthouses, Terres Rouges Lodge has the most sophisticated menu, while Tree Top Ecolodge and Banlung Balcony are also reliable.

To get down with the locals, head to the lakefront near Coconut Shake Restaurant around sunset, plop down on a mat, and order cheap beer and snacks from waterfront shacks.

Night owls don't have much choice. Banlung Balcony has a great bar regularly brimming with backpackers and some local expats.

★**Cafe Alee** INTERNATIONAL $
(mains US$1.50-5.50; ⊘7am-9pm; 🖥📶) 🍴 This
friendly cafe has one of the more interesting
menus in town, including a generous smattering of vegetarian options, a hearty lasagne
and the full gamut of Khmer food. Be sure
to check the exciting specials board. It often
stays open later if there is drinking to be done.

They also run a scholarship to send indigenous kids to college.

★**Green Carrot** INTERNATIONAL $
(mains US$2-6; ⊘7am-10pm; 🖥) A great little
hole-in-the-wall restaurant that turns out
surprisingly sophisticated food, including
healthy salads, sandwiches and wraps, plus
a good range of Khmer favourites. It even
does a decent burger and some very affordable pizzas. Happy hour has two-for-one
cocktails from 6pm to 8pm.

Coconut Shake Restaurant CAMBODIAN $
(Boeng Kansaign; mains 6000-16,000r; ⊘7am-
9pm; 🖥) The best coconut shakes in the
northeast cost just 4000r at this little place
overlooking the lake. It has fried noodles and
other Khmer fare if you're feeling peckish.

Ta Nam CAMBODIAN $
(dishes 6000-12,000r; ⊘6am-8pm; 🖥) Locals
flock to this place for wholesome Cambodian and Chinese breakfasts, including steam-
ing bowls of noodle soup – guaranteed to
give an energy boost ahead of a trek in the
forest. It's a block east of the market.

Rith Any Banh Chav CAMBODIAN $
(dishes US$1; ⊘2-7pm) The owner here spe-
cialises in *banh chav* – a dish of meat,
baby shrimps, sprouts, veggies and spices
wrapped inside a thin egg pancake that's
wrapped inside a lettuce leaf, and dipped in
a zesty sweet-chilli sauce.

Everest INDIAN $
(mains US$3-5; ⊘7am-11pm; 🖥) It's Ban Lung,
not Brick Lane, but the extensive range of
Indian flavours on offer here is a welcome
relief from the over-familiar Ratanakiri
menu of Cambodian dishes, burgers and
pasta.

Pteas Bay Khmer INTERNATIONAL $$
(Boeng Kansaign; mains US$4-15) Ratanakiri
Boutique Hotel's wooden restaurant has an
imposing setting above the shores of Boeng
Kansaign, making it a good stop by day or
night. The menu includes some classic Cam-

bodian dishes, homemade pasta and select
cuts of meat.

ℹ Information

Visitors will find guesthouses or tour compa-
nies to be most useful in their quest for local
knowledge.

Canadia Bank (⊘8.30am-3.30pm Mon-Fri,
ATM 24hr) Full-service bank with an interna-
tional ATM.

Green Net (per hour 4000r; ⊘7am-9pm) Fan-
cooled internet access.

Tourist Office (☎075-974125; NH78; ⊘7.30-
11.30am & 2-5pm Mon-Fri) Official government
office with little in the way of handouts and
irregular opening hours.

**Virachey National Park Eco-Tourism Informa-
tion Centre** (☎097 333 4775; leamsou@gmail.
com; ⊘8-11am & 2-5pm Mon-Fri) The place to
organise trekking in Virachey National Park.

ℹ Getting There & Away

Ban Lung is 510km northeast of Phnom Penh
and 129km east of O Poang Moan, the junction
town 19km south of Stung Treng. Highway NH19
between Ban Lung and O Pong Moan is flat,
empty and fully sealed, but leave early as very
little public transport departs Ban Lung in the
afternoon.

There is a vast **bus station** (NH19) on the west-
ern outskirts of town, 2.5km west of Ban Lung's
main roundabout, but guesthouses and tour
companies can arrange pick-ups in town, which
is much more convenient.

Phnom Penh Sorya (☎077 880062) op-
erates early-morning buses to Phnom Penh
(US$10, 11 to 12 hours) via Kratie and Kompong
Cham, but these take the slow route via Snuol
and take hours longer than express minivans
(US$15, eight hours, frequent). Order the latter
through your guesthouse. Call a tour company or
guesthouse to arrange an express van pick-up if
coming from Phnom Penh.

Express minivans serve Stung Treng at 7.30am
and noon (US$7, two hours), or take a slow
morning local minibus from the bus station
(15,000r). A couple of companies run minivans
to Sen Monorom via the new highway (US$7, two
hours), with departures around 7am and noon.

Long-distance bus services to Siem Reap are
also promoted, but in reality this is a hassle, as
you will be forced to change buses, often with an
overnight, in Kompong Cham. You're better off
going to Stung Treng early in the morning and ar-
ranging onward transport by express minivan to
Siem Reap via Preah Vihear Province. Tree Top
Ecolodge can sort you out with this trip.

Advertised trips to Laos (Don Det and Pakse)
by express minivan depart at 7.30am and involve

ⓘ GETTING TO VIETNAM: BAN LUNG TO PLEIKU

Getting to the border The **O'Yadaw/Le Thanh border crossing** (7am to 5pm) is 70km east of Ban Lung along smooth NH19. From Ban Lung, guesthouses advertise a 7.30am bus to Pleiku in Vietnam (US$11, 4½ hours). The van picks you up at your guest-house for a surcharge, which is easier than trying to arrange a ticket independently. Alternatively, take a local minibus to O'Yadaw from Ban Lung's new bus station, and continue 25km to the border by *moto* (motorcycle taxi).

At the border Formalities are straightforward and lines nonexistent, but make sure you have a Vietnamese visa if required, as visas are not issued at the border.

Moving on Once on the Vietnamese side of the frontier, the road is nicely paved and *motos* await to take you to Duc Co (20km), where there are buses to Pleiku, Quy Nhon and Hoi An.

a van change and a few hours' wait in Stung Treng (to Don Det US$17, seven hours).

Local minibuses and pick-up trucks use the bus station to service Lumphat (10,000r, one hour), O'Yadaw (12,000r, 1½ hours) and more remote villages. Local minibuses also offer cheap transport to Kratie (25,000r) and even Phnom Penh (50,000r) for the adventurous and/or masochistic. Share taxis out of Ban Lung are rare.

Ratanakiri's airport has been closed to commercial flights for years.

ⓘ Getting Around

Bicycles (US$1 to US$3), motorbikes (US$5 to US$7), cars (from US$30) and 4WDs (from US$50) are available for hire from most guest-houses in town.

Cheng Heng (☑088 8516104; ⓒ6am-8pm) has some 250cc trail bikes for rent (US$25) in addition to a stable of well-maintained smaller motorbikes (US$6 to US$8).

Motos hang out around the market and some drivers double as guides. Figure on US$15 to US$20 per day for a good English-speaking driver-guide. A *moto* to Boeng Yeak Lom costs about US$5 return; to Veun Sai it's US$15 return; to any waterfall it's about US$7 or so return.

Remorks are expensive by Cambodian standards, about double what a *moto* costs.

Veun Sai

☑075 / POP 3000

Located on the banks of Tonlé San, Veun Sai (វ៉ុនសៃ) is a cluster of Chinese, Lao and ethnic minority villages. Originally, the town was located on the north bank of the river and known as Virachey, but these days the main settlement is on the south bank. There is not a lot to see on the south side, but there are some interesting settlements on the north bank.

From the south side, cross the river on a small ferry (500/3000r without/with a mo-

torbike) and walk west for a couple of kilometres, passing through the Khmer village, a Lao community and a small minority area, before finally emerging in a wealthy Chinese village complete with large wooden houses and inhabitants who still speak Chinese.

The Veun Sai area is known for Tompuon cemeteries, but most of them are closed to outsiders these days. The bans are at least partially the result of tourists flaunting behavioural protocols.

The closest cemetery to Veun Sai open to visitors is an ethnic Kachah cemetery in Kaoh Paek, a 45-minute boat ride upriver from Veun Sai. Expect to pay around US$40 for the boat trip from Veun Sai, or about half that from Kachon, 10km upriver (east) of Veun Sai. Tour companies in Ban Lung charge US$50 for an excursion here.

There are clusters of food stalls on either side of the ferry dock where you can pick up basic local meals like noodles and rice.

Veun Sai is 39km northwest of Ban Lung on an unsealed but smooth all-weather road. It is easy enough to get here under your own steam on a motorbike or with a vehicle. English-speaking guides ask US$15 or so return to take you out here on a *moto*.

Experienced motorbike riders can ride from Veun Sai to Siem Pang (65km) in Stung Treng via Itub (a few hours' walk south of the gibbon zone) along a scenic trail that begins on the north side of the river.

Virachey National Park

☑075 / POP 1000

Virachey National Park (ឧទ្យានជាតិវីរជ័យ; ☑097 333 4775; leamsou@gmail.com; US$5; ⓒoffice hours 8-11am & 2-5pm Mon-Fri) is one of the largest protected areas in Cambodia, stretching for 3325 sq km east to Vietnam, north to Laos and west to Stung Treng Province. The park has never been fully explored and is home to a number of rare mammals, including elephants, clouded leopards and sun bears, although your chances of seeing any of these creatures are extremely slim. However, you'll probably hear endangered gibbons and you might spot great hornbills, giant ibis and other rare birds. So important is the park to the Mekong region that it was designated an Asean Heritage Park in 2003. It is only possible to visit the park on organised treks booked through the Virachey National Park Eco-Tourism Information Centre in Ban Lung. The usual gateway is Ta Veng District on the Tonlé San, about 57km north of Ban Lung on a rollercoaster of a road.

🏃 Activities

Virachey has one of the most organised ecotourism programs in Cambodia, focusing on small-scale culture, nature and adventure trekking. The program aims to involve and benefit local minority communities. The park offers two- to eight-day treks led by English-speaking rangers. Private operators offer tours in the park buffer zone but are forbidden from taking tourists into the park proper. However, private tour companies can be useful in setting things up in advance with park staff, who are not always responsive.

Phnom Veal Thom Wilderness Trek HIKING
(per person US$236-413) The signature trek in Virachey National Park is this eight-day, seven-night odyssey. The trek goes deep into the heart of the Phnom Veal Thom grasslands, an area rich in wildlife such as sambar deer, gibbons, langurs, wild pigs, bears and hornbills. The price includes transport by *moto* to the trailhead, park admission, food, guides, porters, hammocks and boat transport.

Prices drop the larger the group. The trek starts from Ta Veng with an overnight homestay in a Brau village. Trekkers return via a different route and pass through areas of evergreen forest.

🛏 Sleeping & Eating

Most nights in the park will be spent in hammocks with mosquito-net covers. Minority village homestays are an option on most treks.

All food is carried in by guides and porters, and is included in the price of the trekking tour.

ℹ Getting There & Away

Transport by *moto* (motorcycle taxi) to the trailhead is included in the cost of your tour, or you can pay a bit extra for something more comfortable.

MONDULKIRI PROVINCE

POP 75,000

Mondulkiri Province (ខេត្តមណ្ឌលគិរី), the original wild east, is a world apart from the lowlands with not a rice paddy or palm tree in sight.

Home to the hardy Bunong people and their noble elephants, this upland area is a seductive mix of grassy hills, pine groves and rainforests of jade green. Wild animals, such as bears, leopards and especially elephants, are more numerous here than elsewhere, although sightings are usually limited to birds, monkeys and the occasional wild pig. Conservationists have established several superb ecotourism projects in the province, but are facing off against loggers, poachers, plantations and well-connected speculators.

Mondulkiri means 'Meeting of the Hills', an apt sobriquet for a land of rolling hills. It is the most sparsely populated province in the country, with just four people per square kilometre. At an average elevation of 800m, it can get quite chilly at night, so bring something warm.

Sen Monorom

073 / POP 10,000

The provincial capital of Mondulkiri, Sen Monorom (សែនមនោរម្យ) is really an overgrown village, a charming community set in the spot where the hills that give the province its name meet. In the centre of town are two lakes, leading some dreamers to call it 'the Switzerland of Cambodia'.

The area around Sen Monorom is peppered with minority villages and picturesque waterfalls, making it the ideal place to spend some time. Many of the Bunong people from nearby villages come here to trade: the distinctive baskets they carry on their backs make them easy to distinguish from the immigrant lowlanders.

⊙ Sights & Activities

Not much happens in Sen Monorom itself, but there are a few worthwhile sights within a motorbike ride or a long walk from town, including several waterfalls.

Don't miss gibbon spotting in the Seima Protected Forest (p302), about 30km from Sen Monorom.

Bou Sraa Waterfall   WATERFALL
(ទឹកជ្រោះប៊ូស្រា; US$2.50) Plunging into the dense jungle below, this is one of Cambodia's most impressive falls. Famous throughout the country, this double-drop waterfall has an upper tier of some 10m and a spectacular lower tier with a thundering 25m drop. Getting here is a 33km, one-hour journey east of Sen Monorom on a mostly sealed road.

To get to the bottom of the lower falls, cross the bridge over the river and follow a path to a precipitous staircase that continues to the bottom; it takes about 15 minutes to get down. There are some simple eateries out here if you're in the mood for food, and this is also the sight of the thrilling Mayura Zipline (p296), which now manages the site.

Wat Phnom Doh Kromom   BUDDHIST TEMPLE
(វត្តភ្នំដោះក្រមុំ) FREE Looming over the northeast corner of the air strip, Wat Phnom Doh Kromom has Mondulkiri's best sunset vista, where a wooden platform lets you take in the views over Sen Monorom. Continue another 5km north beyond to the wat for **Samot Cheur** (Ocean of Trees), another viewpoint overlooking an emerald forest to the east.

Dak Dam Waterfall   WATERFALL
(ទឹកជ្រោះដាកដាំ) Dak Dam Waterfall is 25km southeast of Sen Monorom, several kilometres beyond the Bunong village of Dak Dam. It's very difficult to find without assistance, so it's best to take a *moto* or local guide; otherwise, locals are able to lead the way if you can make yourself understood.

Romanear Waterfall   WATERFALL
(ទឹកធ្លាក់រមនា) Romanear is a low, wide waterfall with some convenient swimming holes. Set 18km southeast of Sen Monorom, it's very difficult to find without assistance, so it's best to take a *moto* or local guide.

Romanear II Waterfall   WATERFALL
(ទឹកធ្លាក់រមនាពីរ) The second Romanear Waterfall (p296) is known rather originally as Romanear II. It's near the main road between Sen Monorom and Snuol.

Monorom Falls   WATERFALL
(ទឹកធ្លាក់មនោរម្យ) FREE A 10m drop into a popular swimming hole, Monorom Falls is pretty if you can avoid the crowds and the attendant litter. From the west side of the air strip, head northwest for 2.3km, turn left and proceed 1.5km. There's no legible sign at the turn-off.

🏃 Activities

Several Bunong villages around Sen Monorom make for popular excursions, although the frequently visited villages that appear on tourist maps have assimilated into modern society. In general, the further out you go, the less exposed the village.

Trips to Bunong villages can often be combined with waterfalls or elephant interaction tours (eg walking with or feeding, not riding, the elephants). Each guesthouse has a preferred village to send travellers to, which is a great way to spread the wealth.

For more on Bunong culture check out the website of the Mondulkiri Resource and Documentation Centre at www.mondulkiri -centre.org, run by local NGO Mondulkiri Indigenous People Association for Development (MIPAD). MIPAD also runs the WEHH (p299) tour program, which offers an intimate look at Bunong culture in the Dak Dam community. Itineraries include 'Life on a Bunong Farm', 'The Handicrafts of the Bunong' and a trek into old-growth Bunong forest. Prices start from US$55 per person, subject to the size of the group.

Mayura Zipline   ZIPLINE
(📋 011 79 77 79, 071 888 0800; http://mon dulkresort.com; Bou Sraa Waterfall; US$45; ⊙ 9am-4pm) The Mayura Zipline is an adrenaline rush in the extreme, as the longest 300m-line passes right over the top of the spectacular Bou Sraa falls. The zipline course starts on the far bank of the river; there are a total of six lines to navigate, plus a suspension bridge. The first four zips are warm-ups for the high-speed flight over the waterfall; the course finishes with a short tandem line for couples or new friends.

It takes around one hour or so to navigate for smaller groups. Contact guesthouses and hotels for advance bookings or just show up at the new information centre at the falls. Discounts on the price are sometimes available.

Elephant Encounters
A backlash against riding elephants has led to a proliferation of interactive elephant ex-

Sen Monorom

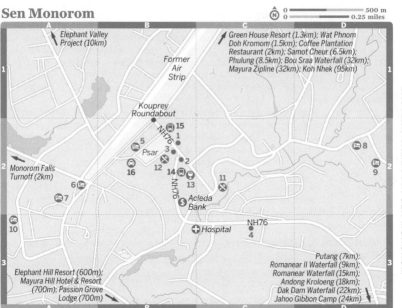

Sen Monorom

⊙ Activities, Courses & Tours
1 Green House	B2
2 Mondulkiri Elephant & Wildlife	
Sanctuary	B2
Mondulkiri Trail	(see 2)
3 Sam Veasna Center	B2
WEHH	(see 3)
4 WWF	C3

⊜ Sleeping
5 Avocado Guesthouse	B2
6 Chantha Srey Pich Guesthouse	A2
7 Happy Elephant	A2
8 Indigenous Peoples Lodge	D2
9 Nature Lodge	D2
10 Tree Lodge	A3

⊗ Eating
11 Café Phka	C2
Green House Restaurant &	
Bar	(see 1)
12 Hefalump Cafe	B2
Khmer Kitchen	(see 1)
Mondulkiri Pizza	(see 11)

⊜ Drinking & Nightlife
Chilli on the Rocks	(see 2)
MK Coffee Shop	(see 5)
13 The Hangout	B2

⊙ Transport
14 Kim Seng Express	B2
15 Rithya Express	B2
16 Taxi Park	B2
Virak Buntham Express	(see 14)

periences in Mondulkiri, with no fewer than four projects now offering tourists a chance to walk and interact with former working elephants in forest sanctuaries around Sen Monorom. Some are better run than others and some ensure more of their income is ploughed into elephant welfare than others, so it pays to do some homework before signing up for an elephant encounter.

★ **Elephant Valley Project** WILDLIFE RESERVE
(EVP; ☑ 099 696041; www.elephantvalleyproject. org; ⊙ Mon-Fri) For an original elephant experience, visit the Elephant Valley Project, a pioneering 'walking with the herd' project in Mondulkiri. The project entices local mahouts to bring their overworked or injured elephants to this 1600-hectare sanctuary. It's very popular, so make sure you book well ahead. You can visit for a whole day (US$85)

TREAD LIGHTLY IN THE HILLS

Tourism can bring many benefits to highland communities: cross-cultural understanding, improved infrastructure, cheaper market goods, employment opportunities and tourist dollars supporting handicraft industries. However, there are also negatives, such as increased litter and pollutants, domination of the tourism business by lowland Khmers at the expense of highland minorities, and the tendency of tourists to disregard local customs and taboos.

One way to offset the negatives in a big way is to hire indigenous guides. Not only does this ensure that your tourist dollars go directly to indigenous communities, it will also enrich your own visit. Indigenous guides can greatly improve your access to the residents of highland communities, who are animists and speak Khmer only as a second language. They also understand taboos and traditions that might be lost on Khmer guides. Their intimate knowledge of the forests is another major asset.

Interaction

➡ Be polite and respectful, especially with elderly people.

➡ Dress modestly.

➡ Taste traditional wine if you are offered it, especially during a ceremony. Refusal will cause offence.

➡ Honour signs discouraging outsiders from entering a village, for instance during a spiritual ceremony. A good local guide will be able to detect these signs.

➡ Learn something about the community's culture and language and demonstrate something good about yours.

Gifts

➡ Individual gifts create jealousy and expectations. Instead, consider making donations to the local school, medical centre or community fund.

➡ If you do give individual gifts, keep them modest (such as pens, pencils and notebooks).

➡ Do not give children sweets or money.

➡ Do not give clothes, as communities are self-sufficient.

Photographs

➡ Don't photograph altars.

➡ Don't use a flash.

➡ Do not photograph without asking permission first, and this includes children. Some hill tribes believe the camera will capture their spirit.

➡ Don't show up for 15 minutes and expect to be granted permission to take photos. Invest some time in getting to know the villagers first.

Shopping

➡ Haggle politely and always pay the agreed (and fair) price.

➡ Do not ask to buy a villager's personal household items, tools, or the jewellery or clothes they are wearing.

➡ Don't buy village treasures, such as altar pieces or totems.

Travel

➡ Make a point of travelling in small, less disruptive groups.

➡ Try to spend some real time in minority villages – at least several hours if not an overnight. If you don't have a few hours to invest, don't go.

or a half day (US$55). It does not take overnight visitors on Friday and Saturday nights and is not open to day visitors on Saturday and Sunday.

Mahouts who bring their elephants here are paid a competitive working wage to retire their elephants full-time to the forest and ecotourism. Mahouts continue to work with their elephants, feeding and caring for them and making sure they are as content as possible. The elephants, for their part, can spend their days blasting through the forest in search of food and hanging out by the river spraying mud on one another.

Visitors are not allowed to ride the elephants here. Instead, you simply walk through the forest with them and observe them in their element. In the process you learn a lot about not only elephant behaviour but also Bunong culture and forest ecology. Other project components include funding forestry protection for wild elephants, health care and other support for Bunong communities in the project area in exchange for use of the forest – and, most importantly, health and veterinary care for all the elephants in Mondulkiri, not just those resident in the valley. The Wildlife Conservation Society lauds the EVP for helping to protect the eastern reaches of the Seima Protected Forest.

The overnight options include a stay in spacious bungalows tucked into the jungle on a ridge overlooking the valley. A two-day package in dorm-style accommodation costs US$125, while private bungalows cost US$145. Longer stays of three days in the dorm/bungalow (US$235/265) and five days (US$405/455) are also available. Prices include full board.

Access to the site is tightly controlled, so don't show up unannounced as there are free-range elephants wandering around. The maximum number of day-trippers allowed per day is 12.

If you are in Mondulkiri at the weekend, you may want to consider an alternative elephant experience, such as visiting a community-owned elephant in the villages of **Putang** or **Phulung** or one of the other elephant experiences on offer, but we actively discourage elephant riding in Cambodia.

Mondulkiri Elephant & Wildlife Sanctuary ECOTOUR
(☑ 011 494449; www.mondulkirisanctuary.org; NH76; day visits per person US$45, 8-14yr US$22.50, under 8s free) 🐾 Established by LEAF (Local

Environmental Awareness Foundation), this is a small wildlife corridor near the Otai River. Overnight trips with camping out in the forest can be arranged. Group numbers are limited to 12 people per day. Volunteers are welcome and tours are run on weekdays and at weekends.

Trekking

Multiday forest treks run by guesthouses and tour operators are popular. Figure on about US$50 per person per day for overnight trips, including all meals, transfer to the trail head by *moto*, and an English-speaking guide. Per-person prices drop for larger groups.

We recommend securing indigenous Bunong guides for these trips: they know the forests intimately and can break the ice with the locals in any Bunong villages you visit. The better guesthouse-based tour operators, such as Nature Lodge and Green House, usually employ Bunong people on longer excursions, but you should request this service.

Yoga

Yoga classes take place on weekdays upstairs at the Hefalump Cafe. Headline activities outside of town include the Elephant Valley Project and the Jahoo Gibbon Camp in Seima Protected Forest.

🐘 Tours

Sam Veasna Center WILDLIFE
(☑ 071 553 9779, 012 520828; www.samveasna. org; Hefalump Cafe, Sen Monorom) 🐾 SVC works with the international NGO Wildlife Conservation Society (WCS; www.wcscambodia. org) in promoting wildlife and birdwatching tours in the Seima Protected Forest, including rare primate spotting at its wonderful Jahoo Gibbon Camp, 25km west of Sen Monorom. In Sen Monorom, ask for Pech.

SVC also runs birdwatching trips in Seima with highly trained guides for around US$100 per person per day; there's also a flat US$30-per-person conservation fee.

WEHH ECOTOUR
(☑ 097 273 9566; from US$55) 🐾 The WEHH tour program offers an intimate look at Bunong culture in Dam Dak community. Itineraries include life on a Bunong farm, the handicrafts of the Bunong and a trek into old-growth Bunong forest. Prices start from US$55 per person, subject to the size of the group.

This worthwhile project is operated by the local NGO Mondulkiri Indigenous People

Association for Development (MIPAD) in partnership with international NGO Nomad RSI. Hefalump Cafe frequently hosts MIPAD-organised exhibitions on Bunong culture.

WWF
ECOTOUR

(☏073-690 0096; www.panda.org; NH76) Involved in a host of ecotourism initiatives around Mondulkiri and runs its own set of tours north of Sen Monorom in the Phnom Prich Wildlife Sanctuary and Mondulkiri Protected Forest.

Mondulkiri Trail
TOURS

(☏088 593 5588; www.mondulkiritourguide.com; NH76; tours per person from US$50) Operated by experienced motorbike driver Monyhong, who can take you deep into the bush either on a day trip out of Sen Monorom or on overnight visits to Kratie, Ratanakiri or beyond.

Green House
TOURS

(☏017 905659; www.greenhouse-tour.blogspot. com; NH76) One of the longest-running tour operators in Mondulkiri, Green House organises the full range of forest treks and waterfall trips, and there are motorbikes for hire (per day US$6 to US$8).

🛏 Sleeping

Hot water is a nice bonus in chilly Mondulkiri, but it usually costs a little more. Places without hot-water showers can usually provide flasks of boiling water for bathing. There is rarely need for air-conditioning in this neck of the woods. The Elephant Valley Project offers an alternative lodging experience in the jungle

★ Nature Lodge
GUESTHOUSE $

(☏012 230272; www.naturelodgecambodia.com; r US$10-30; ☏) Sprawling across a windswept hilltop near town are 30 solid wood bungalows with private porches, hot showers and mosquito nets. Among them are Swiss Family Robinson–style chalets with sunken beds and ante-rooms. The magnificent restaurant has comfy nooks, a pool table and an enviable bar where guests chill out and swap travel tales.

Trek-fuelling burgers and pasta are the speciality, plus plenty of vegetarian options. An array of tours are neatly outlined on the menu, including the affiliated Mondulkiri Elephant & Wildlife Sanctuary.

Indigenous Peoples Lodge
BUNGALOW $

(☏012 725375; indigenouspeopleslodge@gmail. com; d US$5-15, q US$20; @☏) Run by a Bunong family, this is a great place to stay, with a whole range of accommodation set in minority houses, including a traditional thatched Bunong house with an upgrade or two. The cheapest rooms involve a share bathroom, but are good value. Perks include free internet and free drop-offs in town.

Chantha Srey Pich Guesthouse
GUESTHOUSE $

(☏012 550388; dm US$5, r US$6-8; ☏) One of the more popular budget places to stay in town, it offers a mix of dorm beds and affordable private rooms. Upstairs is a small bar with a pool table.

Happy Elephant
GUESTHOUSE $

(☏097 616 4011; dm US$2, r US$5-8; ☏) French-Khmer couple Vivi and Mot are your hosts with the most at this basic backpacker pad, which features sturdy cold-water bungalows cascading down a hill. They also offer tours and treks for those without a game plan.

Tree Lodge
BUNGALOW $

(☏097 723 4177; www.treelodgecambodia.com; d US$7-10, q US$12-15; ☏) Sixteen bungalows of various shapes and sizes drip down a hillside at the back of the reception. Rooms have balconies and attractive open-air bathrooms, but lack any shelf space or furniture besides a bed. Hang out at the restaurant, where hammocks and tasty Khmer food await.

The young family in charge are very welcoming and can help with tour arrangements.

Avocado Guesthouse
GUESTHOUSE $

(☏011 803884; avocado-guest-house@gmail.com; r US$15-20; ❋☏) A smart, modern guesthouse near the market, the rooms here are some of the best equipped in town for this sort of money. Rooms are US$5 cheaper if you forsake the air-con, a wise move in the cooler months of November to February. There's a small cafe downstairs.

Passion Grove Lodge
BUNGALOW $

(☏012 474777; passiongrovelodge@gmail.com; r US$20-25; ☏) Hidden away near the Mayura Hill Hotel, this place offers excellent value thanks to its spacious wooden bungalows with private veranda overlooking the passion fruit orchard. There is real potential when the word gets out.

Green House Resort
BUNGALOW $$

(☏017 905659; dm US$10, r from US$40; ❋☏) This is a lovely little resort on the edge of town which offers a generous air-conditioned dorm and some stylish and spacious rooms. There are extensive gardens, organic vegetables grown on site and a restaurant-bar to soak up the views of the surrounding hills.

Ayana Kandara
Boutique Hotel   BOUTIQUE HOTEL **$$**
(☏ 099 763854; www.ayanakandara.com; Road to Putang Village; r US$40-50; ❄ ⚬ ⚑) Located on a windswept hilltop about 6km from town, this new boutique resort has spectacular views of the Mondulkiri landscape. Rooms

are spacious and stylish for the money and the resort includes a small swimming pool amid the manicured gardens. Best suited to those with private transport given the remote location.

Chuncheat House Eco-Lodge   BUNGALOW **$$**
(☏ 088 800 0046; www.chuncheathouse.com; r US$20-40; ❄ ⚬) A quirky lodge on the outskirts of town, the bungalows here – although they are somewhat more gentrified

RESPONSIBLE ENCOUNTERS WITH ELEPHANTS

According to legend, more than one million elephants were used in the construction of Angkor Wat; in reality the numbers were closer to 6000, but elephants have long played an important role in Cambodian history. They were the tractors and tanks that gave the god-kings of Angkor the means to project their power across the region. Originally these elephants were trapped in the wild by the kingdom's indigenous communities.

This illustrious history was cut short by conflict, as captive elephants were marked as a 'legitimate war target' – they were either killed or their owners fled to neighbouring countries. Contemporary Cambodia has very few captive elephants left – just 73 at the last count – and their numbers are dwindling due to overwork and old age. Most are employed in the tourism industry. The biggest hope for the survival of their species lies with Cambodia's healthy wild population, which stands at around 500 and is protected by Cambodia's remaining forests, as captive elephants are no longer being bred.

The modern-day relationship between elephants and tourism is a complex one. There are now more elephants working to carry tourists around than to haul timber or rice, so their care is dependent on the dollars that tourism generates, and once captured they cannot return to the wild. However, there is increasing evidence that riding is actually damaging to the health of the elephant. There are also ethical concerns, given that these are highly endangered wild animals.

Before you consider signing up for an elephant encounter, ask to take a closer look at the animals and their environment. There are many activities tourists take part in that can unwittingly have a negative effect on the elephants. A few things to consider:

➡ Elephants don't like being ridden, especially by anyone who is not their mahout. Most riding also involves carrying large heavy baskets and hours of exhausting work that is damaging to the animal.

➡ Only mahouts have the training to go into the water with an elephant. Tourists have been injured while swimming with elephants in Asia; elephants can lash out if forced to spend longer in the water for the tourists' experience.

➡ Keep your distance taking photos; if you're turning your back to take a selfie, stand 3m to 5m away. Note also that flash photography can spook elephants, and harsh, unnatural light can upset them.

➡ If feeding an elephant, make sure there is a barrier between you and the animal, and feed to its trunk (not its mouth). Elephants often strike out when they are frustrated by not being fed correctly or quickly enough.

➡ Mahouts have a very close relationship with their elephants, understanding the mood and when it's safe to interact; tourists shouldn't approach an elephant unsupervised.

➡ Elephants in captivity are only a small proportion of the elephant population in Cambodia. Check if some of your money is going to fund wild elephant habitat conservation.

For more on issues with elephant welfare and tourism, check out www.elemotion.org or www.worldanimalprotection.org.

Compiled with assistance from Jack Highwood, Founder, Elephant Valley Project (www.elephantvalleyproject.org).

SEIMA PROTECTED FOREST: MONKEY BUSINESS IN MONDULKIRI

The 3000-sq-km **Seima Protected Forest** (https://cambodia.wcs.org/Saving-Wild-Places/Seima-Forest.aspx; Andong Kroloeng; wildlife spotting tours US$70-125; 🏕) 🖉 hosts the country's greatest treasure trove of mammalian wildlife. Besides unprecedented numbers of black-shanked doucs and yellow-cheeked crested gibbons, an estimated 150 wild elephants – accounting for around half of the total population in Cambodia – roam the park, along with bears and cats.

The **Wildlife Conservation Society** (WCS; www.wcscambodia.org) in partnership with ecotourism specialist Sam Veasna Center (p299) help to manage the forest, and there are a range of ecotourism initiatives under way, including primate spotting in Andong Kroloeng.

A recent WCS study estimated populations of 20,600 black-shanked doucs and more than 1000 yellow-cheeked crested gibbons in Seima Protected Forest; these are the world's largest known populations of both species. Jahoo Gibbon Camp offers the chance to trek into the wild and try to spot these primates. The Jahoo Gibbon Camp provides local villagers with an incentive to conserve the endangered primates and their habitat through providing a sustainable income. Treks wind their way through mixed evergreen forest and waterfalls, with an excellent chance of spotting the doucs and macaques along the way. Gibbons are very shy and harder to see, but thanks to recent field research by WCS and the community the local gibbon families are more used to people than gibbons elsewhere. You'll need to be up before dawn to spot them, however, so sleeping at the camp is highly recommended.

Many other species are present in this area; there is an enormous diversity of birdlife, including the spectacular giant hornbill, as well as chances to find the tracks and signs of more elusive species, such as bears, gaur (wild cattle) and elephants. Well-trained English speaking guides accompany guests on wildlife spotting trips for around US$70 to US$125 per person per day. Overnight stays are possible in the Jahoo Gibbon Camp, located on site. There's a flat US$30-per-person conservation fee for both day and overnight visits.

Sleeping

Jahoo Gibbon Camp (☎063-963710; https://samveasna.org/category/jahoo-gibbon-camp/; Andong Kroloeng; per person incl meals US$125-200) The Jahoo Gibbon Camp offers overnight tented accommodation. Rates include meals and a primate trek in the forest to spot rare yellow-cheeked crested gibbons and more common black-shanked doucs. Overnight trips sleeping in upscale tents, are possible through Sam Veasna Center (p299), based at the Hefalump Cafe in Sen Monorom.

Getting There & Away

The road to Sen Monorom passes right through Seima Protected Forest, so keep an eye out for monkeys if driving through. Andong Kroloeng lies about 5km from the NH76 and about 30km from Sen Monorom. The rates include a 4WD transfer from the NH76 for the last 5km to the camp, as the road can get pretty messy in the wet season. For the latest developments on tours in the park contact the Hefalump Cafe in Sen Monorom.

with ensuite bathrooms and decorative flourishes – are designed in keeping with the architecture of the Bunong and other minority groups. The sweeping views are impressive and there is a small restaurant here.

Elephant Hill Resort　　　　HOTEL **$$**
(☎073-500 0666; http://elephant-hill-resort-kh.book.direct/en-gb/; r US$80; 🌐🖥🛏) Perhaps inspired by their neighbours at Mayura Hill, the rooms here are set in spacious villas that double as suites. Each villa includes a

lounge, a bedroom and an indulgent *two* bathrooms. It's a good option for families looking for a comfortable midrange option.

★ **Mayura Hill Hotel & Resort**　　HOTEL **$$$**
(☎077 980980; www.mayurahillresort.com; incl breakfast r US$100-120, ste US$150; 🌐🖥🛏) Setting the standard for upscale accommodation in Mondulkiri, Mayura Hill is a lovely place to stay for those with the budget. The 14 villa rooms are tastefully appointed with woods and silks and the family villa includes

a bunk for the children. Facilities include a swimming pool and a five-a-side football pitch! The restaurant is the most sophisticated in town.

✖ Eating

Most of the guesthouses here have restaurants, the most noteworthy of which are Nature Lodge and Mayura Hill.

★ Coffee Plantation Resort   CAMBODIAN $
(☑012 666542; www.chormkacafe.com; mains US$2.50-7; ☺7am-9pm; 🛜) As the name suggests, this place is set in the grounds of an extensive coffee plantation, but offers some excellent local flavours, as well as the homegrown coffee. The *banh chaeuv* savoury pancakes are a wholesome meal for just US$2.50. There's also delicious honey-roasted chicken.

Café Phka   BAKERY $
(dishes US$1.50-5; ☺8am-5pm) Taught the art of baking (and meatballs) by some Swedish residents in Sen Monorom, this is the source of the delicious cakes that turn up in the Hefalump Cafe each day. Try carrot cake or banana and cinnamon cake, or go healthy with a sandwich or salad first.

Hefalump Cafe   CAFE $
(www.helalumpcafe-tourismhub.com; NH76; cakes US$1-3; ☺7am-6pm Mon-Fri, 9am-4pm Sun; 🛜)
🌿 A collaboration of various NGOs and conservation groups in town, this cafe doubles as a training centre for Bunong people in hospitality. Local coffee or Lavazza, teas, cakes and healthy breakfasts make this a great spot to plan your adventures over a cuppa.

Green House
Restaurant & Bar   INTERNATIONAL $
(NH76; mains US$2.50-3.50; ☺6.30am-10pm; 🛜) As well as internet access and tour information on the menu, Green House is a popular place for inexpensive Khmer and Western dishes. It also doubles as a bar by night with cheap beer and cheeky cocktails set to a soundtrack of ambient reggae beats.

Khmer Kitchen   CAMBODIAN $
(NH76; mains US$2-5; ☺6am-10pm; 🛜) This unassuming street-side eatery whips up some of the most flavoursome Khmer food in the hills. The *kari saik trey* (fish coconut curry) and other curries are particularly noteworthy, plus they also offer a smattering of international dishes.

Mondulkiri Pizza   PIZZA $
(☑097 522 2219; small/large pizza US$4/9; ☺10am-10pm) The big oven here churns out a steady supply of pizzas. Most are dispatched around town, as they deliver to your door if you're feeling lazy after a long trek.

★ Oromis Restaurant   CAMBODIAN $$
(☑097 884 5559; US$2-10; ☺7am-9pm; 🛜) Set amid lush gardens by the Oromis River about 5km from town, this is a lovely place to join out-of-town Cambodians enjoying the fresh mountain air for an extended lunch session. The extensive menu includes Cambodian and Asian favourites and you can chow down in any of the pavilions dotted about the grounds.

🍺 Drinking & Nightlife

For such a sleepy backwater it is perhaps surprising that Sen Monorom has not one, but two decent bars.

★ The Hangout   BAR
(☑088 721 9991) The bar at this backpacker guesthouse is the most happening spot in town. There are bar sports including table football, occasional jam sessions and some of Sen Monorom's best Western food to complement the Khmer menu. It's run by an affable Tasmanian-Khmer couple and has dorms and private rooms downstairs.

Chilli on the Rocks   BAR
(☺11am-11pm) Run by a friendly Swedish couple, Chilli serves cheap beer, strong cocktails and a menu of international bites, including authentic Swedish meatballs and a tasty tapas platter to go with the drinks. Closing hours are flexible, depending on the crowd, and they shut down for a few months in the rainy season as well.

MK Coffee Shop   COFFEE
(☑070 794939; Market Area; US$1.50-3; ☺7am-9pm; 🛜) Watch out Starbucks, as MK Coffee is in town. It is unlikely MK Coffee will face international competition any time soon given the remoteness of Sen Monorom, but it is ready with this contemporary cafe. This is barista brewed coffee practically from the source – it operates a coffee plantation nearby.

ℹ Information

Acleda Bank (NH76; ☺8.30am-3.30pm, ATM 24hr) Changes major currencies and has a Visa-only ATM.

The local tourist office is rarely open and stocks very limited materials. The leading guesthouses in town are good sources of tourist information.

Hefalump Cafe doubles as a 'drop-in centre' for Bunong people, and is the best source of information on sustainable tourism in Mondulkiri Province, including the Elephant Valley Project, the Seima Protected Forest and responsible tours to Bunong communities. It is advisable to try and book two to three days in advance to best ensure availability.

❶ Getting There & Away

The stretch of NH76 connecting Sen Monorom to Snuol and Phnom Penh (370km) is in fantastic shape and passes through large tracts of protected forest in Mondulkiri Province itself. Hardcore dirt bikers may still prefer the old French road, known as the 'King's Highway', that heads east from Kao Seima, which runs roughly parallel to NH76 and pops out near Andong Kroleng, about 25km from Sen Monorom.

There are no longer any buses to Phnom Penh, so take an express minivan (US$11 to US$12, five hours, frequent). There are several competing companies, but local residents say Virak Buntham have the most spacious seating.

Kim Seng Express (☑ 011 229199; NH76) Up to six minivans daily.

Ritya Express (☑ 092 963243; NH76) Four minivans to Phnom Penh daily.

Virak Buntham Express (www.virakbuntham. com) Two 11-seater vans daily.

Advertised trips to Siem Reap (US$20, 11 hours) usually involve a change of vehicle in Kompong Cham. Express minivans to Ban Lung (US$7, two hours, 8am and 1pm) and Kratie (US$9, three hours) can be booked through your guesthouse.

Local minibuses (departing from the **taxi park**) are another way to Kratie (30,000r, four hours). Count on at least one early morning departure and two or three departures around 12.30pm. Reserve the morning van in advance.

❶ Getting Around

English-speaking *motodups* (*moto* drivers) cost about US$15 to US$20 per day. Sample round-trip *moto* (motorcycle taxi) prices for destinations around Sen Monorom are US$12 to Bou Sraa, US$10 to Dak Dam Waterfall, US$5 to Samot Cheur and US$3 for Monorom Falls.

Most guesthouses rent out motorbikes for US$6 to US$8 per day and a few have bicycles for US$2. Pick-up trucks and 4WDs can be chartered for the day; they cost about US$50 around Sen Monorom in the dry season, and more again in the wet season.

Around Sen Monorom

Koh Nhek

☑ 073 / POP 6000

The final frontier as far as Mondulkiri goes, the village of Koh Nhek (កោះញែក) in the far north of the province is a strategic place on the overland route between Sen Monorom and Ratanakiri Province. This is traditionally where the road from Sen Monorom ended and the cattle track to Lumphat (in Ratanakiri) began. Now it's a rest stop on the new Mondulkiri–Ratanakiri highway, with several guesthouses and restaurants.

On the road north to Ratanakiri, **Phnom Kroal Guesthouse** (☑ 015 779799; penyon@ gmail.com; bungalows US$15; ☎) is the best of the guesthouses in town. Rooms are set in spacious bungalows with tasteful furnishings and a large bathroom, making the price an absolute giveaway, but you do have to put up with the on-site karaoke crooners by night. **Ly Sochea Restaurant** (mains 6000-15,000r), opposite Acleda Bank, offers some tasty Khmer fare. There is no menu as such, but the owners will invite you into the kitchen to point at their well-organised ingredients.

Minivans ply the major highway between Sen Monorom in Mondulkiri and Ban Lung in Ratanakiri. It costs about 10,000r per person to either town, although it is easier to get to Koh Nhek than to get out of town, as most minivans pass through full.

Understand Cambodia

Cambodia Today

Cambodia's political landscape shifted dramatically in the 2013 election, with major gains by the opposition Cambodia National Rescue Party (CNRP) further cemented in the 2017 commune elections. This set the scene for an unpredictable general election, but the Cambodian People's Party (CPP) manoeuvered to protect its future, and the opposition was dissolved in late 2017. Meanwhile, the economy continues to grow at a dramatic pace, but many observers are beginning to question at what cost to the environment.

Best on Film

The Killing Fields (1984) This definitive film on the Khmer Rouge period tells the story of American journalist Sydney Schanberg and Cambodian photographer Dith Pran.

Apocalypse Now (1979) In Francis Ford Coppola's masterpiece, Marlon Brando plays a renegade colonel AWOL in Cambodia and Martin Sheen is the young soldier sent to bring him back.

First They Killed My Father (2017) An adaptation of the bestselling Luong Ung book, which tells the story of her childhood surviving the Khmer Rouge regime.

Best in Print

The Gate (François Bizot; 2003) Bizot was kidnapped by the Khmer Rouge, and later held by them in the French embassy.

River of Time (Jon Swain; 1995) Poetic and personal account of his time caught up in the fall of Phnom Penh, as depicted in *The Killing Fields*.

Hun Sen's Cambodia (Sebastian Strangio; 2014) A no-holds-barred look at contemporary Cambodia and the rule of Prime Minister Hun Sen.

A Dragon Apparent (Norman Lewis; 1951) Classic travelogue of exploring Cambodia and French Indochine on the cusp of independence.

Politics

The Cambodian People's Party (CPP) has dominated the politics of Cambodia since 1979 when it was installed in power by the Vietnamese. Party and state are intertwined and the CPP leadership has been making plans for the future with dynastic alliances between its offspring.

However, this control was shaken recent national and local elections when the united opposition was able to make significant gains. In the 2017 commune elections, the opposition CNRP managed to win 489 communes, a tenfold increase on its performance in 2012, offering them a tangible share in local governance for the first time.

However, the overall political climate has been rapidly deteriorating, beginning in 2015 with the threatened arrest and subsequent self-imposed exile of then-CNRP leader Sam Rainsy. His deputy, Kem Sokha, took over the leadership of the party going into the commune elections, but was himself arrested in late 2017 on treason charges that many claim were politically motivated. To make matters worse for the opposition, the CNRP was officially dissolved by the Supreme Court in November 2017, putting major question marks over the legitimacy of the 2018 election.

There are many heated topics on the national agenda, including the sensitive shared border with Vietnam and land reform. Many rural areas of the country have been allocated to economic land concessions for regional companies to develop plantations, but observers suggest these have been used as a cloak for illegal logging and have led to land grabbing. The government is keen to promote land reform as a populist policy to help boost the rural vote.

Media

The governing Cambodian People's Party (CPP) controls most of the national television stations, radio stations and most newspapers. Opposition demonstrations or antigovernment activities are rarely reported via official channels. However, social media is plugging the gap and a new generation of young Cambodians are avid Facebook and YouTube users.

2017 saw a dramatic clampdown on the free press in Cambodia with the closure of the long-running Cambodia Daily under the duress of an unpaid tax bill. Broadcast licences were also revoked for Voice of America, Radio Free Asia and a slew of local radio stations adding up to the most aggressive assault on independent media in Cambodia since the establishment of a free press in 1993.

Economy

Badly traumatised by decades of conflict, Cambodia's economy was long a gecko amid the neighbouring dragons. This has slowly started to change, as the economy has been liberalised and international investors are circling to take advantage of the new opportunities.

The government, long shunned by international big business, is keen to benefit from these new-found opportunities. China has come to the table to play for big stakes, and annually pledges more money than all the other international donors put together, with no burdensome strings attached. There is huge investment from China and other Asian neighbours changing the urban landscape in the capital Phnom Penh.

Aid was long the mainstay of the Cambodian economy, and NGOs have done a lot to force important sociopolitical issues onto the agenda. However, Cambodia remains one of Asia's poorest countries and income is desperately low for many families, with the official minimum wage set at only US$170 per month.

Development Vs Environment

Cambodia's pristine environment may be a big draw for adventurous ecotourists, but much of it is currently under threat. Ancient forests are being razed to make way for plantations, rivers are being sized up for major hydroelectric power plants and the South Coast is being stripped of sand and explored by leading oil companies. Places like the Cardamom Mountains are on the front line, and it remains to be seen whether the environmentalists or the investors will win the debate. All this economic activity adds up to some impressive statistics, but it's unlikely to encourage the ecotourism that is just starting to take off.

GDP: **US$20.02 BILLION (2016)**

ADULT LITERACY RATE: **80%**

INFANT MORTALITY: **25 PER 1000 BIRTHS**

LIFE EXPECTANCY: **69 YEARS**

POPULATION: **16 MILLION**

if Cambodia were 100 people

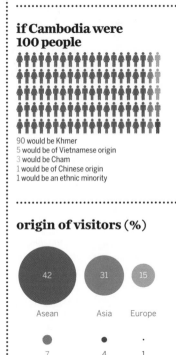

90 would be Khmer
5 would be of Vietnamese origin
3 would be Cham
1 would be of Chinese origin
1 would be an ethnic minority

origin of visitors (%)

42 Asean
31 Asia
15 Europe
7 Americas
4 Australia
1 other

population per sq km

CAMBODIA LAOS VIETNAM

≈ 29 people

History

'The good, the bad and the ugly' is a simple way to sum up Cambodian history. Things were good in the early years, culminating in the vast Angkor empire, unrivalled in the region during four centuries of dominance. Then the bad set in, from the 13th century, as ascendant neighbours chipped away at Cambodian territory. In the 20th century it turned downright ugly, as a brutal civil war culminated in the genocidal rule of the Khmer Rouge (1975–79), from which Cambodia is still recovering today.

The Origin of the Khmers

Like many legends, the story of the origin of Cambodia is historically opaque, but it does say something about the cultural forces that brought Cambodia into existence, in particular its relationship with its great sub-continental neighbour, India. Cambodia's religious, royal and written traditions stemmed from India and began to coalesce as a cultural entity in their own right between the 1st and 5th centuries AD.

Very little is known about prehistoric Cambodia. Much of the southeast was a vast, shallow gulf that was progressively silted up by the mouths of the Mekong, leaving pancake-flat, mineral-rich land ideal for farming. Evidence of cave-dwellers has been found in the northwest of Cambodia, and carbon dating on ceramic pots found in the area shows that they were made around 4200 BC. Examinations of bones dating back to around 1500 BC suggest that the people living in Cambodia at that time resembled the Cambodians of today. Early Chinese records report that the Cambodians were 'ugly' and 'dark' and went about naked. A healthy dose of scepticism may be required, however, when reading the reports of imperial China concerning its 'barbarian' neighbours.

India wasn't the only power to have a major cultural impact on Cambodia. The island of Java was also influential, colonising part of 'water Chenla' in the 8th century.

The Early Cambodian Kingdoms

Cambodian might didn't begin and end with Angkor. There were a number of powerful kingdoms present in this area before the 9th century.

From the 1st century AD, the Indianisation of Cambodia occurred through trading settlements that sprang up on the coastline of what is now southern Vietnam, but was then inhabited by the Khmers. These

TIMELINE	**4200 BC**	**AD 100**	**245**
	Cave-dwellers capable of making pots inhabit caves around Laang Spean; archaeological evidence suggests their vessels were similar to those still made in Cambodia today.	The religions, language and sculpture styles of India start to take root in Cambodia with the arrival of Indian traders and holy men.	The Chinese Wei emperor sends a mission to the countries of the Mekong region and is told that a barbarous but rich country called Funan exists in the Delta region.

settlements were important ports of call for boats following the trading route from the Bay of Bengal to the southern provinces of China. The largest of these nascent kingdoms was known as Funan by the Chinese, and may have existed across an area between modern Phnom Penh and the archaeological site of Oc-Eo in Kien Giang Province in southern Vietnam. Funan would have been a contemporary of Champasak in southern Laos (then known as Kuruksetra) and other lesser fiefdoms in the region.

Funan, a Chinese name, may be a transliteration of the ancient Khmer word *bnam* (mountain). Although very little is known about it, much has been made of its importance as an early Southeast Asian centre of power.

It is most likely that between the 1st and 8th centuries Cambodia was a collection of small states, each with its own elites who strategically intermarried and often went to war with one another. Funan was no doubt one of these states, and as a major sea port would have been pivotal in the transmission of Indian culture into the interior of Cambodia.

The little that historians do know about Funan has mostly been gleaned from Chinese sources. These report that Funan-period Cambodia (1st century to 6th century AD) embraced the worship of the Hindu deities Shiva and Vishnu and, concurrently, Buddhism. The *linga* (phallic totem) appears to have been the focus of ritual and an emblem of kingly might, a feature that was to evolve further in the Angkorian cult of the god-king. The people practised primitive irrigation, which enabled successful cultivation of rice, and traded raw commodities such as spices and precious stones with China and India.

From the 6th century, Cambodia's population gradually concentrated along the Mekong and Tonlé Sap Rivers, where the majority of people remain today. The move may have been related to the development of wet-rice agriculture. Between the 6th and 8th centuries, Cambodia was a collection of competing kingdoms, ruled by autocratic kings who legitimised their rule through hierarchical caste concepts borrowed from India.

This era is generally referred to as the Chenla period. Like Funan, this is a Chinese term and there is little to support the idea that Chenla

THE LEGEND OF KAUNDINYA & THE NAGA PRINCESS

Cambodia came into being, so the legend says, through the union of a princess and a foreigner. The foreigner was an Indian Brahman named Kaundinya and the princess was the daughter of a naga (mythical serpent-being) king who ruled over a watery land. One day, as Kaundinya sailed by, the princess paddled out in a boat to greet him. Kaundinya shot an arrow from his magic bow into her boat, causing the fearful princess to agree to marriage. In need of a dowry, her father drank up the waters of his land and presented them to Kaundinya to rule over. The new kingdom was named Kambuja.

600	802	889	924
The first inscriptions are committed to stone in Cambodia in ancient Khmer, offering historians the only contemporary accounts of the pre-Angkorian period other than from Chinese sources.	Jayavarman II proclaims independence from Java in a ceremony to anoint himself a *devaraja* (god-king) on the holy mountain of Phnom Kulen, marking the birth of the Khmer Empire of Angkor.	Yasovarman I moves the capital from the ancient city of Hariharalaya (Roluos today) to the Angkor area, 16km to the northwest, and marks the location with three temple mountains.	Usurper king Jayavarman IV transfers the capital to Koh Ker and begins a mammoth building spree, but the lack of water sees the capital move back to Angkor just 20 years later.

was a unified kingdom that held sway over all of Cambodia. Indeed, the Chinese themselves referred to 'water Chenla' and 'land Chenla'. Water Chenla was located around Angkor Borei and the temple mount of Phnom Da, near the present-day provincial capital of Takeo, and land Chenla in the upper reaches of the Mekong River and east of Tonlé Sap Lake, around Sambor Prei Kuk, an essential stop on a chronological jaunt through Cambodia's history.

The Rise of the Angkorian Empire

Gradually the Cambodian region was becoming more cohesive. Before long the fractured kingdoms of Cambodia would merge to become the mighty Khmer empire.

A popular place of pilgrimage for Khmers today, the sacred mountain of Phnom Kulen, northeast of Angkor, is home to an inscription that tells of Jayavarman II (r 802–50) proclaiming himself a 'universal monarch', or *devaraja* (god-king) in 802. It is believed that he may have resided in the Buddhist Shailendras' court in Java as a young man and was inspired by the great Javanese temples of Borobudur and Prambanan near present-day Yogyakarta. Upon his return to Cambodia, he instigated an uprising against Javanese control over the southern lands of Cambodia. Jayavarman II then set out to bring the country under his control through alliances and conquests, becoming the first monarch to rule most of what we call Cambodia today.

Jayavarman II was the first of a long succession of kings who presided over the rise and fall of the greatest empire mainland Southeast Asia has ever seen, one that was to bequeath the stunning legacy of Angkor. The key to the meteoric rise of Angkor was a mastery of water and an elaborate hydraulic system that allowed the ancient Khmers to tame the elements. The first records of the massive irrigation works that supported the population of Angkor date to the reign of Indravarman I (r 877–89), who built the *baray* (reservoir) of Indratataka. His rule also marks the flourishing of Angkorian art, with the building of temples in the Roluos area, notably Bakong.

By the turn of the 11th century, the kingdom of Angkor was losing control of its territories. Suryavarman I (r 1002–49), a usurper, moved into the power vacuum and, like Jayavarman II two centuries before, reunified the kingdom through war and alliances, stretching the frontiers of the empire. A pattern was beginning to emerge, which was repeated throughout the Angkorian period: dislocation and turmoil, followed by reunification and further expansion under a powerful king. Architecturally, the most productive periods occurred after times of turmoil, indicating that newly incumbent monarchs felt the need to celebrate, even legitimise, their rule with massive building projects.

Cambodia's turbulent past is uncovered in a series of articles, oral histories and photos on an excellent website called 'Beauty and Darkness: Cambodia in Modern History'. Find it at www.mekong.net/cambodia.

Cambodia's Funan-period trading port of Oc-Eo, now located in Vietnam's Mekong Delta, was a major commercial crossroads between Asia and Europe, and archaeologists there have unearthed Roman coins and Persian pottery.

1002	1112	1152	1177
Suryavarman I comes to power and expands the kingdom by annexing the Buddhist kingdom of Louvo (Lopburi in modern-day Thailand). He also increases trade links with the outside world.	Suryavarman II commences the construction of Angkor Wat, the mother of all temples, dedicated to Vishnu and designed as his funerary temple.	Suryavarman II is killed in a disastrous campaign against the Dai Viet (Vietnamese), provoking this rising northern neighbour and sparking centuries of conflict between the two countries.	The Chams launch a surprise attack on Angkor by sailing up the Tonlé Sap. They defeat the powerful Khmers and occupy the capital for four years.

By 1066, Angkor was again riven by conflict, becoming the focus of rival bids for power. It was not until the accession of Suryavarman II (r 1112–52) that the kingdom was again unified. Suryavarman II embarked on another phase of expansion, waging costly wars in Vietnam and the region of central Vietnam known as Champa. He is immortalised as the king who, in his devotion to the Hindu deity Vishnu, commissioned the majestic temple of Angkor Wat. For an insight into events in this epoch, see the bas-reliefs on the southwest corridor of Angkor Wat, which depict Suryavarman II's reign.

Suryavarman II had brought Champa to heel and reduced it to vassal status, but the Chams struck back in 1177 with a naval expedition up the Mekong and into Tonlé Sap Lake. They took the city of Angkor by surprise and put King Dharanindravarman II to death. The following year a cousin of Suryavarman II rallied the Khmer troops and defeated the Chams in yet another naval battle. The new leader was crowned Jayavarman VII in 1181.

Chinese emissary Chou Ta Kuan lived in Angkor for a year in 1296, and his observations have been republished as *The Customs of Cambodia* (2000), a fascinating insight into life during the height of the empire.

Jayavarman VII

A devout follower of Mahayana Buddhism, Jayavarman VII (r 1181–1219) built the city of Angkor Thom and many other massive monuments. Indeed, many of the temples visited around Angkor today were constructed during Jayavarman VII's reign. However, Jayavarman VII is a figure of many contradictions. The bas-reliefs of the Bayon depict him presiding over battles of terrible ferocity, while statues of the king depict a meditative, otherworldly aspect. His program of temple construction and other public works was carried out in great haste, no doubt bringing enormous hardship to the labourers who provided the muscle, and thus accelerating the decline of the empire. He was partly driven by a desire to legitimise his rule, as there may have been other contenders closer to the royal bloodline, and partly by the need to introduce a new religion to a population predominantly Hindu in faith. However, in many ways he was also Cambodia's first progressive leader, proclaiming the population equal, abolishing castes and embarking on a program of school, hospital and road building.

One of the definitive guides to Angkor is *A Guide to the Angkor Monuments* by Maurice Glaize, first published in the 1940s and now out of print. Download it free at www.theangkorguide.com.

Decline & Fall of Angkor

Angkor was the epicentre of an incredible empire that held sway over much of the Mekong region, but like all empires, the sun was to eventually set.

A number of scholars have argued that decline was already on the horizon at the time Angkor Wat was built, when the Angkorian empire was at the height of its remarkable productivity. There are indications that the irrigation network was overworked and slowly starting to silt up due to the massive deforestation that had taken place in the heavily populated areas to the north and east of Angkor. This was exacerbated

1181	1219	1253	1296
The Chams are vanquished as Jayavarman VII, the greatest king of Angkor and builder of Angkor Thom, takes the throne, changing the state religion to Mahayana Buddhism.	Jayavarman VII dies aged in his nineties, and the empire of Angkor slowly declines due to a choking irrigation network, religious conflict and the rise of powerful neighbours.	The Mongols of Kublai Khan sack the Thai kingdom of Nanchao in Yunnan, sparking an exodus southwards, which brings Thais into direct conflict with the weakening Khmer empire.	Chinese emissary Chou Ta Kuan spends one year living at Angkor and writes *The Customs of Cambodia*, the only contemporary account of life in the great Khmer capital.

by prolonged periods of drought in the 14th century, which was more recently discovered through the advanced analysis of dendrochronology, or the study of tree rings, in the Angkor area.

Massive construction projects such as Angkor Wat and Angkor Thom no doubt put an enormous strain on the royal coffers and on thousands of slaves and common people who subsidised them in hard labour and taxes. Following the reign of Jayavarman VII, temple construction effectively ground to a halt, in large part because Jayavarman VII's public works had quarried local sandstone into oblivion and left the population exhausted.

Another challenge for the later kings was religious conflict and internecine rivalries. The state religion changed back and forth several times during the twilight years of the empire, and kings spent more time engaged in iconoclasm, defacing the temples of their predecessors, than building monuments to their own achievements. From time to time this boiled over into civil war.

Angkor was losing control over the peripheries of its empire. At the same time, the Thais were ascendant, having migrated south from Yunnan, China, to escape Kublai Khan and his Mongol hordes. The Thais, first from Sukothai, later Ayuthaya, grew in strength and made repeated incursions into Angkor before finally sacking the city in 1431 and making off with thousands of intellectuals, artisans and dancers from the royal court. During this period, perhaps drawn by the opportunities for sea trade with China and fearful of the increasingly bellicose Thais, the Khmer elite began to migrate to the Phnom Penh area. The capital shifted several times over the centuries but eventually settled in present-day Phnom Penh.

The commercial metropolis that is now Ho Chi Minh City (Saigon) in Vietnam was, in 1600, a small Cambodian village called Prey Nokor.

From 1500 until the arrival of the French in 1863, Cambodia was ruled by a series of weak kings beset by dynastic rivalries. In the face of such intrigue, they sought the protection – granted, of course, at a price – of either Thailand or Vietnam. In the 17th century, the Nguyen lords of southern Vietnam came to the rescue of the Cambodian king in return for settlement rights in the Mekong Delta region. The Khmers still refer to this region as Kampuchea Krom (Lower Cambodia), even though it is well and truly populated by the Vietnamese today.

In the west, the Thais controlled the provinces of Battambang and Siem Reap from 1794 and held influence over the Cambodian royal family. Indeed, one king was crowned in Bangkok and placed on the throne at Udong with the help of the Thai army. That Cambodia survived through the 18th century as a distinct entity is due to the preoccupations of its neighbours: while the Thais were expending their energy and resources fighting the Burmese, the Vietnamese were wholly absorbed by internal strife. The pattern continued for more than two centuries, the carcass of Cambodia pulled back and forth between two powerful tigers.

1353	1431	1516	1594
Lao prince Chao Fa Ngum ends his Angkor exile and is sponsored by his Khmer father-in-law on an expedition to conquer the new Thai kingdoms, declaring himself leader of Lan Xang (Land of a Million Elephants).	The Thais sack Angkor definitively, carting off most of the royal court to Ayuthaya, including nobles, priests, dancers and artisans.	King Ang Chan I ascends the throne, defeats the Thais in a battle that gives modern-day Siem Reap its name and 'rediscovers' the great walled city of Angkor Thom on a hunting expedition.	The temporary Cambodian capital of Lovek falls when, legend says, the Siamese fire a cannon of silver coins into its bamboo defences. Soldiers cut down the bamboo to retrieve the silver, leaving the city exposed.

The French in Cambodia

The era of yo-yoing between Thai and Vietnamese masters came to a close in 1863, when French gunboats intimidated King Norodom I (r 1860–1904) into signing a treaty of protectorate. Ironically, it really was a protectorate, as Cambodia was in danger of going the way of Champa and vanishing from the map. French control of Cambodia developed as a sideshow to its interests in Vietnam, uncannily similar to the American experience a century later, and initially involved little direct interference in Cambodia's affairs. The French presence also helped keep Norodom on the throne despite the ambitions of his rebellious half-brothers.

By the 1870s, French officials in Cambodia began pressing for greater control over internal affairs. In 1884 Norodom was forced into signing a treaty that turned his country into a virtual colony, sparking a two-year rebellion that constituted the only major uprising in Cambodia before WWII. The rebellion only ended when the king was persuaded to call upon the rebel fighters to lay down their weapons in exchange for a return to the status quo.

During the following decades, senior Cambodian officials opened the door to direct French control over the day-to-day administration of the country, as they saw certain advantages in acquiescing to French power. The French maintained Norodom's court in splendour unseen since the heyday of Angkor, helping to enhance the symbolic position of the monarchy. In 1907 the French were able to pressure Thailand into returning the northwest provinces of Battambang, Siem Reap and Preah Vihear in return for concessions of Lao territory to the Thais. This meant Angkor came under Cambodian control for the first time in more than a century.

King Norodom I was succeeded by King Sisowath (r 1904–27), who was succeeded by King Monivong (r 1927–41). Upon King Monivong's death, the French governor-general of Japanese-occupied Indochina, Admiral Jean Decoux, placed 19-year-old Prince Norodom Sihanouk on the Cambodian throne. The French authorities assumed young Sihanouk would be pliable, but this proved to be a major miscalculation.

During WWII, Japanese forces occupied much of Asia, and Cambodia was no exception. However, with many in France collaborating with the occupying Germans, the Japanese were happy to let their new Vichy France allies control affairs in Cambodia. The price was conceding to Thailand (a Japanese ally of sorts) much of Battambang and Siem Reap Provinces once again, areas that weren't returned until 1947. However, after the fall of Paris in 1944 and with French policy in disarray, the Japanese were forced to take direct control of the territory by early 1945.

After WWII, the French returned, making Cambodia an autonomous state within the French Union, but retaining de facto control. The

The French did very little to encourage education in Cambodia, and by the end of WWII, after 70 years of colonial rule, there were no universities and only one high school in the whole country.

HISTORY THE FRENCH IN CAMBODIA

1772	1834	1863	1884
Cambodia is caught between the powerful Vietnamese and Siamese, and the latter burn Phnom Penh to the ground, another chapter in the story of inflamed tensions, which persist today.	The Vietnamese take control of much of Cambodia during the reign of Emperor Minh Mang and begin a slow revolution to 'teach the barbarians their customs'.	The French force King Norodom I into signing a treaty of protectorate, which prevents Cambodia being wiped off the map and thus begins 90 years of French rule.	Rebellion against French rule in Cambodia erupts in response to a treaty giving French administrators wide-ranging powers. The treaty is signed under the watch of French gunboats in the Mekong River.

immediate postwar years were marked by strife among the country's various political factions, a situation made more unstable by the Franco-Vietminh War then raging in Vietnam and Laos, which spilled over into Cambodia. The Vietnamese, as they were also to do 20 years later in the war against Lon Nol and the Americans, trained and fought with bands of Khmer Issarak (Free Khmer) against the French authorities.

The Sihanouk Years

The postindependence period was one of peace and prosperity. It was Cambodia's golden era, a time of creativity and optimism. Phnom Penh grew in size and stature, the temples of Angkor were the leading tourist destination in Southeast Asia and Sihanouk played host to a succession of influential leaders from across the globe. However, dark clouds were circling, as the American war in Vietnam became a black hole, sucking in neighbouring countries.

In late 1952 King Sihanouk dissolved the fledgling parliament, declared martial law and embarked on his 'royal crusade', a travelling campaign to drum up international support for his country's independence. Independence was proclaimed on 9 November 1953 and recognised by the Geneva Conference of May 1954, which ended French control of Indochina. In 1955, Sihanouk abdicated, afraid of being marginalised amid the pomp of royal ceremony. The 'royal crusader' became 'citizen Sihanouk'. He vowed never again to return to the throne. Meanwhile his father became king. It was a masterstroke that offered Sihanouk both royal authority and supreme political power. His newly established party, Sangkum Reastr Niyum (People's Socialist Community), won every seat in parliament in the September 1955 elections and Sihanouk was to dominate Cambodian politics for the next 15 years.

Although he feared the Vietnamese communists, Sihanouk considered South Vietnam and Thailand – both allies of the mistrusted USA – the greatest threats to Cambodia's security, even survival. In an attempt to fend off these many dangers, he declared Cambodia neutral and refused to accept further US aid, which had accounted for a substantial chunk of the country's military budget. He also nationalised many industries, including the rice trade, which angered many Chinese-Cambodians. In 1965 Sihanouk, convinced that the USA had been plotting against him and his family, broke diplomatic relations with Washington and veered towards the North Vietnamese and China. In addition, he agreed to let the communists use Cambodian territory in their battle against South Vietnam and the USA. Sihanouk was taking sides, a dangerous position in a volatile region.

These moves and his socialist economic policies alienated conservative elements in Cambodian society, including the army brass and the urban elite. At the same time, left-wing Cambodians, many of them ed-

1907	1941	1942	1947
French authorities successfully negotiate the return of the northwest provinces of Siem Reap, Battambang and Preah Vihear, which have been under Thai control since 1794.	A young King Sihanouk ascends the throne aged just 19 years old, beginning an incredible political career that will span about 70 years.	Japanese forces occupy Cambodia, leaving the administration in the hands of Vichy France officials, but fanning the flames of independence as the war draws to a close.	The provinces of Battambang, Siem Reap and Sisophon, seized by the Thais during the Japanese occupation, are returned to Cambodia.

SIHANOUK THE LAST OF THE GOD-KINGS

Norodom Sihanouk was a towering presence in the topsy-turvy world of Cambodian politics. A larger-than-life character of many enthusiasms and shifting political positions, amatory exploits dominated his early life. Later he became the prince who stage-managed the close of French colonialism, led Cambodia during its golden years, was imprisoned by the Khmer Rouge and, from privileged exile, finally returned triumphant as king. He was many things to many people, but whatever else he was, he proved himself a survivor.

Sihanouk, born in 1922, was not an obvious contender for the throne, as he was from the Norodom branch of the royal family. He was crowned in 1941, at just 19, with his education incomplete. In 1955 Sihanouk abdicated and turned his attention to politics, his party winning every seat in parliament that year. By the mid-1960s Sihanouk had been calling the shots in Cambodia for a decade.

The conventional wisdom was that 'Sihanouk is Cambodia', his leadership the key to national success. However, as the country was inexorably drawn into the American war in Vietnam and government troops battled with a leftist insurgency in the countryside, Sihanouk was increasingly seen as a liability.

On 18 March 1970, the National Assembly voted to remove Sihanouk from office. He went into exile in Beijing and joined the communists. Following the Khmer Rouge victory on 17 April 1975, Sihanouk returned to Cambodia as head of the new state of Democratic Kampuchea. He resigned after less than a year and was confined to the Royal Palace as a prisoner of the Khmer Rouge. He remained there until early 1979 when, on the eve of the Vietnamese invasion, he was flown back to Beijing.

Sihanouk never quite gave up wanting to be everything for Cambodia: international statesman, general, president, film director and man of the people. On 24 September 1993, after 38 years in politics, he settled once more for the role of king. On 7 October 2004 he once again abdicated, and his son King Sihamoni ascended the throne.

Norodom Sihanouk died on 15 October 2012 in Beijing and his body was flown back to Cambodia a few days later. More than 1 million Cambodians lined the streets from the airport to the Royal Palace and his body was laid in state for 100 days before an elaborate state funeral. However, Sihanouk's place in history is assured, the last in a long line of Angkor's god-kings.

ucated abroad, deeply resented his domestic policies, which stifled political debate. Compounding Sihanouk's problems was the fact that all classes were fed up with the pervasive corruption in government ranks, some of it uncomfortably close to the royal family. Although most peasants revered Sihanouk as a semidivine figure, in 1967 a rural-based rebellion broke out in Samlot, Battambang, leading him to conclude that the greatest threat to his regime came from the left. Bowing to pressure

1953	1955	1962	1963
Sihanouk's royal crusade for independence succeeds and Cambodia goes it alone without the French on 9 November, ushering in a new era of optimism.	King Sihanouk abdicates the throne to enter a career in politics; he founds the Sangkum Reastr Niyum (People's Socialist Community) party and wins the election with ease.	The International Court rules in favour of Cambodia in the long-running dispute over the dramatic mountain temple of Preah Vihear, perched on the Dangkrek Mountains on the border with Thailand.	Pol Pot and Ieng Sary flee from Phnom Penh to the jungles of Ratanakiri. With training from the Vietnamese, they launch a guerrilla war against Sihanouk's government.

from the army, he implemented a policy of harsh repression against left-wingers.

By 1969 the conflict between the army and leftist rebels had become more serious, as the Vietnamese sought sanctuary deeper in Cambodia. Sihanouk's political position had also decidedly deteriorated – due in no small part to his obsession with film-making, which was leading him to neglect affairs of state. In March 1970, while Sihanouk was on a trip to France, General Lon Nol and Prince Sisowath Sirik Matak, Sihanouk's cousin, deposed him as chief of state, apparently with tacit US consent. Sihanouk took up residence in Beijing, where he set up a government-in-exile in alliance with an indigenous Cambodian revolutionary movement that Sihanouk had nicknamed 'les Khmers Rouges' (Khmer Rouge). This was a definitive moment in contemporary Cambodian history, as the Khmer Rouge exploited its partnership with Sihanouk to draw new recruits into its small organisation. Talk to many former Khmer Rouge fighters and they'll say that they 'went to the hills' (a euphemism for joining the Khmer Rouge) to fight for their king and knew nothing of Mao or Marxism.

For more on the incredible life and times of Norodom Sihanouk, read the biography *Prince of Light, Prince of Darkness* (1994) by Milton Osborne.

Descent into Civil War

The lines were drawn for a bloody era of civil war. Sihanouk was condemned to death in absentia, a divisive move on the part of the new government that effectively ruled out any hint of compromise for the next five years. Lon Nol gave communist Vietnamese forces an ultimatum to withdraw their units within one week, which amounted to a declaration of war, as the Vietnamese did not want to return to the homeland to face the Americans.

On 30 April 1970, US and South Vietnamese forces invaded Cambodia in an effort to flush out thousands of Viet Cong and North Vietnamese troops who were using Cambodian bases in their war to overthrow the South Vietnamese government. As a result of the invasion, the Vietnamese communists withdrew deeper into Cambodia, further destabilising the Lon Nol government. Cambodia's tiny army never stood a chance and within the space of a few months, Vietnamese forces and their Khmer Rouge allies overran almost half the country. The ultimate humiliation came in July 1970 when the Vietnamese occupied the temples of Angkor.

During the 1960s, Cambodia was an oasis of peace while wars raged in neighbouring Vietnam and Laos. By 1970 that had all changed. For the full story, read *Sideshow: Kissinger, Nixon and the Destruction of Cambodia,* by William Shawcross (1979).

In 1969 the USA launched Operation Menu, the secret bombing of suspected communist base camps in Cambodia. For the next four years, until bombing was halted by the US Congress in August 1973, huge areas of the eastern half of the country were carpet-bombed by US B-52s, killing what is believed to be many thousands of civilians and turning hundreds of thousands more into refugees. Undoubtedly, the bombing campaign helped the Khmer Rouge in their recruitment drive, as more and more peasants were losing family members to the aerial assaults.

1964	1969	1970	1971
After the US-sponsored coup against President Diem in South Vietnam, Sihanouk veers left, breaking diplomatic ties with the USA and nationalising the rice trade, antagonising the ethnic Chinese business community.	US President Nixon authorises the secret bombing of Cambodia, which starts with the carpet bombing of border zones, but spreads to the whole country, continuing until 1973 and killing up to 250,000 Cambodians.	Marking the start of a five-year civil war, Sihanouk throws in his lot with the Khmer Rouge after being overthrown by his cousin Prince Sirik Matak and military commander Lon Nol, and sentenced to death in absentia.	Lon Nol, leader of the Khmer Republic, launches the disastrous Chenla offensive against Vietnamese communists and their Khmer Rouge allies in Cambodia. He suffers a stroke, but struggles on as leader until 1975.

While the final, heaviest bombing in the first half of 1973 may have saved Phnom Penh from a premature fall, its ferocity also helped to harden the attitude of many Khmer Rouge cadres and may have contributed to the later brutality that characterised their rule.

Savage fighting engulfed the country, bringing misery to millions of Cambodians; many fled rural areas for the relative safety of Phnom Penh and provincial capitals. Between 1970 and 1975, several hundred thousand people died in the fighting. During these years, the Khmer Rouge came to play a dominant role in trying to overthrow the Lon Nol regime, strengthened by the support of the Vietnamese, although the Khmer Rouge leadership would vehemently deny this from 1975 onwards.

The leadership of the Khmer Rouge, including Paris-educated Pol Pot and Ieng Sary, had fled into the countryside in the 1960s to escape the summary justice then being meted out to suspected leftists by Sihanouk's security forces. They consolidated control over the movement and began to move against opponents before they took Phnom Penh. Many of the Vietnamese-trained Cambodian communists who had been based in Hanoi since the 1954 Geneva Accords returned down the Ho Chi Minh Trail to join their 'allies' in the Khmer Rouge in 1973. Many were dead by 1975, executed on the orders of the anti-Vietnamese Pol Pot faction. Likewise, many moderate Sihanouk supporters who had joined the Khmer Rouge as a show of loyalty to their fallen leader rather than a show of ideology to the radicals were victims of purges before the regime took power. This set a precedent for internal purges and mass executions that were to eventually bring the downfall of the Khmer Rouge.

It didn't take long for the Lon Nol government to become very unpopular as a result of unprecedented greed and corruption in its ranks. As the USA bankrolled the war, government and military personnel found lucrative means to make a fortune, such as inventing 'phantom soldiers' and pocketing their pay, or selling weapons to the enemy. Lon Nol was widely perceived as an ineffectual leader, obsessed by superstition, fortune tellers and mystical crusades. This perception increased with his stroke in March 1971 and for the next four years his grip on reality seemed to weaken as his brother Lon Non's power grew.

Despite massive US aid, Lon Nol never succeeded in gaining the initiative against the Khmer Rouge. Large parts of the countryside fell to the rebels and many provincial capitals were cut off from Phnom Penh. Lon Nol fled the country in early April 1975, leaving Sirik Matak, who refused evacuation to the end, in charge. 'I cannot alas leave in such a cowardly fashion...I have committed only one mistake, that of believing in you, the Americans' were the words he poignantly penned to US ambassador John Gunther Dean. On 17 April 1975 – two weeks before the fall of Saigon (now Ho Chi Minh City) – Phnom Penh surrendered to the Khmer Rouge.

Lon Nol's military press attaché was known for his colourful, even imaginative media briefings that painted a rosy picture of the increasingly desperate situation on the ground. With a name like Major Am Rong, few could take him seriously.

During the US bombing campaign, more bombs were dropped on Cambodia than were used by all sides during WWII.

HISTORY DESCENT INTO CIVIL WAR

1973	1975	1977	1979
Sihanouk and his wife, Monique, travel down the Ho Chi Minh Trail to visit Khmer Rouge allies at the holy mountain of Phnom Kulen near Angkor, a propaganda victory for Pol Pot.	The Khmer Rouge march into Phnom Penh on 17 April and turn the clocks back to Year Zero, evacuating the capital and turning the whole nation into a prison without walls.	The Pol Pot faction of the Khmer Rouge launches its bloodiest purge against the Eastern Zone of the country, sparking a civil war along the banks of the Mekong and drawing the Vietnamese into the battle.	Vietnamese forces liberate Cambodia from Khmer Rouge rule on 7 January 1979, just two weeks after launching the invasion, and install a friendly regime in Phnom Penh.

The Khmer Rouge Revolution

Upon taking Phnom Penh, the Khmer Rouge implemented one of the most radical and brutal restructurings of a society ever attempted; its goal was a pure revolution, untainted by those that had gone before, to transform Cambodia into a peasant-dominated agrarian cooperative. Within days of the Khmer Rouge coming to power, the entire population of Phnom Penh and provincial towns, including the sick, elderly and infirm, was forced to march into the countryside and work as slaves for 12 to 15 hours a day. Disobedience of any sort often brought immediate execution. The advent of Khmer Rouge rule was proclaimed Year Zero. Currency was abolished and postal services ground to a halt. The country cut itself off from the outside world.

In the eyes of Pol Pot, the Khmer Rouge was not a unified movement, but a series of factions that needed to be cleansed. This process had already begun with attacks on Vietnamese-trained Khmer Rouge and Sihanouk's supporters, but Pol Pot's initial fury upon seizing power was directed against the former regime. All of the senior government and military figures who had been associated with Lon Nol were executed within days of the takeover. Then the centre shifted its attention to the outer regions, which had been separated into geographic zones. The loyalist Southwestern Zone forces, under the control of one-legged general Ta Mok, were sent into region after region to 'purify' the population, a process that saw thousands perish.

The cleansing reached grotesque heights in the final and bloodiest purge against the powerful and independent Eastern Zone. Generally considered more moderate than other Khmer Rouge factions, the Eastern Zone was ideologically, as well as geographically, closer to Vietnam. The Pol Pot faction consolidated the rest of the country before moving against the east from 1977 onwards. Hundreds of leaders were executed before open rebellion broke out, sparking a civil war in the east. Many Eastern Zone leaders fled to Vietnam, forming the nucleus of the government installed by the Vietnamese in January 1979. The people were defenceless and distrusted – 'Cambodian bodies with Vietnamese minds' or 'duck's arses with chicken's heads' – and were deported to the northwest with new, blue *kramas* (scarves). Had it not been for the Vietnamese invasion, all would have perished, as the blue *krama* was a secret party sign indicating an eastern enemy of the revolution.

Hundreds of thousands of people were executed by the Khmer Rouge leadership, while hundreds of thousands more died of famine and disease. Meals consisted of little more than watery rice porridge twice a day, but were meant to sustain men, women and children through a back-breaking day in the fields. Disease stalked the work camps, malaria and dysentery striking down whole families; death was a relief for

To the End of Hell: One Woman's Struggle to Survive Cambodia's Khmer Rouge is the incredible memoir of Denise Affonço, one of the only foreigners to live through the Khmer Rouge revolution, due to her marriage to a senior intellectual in the movement.

1980	1982	1984	1985
Cambodia is gripped by a terrible famine, as the dislocation of the previous few years means that no rice has been planted or harvested, and worldwide 'Save Kampuchea' appeals are launched.	Sihanouk is pressured to join the Khmer Rouge as head of the Coalition Government of Democratic Kampuchea (CGDK), a new military front against the Vietnamese-backed government in Phnom Penh.	The Vietnamese embark on a major offensive in the west of Cambodia and the Khmer Rouge and its allies are forced to retreat to refugee camps and bases inside Thailand.	There is a changing of the guard at the top and Hun Sen becomes Prime Minister of Cambodia, a title he still holds today with the Cambodian People's Party (CPP).

many from the horrors of life. Some zones were better than others, some leaders fairer than others, but life for the majority was one of unending misery and suffering in this 'prison without walls'.

As the centre eliminated more and more moderates, Angkar (the organisation) became the only family people needed and those who did not agree were sought out and crushed. The Khmer Rouge detached the Cambodian people from all they held dear: their families, their food, their fields and their faith. Even the peasants who had supported the revolution could no longer blindly follow such insanity. Nobody cared for the Khmer Rouge by 1978, but nobody had an ounce of strength to do anything about it...except the Vietnamese.

Enter the Vietnamese

Relations between Cambodia and Vietnam have historically been tense, as the Vietnamese have slowly but steadily expanded southwards, encroaching on Cambodian territory. Despite the fact the two communist parties had fought together as brothers in arms, old tensions soon came to the fore.

From 1976 to 1978, the Khmer Rouge instigated a series of border clashes with Vietnam, and claimed the Mekong Delta, once part of the Khmer empire. Incursions into Vietnamese border provinces left hundreds of Vietnamese civilians dead. On 25 December 1978 Vietnam launched a full-scale invasion of Cambodia, toppling the Pol Pot government two weeks later. As Vietnamese tanks neared Phnom Penh, the Khmer Rouge fled westward with as many civilians as it could seize, taking refuge in the jungles and mountains along the Thai border.

The Vietnamese installed a new government led by several former Khmer Rouge officers, including current Prime Minister Hun Sen, who had defected to Vietnam in 1977. The Khmer Rouge's patrons, the Chinese communists, launched a massive reprisal raid across Vietnam's northernmost border in early 1979 in an attempt to buy their allies time. It failed and after 17 days the Chinese withdrew, their fingers badly burnt by their Vietnamese enemies. The Vietnamese then staged a show trial in Cambodia in which Pol Pot and Ieng Sary were condemned to death in absentia for their genocidal acts.

A traumatised population took to the road in search of surviving family members. Millions had been uprooted and had to walk hundreds of kilometres across the country. Rice stocks were decimated, the harvest left to wither and little rice planted, sowing the seeds for a widespread famine in 1979 and 1980.

As the conflict in Cambodia raged, Sihanouk agreed in 1982, under pressure from China, to head a military and political front opposed to the Phnom Penh government. The Sihanouk-led resistance coalition brought together – on paper, at least – Funcinpec (the French acronym

Only a handful of foreigners were allowed to visit Cambodia during the Khmer Rouge period of Democratic Kampuchea. US journalist Elizabeth Becker was one who travelled there in late 1978; her book *When the War Was Over* (1986) tells her story.

1989	1991	1993	1994
As the effects of President Gorbachev's perestroika (restructuring) begin to impact on communist allies, Vietnam feels the pinch and announces the withdrawal of its forces from Cambodia.	The Paris Peace Accords are signed, in which all parties, including the Khmer Rouge, agree to participate in free and fair elections supervised by the UN.	The pro-Sihanouk royalist party Funcinpec, under the leadership of Prince Ranariddh, wins the popular vote, but the communist CPP threatens secession in the east to muscle its way into government.	The Khmer Rouge targets foreign tourists in Cambodia, kidnapping and killing groups travelling by taxi and train to the South Coast, reinforcing Cambodia's overseas image as a dangerous country.

The Documentation Center of Cambodia is an organisation established to document the crimes of the Khmer Rouge as a record for future generations. Its excellent website has a wealth of information about Cambodia's darkest hour. Take your time to visit www.dccam.org.

The Killing Fields (1985) is the definitive film on the Khmer Rouge period in Cambodia. It tells the story of American journalist Sydney Schanberg and his Cambodian assistant Dith Pran during and after the war.

for the National United Front for an Independent, Neutral, Peaceful and Cooperative Cambodia), which comprised a royalist group loyal to Sihanouk; the Khmer People's National Liberation Front, a noncommunist grouping under former prime minister Son Sann; and the Khmer Rouge, officially known as the Party of Democratic Kampuchea and by far the most powerful of the three. The crimes of the Khmer Rouge were swept aside to ensure a compromise that suited the realpolitik of the day.

For much of the 1980s Cambodia remained closed to the Western world, save for the presence of some humanitarian aid groups. Government policy was effectively under the control of the Vietnamese, so Cambodia found itself very much in the Eastern-bloc camp. The economy was in tatters for most of this period, as Cambodia, like Vietnam, suffered from the effects of a US-sponsored embargo.

In 1984, the Vietnamese overran all the major rebel camps inside Cambodia, forcing the Khmer Rouge and its allies to retreat into Thailand. From this time the Khmer Rouge and its allies engaged in guerrilla warfare aimed at demoralising its opponents. Tactics used by the Khmer Rouge included shelling government-controlled garrison towns, planting thousands of mines in rural areas, attacking road transport, blowing up bridges, kidnapping village chiefs and targeting civilians. The Khmer Rouge also forced thousands of men, women and children living in the refugee camps it controlled to work as porters, ferrying ammunition and other supplies into Cambodia across heavily mined sections of the border.

The Vietnamese, for their part, laid the world's longest minefield, known as K-5 and stretching from the Gulf of Thailand to the Lao border, in an attempt to seal out the guerrillas. They also sent Cambodians into the forests to cut down trees on remote sections of road to prevent ambushes. Thousands died of disease and from injuries sustained from land mines. The Khmer Rouge was no longer in power, but for many the 1980s were almost as tough as the 1970s – it was one long struggle to survive.

The Politics of Disaster Relief

The Cambodian famine became a new front in the Cold War, as Washington and Moscow jostled for influence from afar. As hundreds of thousands of Cambodians fled to Thailand, a massive international famine relief effort, sponsored by the UN, was launched. The international community wanted to deliver aid across a land bridge at Poipet, while the new Vietnamese-backed Phnom Penh government wanted all supplies to come through the capital via Kompong Som (Sihanoukville) or the Mekong River. Both sides had their reasons – the new government did not want aid to fall into the hands of its Khmer Rouge enemies, while

1995	1996	1997	1998
Prince Norodom Sirivudh is arrested and exiled for allegedly plotting to kill Prime Minister Hun Sen, removing another potential rival from the scene.	British deminer Christopher Howes, working in Cambodia with the Mines Advisory Group (MAG), is kidnapped by the Khmer Rouge and later killed, together with his interpreter Houn Hourth.	Second Prime Minister Hun Sen overthrows First Prime Minister Norodom Ranariddh in a military coup, referred to as 'the events of 1997' in Cambodia.	Pol Pot dies on 15 April as Anlong Veng falls to government forces, and many observers ponder whether the timing is coincidental.

the international community didn't believe the new government had the infrastructure to distribute the aid – and both fears were right.

Some agencies distributed aid the slow way through Phnom Penh, and others set up camps in Thailand. The camps became a magnet for half of Cambodia, as many Khmers still feared the return of the Khmer Rouge or were seeking a new life overseas. The Thai military convinced the international community to distribute all aid through their channels and used this as a cloak to rebuild the shattered Khmer Rouge forces as an effective resistance against the Vietnamese. Thailand demanded that, as a condition for allowing international food aid for Cambodia to pass through its territory, food had to be supplied to the Khmer Rouge forces encamped in the Thai border region as well. Along with weaponry supplied by China, this international assistance was essential in enabling the Khmer Rouge to rebuild its military strength and fight on for another two decades.

For the full flavour of Cambodian history, from humble beginnings in the prehistoric period through the glories of Angkor and right up to the present day, grab a copy of *The History of Cambodia* (1994), by David Chandler.

The UN Comes to Town

The arrival of Mikhail Gorbachev in the Kremlin saw the Cold War draw to a close. It was the furthest-flung Soviet allies who were cut adrift first, leaving Vietnam internationally isolated and economically crippled. In September 1989, Vietnam announced the withdrawal of all its troops from Cambodia. With the Vietnamese gone, the opposition coalition, still dominated by the Khmer Rouge, launched a series of offensives, forcing the now-vulnerable government to the negotiating table.

Diplomatic efforts to end the civil war began to bear fruit in September 1990, when a peace plan was accepted by both the Phnom Penh government and the three factions of the resistance coalition. According to the plan, the Supreme National Council (SNC), a coalition of all factions, would be formed under the presidency of Sihanouk. Meanwhile, the UN Transitional Authority in Cambodia (Untac) would supervise the administration of the country for two years, with the goal of free and fair elections.

Untac undoubtedly achieved some successes, but for all of these, it is the failures that were to cost Cambodia dearly in the 'democratic' era. Untac was successful in pushing through many international human-rights covenants; it opened the door to a significant number of nongovernmental organisations (NGOs); and, most importantly, on 25 May 1993, elections were held with an 89.6% turnout. However, the results were far from decisive. Funcinpec, led by Prince Norodom Ranariddh, took 58 seats in the National Assembly, while the Cambodian People's Party (CPP), which represented the previous communist government, took 51 seats. The CPP had lost the election, but senior leaders threatened a secession of the eastern provinces of the country. As a result, Cambodia ended up with two prime ministers: Norodom Ranariddh as first prime minister, and Hun Sen as second prime minister.

Journalist Henry Kamm spent many years filing reports from Cambodia in the 1970s and 1990s, and his book *Cambodia: Report from a Stricken Land* is a fascinating insight into recent events.

1999	2000	2002	2003
Cambodia finally joins Asean after a two-year delay, taking its place among the family of Southeast Asian nations, which welcome the country back onto the world stage.	The Cambodian Freedom Fighters (CFF) launch an 'assault' on Phnom Penh. Backed by Cambodian-American dissidents, the attackers are lightly armed, poorly trained and politically inexperienced.	Cambodia holds its first ever local elections at commune level, a tentative step towards dismantling the old communist system of control and bringing grass-roots democracy to the country.	The CPP wins the election, but political infighting prevents the formation of the new government for almost a year until the old coalition with Funcinpec is revived.

THE NAME GAME

Cambodia has changed its name so many times over the last few decades that there are understandable grounds for confusion. To the Cambodians, their country is Kampuchea. The name is derived from the word 'Kambuja', meaning 'those born of Kambu', the mythical founder of the country. It dates back as far as the 10th century. The Portuguese 'Camboxa' and the French 'Cambodge', from which the English name 'Cambodia' is derived, are adaptations of 'Kambuja'.

It was the Khmer Rouge that insisted the outside world use the name Kampuchea. Changing the country's official English name back to Cambodia was intended as a symbolic move to distance the present government in Phnom Penh from the bitter connotations of the name Kampuchea, which Westerners associate with the Khmer Rouge regime.

Even today, Untac is heralded as one of the UN's success stories. Another perspective is that it was an ill-conceived and poorly executed peace because so many of the powers involved in brokering the deal had their own agendas to advance. To many Cambodians who had survived the 1970s, it was unthinkable that the Khmer Rouge would be allowed to play a part in the electoral process after presiding over a genocide.

The UN's disarmament program took weapons away from rural militias who for so long provided the backbone of the government's provincial defence network against the Khmer Rouge and this left communities throughout the country vulnerable to attack. Meanwhile the Khmer Rouge used the veil of legitimacy conferred upon it by the peace process to re-establish a guerrilla network throughout Cambodia. By 1994, when it was finally outlawed by the government, the Khmer Rouge was arguably a greater threat to the stability of Cambodia than at any time since 1979.

Untac's main goals had been to 'restore and maintain peace' and 'promote national reconciliation', and in the short term it achieved neither. It did oversee free and fair elections, but these were later annulled by the actions of Cambodia's politicians. Little was done during the UN period to try to dismantle the communist apparatus of state set up by the CPP, a well-oiled machine that continues to ensure that former communists control the civil service, judiciary, army and police today.

During much of the 1980s, the second-largest concentration of Cambodians outside Phnom Penh was in the Khao-I-Dang refugee camp on the Thai border.

The Slow Birth of Peace

When the Vietnamese toppled the Pol Pot government in 1979, the Khmer Rouge disappeared into the jungle. The guerrillas eventually boycotted the 1993 elections and later rejected peace talks aimed at establishing a ceasefire. In 1994, the Khmer Rouge resorted to a new tactic of targeting

2004	2005	2006	2007
In a move that catches observers by surprise, King Sihanouk abdicates the throne and is succeeded by his son King Sihamoni, a popular choice as Sihamoni has steered clear of politics.	Cambodia joins the WTO, opening its markets to free trade, but many commentators feel it could be counterproductive, as the economy is so small and there is no more protection for domestic producers.	Lawsuits and counter lawsuits see political leaders moving from conflict to courtroom in the new Cambodia. The revolving doors stop with opposition leader Sam Rainsy back in the country and Prince Ranariddh out.	Royalist party Funcinpec continues to implode in the face of conflict, intrigue and defections, with democrats joining Sam Rainsy, loyalists joining the new Norodom Ranariddh Party and others joining the CPP.

tourists, with horrendous results for a number of foreigners in Cambodia. During 1994, three people were taken from a taxi on the road to Sihanoukville and subsequently shot. A few months later another three foreigners were seized from a train bound for Sihanoukville and in the ransom drama that followed they were executed as the army closed in.

The government changed course during the mid-1990s, opting for more carrot and less stick in a bid to end the war. The breakthrough came in 1996 when Ieng Sary, Brother Number Three in the Khmer Rouge hierarchy and foreign minister during its rule, was denounced by Pol Pot for corruption. He subsequently led a mass defection of fighters and their dependants from the Pailin area, and this effectively sealed the fate of the remaining Khmer Rouge. Pailin, rich in gems and timber, had long been the economic crutch that kept the Khmer Rouge hobbling along. The severing of this income, coupled with the fact that government forces now had only one front on which to concentrate their resources, suggested the days of civil war were numbered.

By 1997, cracks were appearing in the coalition and the fledgling democracy once again found itself under siege. But it was the Khmer Rouge that again grabbed the headlines. Pol Pot ordered the execution of Son Sen, defence minister during the Khmer Rouge regime, and many of his family members. This provoked a putsch within the Khmer Rouge leadership, and the one-legged hardliner general Ta Mok seized control, putting Pol Pot on 'trial'. Rumours flew about Phnom Penh that Pol Pot would be brought there to face international justice, but events dramatically shifted back to the capital.

A lengthy courting period ensued in which both Funcinpec and the CPP attempted to win the trust of the remaining Khmer Rouge hardliners in northern Cambodia. Ranariddh was close to forging a deal with the jungle fighters and was keen to get it sewn up before Cambodia's accession to Asean, as nothing would provide a better entry fanfare than the ending of Cambodia's long civil war. He was outflanked and subsequently outgunned by Second Prime Minister Hun Sen. On 5 July 1997, fighting again erupted on the streets of Phnom Penh as troops loyal to the CPP clashed with those loyal to Funcinpec. The heaviest exchanges were around the airport and key government buildings, but before long the dust had settled and the CPP once again controlled Cambodia. Euphemistically known as 'the events of 1997' in Cambodia, much of the international community condemned the violence as a coup.

As 1998 began, the CPP announced an all-out offensive against its enemies in the north. By April it was closing in on the Khmer Rouge strongholds of Anlong Veng and Preah Vihear, and amid this heavy fighting Pol Pot evaded justice by dying a natural death on 15 April in the captivity of his former Khmer Rouge comrades. The fall of Anlong Veng in April was

Western powers, including the USA and UK, ensured the Khmer Rouge retained its seat at the UN general assembly in New York until 1991, a scenario that saw those responsible for the genocide representing their victims on the international stage.

HISTORY THE SLOW BIRTH OF PEACE

2008	2009	2010	2011
Elections are held and the CPP increases its share of the vote to 58%, while the opposition vote is split across several parties.	Comrade Duch, aka Kaing Guek Eav, commandant of the notorious S-21 prison, goes on trial for crimes committed during the Khmer Rouge regime.	As the annual Bon Om Tuk (Water Festival) draws to a close on 22 November, more than 350 people die as revellers swarm across a narrow bridge in huge numbers.	The simmering border conflict over the ancient temple of Preah Vihear spills over into actual fighting between Cambodia and Thailand. A ceasefire is negotiated by Asean chair Indonesia.

followed by the fall of Preah Vihear in May, and the surviving big three, Ta Mok, Khieu Samphan and Nuon Chea, were forced to flee into the jungle near the Thai border with their remaining troops.

The 1998 election result reinforced the reality that the CPP was now the dominant force in the Cambodian political system and on 25 December Hun Sen received the Christmas present he had been waiting for: Khieu Samphan and Nuon Chea were defecting to the government side. The international community began to pile on the pressure for the establishment of some sort of war-crimes tribunal to try the remaining Khmer Rouge leadership. After lengthy negotiations, agreement was finally reached on the composition of a court to try the surviving leaders of the Khmer Rouge. The CPP was suspicious of a UN-administered trial as the UN had sided with the Khmer Rouge–dominated coalition against the government in Phnom Penh, and the ruling party wanted a major say in who was to be tried and for what. The UN for its part doubted that the judiciary in Cambodia was sophisticated or impartial enough to fairly oversee such a major trial. A compromise solution – a mixed tribunal of three international and four Cambodian judges requiring a super majority of two plus three for a verdict – was eventually agreed upon.

Will Democracy Prevail?

In 2002 Cambodia's first-ever local elections were held to select village- and commune-level representatives, an important step in bringing grass-roots democracy to the country. Despite national elections since 1993, the CPP continued to monopolise political power at local and regional levels and only with commune elections would this grip be loosened. The national elections of July 2003 saw a shift in the balance of power, as the CPP consolidated its grip on Cambodia and the Sam Rainsy–led CNRP overtook Funcinpec as the second party. This trend continued into the 2008 election when the CPP's majority grew. However, the 2013 election saw a massive reversal in the trend as the opposition managed to stay united through the election campaign. The return of Cambodia National Rescue Party (CNRP) leader Sam Rainsy from self-imposed exile saw his party come close to victory over the CPP. However, in the subsequent years, the CPP has been cracking down hard on the opposition, which was officially dissolved in late 2017. Whether this is a 'descent into outright dictatorship' – to quote a final edition headline of newspaper Cambodia Daily before it was shut down by the government – remains to to seen.

When Jemaah Is-lamiyah (affiliated with Al Qaeda) bomber Hambali was arrested in Thailand in August 2003, it later surfaced that he had been living in a backpacker hostel on Boeng Kak Lake for about six months.

2012	2013	2016	2017
Cambodia assumes the chair of Asean and hosts the Asia-Pacific Economic Cooperation (APEC) summit. US President Obama flies into Phnom Penh, but doesn't meet with Prime Minister Hun Sen.	In Cambodia's fifth postwar election the united opposition Cambodia National Rescue Party (CNRP) wins 55 seats in the National Assembly. CNRP cites voting irregularities but the CPP ignores calls for an investigation.	Opposition leader Sam Rainsy once again chooses exile ahead of imprisonment as the CPP press defamation charges and he is formally barred from returning to the country in October.	Commune elections are held countrywide and although the CPP claim overall victory, they lose almost one third of their seats as the CNRP appoint 449 commune chiefs.

Pol Pot & the Khmer Rouge Trials

The Khmer Rouge controlled Cambodia for three years, eight months and 20 days, a period etched into the consciousness of the Khmer people. The Vietnamese ousted the Khmer Rouge on 7 January 1979, but Cambodia's civil war rumbled on for another two decades before drawing to a close in 1999. More than 20 years after the collapse of the Khmer Rouge regime, trials commenced to bring those responsible for the deaths of about two million Cambodians to justice.

The Khmer Rouge Tribunal
Case 001
Case 001, the trial of Kaing Guek Eav, aka Comrade Duch, began in 2009. Duch was seen as a key figure as he provided the link between the regime and its crimes in his role as head of S-21 prison. Duch was sentenced to 35 years in 2010, but this was reduced to just 19 years in lieu of time already served and his cooperation with the investigating team. For many Cambodians this was a slap in the face, as Duch had already admitted overall responsibility for the deaths of about 17,000 people. Convert this into simple numbers and it equates to about 10 hours of prison time per victim. However, an appeal verdict announced on 3 February 2012 extended the sentence to life imprisonment.

Case 002
Case 002 began in November 2011, involving the most senior surviving leaders of the Democratic Kampuchea (DK) era: Brother Number Two Nuon Chea (now in his 90s), former DK head of state Khieu Samphan (in his 80s) and former DK Foreign Minister Ieng Sary, who died on 14 March 2013. Ieng Sary's wife and former DK Minister of Social Affairs Ieng Thirith was ruled unfit to stand trial due to the onset of dementia (she later died as well). Both Nuon Chea and Khieu Samphan received life sentences for crimes against humanity in August 2014 and are currently facing additional charges of genocide.

Case 003
Case 003 was lodged in 2009 against head of the DK navy, Meas Muth, and head of the DK air force, Sou Met. The latter died in 2014, leaving Meas Muth as the lone accused in this case. Case 003 has been politically charged from the get-go and threatened to derail the entire tribunal during 2011. Investigations into this case stalled almost immediately back in 2009 under intense pressure from the Cambodian government, which wanted to draw a line under proceedings with the completion of Case 002. Prime Minister Hun Sen made several public statements objecting to the continuation of Case 003 and the subsequent impasse has led to criticism from many quarters including Human Rights Watch. Meas Muth was eventually charged with crimes against humanity and genocide in late-2015 and the case remains under investigation.

To learn more about the origins of the Khmer Rouge and the Democratic Kampuchea regime, read *How Pol Pot Came to Power* (1985) and *The Pol Pot Regime* (1996), both written by Yale University academic Ben Kiernan.

Pol Pot travelled up the Ho Chi Minh Trail to visit Beijing in 1966, at the height of the Cultural Revolution there. He was obviously inspired by what he saw, as the Khmer Rouge went even further than the Red Guards in severing links with the past.

Cost

Around US$300 million has been spent to date, against a backdrop of allegations of corruption and mismanagement on the Cambodian side. Some Cambodians feel the trial will send an important political message about accountability that may resonate with some of the Cambodian leadership today. However, others argue that the trial is a major waste of money, given the overwhelming evidence against surviving senior leaders, and that a truth and reconciliation commission may have provided more compelling answers for Cambodians who want to understand what motivated the average Khmer Rouge cadre.

Pol Pot & His Comrades

Pol Pot: Brother Number One

Pol Pot is a name that sends shivers down the spines of Cambodians and foreigners alike. It is Pol Pot who is most associated with the bloody madness of the regime he led between 1975 and 1979, and his policies heaped misery, suffering and death on millions of Cambodians.

Pol Pot was born Saloth Sar in a small village near Kompong Thom in 1925. As a young man he won a scholarship to study in Paris, where he came into contact with the Cercle Marxiste and communist thought, which he later transformed into a politics of extreme Maoism.

In 1963, Sihanouk's repressive policies sent Saloth Sar and his comrades fleeing to the jungles of Ratanakiri. It was from this moment that Saloth Sar began to call himself Pol Pot. Once the Khmer Rouge was allied with Sihanouk, following his overthrow by Lon Nol in 1970 and subsequent exile in Beijing, its support soared and the faces of the leadership became familiar. However, Pol Pot remained a shadowy figure, leaving public duties to Khieu Samphan and Ieng Sary.

When the Khmer Rouge marched into Phnom Penh on 17 April 1975, few people could have anticipated the hell that was to follow. Pol Pot and his clique were the architects of one of the most radical and brutal revolutions in the history of humankind. It was Year Zero and Cambodia was on a self-destructive course to sever all ties with the past.

Pol Pot was not to emerge as the public face of the revolution until the end of 1976, after he returned from a trip to see his mentors in Beijing. He granted almost no interviews to foreign media and was seen only on propaganda movies produced by government TV. Such was his aura and reputation that, by the last year of the regime, a cult of personality was developing around him.

After being ousted by the Vietnamese, Pol Pot spent much of the 1980s living in Thailand and was able to rebuild his shattered forces and once again threaten Cambodia. His enigma increased as the international media speculated on his real fate. His demise was reported so often that when he finally died on 15 April 1998, many Cambodians refused to believe it until they had seen his body on TV or in newspapers. Even then, many were sceptical and rumours continue to circulate about exactly how he met his end. Officially, he was said to have died from a heart attack, but a full autopsy was not carried out before his body was cremated on a pyre of burning tyres.

For more on the life and times of Pol Pot, pick up one of the excellent biographies written about him: *Brother Number One* by David Chandler or *Pol Pot: The History of a Nightmare* by Phillip Short.

Nuon Chea: Brother Number Two

Long considered one of the main ideologues and architects of the Khmer Rouge revolution, Nuon Chea studied law at Bangkok's Thammasat University before joining the Thai Communist Party. He was appointed Dep-

Brother Number One (2011) is a feature-length documentary that follows New Zealand rower Rob Hamill on a personal journey to discover who was responsible for the murder of his brother Kerry Hamill in S-21 prison in 1978.

Pick up a copy of *When Clouds Fell From the Sky* (2015) by Robert Carmichael, a book that tells the story of a Cambodian diplomat's disappearance on his return to Cambodia in 1977 and his family's search for justice more than 30 years later.

uty Secretary of the Communist Party of Kampuchea upon its secretive founding in 1960 and remained Pol Pot's second in command throughout the regime's rule, with overall responsibility for internal security. He was sentenced to life imprisonment in 2014, a verdict that was upheld on appeal in November 2016, and he now awaits further trial at the ECCC for additional charges of genocide as part of Case 002.

Ieng Sary: Brother Number Three

One of Pol Pot's closest confidants, Ieng Sary fled to the jungles of Ratanakiri in 1963, where he and Pol Pot both underwent intensive guerrilla training in the company of North Vietnamese communist forces. Ieng Sary was one of the public faces of the Khmer Rouge and became foreign minister of Democratic Kampuchea. Until his death in 2013, he maintained that he was not involved in the planning or execution of the genocide. However, he did invite many intellectuals, diplomats and exiles to return to Cambodia from 1975, the majority of whom were subsequently tortured and executed in S-21 prison. He helped hasten the demise of the Khmer Rouge as a guerrilla force with his defection to the government side in 1996 and was given an amnesty for his earlier crimes.

Khieu Samphan: Brother Number Nine

Khieu Samphan studied economics in Paris and some of his theories on self-reliance were credited with inspiring Khmer Rouge economic policies. During the Sihanouk years of the 1960s, Khieu Samphan spent several years working with the Sangkum government and putting his more moderate theories to the test. During a crackdown on leftists in 1967, he fled to the jungle to join Pol Pot and Ieng Sary. During the Democratic Kampuchea (DK) period, he was made head of state from 1976 to 1979. Along with Nuon Chea, he was sentenced to life imprisonment in 2014, a verdict that was upheld on appeal in November 2016. He now awaits further trial for genocide charges as part of Case 002.

Comrade Duch: Commandant of S-21

Born Kaing Guek Eav in Kompong Thom in 1942, Duch initially worked as a teacher before joining the Khmer Rouge in 1967. Based in the Cardamom Mountains during the civil war of 1970–75, he was given responsibility for security and political prisons in his region, where he refined his interrogation techniques. Following the Khmer Rouge takeover, he was moved to S-21 prison and was responsible for the interrogation and execution of thousands of prisoners. He fled Phnom Penh as Vietnamese forces surrounded the city, and his whereabouts were unknown until he was discovered living in Battambang Province by British photojournalist Nic Dunlop. The first to stand trial and be sentenced in Case 001, Comrade Duch cooperated through the judicial process. He was sentenced to life imprisonment in early 2012.

The Future

It remains to be seen whether the wheels of justice will turn fast enough to deliver a verdict on the remaining Khmer Rouge leaders on trial. However, that justice has already been served in the case of Comrade Duch (and at least partially for Brothers Two and Nine) has provided a measure of closure for some victims. Keep up to date with the latest developments in the trial by visiting the official website of the Cambodian Tribunal Monitor (www.cambodiatribunal.org) and the official ECCC site (www.eccc.gov.kh/en).

Enemies of the People (2010) follows Cambodian journalist and genocide survivor Thet Sambath as he wins the confidence of Brother Number Two in the Khmer Rouge, Nuon Chea, eventually coaxing him to give new testimony on his role in the genocidal regime.

Khieu Samphan tries to exonerate himself in his 2004 publication, *Cambodia's Recent History and the Reasons Behind the Decisions I Made.*

The Khmer Rouge period is politically sensitive in Cambodia, due in part to the connections the current leadership has with the communist movement – so much so that the history of the genocide was not taught in high schools until 2009.

People & Culture

A tumultuous history, an incredible heritage of architecture, sculpture and dance, a modern arts scene, and a fascinating mosaic of people and faiths all go towards making Cambodia's rich national character.

The National Psyche

Since the glory days of the Angkorian empire, the Cambodian people have been on the losing side of many a battle – their country all too often a minnow amid the circling sharks – and popular attitudes have been shaped by this history. At first glance, Cambodia appears to be a nation of shiny, happy people, but look deeper and it is a country of evident contradictions. Light and dark, rich and poor, love and hate, life and death – all are visible on a journey through the kingdom. Most telling of all is the evidence of the nation's glorious past set against the more recent tragedy of its present.

Angkor is everywhere: on the flag, the national beer, cigarettes, hotels and guesthouses – anything and everything. It's a symbol of nationhood and fierce pride – no matter how ugly things got in the bad old days, the Cambodians built Angkor Wat and it doesn't get bigger than that.

Contrast this with the abyss into which the nation was sucked during the years of the Khmer Rouge. 'Pol Pot' is a dirty word in Cambodia due to the death and suffering he inflicted on the country.

As for Cambodian attitudes towards their regional neighbours, these are complex. Thais aren't always popular, as some Cambodians feel they fail to acknowledge their cultural debt to Cambodia and generally look down on their less affluent neighbour. Cambodian attitudes towards the Vietnamese are more ambivalent. There is a certain level of mistrust, as many feel the Vietnamese aspire to colonise their country. (Many Khmers still call the lost Mekong Delta 'Kampuchea Krom', meaning 'Lower Cambodia'.) However, this mistrust is balanced with a grudging respect for the Vietnamese role in Cambodia's 'liberation' from the Khmer Rouge in 1979. But when liberation became occupation in the 1980s, the relationship soured once more.

Jayavarman VII was a Mahayana Buddhist who directed his faith towards improving the lot of his people, with the construction of hospitals, universities, roads and shelters.

THE POPULATION OF CAMBODIA

Cambodia's second postwar population census was carried out in 2008 and put the country's population at about 13.5 million. The current population is estimated at around 16 million and, with a rapid growth rate of about 2% per year, it's predicted to reach 20 million by 2025.

Phnom Penh is the largest city, with a population of about two million. Other major population centres include the boom towns of Siem Reap, Sihanoukville, Battambang and Poipet.

The much-discussed imbalance of men to women due to years of conflict is not as serious as it was in 1980, but it's still significant: there are about 95 males to every 100 females, up from 86.1 to 100 in 1980. There is, however, a marked imbalance in age groups: more than 40% of the population is under the age of 16.

CAMBODIAN GREETINGS

Cambodians traditionally greet each other with the *sompiah*, which involves pressing the hands together in prayer and bowing, similar to the *wai* in Thailand. The higher the hands and the lower the bow, the more respect is conveyed – important to remember when meeting officials or the elderly. In recent times this custom has been partly replaced by the handshake but, although men tend to shake hands with each other, women usually use the traditional greeting with both men and women. It is considered acceptable (or perhaps excusable) for foreigners to shake hands with Cambodians of both sexes.

The Cambodian Way of Life

For many older Cambodians, life is centred on family, faith and food, an existence that has stayed the same for centuries. Family is more than the traditional nuclear family, it's the extended family of third cousins and obscure aunts – as long as there is a bloodline, there is a bond. Families stick together, solve problems collectively, listen to the wisdom of the elders and pool resources. The extended family comes together during times of trouble and times of joy, celebrating festivals and successes, mourning deaths and disappointments. Whether the Cambodian house is big or small, there will be a lot of people living inside.

For the majority of the population still living in the countryside, these constants carry on as they always have: several generations sharing the same roof, the same rice and the same religion. But during the dark decades of the 1970s and 1980s, this routine was ripped apart by war and ideology, as the peasants were dragged into a bloody civil war and later forced into slavery. The Khmer Rouge organisation Angkar took over as the moral and social beacon in the lives of the people. Families were forced apart, children turned against parents, brothers against sisters. The bond of trust was broken and is only slowly being rebuilt today.

For the younger generation, brought up in a postconflict, postcommunist period of relative freedom, it's a different story – arguably thanks to their steady diet of MTV and steamy soaps. Cambodia is experiencing its very own '60s swing, as the younger generation stands ready for a different lifestyle to the one their parents had to swallow. This creates plenty of friction in the cities, as rebellious teens dress as they like, date whoever they wish and hit the town until all hours. More recently this generational conflict has spilled over into politics as the Facebook generation helped deliver some shock results that has seen the governing Cambodian People's Party (CPP) grip on power much weakened.

Cambodia is set for major demographic shifts in the next couple of decades. Currently, just 25% of the population lives in urban areas, which contrasts starkly with the country's more developed neighbours, such as Malaysia and Thailand. Increasing numbers of young people are likely to migrate to the cities in search of opportunity, forever changing the face of contemporary Cambodian society. However, for now at least, Cambodian society remains much more traditional than that of Thailand and Vietnam, and visitors need to keep this in mind.

Lowland Khmers are being encouraged to migrate to Cambodia's northeast where there is plenty of available land. But this is home to the country's minority peoples, who have no indigenous concepts of property rights or land ownership, so this may see their culture marginalised in coming years.

Multiculturalism

According to official statistics, more than 90% of the people who live in Cambodia are ethnic Khmers, making the country the most ethnically homogeneous in Southeast Asia. However, unofficially, the figure is probably smaller due to a large influx of Chinese and Vietnamese in the past century. Other ethnic minorities include Cham, Lao and the indigenous peoples of the rural highlands.

THE HIDDEN COST OF ORPHAN TOURISM

In recent years, visiting orphanages in the developing world – Cambodia in particular – has become a popular activity, but is it always good for the children and the country in the longer run? Tough question. 'Orphan tourism' and all the connotations that come with it is a disturbing development that has brought unscrupulous elements into the world of caring for Cambodian children. There have already been reports of new orphanages opening up with a business model to bring in a certain number of visitors per month. In other cases, the children are not orphans at all, but are 'borrowed' from the local school for a fee.

Save the Children have said that most children living in orphanages throughout the developing world have at least one parent still alive. More than eight million children worldwide are living in institutions, with most sent there by their families because of poverty rather than the death of a parent. Many are in danger of abuse and neglect from carers, as well as exploitation and international trafficking, with children aged under three most at risk.

The Save the Children report stated: 'One of the biggest myths is that children in orphanages are there because they have no parents. This is not the case. Most are there because their parents simply can't afford to feed, clothe and educate them'. From 2005 to 2010, the number of orphanages in Cambodia almost doubled from 153 to 269. Of the 12,000 Cambodian children in institutions, only about 28% are genuine orphans without both parents.

Many orphanages in Cambodia are doing a good job in tough circumstances. Some are world class, enjoy funding and support from wealthy benefactors, and don't need visitors; others are desperate places that need all the help they can get. However, if a place is promoting orphan tourism, then proceed with caution, as the adults may not always have the best interests of the children at heart.

Child-welfare experts also recommend that any volunteering concerning children should involve a minimum three-month commitment – having strangers drop in and out of their lives on short visits can be detrimental to a child's emotional well-being and development. Some organisations, such as Friends International and Unicef, recommend travellers never volunteer at orphanages. Friends International and Unicef joined forces in 2011 to launch the 'Think Before Visiting' campaign. Learn more at www.thinkchildsafe. org/thinkbeforevisiting before you inadvertently contribute to the problem.

Ethnic Khmers

The Khmers have inhabited Cambodia since the beginning of recorded regional history (around the 2nd century), many centuries before Thais and Vietnamese migrated to the region. Over the centuries, the Khmers have mixed with other groups residing in Cambodia, including Javanese and Malays (8th century), Thais (10th to 15th centuries), Vietnamese (from the early 17th century) and Chinese (since the 18th century).

Ethnic Vietnamese

Look out for Chinese and Vietnamese cemeteries dotting the rice fields of provinces to the south and east of Phnom Penh. Khmers do not bury their dead, but practise cremation, and the ashes may be interred in a stupa in the grounds of a wat.

The Vietnamese are one of the largest non-Khmer ethnic groups in Cambodia. According to government figures, Cambodia is host to around 100,000 Vietnamese, though unofficial observers claim the real figure may be somewhere between half a million and one million. The Vietnamese play a big part in the fishing and construction industries in Cambodia. There is still some distrust between the Cambodians and the Vietnamese, though, even of the Vietnamese who have been living in Cambodia for generations.

Ethnic Chinese

The government claims there are around 50,000 ethnic Chinese in Cambodia, however informed observers estimate half a million to one million

KHMER KROM

The Khmer Krom people of southern Vietnam are ethnic Khmers separated from Cambodia by historical deals and Vietnamese encroachment on what was once Cambodian territory. Nobody is sure just how many of them there are and estimates vary from one million to seven million, depending on who is doing the counting.

The history of Vietnamese expansion into Khmer territory has long been a staple of Khmer textbooks. King Chey Chetha II of Cambodia, in keeping with the wishes of his Vietnamese queen, first allowed Vietnamese to settle in the Cambodian town of Prey Nokor in 1623. It was obviously the thin end of the wedge, as Prey Nokor is now better known as Ho Chi Minh City (Saigon).

The Vietnamese government has pursued a policy of forced assimilation since independence, which has involved ethnic Khmers taking Vietnamese names and studying in Vietnamese. According to the Khmer Kampuchea Federation (KKF), the Khmer Krom continue to suffer persecution, including lack of access to health services, religious discrimination and outright racism. Several monks have been defrocked for nonviolent protests in recent years and the Cambodian government has even assisted in deporting some agitators, according to Human Rights Watch.

Many Khmer Krom would like to see Cambodia act as a mediator in the quest for greater autonomy and ethnic representation in Vietnam, but the Cambodian government takes a softly, softly approach towards its more powerful neighbour, perhaps born of the historic ties between the two political dynasties.

For more about the ongoing struggles of the Khmer Krom, visit www.khmerkrom.org.

in urban areas. Many Chinese Cambodians have lived in Cambodia for generations and have adopted the Khmer culture, language and identity. Until 1975, the ethnic Chinese controlled the economic life of Cambodia and in recent years they have re-emerged as a powerful economic force, mainly due to increased investment by overseas Chinese.

Ethnic Cham

Cambodia's Cham Muslims (known locally as the Khmer Islam) officially number around 200,000. Unofficial counts put the figure higher at around 500,000. The Cham live in villages on the banks of the Mekong and Tonlé Sap Rivers, mostly in the provinces of Kompong Cham, Kompong Speu and Kompong Chhnang. They suffered vicious persecution between 1975 and 1979, when a large part of their community was targeted. Many Cham mosques that were destroyed under the Khmer Rouge have since been rebuilt.

Ethnolinguistic Minorities

Cambodia's diverse Khmer Leu (Upper Khmer) or *chunchiet* (ethnic minorities), who live in the country's mountainous regions, probably number around 100,000.

The majority of these groups live in the northeast of Cambodia, in the provinces of Ratanakiri, Mondulkiri, Stung Treng and Kratie. The largest group is the Tompuon (many other spellings are also used), who number nearly 20,000. Other groups include the Bunong, Kreung, Kavet, Brau and Jarai.

The hill tribes of Cambodia have long been isolated from mainstream Khmer society, and there is little in the way of mutual understanding. They practise shifting cultivation, rarely staying in one place for long. Finding a new location for a village requires a village elder to mediate with the spirit world. Very few of the minorities retain the sort of colourful traditional costumes found in Thailand, Laos and Vietnam.

Religion

Buddhism

Buddhism arrived in Cambodia with Hinduism but only became the official religion from the 13th and 14th centuries. Most Cambodians today practise Theravada Buddhism. Between 1975 and 1979 many of Cambodia's Buddhist monks were murdered by the Khmer Rouge and nearly all of the country's wats (more than 3000) were damaged or destroyed. In the late 1980s, Buddhism once again became the state religion and today young monks are a common sight throughout the country. Many wats have been rebuilt or rehabilitated and money-raising drives for this work can be seen on roadsides across the country.

The ultimate goal of Theravada Buddhism is nirvana – 'extinction' of all desire and suffering to reach the final stage of reincarnation. By feeding monks, giving donations to temples and performing regular worship at the local wat, Buddhists hope to improve their lot, acquiring enough merit to reduce their number of rebirths.

Every Buddhist male is expected to become a monk for a short period in his life, optimally between the time he finishes school and starts a career or marries. Men or boys under 20 years of age may enter the *sangha* (monastic order) as novices. Nowadays men may spend as little as 15 days to accrue merit as monks.

> The purest form of animism is practised among the minority people known as Khmer Leu. Some have converted to Buddhism, but the majority continue to worship spirits of the earth and skies and their forefathers.

Hinduism

Hinduism flourished alongside Buddhism from the 1st century AD until the 14th century. During the pre-Angkorian period, Hinduism was represented by the worship of Harihara (Shiva and Vishnu embodied in a single deity). During the time of Angkor, Shiva was the deity most in favour with the royal family, although in the 12th century he was superseded by Vishnu. Today some elements of Hinduism are still incorporated into important ceremonies involving birth, marriage and death.

> The famous Hindu epic the *Ramayana* is known as the *Reamker* in Cambodia. Reyum Publishing issued a beautifully illustrated book, *The Reamker* (1999), telling the story.

Animism

Both Hinduism and Buddhism were gradually absorbed from beyond the borders of Cambodia, fusing with the animist beliefs already present among the Khmers before Indianisation. Local beliefs didn't disappear but were incorporated into the new religions to form something uniquely Cambodian. The concept of Neak Ta has its foundations in animist beliefs regarding sacred soil and the sacred spirit around us. Neak Ta can be viewed as a mother-earth concept, an energy force uniting a community with its earth and water. It can be represented in many forms, from stone or wood to termite hills – anything that symbolises both a link between the people and the fertility of their land. The sometimes phallic representation of Neak Ta helps explain the popularity of Hinduism and the worship of the *lingam* (phallic symbol).

Islam

Cambodia's Muslims are descendants of Chams, who migrated from what is now central Vietnam after the final defeat of the kingdom of Champa by the Vietnamese in 1471. Like Buddhists in Cambodia, the Cham Muslims call the faithful to prayer by banging a drum, rather than with the call of the muezzin.

Christianity

Christianity has made limited headway into Cambodia compared with neighbouring Vietnam. There were a number of churches in Cambodia before the war, but many of these were systematically destroyed by the Khmer Rouge, including Notre Dame Cathedral in Phnom Penh. Christianity made a comeback of sorts throughout the refugee camps on the Thai border in the 1980s, as a number of food-for-faith-type charities set up shop dispensing religion with every meal. Many Cambodians changed their public faith for survival, before converting back to Buddhism on their departure from the camps, earning the moniker 'rice Christians'.

The Arts

Architecture

Khmer architecture reached its peak during the Angkorian era (9th to 14th centuries). Some of the finest examples of architecture from this period are Angkor Wat and the structures of Angkor Thom.

Today, most rural Cambodian houses are built on high wood pilings (if the family can afford it) and have thatched roofs, walls made of palm mats and floors of woven bamboo strips resting on bamboo joists. The shady space underneath is used for storage and for people to relax at midday. Wealthier families have houses with wooden walls and tiled roofs, but the basic design remains the same.

The French left their mark in Cambodia in the form of some handsome villas and government buildings built in neoclassical style, Romanesque pillars and all. Some of the best architectural examples are in Phnom Penh, but most of the provincial capitals have at least one or two examples of architecture from the colonial period. Battambang and Kampot are two of the best-preserved colonial-era towns, with handsome rows of shophouses and the classic governors' residences.

During the 1950s and 1960s, Cambodia's so-called golden era, a group of young Khmer architects shaped the capital of Cambodia in their own image, experimenting with what is now called New Khmer Architecture. Vann Molyvann was the most famous proponent of this school of architecture, designing a number of prominent Phnom Penh landmarks such as the Olympic Stadium, the Chatomuk Theatre and Independence Monument. The beach resort of Kep was remodelled at this time, as the emergent Cambodian middle class flocked to the beach, and there are some fantastic if dilapidated examples of New Khmer Architecture around the small town. Boutique hotels Knai Bang Chatt and Villa Romonea in Kep are both restored examples from this period.

To discover examples of New Khmer Architecture, visit the website of Khmer Architecture Tours (www.ka-tours.org) or sign up for one of its walking tours of Phnom Penh or Battambang. The website includes downloadable printouts for DIY tours of each city.

Cinema

Back in the 1960s, the Cambodian film industry was booming. Between 1960 and 1975, more than 300 films were made, some of which were exported all around Asia, including numerous films by then head-of-state Norodom Sihanouk. However, the advent of Khmer Rouge rule saw the film industry disappear overnight and it didn't recover for more than a quarter of a century.

The film industry in Cambodia was given a new lease of life in 2000 with the release of *Pos Keng Kong* (The Giant Snake). A remake of a 1960s Cambodian classic, it tells the story of a powerful young girl born from a rural relationship between a woman and a snake king. It's an interesting love story, albeit with dodgy special effects, and achieved massive box-office success around the region.

The success of *Pos Keng Kong* heralded a minirevival in the Cambodian film industry and local directors now turn out several films a year. However, many of these are amateurish horror films of dubious artistic value.

To learn more about New Khmer Architecture, pick up a copy of *Building Cambodia: New Khmer Architecture 1953–1970* by Helen Grant Ross and Darryl Collins.

PEOPLE & CULTURE THE ARTS

Friends of Khmer Culture (www.khmerculture.net) is dedicated to supporting Khmer arts and cultural organisations, and Meta House, an exhibition space in Phnom Penh, promotes Khmer arts and culture.

SIHANOUK & THE SILVER SCREEN

Between 1965 and 1969 Sihanouk (former king and head of state of Cambodia) wrote, directed and produced nine feature films, a figure that would put the average workaholic Hollywood director to shame. Sihanouk took the business of making films very seriously, and family and officials were called upon to play their part: the minister of foreign affairs acted as the male lead in Sihanouk's first feature, *Apsara* (1965), and his daughter, Princess Bopha Devi, the female lead. When, in the same movie, a show of military hardware was required, the air force was brought into action.

Sihanouk often took on the leading role himself. Notable performances saw him as a spirit of the forest and as a victorious general. Perhaps it was no surprise, given the king's apparent addiction to the world of celluloid dreams, that Cambodia should challenge Cannes with its Phnom Penh International Film Festival. The festival was held twice, in 1968 and 1969. Also perhaps unsurprisingly, Sihanouk won the grand prize on both occasions. He continued to make movies in later life and made around 30 films during his remarkable career.

At least one overseas Cambodian director has enjoyed major success in recent years: Rithy Panh. His *The Missing Picture,* which used clay figurines to tell his personal story of survival under the Khmer Rouge, was nominated for an Academy Award for Best Foreign Language Film in 2014. His success goes back to 1995, when *People of the Rice Fields* was nominated for the Palme d'Or at the Cannes Film Festival. His other films include *One Night after the War* (1997), the story of a young Khmer kickboxer falling for a bar girl in Phnom Penh; and the award-winning *S-21: The Khmer Rouge Killing Machine* (2003), a powerful documentary in which survivors from Tuol Sleng are brought back to confront their guards.

The Last Reel (2014; www. thelastreel.info) is an award-winning film from Cambodia that explores the impact of Cambodia's dark past on the next generation. Michael Moore awarded it his Grand Founder's Prize at the 2016 Traverse City Film Festival.

The definitive film about Cambodia is *The Killing Fields* (1985), which tells the story of American journalist Sydney Schanberg and his Cambodian assistant Dith Pran. Most of the footage was actually shot in Thailand, as it was filmed in 1984 when Cambodia was effectively closed to the West.

Quite a number of international films have been shot in Cambodia in recent years, including *Tomb Raider* (2001), *City of Ghosts* (2002) and *Two Brothers* (2004), all worth seeking out for their beautiful Cambodian backdrops. Angelina Jolie returned to Cambodia in 2015–16 to film *First They Killed My Father,* a full-length feature film based on the book by Luong Ung, available on Netflix since September 2017.

For more on Cambodian films and cinema, pick up a copy of *Kon: The Cinema of Cambodia* (2010), published by the Department of Media and Communication at the Royal University of Cambodia. Also look out for the Cambodia International Film Festival (www.cambodia-iff.com), held in Phnom Penh every year.

Dance

Rithy Panh's The Missing Picture (2013) became the first Cambodian film to be shortlisted for 'Best Foreign Language Film' at the 2014 Oscars.

More than any of the other traditional arts, Cambodia's royal ballet is a tangible link with the glory of Angkor. Its traditions stretch long into the past, when the dance of the *apsara* (heavenly nymph) was performed for the divine king. Early in his reign, King Sihanouk released the traditional harem of royal *apsara* that came with the crown.

Dance fared particularly badly during the Pol Pot years. Very few dancers and teachers survived. In 1981, with a handful of teachers, the University of Fine Arts was reopened and the training of dance students resumed.

Much of Cambodian royal dance resembles that of India and Thailand (the same stylised hand movements, the same sequined, lamé costumes and the same opulent stupa-like headwear), as the Thais incorporated techniques from the Khmers after sacking Angkor in the 15th century. Although royal dance was traditionally an all-female affair (with the exception of the role of the monkey), more male dancers are now featured. Known as *robam preah reachtrop* in Khmer, the most popular classical dances are the Apsara dance and the Wishing dance.

Folk dance is another popular element of dance performances that are regularly staged for visitors in Phnom Penh and Siem Reap. Folk dances draw on rural lifestyle and cultural traditions for their inspiration. One of the most popular folk dances is *robam kom arek,* involving bamboo poles and some nimble footwork. Also popular are fishing and harvest-themed dances that include plenty of flirtatious interaction between male and female performers.

Other celebrated dances are only performed at certain festivals or at certain times of the year. The *trot* is very popular at Khmer New Year to ward off evil spirits from the home or business. A dancer in a deer costume runs through the property pursued by a hunter and is eventually slain.

Chinese New Year (*Tet* to the Vietnamese in Cambodia) sees elaborate lion dances performed all over Phnom Penh and other major cities in Cambodia.

Contemporary dances include the popular *rom vong* or circle dance, which is likely to have originated in neighbouring Laos. Dancers move around in a circle taking three steps forward and two steps back. Hiphop and breakdancing is fast gaining popularity among urban youngsters and is regularly performed at outdoor events.

Music

The bas-reliefs on some of the monuments in the Angkor region depict musicians and *apsara* holding instruments similar to the traditional Khmer instruments of today, demonstrating that Cambodia has a long musical tradition all of its own.

Customarily, music was an accompaniment to a ritual or performance that had religious significance. Musicologists have identified six types of Cambodian musical ensemble, each used in different settings. The most traditional of these is the *areak ka,* an ensemble that performs at weddings. The instruments of the *areak ka* include a *tro khmae* (three-stringed fiddle), a *khsae muoy* (single-stringed bowed instrument) and *skor areak* (drums), among others. *Ahpea pipea* is another type of wedding music that accompanies the witnessing of the marriage and *pin peat* is the music that is heard at ballet performances and shadow-puppet displays.

SPORT IN CAMBODIA

The national sport of Cambodia is *pradal serey* (Cambodian kickboxing). It's similar to kickboxing in Thailand (don't make the mistake of calling it 'Thai boxing' over here, though) and there are regular weekend bouts on CTN and TV5. It's also possible to go to the TV arenas and watch the fights live.

Football is another national obsession, although the Cambodian team is a real minnow, even by Asian standards. Many Cambodians follow the English Premier League religiously and regularly bet on games.

The French game of *pétanque,* also called boules, is also very popular here and the Cambodian team has won several medals in regional games.

Much of Cambodia's golden-era music from the pre-war period was lost during the Pol Pot years. The Khmer Rouge targeted singers, and the great Sinn Sisamouth, Ros Sereysothea and Pen Ron, Cambodia's most famous songwriters and performers, all disappeared in the early days of the regime.

After the war, many Khmers settled in the USA, where a lively Khmer pop industry developed. Influenced by US music and later exported back to Cambodia, it has been enormously popular. Cambodians are now returning to the homeland raised on a diet of rap in the US or France, and lots of artists are breaking through, such as the KlapYaHandz collective started by Sok 'Cream' Visal.

There's also a burgeoning local pop industry, many of whose stars perform at outdoor concerts in Phnom Penh. It's easy to join in the fun by visiting one of the innumerable karaoke bars around the country. Preap Sovath is the Robbie Williams of Cambodia and if you flick through the Cambodian channels for more than five minutes chances are he will be performing. Meas Soksophea is the most popular female singer, with a big voice, but it's a changeling industry and new stars are waiting in the wings.

Dengue Fever is the ultimate fusion band, rapidly gaining a name for itself beyond the USA and Cambodia. Cambodian singer Chhom Nimol fronts five American prog rockers who dabble in psychedelic sounds. Another fusion band fast gaining a name for itself is the Cambodian Space Project, comprising a mix of Cambodians and expats. They regularly play in Phnom Penh and are well worth catching if you're in town at the same time.

One form of music unique to Cambodia is *chapaye,* a sort of Cambodian blues sung to the accompaniment of a two-stringed wooden instrument, similar in sound to a bass guitar played without an amplifier. There are few old masters, such as Kong Nay (the Ray Charles of Cambodia), left alive, but *chapaye* is still often shown on late-night Cambodian TV before transmission ends. Kong Nay has toured internationally in countries such as Australia and the US, and has even appeared with Peter Gabriel at the WOMAD music festival in the UK.

For more on Cambodian music, pick up a copy of *Dontrey: The Music of Cambodia* (2011), published by the Department of Media and Communication at the Royal University of Cambodia. There is also an excellent rockumentary feature called *Don't Think I've Forgotten,* which is about Cambodia's lost rock-and-roll era; watch it at www.dtifcambodia.com.

Sculpture

The Khmer empire of the Angkor period produced some of the most exquisite carved sculptures found anywhere on earth. Even in the pre-Angkorian era, the periods generally referred to as Funan and Chenla, the people of Cambodia were producing masterfully sensuous sculpture that was more than just a copy of the Indian forms on which it was modelled. Some scholars maintain that the Cambodian forms are unrivalled, even in India itself.

The earliest surviving Cambodian sculpture dates from the 6th century AD. Most of it depicts Vishnu with four or eight arms. A large eight-armed Vishnu from this period is displayed at the National Museum in Phnom Penh.

Also on display at the National Museum is a statue of Harihara from the end of the 7th century, a divinity who combines aspects of both Vishnu and Shiva but looks more than a little Egyptian with his pencil moustache and long, thin nose – a reminder that Indian sculpture drew from the Greeks, who in turn were influenced by the Pharaohs.

One of the greatest '70s legends to seek out is Yos Olarang with his screaming vocals and wah-wah pedals. His most famous song, 'Jis Cyclo', is an absolute classic.

Check out www.tinytoones.org for info about a hip-hop cooperative seeking to inspire Cambodian youth to adopt a healthier lifestyle free of drugs and exposure to HIV. Keep an eye out for its performances around Phnom Penh.

Cambodia's great musical tradition was almost lost during the Khmer Rouge years, but the Cambodian Master Performers Program is dedicated to reviving the country's musical tradition. Visit its website at www.cambodianmasters.org.

Innovations of the early Angkorian era include freestanding sculpture that dispenses with the stone aureole that in earlier works supported the multiple arms of Hindu deities. The faces assume an air of tranquillity, and the overall effect is less animated.

The Banteay Srei style of the late 10th century is commonly regarded as a high point in the evolution of Southeast Asian art. The National Museum has a splendid piece from this period: a sandstone statue of Shiva holding Uma, his wife, on his knee. Sadly, Uma's head was stolen some time during Cambodia's turbulent years. The Baphuon style of the 11th century was inspired to a certain extent by the sculpture of Banteay Srei, producing some of the finest works to have survived today.

The statuary of the Angkor Wat period is felt to be conservative and stilted, lacking the grace of earlier work. The genius of this period manifests itself more clearly in the immense architecture and incredible bas-reliefs of Angkor Wat itself.

The final high point in Angkorian sculpture is the Bayon period from the end of the 12th century to the beginning of the 13th century. In the National Museum, look for the superb representation of Jayavarman VII, an image that projects both great power and sublime tranquillity.

As the state religion swung back and forth between Mahayana Buddhism and Hinduism during the turbulent 13th and 14th centuries, Buddha images and bodhisattvas were carved only to be hacked out by militant Hindus on their return to power. By the 15th century stone was generally replaced by polychromatic wood as the material of choice for Buddha statues. A beautiful gallery of post-16th-century Buddhas from around Angkor is on display at the National Museum.

Cambodian sculptors are rediscovering their skills now that there is a ready market among visitors for reproduction stone carvings of famous statues and busts from the time of Angkor.

Even the destructive Khmer Rouge paid homage to the mighty Angkor Wat on its flag, with three towers of the temple in yellow, set against a blood-red background.

PEOPLE & CULTURE THE ARTS

Food & Drink

Cambodia is a crossroads in Asia, the meeting point of the great civilisations of India and China, and, just as its culture has drawn on both, so too has its cuisine. It boasts a great variety of national dishes, some similar to the cuisine of neighbouring Thailand and Laos, others closer to Vietnamese cooking, but all with a unique Cambodian twist. You're bound to find something that takes your fancy, whether your tastes run to spring rolls or curry. Add to this a world of dips and sauces to complement the cooking and a culinary journey through Cambodia becomes as rich a feast as any in Asia. Just as Angkor has put Cambodia on the tourist map, so too amok (baked fish with lemongrass-based kreung paste, coconut and chilli in banana leaf) could put it on the gourmet's map.

Staples & Specialities

No matter what part of the world you come from, if you travel much in Cambodia, you are going to encounter food that is unusual, strange, maybe even immoral, or just plain weird. The fiercely omnivorous Cambodians find nothing strange in eating insects, algae, offal or fish bladders. They will dine on a duck foetus, brew up some brains or snack on some spiders. They will peel live frogs to grill on a barbecue or down wine infused with snake to increase their virility.

To the Khmers there is nothing 'strange' about anything that will sustain the body. To them a food is either wholesome or it isn't; it's nutritious or it isn't; it tastes good or it doesn't. And that's all they worry about. They'll try anything once, even a burger.

Rice, Fish & Soup

Cambodia's abundant waterways provide the fish that is fermented into *prahoc* (fermented fish paste), which forms the backbone of Khmer cuisine. Built around this are the flavours that give the cuisine its kick: the secret roots, the welcome herbs and the aromatic tubers. Together they give the salads, snacks, soups and stews a special aroma and taste that smacks of Cambodia.

Rice from Cambodia's lush fields is the principal staple, enshrined in the Khmer word for 'eating' or 'to eat', *nyam bai* – literally 'eat rice'. Many a Cambodian, particularly drivers, will run out of steam if they run out of rice. It doesn't matter that the same carbohydrates are available in

COOKING COURSES

If you are really taken with Cambodian cuisine, it's possible to learn some tricks of the trade by signing up for a cooking course. This is a great way to introduce your Cambodian experience to your friends – no one wants to sit through the slide show of photos, but offer them a mouth-watering meal and they will all come running. There are courses available in Phnom Penh, Siem Reap, Battambang and Sihanoukville, and more are popping up all the time.

other foods, it is rice and rice alone that counts. Battambang Province is Cambodia's rice bowl and produces the country's finest yield.

For the taste of Cambodia in a bowl, try the local *kyteow,* a rice-noodle soup that will keep you going all day. This full, balanced meal will cost you just 5000r in markets and about US$2 in local restaurants. Don't like noodles? Then try the *bobor* (rice porridge), a national institution, for breakfast, lunch and dinner, and best sampled with some fresh fish and a splash of ginger.

A Cambodian meal almost always includes a *samlor* (traditional soup), which will appear at the same time as the other courses. *Samlor machou bunlay* (hot and sour fish soup with pineapple and spices) is popular.

Freshwater fish forms a huge part of the Cambodian diet thanks to the natural phenomenon that is the Tonlé Sap lake. The fish come in every shape and size, from the giant Mekong catfish to teeny-tiny whitebait, which are great beer snacks when deep-fried. *Trey ahng* (grilled fish) is a Cambodian speciality (*ahng* means 'grilled' and can be applied to many dishes). Traditionally, the fish is eaten as pieces wrapped in lettuce or spinach leaves and then dipped into *teuk trey,* a fish sauce that is a close relative to Vietnam's *nuoc mam,* but with the addition of ground peanuts.

Teuk trey (fish sauce), one of the most popular condiments in Cambodian cooking, cannot be taken on international flights, in line with regulations on carrying strong-smelling or corrosive substances.

Salads

Cambodian salad dishes are popular and delicious, although they're quite different from the Western idea of a cold salad. *Phlea sait kow* is a beef-and-vegetable salad flavoured with coriander, mint and lemongrass. These three herbs find their way into many Cambodian dishes.

Desserts & Fruit

Desserts can be sampled cheaply at night markets around the country. One sweet snack to look out for is the ice-cream sandwich. Popular with the kids, it involves putting a slab of homemade ice cream into a piece of sponge or bread.

Cambodia is blessed with many tropical fruits and sampling these is an integral part of a visit to the country. All the common fruits can be found in abundance, including *chek* (banana)*, menoa* (pineapple) and *duong* (coconut). Among the larger fruit, *khnau* (jackfruit) is very common, often weighing more than 20kg. The *tourain* (durian) usually needs no introduction, as you can smell it from a mile off; the exterior is green with sharp spikes, while inside is a milky, soft interior regarded by the Chinese as an aphrodisiac.

The fruits most popular with visitors include the *mongkut* (mangosteen) and *sao mao* (rambutan). The small mangosteen has a purple skin that contains white segments with a divine flavour, while the rambutan has an interior like a lychee and an exterior covered in soft red and green spikes.

Best of all, although common throughout the world, is the *svay* (mango). The Cambodian mango season is from March to May. Other varieties of mango are available year-round, but it's the hot-season ones that are a taste sensation.

Drinks

Beer

It's never a challenge to find a beer in Cambodia and even the most remote village usually has a stall selling a few cans. Angkor is the national beer, produced in vast quantities in a big brewery down in Sihanoukville. It costs around US$2 to US$3 for a 660mL bottle in most restaurants and bars. Draught Angkor is available for around US$0.50 to US$1.50 in the

As well as eating the notorious tarantulas of Skuon, Cambodians also like to eat crickets, beetles, larvae and ants. Some scientists have suggested insect farms as a way to solve food problems of the future. This time, Cambodia might be ahead of the curve.

main tourist centres. Other popular local brands include Cambodia Beer, aiming to topple Angkor as the beer of choice, and provincial favourite Crown Lager.

A beer brand from neighbouring Laos, Beerlao, is very drinkable and is also one of the cheapest ales available. Tiger Beer is produced locally and is a popular draught in the capital. Some Khmer restaurants have a bevy of 'beer girls', each promoting a particular beer brand. They are always friendly and will leave you alone if you prefer not to drink.

Craft beer is taking off in Phnom Penh and there are now around a dozen microbreweries in the city. Try Cerevisia Craft Brewhouse aka Botanico (p77) or Hops (p76).

A word of caution for beer seekers in Cambodia: while the country is awash with good brews, there's a shortage of refrigeration in the countryside. Go native and learn how to say, '*Som teuk koh*' (ice, please).

Wine & Spirits

Local wine in Cambodia generally means rice wine; it is popular with the minority peoples of the northeast. Some rice wines are fermented for months and are super strong, while other brews are fresher and taste more like a demented cocktail. Either way, if you are invited to join a session in a minority village, it's rude to decline. Other local wines include light sugar-palm wine and ginger wine.

In Phnom Penh and Siem Reap, foreign wines and spirits are sold in supermarkets at bargain prices, given how far they have to travel. Wines from Europe and Australia start at about US$5, while the famous names of the spirit world cost between US$5 and US$15.

Tea & Coffee

Chinese-style *tai* (tea) is a bit of a national institution, and in most Khmer and Chinese restaurants a pot will automatically appear for no extra charge as soon as you sit down. *Kaa fey* (coffee) is sold in most restaurants. It is either black or *café au lait,* served with dollops of condensed milk.

Water & Soft Drinks

Drinking tap water *must* be avoided, especially in the provinces, as it is rarely purified and may lead to stomach complaints. Locally produced mineral water starts at 1000r per bottle at shops and stalls.

Although tap water should be avoided, it is generally OK to have ice in your drinks. Throughout Cambodia, *teuk koh* (ice) is produced with treated water at local ice factories, a legacy of the French.

All the well-known soft drinks are available in Cambodia. Bottled drinks are about 1000r, while canned drinks cost about 2000r, more again in restaurants or bars.

Teuk kalohk are popular throughout Cambodia. They are a little like fruit smoothies and are a great way to wash down a meal.

Dining Out

Whatever your tastes, some eatery in Cambodia is sure to help out, be it the humble peddler, a market stall, a local diner or a slick restaurant.

It's easy to sample inexpensive Khmer cuisine throughout the country, mostly at local markets and cheap restaurants. For more refined Khmer dining, the best restaurants are in Phnom Penh and Siem Reap, where there is also the choice of excellent Thai, Vietnamese, Chinese, Indian, French and Mediterranean cooking. Chinese and Vietnamese food is available in towns across the country due to the large urban populations of both of these ethnic groups.

Some Cambodian nightclubs allow guests to rent premium bottles of spirits, such as Johnnie Walker Blue Label, to display on the table – a way of maintaining face despite the fact it's actually Johnnie Walker Red Label in the glass.

The local brew for country folk is sugar-palm wine, distilled daily direct from the trees and fairly potent after it has settled. Sold in bamboo containers off the back of bicycles, it's tasty and cheap, although only suitable for those with a cast-iron stomach.

Friends is one of the best-known restaurants in Phnom Penh, turning out a fine array of tapas, shakes and specials to help street children in the capital. Its cookbook *The Best of Friends* is a visual feast showcasing its best recipes.

There are often no set hours for places to eat but, as a general rule of thumb, street stalls are open from very early in the morning until early evening, although some stalls specialise in the night shift. Most restaurants are open all day, while some of the fancier places are only open for lunch (usually 11am to 2.30pm) and dinner (usually 5pm to 10pm).

Dining Out With Kids

Both Phnom Penh and Siem Reap have child-friendly eateries, although most restaurants in Cambodia are pretty friendly towards children. Some international restaurants have a children's menu available. High chairs are generally only found at international restaurants and fast-food outlets. Baby-changing facilities are almost nonexistent in Cambodian restaurants.

Street Snacks

Street food is an important part of everyday Cambodian life. Like many Southeast Asians, Cambodians are inveterate snackers. They can be found at impromptu stalls at any time of the day or night, delving into a range of unidentified frying objects. Drop into the markets for an even greater range of dishes and the chance of a comfortable seat. It's a cheap, cheerful and cool way to get up close and personal with Khmer cuisine.

Here's a list of five top street snacks to look out for:

Banh chev Rice pancake stuffed with yummy herbs, bean sprouts and a meat or fish staple.

Bobor Rice porridge, like congee in China, popular with dried fish and egg or zip it up with chilli and black pepper.

Chek chien Deep-fried bananas; these are a popular street snack at any time of day.

Nam ben choc Thin rice noodles served with a red chicken curry or a fish-based broth.

Loat Small white noodles that almost look like bean sprouts; they taste delicious fried up with beef.

In the Cambodian Kitchen

Enter the Cambodian kitchen and you will learn that fine food comes from simplicity. Essentials consist of a strong flame, clean water, basic cutting utensils, a mortar and pestle, and a well-blackened pot or two.

Cambodians eat three meals a day. Breakfast is either *kyteow* or *bobor*. Baguettes are available at any time of day or night, and go down well with a cup of coffee.

Lunch starts early, around 11am. Traditionally, lunch is taken with the family, but in towns and cities many workers now eat at local restaurants or markets.

Dinner is the time for family bonding. Dishes are arranged around the central rice bowl and diners each have a small eating bowl. The procedure is uncomplicated: spoon some rice into your bowl, and lay 'something else' on top of it.

When ordering multiple courses from a restaurant menu, don't worry – don't even think – about the proper succession of courses. All dishes are placed in the centre of the table as soon as they are ready. Diners then help themselves to whatever appeals to them, regardless of who ordered what.

Table Etiquette

Sit at the table with your bowl on a small plate, chopsticks or fork and spoon at the ready. Some Cambodians prefer chopsticks, some prefer fork and spoon, but both are usually available. Each place setting will include a small bowl, usually located at the top right-hand side for the dipping sauces.

Before it became a member of the World Trade Organization (WTO), copyright protection was almost unknown in Cambodia. During that period there were a host of copycat fast-food restaurants, including Khmer Fried Chicken, Pizza Hot and Burger Queen, all now sadly defunct.

One of the most popular street snacks in Cambodia is the unborn duck foetus. The white duck eggs contain a little duckling, feathers and all. Don't order *kaun pong tier* if you want to avoid this.

FOOD & DRINK IN THE CAMBODIAN KITCHEN

BOTTOMS UP

When Cambodians propose a toast, they usually stipulate what percentage must be downed. If they are feeling generous, it might be just *ha-sip pea-roi* (50%), but more often than not it is *moi roi pea-roi* (100%). This is why they love ice in their beer, as they can pace themselves over the course of the night. Many a *barang* (foreigner) has ended up face down on the table at a Cambodian wedding when trying to outdrink the Khmers without the aid of ice.

When serving yourself from the central bowls, use the communal serving spoon so as not to dip your chopsticks or spoon into the food. To begin eating, just pick up your bowl with your left hand, bring it close to your mouth and spoon in the food.

Some dos and don'ts:

➡ *Do* wait for your host to sit first.

➡ *Don't* turn down food placed in your bowl by your host.

➡ *Do* learn to use chopsticks.

➡ *Don't* leave chopsticks in a V-shape in the bowl, a symbol of death.

➡ *Do* tip about 5% to 10% in restaurants, as wages are low.

➡ *Don't* tip if there is already a service charge on the bill.

➡ *Do* drink every time someone offers a toast.

➡ *Don't* pass out face down on the table if the toasting goes on all night.

For the scoop on countryside cooking in Cambodia, pick up *From Spiders to Waterlilies* (2009), a cookbook produced by Romdeng restaurant in Phnom Penh.

Vegetarians & Vegans

Few Cambodians understand the concept of strict vegetarianism and many will say something is vegetarian to please the customer when in fact it is not. If you are not a strict vegetarian and can deal with fish sauces and the like, you should have few problems ordering meals, and those who eat fish can sample Khmer cooking at its best. In the major tourist centres, many of the international restaurants feature vegetarian meals, although these are not budget options.

In Khmer and Chinese restaurants, stir-fried vegetable dishes are readily available, as are vegetarian fried-rice dishes, but it is unlikely these 'vegetarian' dishes have been cooked in separate woks from other fish- and meat-based dishes. Indian restaurants in the popular tourist centres can cook up genuine vegetarian food, as they usually understand the vegetarian principle better than the *prahoc*-loving Khmers.

Environment

Cambodia's landscape ranges from the highs of the Cardamom Mountains to the lows of the Tonlé Sap basin, and includes some critically endangered species clinging on in the protected areas and national parks. However, these species and their habitat are under threat from illegal logging, agricultural plantations and hydroelectric dams for electricity. Cambodia faces a challenge to balance the economy and its need for electricity against the desire to develop sustainable ecotourism.

The Land

Cambodia's borders as we know them today are the result of a classic historical squeeze. As the Vietnamese moved south into the Mekong Delta and the Thais pushed west towards Angkor, Cambodia's territory, which in Angkorian times stretched from southern Burma to Saigon and north into Laos, began to shrink. Only the arrival of the French prevented Cambodia from going the way of the Chams, who became a people without a state. In that sense, French colonialism created a protectorate that actually protected.

Modern-day Cambodia covers 181,035 sq km, making it a little more than half the size of Vietnam or about the same size as England and Wales combined. To the west and northwest it borders Thailand, to the northeast Laos, to the east Vietnam, and to the south is the Gulf of Thailand.

Cambodia's two dominant geographical features are the mighty Mekong River and a vast lake, the Tonlé Sap. At Phnom Penh the Mekong splits into three channels: the Tonlé Sap River, which flows into, and out of, the Tonlé Sap lake; the Upper River (usually called simply the Mekong or, in Vietnamese, Tien Giang); and the Lower River (the Tonlé Bassac, or Ha u Giang in Vietnamese). The rich sediment deposited during the Mekong's annual wet-season flooding has made central Cambodia incredibly fertile. This low-lying alluvial plain is where the vast majority of Cambodians live – fishing and farming in harmony with the rhythms of the monsoon.

In Cambodia's southwest quadrant, much of the landmass is covered by mountains: the Cardamom Mountains (Chuor Phnom Kravanh), covering parts of the provinces of Koh Kong, Battambang, Pursat and Krong Pailin, which are now opening up to ecotourism; and, southeast of there, the Elephant Mountains (Chuor Phnom Damrei), situated in the provinces of Kompong Speu, Koh Kong and Kampot.

Cambodia's 435km coastline is a big draw for visitors on the lookout for isolated tropical beaches. There are islands aplenty off the coast of Sihanoukville, Kep and Koh Kong.

Along Cambodia's northern border with Thailand, the plains collide with a striking sandstone escarpment more than 300km long that towers up to 550m above the lowlands: the Dangkrek Mountains (Chuor Phnom Dangkrek). One of the best places to get a sense of this area is Prasat Preah Vihear.

TONLÉ SAP HEARTBEAT OF CAMBODIA

The Tonlé Sap, the largest freshwater lake in Southeast Asia, is an incredible natural phenomenon that provides fish and irrigation waters for half the population of Cambodia. It is also home to 90,000 people, many of them ethnic Vietnamese, who live in 170 floating villages.

Linking the lake with the Mekong at Phnom Penh is a 100km-long channel known as the Tonlé Sap River. From June to early October, wet-season rains rapidly raise the level of the Mekong, backing up the Tonlé Sap River and causing it to flow northwestward into the Tonlé Sap lake. During this period, the lake surface increases in size by a factor of four or five, from 2500 sq km to 3000 sq km up to 10,000 sq km to 16,000 sq km, and its depth increases from an average of about 2m to more than 10m. An unbelievable 20% of the Mekong's wet-season flow is absorbed by the Tonlé Sap. In October, as the water level of the Mekong begins to fall, the Tonlé Sap River reverses direction, draining the waters of the lake back into the Mekong.

This extraordinary process makes the Tonlé Sap an ideal habitat for birds, snakes and turtles, as well as one of the world's richest sources of freshwater fish: the flooded forests make for fertile spawning grounds, while the dry season creates ideal conditions for fishing. Experts believe that fish migrations from the lake help to restock fisheries as far north as China.

This unique ecosystem was declared a Unesco Biosphere Reserve in 2001, but this may not be enough to protect it from the twin threats of upstream dams and rampant deforestation. Dams are already in operation on the Chinese section of the Mekong, known locally as the Lancang, and the massive new Xayaboury Dam in Laos is now under construction, the first major dam on the Middle or Lower Mekong.

You can learn more about the Tonlé Sap and its unique ecosystem at the Gecko Centre (p130) near Siem Reap.

In the northeastern corner of the country, the plains give way to the Eastern Highlands, a remote region of densely forested mountains that extends east into Vietnam's Central Highlands and north into Laos. The wild provinces of Ratanakiri and Mondulkiri provide a home for many minority (hill-tribe) peoples and are taking off as an ecotourism hot spot.

Flora & Fauna

Cambodia's forest ecosystems were in excellent shape until the 1990s and, compared with its neighbours, its habitats are still relatively healthy. The years of war took their toll on some species, but others thrived in the remote jungles of the southwest and northeast. Ironically, peace brought increased threats as loggers felled huge areas of primary forest and the illicit trade in wildlife targeted endangered species. Due to years of inaccessibility, scientists have only relatively recently managed to research and catalogue the country's plant and animal life.

Animals

The Tonlé Sap provides a huge percentage of Cambodians' protein intake, 70% of which comes from fish. The volume of water in the Tonlé Sap can expand by up to a factor of 70 during the wet season.

Cambodia is home to an estimated 212 species of mammal, including tigers, elephants, bears, leopards and wild oxen. Some of the biggest characters, however, are the smaller creatures, including the binturong (nicknamed the bear cat), the pileated gibbon (the world's largest populations live in the Cardamoms and the Seima Protected Forest in Mondulkiri) and the slow loris, which hangs out in trees all day. The country also has a great variety of butterflies.

Most of Cambodia's fauna is extremely hard to spot in the wild. The easiest way to see a healthy selection is to visit the Phnom Tamao Wildlife Rescue Centre (p93) near Phnom Penh, which provides a home for rescued animals and includes all the major species.

A whopping 720 bird species find Cambodia a congenial home, thanks in large part to its year-round water resources. Relatively common birds include ducks, rails, cranes, herons, egrets, cormorants, pelicans, storks and parakeets, with migratory shorebirds, such as waders, plovers and terns, around the South Coast estuaries. Serious twitchers should consider a visit to Prek Toal Bird Sanctuary (p127); Ang Trapeng Thmor Reserve (p131), home to the extremely rare sarus crane, depicted on the bas-reliefs at Angkor; or the Tmatboey Ibis Project (p264), where the critically endangered giant ibis, Cambodia's national bird, can be seen. For details on birdwatching in Cambodia, check out the Siem Reap–based Sam Veasna Center (p361).

Cambodia is home to about 240 species of reptile, including several species of snake whose venom can be fatal, including members of the cobra and viper families.

Cambodia's highest mountain, at 1813m, is Phnom Aural in Pursat Province.

Endangered Species

Unfortunately, it is getting mighty close to checkout time for a number of species in Cambodia. The kouprey (wild ox), declared Cambodia's national animal by King Sihanouk back in the 1960s, and the Wroughton's free-tailed bat, previously thought to exist in only one part of India but discovered in Preah Vihear Province in 2000, are on the 'Globally Threatened: Critical' list, the last stop before extinction.

Other animals under serious threat in Cambodia include the Asian elephant, banteng, gaur, Asian golden cat, black gibbon, clouded leopard, fishing cat, marbled cat, sun bear, pangolin, giant ibis and Siamese crocodile. Tigers have been declared functionally extinct in Cambodia, although in 2016 conservation groups announced plans to reintroduce the big cats to Mondulkiri Province's eastern plains.

Cambodia has some of the last remaining freshwater Irrawaddy dolphins (*trey pisaut* in Khmer), instantly identifiable thanks to their bulging forehead and short beak. Viewing them at Kampi, near Kratie, is a popular activity.

In terms of fish biodiversity, the Mekong is second only to the Amazon, but dam projects threaten migratory species. The Mekong giant catfish, which can weigh up to 300kg, is critically endangered due to habitat loss and overfishing.

Despite responsibility for nearly 20% of the Mekong River's waters, China is not a member of the Mekong River Commission (MRC). However, it began discussing its extensive dam developments with downstream MRC members in 2007.

The following environmental groups – staffed in Cambodia mainly by Khmers – are playing leading roles in protecting Cambodia's wildlife:

➡ **Birdlife International** (www.birdlife.org)

➡ **Conservation International** (www.conservation.org)

➡ **Fauna & Flora International** (www.fauna-flora.org)

➡ **Wildlife Alliance** (WildAid; www.wildlifealliance.org)

➡ **Wildlife Conservation Society** (www.wcs.org)

➡ **WWF** (www.worldwildlife.org)

Plants

No one knows how many plant species are present in Cambodia because no comprehensive survey has ever been conducted, but it's estimated that the country is home to 15,000 species, at least a third of them endemic.

In the southwest, rainforests grow to heights of 50m or more on the rainy southern slopes of the mountains, with montane (pine) forests in cooler climes above 800m and mangrove forests fringing the coast. In the northern mountains there are broadleaved evergreen forests, with trees soaring 30m above a thick undergrowth of vines, bamboos, palms and assorted woody and herbaceous ground plants. The northern plains support dry dipterocarp forests, while around the Tonlé Sap there are

Researchers estimate that there are about 500 wild elephants in Cambodia, mainly concentrated in Mondulkiri Province and the Cardamom Mountains.

flooded (seasonally inundated) forests. The Eastern Highlands are covered with deciduous forests and grassland. Forested upland areas support many varieties of orchid.

The sugar palm, often seen towering over rice fields, provides fronds to make roofs and walls for houses, and fruit that's used to produce medicine, wine and vinegar. Sugar palms grow taller over the years, but their barkless trunks don't get any thicker, hence they retain shrapnel marks from every battle that has ever raged around them.

National Parks

In the late 1960s Cambodia had six national parks, together covering 22,000 sq km (around 12% of the country). The long civil war effectively destroyed this system and it wasn't reintroduced until 1993, when a royal decree designated 23 areas as national parks, wildlife sanctuaries, protected landscapes and multiple-use areas. Several more protected forests were added to the list in the last decade, bringing the area of protected land in Cambodia to over 43,000 sq km, or around 25% of the country.

This is fantastic news in principle, but in practice the authorities don't always protect these areas in any way other than drawing a line on a map. The government has enough trouble finding funds to pay the rangers who patrol the most popular parks, let alone to recruit staff for the remote sanctuaries, though in recent years a number of international NGOs have been helping to train and fund teams of enforcement rangers.

The Mondulkiri Protected Forest, at 4294 sq km, is now the largest protected area in Cambodia and is contiguous with Yok Don National Park in Vietnam. The Central Cardamoms Protected Forest, at 4013 sq km, borders the Phnom Samkos Wildlife Sanctuary to the west and the Phnom Aural Wildlife Sanctuary to the east, creating almost 10,000 sq km of designated protected land. The noncontiguous Southern Cardamoms Protected Forest (1443 sq km) is along the Koh Kong Conservation Corridor, whose ecotourism potential is as vast as its jungles are impenetrable.

Environmental Issues

Doing Your Bit

Every visitor to Cambodia can make at least a small contribution to the country's ecological sustainability.

➡ Dispose of your rubbish responsibly.

➡ Drink fresh coconuts, in their natural packaging, rather than soft drinks in throwaway cans and bottles.

➡ Buy a 'Refill Not Landfill' water bottle in Siem Reap and use it in your travels.

➡ Choose trekking guides who respect both the ecosystem and the people who live in it.

➡ Avoid eating wild meat, such as bat, deer and shark fin.

➡ Don't touch live coral when snorkelling or diving, and don't buy coral souvenirs.

➡ If you see wild animals being killed, traded or eaten, take down details of what and where, and contact the **Wildlife Alliance** (☎ rescue hotline 012 500094; www.wildlifealliance.org/cambodia), an NGO that helps manage the government's Wildlife Rapid Rescue Team. Rescued animals are either released or taken to the Phnom Tamao Wildlife Rescue Centre.

Logging

The greatest threat to Cambodia's globally important ecosystems is logging for charcoal and timber and to clear land for cash-crop plantations. During the Vietnamese occupation, troops stripped away swaths of for-

Snake bites are responsible for a similar number of amputations to landmines these days. Many villagers go to their local medicine man for treatment and end up with an infection or gangrene; some even die.

Cambodia became the first Southeast Asian country to establish a national park when it created a protected area in 1925 to preserve the forests around the temples of Angkor.

The *khting vor* (spiral-horned ox), so rare that no one had ever seen a live specimen, was considered critically endangered until DNA analysis of its distinctive horns showed that the creature had never existed – the 'horns' belonged to ordinary cattle and buffalo!

est to prevent Khmer Rouge ambushes along highways. The devastation increased in the 1990s, when the shift to a capitalist market economy led to an asset-stripping bonanza by well-connected businessmen.

International demand for timber is huge and, as neighbouring countries such as Thailand and Vietnam began to enforce much tougher logging regulations, foreign logging companies flocked to Cambodia. At the height of the country's logging epidemic in the late 1990s, just under 70,000 sq km of the country's land area, or about 35% of its total surface area, had been allocated as concessions, amounting to almost all of Cambodia's forest land except national parks and protected areas. However, even in these supposed havens, illegal logging continued. According to environmental watchdog Global Witness (www.globalwitness.org), the Royal Cambodian Armed Forces (RCAF) is the driving force behind much of the recent logging in remote border regions.

In the short term, deforestation is contributing to worsening floods along the Mekong, but the long-term implications of logging are hard to assess. Without trees to cloak the hills, rains will inevitably carry away large amounts of topsoil during future monsoons and in time this will have a serious effect on Tonlé Sap.

From 2002 things improved for a time. Under pressure from donors and international institutions, all logging contracts were effectively frozen, pending further negotiations with the government. However, small-scale illegal logging continued, including cutting for charcoal production and slash-and-burn for settlement.

According to Global Forest Watch (GFW; www.globalforestwatch.org), Cambodia lost a total of 2379 sq km of tree cover in 2010. Since then, the numbers have declined, though the country still recorded a loss of 1780 sq km in 2014.

The latest threat to Cambodia's forests comes from 'economic land concessions' granted to establish plantations of cash crops such as rubber, mango, cashew and jackfruit, or agro-forestry groves of acacia and eucalyptus to supply wood chips for the paper industry. The government argues these plantations are necessary for economic development and counts them as reforestation, but in reality the damage to the delicate ecosystem is irreparable and on a massive scale.

For a close encounter with tigers at the temples of Angkor, watch Jean-Jacques Annaud's 2004 film *Two Brothers*, the story of two orphaned tiger cubs during the colonial period.

Banned in Cambodia, the damning 2007 report *Cambodia's Family Trees*, by the UK-based environmental watchdog Global Witness (www.globalwitness.org), exposes Cambodia's most powerful illegal-logging syndicates.

CAMBODIA'S TOP NATIONAL PARKS

PARK	SIZE	FEATURES	ACTIVITIES	BEST TIME TO VISIT
Bokor	1581 sq km	hotel-casino, ghost town, views, waterfalls	trekking, cycling, wildlife watching	Nov–May
Kirirom	350 sq km	waterfalls, vistas, pine forests	hiking, mountain biking, wildlife watching	Nov–Jun
Seima Protected Forest	3000 sq km	waterfalls, gibbons, elephants	trekking, wildlife watching	Nov–May
Southern Cardamoms Protected Forest	1443 sq km	rivers, waterfalls, jungle, elephants	hiking, cycling, wildlife watching	Nov–Jun
Virachey	3325 sq km	unexplored jungle, waterfalls	trekking, adventure, wildlife watching	Nov–Apr

Pollution

Phnom Penh's air isn't as bad as Bangkok's, but as vehicles multiply it's getting worse. In provincial towns and villages, the smoke from garbage fires can ruin your dinner or lead to breathing difficulties and dry coughs.

Detritus of all sorts, especially plastic bags and bottles, can be seen in distressing quantities on beaches, around waterfalls, along roads and carpeting towns, villages and hamlets.

Cambodia has extremely primitive sanitation systems in urban areas, and nonexistent sanitary facilities in rural areas, with only a tiny percentage of the population having access to proper facilities. These conditions breed and spread disease: epidemics of diarrhoea are not uncommon and it is the number-one killer of young children in Cambodia.

In the mid-1960s Cambodia was reckoned to have around 90% of its original forest cover intact. Estimates today vary, but 25% is common.

Damming the Mekong

The Mekong rises in Tibet and flows for 4800km before continuing through southern Vietnam into the South China Sea. This includes almost 500km in Cambodia, where it can be up to 5km wide. With energy needs spiralling upwards throughout the region, it is very tempting for developing countries like Cambodia and its upstream neighbours to build hydroelectric dams on the Mekong and its tributaries.

Environmentalists fear that damming the mainstream Mekong may be nothing short of catastrophic for the flow patterns of the river, the migratory patterns of fish, the survival of the freshwater Irrawaddy dolphin and the very life of the Tonlé Sap. Plans currently under consideration include the Sambor Dam, a massive 3300MW project 35km north of Kratie. Work is also underway on the Don Sahong (Siphandone) Dam, just north of the Cambodia–Laos border.

Also of concern is the potential impact of dams on the annual monsoon flooding of the Mekong, which deposits nutrient-rich silt across vast tracts of land used for agriculture. A drop of just 1m in wet-season water levels on the Tonlé Sap would result in the flood area decreasing by around 2000 sq km, with potentially disastrous consequences for Cambodia's farmers.

Overseeing development plans for the river is the Mekong River Commission (MRC; www.mrcmekong.org). Formed by the United Nations Development Programme and involving Cambodia, Thailand, Laos and Vietnam, it is ostensibly committed to sustainable development.

In September 2005, three enforcement rangers working in the Cardamom Mountains were murdered in two separate incidents, apparently by poachers. Then in 2012, popular environmental activist Chhut Vuthy was shot dead in Koh Kong Province.

Sand Extraction

Sand dredging in the estuaries of Koh Kong Province, including inside the protected Peam Krasaop Wildlife Sanctuary, threatens delicate mangrove ecosystems and the sea life that depends on them. Much of the sand is destined for Singapore. For details, see Global Witness' 2009 report *Country for Sale* (www.globalwitness.org/reports/country-sale). Sand extraction from the Mekong River is also having an impact on local communities, as many riverbank collapses have been reported in recent years.

Survival Guide

Directory A-Z

Accommodation

Hotels & Guesthouses

In Phnom Penh, Siem Reap and the South Coast, which see a steady flow of tourist traffic, hotels improve significantly once you start spending more than US$15 a night. If you spend between US$20 and US$50 it is possible to arrange something very comfortable with the potential bonus of a swimming pool. There has also been an explosion of boutique hotels in Phnom Penh, Siem Reap, Sihanoukville, Kep and Battambang and these are atmospheric and charming places to stay in the US$50 to US$100 range. Most smaller provincial cities also offer air-conditioned comfort in the US$10 to US$20 range.

There is now a host of international-standard hotels in Siem Reap, several in Phnom Penh and a couple on the coast in Sihanoukville and Kep. Most quote hefty walk-in rates and whack 10% tax and 10% service on as well. Book online for a lower rate, including taxes and service.

Hotel rates in tourist centres such as Siem Reap, Sihanoukville, the southern islands and Phnom Penh tend to be substantially discounted in the low season (May through September). Discounts of 50% are common, as are specials such as 'stay three, pay two'. Check hotel websites for details on any promos or offers.

While many of the swish new hotels have lifts, older hotels often don't and the cheapest rooms are at the top of several flights of stairs.

Budget guesthouses used to be restricted to Phnom Penh, Siem Reap and Sihanoukville, but as tourism takes off in the provinces, they are turning up in most of the other provincial capitals. Costs hover around US$5 to US$10 for a bed, usually with fan, bathroom and satellite TV. Most guesthouses in this range do not have hot water, but may offer at least a few more expensive rooms where it is available.

Hostels

There has been a surge in backpacker hostels in recent years, particularly in popular destinations such as Phnom Penh, Siem Reap and Sihanoukville. These are lively and well-run, but the dorms are not always the best value and are often the same price as a private room in a locally owned guesthouse. However, most hostels also offer private rooms and some have bonus draws like a swimming pool.

Homestays

There are several organised homestays around the country in provinces including Kompong Cham and Kompong Thom, as well as lots of informal homestays in out-of-the-way places such as Preah Vihear. The Mekong Discovery Trail includes several homestays between Kratie and the Lao border. There are also plenty of easily accessible homestays in Siem Reap Province.

Activities

For more on the wide range of activities in Cambodia, see p32.

Children

Children can live it up in Cambodia, as they are always the centre of attention and almost everybody wants

PRACTICALITIES

Newspapers The *Phnom Penh Post* (www.phnompenhpost.com) offers the best balance of Cambodian and international news, including business and sport.

Magazines *AsiaLife* (www.asialifemagazine.com/Cambodia) is a free monthly listings magazine (a sort of *Time Out: Phnom Penh*). A variety of international magazines and newspapers is also widely available in Phnom Penh and Siem Reap.

Radio BBC World Service broadcasts on 100.00FM in Phnom Penh. Cambodian radio stations are mainly government-controlled and specialise in phone-ins and product placements.

TV Cambodia has a dozen or so local Khmer-language channels, but most of them support the ruling CPP and churn out a mixture of karaoke videos, soap operas and ministers going about their business. Most midrange hotels have cable TV with access to between 20 and 120 channels, including some obscure regional channels, international movie channels and the big global news and sports channels such as BBC and ESPN.

Smoking All hotels and most guesthouses offer non-smoking rooms these days. Smoking was officially banned in some public places such as cafes, restaurants and bars in 2016, but in practice its enforcement seems down to the individual businesses.

Weights & Measures Cambodians use the metric system for everything except precious metals and gems, where they prefer Chinese units of measurement.

to play with them. This is great news when it comes to babes in arms and little toddlers, as everyone wants to entertain them for a time or babysit while you tuck into a plate of noodles. For the full picture on surviving and thriving on the road, check out Lonely Planet's *Travel with Children*, which contains useful advice on how to cope while travelling. There is also a rundown on health precautions for kids and advice on travel during pregnancy.

Practicalities

Child-friendly amenities such as high chairs in restaurants, car seats, and changing facilities in public restrooms are not that common in Cambodia, with the exception of some hotels, restaurants and malls in Phnom Penh and Siem Reap. Car seats are available on request if you book through a tour operator. Parents travelling independently will have to be extra resourceful in seeking out substitutes or follow the example of Khmer families, which means holding smaller children on their laps much of the time.

Baby formula and nappies (diapers) are available at minimarts in the larger towns and cities, but bring along a sufficient supply to rural areas. For the most part parents needn't worry too much about health concerns, although it pays to lay down a few ground rules – such as regular hand-washing or using hand-cleansing gel – to head off potential medical problems. All the usual health precautions apply. Children should especially be warned not to play with animals encountered along the way, as rabies is present in Cambodia.

Do not let children stray from the path in remote areas of Cambodia, as there are landmines in remote areas near the Thai border and other parts of the country.

Electricity

Type A
120V/60Hz

SLEEPING PRICE RANGES

The following price ranges refer to a double room in high season. Prices in Phnom Penh and Siem Reap tend to be a little higher.

$ less than US$25

$$ US$25-80

$$$ more than US$80

Type C
220V/50Hz

Embassies & Consulates

Many countries now have embassies in Phnom Penh, though some travellers will find that their nearest embassy is in Bangkok.

In genuine emergencies assistance may be available, but only if all other channels have been exhausted. If you have all your money and documents stolen, the embassy can assist with getting a new passport, but a loan for onward travel is out of the question.

Australian Embassy (☑023-213470; 16 National Assembly St, Phnom Penh)

Chinese Embassy (☑023-720920; 256 Mao Tse Toung Blvd, Phnom Penh)

EATING PRICE RANGES

The following price ranges refer to a standard main course. Unless otherwise stated, tax is included in the price.

$ less than US$5

$$ US$5–15

$$$ more than US$15

French Embassy (☑023-430020; 1 Monivong Blvd, Phnom Penh)

German Embassy (☑023-216381; 76-78 St 214, Phnom Penh)

Indian Embassy (☑023-210912; 5 St 466, Phnom Penh)

Indonesian Embassy (☑023-217934; 1 St 466, Phnom Penh)

Japanese Embassy (☑023-217161; 194 Norodom Blvd, Phnom Penh)

Lao Embassy (☑023-997931; 15-17 Mao Tse Toung Blvd, Phnom Penh)

Malaysian Embassy (☑023-216177; 220 Norodom Blvd, Phnom Penh)

Myanmar Embassy (☑023-223761; 181 Norodom Blvd, Phnom Penh)

Philippine Embassy (☑023-222303; 128 Norodom Blvd, Phnom Penh)

Singaporean Embassy (☑023-221875; 92 Norodom Blvd, Phnom Penh)

Thai Embassy (☑023-726306; 196 Norodom Blvd, Phnom Penh)

UK Embassy (☑023-427124; 27-29 St 75, Phnom Penh)

US Embassy (☑023-728000; 1 St 96, Phnom Penh)

Vietnamese Embassy (☑023-726274; 436 Monivong Blvd, Phnom Penh) Also has consulates in **Battambang** (☑097 332 1188, 053-952894; St 3; ☺8.30-11am & 2-5pm Mon-Fri), issuing visas in a day; and **Sihanoukville** (☑034-934039; 310 Ekareach St; ☺8am-noon & 2-4pm Mon-Sat), also with speedy visa processing.

Food

See the Food & Drink section on p338 for more on Cambodian cuisine.

Insurance

Health insurance is essential. Make sure your policy covers emergency evacuation: limited medical facilities mean evacuation by air to Bangkok in the event of serious injury or illness.

Worldwide travel insurance is available at www.lonelyplanet.com/travel-insurance. You can buy, extend and claim online any-time – even if you're already on the road.

Internet Access

Internet access is widespread, but there are not as many internet shops as there used to be now that wi-fi is more prevalent. Charges range from 1500r to US$2 per hour. Many hotels, guesthouses, restaurants and cafes now offer free wi-fi, even in the most out-of-the-way provincial capitals.

Language Courses

The only language courses available in Cambodia at present are in Khmer and are aimed at expat residents of Phnom Penh rather than travellers. Try the Institute of Foreign Languages at the **Royal University of Phnom Penh** (☑012 866826; www.rupp.edu.kh; Russian Blvd). Also check out the noticeboards at popular guesthouses, restaurants and bars, where one-hour lessons are often advertised by private tutors. There are also regular listings under the classifieds in the *Phnom Penh Post*.

Legal Matters

Marijuana is not legal in Cambodia and the police are beginning to take a harder line on it. There have been several busts (and a few set-ups) of foreigner-owned bars and restaurants where ganja was smoked, so the days of free bowls in guesthouses are definitely history. Marijuana is traditionally used in some Khmer dishes, so it will continue to be around for a long time, but if you are a smoker, be discreet.

This advice applies equally to other narcotic substances, which are also illegal. And think twice about buying any pills from a 'friendly' street dealer, as they may turn out to be tranquillisers and you'll wake up as a robbery victim.

Travellers should note that they can be prosecuted under the law of their home country regarding age of consent, even when abroad.

LGBT Travellers

While Cambodian culture is tolerant of homosexuality, the gay and lesbian scene here is certainly nothing like that in Thailand. Both Phnom Penh and Siem Reap have a few gay-friendly bars, but it's a low-key scene compared with some parts of Asia.

With the vast number of same-sex travel partners – gay or otherwise – checking into hotels across Cambodia, there is little consideration over how travelling foreigners are related. However, it is prudent not to announce your sexuality. As with heterosexual couples, passionate public displays of affection are considered a basic no-no.

Recommended websites when planning a trip:

Cambodia Gay (www.cambodia-gay.com) Promoting the LGBT community in Cambodia.

Sticky Rice (www.stickyrice. ws) Gay travel guide covering Cambodia and Asia.

Utopia (www.utopia-asia.com) Gay travel information and contacts, including some local gay terminology.

Maps

The best all-rounder for Cambodia is the Gecko *Cambodia Road Map*. At 1:750,000 scale, it has lots of detail and accurate place names. Other popular foldout maps include Nelles *Cambodia, Laos and Vietnam Map* at 1:1,500,000,

although the detail is limited, and the Periplus *Cambodia Travel Map* at 1:1,000,000, with city maps of Phnom Penh and Siem Reap.

Lots of free maps, subsidised by advertising, are available in Phnom Penh and Siem Reap at leading hotels, guesthouses, restaurants and bars.

Money

Cambodia's currency is the riel, abbreviated in our listings to a lower-case 'r' written after the sum. Cambodia's second currency (some would say its first) is the US dollar, which is accepted everywhere and by everyone, though small amounts of change may arrive in riel. Businesses may quote prices in US dollars or riel, but in towns bordering on Thailand in the north and west it is sometimes Thai baht (B).

If three currencies seems a little excessive, perhaps it's because the Cambodians are making up for lost time: during the Pol Pot era, the country had *no* currency. The Khmer Rouge abolished money and blew up the National Bank building in Phnom Penh.

The Cambodian riel comes in notes of the following denominations: 100r, 200r, 500r, 1000r, 2000r, 5000r, 10,000r, 20,000r, 50,000r and 100,000r.

Dollar bills with a small tear are unlikely to be accepted by Cambodians, so it's worth scrutinising the change you are given to make sure you don't have bad bills.

ATMs

There are credit-card-compatible ATMs (Visa, MasterCard, JCB, Cirrus) in most major cities. There are also ATMs at the Cham Yeam, Poipet and Bavet borders if arriving by land from Thailand or Vietnam. Machines usually give you the option of withdrawing in US dollars or riel. Single

withdrawals of up to US$500 at a time are usually possible, providing your account can handle it. Stay alert when using ATMs late at night.

ANZ Royal Bank has the most extensive network, including ATMs at petrol stations, and popular hotels, restaurants and shops, closely followed by Canadia Bank. Acleda Bank has the widest network of branches in the country, including all provincial capitals, but their ATMs generally only take Visa-affiliated cards. Most ATM withdrawals incur a charge of US$4 to US$5.

Bargaining

It's important to haggle in markets in Cambodia, otherwise the stallholder may 'shave your head' (local vernacular for 'rip you off'). As well as in markets, bargaining is the rule when arranging share taxis and pick-ups, and in some guesthouses. The Khmers are not ruthless hagglers, so a persuasive smile and a little friendly quibbling is usually enough to get a price that's acceptable to both you and the seller.

Cash

The US dollar remains king in Cambodia. Armed with enough cash, you won't need to visit a bank at all because it is possible to change small amounts of dollars for riel at hotels, restaurants and markets. It is always handy to have about US$10 worth of riel kicking around, as it is good for *motos* (unmarked motorcycle taxis), *remork-motos (tuk tuks)* and markets. Pay for something cheap in US dollars and the change comes in riel.

The only other currency that can be useful is Thai baht, mainly in the west of the country. Prices in towns such as Koh Kong, Poipet and Sisophon are often quoted in baht, and even in Battambang it is common.

In the interests of making life as simple as possible when travelling overland, organise a supply of US dollars before arriving in Cambodia. Cash in other major currencies can be changed at banks or markets in major cities. However, most banks tend to offer a poor rate for any non-dollar transaction so it can be better to use moneychangers, which are found in and around every major market.

Western Union and MoneyGram are both represented in Cambodia for fast, if more expensive, money transfers. Western Union is represented by Acleda Bank, and MoneyGram by Canadia Bank.

Credit Cards

Top-end hotels, airline offices and upmarket boutiques and restaurants generally accept most major credit cards (Visa, MasterCard, JCB and sometimes American Express), but many pass the charges straight on to the customer, meaning an extra 2% to 3% on the bill.

Cash advances on credit cards are available in Phnom Penh, Siem Reap, Sihanoukville, Kampot, Battambang, Kompong Cham and other major towns. Most banks advertise a minimum charge of US$5.

Several travel agents and hotels in Phnom Penh and Siem Reap can arrange cash advances for about 5% com-

mission; this can be particularly useful if you get caught short at the weekend.

Tipping

Tipping is not traditionally expected, but in a country as poor as Cambodia, tips can go a long way.

➡ **Hotels** Not expected outside the fanciest hotels, but 2000r to US$1 per bag plus a small tip for the cleaner will be a nice surprise.

➡ **Restaurants** A few thousand riel at local restaurants will suffice; at fancier restaurants you might leave 10% on a small bill, 5% on a big bill.

➡ **Remorks & Moto Drivers** Not expected for short trips, but leave a dollar or two for half-day or full-day rentals if the service was noteworthy.

➡ **Temples** Most wats have contribution boxes – drop a few thousand riel in at the end of a visit, especially if a monk has shown you around.

➡ **Service Charges** Many of the upmarket hotels levy a 10% service charge, but this doesn't always make it to the staff.

Opening Hours

Everything shuts down during the major holidays: Chaul Chnam Khmer (Khmer New Year), P'chum Ben (Festival of the Dead) and Chaul Chnam Chen (Chinese New Year).

Banks 8am to 3.30pm Monday to Friday, Saturday mornings

Bars 5pm to late

Government offices 7.30am to 11.30am and 2pm to 5pm Monday to Friday

Museums Hours vary, but usually open seven days a week

Restaurants (international) 7am to 10pm or meal times

Restaurants (local) 6.30am to 9pm

Shops 8am to 6pm daily

Local markets 6.30am to 5.30pm daily

Photography

Be polite about photographing people, don't push cameras into their faces, and show respect for monks and people at prayer. In general, the Khmers are remarkably courteous people and if you ask nicely, they'll agree to have their photograph taken. The same goes for filming, although in rural areas you will often find children desperate to get in front of the lens and astonished at seeing themselves played back on an LCD screen. Some people will expect money in return for their photo being snapped; be sure to establish this before clicking away.

While there are no official restrictions on taking photographs at border crossings or military bases, use discretion and your own best judgement. If the officials are unfriendly, then they probably won't appreciate you snapping away.

Post

The postal service is hit and miss from Cambodia; send anything valuable by courier or from another country. Ensure postcards and letters are franked before they vanish from your sight.

Letters and parcels sent further afield than Asia can take up to two or three weeks to reach their destination. Use a courier to speed things up; **EMS** (☎023-723511; www.ems.com.kh; Main Post Office, St 13, Phnom Penh) has branches at every major post office in the country. DHL and Fed Ex are present in major cities such as Phnom Penh, Siem Reap and Sihanoukville.

Public Holidays

Banks, ministries and embassies close down during public holidays and festivals, so plan ahead if visiting Cambodia during these times. Cambodians also roll over holidays if they fall on a weekend and take a day or two extra during major festivals. Add to this the fact that they take a holiday for international days here and there, and it soon becomes apparent that Cambodia has more public holidays than any other nation on earth!

International New Year's Day 1 January

Victory over the Genocide 7 January

International Women's Day 8 March

International Workers' Day 1 May

International Children's Day 8 May

King's Birthday 13–15 May

King Mother's Birthday 18 June

Constitution Day 24 September

Commemoration Day 15 October

Independence Day 9 November

International Human Rights Day 10 December

DANGEROUS DRUGS 101

Watch out for *yaba*, the 'crazy' drug from Thailand, known rather ominously in Cambodia as *yama* (the Hindu god of death). Known as ice or crystal meth elsewhere, it's not just any old diet pill from the pharmacist but homemade methamphetamines produced in labs in Cambodia and the region beyond. The pills are often laced with toxic substances, such as mercury, lithium or whatever else the maker can find. *Yama* is a dirty drug and more addictive than users would like to admit, provoking powerful hallucinations, sleep deprivation and psychosis. Steer clear of the stuff unless you plan on an indefinite extension to your trip.

Safe Travel

➡ Cambodia is a pretty safe country for travellers these days, with few incidences of petty crime.

➡ Remember the golden rule: stick to marked paths in remote areas (due to the possible presence of landmines).

➡ *Phnom Penh Post* (www.phnompenhpost.com) is a good source for breaking news, so check its website before you hit the road to check the political pulse and catch up with any recent events on the ground such as demonstrations.

➡ Take care with some of the electrical wiring in guesthouses around the country, as it can be pretty amateurish.

Crime & Violence

Given the number of guns in Cambodia, there is less armed theft than one might expect. Still, holdups and drive-by theft by motorcycle-riding tandems are a potential danger in Phnom Penh and Sihanoukville. There is no need to be paranoid, just cautious. Walking or riding alone late at night is not ideal, certainly not in rural areas.

There have been incidents of bag snatching in Phnom Penh in the last few years and the motorbike thieves don't let go, dragging passengers off *motos* and endangering lives. Smartphones are a particular target, so avoid using your smartphone in public, especially at night, as you'll be susceptible to drive-by thieves.

Should anyone be unlucky enough to be robbed, it is important to note that the Cambodian police are the best that money can buy! Any help, such as a police report, is going to cost you. The going rate depends on the size of the claim, but anywhere from US$5 to US$50 is possible.

Violence against foreigners is extremely rare, but it pays to take care in crowded bars or nightclubs

---

FESTIVAL WARNING

In the run-up to major festivals such as P'chum Ben or Chaul Chnam Khmer, there is a palpable increase in the number of robberies, particularly in Phnom Penh. Cambodians need money to buy gifts for relatives or to pay off debts, and for some individuals theft is the quickest way to get this money. Be more vigilant at night at these times. Guard your smartphone vigilantly and don't take valuables out with you unnecessarily.

in Phnom Penh. If you get into a stand-off with rich young Khmers in a bar or club, swallow your pride and back down. Many carry guns and have an entourage of bodyguards.

Mines, Mortars & Bombs

Never touch any rockets, artillery shells, mortars, mines, bombs or other war material you may come across. The most heavily mined part of the country is along the Thai border area, but mines are a problem in much of Cambodia. In short: *do not stray from well-marked paths under any circumstances*. If you are planning any walks, even in safer areas such as the remote northeast, it is imperative you take a guide as there may still be unexploded ordnance (UXO) from the American bombing campaign of the early 1970s.

Scams

Most scams are fairly harmless, involving a bit of commission here and there for taxi, *remork* or *moto* drivers, particularly in Siem Reap.

There have been one or two reports of police set-ups in Phnom Penh, involving planted drugs. This seems to be very rare, but if you fall victim to the ploy, it may be best to pay them off before more police get involved at the local station, as the price will only rise when there are more mouths to feed.

There is quite a lot of fake medication floating about the region. Safeguard yourself by only buying prescription drugs from reliable pharmacies or clinics.

Beware the Filipino blackjack scam: don't get involved in any gambling with seemingly friendly Filipinos unless you want to part with plenty of cash.

Beggars in places such as Phnom Penh and Siem Reap may ask for milk powder for an infant in arms. Some foreigners succumb to the urge to help, but the beggars usually request the most expensive milk formula available and return it to the shop to split the proceeds after the handover.

Telephone

To place a long-distance domestic call from a landline, or to dial a mobile (cell) number, dial zero, the area code (or mobile prefix) and the number. Leave out the zero and the area code if you are making a local call. Drop the zero from the mobile prefix or regional (city) code when dialling into Cambodia from another country.

For telephone listings of businesses and government offices, check out www. yp.com.kh.

| Country code | ☎855 |
| International Access Code | ☎001 |

Mobile Phones

Roaming is possible but it is expensive. Local SIM cards and unlocked mobile phones are readily available.

Mobile phones, whose numbers start with 01, 06, 07, 08 or 09, are hugely popular with both individuals and commercial enterprises.

Cambodian roaming charges are extraordinarily high. Wi-fi is widely available and is useful for saving money on data as you travel around the country.

Those who plan on spending longer in Cambodia should arrange a SIM card for one of the local service providers. Foreigners need to present a valid passport to get a local SIM card, but they are available free on arrival at international airports.

Most mobile companies now offer cheap internet-based phone calls accessed through a gateway number. Look up the cheap prefix and calls will be around US5¢ per minute.

Time

Cambodia is in the Indochina time zone, which means GMT/UTC plus seven hours. Thus, noon in Phnom Penh is midnight the previous day in New York, 5am in London, 1pm in Hong Kong and 3pm in Sydney. There is no daylight saving time.

Toilets

Cambodian toilets are mostly of the sit-down 'throne' variety. The occasional squat toilet turns up here and there, particularly in the most budget of budget guesthouses in the provinces or out the back of provincial restaurants.

The issue of toilets and what to do with used toilet paper is a cause for concern. Generally, if there's a wastepaper basket next to the toilet, that is where the toilet paper goes, as many sewerage systems cannot handle toilet paper. Toilet paper is seldom provided in the toilets at bus stations or in other public buildings, so keep a stash with you at all times.

Many Western toilets also have a hose spray in the bathroom, aptly named the 'bum gun' by some. Think of this as a flexible bidet, used for cleaning and ablutions as well as hosing down the loo.

Public toilets are rare, the only ones in the country being along Phnom Penh's riverfront and some beautiful wooden structures dotted about the temples of Angkor. The charge is usually 500r for a public toilet, although they are free at Angkor on presentation of a temple pass. Most local restaurants have some sort of toilet.

Should you find nature calling in remote border areas, don't let modesty drive you into the bushes: *there may be landmines near the road or track*. Do it near the roadside, or wait until the next town.

Tourist Information

Cambodia has only a handful of tourist offices, and those encountered by the independent traveller in Phnom Penh and Siem Reap are generally of limited help. However, in the provinces the staff are sometimes happy to see visitors, if the office happens to be open. These offices generally have little in the way of brochures or handouts though. Generally speaking, fellow travellers, guesthouses, hotels and free local magazines are more useful than tourist offices. The official tourism website for Cambodia is www.tourismcambodia.org.

Travellers with Disabilities

Broken pavements, potholed roads and stairs as steep as ladders at Angkor ensure that for most people with mobility impairments, Cambodia is not going to be an easy country in which to travel. Few buildings have been designed with people with a disability in mind, although new projects, such as the international airports at Phnom Penh and Siem Reap, and top-end hotels, include ramps for wheelchair access. Transport in the provinces is usually very overcrowded, but taxi hire from point to point is an affordable option.

On the positive side, the Cambodian people are usually very helpful towards all foreigners, and local labour is cheap if you need someone to accompany you at all times. Most guesthouses and small hotels have ground-floor rooms that are reasonably easy to access.

The biggest headache also happens to be the main attraction: the temples of Angkor. Causeways are uneven, obstacles common and staircases daunting, even for able-bodied people. It is likely to be some years before things improve, although some ramping has been introduced at major temples.

Wheelchair travellers will need to undertake a lot of research before visiting Cambodia. There is a growing network of information sources that can put you in touch with others who have wheeled through Cambodia before. Try contacting the following organisations:

Disability Rights UK (http://disabilityrightsuk.org)

Mobility International USA (www.miusa.org)

Society for Accessible Travel & Hospitality (SATH; www.sath.org)

Download Lonely Planet's free Accessible Travel guide from http://lptravel.to/AccessibleTravel.

Visas

A one-month tourist visa costs US$30 on arrival and requires one passport-sized photo. Easily extendable business visas are available for US$35.

Most visitors to Cambodia require a one-month tourist visa (US$30). Most nationalities receive this on arrival at Phnom Penh, Siem Reap or Sihanoukville airports, and at land borders, but citizens of Afghanistan, Algeria, Bangladesh, Iran, Iraq, Nigeria, Pakistan, Saudi Arabia, Sri Lanka and Sudan need to make advance arrangements. One passport-sized photo is required and you'll be 'fined' US$2 if you don't have one. It is also possible to arrange a visa through Cambodian embassies overseas or an online e-visa (US$30, plus a US$7 processing fee) through the Ministry of Foreign Affairs (www.mfaic.gov.kh). However, e-visas are only accepted at Phnom Penh and Siem Reap airports (they are not accepted in Sihanoukville), and at the three main land borders: Poipet/Aranya Prathet and Cham Yeam/Hat Lek (both Thailand) and Bavet/Moc Bai (Vietnam).

Passport holders from Asean member countries do not require a visa to visit Cambodia.

Those seeking work in Cambodia should opt for the business visa (US$35) as it is easily extended for longer periods, including multiple entries and exits. A tourist visa can be extended only once and only for one month, and does not allow for re-entry.

Travellers are sometimes overcharged when crossing at land borders with Thailand, as immigration officials demand payment in baht and round up the figure

GOVERNMENT TRAVEL ADVICE

Australian Department of Foreign Affairs (www.smartraveller.gov.au)

Canadian Government (www.voyage.gc.ca)

German Foreign Office (www.auswaertiges-amt.de)

Japanese Ministry of Foreign Affairs (www.anzen.mofa.go.jp)

Netherlands Government (www.minbuza.nl)

New Zealand Ministry of Foreign Affairs (www.safetravel.govt.nz/cambodia)

UK Foreign Office (www.gov.uk/foreign-travel-advice/cambodia)

US Department of State (travel.state.gov/content/passports/en/country/cambodia.html)

considerably. Overcharging is also an issue at the Laos border, but not usually at Vietnam borders. Arranging a visa in advance can help avoid overcharging.

Overstaying a visa currently costs US$5 a day.

For visitors continuing to Vietnam, one-month single-entry visas cost US$55 and take two days in Phnom Penh, or just one day via the Vietnamese consulate in Sihanoukville. Most visitors to Laos can obtain a visa on arrival (US$30 to US$42) and most visitors heading to Thailand do not need a visa.

Visa Extensions

Visa extensions are issued by the large immigration office located directly across the road from Phnom Penh International Airport.

Extensions are easy to arrange, taking just a couple of days. It costs US$45 for one month (for both tourist and business visas), US$75 for three months, US$155 for six months and US$285 for one year (the latter three prices relate to business visas only). It's pretty straightforward to extend business visas ad infinitum. Travel agencies and some motorbike-rental shops in Phnom Penh can help with arrangements, sometimes at a discounted price.

Volunteering

There are fewer opportunities for volunteering than one might imagine in a country as impoverished as Cambodia. This is partly due to the sheer number of professional development workers based here, and development is a pretty lucrative industry these days.

Cambodia hosts a huge number of NGOs, some of which do require volunteers from time to time. The best

way to find out who is represented in the country is to drop in at the **Cooperation Committee for Cambodia** (CCC; ☎023-214152; www. ccc-cambodia.org; 9-11 St 476) in Phnom Penh. This organisation has a handy list of all NGOs, both Cambodian and international, and is extremely helpful. Siem Reap–based organisation **ConCERT** (www.concertcambodia.org) has a 'responsible volunteering' section on its website that offers some sound advice on preparing for a stint as a volunteer.

The other avenue is professional volunteering through an organisation back home that offers one- or two-year placements in Cambodia. One of the largest organisations is Voluntary Service Overseas (www. vsointernational.org) in the UK, but other countries also have their own organisations, including Australian Volunteers International (www.avi.org.au) and New Zealand's Volunteer Service Abroad (www.vsa.org.nz). The UN also operates its own volunteer program; details are available at www.unv.org. Other general volunteer sites with links all over the place include www.voluntourism. org and www.goabroad.com/volunteer-abroad.

Women Travellers

Women will generally find Cambodia a hassle-free place to travel, although some of the guys in the guesthouse industry will try their luck from time to time. Foreign women are unlikely to be targeted by local men, and will probably find Khmer men to be courteous and polite. At the same time it pays to be careful. As is the case in many places, walking or riding a bike alone late at night can be risky.

Khmer women dress fairly conservatively, in general preferring long-sleeved shirts and long trousers or skirts. It is worth having trousers for heading out at night on *motos*, as short skirts aren't very practical.

Tampons and sanitary napkins are widely available in the major cities and provincial capitals, but if you are heading into very remote areas for a few days, it is worth having your own supply.

Work

Jobs are available throughout Cambodia, but apart from teaching English or helping out in guesthouses, bars or restaurants, most are for professionals and are arranged in advance. There is a lot of teaching work available for English-language speakers and salary is directly linked to experience. Anyone with an English-language teaching certificate can earn considerably more than those with no qualifications.

For information about work opportunities with NGOs, call into Phnom Penh's **Cooperation Committee for Cambodia** (CCC; ☎023-214152; www.ccc-cambodia.org; 9-11 St 476), which has a noticeboard for positions vacant. If you are thinking of applying for work with NGOs, you should bring copies of your education certificates and work references. However, most of the jobs available are likely to be on a voluntary basis, as most recruiting for specialised positions is done in home countries or through international organisations.

Other places to look for work include the classifieds section of the *Phnom Penh Post* and on noticeboards at guesthouses and restaurants in Phnom Penh.

Transport

GETTING THERE & AWAY

The majority of visitors enter or exit Cambodia by air through the popular international gateways of Phnom Penh or Siem Reap. Lots of independent travellers enter or exit the country via the numerous land borders shared with Thailand, Vietnam and Laos. There is also the option to cross via the Mekong River between Vietnam and Cambodia. Flights, cars and tours can be booked online at lonelyplanet.com/bookings.

Entering the Country

Cambodia has three international gateways for arrival by air – Phnom Penh, Siem Reap and Sihanoukville – and a healthy selection of land borders with neighbouring Thailand, Vietnam and Laos. Formalities at Cambodia's international airports are tra-

ditionally smoother than at land borders, as the volume of traffic is greater. Crossing at land borders is relatively easy, but immigration officers may try to wangle some extra cash, either for the visa or via some other scam. Anyone without a photo for their visa form will be charged about US$2 at the airport, and around 100B at land borders with Thailand.

Arrival by air is popular for those on a short holiday, as travelling overland to or from Cambodia puts a dent in the time in-country. Travellers on longer trips usually enter and exit by land, as road and river transport is very reasonably priced in Cambodia.

Passport

A passport essential needs to be valid for at least six months or Cambodian immigration will not issue a visa.

It's also important to make sure that there is plenty of space left in the passport, as a Cambodian visa alone takes up one page.

Air

Airports & Airlines

Phnom Penh International Airport (PNH; ☏023-862800; www.cambodia-airports.com) Gateway to the Cambodian capital.

Siem Reap International Airport (Map p134; ☏063-962400; www.cambodia-airports.com) Serves visitors to the temples of Angkor. Both major airports have a good range of services, including restaurants, bars, shops and ATMs.

Sihanoukville International Airport (☏012-333524; www.cambodia-airports.com) Very limited international connections. E-visas are not accepted at Sihanoukville's airport.

Flights to Cambodia are expanding, but most connect only as far as regional capitals. **Cambodia Angkor Airways** (www.cambodiaangkorair.com) is the national airline and offers

---

CLIMATE CHANGE & TRAVEL

Every form of transport that relies on carbon-based fuel generates CO_2, the main cause of human-induced climate change. Modern travel is dependent on aeroplanes, which might use less fuel per kilometre per person than most cars but travel much greater distances. The altitude at which aircraft emit gases (including CO_2) and particles also contributes to their climate change impact. Many websites offer 'carbon calculators' that allow people to estimate the carbon emissions generated by their journey and, for those who wish to do so, to offset the impact of the greenhouse gases emitted with contributions to portfolios of climate-friendly initiatives throughout the world. Lonely Planet offsets the carbon footprint of all staff and author travel.

DEPARTURE TAX

International departure tax of US$25 is included in the ticket price at the point of purchase so there is no need for cash dollars when you leave the country.

the most international flight connections to destinations around the region, including Bangkok, Danang, Guangzhou, Ho Chi Minh City, Seoul and Shanghai. **Thai Airways** (www.thaiair.com) and **Bangkok Airways** (www.bangkokair.com) offer the most daily international flights connections, all via Bangkok. **Vietnam Airlines** (www.vietnamairlines.com) has several useful connections, including from both Phnom Penh and Siem Reap to both Hanoi and Ho Chi Minh City, as well from Phnom Penh to Vientiane and Siem Reap to Luang Prabang, Danang and Phu Quoc.

Useful budget airlines include **Air Asia** (www.airasia.com), with daily flights connecting Phnom Penh and Siem Reap to Kuala Lumpur and Bangkok; **Jetstar** (www.

jetstar.com), with daily flights from both Phnom Penh and Siem Reap to Singapore; and **Cebu Pacific** (www.cebupacificair.com), with three or four weekly flights from Siem Reap to Manila.

Other regional centres with direct flights to Cambodia include Pakse, Hong Kong and Taipei. Longer-haul flights are currently limited to Doha and Tokyo.

Land

Border Crossings

Cambodian visas are now available at all the land crossings with Laos, Thailand and Vietnam.

Visas on arrival are available in Laos, while most nationalities enjoy 15 to 30 days

visa-free access to Thailand. Vietnam grants visas on arrival only to limited nationalities, so check before heading to the border. Most borders are open during the core hours of 7am to 5pm. However, some of the most popular crossings stay open later and other more remote crossings close for lunch.

There are few legal money-changing facilities at the more remote border crossings, so be sure to have some small-denomination US dollars handy.

Tourist visas are available at all crossings for US$30, but Cambodian immigration officers at the border crossings, especially with Thailand and Laos, have a reputation for petty extortion. Travellers are occasionally asked for a small 'immigration fee' or some sort of bogus health certificate costing US$1. More serious scams include overcharging for visas by demanding payment in Thai baht and forcing tourists to change US dollars into riel at a poor rate.

POPULAR LAND CROSSINGS

Laos

For Laos, the Trapeang Kriel/Nong Nok Khiene (p362) crossing connects Stung Treng in Cambodia with Don Det in Laos.

Thailand

BORDER CROSSING	CAMBODIAN TOWN	CONNECTING TOWN
Poipet/Aranya Prathet (p254)	Siem Reap	Bangkok
Cham Yeam/Hat Lek (p181)	Koh Kong City	Trat
O Smach/Chong Chom (p255)	Samraong	Surin
Psar Pruhm/Pong Nam Ron (p253)	Pailin	Chanthaburi
Choam/Chong Sa-Ngam (p259)	Anlong Veng	Phusing

Vietnam

BORDER CROSSING	CAMBODIAN TOWN	CONNECTING TOWN
Bavet/Moc Bai (p86)	Phnom Penh	Ho Chi Minh City
Kaam Samnor/Vinh Xuong (p86)	Phnom Penh	Chau Doc
Prek Chak/Xa Xia (p228)	Kep, Kampot	Ha Tien, Phu Quoc
Phnom Den/Tinh Bien (p230)	Takeo	Chau Doc
O'Yadaw/Le Thanh (p294)	Ban Lung	Pleiku
Trapeang Plong/Xa Mat (p278)	Kompong Cham	Tay Ninh
Trapeang Sre/Loc Ninh (p283)	Kratie	Binh Long

Cambodia Border Crossings

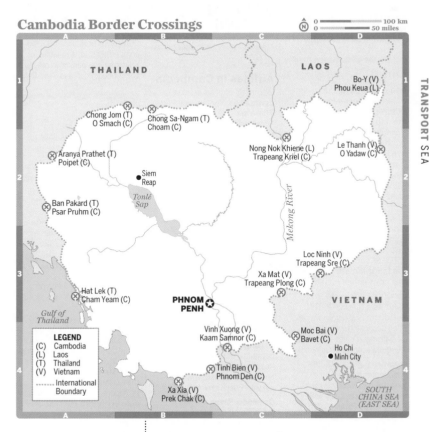

Hold your breath, stand your ground, and don't let this experience flavour your impression of Cambodians overall.

Be aware of border closing times, visa regulations and transport scams. Border details change regularly, so ask around or check the Lonely Planet Thorn Tree (lonelyplanet.com/thorntree).

LAOS

Cambodia and Laos share a remote frontier that includes some of the wildest areas of both countries. There is only one border crossing open to foreigners.

THAILAND

Cambodia and Thailand share an 805km border and there are now five legal internation-al border crossings, and many more options for locals.

VIETNAM

Cambodia and Vietnam share a long frontier with a bevy of border crossings. Foreigners are currently permitted to cross at seven places. Cambodian visas are now available at all crossings, but for entry to Vietnam, 15- to 30-day visa-free entry is available on arrival for citizens from Asean countries, Japan, South Korea, Scandinavian countries, France, Germany, Italy, Spain and the UK.

Car & Motorcycle

Car drivers and motorcycle riders will need registration papers, insurance documents and an International Driving Licence (although not officially recognised) to bring vehicles into Cambodia. It is complicated to bring in a car but relatively straightforward to bring in a motorcycle, as long as you have a *carnet de passage* (vehicle passport). This acts as a temporary import-duty waiver and should save a lot of hassles with Cambodian customs.

Sea

There are no official sea borders between Cambodia and its neighbours, although Sihanoukville is an international port and Asian cruise ships regularly dock there.

There are plans to set up an international port near Kampot for sea connections to Phu Quoc Island in Vietnam.

Tours

In the early days of tourism in Cambodia, organised tours were a near necessity. The situation has changed dramatically and it is now much easier to organise your own trip.

If you do decide to go with a tour, shop around, as there is lots of competition and some companies offer more interesting itineraries than others and/or do more to support responsible travel. Tours as well as flights can be booked online at lonelyplan et.com/bookings. The following are reliable tour companies based in Cambodia:

About Asia (☑063-760190; www.aboutasiatravel.com) ✈ Small bespoke travel company specialising in Siem Reap. Profits help build schools in Cambodia.

Hanuman (☑023-218396; www.hanumantravel.com) Long-running, locally owned and operated company with tours such as Temple Safari. A supporter of responsible tourism initiatives.

Journeys Within (☑063-968782; www.journeys-within. com) A boutique tourism company based in Siem Reap that offers various cross-border trips in addition to appealing tours within Cambodia. Operates a charitable arm helping schools and communities.

Sam Veasna Center (SVC; Map p100;☑063-963710; www. samveasna.org; St 26; per person from US$100) ✈ Genuine ecotourism operator offering one- to several-day birdwatching and wildlife watching tours that contribute directly to forest and species preservation.

GETTING AROUND

Air
Airlines in Cambodia

Domestic airlines seem to come and go pretty quickly. There are currently five in Cambodia, operating flights between Phnom Penh and Siem Reap and Sihanoukville. There are up to 10 flights a day between Phnom Penh and Siem Reap and it is usually possible to get on a flight at short notice. Book ahead in peak season. There are currently about five flights per day between Siem Reap and Sihanoukville in peak season.

Bassaka Air (☑023-217613; www.bassakaair.com) At least one flight daily between Phnom Penh and Siem Reap and Siem Reap and Sihanoukville.

Cambodia Angkor Air (☑023-212564; www.cambodiaangkor air.com) Several flights a day between Phnom Penh and Siem Reap and up to two flights a day between Siem Reap and Sihanoukville. Prices generally higher.

Cambodia Bayon Airlines (☑023-231555; www.bayonair lines.com) At least one flight daily between Phnom Penh and Siem Reap and one or two daily between Siem Reap and Sihanoukville.

JC International Airlines (☑023-989707; www.jcairline. com) New airline with daily discounted flights between Phnom Penh and Siem Reap.

Sky Angkor Airlines (☑063-967300; www.skyangkorair. com) Has several weekly flights between Siem Reap and Sihanoukville.

Helicopter

Two private helicopter companies offer scenic flights over the temples of Angkor and charter flights.

Helicopters Cambodia (☑012 814500; www.helicopterscam bodia.com) Has offices in Phnom Penh and Siem Reap; affiliated with Helicopters New Zealand.

Helistar (Map p128;☑088 888 0016; www.helistarcambodia. com; Airport Rd) A reliable helicopter company with offices in both Phnom Penh and Siem Reap.

Bicycle

Cambodia is a great country for experienced cyclists to explore. A mountain bike is recommended thanks to the notorious state of the roads. Most roads have a flat unpaved trail along the side, which is useful for cyclists.

Much of Cambodia is pancake flat or only moderately hilly. Safety, however, is a considerable concern on the newer surfaced roads, as local traffic travels at high speed. Bicycles can be transported around the country in the back of pick-ups or on the roof of minibuses.

Guesthouses and hotels rent out bicycles for US$1 to US$2 per day, or US$7 to US$15 for an imported brand such as Giant or Trek.

Top bikes, safety equipment and authentic spare parts are now readily available in Phnom Penh at very reasonable prices.

PEPY Tours (☑023-222804; www.pepytours.com) ✈ is a bicycle and volunteer tour company offering adventures throughout Cambodia. PEPY promotes 'adventurous living, responsible giving' and puts funds put back into community education and other projects.

Boat

North of Phnom Penh, the Mekong is easily navigable as far as Kratie, but there are no longer regular passenger services on these routes. There are scenic boat services between Siem Reap and Battambang, and the Tonlé Sap lake is also navigable year-round, although only by smaller boats between March and July.

Traditionally the most popular boat services with foreigners are those that run between Phnom Penh and Siem Reap. The express services do the trip in as little as five hours. The first couple of hours out of Phnom Penh along the Tonlé Sap River are scenic, but it becomes less interesting when the river morphs into the Tonlé Sap lake, which is like a vast sea, offering little scenery. It's more popular (and much cheaper) to take a bus on the paved road instead.

The small boat between Siem Reap and Battambang is more rewarding, as the river scenery is truly memorable, but it can take as long as a whole day with delays.

Bus

The range of road transport is extensive. On sealed roads, large air-conditioned buses and speedy express minivans are the most popular choices. Elsewhere, a shared taxi or local minibus is the way to go.

All major cities are now well-linked by bus to Phnom Penh along sealed roads, but if you're travelling from one end of the country to the other you may have to change buses.

While it doesn't cover all bus companies, **bookmebus** (www.bookmebus.com) is a reliable bus-ticket booking site, including for more obscure routes and cross-border trips.

Buses are reasonably safe but accidents can happen on Cambodia's dicey roads, and there have been several big accidents involving buses or express minivans where tourists were killed.

Express minivans, usually modern Ford Transits or Toyota Hiaces, operate a one seat/ one passenger policy and are reasonably comfortable, but they are sometimes driven by maniacs, so check the reviews.

Older local minibuses serve most provincial routes but are not widely used by Western visitors. They are very cheap but painfully slow and often uncomfortably overcrowded; only really consider them if there is no alternative.

Car & Motorcycle

Many visitors rent a car or bike for greater flexibility to visit out-of-the-way places and to stop when they choose. Almost all car rental in Cambodia includes a driver, although self-drive rentals are also available in Phnom Penh.

Driving Licenses

According to official rules, to drive a car you need a Cambodian licence, but the law is seldom applied. Local travel agents and some motorbike renters can arrange a Cambodian licence in less than a week for around US$35.

For renting motorcycles, no licence is required. If you can drive the bike out of the shop, you can drive it anywhere, or so the logic goes.

Fuel & Spare Parts

Fuel is relatively expensive in Cambodia compared with other staples. Fuel prices are generally much higher in central Phnom Penh and Siem Reap (4000r to 5000r, or US$1 to US$1.25, per litre) than elsewhere because of high rents. Highway petrol stations in the provinces are a good bet for cheap fuel (as low as 3000r per litre for gasoline, or 2200r per litre for diesel).

Fuel is readily available throughout the country. Even the most isolated communities usually have someone selling petrol out of Fanta or Johnnie Walker bottles. Some sellers mix this fuel with kerosene to make a quick profit, so use it sparingly, in emergencies only.

When it comes to spare parts, Cambodia is flooded with Chinese, Japanese and Korean motorcycles, so it's easy to get parts for Hondas, Yamahas or Suzukis, but finding a part for a specialist make is another matter. The same goes for cars. Spares for Japanese cars are easy to come by, but if you are driving something obscure, bring substantial spares.

Hire

CAR

Car hire is generally only available with a driver and is most useful for sightseeing around Phnom Penh and Angkor, and for conveniently travelling between cities. Some tourists with a healthy budget also arrange cars or 4WDs with drivers for touring the provinces. Hiring a car with a driver is about US$30 to US$35 for a day in and around Cambodia's towns. Heading into the provinces it rises to US$50 or more, plus petrol, depending on the destination. Hiring 4WDs will cost around US$60 to US$120 a day, depending on the model and the distance travelled. Self-drive car rentals are available in Phnom Penh, but think twice about driving yourself due to chaotic road conditions and personal liability in the case of an accident.

MOTORCYCLE

It is possible to explore Cambodia by motorbike. Anyone planning a longer ride should try out the bike around town for a day or so first to make sure it is in good health.

Motorcycles are available for hire in Phnom Penh and other provincial capitals. In Siem Reap motorcycle rental is still technically forbidden, but of late authorities are taking a relaxed view and a growing number of places now hire out motorbikes to tourists. It is usually possible to rent a 100cc motorbike for between US$4 and US$10 per day; costs are around US$15 to US$25 for a 250cc dirt bike.

Motorcycle tours are a great way to get way off the beaten track and there are some experienced operators in Cambodia.

ROAD SAFETY

Many more people are now killed and injured each month in traffic accidents than by landmines. Be extremely vigilant when travelling under your own steam. It's best not to travel on the roads at night, especially by bike, due to a higher prevalence of accidents at this time.

Cambodia has some of the best roads (read worst roads) in the world for dirt biking, but only experienced off-road bikers should ride them. Cambodia is not the ideal place to start riding a bike. If you're jumping in at the deep end, make sure you are under the supervision of someone who knows how to ride.

When travelling on *motos*, beware of nasty burns from the exhaust pipe.

Dancing Roads (✆012 822803; www.dancingroads.com) Offers motorbike tours around the capital and gentle tours further afield to the South Coast. Based in Phnom Penh, the driver-guides are fun and friendly.

Hidden Cambodia (Map p106; www.hiddencambodia.com) A Siem Reap–based company specialising in motorcycle trips throughout the country, including the remote temples of northern Cambodia and beyond.

Red Raid Cambodia (Map p54; www.motorcycletourscambodia. com; 31 St 302) More expensive but experienced French-run outfit offering trips through-out Cambodia, including the Cardamoms.

Insurance

If you are travelling in a tour-ist vehicle with a driver, then the car is usually insured. When it comes to motor-cycles, many rental bikes are not insured and you will have to sign a contract agreeing to a valuation for the bike if it is stolen. Make sure you have a strong lock and always leave the bike in guarded parking where available.

Do not even consider hiring a motorcycle if you are travelling in Cambodia with-out medical insurance. The cost of treating serious inju-ries, especially if you require an evacuation, is bankrupting for budget travellers.

Road Conditions & Hazards

Whether travelling or living in Cambodia, it is easy to lull yourself into a false sense of security and assume that down every rural road is yet another friendly village. How-ever, even with the demise of the Khmer Rouge, odd incidents of banditry and robbery do occur in rural areas. There have also been some nasty bike-jackings in Sihanoukville. When travel-ling in your own vehicle, and particularly by motorcycle in rural areas, make certain you check the latest security information in communities along the way.

Be particularly careful about children on the road, as you'll sometimes find kids hanging out in the middle of a major highway. Livestock on the road is also a menace.

Other general security suggestions for those travel-ling by motorcycle:

➡ Try to get hold of a good-quality helmet for long journeys or high-speed riding.

➡ Carry a basic repair kit, including some tyre levers, a puncture-repair kit and a pump.

➡ Always carry a rope for towing on longer journeys in case you break down.

➡ In remote areas always carry several litres of water, as you never know when you will run out.

➡ Travel in small groups, not alone, and stay close together.

➡ Don't be cheap with the petrol, as running out of fuel in a rural area could jeopardise your health, especially if water runs out too.

➡ Do not smoke marijuana or drink alcohol and drive.

➡ Keep your eyes firmly fixed on the road; Cambodian potholes eat people for fun.

Road Rules

If there are road rules in Cambodia it is doubtful that anyone is following them. Size matters and the biggest vehicle wins by default. The best advice if you drive a car or ride a motorcycle in Cam-bodia is to take nothing for granted.

In Cambodia traffic drives on the right. There are some traffic lights at junctions in Phnom Penh, Siem Reap and Sihanoukville, but where there are no lights, most traf-fic turns left into the oncom-ing traffic, edging along the wrong side of the road until a gap becomes apparent. Cambodians are quite used to the system. Foreigners should stop at crossings and develop a habit of constant vigilance. Never assume that other drivers will stop at red lights; these are considered optional by most Cambodi-ans, especially at night.

Phnom Penh is the one place where, amid all the chaos, traffic police take issue with Westerners break-ing even the most trivial road rules. Make sure you don't turn left at a 'no left turn' sign or travel with your headlights on during the day (although, strangely, it doesn't seem to be illegal for Cambodians to travel without headlights at night). Laws requiring that bikes have mirrors and that drivers (not passengers, even children) wear helmets, are being enforced around the country by traffic police eager to levy fines. Foreigners are popular targets.

Local Transport

Boat

Outboards (pronounced 'outboor') are the equivalent of Venice's vaporetto, a sort of local river-bus or taxi. Found all over the country, they are small fibreglass boats with 15HP or 40HP engines, and can carry up to six people for local or longer trips. They rarely run to schedules, but locals wait patiently for them to fill up or you can charter the whole boat and take off. Another variation are the longtail rocket boats that connect small villages on the upper stretches of the Mekong. Rocket is the definitive word and their safety is questionable.

Bus

Phnom Penh has several public city bus routes that are proving popular with local students, but are not yet widely used by visitors. Elsewhere there are no public bus networks.

Cyclo

As in Vietnam and Laos, the cyclo (bicycle rickshaw or pedicab) is a cheap way to get around urban areas. In Phnom Penh cyclo drivers can either be flagged down on main roads or found waiting around markets and major hotels. It is necessary to bargain the fare if taking a cyclo from outside an expensive hotel or popular restaurant or bar. Fares range from US$1 to US$3. There are few cyclos in the provinces, and in Phnom Penh the cyclo has almost been driven to extinction by the moto (motorcycle taxi).

Moto

Motos, also known as motodups (meaning moto driver), are small motorcycle taxis. They are a quick way of making short hops around towns and cities.

Prices range from 2000r to US$1.50 or more, depending on the distance and the town; expect to pay more at night. In the past it was rare for prices to be agreed in advance, but with the increase in visitor numbers, a lot of drivers have got into the habit of overcharging. It's probably best to negotiate up front, particularly in the major tourist centres, outside fancy hotels or at night.

Remork-moto

The remork-moto (tuk tuk) is a large trailer hitched to a motorcycle and pretty much operates as a low-tech local bus with oh-so-natural air-conditioning. They are used throughout rural Cambodia to transport people and goods, and are often seen on the edge of towns ready to ferry farmers back to the countryside.

Most popular tourist destinations, including Phnom Penh, Siem Reap and the South Coast, have their very own tourist versions of the remork, with a canopied trailer hitched to the back of the motorbike for two people in comfort or as many as you can pile on at night. Often referred to as tuk tuks by foreigners travelling in Cambodia, they're a great way to explore temples, as you get the breeze of the bike but some protection from the elements.

Rotei Ses

Rotei means 'cart' or 'carriage' and ses is 'horse', but the term is used for any cart pulled by an animal. Cambodia's original 4WD, ox carts, usually pulled by water buffalo or cows, are a common form of transport in remote parts of the country, as only they can get through thick mud in the height of the wet season. Some local community-tourism initiatives now include cart rides.

Share Taxi

In these days of improving roads, share taxis are losing ground to express minivans. When using share taxis, it is an advantage to travel in numbers, as you can buy spare seats to make the journey more comfortable. Double the price for the front seat and quadruple it for the entire back row. It is important to remember that there aren't necessarily fixed prices on every route, so you have to negotiate. For major destinations they can be hired individually, or you can pay for a seat and wait for other passengers to turn up. Guesthouses are also very helpful when it comes to arranging share taxis, albeit at a price.

Taxi

Taxi hire in towns and cities is getting easier, but there are still very few metered taxis, with just a handful of operators in Phnom Penh. Guesthouses, hotels and travel agents can arrange cars for sightseeing in and around towns. Big online players such as Uber have now entered the market.

Train

Mothballed for years, Cambodia's rail system has been rehabilitated in recent years and limited passenger services resumed in 2016 through national carrier **Royal Railways** (☑078 888583; www.royal-railway. com). Currently the only service links Phnom Penh with Sihanoukville via Kampot, with departures on weekend mornings. Plans call for plugging the Cambodian line into the Trans-Asian Railway network, which will link Singapore and China, but connecting Phnom Penh with Ho Chi Minh City via a Mekong bridge will take a few years yet. The 385km northwestern line, which links Phnom Penh with Pursat and Battambang and was built before WWII, is next in line to open.

Health

General health is more of a concern in Cambodia than most other parts of Southeast Asia, due to a lack of international-standard medical-treatment facilities, a prevalence of tropical diseases and poor sanitation. Once you venture into rural areas you are very much on your own, although most provincial capitals have a reasonable clinic these days.

If you feel particularly unwell, try to see a doctor rather than visit a hospital; hospitals in rural areas are pretty primitive and diagnosis can be hit and miss. If you fall seriously ill in Cambodia you should head to Phnom Penh or Siem Reap, as these are the only places in the country with decent emergency treatment. Pharmacies in the larger towns are remarkably well stocked and you don't need a prescription to get your hands on anything from antibiotics to antimalarials. Prices are also very reasonable, but do check the expiry date, as some medicine may be out of date.

While the potential dangers can seem quite unnerving, in reality few travellers experience anything more than an upset stomach. Don't let these warnings make you paranoid.

BEFORE YOU GO

Health Insurance

Do not visit Cambodia without medical insurance. Hospitals are extremely basic in the provinces and even in Phnom Penh the facilities are not necessarily what you may be used to at home. Anyone who has a serious injury or illness while in Cambodia may require emergency evacuation to Bangkok. With an insurance policy costing no more than the equivalent of a bottle of beer a day, this evacuation is free. Without an insurance policy, it will cost between US$10,000 and US$20,000. Don't gamble with your health in Cambodia or you may end up another statistic.

Medical Checklist

Following is a list of items to consider including in a medical kit:

➡ aspirin or paracetamol – for pain or fever

➡ antihistamine – for allergies, or to ease the itch from insect bites or stings

➡ cold and flu tablets, throat lozenges and nasal decongestant

➡ multivitamins – especially for long trips, when dietary vitamin intake may be inadequate

➡ loperamide or diphenoxylate – 'blockers' for diarrhoea

➡ rehydration mixture – to prevent dehydration, which may occur during bouts of diarrhoea

➡ insect repellent, sunscreen, lip balm and eye drops

➡ calamine lotion or aloe vera – to ease irritation from sunburn

➡ antifungal cream or powder – for fungal skin infections and thrush

➡ antiseptic (such as povidone-iodine) – for cuts and grazes

EVERYDAY HEALTH

Normal body temperature is up to 37°C (98.6°F); more than 2°C (4°F) higher indicates a high fever. The normal adult pulse rate is 60 to 100 beats per minute (children 80 to 100, babies 100 to 140). As a general rule, the pulse increases about 20 beats per minute for each 1°C (2°F) rise in fever.

CONTACT LENSES

People wearing contact lenses should be aware that Cambodia is an extremely dusty country and this can cause much irritation when travelling. It is generally bearable in cars, but when travelling by motorcycle or pick-up, it is most definitely not. Pack a pair of glasses.

➡ bandages, plasters and other wound dressings

➡ water-purification tablets or iodine

➡ sterile kit (sealed medical kit containing syringes and needles) – highly recommended, as Cambodia has potential medical-hygiene issues

IN CAMBODIA

Availability & Cost of Healthcare

Self-diagnosis and treatment of health problems can be risky, so always seek professional medical help.

Antibiotics should ideally be administered only under medical supervision. Take only the recommended dose at the prescribed intervals and use the whole course, even if the illness seems to be cured earlier. Stop immediately if there are any serious reactions.

The best clinics and hospitals in Cambodia are found in Phnom Penh and Siem Reap. A consultation usually costs in the region of US$20 to US$50, plus medicine. Elsewhere, facilities are more basic, although a private clinic is usually preferable to a government hospital. For serious injuries, seek treatment in Bangkok.

Infectious Diseases

Dengue Fever

This viral disease is transmitted by mosquitoes. There is only a small risk to travellers, except during epidemics, which usually occur during and just after the wet season.

Unlike the malaria mosquito, the *Aedes aegypti* mosquito, which transmits the dengue virus, is most active during the day and is found mainly in urban areas.

Signs and symptoms of dengue fever include a sudden onset of high fever, headache, joint and muscle pains (hence its old name, 'breakbone fever'), plus nausea and vomiting. A rash of small red spots appears three to four days after the onset of fever.

Seek medical attention if you think you may be infected. A blood test can diagnose infection, but there is no specific treatment for the disease. Aspirin should be avoided, as it increases the risk of haemorrhaging, but plenty of rest is advised.

There is no vaccine against dengue fever. The best prevention is to avoid mosquito bites at all times.

Fungal Infections

Fungal infections occur more commonly in hot weather and are usually on the scalp, between the toes (athlete's foot) or fingers, in the groin and on the body (ringworm). Ringworm, a fungal infection, not a worm, is contracted from infected animals or other people. Moisture encourages these infections.

To prevent fungal infections wear loose, comfortable clothes, avoid artificial fibres, wash frequently and dry yourself carefully.

Hepatitis

Hepatitis is a general term for inflammation of the liver. Several different viruses cause hepatitis, and they differ in the way that they are transmitted. The symptoms are similar in all forms of the illness, and include fever, chills, headache, fatigue, feelings of weakness, and aches and pains, followed by loss of appetite, nausea, vomiting, abdominal pain, dark urine, light-coloured faeces, jaundiced (yellow) skin and yellowing of the whites of the eyes.

Hepatitis A and E are both transmitted by ingesting contaminated food or water. Seek medical advice, but there is not much you can do apart from resting, drinking lots of fluids, eating lightly and avoiding fatty foods.

There are almost 300 million chronic carriers of hepatitis B in the world. It is spread through contact with infected blood, blood products or body fluids; for example, through sexual contact, unsterilized needles, blood transfusions or contact with blood via small breaks in the skin. Hepatitis C and D are spread in the same way as hepatitis B and can also lead to long-term complications.

HIV & AIDS

Infection with the human immunodeficiency virus (HIV) may lead to acquired immune deficiency syndrome (AIDS), which is a fatal disease. Any exposure to blood, blood products or body fluids may put the individual at risk.

The disease is often transmitted through sexual contact or dirty needles, so vaccinations, acupuncture, tattooing and body piercing can be potentially as dangerous as intravenous drug use.

Intestinal Worms

These parasites are most common in rural Cambodia. The various worms have different ways of infecting people. Some may be ingested in food such as undercooked meat (eg tapeworms) and some enter through your skin (eg hookworms). Consider having a stool test when you

RECOMMENDED VACCINATIONS

Plan ahead for getting your vaccinations, as some of them require more than one injection over a period of time, while others should not be given in combination.

Record all vaccinations on an International Certificate of Vaccination, available from your doctor. It is a good idea to carry this as proof of your vaccinations when travelling in Cambodia.

Recommended vaccinations for a trip to Cambodia are listed here, but it is imperative that you discuss your needs with your doctor:

Diphtheria and tetanus Vaccinations for these two diseases are usually combined.

Hepatitis A This vaccine provides long-term immunity after an initial injection and a booster at six to 12 months. The hepatitis A vaccine is also available in a combined form with the hepatitis B vaccine – three injections over a six-month period are required.

Hepatitis B Vaccination involves three injections, with a booster at 12 months.

Polio A booster every 10 years maintains immunity.

Tuberculosis Vaccination against TB (BCG vaccine) is recommended for children and young adults who will be living in Cambodia for three months or more.

Typhoid Vaccination against typhoid may be required if you are travelling for more than a few weeks in Cambodia.

return home to check for worms and to determine the appropriate treatment.

Malaria

This serious and potentially fatal disease is spread by mosquitoes. If you are travelling in endemic areas it is extremely important to avoid mosquito bites and to take tablets to prevent the disease developing if you become infected. There is no malaria in Phnom Penh, Siem Reap and most other major urban areas in Cambodia, so visitors on short trips to the most popular places do not need to take medication. The areas where malaria is most prevalent is along remote areas of the Thai border and on some offshore islands. Malaria self-test kits are widely available in Cambodia, but are not that reliable.

Symptoms of malaria include fever, chills and sweating, headache, aching joints, diarrhoea and stomach pains, usually preceded by a vague feeling of ill health. Seek medical help immediately if malaria is suspected, as, without treatment, the disease can rapidly become more serious or even fatal.

Sexually Transmitted Infections (STIs)

Gonorrhoea, herpes and syphilis are among these infections. Sores, blisters or a rash around the genitals and discharges or pain when urinating are common symptoms. With some STIs, such as wart virus or chlamydia, symptoms may be less marked or not observed at all, especially in women. Reliable condoms are widely available throughout urban areas of Cambodia.

Traveller's Diarrhoea

Simple things like a change of water, food or climate can all cause a mild bout of diarrhoea, but a few rushed toilet trips with no other symptoms are not indicative of a major problem. Almost everyone gets a mild bout of the runs on a longer visit to Cambodia.

Dehydration is the main danger with diarrhoea, particularly in children or the elderly as it can occur quite quickly. Under all circumstances *fluid replacement* is the most important thing to remember. Stick to a bland diet as you recover.

Commercially available oral rehydration salts are very useful; add them to boiled or bottled water.

Gut-paralysing drugs such as Lomotil or Imodium can be used to bring relief from the symptoms of diarrhoea, although they do not actually cure the problem. Only use these drugs if you do not have access to toilets and *must* travel.

Typhoid

Typhoid fever is a dangerous gut infection caused by contaminated water and food. Medical help must be sought.

In its initial stages sufferers may feel they have a bad cold or flu on the way, as early symptoms are a headache, body aches and a fever that rises a little each day until it is around 40°C (104°F) or higher. There may also be vomiting, abdominal pain, diarrhoea or constipation.

In the second week, the high fever continues and a few pink spots may appear on the body; trembling, delirium, weakness, weight loss and dehydration may occur.

TAP WATER

The number-one rule is *be careful of water and ice*, although both are usually factory produced, a legacy of the French. If you don't know for certain that the water is safe, assume the worst. Reputable brands of bottled water or soft drinks are usually fine, but you can't safely drink tap water. Only use water from containers with a serrated seal. Tea and coffee are generally fine, as they're made with boiled water.

Environmental Hazards

Food

There is an adage that says, 'If you can cook it, boil it or peel it you can eat it...otherwise forget it'. This is slightly extreme, but many travellers have found it is better to be safe than sorry. Vegetables and fruit should be washed with purified water or peeled where possible. Beware of ice cream that is sold in the street (or anywhere), as it might have melted and refrozen. Shellfish such as mussels, oysters and clams should be avoided, as should undercooked meat, particularly in the form of mince.

Heat Exhaustion

Dehydration and salt deficiency can cause heat exhaustion. Take time to acclimatise to high temperatures, drink sufficient liquids and do not do anything too physically demanding.

Salt deficiency is characterised by fatigue, lethargy, headaches, giddiness and muscle cramps; salt tablets may help, but adding extra salt to your food is better.

Heatstroke can occur if the body's heat-regulating mechanism breaks down, causing the body temperature to rise to dangerous levels. Long, continuous periods of exposure to high temperatures and insufficient fluids can leave you vulnerable to heatstroke.

Insect Bites & Stings

Bedbugs live in various places, but particularly in dirty mattresses and bedding, and are evidenced by spots of blood on bedclothes or on the wall. Bedbugs leave itchy bites in neat rows. Calamine lotion or Stingose spray may help.

All lice cause itching and discomfort. They make themselves at home in your hair (head lice), your clothing (body lice) or in your pubic hair (crabs). You catch lice through direct contact with infected people or by sharing combs, clothing and the like. Powder or shampoo treatment will kill the lice, and infected clothing should be washed in very hot, soapy water and left to dry in the sun.

Leeches may be present in damp rainforest conditions; they attach themselves to your skin to suck your blood. Trekkers often get them on their legs or in their boots. Salt or a lighted cigarette end will make them fall off.

Sandflies inhabit beaches (usually the more remote ones) across Southeast Asia. They have a nasty bite that is extremely itchy and can easily become infected. Use an antihistamine to quell the itching, and, if you have to itch, use the palm of your hand and not your nails or infection may follow.

Prickly Heat

Prickly heat is an itchy rash caused by excessive perspiration trapped under the skin. It usually strikes people who have just arrived in a hot climate. Keeping cool, bathing often, drying the skin, using a mild talcum or prickly heat powder, or finding air-conditioning may help.

Snakes

To minimise the chances of being bitten by a snake, always wear boots, socks and long trousers when walking through undergrowth where snakes may be present.

Traditional Medicine

Traditional medicine or *thnam boran* is very popular in rural Cambodia. There are *kru Khmer* (traditional medicine men) in most districts of the country and some locals trust them more than modern doctors and hospitals. Working with tree bark, roots, herbs and plants, they boil up brews to supposedly cure all ills. However, when it comes to serious conditions such as snake bites, their treatments can be counterproductive.

Language

The Khmer language is spoken by approximately nine million people in Cambodia, and is understood by many in neighbouring countries. Although Khmer as spoken in Phnom Penh is generally intelligible to Khmers nationwide, there are several distinct dialects in other parts of the country. Most notably, inhabitants of Takeo Province tend to modify or slur hard consonant/vowel combinations, especially those with 'r'. For example, *bram* (five) becomes *pe-am*, *sraa* (alcohol) becomes *se-aa*, and *baraang* (French for foreigner) becomes *be-ang*. In Siem Reap there's a Lao-sounding lilt to the local speech – some vowels are modified, eg *poan* (thousand) becomes *peuan*, and *kh'sia* (pipe) becomes *kh'seua*.

Though English is fast becoming Cambodia's second language, the Khmer population still clings to the Francophone pronunciation of the Roman alphabet and most foreign words. This is helpful to remember when spelling Western words and names aloud – 'ay-bee-see' becomes 'ah-bey-sey' and so on.

The pronunciation guides in this chapter are designed for basic communication rather than linguistic perfection. Read them as if they were English, and you shouldn't have problems being understood. Some consonant combinations are separated with an apostrophe for ease of pronunciation, eg 'j-r' in j'rook (pig) and 'ch-ng' in ch'ngain

WANT MORE?

For in-depth language information and handy phrases, check out Lonely Planet's *Southeast Asia Phrasebook*. You'll find it at **shop.lonelyplanet.com**, or you can buy Lonely Planet's iPhone phrasebooks at the Apple App Store.

(delicious). Also note that k is pronounced as the 'g' in 'go'; kh as the 'k' in 'kind'; p as the final 'p' in 'puppy'; ph as the 'p' in 'pond'; r as in 'rum' (hard and rolling); t as the 't' in 'stand'; and th as the 't' in 'two'.

Vowels and vowel combinations with an h at the end are pronounced with a puff of air at the end. Vowels are pronounced as follows:

a and ah shorter and harder than aa
aa as the 'a' in 'father'
ae as the 'a' in 'cat'
ai as in 'aisle'
am as the 'um' in 'glum'
av like a nasal ao (without the'v')
aw as the 'aw' in 'jaw'
awh as the 'aw' in 'jaw' (short and hard)
ay as ai (slightly nasal)
e as in 'they'
eh as the 'a' in 'date' (short and hard)
eu like 'oo' (with flat lips)
euh as eu (short and hard)
euv like a nasal eu (without the 'v')
ey as in 'prey'
i as in 'kit'
ia as the 'ee' in 'beer' (without the 'r')
ih as the 'ee' in 'teeth' (short and hard)
ii as the 'ee' in 'feet'
o as the 'ow' in 'cow'
œ as 'er' in 'her' (more open)
oh as the 'o' in 'hose' (short and hard)
ohm as the 'ome' in 'home'
ow as in 'glow'
u as the 'u' in 'flute' (short and hard)
ua as the 'ou' in 'tour'
uah as ua (short and hard)
uh as the 'u' in 'but'
uu as the 'oo' in 'zoo'

BASICS

The Khmer language reflects the social standing of the speaker and the subject through personal pronouns and 'politeness words'. These range from the simple *baat* for men and *jaa* for women, placed at the end of a sentence and meaning 'yes' or 'I agree', to the very formal and archaic *Reachasahp* or 'royal language', a separate vocabulary reserved for addressing the king and very high officials. Many of the pronouns are determined on the basis of the subject's age and gender in relation to the speaker.

Foreigners are not expected to know all of these forms. The easiest and most general personal pronoun is *niak* (you), which may be used in most situations, for either gender. Men of your age or older can be called *lowk* (Mister). Women of your age or older can be called *bawng srei* (older sister) or, for more formal situations, *lowk srei* (Madam). *Bawng* is an informal, neutral pronoun for men or women who are (or appear to be) older than you. For the third person (he/she/they), male or female, singular or plural, the respectful form is *koat* and the common form is *ke*.

Hello.	ជម្រាបសួរ	johm riab sua
Goodbye.	លាសិនហើយ	lia suhn hao-y
Excuse me./ Sorry.	សូមទោស	sohm toh
Please.	សូម	sohm
Thank you.	អរគុណ	aw kohn
You're welcome.	អត់អីទេ/ សូមអញ្ជើញ	awt ei te/ sohm onh-jernh
Yes.	បាទ/ចាស	baat/jaa (m/f)
No.	ទេ	te

How are you?
អ្នកសុខសប្បាយទេ? niak sohk sabaay te

I'm fine.
ខ្ញុំសុខសប្បាយ kh'nyohm sohk sabaay

What's your name?
អ្នកឈ្មោះអី? niak ch'muah ei

My name is ...
ខ្ញុំឈ្មោះ... kh'nyohm ch'muah ...

Does anyone speak English?
ទីនេះមានអ្នកចេះ tii nih mian niak jeh
ភាសាអង់គ្លេសទេ? phiasaa awngle te

I don't understand.
ខ្ញុំមិនយល់ទេ/ kh'nyohm muhn yuhl te/
ខ្ញុំស្ដាប់មិនបាន kh'nyohm s'dap muhn baan te

ACCOMMODATION

Where's a hotel?
អូតែលនៅឯណា? ohtail neuv ai naa

I'd like a room ...	ខ្ញុំសុំបន្ទប់...	kh'nyohm sohm bantohp ...
for one person	សម្រាប់ មួយនាក់	samruhp muy niak
for two people	សម្រាប់ ពីរនាក់	samruhp pii niak
with a bathroom	ដែលមាន បន្ទប់ទឹក	dail mian bantohp tuhk
with a fan	ដែលមាន កង្ហារ	dail mian kawnghahl
with a window	ដែលមាន បង្អួច	dail mian bawng uoch

How much is it per day?
តម្លៃមួយថ្ងៃ damlay muy th'ngay
ប៉ុន្មាន? ponmaan

DIRECTIONS

Where is a/the ...?
...នៅឯណា? ... neuv ai naa

How can I get to ...?
ផ្លូវណាទៅ...? phleuv naa teuv ...

Go straight ahead.
ទៅត្រង់ teuv trawng

Turn left.
បត់ឆ្វេង bawt ch'weng

Turn right.
បត់ស្ដាំ bawt s'dam

at the corner
នៅកាច់ជ្រុង neuv kait j'rohng

behind
នៅខាងក្រោយ neuv khaang krao-y

in front of
នៅខាងមុខ neuv khaang mohk

next to
នៅជាប់ neuv joab

opposite
នៅទល់មុខ neuv tohl mohk

EATING & DRINKING

Where's a ...?	...នៅឯណា?	... neuv ai naa
food stall	កន្លែងលក់ម្ហូប	kuhnlaing loak m'howp
market	ផ្សារ	psar
restaurant	ភោជនីយដ្ឋាន	resturawn

Do you have a menu in English?

មានម៉ឺនុយជា ភាសាអង់គ្លេសទេ?	mien menui jea piasaa awnglay te

What's the speciality here?

ទីនេះមានម្ហូប អ្វីពិសេសទេ?	tii nih mien m'howp ei piseh te

I'm vegetarian.

ខ្ញុំតមសាច់	kh'nyohm tawm sait

I'm allergic to (peanuts).

កុំដាក់ (សណ្ដែកដី)	kohm dak (sandaik dei)

Not too spicy, please.

សូមកុំធ្វើហឹរពេក	sohm kohm twœ huhl pek

This is delicious.

អានេះឆ្ងាញ់ណាស់	nih ch'ngain nah

The bill, please.

សូមគិតលុយ	sohm kuht lui

Fruit & Vegetables

apple	ផ្លែប៉ោម	phla i powm
banana	ចេក	chek
coconut	ដូង	duong
custard apple	ទៀប	tiep
dragonfruit	ផ្លែស្រកានាគ	phlai srakaa neak
durian	ធូរេន	tourain
grapes	ទំពាំងបាយជូរ	tompeang baai juu
guava	ត្របែក	trawbaik
jackfruit	ខ្នុរ	khnau
lemon	ក្រូចឆ្មារ	krow-it ch'maa
longan	មៀន	mien
lychee	ផ្លែគូលែន	phlai kuulain
mandarin	ក្រូចខ្វិច	krow-it khwait
mango	ស្វាយ	svay
mangosteen	មង្ឃុត	mongkut

orange	ក្រូចពោធិ៍សាត់	kroch pow saat
papaya	ល្ហុង	l'howng
pineapple	ម្នាស់	menoa
pomelo	ក្រូចថ្លុង	kroch th'lohng
rambutan	សាវម៉ាវ	sao mao
starfruit	ស្ពឺ	speu
vegetables	បន្លែ	buhn lai
watermelon	ឪឡឹក	euv luhk

Meat & Fish

beef	សាច់គោ	sach kow
chicken	សាច់មាន់	sach moan
crab	ក្ដាម	k'daam
eel	អន្ទង់	ahntohng
fish	ត្រី	trey
frog	កង្កែប	kawng kaip
lobster	បង្កង	bawng kawng
pork	សាច់ជ្រូក	sach j'ruuk
shrimp	បង្គា	bawngkia
snail	ខ្យង	kh'jawng
squid	មឹក	meuk

Other

bread	នំប៉័ង	nohm paang
butter	ប៊ឺរ	bœ
chilli	ម្ទេស	m'teh
curry	ការី	karii
fish sauce	ទឹកត្រី	teuk trey
fried	ចៀន/ឆា	jien/chaa
garlic	ខ្ទឹមស	kh'tuhm saw
ginger	ខ្ញី	kh'nyei
grilled	អាំង	ahng
ice	ទឹកកក	teuk koh
lemongrass	ស្លឹកគ្រៃ	sluhk krey
noodles (egg/rice)	មី/គុយទាវ	mii/kyteow
pepper	ម្រេច	m'rait

rice	បាយ	bai
salt	អំបិល	uhmbuhl
soup	ស៊ុប	sup
soy sauce	ទឹកស៊ីអ៊ីវ	teuk sii iw
spring rolls (fresh/fried)	ណែម/ឆាយ៉	naim/chaa yaw
steamed	ចំហុយ	jamhoi
sugar	ស្ករ	skaw

Drinks

beer	ប៊ីយ៉ែរ	bii-yœ
coffee	កាហ្វេ	kaa fey
lemon juice	ទឹកក្រូច ឆ្មា	teuk kroch ch'maa
orange juice	ទឹកក្រូច ពោធិ៍សាត់	teuk kroch pow sat
tea	តែ	tai
water	ទឹក	teuk

EMERGENCIES

Help!
ជួយខ្ញុំផង!   juay kh'nyohm phawng

Call the police!
ជួយហៅប៉ូលិសមក!   juay hav police mok

Call a doctor!
ជួយហៅ   juay hav
គ្រូពេទ្យមក!   kruu paet mok

I've been robbed.
ខ្ញុំត្រូវចោរប្លន់   kh'nyohm treuv jao plawn

I'm ill.
ខ្ញុំឈឺ   kh'nyohm cheu

I'm allergic to (antibiotics).
ខ្ញុំមិនត្រូវជាតុ   kh'nyohm muhn treuv thiat
(អង់ទីប៊ីយ៉ូទិក)   (awntiibiowtik)

Where are the toilets?
បង្គន់នៅឯណា?   bawngkohn neuv ai naa

SHOPPING & SERVICES

I want to see the ...
ខ្ញុំចង់ទៅមើល...   kh'nyohm jawng teuv mœl ...

What time does it open?
វាបើកម៉ោងប៉ុន្មាន?   wia baok maong pohnmaan

What time does it close?
វាបិទម៉ោងប៉ុន្មាន?   wia buht maong pohnmaan

I'm looking for the ...   ខ្ញុំរក...   kh'nyohm rohk ...

   bank   ធនាគារ   th'niakia

   post office   ប្រៃសណីយ៍   praisuhnii

   public telephone   ទូរស័ព្ទ សាធារណៈ   turasahp saathiaranah

   temple   វត្ត   wawt

How much is it?
នេះថ្លៃប៉ុន្មាន?   nih th'lay pohnmaan

That's too much.
ថ្លៃពេក   th'lay pek

No more than ...
មិនលើសពី...   muhn lœh pii ...

What's your best price?
អ្នកដាច់ប៉ុន្មាន?   niak dach pohnmaan

I want to change US dollars.
ខ្ញុំចង់ដូរ   kh'nyohm jawng dow
ដុល្លារអាមេរិក   dolaa amerik

What is the exchange rate for US dollars?
មួយដុល្លារ   muy dolaa
ដូរបានប៉ុន្មាន?   dow baan pohnmaan

TIME & DATES

What time is it?
ឥឡូវនេះម៉ោងប៉ុន្មាន?   eileuv nih maong pohnmaan

in the morning	ពេលព្រឹក	pel pruhk
in the afternoon	ពេលរសៀល	pel r'sial
in the evening	ពេលល្ងាច	pel l'ngiach
at night	ពេលយប់	pel yohp
yesterday	ម្សិលមិញ	m'suhl mein
today	ថ្ងៃនេះ	th'ngay nih
tomorrow	ថ្ងៃស្អែក	th'ngay s'aik

Monday	ថ្ងៃចន្ទ	th'ngay jahn
Tuesday	ថ្ងៃអង្គារ	th'ngay ahngkia
Wednesday	ថ្ងៃពុធ	th'ngay poht
Thursday	ថ្ងៃព្រហស្បតិ៍	th'ngay prohoah
Friday	ថ្ងៃសុក្រ	th'ngay sohk
Saturday	ថ្ងៃសៅរ៍	th'ngay sav
Sunday	ថ្ងៃអាទិត្យ	th'ngay aatuht

TRANSPORT

Where's the ...?	...នៅឯណា?	... neuv ai naa
airport	វាលយន្ត	wial yohn
	ហោះ	hawh
bus stop	ចំណត	jamnawt
	ឡានឈ្នួល	laan ch'nual
train station	ស្ថានីយ	s'thaanii
	រថភ្លើង	roht plœng

When does the ... leave?	...ចេញម៉ោង ប៉ុន្មាន?	... jeinh maong pohnmaan
boat	ទូក	duk
bus	ឡានឈ្នួល	laan ch'nual
train	រថភ្លើង	roht plœng
plane	យន្តហោះ	yohn hawh

What time does the last bus leave?

ឡានឈ្នួលចុងក្រោយ
ចេញទៅម៉ោងប៉ុន្មាន?

laan ch'nual johng krao-y jein teuv maong pohnmaan

I want to get off (here).

ខ្ញុំចង់ចុះ(ទីនេះ)

kh'nyohm jawng joh (tii nih)

How much is it to ...?

ទៅ...ថ្លៃប៉ុន្មាន?

teuv ... th'lay pohnmaan

Please take me to (this address).

សូមជូនខ្ញុំទៅ
(អាសយដ្ឋាននេះ)

sohm juun kh' nyohm teuv (aasayathaan nih)

Here is fine, thank you.

ឈប់នៅទីនេះក៏បាន

chohp neuv tii nih kaw baan

Numbers

Khmers count in increments of five – after reaching the number five *(bram)*, the cycle begins again with the addition of one, ie 'five-one' *(bram muy)*, 'five-two' *(bram pii)* and so on to 10, which begins a new cycle. For example, 18 has three parts: 10, five and three.

There's also a colloquial form of counting that reverses the word order for numbers between 10 and 20 and separates the two words with *duhn: pii duhn dawp* for 12, *bei duhn dawp* for 13 and so on. This form is often used in markets, so listen keenly.

1	មួយ	muy
2	ពីរ	pii
3	បី	bei
4	បួន	buan
5	ប្រាំ	bram
6	ប្រាំមួយ	bram muy
7	ប្រាំពីរ	bram pii
8	ប្រាំបី	bram bei
9	ប្រាំបួន	bram buan
10	ដប់	dawp
11	ដប់មួយ	dawp muy
12	ដប់ពីរ	dawp pii
16	ដប់ប្រាំមួយ	dawp bram muy
20	ម្ភៃ	m'phei
21	ម្ភៃមួយ	m'phei muy
30	សាមសិប	saamsuhp
40	សែសិប	saisuhp
100	មួយរយ	muy roy
1000	មួយពាន់	muy poan
1,000,000	មួយលាន	muy lian

1st	ទីមួយ	tii muy
2nd	ទីពីរ	tii pii
3rd	ទីបី	tii bei
4th	ទីបួន	tii buan
10th	ទីដប់	tii dawp

GLOSSARY

apsara – heavenly nymph or angelic dancer, often represented in Khmer sculpture

Asean – Association of Southeast Asian Nations

Avalokiteshvara – Bodhisattva of Compassion and the inspiration for Jayavarman VII's Angkor Thom

baray – reservoir

boeng – lake

Chenla – pre-Angkorian period, 6th to 8th centuries

chunchiet – ethnic minorities

CNRP – Cambodia National Rescue Party

CPP – Cambodian People's Party

cyclo – pedicab; bicycle rickshaw

devaraja – cult of the god-king, established by Jayavarman II, in which the monarch has universal power

devadas – goddesses

EFEO – École Française d'Extrême Orient

essai – wise man or traditional medicine man

Funan – pre-Angkorian period, 1st to 5th centuries

Funcinpec – National United Front for an Independent, Neutral, Peaceful and Cooperative Cambodia; royalist political party

garuda – mythical half-man, half-bird creature

gopura – entrance pavilion in traditional Hindu architecture

Hun Sen – Cambodia's prime minister (1985–present)

Jayavarman II – the king (r 802–50) who established the cult of the god-king, kicking off a period of amazing architectural productivity that resulted in the extraordinary temples of Angkor

Jayavarman VII – the king (r 1181–1219) who drove the Chams out of Cambodia before embarking on an ambitious

construction program, including the walled city of Angkor Thom

Kampuchea – the name Cambodians use for their country; to non-Khmers, it is associated with the bloody rule of the Khmer Rouge, which insisted that the outside world adopt for Cambodia the name Democratic Kampuchea from 1975 to 1979

Khmer – a person of Cambodian descent; the language of Cambodia

Khmer Krom – ethnic Khmers living in Vietnam

Khmer Rouge – a revolutionary organisation that seized power in 1975 and implemented a brutal social restructuring, resulting in the suffering and death of millions of Cambodians during its four-year rule

krama – scarf

linga – phallic symbols

Mahayana – literally, 'Great Vehicle'; a school of Buddhism (also known as the Northern School) that built upon and extended the early Buddhist teachings; see also Theravada

moto – small motorcycle with driver; a common form of transport in Cambodia

naga – mythical serpent, often multiheaded; a symbol used extensively in Angkorian architecture

nandi – sacred ox, vehicle of Shiva

NGO – nongovernmental organisation

NH – national highway

Norodom Ranariddh, Prince – son of King Sihanouk and former leader of Funcinpec

Norodom Sihanouk, King – former king, head of state, film director and a towering figure in modern-day Cambodia

Pali – ancient Indian language that, along with Sanskrit, is the root of modern Khmer

phnom – mountain or hill

Pol Pot – the former leader of the Khmer Rouge; responsible for the suffering and deaths of

millions of Cambodians; previously known as Saloth Sar

prasat – stone or brick hall with religious or royal significance

preah – sacred

psar – market

Ramayana – an epic Sanskrit poem composed around 300 BC featuring the mythical Ramachandra, the incarnation of the god Vishnu

remork-moto – trailer pulled by a motorcycle; often shortened to *remork*

rom vong – Cambodian circle dancing

Sangkum Reastr Niyum – People's Socialist Community; a national movement, led by King Sihanouk, that ruled the country during the 1950s and 1960s

Sanskrit – ancient Hindu language that, along with Pali, is the root of modern Khmer language

stung – river

Suryavarman II – the king (r 1112–52) responsible for building Angkor Wat and for expanding and unifying the Khmer empire

Theravada – a school of Buddhism (also known as the Southern School or Hinayana) found in Myanmar (Burma), Thailand, Laos and Cambodia; this school confined itself to the early Buddhist teachings; see also Mahayana

tonlé – large river

UNDP – UN Development Programme

Unesco – UN Educational Scientific and Cultural Organization

Untac – UN Transitional Authority in Cambodia

vihara – temple sanctuary

WHO – World Health Organization

Year Zero – 1975; the year the Khmer Rouge seized power

yoni – female fertility symbol

Behind the Scenes

SEND US YOUR FEEDBACK

We love to hear from travellers – your comments keep us on our toes and help make our books better. Our well-travelled team reads every word on what you loved or loathed about this book. Although we cannot reply individually to your submissions, we always guarantee that your feedback goes straight to the appropriate authors, in time for the next edition. Each person who sends us information is thanked in the next edition – the most useful submissions are rewarded with a selection of digital PDF chapters.

Visit **lonelyplanet.com/contact** to submit your updates and suggestions or to ask for help. Our award-winning website also features inspirational travel stories, news and discussions.

Note: We may edit, reproduce and incorporate your comments in Lonely Planet products such as guidebooks, websites and digital products, so let us know if you don't want your comments reproduced or your name acknowledged. For a copy of our privacy policy visit lonelyplanet.com/privacy.

OUR READERS

Many thanks to the travellers who used the last edition and wrote to us with helpful hints, useful advice and interesting anecdotes:

Annemarie Sagoi, Aryeh Levenson, Daniela, Francois Depierreux, Frank Boyce, Graham Sutherland, Jason Blackwell, Joan Hellmann, Lucy Marris, Maria Fera, Michaela Benešová, Peter Herd, Roman Cattaneo, Samantha Farinella, Stephen Johnson, Suzi Park, Veronika Stalz, Will Hazell

WRITER THANKS
Nick Ray

A huge and heartfelt thanks to the people of Cambodia, whose warmth and humour, stoicism and spirit make it such a fascinating place to live. Biggest thanks are reserved for my lovely wife Kulikar Sotho and our children Julian and Belle, as without their support and encouragement the adventures would not be possible. Thanks also to Mum and Dad for giving me a taste for travel from a young age.

Thanks to fellow travellers and residents, friends and contacts in Cambodia who have helped shaped my knowledge and experience in this country. There is no room to thank everyone, but you all know who you are, as we meet for anything from beers to ecotourism conferences regularly enough.

Thanks also to my co-author Ashley Harrell for going the distance to ensure this is a worthy new edition. Finally, thanks to the Lonely Planet team who have worked on this title. The author may be the public face, but a huge amount of work goes into making this a better book behind the scenes and I thank everyone for their hard work.

Ashley Harrell

Thanks to editor Laura Crawford and co-author Nick Ray for the faith and guidance; Lauren Gurfein for introducing me to Cambodia; Andy Lavender for the dog-sitting; Peyton Bowsher for the dog-tolerating; Jess in Kampot for going above and beyond; Nicole and Alex for excellent company on Koh Totang; Ben, Sharyon, Amelie, Jarrah and Georgie for my favourite 'research' day, Lim for the hospitality/volcano sauce and Nick Berry for showing me the real Cambodia and teaching me to ride a motorbike.

ACKNOWLEDGEMENTS

Climate map data adapted from Peel MC, Finlayson BL & McMahon TA (2007) 'Updated World Map of the Köppen-Geiger Climate Classification', Hydrology and Earth System Sciences, 11, 163344.

Cover photograph: Ta Prohm temple, Stuart Westmorland/Getty Images ©

Illustration p138-9 by Michael Weldon.

THIS BOOK

This 11th edition of Lonely Planet's *Cambodia* guidebook was researched and written by Nick Ray and Ashley Harrell. The 10th edition was written by Nick Ray and Jessica Lee, and the 9th by Nick Ray and Greg Bloom. This guidebook was produced by the following:

Destination Editor Laura Crawford

Product Editors Bruce Evans, Ross Taylor

Senior Cartographer Diana Von Holdt

Book Designer Michael Weldon

Assisting Editors James Bainbridge, Katie Connolly, Melanie Dankel, Jennifer Hattam, Gabrielle Innes, Jodie Martire, Louise McGregor

Cartographer Julie Dodkins

Cover Researcher Naomi Parker

Thanks to Shona Gray, Liz Heynes, Mao Monkolransey, Mazzy Prinsep, Victoria Smith, Tracy Whitmey

Index